THE COMPANY OF PREACHERS

THE COMPANY OF PREACHERS

Wisdom on Preaching,
Augustine to the Present

*   *

Edited by

RICHARD LISCHER

WILLIAM B. EERDMANS PUBLISHING COMPANY
GRAND RAPIDS, MICHIGAN / CAMBRIDGE, U.K.

Wm. B. Eerdmans Publishing Co.
2140 Oak Industrial Drive N.E., Grand Rapids, Michigan 49505 /
P.O. Box 163, Cambridge CB3 9PU U.K.

Printed in the United States of America

13 12 11 10 09   9 8 7 6 5 4

Library of Congress Cataloging-in-Publication Data

The company of preachers: wisdom on preaching, Augustine to the present /
edited by Richard Lischer.
p.   cm.
Includes bibliographical references.
ISBN 978-0-8028-4609-9 (paper: alk. paper)
1. Preaching — History of doctrines.   I. Lischer, Richard.

BV4207.C66   2002
251 — dc21

2002024468

www.eerdmans.com

To
The Great Company of My Students
Duke Divinity School, 1979–

Partners in the Gospel,
Fellow Pilgrims,
Preachers

CONTENTS

Preface   xi

Introduction: The Promise of Renewal   xiii

Epigraph: "Listen, Lord — A Prayer"   xvii

I. WHAT IS PREACHING?

ALAN OF LILLE	*The Seventh Rung*	3
FRIEDRICH SCHLEIERMACHER	*Religious Discourse*	8
PHILLIPS BROOKS	*Truth and Personality*	15
C. H. DODD	*The Primitive Preaching*	23
DIETRICH BONHOEFFER	*The Proclaimed Word*	31
CARL MICHALSON	*Communicating the Gospel*	38
BARBARA BROWN TAYLOR	*Preaching*	46

II. THE PREACHER

JOHN CHRYSOSTOM	*The Temptations of Greatness*	57
GEORGE HERBERT	*The Parson Preaching*	64
RICHARD BAXTER	*On the Making of the Preacher*	69
JARENA LEE	*My Call to Preach the Gospel*	75
HORACE BUSHNELL	*Pulpit Talent*	83

PHOEBE PALMER	*The Great Army of Preaching Women*	90
P. T. FORSYTH	*The Authority of the Preacher*	98
GARDNER C. TAYLOR	*Portrait of a Prophet*	104

III. PROCLAIMING THE WORD

MARTIN LUTHER	*Proclamation versus Moralism*	115
JONATHAN EDWARDS	*Preaching the Terrors*	120
JOHN WESLEY	*Mixing Law and Gospel*	126
CHARLES GRANDISON FINNEY	*Preaching for Conversion*	132
H. H. FARMER	*The I-Thou Encounter*	142
HENRY H. MITCHELL	*Preaching as Celebration*	149
WALTER BRUEGGEMANN	*Prophetic Energizing*	156

IV. BIBLICAL INTERPRETATION

AUGUSTINE	*Literal and Figurative Interpretation*	169
JOHN CASSIAN	*The Fourfold Reading*	182
MARTIN LUTHER	*The Letter and the Spirit*	188
RUDOLF BULTMANN	*Is Exegesis without Presuppositions Possible?*	196
GERHARD EBELING	*Word of God and Hermeneutics*	204
PAUL RICOEUR	*The Hermeneutic Question*	211
JAMES A. SANDERS	*Contextual Hermeneutics*	218
NICHOLAS LASH	*Performing the Scriptures*	230
KATHARINE DOOB SAKENFELD	*Feminist Uses of Biblical Materials*	238

Contents

JUSTO GONZÁLEZ AND *The Neglected Interpreters* 248
CATHERINE G. GONZÁLEZ

RICHARD B. HAYS *A Hermeneutic of Trust* 265

V. RHETORIC

AUGUSTINE *The Uses of Rhetoric* 277

ROBERT OF BASEVORN *Ornamentation* 293

WILLIAM PERKINS *The Art of Prophesying* 298

FRANÇOIS FÉNELON *Natural Communication* 305

JOHN BROADUS *Rhetoric and Homiletics* 311

CHARLES HADDON SPURGEON *Illustrations in Preaching* 316

AMOS N. WILDER *The New Utterance* 324

JOSEPH SITTLER *Imagining a Sermon* 331

DAVID BUTTRICK *Designing Moves* 337

VI. THE HEARER

GREGORY THE GREAT *A Catalogue of Hearers* 355

JOHN CALVIN *The Internal Testimony of the Spirit* 362

PHILIP JACOB SPENER *Listening with the Heart* 369

JONATHAN EDWARDS *The Inner Turmoil of the Awakened* 375

JOHN HENRY NEWMAN *University Preaching* 380

PHILLIPS BROOKS *The Congregation* 389

HARRY EMERSON FOSDICK *Preaching as Personal Counseling* 395

FRED B. CRADDOCK *By Way of the Hearer* 401

VII. PREACHING AND THE CHURCH

P. T. FORSYTH	*The One Great Preacher*	411
FRANK BARTLEMAN	*Power in a Pentecostal Congregation*	417
KARL BARTH	*Preaching, Revelation, and the Church*	423
OSCAR ROMERO	*A Pastor's Last Homily*	433
GEOFFREY WAINWRIGHT	*Preaching and Eucharist*	443
WILLIAM H. WILLIMON	*Baptismal Speech*	453
CHARLES L. CAMPBELL	*Building Up the Church*	459
	Acknowledgments	468
	Index	471

PREFACE

The present book began as a modest revision of an earlier work, *Theories of Preaching*. Three years and too many cups of coffee later, as such projects usually go, it appears as a thoroughly reorganized and re-titled collection of sustained theological and biographical reflections on the art of preaching. *The Company of Preachers* is arranged in seven divisions with between six and eleven selections under each division. I have provided a brief introduction to each selection and attempted to maintain a conversation between the positions represented in the various selections. As a help to the reader, certain matters of spelling, punctuation, and the like have been made uniform. Our forebears were great Capitalizers. If a word wasn't capitalized, it probably wasn't important. I understand what they were conveying when they put into caps the essential symbols, events, and virtues associated with the Christian faith. Nevertheless, I have reined them in in order to conform with the contemporary reader's expectations. Omissions are marked by an ellipsis. In some cases footnotes have been placed in brackets in the text; for the sake of clarity and brevity many other footnotes have been eliminated.

A theological and historical cross section of the church's homiletics offers an exciting depth of riches, but also several painful limitations. One such limit is the foreshortened perspective on preaching that in most selections restricts that office to males. At times the "manliness" of preaching, as it is represented in some authors, may be oppressive to the reader, whether female or male. It is my judgment that to change the language is to tamper with matters over which I have no jurisdiction and, ultimately, to rewrite history. Thus in every case the author's language stands.

The title after each author's name is usually my own distillation of the material, though in some cases I have used the exact chapter titles or subheadings of the original work. At the end of each introduction, the source and original title of the selection is indicated as precisely as possible and, where applicable, according to the directions of the publisher holding the copyright. In the page references I have not tried to account for the occasional paragraph or page that has been elided from the selection.

Much of the material used in *The Company of Preachers* and its predecessor volume lies in the public domain, but the book would not have been possible without the permission granted by the holders of copyright material. Some of the publishers and individuals have been exceptionally generous with their permissions. My gratitude to them is heartfelt.

I also wish to thank several individuals for their invaluable assistance: On the first edition, Harriet Leonard, Emerson Ford, Judy Owens, Christopher Walters-Bugbee, Ted Campbell, Elizabeth Achtemeier, and Grant Wacker. Also: The Association of Theological Schools and the Duke University Research Council for their generous grants. My original editor was David Steinmetz.

For their assistance with *The Company of Preachers* I wish to thank Dean L. Gregory Jones for a generous grant from the Jameson Jones Endowment Fund at Duke Divinity School. The former director of the graduate program in religion at Duke, David Steinmetz, always managed to find money for research assistants. Some who helped with this project were Leslie Pardue, David McCarthy, and Christopher Franks. At its penultimate stage, Jennifer Trafton offered invaluable assistance by collecting materials, proofreading copy, and writing the first draft of several of the introductions. At the end, Kathryn Blanchard and Carol Shoun added their editorial expertise, and Alex Sider prepared the index. At Eerdmans, editor Hannah Timmermans guided this study from manuscript to completed book.

Finally, I wish to thank Bill Eerdmans of Wm. B. Eerdmans Publishing Co., who agreed that this would be a valuable book and then waited patiently for me to deliver it.

Richard Lischer
The Divinity School
Duke University

INTRODUCTION

The Promise of Renewal

The Company of Preachers takes its title from the mistranslation of Psalm 68:11 in the *Great Bible* of 1560 later immortalized by Handel in *The Messiah:* "The Lord gave the word: great was the company of the preachers." This book makes available to the student fifty or so of the great company of voices that constitutes the church's homiletical tradition.

When students and pastors want to learn more about that tradition, they find the original documents somewhat scattered and inaccessible. In the absence of theological and historical sources, they are left to formulate their own theories of preaching, as if they were the first on whom the responsibility of proclaiming the word of God had fallen.

The main criterion for selection in this anthology is theological. Does the piece contribute to a clearer theological understanding of preaching? Much could have been chosen from the fields of rhetoric, communications, cultural studies, and history, but to have done so would have created a very different book, one that focused on the sermon's satellites rather than the integrated act of preaching itself.

I have organized the church's wisdom on preaching around the following themes: (1) What Is Preaching? (2) The Preacher; (3) Proclaiming the Word; (4) Biblical Interpretation; (5) Rhetoric; (6) The Hearer; (7) Preaching and the Church.

The matter of definition is not as formulaic as it first appears. How one defines any activity will dictate one's attitude toward the task and its execution. Since preaching presents an eternal triangle of message, speaker, and audience, the choice of a point of departure for its definition — the text, the gospel, the preacher's character, or the ecclesial or social situation — does much to determine the shape and character of the sermon. Almost all the succeeding categories are implicitly contained in the choice of definition.

The reader will notice considerable overlap between categories. Overlap is necessary because preaching is a unified event that takes place in the fusion of elements represented by these categories and others not named. The act can be divided and analyzed only conceptually. For example, one might want separate categories for the content of the gospel and its oral performance, but in the New Testament the gospel is both. The same is true for the Holy Spirit, the sacraments, and the church. In the section titled "Preaching and the Church," the reader will find discussions of the sacraments, the Holy Spirit, and theology, all of which are present within the life of the church.

A thematic and historical collection such as this presents a fascinating case study in continuity and discontinuity in theology. On some issues the church's theologians once spoke continuously but now are silent. Some controversies the church actually resolved before moving on to new challenges. Others were temporarily quieted only to emerge in different forms in new generations.

The person of the preacher is a good example of a topic that was of great importance to the medieval church but is now seldom discussed in homiletics. Most homiletical treatises from Augustine through the Middle Ages deal with the formation and holiness of the one appointed to preach. The same concerns are evident in seventeenth-, eighteenth-, and nineteenth-century classic texts, whether by Baxter, Herbert, Spener, or Schleiermacher. Despite the interest in spirituality in both the church and popular culture today, however, one does not discern a revival of the classical preoccupation with the holiness of the preacher.

The practice of allegory in interpretation and preaching is an example of an issue that appears to have been resolved, first by the sixteenth-century Reformers and later by modern, nineteenth- and twentieth-century historical methods of interpretation. Yet the debate over "meaning" in texts is far from over, as postmodern interpreters have made clear. Literary criticism has opened our eyes to the unity of genres and the multivalency of texts; and theological interpretation is once again displaying the riches of patristic exegesis, including allegory.

For more than a millennium it appeared that Augustine had relieved the church's agony over the use of secular rhetoric by "baptizing" Cicero in Book 4 of *On Christian Doctrine*. But the issue was revived among the Puritans, whose corrective — "plain and perspicuous" English — was itself yet another rhetoric of preaching. In the late twentieth- and early twenty-first centuries the concern has resurfaced in a different form, namely, in the debate over technology and religious values. Television can simulate "church" in the family rooms of millions of television viewers. How is this modern communications technique — and the preaching it conveys — to be evaluated over against traditional ecclesiology, which presupposes the fellowship of word and table? How has television had an impact on the Sunday sermon?

Another, related, issue has to do with the relation of God and what might be called "technique" in preaching. Theologians perennially debated the proportions of the human versus divine operations in conversion. For Puritans such as Jonathan Edwards the sermon's effectiveness was controlled by the sovereignty of God. Nineteenth-century revivalists such as Charles Grandison Finney, however, vanquished Puritan qualms about human freedom by suggesting another form of sovereignty, that of the "laws" of spiritual communication. The question, once hotly debated, seldom comes up in contemporary homiletics.

Nor does the question of law and gospel in preaching, at least not as pervasively as it once did. Luther's passion for the gospel ignited the discussion, and the abiding danger of moralism — the confusion of God's grace with the moral, religious, social, or political rectitude of its recipients — keeps the question alive in some (Lutheran) quarters. The law-gospel debate was taken up by Wesley, Edwards, Finney, Barth, and many others who attempted to define the terms and formulate their co-existence in the sermon. It continued less explicitly in Bultmann and the school of the New Hermeneutic (represented in this book by Gerhard Ebeling), and one still hears its echoes in courageous treatises and sermons of liberation (see Oscar Romero, "A Pastor's Last Homily").

But on the whole, the newer interest in narrative preaching has changed the terms of the law-gospel controversy. For in narrative the mode is less proclamatory, less existentially decisive. The preacher does not explicitly rivet the hearer with God's judgment in preparation for the gracious news of the promise. Instead, many contemporary preachers and homileticians, represented in this book by thinkers as disparate as Barbara Brown Taylor, Nicholas Lash, Fred B. Craddock, and Charles L. Campbell, envision the sermon as a means of enrolling the listener into a larger consciousness or group. The sermon is better viewed as a narrative process than a proclamation, whose end is self-recognition, repentance, and participation in the church. The word does not knife downward through history toward its target as much as it rises out of the shared humanity and Christian identity of its hearers.

A final issue has to do with the response to the sermon. The word of God promises results, and preachers have always wanted to see them with their own eyes. What then is the most appropriate response to the preached word? Is it the life of Christian freedom in service enjoyed by one who, said Luther, is *semper justificandi,* always under the necessity of being justified? Is it sanctification and the pursuit of perfection, as Wesley preached, or the solution of personal and social problems, as counseled by Harry Emerson Fosdick? Or are the results of preaching more immediately and dramatically manifest in the terrors to the affections induced by one of Edwards's sermons, the mass conversions of a Finney revival, or the ecstasy of a Pentecostalist meeting? Or is the goal of the sermon more modest (and more profound), namely, as Geoffrey Wainwright argues, the interpretation of the Eucharist for those who would be Christ's body in the world?

Whatever the answers proposed, many in *The Company of Preachers* breathe a longing for the renewal of preaching. In every era of the church's history we hear voices decrying the corruption of the pulpit and calling for its reform. If the church is to achieve that renewal, it will find it where it has always found it, in the reappropriation of the gospel. Almost every reform movement in the church, whether the Franciscan, Dominican, Lollard, Brethren, Lutheran, Presbyterian, or Methodist, has meant not only a revival of preaching but a reforming of its method of presentation. But in no case did the redesign work precede the theological earthquake that made it necessary. Neither the New Testament evangelists, nor Augustine, Luther, or Wesley, created new forms of preaching for rhetorically motivated reasons. The notion of *ars gratia artis* is as foreign to the great preachers as it is to the New Testament.

"The New Utterance," as Amos Wilder names the gospel, has always depended on its own inner logic and the demands of the church to give rhetorical shape to its expression in preaching. The many studies of form and design that so dominated our generation's homiletical thinking, as well as more recent theories of culture and human consciousness, cannot produce the renewal promised by the gospel. Instead of seeking a scheme by which to clothe and communicate a religious idea, preachers will eventually ask the more integrated, theological question: What is it about the *gospel* that demands this particular expression? It is that question, and no other, that holds the promise of the renewal of preaching.

Revised
Sts. Peter and Paul, Apostles
June 29, 2001

Listen, Lord — A Prayer

O Lord, we come this morning
Knee-bowed and body-bent
Before thy throne of grace.
O Lord — this morning —
Bow our hearts beneath our knees,
And our knees in some lonesome valley.
We come this morning —
Like empty pitchers to a full fountain,
With no merits of our own.
O Lord — open up a window of heaven,
And lean out far over the battlements of glory,
And listen this morning.

Lord, have mercy on proud and dying sinners —
Sinners hanging over the mouth of hell,
Who seem to love their distance well.
Lord — ride by this morning —
Mount your milk-white horse,
And ride-a this morning —
And in your ride, ride by old hell,
Ride by the dingy gates of hell,
And stop poor sinners in their headlong plunge.

And now, O Lord, this man of God,
Who breaks the bread of life this morning —
Shadow him in the hollow of thy hand,
And keep him out of the gunshot of the devil.
Take him, Lord — this morning —
Wash him with hyssop inside and out,
Hang him up and drain him dry of sin.
Pin his ear to the wisdom-post,
And make his words sledge hammers of truth —
Beating on the iron heart of sin.
Lord God, this morning —
Put his eye to the telescope of eternity,
And let him look upon the paper walls of time.
Lord, turpentine his imagination,
Put perpetual motion in his arms,

Fill him full of the dynamite of thy power,
Anoint him all over with the oil of thy Salvation,
And set his tongue on fire.

And now, O Lord —
When I've done drunk my last cup of sorrow —
When I've been called everything but a child of God —
When I've done travelling up the rough side of the mountain —
O — Mary's Baby —
When I start down the steep and slippery steps of Death —
When this old world begins to rock beneath my feet —
Lower me to my dusty grave in peace
To wait for that great gittin' up morning — Amen.

from *God's Trombones*
by James Weldon Johnson

· I ·

WHAT IS PREACHING?

ALAN OF LILLE

The Seventh Rung

The universal association of preaching with the Christian faith has not led to a uniform definition of the task. Some theologians have begun their definition from the nature of the message, others from the character or holiness of the preacher. The Cistercian scholar and religious, Alan of Lille (c. 1128-1202), forsakes one key element in the classical definition of oratory, namely, persuasion, and instead speaks pastorally of "formation" as the goal of Christian preaching. "Persuasion" indicates a sudden change of attitude; "formation" implies a lifelong process, which the author compares to climbing a ladder. Alan is an influential figure in the so-called Renaissance of the twelfth century as well as in the whole history of preaching. Not for eight hundred years — since Augustine — had a Christian author attempted a systematic treatment of homiletics. According to James J. Murphy, the definition of preaching with which Alan begins his *Compendium* marks "the first formal definition in the 1200-year history of the church" (*Rhetoric in the Middle Ages* [Berkeley: University of California Press, 1974], p. 307). From that definition, reprinted below, Alan elaborates forty-seven sermonettes exemplifying the various purposes and audiences of preaching. These he concludes with a humorous message directed "To Sleepyheads *[Ad somnolentes]*." Alan did not invent the complex "university sermon," nor did he insist on specific rules of sermon construction. Yet his work does reveal his century's interest in the logical *division* of ideas (usually into threes) and its overwhelming reliance on the biblical *authorities* in homiletics and preaching. Within twenty years of Alan the traits suggested by his treatise had become a torrent of technical manuals on preaching, representing nothing less than a homiletical and rhetorical "revolution" in Europe (see Murphy, p. 310).

Alan of Lille, *The Art of Preaching*, Cistercian Fathers Series, Number 23, trans. Gilian R. Evans (Kalamazoo: Cistercian Publications, 1981), pp. 15-22.

Jacob beheld a ladder reaching from earth to heaven, on which angels were ascending and descending. The ladder represents the progress of the catholic man in his ascent from the beginning of faith to the full development of the perfect man. The first rung of this ladder is confession; the second, prayer; the third, thanksgiving; the fourth, the careful study of the Scriptures; the fifth, to inquire of someone more experienced if one comes upon any point in Scripture which is not clear; the sixth, the expounding of Scripture; the seventh, preaching.

The man who repents his sin then should first set his foot on the first rung of this ladder by confessing his sin. He should mount to the second rung by praying to God that grace may be bestowed on him. The third rung is reached through thanksgiving for the grace which is given. The ascent to the fourth rung is made by studying Scripture so as to preserve the gift of grace — for Holy Scripture teaches how grace, once given, may be held fast. In this way the fifth rung is seen in sight when a doubtful point arises and the reader asks someone senior to help him understand it. The sixth rung is reached when the reader himself expounds Holy Scripture to others. He climbs the seventh rung when he preaches in public what he has learned from Scripture.

Various writers have composed treatises on the other "rungs," how and when one must "mount" them. Little has been said up to now about preaching: its nature, by whom and to whom it should be delivered, on what subjects and in what manner, at what time or in what place. We have thought it worthwhile to compile a treatise on the subject, for the edification of our "neighbors."

First, then, we must see what preaching is, what form it should take — in the surface aspect of its words, and in the weight of its thoughts — and how many kinds of preaching there are. Secondly, we must consider who the preachers should be; thirdly, to whom the sermon should be delivered; fourthly, for what reasons, and fifthly, in what place.

Preaching is an open and public instruction in faith and behavior, whose purpose is the forming of men; it derives from the path of reason and from the fountainhead of the "authorities." Preaching should be public, because it must be delivered openly. That is why Christ says: "What I say to you in your ear, preach upon the housetops." For if preaching were hidden, it would be suspect; it would seem to smell of heretical dogmas. The heretics preach secretly in their assemblies, so that they may the more easily deceive others. Preaching should be public because it must be delivered not to one, but to many; if it were given to a single man, it would not be preaching but teaching — for that is where the distinction lies between preaching, teaching, prophecy, and public speaking. Preaching is that instruction which is offered to many, in public, and for their edification. Teaching is that which is given to one or to many to add to their knowledge. Prophecy gives warning of what is to come, through the revelation of future events. Public speaking is the admonishing of the people to maintain the well-being of the community. By means of what is called "preaching" — instruction in matters of faith and behavior — two aspects of theology may be introduced: that which appeals to the reason and deals with the knowledge of spiritual matters, and the ethical, which offers teaching on the living of a good life. For preaching sometimes teaches about holy things, sometimes about conduct. This is what is meant by the angels ascending and descending. Preachers are the "angels," who "ascend" when they preach about heavenly matters, and "descend" when they bend themselves to earthly things in speaking of behavior.

In the remainder of our definition, the ultimate reason for preaching — the benefit it brings — is implied in: "whose purpose is the forming of men." Because preaching must be dependent on reasoning and corroborated by authoritative texts, we have: "it derives from the path of reason and from the fountainhead of the 'authorities.'"

Preaching should not contain jesting words, or childish remarks, or that melodiousness and harmony which result from the use of rhythm or metrical lines; these are better fitted to delight the ear than to edify the soul. Such preaching is theatrical and full of buffoonery, and in every way to be condemned. Of such preaching the prophet says: "Your innkeepers mix water with the wine." Water is mingled with wine in the preaching in which childish and mocking words — what we may call "effeminacies" — are put into the minds of the listeners. Preaching should not glitter with verbal trappings, with purple patches, nor should it be too much enervated by the use of colorless words: the blessed keep to a middle way. If it were too heavily embroidered, [the sermon] would seem to have been contrived with excessive care, and elaborated to win the admiration of man, rather than for the benefit of our neighbors, and so it would move less the hearts of those who heard it. Those who preach in this way are to be compared with the Pharisees, who made the tassels of their garments long and wore large phylacteries. Such preaching may be said to be suspect, yet it is not to be wholly condemned, but rather tolerated. For St. Paul says: "On whatever occasion Christ is preached, I rejoice in it and shall rejoice." It serves no purpose to interpolate at intervals the phrase, "to the greater glory of Christ," for Christ is no less angered by false praise than by a denial of the truth. Such — as a rule — is the teaching of heretics, who propound truths and introduce falsehoods among them. It is said of them: "even jackals bare their breasts and feed their young." These jackals have the faces of young girls, but the feet of horses. Horses' hooves are not cloven, but stand squarely on the ground. By "jackals," therefore, we should understand "heretics," who have the faces of young girls, but whose bodies end in the scorpion's sting. For first they propound the truth and then they draw false conclusions from it. They have indeed the feet of horses, for they do not divide their hearts' desire between the love of God and the love of their neighbor, but they set all their desires on earthly pleasures. Such preaching must be wholly rejected, because it is full of vices and dangers. There should be some weight in the thought of a good sermon, so that it may move the spirits of its hearers, stir up the mind, and encourage repentance. Let the sermon rain down doctrines, thunder forth admonitions, soothe with praises, and so in every way work for the good of our neighbors. There are some who make earthly gain the motive for their preaching, but their preaching is extravagant; such are rather merchants than preachers, and so their preaching is to be heard and endured. That is why the Lord says: "Do what they tell you to do, but do not follow the example they set."

There are three kinds of preaching: That which is by the spoken word, of which it is said: "Go, preach the gospel to every creature." Another is by means of the written word, as when the Apostle says that he has "preached" to the Corinthians because he has written them a letter. The third is by deed, as it is said: "Every work of Christ is our instruction."

This should be the form of preaching: it should develop from, as it were, its own proper foundation, from a theological authority — especially a text from the Gospels, the Psalms, the epistles of Paul, or the Books of Solomon, for in these, in particular, edifying instruction resounds. Texts should also be taken from other books of Holy Writ if necessary, and if they have a bearing on the theme in hand.

And so the preacher must win the goodwill of his audience through the humility he shows in his own person, and through the profitableness of his subject matter. He must say that he propounds the word of God to his listeners so that it may bring forth fruit in their minds, not for any earthly gain, but to set them on their way and to help them make progress. He must make it clear that the sermon is not designed to arouse the foolish acclaim of the mob, nor tempered to win popular favor, nor shaped to evoke applause, as in a theater. It is composed to instruct the souls of the listeners, so that they may concentrate, not on who is speaking to them, but on what he is saying. It is not the sharpness of the thorn that we should dwell on, but the sweetness of the rose. Honey can be sucked from the broken reed, and fire may be struck from a stone. Thus, if he is committed to his task, [the preacher] should show how profitable it is to hear the word of God.

He should also assure his listeners that he will speak briefly and to their profit, and that he has been led to speak only by his love for his listeners; that he does not speak as one greater in knowledge or in wisdom, or as one who lives a better life, but because things are sometimes revealed to the little ones which are not shown to the great; and at such a time, the great ought to be silent. And because sometimes the great do not wish to preach, it is not surprising if lesser men then prattle. For if the learned are silent, the very stones will speak and cry out. So the preacher should come to the exposition of the proposed text and bend everything he says to the edification of the listener. Let him not begin with a text which is too obscure or too difficult, in case his listeners are put off by it and so listen less attentively. Nor, in the expounding of his authority, should he move too quickly away from his text, in case the beginning should be out of keeping with the middle and the middle with the end. He should also bring in other authorities to corroborate the first, especially those which are relevant to his subject. He may also, on occasion, insert sayings of the pagan writers — just as the apostle Paul sometimes introduces quotations from the philosophers into his epistles, for he will make an apt point if he provides a fresh illumination by such a skillful juxtaposition. He may also introduce moving words which soften hearts and encourage tears. But let the sermon be brief, in case prolixity should cause boredom. When the preacher sees that his hearers' minds are moved, and that they weep freely, and that their expressions are downcast, he should hold back a little, but not too much, for, as Lucretius says: "Nothing dries up faster than a tear." Finally, he should make use of examples to prove what he says, because teaching by means of examples is a familiar method.

FRIEDRICH SCHLEIERMACHER

Religious Discourse

Friedrich Schleiermacher (1768-1834) is justly acclaimed as the father of modern theology. From his chair at the University of Berlin and his Reformed pulpit in Berlin's Trinity Church, he presided over theology's encounter with Romanticism and psychology. He is venerated as the modern discoverer of the hermeneutical basis of all theology. Although he insisted on the "grammatical" basis of preaching in the text itself, he is remembered for shifting the weight of the hermeneutical and homiletical task from the objectivity of dogma to the subjectivities of the God-consciousness of the preacher and the life-situation of the hearer. In hermeneutics, he mediated between the authority of the text and "divinatory" powers of the interpreter. In apologetics, he acted as an intermediary between orthodoxy and the Hegelian philosophy of Christianity's "cultured despisers," whom he addressed in his famous *Speeches*. Schleiermacher was the foremost preacher in the city of Berlin, but in his homiletics he sought, in Hegelian fashion, a broader and more universal grounding for religious discourse. He mediated between Scripture and the capacities of the listener, between the written and spoken word, and between the technical language of theology and the human language of the heart. He single-handedly reinvented the sermon as a medium through which the speaker imaginatively imparts his or her own experience of God to those who are receptive to it. The following selection is drawn from his lectures on practical theology. Although it makes much of the religious "moment," the notion of feeling for Schleiermacher was not a generalized and contentless religiosity. Certainly "the main thing always remains the animation of the religious consciousness," but in the evangelical church this happens only through an effective communication of Jesus Christ (see *Servant of the Word: Selected Sermons of Friedrich Schleiermacher*, translated and with an introduction by Dawn DeVries [Philadelphia: Fortress, 1987], pp. 11ff.).

Friedrich Schleiermacher, *Praktische Theologie, Sämtliche Werke*, First Part, Vol. 13, Berlin, 1850, photo-reproduced, Walter De Gruyter, 1983, pp. 239-49, selection trans. B. Maurice Ritchie.

How does one arrive at unity in the formulation of a religious speech? We connect here with something we have already noted, that every artistic creation proceeds from a heightened stimulation of the mind, but not in such a way that both the creation and the stimulation always come together in one and the same moment. Rather, one regards all these heightened mental states, as they emerge in intermittent moments, as one, and every artistic conception also as one, viewing the latter as grounded in the former. The religious speaker can only be religious by an intention and purity of the religious element in him that transcends the ordinary. Out of this permanent state proceed particular creations. How does the active minister emerge from this general state to a particular creation? How does the unity of speech arise out of it for him?

We are directed toward two points. The first is this: The minister lives in and with his congregation. This is his official and particular point of view. Insofar as he bears within himself the religious life of his congregation, with both its perfections and its deficiencies, he can find a sense of direction for his sermon. When the minister's thought progression arises from his knowledge of the needs of the congregation, it emerges in a most legitimate and immediate way. It proceeds out of the common life of the congregation. If it arises only out of his personal state of mind, the issue is no longer the same. As a result, the speech can lose its popular character whenever the speaker does not find himself at one with the situation of the congregation. But as soon as his thought is examined in light of this other dimension and is brought in line with the religious and congregational mind, there will be nothing to find fault with in the sermon.

It is significantly different when the sermon arises from the knowledge of the needs of the parish (but) the speaker does not share the same need, *or* when this need simultaneously stirs his own soul. In the latter case, the speech will be warmer and more lively. But in the former, the speech will have a colder tone, which can only be remedied in an artificial way.

The minister must be able to transport himself into the mind of the parish to the extent that it becomes his own mind. If he is unable to do so, the impetus of his speech will remain valid because it relates totally to the life of the congregation. Yet there will be something missing in its development. At its conception, the fundamental prerequisite for the proper character of an address depends on this: the minister must have personal interest in a matter which is at the same time an issue in the life of his congregation. However, this will clearly happen in only a few cases, for in most instances where the minister is to produce a sermon, he will be subject to too many stimuli and will lack a firm direction.

Now there is another point from which we must construct a religious speech. In addition to his particular relationship to the local congregation, the minister is first of all himself a Christian and then a theologian. In both these roles we must think of him as one who is in constant dialogue with Scripture. Every Christian stands in relation to and [in] lively dialogue with Scripture. For many the relationship is one-sided. The minister should discard this one-sidedness. By virtue of his office he is bound to the whole of Scripture from which alone he can build the congregation.

As a minister, he is also a theologian, and to him alone Scripture is comprehensible in its total context. In this interaction, individual questions will stand out, and, in the uncertainty which remains, constant contact with Scripture will offer firm direction toward total understanding.

Let us now look at the reverse side, where the speaker's impulse begins with the text (rather than [with] his relationship to the congregation). How does that happen? Obviously, it is quite possible that seeds of thought germinate in the minister's own situation or in the religious situation of his congregation. He then happens upon a text which relates to the situation. The text presents itself as a consequence of his consciousness. But that procedure does not belong here [in text-centered preaching]. If the preacher's thinking arises solely from the text, it emerges from engagement with the Bible, which, again, is of a very different order. . . .

Engagement with Scripture can be a learned and theological enterprise, and thus the minister stands in danger of delivering a theological treatise instead of a sermon. There must always be a reflective step between the text and the religious situation of the congregation. Only the right step will be appropriate. The appropriateness of the relationship is thus contingent upon the relation of the two.

It is well nigh impossible to conceive of a proper execution of the ministerial office without industrious engagement with the Bible, though not forced reading on a fixed schedule; but the Bible must become the center of the minister's conceptual thinking. It is appropriate that it always be there at the center. The biblical content must penetrate our ongoing consciousness to the extent that no noble moment in life occurs in which we do not return to Scripture.

We must of necessity presuppose an intimate familiarity with and an inward and lively grasp of the New Testament. Given this, when an impulse for a series of thoughts comes, an apt passage will also occur that has the potential to become the central focus of the sermon. Many make chance their master, a poor resource. One must not make the choosing of a text a special practice, and one should certainly not believe there is a special providence governing it. That is pure superstition. Obviously, such chance procedure suggests an inner deficiency from which one can expect nothing of a superior nature.

I think the issue itself suggests its own solution. It can happen that during the week no sermon idea presents itself. That has to be assumed. But certainly over four weeks it does; thus one must formulate a *series* of themes. That is a normal practice. When a particularly stimulating moment occurs in life, it is accompanied by a desire to present its content. When we compare a single sermon with the general conduct of the minister's office over its annual cycle, one clearly sees either an unevenness in the minister's life or a certain sameness. The variable lies in the quality of the minister's own life. A minister should never suffer the embarrassment of uncertainty about the coherence of the sermon. Therefore the first stipulation for a successful address is that a minister be sure of his text and theme [via long-range planning of themes].

If one of these two factors is missing — either the pastor's common life with his congregation or his dialogue with Scripture — the pastor will find himself in great difficulty selecting a text. Further development of the sermon will be impossible because the desired coherence has not been appropriately interiorized. No worse situation for the minister exists than to have to prepare a sermon, only to be stymied over what to preach. In this instance, one of the two above factors is absent. The less the minister trusts himself, the more difficult it is for him to choose a text. When we consider the usual custom that each worship service has its own appointed lesson, the solution seems quite simple: take the appointed pericope as a text.

Then the issue is how to handle that text, whether homiletically or thematically. If the speaker simply chooses the theme he can best execute, the choice is already made. We hope this practice is no longer widespread because it does an injustice to the rest of the Bible by giving priority to an arbitrarily selected portion of Scripture. . . .

[But] when the pastor lives in his vocation . . . a host of topics, all competing for priority, will emerge from life. One thinks first of religious instruction the minister has to render, as a source for preaching topics. There he has something very specific to deal with. Then of course there is the rest of life that is also a rich source of ideas! Thus one imagines the minister continually formulating his thoughts more or less directly from life and reflecting on them before the congregation.

One certainly sees a great difference among individual personalities. One minister can generate ideas more readily than another. One minister contends well with a wealth of ideas. Another has trouble deciding anything. When we consider the very beginning, or the kernel, of a speech clear through to its delivery as a progression . . . , we shall have to propose that there can be no absolute beginning. Everything depends on how much one can trust himself to hold fast to what has arisen from within. Timing varies in this regard. On other occasions the speaker may be short on ideas. He has only to hold on to the nuclei of experience in order to mine the rich treasure. *Thus the first practical rule: try to hold fast to kernels of thought as they arise, in order to come as infrequently as possible to the point of beginning with nothing.*

In the customary treatment of this subject we find the traditional distinctions used to classify the nature of a sermon. Some are taken from the subjective side [the preacher]; others from the objective side of a speech. Our critique of these will clarify several things.

One distinguishes the instructive speech from the one that moves. We cannot accept this absolute distinction as appropriate, for instructing and convincing, considered entirely separately, are both the vocation of the preacher. Moving, in itself, is also a calling and proceeds from the essential character of religious speech. . . .

Further, one often distinguishes between dogmatic and moral sermons. That is a contrast which does not rest on either of the two distinctions indicated above; rather, they can cross over: a dogmatic sermon can be either instructive or moving. . . . A purely dogmatic speech proceeds from the essential nature of religious discourse, as does a purely moral address, because both belong in the religious consciousness: the theoretical and the practical mutually penetrate and do not allow for separation. When one is separated from the other, things are not as they should be in religious speech. At the core of every religious moment, which a sermon should convey, lies the relationship of the human being with God as classical Christianity has determined it, expressed in a variety of ways. Every theoretical dogma is an expression of that relationship. . . . The sum total of such expressions is dogmatics.

But in the religious moment itself one always sees a movement from knowledge toward will, for there is no feeling (of truth) which does not cross over into activity. Such a religious moment cannot be adequately described if this crossover is not also accounted for. Even if the sermon wishes to present only the first element — [the display of knowledge] — it still wouldn't be accurate [*wissenschaftlich*]. It would never achieve its end. The transition from feeling to action has to be conveyed. If, on the other hand, the minister were to discuss only the action component, it could not be considered as truly arising from religious consciousness. . . .

In earlier days, the formula for a sermon included a dogma followed by a *usus,* a practical application. The theoretical argument was always glaringly divided from its practical application. The more the latter is interwoven with the former, however, the more complete the sermon will be.

Still another antithesis is not so much related to theme as to the text. We divide Holy Scripture into the historical and the didactic, a division which is not completely antithetical, though it can be demonstrated in particular instances, for there are sections of Scripture where the historical or the didactic predominates. . . .

What is historical in this area but a religious moment, which is nothing more than a mode of action proceeding from the religious consciousness and presenting itself in a particular instance? And what is didactic but, on the other hand, a religious mode of thought and action which has significance here insofar as it emerges in the particular moment, forming a part of the religious life. *That means the historical can only be useful if it is understood didactically and the didactic only insofar as it is introduced into life and the historical. The difference is this: a historical text expresses a particular instance while a didactic text expresses something universal.*

In the first instance there is a transition from the particular to the universal; in the second from the universal to the particular. . . .

We have assumed distinctions in religious discourse which rest in turn upon its fundamental coherence, whether this be greater or lesser. The greater unity can be constructed in such a way that variety is emphasized within the unity. It seems that a didactic text is more suited as a basis for a sermon with strict unity and the historical mode better suited for the sermon that deals with multiplicity. But this distinction, too, is an illusion.

If the historical text is not of a certain scope, the weights of whose facts do not emerge with certainty, it will not be easy to base a sermon on it.

If the didactic text is of a larger scope, it will be equally well suited for preaching. One could say, a text of lesser scope is more suited as a foundation for a proper sermon, a text of larger scope for a homily. This distinction is by no means definitive. One can develop a strong thematic unity from a text of larger scope, and from a text of lesser scope a sermon whose individual parts vary and allow for extensive development. . . .

The minister has two perspectives. On the one hand, he goes back to the context in the biblical passage. But with his congregation in mind, he also has to see what they are accustomed to. Because his own exploration in the text is quite extensive, he must remember the capacities of his congregation.

The method is by nature a dialogical one. It is a dialogue with the biblical passage which the minister queries and which answers him, and a dialogue with his congregation. If we ask, May we exempt the pastor from one of these two activities? the answer is no. Whoever is incapable of thoughtful decisions in biblical interpretation is not fit to be the voice of the whole congregation. But one who is not sensitive to how the congregation's consciousness is shaped is scarcely fit for pastoral care. Both must be joined, and I want to emphasize again that neither skill is sufficient if the minister is not the master of both.

Such skills are acquired only through practice. Biblical interpretation and pastoral care are necessary for the minister, and only their coupling will produce the wholeness so beneficial to the congregation.

PHILLIPS BROOKS

Truth and Personality

The most durable of all definitions of preaching was given by Phillips Brooks (1835-1893) in his Lyman Beecher Lectures at Yale University in 1877. The twin essentials of preaching are the truth of the message and the personality of the messenger, neither of which may be "repressed," as Brooks puts it, without undermining the sermon. Christian truth takes the form of a message which, through the particular attributes of the preacher, is transmuted into a witness. The very character of the gospel requires a breadth and liberality of the human spirit with which to convey it. Where earlier centuries of preachers strove to form communities of faith, Brooks reminds his hearers that the preacher must first touch the individual soul. "Truth through personality" was the logical extension of Horace Bushnell's theory of Christian experience as the authority for truth. The phrase was epigraph to an era of Christian liberalism exemplified by the urban and urbane ministry of Brooks himself. His sympathy for personality — "manliness" is a frequent term in Brooks — as well as his sensitivity to the needs of the listener, take him well out of the orbit of Calvinism. But his intellectual confidence in "the truth" is even further removed from the mass manipulations of nineteenth-century revivalism. If the successes of his contemporary Dwight Moody threatened him, he never said so. Brooks's *Lectures* have traveled the century more effectively than any nineteenth-century treatise on preaching, perhaps because the temper of his times and personality is so much like our own. At the time of the lectures Brooks was rector of Trinity Church, Boston. When he died as bishop of Massachusetts, the Boston Stock Exchange closed and twenty thousand people came to mourn America's most influential preacher.

Phillips Brooks, *Lectures on Preaching* (New York: E. P. Dutton & Company, 1907 [1877]), pp. 5-26.

Preaching is the communication of truth by man to men. It has in it two essential elements, truth and personality. Neither of those can it spare and still be preaching. The truest truth, the most authoritative statement of God's will, communicated in any other way than through the personality of brother man to men is not preached truth. Suppose it written on the sky, suppose it embodied in a book which has been so long held in reverence as the direct utterance of God that the vivid personality of the men who wrote its pages has well-nigh faded out of it; in neither of these cases is there any preaching. And on the other hand, if men speak to other men that which they do not claim for truth, if they use their powers of persuasion or of entertainment to make other men listen to their speculations, or do their will, or applaud their cleverness, that is not preaching either. The first lacks personality. The second lacks truth. And preaching is the bringing of truth through personality. It must have both elements. It is in the different proportion in which the two are mingled that the difference between two great classes of sermons and preaching lies. It is in the defect of one or the other element that every sermon and preacher falls short of the perfect standard. It is in the absence of one or the other element that a discourse ceases to be a sermon, and a man ceases to be a preacher altogether....

This was the method by which Christ chose that his gospel should be spread through the world. It was a method that might have been applied to the dissemination of any truth, but we can see why it was especially adapted to the truth of Christianity. For that truth is preeminently personal. However the gospel may be capable of statement in dogmatic form, its truest statement we know is not in dogma but in personal life. Christianity is Christ; and we can easily understand how a truth which is of such peculiar character that a person can stand forth and say of it, "I am the truth," must always be best conveyed through, must indeed be almost incapable of being perfectly conveyed except through, personality. And so some form of preaching must be essential to the prevalence and spread of the knowledge of Christ among men. There seems to be some such meaning as this in the words of Jesus when he said to his disciples, "As my Father has sent me into the world even so have I sent you into the world." It was the continuation, out to the minutest ramifications of the new system of influence, of that personal method which the incarnation itself had involved.

If this be true, then, it establishes the first of all principles concerning the ministry and preparation for the ministry. Truth through personality is our description of real preaching. The truth must come really through the person, not merely over his lips, not merely into his understanding and out through his pen. It must come through his character, his affections, his whole intellectual and moral being. It must come genuinely through him. I think that, granting

16

equal intelligence and study, here is the great difference which we feel between two preachers of the word. The gospel has come *over* one of them and reaches us tinged and flavored with his superficial characteristics, belittled with his littleness. The gospel has come *through* the other, and we receive it impressed and winged with all the earnestness and strength that there is in him. In the first case the man has been but a printing machine or a trumpet. In the other case he has been a true man and a real messenger of God. . . .

Let us look now for a few moments at these two elements of preaching — truth and personality; the one universal and invariable, the other special and always different. There are a few suggestions that I should like to make to you about each.

And first with regard to the truth. It is strange how impossible it is to separate it and consider it wholly by itself. The personalness will cling to it. There are two aspects of the minister's work, which we are constantly meeting in the New Testament. They are really embodied in two words, one of which is "message," and the other is "witness." "This is the message which we have heard of him and declare unto you," says St. John in his first epistle. "We are his witnesses of these things," says St. Peter before the council at Jerusalem. In these two words together, I think, we have the fundamental conception of the matter of all Christian preaching. It is to be a message given to us for transmission, but yet a message which we cannot transmit until it has entered into our own experience and we can give our own testimony of its spiritual power. The minister who keeps the word "message" always written before him, as he prepares his sermon in his study, or utters it from his pulpit, is saved from the tendency to wanton and wild speculation, and from the mere passion of originality. He who never forgets that word "witness" is saved from the unreality of repeating by rote mere forms of statement which he has learned as orthodox, but never realized as true. If you and I can always carry this double consciousness, that we are messengers, and that we are witnesses, we shall have in our preaching all the authority and independence of assured truth, and yet all the appeal and convincingness of personal belief. It will not be we that speak, but the spirit of our Father that speaketh in us, and yet our sonship shall give the Father's voice its utterance and interpretation to his other children.

I think that nothing is more needed to correct the peculiar vices of preaching which belong to our time, than a new prevalence among preachers of this first conception of the truth which they have to tell as a message. I am sure that one great source of the weakness of the pulpit is the feeling among the people that these men who stand up before them every Sunday have been making up trains of thought, and thinking how they should "treat their subject," as the phrase runs. There is the first ground of the vicious habit that our congregations have of talking about the preacher more than they think about the truth. The minstrel who sings before you to show his skill will be praised for his wit, and rhymes, and voice. But the courier who hurries in, breathless, to bring you a message, will be forgotten in the message that he brings. . . .

Whatever else you count yourself in the ministry, never lose this fundamental idea of yourself as a messenger. As to the way in which one shall best keep that idea, it would not be hard to state; but it would involve the whole story of the Christian life. Here is the primary necessity that the Christian preacher should be a Christian first, that he should be deeply cognizant of God's authority, and of the absoluteness of Christ's truth. That was one of the first principles which I ventured to assume as I began my lecture. But without entering so wide a field, let me say one thing about this conception of preaching as the telling of a message which constantly impresses me. I think that it would give to our preaching just the quality which it appears to me to most lack now. That quality is breadth. I do not mean liberality of thought, not tolerance of opinion, nor anything of that kind. I mean largeness of movement, the great utterance of great truths, the great enforcement of great duties, as distinct from the minute, and subtle, and ingenious treatment of little topics, side issues of the soul's life, bits of anatomy, the bric-a-brac of theology. . . .

And then another result of this conception of preaching as the telling of a message is that it puts us into right relations with all historic Christianity. The message never can be told as if we were the first to tell it. It is the same message which the church has told in all the ages. He who tells it today is backed by all the multitude who have told it in the past. He is companied by all those who are telling it now. The message is his witness; but a part of the assurance with which he has received it, comes from the fact of its being the identical message which has come down from the beginning. Men find on both sides how difficult it is to preserve the true poise and proportion between the corporate and the individual conceptions of the Christian life. But all will own today the need of both.

The identity of the church in all times consists in the identity of the message which she had always had to carry from her Lord to men. All outward utterances of the perpetual identity of the church are valuable only as they assert this real identity. There is the real meaning of the perpetuation of old ceremonies, the use of ancient liturgies, and the clinging to what seem to be apostolic types of government. The heretic in all times has been not the errorist as such, but the self-willed man, whether his judgments were right or wrong. "A man may be a heretic in the truth," says Milton. He is the man who, taking his ideas not as a message from God, but as his own discoveries, has cut himself off from the message-bearing church of all the ages. I am sure that the more fully you come to count your preaching the telling of a message, the more valuable and real the church will become to you, the more true will seem to you your brotherhood with all messengers of that same message in all strange dresses and in all strange tongues.

I should like to mention, with reference to the truth which the preacher has to preach, two tendencies which I am sure you will recognize as very characteristic of our time. One is the tendency of criticism, and the other is the tendency of mechanism. Both tendencies are bad. By the tendency of criticism I mean the disposition that prevails everywhere to deal with things from outside, discussing their relations, examining their nature, and not putting ourselves into their power. Preaching in every age follows, to a certain extent, the changes which come to all literature and life. The age in which we live is strangely fond of criticism. It takes all things to pieces for the mere pleasure of examining their nature. It studies forces, not in order to obey them, but in order to understand them. It talks about things for the pure pleasure of discussion. Much of the poetry and prose about nature and her wonders, much of the investigation of the country's genius and institutions, much of the subtle analysis of human nature is of this sort. It is all good; but it is something distinct from the cordial sympathy by which one becomes a willing servant of any of these powers, a real lover of nature, or a faithful citizen, or a true friend.

Now it would be strange if this critical tendency did not take possession of the preaching of the day. And it does. The disposition to watch ideas in their working, and to talk about their relations and their influence on one another, simply as problems, in which the mind may find pleasure without any real entrance of the soul into the ideas themselves, this, which is the critical tendency, invades the pulpit, and the result is an immense amount of preaching which must be called preaching about Christ as distinct from preaching Christ. There are many preachers who seem to do nothing else, always discussing Christianity as a problem instead of announcing Christianity as a message and proclaiming Christ as a Savior. I do not undervalue their discussions. But I think we ought always to feel that such discussions are not the type or ideal of preaching. They may be necessities of the time, but they are not the work which the great apostolic preachers did, or which the true preacher will always most desire. Definers and defenders of the faith are always needed, but it is bad for a church when its ministers count it their true work to define and defend the faith rather than to preach the gospel.

Beware of the tendency to preach about Christianity, and try to preach Christ. To discuss the relations of Christianity and science, Christianity and society, Christianity and politics, is good. To set Christ forth to men so that they shall know him, and in gratitude and love become his, that is far better. It is good to be a Herschel who describes the sun; but it is better to be a Prometheus who brings the sun's fire to the earth.

I called the other tendency the tendency of mechanism. It is the disposition of the preacher to forget that the gospel of Christ is primarily addressed to individuals, and that its ultimate purpose is the salvation of multitudes of men. Between the time when it first speaks to a man's soul, and the time when that man's soul is gathered into heaven, with the whole host of the redeemed, the gospel uses a great many machineries which are more or less impersonal. The church, with all its instrumentalities, comes in. The preacher works by them. But if the preacher ever for a moment counts them the purpose of his working, if he takes his eye off the single soul as the prize he is to win, he falls from his highest function and loses his best power. All successful preaching, I more and more believe, talks to individuals. The church is for the soul. . . .

Of the second element in preaching, namely, the preacher's personality, there will be a great deal to say, especially in the next lecture. But there are two or three fundamental things which I wish to say today.

The first is this, that the principle of personality once admitted involves the individuality of every preacher. The same considerations which make it good that the gospel should not be written on the sky, or committed merely to an almost impersonal book, make it also most desirable that every preacher should utter the truth in his own way, and according to his own nature. It must come not only through man but through men. If you monotonize men you lose their human power to a large degree. If you could make all men think alike it would be very much as if no man thought at all, as when the whole earth moves together with all that is upon it, everything seems still.

Now the deep sense of the solemnity of the minister's work has often a tendency to repress the free individuality of the preacher and his tolerance of other preachers' individualities. His own way of doing his work is with him a matter of conscience, not of taste, and the conscience when it is thoroughly awake is more intolerant than the taste is. Or, working just the other way, his conscience tells him that it is not for him to let his personal peculiarities intrude in such a solemn work, and so he tries to bind himself to the ways of working which the most successful preachers of the word have followed.

I have seen both these kinds of ministers: those whose consciences made them obstinate, and those whose consciences made them pliable; those whose consciences hardened them to steel or softened them to wax. However it comes about, there is an unmistakable tendency to the repression of the individuality of the preacher. It is seen in little things: in the uniform which preachers wear, and the disposition to a uniformity of language. It is seen in great things: in the disposition which all ages have witnessed to draw a line of orthodoxy inside the lines of truth. Wisely and soberly let us set ourselves against this influence. The God who sent men to preach the gospel of his Son in their humanity, sent each man distinctively to preach it in his humanity. Be yourself by all means, but let that good result come not by cultivating merely superficial peculiarities and oddities. Let it be by winning a true self full of your own faith and your own love. The deep originality is noble, but the surface originality is miserable. It is so easy to be a John the Baptist, as far as the desert and camel's hair and locusts and wild honey go. But the devoted heart to speak from, and the fiery words to speak, are other things.

Again, we can never forget in thinking of the preacher's personality that he is one who lives in constant familiarity with thoughts and words which to other men are occasional and rare, and which preserve their sacredness mainly by their rarity. That fact must always come in when we try to estimate the influences of a preacher's life. What will the power of that fact be? I am sure that often it weakens the minister. I am sure that many men who, if they came to preach once in a great while in the midst of other occupations, would preach with reality and fire, are deadened to their sacred work by their constant intercourse with sacred things. Their constant dealing with the truth makes them less powerful to bear the truth to others, as a pipe through which the water always flows collects its sediment, and is less fit to let more water through.

And besides this, it ministers to self-deception and to an exaggeration or distortion of our own history. The man who constantly talks of certain experiences, and urges other men to enter into them, must come in time, by very force of describing those experiences, to think that he has undergone them. You beg men to repent, and you grow so familiar with the whole theory of repentance that it is hard for you to know that you yourself have not repented. You exhort to patience till you have no eyes or ears for your own impatience. It is the way in which the man who starts the trains at the railroad station must come in time to feel as if he himself had been to all the towns along the road whose names he has always been shouting in the passengers' ears, and to which he has for years sold them their tickets, when perhaps he has not left his own little way-station all the time.

I know that all this is so, and yet certainly the fault is in the man, not in the truth. The remedy certainly is not to make the truth less familiar. There is a truer relation to preaching, in which the constancy of it shall help instead of harming the reality and earnestness with which you do it. The more that you urge other people to holiness the more intense may be the hungering and thirsting after holiness in your own heart. Familiarity does not breed contempt except of contemptible things or in contemptible people. The adage, that no man is a hero to his *valet de chambre,* is sufficiently answered by saying that it is only to a *valet de chambre* that a truly great man is unheroic. You must get the impulse, the delight, and the growing sacredness of your life out of your familiar work. You are lost as a preacher if its familiarity deadens and encrusts, instead of vitalizing and opening your powers. And it will all depend upon whether you do your work for your Master and his people or for yourself. The last kind of labor slowly kills, the first gives life more and more.

C. H. DODD

The Primitive Preaching

Soon after its publication in 1936, *The Apostolic Preaching and Its Developments* was recognized as a seminal work in the field of biblical studies and homiletics. At a time when the academic world had begun dissecting the Bible by means of form and source criticism, C. H. Dodd (1884-1973), the consummate British scholar and theologian, announced the unity of the church's proclamation, its *kerygma*. He cautioned both church and academy to avoid two pitfalls: the preoccupation with purely historical questions about Jesus, on the one hand, and the substitution of eschatology with liberal truisms, such as "the fatherhood of God and the brotherhood of man," on the other. He sharply distinguished *kerygma*, or missionary preaching, from *didache* or instruction, asserting that only the former belonged to the preaching of the primitive church. His ideas drew fire from many quarters. Many biblical scholars disputed his absolute distinction between preaching and teaching, as well as his dogmatic insistence upon "realized eschatology" as the exclusive position of the first church. Liberals, for whom the timeless teachings of Jesus represented the essence of Christianity, were offended by the eschatological strangeness of the message Dodd delineated. What optimists remained after the Great War were also dismayed by the subsidiary place of ethics in Dodd's kerygma. Finally, preachers of succeeding decades have been sobered and challenged by Dodd's admonition: "Much of our preaching in church at the present day would not have been recognized by the early Christians as *kerygma*." As did no other statement of the twentieth century, *The Apostolic Preaching* forced preachers to examine their own work and to ask, What is preaching?

C. H. Dodd, *The Apostolic Preaching and Its Developments* (Grand Rapids: Baker, 1980 [1936]), pp. 13, 16-17, 21-24, 74-78.

The Pauline *kerygma*, therefore, is a proclamation of the facts of the death and resurrection of Christ in an eschatological setting which gives significance to the facts. They mark the transition from "this evil age" to the "age to come." The "age to come" is the age of fulfillment. Hence the importance of the statement that Christ died and rose "according to the Scriptures." Whatever events the Old Testament prophets may indicate as impending, these events are for them significant as elements in the coming of "the day of the Lord." Thus the fulfillment of prophecy means that the day of the Lord has dawned: the age to come has begun. The death and resurrection of Christ are the crucial fulfillment of prophecy. By virtue of them believers are already delivered out of this present evil age. The new age is here, of which Christ, again by virtue of his death and resurrection, is Lord. He will come to exercise his lordship both as judge and as savior at the consummation of the age.

We have now to ask how far this form of *kerygma* is distinctively Pauline, and how far it provides valid evidence for the apostolic preaching in general.

Paul himself at least believed that in essentials his gospel was that of the primitive apostles; for although in Galatians 1:11-18 he states with emphasis that he did not derive it from any human source, nevertheless in the same epistle (2:2) he says that he submitted "the gospel which I preach" to Peter, James, and John at Jerusalem, and that they gave their approval. Not only so, but in the *locus classicus*, 1 Corinthians 15:1ff., he expressly declares that this summary of the gospel is what he had "received" as tradition; and after referring to other witnesses to the facts, including Peter, James, and "all the apostles," he adds with emphasis, "Whether I or they, it was thus that we preached and thus that you believed." . . .

We see emerging the outlines of an apostolic gospel which Paul believed to be common to himself and other Christian missionaries. As the epistles from which we have quoted belong to the fifties of the first century, they are evidence of prime value for the content of the early *kerygma*. And this evidence is in effect valid for a much earlier date than that at which the epistles themselves were written. When did Paul "receive" the tradition of the death and resurrection of Christ? His conversion can, on his own showing, be dated not later than about A.D. 33-34. His first visit to Jerusalem was three years after this (possibly just over two years on our exclusive reckoning); at the utmost, therefore, not more than seven years after the crucifixion. At that time he stayed with Peter for a fortnight, and we may presume they did not spend all the time talking about the weather. After that he had no direct contact with the primitive church for fourteen years, that is to say, almost down to the period to which our epistles belong, and it is difficult to see how he could during this time have had any opportunity of further instruction in the apostolic traditions.

The date, therefore, at which Paul received the fundamentals of the gospel cannot well be later than some seven years after the death of Jesus Christ. It may be earlier, and, indeed, we must assume some knowledge of the tenets of Christianity in Paul even before his conversion. Thus Paul's preaching represents a special stream of Christian tradition which was derived from the main stream at a point very near to its source. No doubt his own idiosyncrasy counted for much in his presentation of the gospel, but anyone who should maintain that the primitive Christian gospel was fundamentally different from that which we have found in Paul must bear the burden of proof.

It is true that the *kerygma* as we have recovered it from the Pauline epistles is fragmentary. No complete statement of it is, in the nature of the case, available. But we may restore it in outline somewhat after this fashion:

> The prophecies are fulfilled, and the new age is inaugurated by the coming of Christ.
> He was born of the seed of David.
> He died according to the Scriptures, to deliver us out of the present evil age.
> He was buried.
> He rose on the third day according to the Scriptures. He is exalted at the right hand of God, as Son of God and Lord of quick and dead.
> He will come again as judge and savior of men.

The apostolic preaching as adopted by Paul may have contained, almost certainly did contain, more than this. Comparison with other forms of the *kerygma* may enable us to expand the outline with probability; but so much of its content can be demonstrated from the epistles, and the evidence they afford is of primary value. . . .

The first four speeches of Peter [in the Book of Acts] cover substantially the same ground. The phraseology and the order of presentation vary slightly, but there is no essential advance from one to another. They supplement one another, and taken together they afford a comprehensive view of the content of the early *kerygma*. This may be summarized as follows:

First, the age of fulfillment has dawned. "This is that which was spoken by the prophet" (Acts 2:16). "The things which God foreshewed by the mouth of all the prophets, he thus fulfilled" (3:18). "All the prophets from Samuel and his successors told of these days" (3:24). It was a standing principle of Rabbinic exegesis of the Old Testament that what the prophets predicted had reference to the "days of the Messiah," that is to say, to the expected time when God, after long centuries of waiting, should visit his people with judgment and blessing, bringing to a climax his dealings with them in history. The apostles, then, declare that the messianic age has dawned.

Secondly, this has taken place through the ministry, death, and resurrection of Jesus, of which a brief account is given, with proof from the Scriptures that all took place through "the determinate counsel and foreknowledge of God": *(a)* His Davidic descent. "David, being a prophet, and knowing that God had sworn to set one of the fruit of his loins upon his throne, foresaw (Christ)," who is therefore proclaimed, by implication, to have been born "of the seed of David" (2:30-31, citing Ps. 132:11). *(b)* His ministry. "Jesus of Nazareth, a man divinely accredited to you by works of power, prodigies, and signs which God did through him among you" (Acts 2:22). "Moses said, the Lord your God will raise up a prophet like me; him you must hear in everything that he may say to you" (Acts 3:22, apparently regarded as fulfilled in the preaching and teaching of Jesus). *(c)* His death. "He was delivered up by the determinate counsel and foreknowledge of God, and you, by the agency of men without the law, killed him by crucifixion" (2:23). "You caused him to be arrested, and denied him before Pilate, when he had decided to acquit him. You denied the Holy and Righteous One, and asked for a murderer to be granted to you, while you killed the Prince of Life" (3:13-14). *(d)* His resurrection. "God raised him up, having loosed the pangs of death, because it was not possible for him to be held by it. For David says with reference to him, 'Thou wilt not leave my soul in Hades, nor give thy Holy One to see corruption'" (2:24-31). "God raised him from the dead, whereof we are witnesses" (3:15). "Jesus of Nazareth, whom you crucified, whom God raised from the dead" (4:10).

Thirdly, by virtue of the resurrection, Jesus has been exalted at the right hand of God, as messianic head of the new Israel. "Being exalted at the right hand of God" . . . "God has made him Lord and Christ" (2:33-36). "The God of our fathers has glorified his servant Jesus" (3:13). "He is the stone which was rejected by you builders, and has become the top of the corner" (4:11, citing Ps. 118:22). . . . . Fourthly, the Holy Spirit in the church is the sign of Christ's present power and glory. "Being exalted at the right hand of God, and having received the promise of the Holy Spirit from the Father, he poured out this which you see and hear" (Acts 2:33). This is documented from Joel 2:28-32 (Acts 2:17-21). . . .

Fifthly, the messianic age will shortly reach its consummation in the return of Christ. "That he may send the messiah appointed beforehand for you, Jesus, whom heaven must receive until the times of the restoration of all things, of which God spoke through the mouth of his prophets from of old" (3:20-21). This is the only passage in Acts 1-4 which speaks of the second advent of Christ. In Acts 10 this part of the *kerygma* is presented in these terms: "This is he who is appointed by God as judge of living and dead" (10:42). There is no other explicit reference to Christ as judge in these speeches.

Finally, the *kerygma* always closes with an appeal for repentance, the offer of forgiveness and of the Holy Spirit, and the promise of "salvation," that is, of "the life of the age to come," to those who enter the elect community. "Repent and be baptized, each of you, upon the name of Jesus Christ for the remission of your sins, and you will receive the gift of the Holy Spirit. For the promise is for you and your children, and for all those far off, whom the Lord your God may call" (Acts 2:38-39, referring to Joel 2:32; Isa. 57:19). "Repent therefore and be converted for the blotting out of your sins. . . . You are the sons of the prophets and of the covenant which God made with your fathers, saying to Abraham, 'And in thy seed shall all families of the earth be blessed.' For you in the first place God raised up his servant Jesus and sent him to bless you by turning each of you away from your sins" (Acts 3:19, 25-26, citing Gen. 12:3). "In no other is there salvation, for there is no other name under heaven given among men by which you must be saved" (Acts 4:12).

✳   ✳   ✳

In this survey of the apostolic preaching and its developments two facts have come into view: first, that within the New Testament there is an immense range of variety in the interpretation that is given to the *kerygma;* and, secondly, that in all such interpretation the essential elements of the original *kerygma* are steadily kept in view. Indeed, the farther we move from the primitive modes of expression, the more decisively is the central purport of it affirmed. With all the diversity of the New Testament writings, they form a unity in their proclamation of the one gospel.

At a former stage of criticism, the study of the New Testament was vitalized by the recognition of the individuality of its various writers and their teachings. The results of this analytical stage of criticism are of permanent value. With these results in mind, we can now do fuller justice to the rich many-sidedness of the central gospel which is expressed in the whole. The present task of New Testament criticism, as it seems to me, is the task of synthesis. Perhaps, however, "synthesis" is not quite the right word, for it may imply the creation of unity out of originally diverse elements. But in the New Testament the unity is original. We have to explore, by a comparative study of the several writings, the common faith which evoked them, and which they aimed at interpreting to an ever-widening public. . . .

There is one further part of the task, to which in these lectures I have done no more than allude, and that is, to ascertain the relation between the apostolic preaching and that of Jesus Christ himself. I have said something about it elsewhere. I will here only state my belief that it will be found that the primitive *kerygma* arises directly out of the teaching of Jesus about the kingdom of God and all that hangs upon it; but that it does only partial justice to the range and depth of his teaching, and needs the Pauline and Johannine interpretations before it fully rises to the height of the great argument. It is in the Fourth Gospel, which in form and expression, as probably in date, stands farthest from the original tradition of the teaching, that we have the most penetrating exposition of its central meaning.

In conclusion, I would offer some brief reflections upon the relation of this discussion to the preaching of Christianity in our own time.

What do we mean by preaching the gospel? At various times and in different circles the gospel has been identified with this or that element in the general complex of ideas broadly called Christian; with the promise of immortality, with a particular theory of the atonement, with the idea of "the fatherhood of God and the brotherhood of man," and so forth. What the gospel was, historically speaking, at the beginning, and during the New Testament period, I hope these lectures have in some measure defined. No Christian of the first century had any doubt what it was, or any doubt of its relevance to human need. How far can it be preached in the twentieth century?

A well-known New Testament scholar has expressed the opinion that "the modern man does not believe in any form of salvation known to ancient Christianity" [Kirsopp Lake, *Landmarks in the History of Early Christianity* (New York: Macmillan, 1922), p. 77]. It is indeed clear that the primitive formulation of the gospel in eschatological terms is as strange as it could well be to our minds. It is no wonder that it has taken a long time, and stirred up much controversy, to reach the frank conclusion that the preaching of the early church, and of Jesus himself, had its being in this strange world of thought. For many years we strove against this conclusion. We tried to believe that criticism could prune away from the New Testament those elements in it which seemed to us fantastic, and leave us with an original "essence of Christianity," to which the modern man could say, "This is what I have always thought." But the attempt has failed. At the center of it all lies this alien, eschatological gospel, completely out of touch, as it seems, with our ways of thought.

But perhaps it was not much less out of touch with the thought of the Hellenistic world to which the earliest missionaries appealed. Paul at least found that the gospel had in it an element of "foolishness" and "scandal" for his public. But he and others succeeded in reinterpreting it to their contemporaries in terms which made its essential relevance and truth clear to their minds. It is this process of reinterpretation that we have been studying. Some similar process is clearly demanded of the preachers of the gospel in our time. If the primitive "eschatological" gospel is remote from our thought, there is much in Paul and John which as it stands is almost equally remote, and their reinterpretations, profound and conclusive though they are, do not absolve us from our task.

But the attempt at reinterpretation is always in danger of becoming something quite different; that which Paul called, "preaching another Jesus and another gospel." We have seen that the great thinkers of the New Testament period, while they worked out bold, even daring ways of restating the original gospel, were so possessed by its fundamental convictions that their restatements are true to its first intention. Under all variations of form, they continued to affirm that in the events out of which the Christian church arose there was a conclusive act of God, who in them visited and redeemed his people; and that in the corporate experience of the church itself there was revealed a new quality of life, arising out of what God had done, which in turn corroborated the value set upon the facts.

The real problem for the student of the New Testament is not whether this or that incident in the life of Jesus is credibly reported, this or that saying rightly attributed to him; nor yet whether such and such a doctrine in Paul or John can be derived from Judaism or the "mystery religions." It is, whether the fundamental affirmations of the apostolic preaching are true and relevant. We cannot answer this question without understanding the preaching, nor understand it without painstaking study of material which in some of its forms is strange and elusive; but without answering this question, we cannot confidently claim the name of Christian for that which we preach. To select from the New Testament certain passages which seem to have a "modern" ring, and to declare that these represent the "permanent element" in it, is not necessarily to preach the gospel. It is, moreover, easy to be mistaken, on a superficial reading, about the true meaning of passages which may strike us as congenial. Some of them may not be as "modern" as they sound. The discipline of confronting the gospel of primitive Christianity, in those forms of statement which are least congenial to the modern mind, compels us to re-think, not only the gospel, but our own prepossessions.

It is for this reason that I conceive the study of the New Testament, from the standpoint I have indicated, to be of extreme importance just now. I do not suggest that the crude early formulation of the gospel is our exclusive standard. It is only in the light of its development all through the New Testament that we learn how much is implied in it. But I would urge that the study of the Synoptic Gospels should be more than an exercise in the historical critic's art of fixing the irreducible minimum of bare fact in the record; and that the study of Paul and John should be more than either a problem in comparative religion or the first chapter in a history of dogma. Gospels and Epistles alike offer a field of study in which the labor of criticism and interpretation may initiate us into the "many-sided wisdom" which was contained in the apostolic preaching, and make us free to declare it in contemporary terms to our own age.

DIETRICH BONHOEFFER

The Proclaimed Word

At about the same time that C. H. Dodd was lecturing at King's College, London, Dietrich Bonhoeffer (1906-1945) was directing the tiny Confessing Church seminary at Finkenwalde and offering a course in homiletics. Seminary life included daily worship and Bonhoeffer's active participation in the hearing and critiquing of sermons. *Hearing* the word of God even in the most unaccomplished effort was as important as artful proclamation. At Finkenwalde Bonhoeffer reassessed the ground of homiletics, moving from ecclesiology to radical Christology. The sermon neither contains the word of God nor points to the Lord. In its entirety it *is* the incarnate yet often hidden Christ and is thus clothed in Christ's own humility and power. It participates in the same God who, as Bonhoeffer says elsewhere, allows himself to be pushed out of the world and onto a cross. Such a word cannot be *made* relevant or validated by the preacher's experience. Given his radical view of the incarnation (and preaching) in 1937, Bonhoeffer's shift to so-called religionless language in 1944-45 is far from abrupt. His *Homiletics* of 1937 prepared the way for the following prediction in a sermon written from prison in 1944: "It is not for us to prophesy the day (though the day will come) when men will once more be called so to utter the word of God that the world will be changed and renewed by it. It will be a new language, perhaps quite non-religious, but liberating and redeeming — as was Jesus' language; it will shock people and yet overcome them by its power; it will be the language of a new righteousness and truth, proclaiming God's peace with men and the coming of his kingdom" (*Letters and Papers from Prison* [New York: Macmillan, 1953], p. 300).

Dietrich Bonhoeffer, *Worldly Preaching*, ed. Clyde E. Fant (Nashville and New York: Thomas Nelson Inc., 1975), pp. 123-30.

Historical Considerations

The New Testament contains several expressions for preaching: *kerussein, euaggelizein, -esthai, didaskein, marturein, presbeuein,* each with its own distinctive emphasis. *Kerussein* refers to public proclamation, such as the announcements of an ancient herald on a foreign assignment. It suggests an element of newness, the announcing of something that has not been heard before. *Euaggelizein* expresses more strongly its connection with the subject matter of proclamation, with the joyful content of the message, the *euaggelion.* Its similarity to the word *aggelos,* or messenger, underscores the element of mission in the message and indicates that we allow ourselves to become the bearers of good news. It is in this spirit that the preacher should enter the pulpit, as the messenger from Marathon with his exultant cry — "The victory is won!"

Didaskein and *didache* suggest the content of the message, the clear facts of the case, the report of something worth knowing. *Kerussein* and *euaggelizesthai* are related to the mission sermon or to evangelistic preaching. *Didaskein* connotes the building up of an existing congregation through daily instruction in previously unknown doctrine. *Marturein* and *marturia* suggest the testimony of Jesus before Pilate, as well as the testimony of Timothy before many witnesses. These two words connote the closest possible relationship between the proclamation and its proclaimer; in other words, that as I preach, I allow myself to become a witness for something else, something outside of myself — but nevertheless that the witness that I give is also my own, my personal testimony. In these words the distinction between ministry and person is the least suggested. This concept is found often in Acts and in the Pastoral Epistles, in which the separation of ministry and person moves completely into the background. "Perform your ministry, that you may be saved" (1 Tim. 4:16). Only in one place, 2 Timothy 2:9, is the separation noticeable. Reformation theology differs somewhat in this respect.

Homilein in the New Testament does not refer to public preaching but rather to speaking confidentially with one another. (For example, the conversation of the disciples at Emmaus, Luke 24:14-15; 1 Cor. 15:33.) Only later, in the seventeenth century, did this expression come to be the designation for the science of preaching (homiletics).

Besides the public *kerygma,* private assembly of Christians in homes was practiced in early Christianity (Acts 2:46, and in other places). In these small circles the actual practice of preaching to a congregation began. The first evidence for such services stems from Justin Martyr. After the reading of a text (probably the *lectio continua*), an elder of the congregation addressed a short exhortation to the gathered congregation. This exhortation later became the homily, which had the purpose of warning the congregation against false teachings. The first preserved homily is known as the Second Epistle of Clement. The homily then became an exposition of Scripture in connection with the reading of a text, and thus the sermon was born. By the time of Origen the homily was no longer a speech before a closed circle of Christians, but catechumens and heathen as well were allowed to attend this part of the assembly. Under Origen, however, the "secret discipline" also began, that is, the holding of a private meeting to receive the sacraments and to recite the confession of faith (the creed) and the Lord's Prayer. This closed meeting was begun to provide protection for the church against the mockery of the world. The sermon then became separated from this inner worship service; it was conducted publicly so that catechumens and heathen could attend. It should be noticed, however, that in the New Testament the possibility of the admittance of the heathen to preaching was already considered (1 Cor. 14:23).

After the time of Origen the simple sermon developed into the artistic homily, that is, into synthetic sermon arrangement or theme-preaching. The thematic sermon is one in which a subject is set forth as well as a text; as, for example, in the early sermons concerning Mary, the great saints, or specific matters of interest to the congregation. Examples of thematic preaching are to be found in the preaching of the Church Fathers. . . .

Preaching has the dual objectives of establishing the Christian congregation and building it up. In the early centuries the separation of believers and unbelievers in worship was clear and meaningful, and this division at first did not represent any particular problem for these objectives of preaching. The matter first became problematical under Constantine and with the development of the mission, or evangelistic, sermon. Even today we are still occupied with the proper connection between the missionary and congregational character of the sermon. Schleiermacher saw the sermon as an expression of the religious self-awareness of the preacher and a presentation of the pious convictions of the congregation, as if there really were such; he consciously ignored any empirical evidence. The Church of England has lost hundreds of thousands of members to the Methodists because it no longer paid attention to these dual objectives of preaching, or else no longer distinguished between them, and quit evangelizing — or perhaps because it only taught in its preaching and presupposed a mindset in the congregation that was not there.

Our question now is how we may come to the proper kind of sermon, one in which both the establishment and the building up of the congregation may be accomplished, one in which *kerussein, didaskein, euaggelizesthai,* and *marturein* may be realized and kept in proper relationship to one another.

The Proclaimed Word

1. The proclaimed word has its origin in the incarnation of Jesus Christ. It neither originates from a truth once perceived nor from personal experience. It is not the reproduction of a specific set of feelings. Nor is the word of the sermon the outward form for the substance which lies behind it. The proclaimed word is the incarnate Christ himself. As little as the incarnation is the outward shape of God, just so little does the proclaimed word present the outward form of a reality; rather, it is the thing itself. The preached Christ is both the Historical One and the Present One. (Kähler: the preached Christ is the so-called historical Jesus.) He is the access to the historical Jesus. Therefore the proclaimed word is not a medium of expression for something else, something which lies behind it, but rather it is the Christ himself walking through his congregation as the word.

2. In the incarnation the Word became flesh. God, the Son, took on human form. So he accepts all of mankind and bears it in himself, in that he is fleshly. He embraces the whole of humanity with its genuinely sinful nature. That he wears this humanness is the whole mystery of the Gospels. It is not enough to say that he suffers with mankind — he actually takes mankind upon himself. It is false to say that the Logos accepted, that is, adopted, man; instead, he has taken on human nature, my nature and your nature. His flesh is our flesh and our flesh is his flesh. This also means that in the incarnation the new mankind is established. Mankind has become one through the incarnation. The congregation is already present in the embodied Christ; his body is "we ourselves." The church is included in the incarnation as the *sanctorum communio.*

3. The proclaimed word is the Christ bearing human nature. This word is no new incarnation, but the Incarnate One who bears the sins of the world. Through the Holy Spirit this word becomes the actualization of his acceptance and sustenance. The word of the sermon intends to accept mankind, nothing else. It wants to bear the whole of human nature. In the congregation all sins should be cast upon the word. Preaching must be so done that the hearer places all of his needs, cares, fears, and sins upon the word. The word accepts all of these things. When preaching is done in this way, it is the proclamation of Christ. This proclamation of the Christ does not regard its primary responsibility to be giving advice, arousing emotions, or stimulating the will — it will do these things, too — but its intention is to sustain us. The word is there that burdens might be laid upon it. We are all borne up by the word of Christ. Because it does so, it creates fellowship. Because the word includes us into itself, it makes of us members of the body of Christ. As such we share in the responsibility of upholding one another. Thus the word of Christ also presupposes Christian

brotherhood. The word intends that no one should remain alone, for in him no one remains alone. The word makes individuals part of one body.

4. Word and congregation. Because the word conveys the new humanity, by its very nature it is always directed toward the congregation. It seeks community, it needs community, because it is already laden with humanity. At this point it is significant to notice that the word produces its own momentum. It proceeds from itself toward the congregation in order to sustain it. The preacher does not therefore accomplish the application of the word; he is not the one who shapes it and forms it to suit the congregation. With the introduction of the biblical word the text begins moving among the congregation. Likewise the word arises out of the Bible, takes shape as the sermon, and enters into the congregation in order to bear it up. This self-movement of the word to the congregation should not be hindered by the preacher, but rather he should acknowledge it. He should not allow his own efforts to get in its way. If we attempt to give impetus to the word, then it becomes distorted into words of instruction or education or experience. As such it can no longer uphold the congregation nor sustain it. Upon Christ, however, who is the proclaimed word, should fall all of the need, the sin, and death of the congregation.

5. The form of the proclaimed word. The form of the preached word is different from every other form of speech. Other speeches are structured so that they have some truth which they wish to communicate either behind them or beneath them or over them, or else they are arranged so as to express an emotion or teach a concept. These human words communicate something else besides what they are of themselves. They become means to an end. The meaning of the proclaimed word, however, does not lie outside of itself; it is the thing itself. It does not transmit anything else, it does not express anything else, it has no external objectives — rather, it communicates that it is itself: the historical Jesus Christ, who bears humanity upon himself with all of its sorrows and its guilt. The sustaining Christ is the dimension of the preached word. The biblical content of the proclaimed word makes clear this distinction from all other forms of speech. Cultic expressions only make it unclear. How can our words again become the proclaimed word in this original sense?

6. The unique dignity of the word. The promise to be able to accept men and sustain them has been given to the spoken word. Nothing is equal in dignity to the spoken word. As the Logos has adopted human nature, so the spoken word actualizes our adoption. It is *that word* which the Logos honors, not some magical transaction. Therefore our adoption is not a matter of some kind of psychi-magical act through which we are adopted and included into Christ. What really happens is that we are accepted through the clearly heard and understood word of Christ. Cult and liturgy can therefore only serve as adoration,

celebration, and praise of the clearly spoken word of God. Proclamation, therefore, in the strictest sense, does not issue from cultic ritual but from the testimony of the word. Liturgy and cultic acts serve proclamation. In the proclaimed word, according to the promise, Christ enters into his congregation which in its liturgy adores him, calls unto him, and awaits him. In the proclaimed word Christ is alive as the word of the Father. In the proclaimed word he receives the congregation unto himself. Through the Word the world was created. The Word became incarnate. The incarnate Word continues to exist for us in the Scripture. Through the Holy Spirit, the incarnate Word comes to us from the Scripture in the sermon. And it is one and the same word: the word of creation, the word of the incarnation, the word of the Holy Scripture, the word of the sermon. It is the creating, accepting, and reconciling word of God, for whose sake the world exists.

7. Because we were created by the word and are daily kept by it, because we have been reconciled through the word before we knew it, therefore only through this word are we able to recognize God. Through this word we find certainty. This word alone affects our will. Only this word keeps on being clear to us in its accusations and its promises. Only this word makes us without excuse. Music and symbols (as the Berneuchen movement believed) do not make us without excuse; they are not unequivocal and do not break down the will! Music and symbols do not create the *anthropos pneumatikos* [spiritual person], but likely the *psychikos* [soulful, personal]. The word, however, conveys the Spirit and does accomplish this. With cultic endeavors we are in danger of wanting to add something to the preached word, of attempting to lend a particular style of expression to it. But it may not be and does not need to be so undergirded. The word of the sermon is not one species of the genus "word," but rather it is just the opposite: all of our words are species of the one, original word of God which both creates and sustains the world.

For the sake of the proclaimed word the world exists with all of its words. In the sermon the foundation for a new world is laid. Here the original word becomes audible. There is no evading or getting away from the spoken word of the sermon; nothing releases us from the necessity of this witness, not even cult or liturgy. Everything revolves about the accepting and sustaining witness of Christ. This is the way we must learn to look at the sermon again.

8. While the word accepts and sustains us, there is nevertheless no fusion of God's being with ours, no identification of the godly nature with human nature. The word accepts and bears us in that he forgives sin and keeps us in the commandments of God. The relationship of the word to us is one of providing forgiveness and assurance along the pathways of our lives. There is no mystical metamorphosis which occurs, but rather faith and sanctification.

9. The sacrament of the word *(Sacramentum verbi)*. Because the word is the Christ accepting men, it is full of grace but also full of judgment. Either we will let ourselves be accepted and be forgiven and be borne up by Christ, or we remain unaccepted. If we ignore the spoken word of the sermon, then we ignore the living Christ. There is a sacrament of the word.

10. Therefore the preacher needs to approach the sermon with the utmost certainty. The word of Scripture is certain, clear, and plain. The preacher should be assured that Christ enters the congregation through those words which he proclaims from the Scripture. Luther could say that the preacher did not have to pray the fifth request of the Lord's Prayer after his sermon ["Forgive us our trespasses"]. The sermon should not leave the preacher despairing and perplexed, but rather it should make him joyful and certain.

CARL MICHALSON

Communicating the Gospel

Carl Michalson (1915-1965) was professor of systematic theology in the Theological School of Drew University, where he maintained a lively interest in preaching. He was not concerned with technical homiletics but with preaching as the essential bearer of Christian meaning. He came to this "high" view of preaching by way of his own radically historical theology with its universal, biblical, existential, and eschatological dimensions. Following Bultmann and the school of the New Hermeneutic, he made a sharp distinction between the events of world history, or outer history, and the meaning of history for the person, or inner history. Michalson believed that the only language capable of bringing coherence to these is the language of Jesus, who as a genuinely historical figure and the source of history's meaning can be understood as the "hinge of history." Likewise the message of Jesus participates in both these worlds; it affords the only clue to what is normative in our preaching. As the following selection makes clear, the preached gospel addresses the ultimate concerns of its hearers. It expands upon the narrative kerygma, crystalized by Dodd and others, confronting death, alienation, anxiety, and all other human regions that await the resurrection of meaning. Contemporary preaching, then, is not concerned with proving the historical Jesus or reciting historical or dogmatic facts about him. Rather, it strives to reactivate the language of the gospel in such a way that preaching may once again be true to Jesus and therefore to history in all its dimensions. Michalson owed much to Luther, Kierkegaard, Bultmann, and the existentialists, but, with regard to the *language* of the gospel, his work was begun by the prisoner, Bonhoeffer.

Carl Michalson, "Communicating the Gospel," *Theology Today* 14, no. 3 (October 1957): 321-33.

The gospel is the story of God's turning to man in Jesus of Nazareth. In a single report it tells us to whom we really belong and saves us from being lost. Part of the gospel is the good news that God has appointed a people called the church for the purpose of enjoying the story and telling it to others. It is as if Christians have witnessed a mysterious event. God has turned to man in Jesus of Nazareth, and Christians are those who have seen that this is what Jesus was about. From now on, what others will know about that event depends on whether or not some witness is willing to testify. A Christian is one who acknowledges that God has turned to man in Jesus and who takes upon himself the responsibility of turning to the world with that report. Hence, to be a Christian is to be involved in the problem of the communication of the gospel.

How, then, shall we turn to the world? The best answers to that question are to be found in the nature of the message itself. One appeals in vain to methods of communication if they are not enlightened by the message. Public relations bureaus can catalogue every soft spot in the public's sales resistance and never have a positive suggestion for Christian communication. Writers may know every literary strategy from Aeschylus to Yeats and yet be powerless to evoke an act of Christian faith. Artists may be able to see beneath the surface of ordinary affairs to the turbulence and formlessness beneath, yet lack the authority to say, "Peace, be still," or the one perspective that makes "all things cohere." Before the physicist Helmholtz could arrive at the nature of vision, he had to do more than study the human eye. He had to study the properties of light. Similarly, the clue to the strategy of Christian communication is best found in the nature of the message itself.

The gospel is the good news about who God is and to whom therefore we belong. As such it speaks to our needs and longing from out of the ultimate depth of reality. It is easy to be misled about the meaning of the gospel by the fact that the first four books of the New Testament are named "Gospels." The four Gospels appear to be narrations of the history of Jesus' life and teachings, so that the word "gospel" takes on the connotation of a short historical narrative. The Gospels are not so much histories, however, as they are propaganda contrived to elicit faith in Jesus as the revealer of God. They engage in evangelism, not biography. "These are written that you may believe that Jesus is the Christ, the Son of God, and that believing you may have life in his name" (John 20:31).

The communication of the gospel is not directed, then, to just any old question people happen to be asking. It is directed to the question about the ultimate meaning of life and a man's relation to it. As Gabriel Marcel has observed, one can spend a whole day in an art museum and appreciate nothing if he has asked the wrong questions. "Will I recognize these paintings when I see them again?" "Is this a profitable experience I am having?" The realm of beauty and meaning is dumb before such queries. A schoolboy may simply study the answers at the back of his book, as Kierkegaard points out. But he should know that in the process he will never learn to solve a problem.

People who are confronting the message of Christianity with questions which the gospel is not really attempting to answer, or digging out answers to questions which they themselves have not yet asked, violate a basic condition for Christian communication: namely, the truth about God and the truth about man involve each other.

But human questions which do not pertain to the mystery of man's ultimate significance will never open the way for the coming of the divine answers. Cervantes' Don Quixote may not be any nearer the kingdom of heaven simply by virtue of his painful sense of being a stranger in this world, nor Dostoevsky's Ivan by virtue of his burdening sense of guilt. But at least the gospel can be addressed to such questions. The gospel is God's answer to questions of a certain quality. "What must I do to be saved?" "Who will deliver me from the body of this death?" "Why am I something and not nothing?"

It would be sheer vanity, then, to attempt to accommodate the gospel answer to other kinds of questions. It would be roughly parallel to attempting to solve lessons in French grammar by solutions at the back of an algebra text. Christians can be made to feel needlessly stupid by their quandary in the presence of the kinds of questions others raise. "Can you prove it?" "What makes you think it's better than other faiths?" "How could God create the world in six days?" "Is the Bible the inspired word of God?" "Is a belief in bodily resurrection something we can hold today?" Christians can invent answers to any of these questions. But the answers are usually not gospel, for they do not communicate the knowledge of who God is and to whom therefore man belongs.

Not all questions are equally deserving of answers. Questions asked from mere curiosity or intellectual acquisitiveness are not the questions which draw upon the wisdom of the Christian message. Some answer to such questions should probably be given, if only in the interests of fair play. However, both parties of the dialogue should know to what extent they are putting off the real issue. The gospel is the answer to the question men ought to be asking because of their destiny as men. And as Kierkegaard has said, it is untrue to answer a question in a medium in which it has not been asked. How ironical, then, for a Christian to prepare himself as a debater in the interests of the promulgation of the Christian faith, only to discover his vocation to be more that of the town crier. Or consider the irony of training the Christian witness in the arts of persuasion, only to discover it is the task of the witness not to convince his hearers but to "transport them out of themselves" (Longinus).

THE GOSPEL is the good news about God and man which comes in a certain form, the form of proclamation. Now proclamation is basically an auditory phenomenon. The witness or the preaching is an appeal more to the ear than to the eye. It was the apostle Paul who laid down this formula. "How are they to believe in him of whom they have never heard? . . . So faith comes from what is heard, and what is heard comes by the preaching of Christ" (Rom. 10:14, 17). Or, as Luther says it in his commentary on this passage, "Faith is an acoustical affair." Peter verified the method when he claimed that it was "*by my mouth* the Gentiles should hear the word of the gospel and believe." . . .

What, then, does one proclaim when he communicates the gospel? The New Testament does not leave us in doubt about that. Everywhere the apostles were saying substantially the same thing. They were uttering short, terse, summary statements about the significance of the appearance of Jesus of Nazareth as the Christ. "The God of our fathers raised Jesus whom you killed by hanging him on a tree. God exalted him at his right hand as leader and savior, to give repentance to Israel and forgiveness of sins. And we are witnesses to these things, and so is the Holy Spirit whom God has given to those who obey him" (Acts 5:30-32). The rather extensive history of the short life of Jesus was summarized in just such pithy proclamations, called in the Greek language, *kerygma.*

By now the meaning of the Christian faith extends itself into vast and voluminous accounts which occupy great lengths of shelf space. Yet it is known that the rudiments of communication are present in these early reductions. The task of the theologian is to sift through the voluminous account for the authentic kerygma. The task of the witness is to proclaim the kerygma.

Such an emphasis on the summation of the gospel in short sentences could, of course, convey a false impression. While the witness of the church took the form of propositions, with acoustical concomitants, essentially the communication was not the spoken word but the event of speaking the word. The revelation of God came originally in the event of Jesus of Nazareth preaching himself as the revelation of God. Judged by any ordinary standard, Jesus was not different from anyone else. But Jesus himself provided the standard by which to judge who he was; for example, Luke 4:18 and 21. Jesus came preaching himself as the preacher, as the revealer, as the truth. Jesus came as the event in which God turns decisively to his people. His words are a part of that larger but more significant event which is Jesus as the Word of God. Everything recorded in the Gospels is a reflection of this basic gospel, as dewdrops on grass record the simplicity of the rising sun. It is possible to read the Gospels and to become enamored of the details of Jesus' amazing life. But that could be to miss the synoptic event which is his very significance as revealer of God.

When the friends and followers of Francis Xavier sorted through his letters with the intention of collecting them in a single memorial volume, they hit upon a device reminiscent of the apostolic preaching. They cut the letters in pieces and arranged them in the form of a cross. In this same way, embracing the events and sayings of the life and ministry of Jesus there is the single event of his witness to the truth that in him God was turning decisively to man. The Bible catches this event in short phrases which, when sounded through God's vocal apparatus in the church, renew the event. "Jesus is Lord!" "Christ died for our sins." "The word became flesh and dwelt among us, full of grace and truth." "God was in Christ reconciling the world unto himself."

Now God has entrusted to us the message of reconciliation. "So we are ambassadors for Christ, God making his appeal through us" (2 Cor. 5:19, 20). The event of God's revelation in Christ which is the gospel, continues to take place among us when the people of God witness to that event. The witness is itself an event in which God turns again to his people, drawing them into the new age of his presence. The emphasis in the witness is not upon the voluminous account, but upon the fidelity to the vocation as witness.

When Jesus preached himself as the revelation of the Father, the saving event took place in which men knew who God is and to whom therefore they belong. The emphasis here is not upon extensive intellectual content requiring studied consideration, nor upon ideas. Ideas can be pigeonholed. The emphasis is upon a sudden breaking through of divine illumination into the human scene. To that one can only react with the decision of obedience or disobedience. A man's destiny hangs upon his decision.

There is more communication of the gospel in the event of the witness to the lordship of Christ than in theories about Christ's nature. There is more communication of the gospel in the act of preaching than in the content of the sermon. The gospel is communicated more efficiently in the fact of the church's existence than in statements about the nature of the church. And there is more gospel in the phenomenon of a Bible than in the defense of its authority.

Someone recently gave my son a compass. I see it almost anywhere around the house amid the rest of our clutter. Nothing in our house seems to stay in the same place, not even that compass. But the compass always seems to know where it is. Every time I see it, it is pointing in the same direction. This is the impressive thing about the Christian witness. In a world of voluminous accounts and miscellaneous directions it is the event which, wherever it occurs, signifies the polar event in the destiny of man. No man is irremediably lost so long as there is a Christian witness. And now that there is, men who seek God through other media "are like mariners who voyaged before the invention of the compass" (John Donne).

WHAT IS being suggested here is that there is more communication of the gospel in the steady, faithful witness of the worshiping community — in its reading of the Scriptures, its conduct of the sacraments, and its unending chain of prayer — than there is in the effort to establish beachheads for the Christian message on the soil of alien faiths and philosophies. There is more justification for such a position than has yet met the eye. For the Christian gospel is not simply good news which must be proclaimed to be heard. It is *new* news. The gospel is a *new testament,* related to the old not as something more recent but as something *different.* If it were simply more recent chronologically, there would scarcely be any point at this late date in considering it as something new. However, the gospel still remains new, in the sense of shockingly different. The gospel should still be expected to meet with the reaction it evoked in its earliest form: the sense of scandal, paradox, enmity, and mystery. . . .

The gospel itself provides for the possibility of its own understanding. Therefore, one does not testify to others with the expectation that their prior acquaintance with the subject will help them understand. One rather testifies with the expectation that what he is saying is providing the conditions for the very understanding of the truth.

And what if others still do not understand? Here the temptations are perilously distressing. In desperation or, what is worse, embarrassment, you panic and step outside the language of your faith for the explanation of your faith. In the act, you lose the very hope one has of understanding you. What do you do if you have just played your original composition and no one understands it? Do you give a lecture on modern music? If you are communicatively efficient, you will simply play it again — not in despair, but joyfully, for you know that the hope for its understanding is in the playing of it, not in abstract explanations. . . . The communication of the Christian gospel continually waits upon the breaking in of illumination where darkness formerly prevailed. And every time it happens, it is a miracle of the moment.

THE GOSPEL, which is the good news proclaimed by Christians as something new every day, is at the same time the once-for-all news (Rom. 6:10; Heb. 7:27). It is the *final* edition. One who hears it should have the same sensations once felt when hearing the voice of a newsboy cracking the night with the latest headline on the war, the elections, or the fights.

If the once-for-all character of the Christian gospel were tied to the sheer fact of a happening in the past, it would be a bit difficult for the Christian communication to sound up-to-the-minute. The truth is, as Luther said, that the gospel is not historical in the sense of a picture which hangs on the wall. It is more like what is known in Marcel Proust's *Remembrance of Things Past* as the "metaphoric memory." It does for time what time does for space: transcends it. Time is telescoped in such a way as to make the event of God's turning to us in Christ a reality of the present moment. The gospel, then, is once-for-all, not in the sense of being located in the irrevocable and irrecoverable past, not in the sense that it can never be repeated. It is final in the sense that it is so full and complete that it can never be rivaled or superseded.

It is fortunate for the Christian witness that this is so. For the event of the witness depends to a great extent on the use of words, and words suffer by the passage of time. Take, for instance, Hegel's illustration. At this moment I jot down the sentence, "Now it is night!" How does this sentence sound when read tomorrow morning? The meaning of the sentence has suffered by the passage of time. But then how do the once-for-all passages in the New Testament sound when put to the same test? "Now is the accepted time!" "I am the way, the truth, and the life." To say that the gospel is the final news is to say that time never stales this event. It is historical in a very unusual sense: not that it is done for, once for all, in the past; it is the repeatable event *par excellence*.

But if the gospel is final in this sense, its language is cast less in the matrix of chronological history and more in the dynamics of present address. The event of God's turning to us in Christ, when expressed propositionally, would sound less like "Washington crossed the Delaware" and more like "I love you." The gospel is the final news in the sense in which a wedding ceremony is final: you date it, as you date Washington's crossing the Delaware; but you commit your future, as in the marriage covenant, and you keep the commitment up-to-date by the repetition of the covenant in daily whispers of self-surrender.

Nor is the gospel final in the sense of being the last truth, as if one thereafter need not seek further for truth. It is not all the news there is; it is simply the best news, the saving truth. For it is the beginning of all truth. It is the perspective that redeems all other truth for us. It is the source and orientation of the meaning of the other truths we hold. Hence, a Christian is not one who deliberately blinds his eyes to the existence of other truths because he has the once-for-all truth. The finality of the Christian truth is rather to him as a lens by which all other truth comes into meaningful focus and coherence. The Christian student does not abandon the university library because he has the truth. The truth in Christ becomes a reading-glass which brings the deceptively fragmentary perspectives of a university library into a single focus.

The net results of witnessing to the final news will be the evoking of decision. The preaching of the gospel requires decision (Rom. 10:16). When this news is heard, filibuster is ruled out and the time for decision is at hand. In the presence of the sudden illumination of the gospel one cannot respond as a character in a Chekhov play, longing wistfully but never acting. "No one who puts his hand to the plow and looks back is fit for the kingdom of God" (Luke 9:62). . . .

FINALLY, the gospel to which Christians witness is official news. It is not invented out of the top of the head and it does not spring from the current situation. It is as venerable as the apostolic witness. The history of the living church is the history of the will to maintain continuity with that witness. When one is called to witness to the gospel, he is called into a community of interpretation which presupposes an entire history of Christian witness. And at the source of this history is the apostolic tradition, the official news, whose mark and authority resides in the way in which it recognizes that the good news is the event of God's turning to us in Jesus of Nazareth.

The meaning of this for Christian communication is not always fully appreciated. It is simply that Christians, for whom witness is an essential part of their lives, are called upon to witness not to their particular experience of the gospel, and least of all to their private opinions about what constitutes the truth. They are called upon in announcing Jesus as Lord to mingle their voices with the prophets and apostles. . . .

[T]he principal actor in Christian communication is not the witness who enunciates the word of truth, but the Spirit of the resurrected Christ who animates the word with life and meaning. If this were not the case, the little story which Kierkegaard tells would have the last word. There was once a circus which caught fire. The director of the circus sent his clown to tell the crowd about the fire. The people, hearing the report from the lips of a clown, believed he was just telling one of his jokes. So they simply sat there, a bit burned up over their inability to tell a prophet from a clown.

Part of the mystery of the gospel is that God always seems to choose some clown to bear witness to it. God, however, unlike the director of the circus, does not leave us clowns to go it alone. He has pledged to make himself heard through the standardized poverty of our vocabularies. When Jeremiah resisted God's call to be a witness, God caused an almond tree to spring up before him. The witness, like the tree, is rooted in vital forces that exceed his own inherent capacity. When Ezekiel was on the verge of saying "No" to God's invitation to a life of witness, God caused him to see wheels within wheels. A technological impossibility! But with God nothing is impossible. It seems paradoxical that God makes his Word known through human words. But that paradox is a paradigm of the power of the Spirit.

BARBARA BROWN TAYLOR

Preaching

"Whenever I hear about manna, I think of grits," says Barbara Brown Taylor as she begins her sermon "Bread of Angels." The comment functions as an introduction to the preacher as well as to her sermon, for it captures both her homiletical and her literary genius for grounding the biblical message in the ordinary experiences of life. Taylor, who formerly served as rector of Grace-Calvary Episcopal Church in Clarkesville, Georgia, currently holds the Harry R. Butman Chair in Religion and Philosophy at Piedmont College in Demorest, Georgia. She has written many books of sermons, including *Bread of Angels* and *Gospel Medicine,* as well as several books of lectures, including *The Luminous Web* (reflections on the relation of science and religion) and her Yale Beecher Lectures, *When God Is Silent.* Barbara Brown Taylor offers several alternatives to traditional pulpit eloquence. She does not attempt to be persuasive in the classical sense of stating a point and arguing vigorously in its defense. In place of "heroic," topical, or literary proofs, her Anglican spirituality dwells on the more universal apprehensions of God in nature and common life. If the traditional orator's skill tended to separate him from the audience, Taylor's style collapses the distance between speaker and audience by closely associating her quest for God with that of her hearers. Traditional homiletics drew formal distinctions between exegesis, exposition of the text, and its application. Taylor skillfully weaves the three into one elegant conversation from which insight never fails to emerge. She is not a narrative preacher or a storyteller, but a narrative *thinker* whose sermons trace the winding path of discovery through her own heart, the lives of her hearers, and on to the printed page.

Barbara Brown Taylor, *The Preaching Life* (Boston: Cowley, 1993), pp. 76-86.

Watching a preacher climb into the pulpit is a lot like watching a tightrope walker climb onto the platform as the drumroll begins. The first clears her throat and spreads out her notes; the second loosens his shoulder and stretches out one rosin-soled foot to test the taut rope. Then both step out into the air, trusting everything they have done to prepare for this moment as they surrender themselves to it, counting now on something beyond themselves to help them do what they love and fear and most want to do. If they reach the other side without falling, it is skill but it is also grace — a benevolent God's decision to let these daredevils tread the high places where ordinary mortals have the good sense not to go.

No other modern public speaker does what the preacher tries to do. The trial attorney has glossy photographs and bagged evidence to hand around; the teacher has blackboards and overhead projectors; the politician has brass bands and media consultants. All the preacher has is words. Climbing into the pulpit without props or sound effects, the preacher speaks — for ten or twenty or thirty minutes — to people who are used to being communicated with in very different ways. Most of the messages in our culture are sent and received in thirty seconds or less and no image on a television screen lasts more than twenty, yet a sermon requires sustained and focused attention. If the topic is not appealing, there are no other channels to be tried. If a phrase is missed, there is no replay button to be pressed. The sermon counts on listeners who will stay tuned to a message that takes time to introduce, develop, and bring to a conclusion. Listeners, for their part, count on a sermon that will not waste the time they give to it.

This is only one of the many ways in which the sermon proves to be a communal act, not the creation of one person but the creation of a body of people for whom and to whom one of them speaks. A congregation can make or break a sermon by the quality of their response to it. An inspired sermon can wind up skewered somewhere near the second pew by a congregation of people who sit with their arms crossed and their eyes narrowed, coughing and scuffing their feet as the preacher struggles to be heard. Similarly, a weak sermon can grow strong in the presence of people who attend carefully to it, leaning forward in their pews and opening their faces to a preacher from whom they clearly expect to receive good news.

If the preacher is also their priest and pastor, then the sermon is theirs in another way. The quality of their life together — the memories, conversations, experiences, and hopes they share — is the fabric from which the sermon is made. The preacher is their parson, their representative person, who never gets into the pulpit without them. Whatever else the sermon is about, it is first of all about them, because they are the community in whose midst the preacher stands. In a very real way, the preacher would have no voice without them. By calling someone to preach to them and by listening to that person week after week, a congregation gives their minister both the authority to speak and a relationship from which to speak, so that every sermon begins and ends with them.

If that sounds too narrow, let me say that I also believe every sermon begins and ends with God. Because the word of God is what a preacher wrestles with in the pulpit, and because it is a living word, every sermon is God's creation as well as the creation of the preacher and the congregation. All three participate in the making of it, with the preacher as their designated voice. It is a delicate job for the one in the pulpit, a balancing act between the text, the congregation, and the self. If the preacher leans too far one way, he will side with the text against the congregation and deliver a finger-pointing sermon from on high. If the preacher leans too far the other way, she will side with the congregation against the text and deliver a sermon that stops short of encountering God.

What is called for, instead, is a sermon that honors all of its participants, in which preachers speak in their own voices out of their own experience, addressing God on the congregation's behalf and — with great care and humility — the congregation on God's behalf. When I preach sometimes I feel like Cyrano de Bergerac in the pulpit, passing messages between two would-be lovers who want to get together but do not know how. The words are my own, but I do not speak for myself. Down in the bushes with a congregation who have elected me to speak for them, I try to put their longing into words, addressing the holy vision that appears on the moonlit balcony above our heads. Then the vision replies, and it is my job to repeat what I have heard, bringing the message back to the bushes for a response. As a preacher I am less a principal player than a go-between, a courier who serves both partners in this ancient courtship.

But I am also in love myself, which means that I am deeply involved in the messages I bear. I do not speak for myself, but I do. I am one of the crowd down in the bushes, and the longing I put into words is my own. When the holy vision speaks, it is my own heart that is pierced. While I may struggle to make sure that my response is true to those whom I represent, I cannot stay out of it myself. Every word I choose, every image, every rise in my voice reveals my own involvement in the message. That is why I have never understood preachers who claim to "stay out of" their sermons, preaching the word of God and the word of God alone. It is not possible, but there is no reason why it should be.

By choosing Christ to flesh out the word, God made a lasting decision in favor of incarnation. Those of us who are his body in the world need not shy away from the fact that our own flesh and blood continue to be where the word of God is made known. We are living libraries of God's word. Our stories are God's stories. Sometimes they are comedies and sometimes they are tragedies;

sometimes faith shines through them and other times they end in darkness, but every one of them bears witness to the truth of God's word. Preachers cannot "stay out of" their sermons any more than singers can stay out of their songs. Our words are embodied, which means we bring all that we are to their expression.

But this does not mean we are free to turn the sermon into personal show-and-tell time. Those of us who preach do so as representatives. We speak as members of a body and not for ourselves alone, which means that we may not dominate the sermon any more than we may be absent from it. When I speak out of my humanity, I want my listeners to recognize their own. When I say "I" from the pulpit, I want them to say, "Me too." The sermon is no place for a virtuoso performance; it is a place for believers to explore together their common experience before God. The stories I tell from the pulpit are not just "my" stories but "our" stories, which are God's stories too. The stool of my sermon rests evenly on those three legs. If any one of them is missing (or too long or too short), the whole thing will wobble and fall.

Preaching is, above all else, an act of faith. Every time I put a sermon together, I rehearse the reasons why and the ways in which I believe in God. Given the world we live in, the case cannot be made too often. Most of us would be hard pressed on Sunday morning to say whether we are in church because we believe or because we want to believe. Like the father of the epileptic boy in Mark's Gospel, we do both: "I believe; help my unbelief!" (9:24). The preacher balances on the round top of that semicolon along with the rest of the world. I cannot preach without belief, but neither can I preach without some experience of unbelief. Both are built into the human experience of the divine, and each tests the strength of the other. The movement of the sermon, like the movement of Christ in the world, is meant to lead from doubt to faith. We may begin by knocking on God's door, unsure whether anyone is now or has ever been at home, but when the door opens and we are led inside, doubt becomes moot. Our host takes it from us and hangs it in the closet with the dustpan and galoshes.

When the door opens in a sermon, it is because God has consented to be present. Sometimes it happens and sometimes it doesn't. When it does, there is no mistaking it. Fresh air pours into a stale room. Light crowds out all shadows. When it doesn't, that may have as much to do with our own failure to be present as with God's. Some preachers will pound away at a sermon without ever finding the handle to it, and some congregations will sit and stare at an open door without ever walking through it, but even our incompetence cannot shut God out for long. The living word of God is more able than we are. If we will remain with it, it will heal us, because God is in it.

Every preacher has a different routine for preparing a sermon. My own begins with a long sitting spell with an open Bible on my lap, as I read and read and read the text. What I am hunting for is the God in it, God for me and for my congregation at this particular moment in time. I am waiting to be addressed by the text by my own name, to be called out by it so that I look back at my human situation and see it from a new perspective, one that is more like God's. I am hoping for a moment of revelation I can share with those who will listen to me, and I am jittery, because I never know what it may show me. I am not in control of the process. It is a process of discovery, in which I run the charged rod of God's word over the body of my own experience and wait to see where the sparks will fly. Sometimes the live current is harder to find than others but I keep at it, knowing that if there is no electricity for me, there will be none for the congregation either.

This means that I never know ahead of time what I will preach. If I did, then my sermons would be little more than lessons, expositions of things I already know that I think my listeners ought to know too. While there are preachers who do this sort of thing well, I am not one of them. I do not want to scatter pearls of wisdom from the pulpit; I want to discover something fresh — even if I cannot quite identify it yet, even if it is still covered with twigs and mud. I want to haul it into the pulpit and show others what God has shown me, while I am still shaking with excitement and delight.

The process of discovery begins with the text. Whether I like it or not, I approach it believing that God is in it and I commence the long, careful discipline of panning for gold. There are translations to be compared, words to be studied, and puzzles to be solved. What is corban? How much is a talent? Where was Emmaus? More important, what did this passage mean to the one who first wrote it down? I am not free to pluck it out and use it in my own design. It has its own integrity. It is part of someone else's design, and the respectful preacher will work to discern its original meaning before imposing any other on it.

This is one of the hardest and most rewarding aspects of the job. We do not make sermons out of air: our creations, poor or brilliant as they may be, are always variations on someone else's theme. The main melody is always a given, and even when we launch into our own bold improvisations we are limited to a scale of eight notes. Our words are not ends in themselves; they exist to serve other words, which means that we never work alone. Sitting all by ourselves in our rooms with bitten pencils in our hands, we compose our sermons in partnership with all those who have done so before us. Together we explore the parameters of our common faith, testing the truth of one another's discoveries and holding each other accountable so that what we offer those who listen to us will not aim to dazzle but to nourish them.

Once I have done all my homework and have a decent idea what the text means, I give it a rest. Understanding is not enough. I do not want to pass on knowledge from the pulpit; I want to take part in an experience of God's living word, and that calls for a different kind of research. It is time to tuck the text into the pocket of my heart and walk around with it inside of me. It is time to turn its words and images loose on the events of my everyday life and see how they mix. It is time to daydream, whittle, whistle, pray. This is the gestation period of a sermon, and it cannot be rushed. It is a time of patient and impatient waiting for the stirring of the Holy Spirit, that bright bird upon whose brooding the sermon depends. Over and over again I check the nest of my notes and outlines, searching through them for some sign of life. I scan the text one more time and all of a sudden there is an egg in plain view, something where there had been nothing just a moment before, and the sermon is born.

What the egg contains is a connection, a likeness, between the life of the text and the life of the world. Sometimes it seems a brand new one, like the connection between Holy Communion and an infant's nursing, but more often it is an ancient one that suddenly catches the light. "God is love" (1 John 4:8). What could be more elementary? Everyone understands that; it is so simple that people put it on their car bumpers, right next to "Have a nice day." A preacher might explain that it means God is kindly disposed toward us, and that would be correct. But if, in the process of composing a sermon, a preacher discovers the visceral connection between the word "God" and the heart-pounding experience of authentic love, then the sermon will be more than correct. It will be true, not at the level of explanation but at the level of experience, where all our deepest truths are tested.

This is where a sermon becomes art. It is not enough to tell a congregation what they need to know about God, or Scripture, or life. The preacher who delivers airtight conclusions from the pulpit leaves the congregation with only two choices: they may agree with what they have heard or they may not, but they are prevented from drawing their own conclusions. The preacher has judged them incapable of that hard work and has done it for them. So when the sermon is over, it is over, unless they wish to praise or reject it as they shake hands at the door.

There is another way to preach, in which the preacher addresses the congregation not as mute students but as active partners in the process of discovering God's word. The sermon traces the preacher's own process of discovery, inviting the congregation to come along and providing them with everything they need to make their own finds. The movement of the sermon leads them past new vantage points on their common experience, so that they look at old landmarks from new perspectives. At each stop, the preacher pauses, pointing in a certain direction without telling the congregation what they should see when they look. It is up to them to discern what the landscape holds. The preacher's job is not to make the trip for them or to block their view, but to take them to the spot where they may best see for themselves. With any luck, where the sermon finally leads both preacher and congregation is into the presence of God, a place that cannot be explained but only experienced. When a sermon like this is over, it is not over. Everyone involved in it goes away with images, thoughts, and emotions that change and grow as the process of discovery goes on and on and on.

It is as hard for a preacher to say how this is done as it is for a painter to say how a tree takes shape on a canvas. Do the leaves come first or the branches? What combination of yellow and blue makes such a bright green? How do you make it look so real? All the parts of preaching can be taught: exegesis, language, metaphor, development, delivery. What is hard to teach is how to put them all together, so that what is true is also beautiful, and evocative, and alive. Life itself is the best teacher. Preachers who are attuned to God's presence and movement in the world do not have to invent much. All we have to learn is how to say what we see. We are not abstract artists, after all. We are God's impressionists, whose sermons reveal our hearts and minds as clearly as fingerprints. Every word choice, every illustration, every question our sermons ask tells the congregation who we are, but our self-disclosure goes even further than that.

"You are a word about the Word before you ever speak a word," Alan Jones said once. Everything we have ever done and everything we have become follows us into the pulpit when we preach. The way we stand there, the way we hold ourselves, what we do with our hands, where we focus our eyes — all of these preach sermons of their own, whatever we happen to be saying with our mouths. This makes preaching a form of prayer for me, an act of conscious self-offering in which I stand exposed before God and my neighbor, seeking relationship with them both. "Do you still get nervous?" a teenager asks me. Is the world still round? But my nervousness has less to do with performance anxiety than it does with standing so close to the truth of who I am before God. The success or failure of any particular sermon seems less important to me than the ongoing process of placing myself in God's hands.

The worst sermon I ever preached was in Canajoharie, New York, chewing-gum capital of the world, where I was invited to address what was described to me as an ailing congregation. The gospel lesson for that Trinity Sunday was John's story about Nicodemus' search for new birth. It was a promising sign, I thought, and proceeded to construct an eight-page masterpiece on faith and doubt. Sunday morning arrived, the processional hymn began, and I marched into a church with three people in it — five, including me and my host. Two of them were elderly women, still weepy over the loss of a friend the day before. The third was a heavy, angry-looking man who occupied the other side of the church all by himself. Time came for the sermon and I crept into the pulpit, wondering what in the world to do. I tried the first page of my manuscript and abandoned it; it was like reciting poetry to a wall. With a fast prayer to the Holy Spirit for guidance, I put my notes away and tried to summarize what I had planned to say without them. The result was five minutes of pure gibberish. The Holy Spirit never showed up, and as my congregation stared blankly up at me I rapidly confirmed all their worst fears about women preachers.

One of the best sermons I ever preached was at the funeral of a baby girl. Her death, which came just three months after her complicated birth, tried the faith of everyone who knew her and her parents, including me. I worked and worked at something to say, but everywhere I turned I ran into the dead end of my own grief. Finally it came time to do the service and I walked into a full church with nothing but half a page of notes. When it was my turn to speak, I stood plucking the words out of thin air as they appeared before my eyes. Somehow, they worked. God consented to be present in them. But when I received a transcript of the sermon later from someone who had recorded the service, it was as if it had been written in disappearing ink. There was nothing there but a jumble of phrases and images, trailing off at the end into awkward silence. While the Holy Spirit was in them, they lived. Afterward, they were no more than empty boxes, lying where the wind had left them.

These two experiences remind me not to take myself too seriously. They also make me reluctant to talk about "best" and "worst" sermons. Something happens between the preacher's lips and the congregation's ears that is beyond prediction or explanation. The same sermon sounds entirely different at 9:00 and 11:15 A.M. on a Sunday morning. Sermons that make me weep leave my listeners baffled, and sermons that seem cold to me find warm responses. Later in the week, someone quotes part of my sermon back to me, something she has found extremely meaningful — only I never said it.

There is more going on here than anyone can say. Preaching is finally more than art or science. It is alchemy, in which tin becomes gold and yard rocks become diamonds under the influence of the Holy Spirit. It is a process of transformation for both preacher and congregation alike, as the ordinary details of their everyday lives are translated into the extraordinary elements of God's ongoing creation. When the drumroll begins and the preacher steps into place, we can count on that. Wherever God's word is, God is — loosening our tongues, tuning our ears, thawing our hearts — making us a people who may speak and hear the Word of Life.

· II ·

THE PREACHER

JOHN CHRYSOSTOM

The Temptations of Greatness

The classical ideal of oratory was that of "the good person speaking well."
Preaching in the post-classical age was also concerned with the speaker's
character, not merely in the Aristotelian sense of *ethos,* which is the speaker's
character as perceived by the audience, but with holiness of heart, prayer, and
conformity to the message. John surnamed Chrysostom, or "Golden-Mouth"
(347-407), epitomizes the church's ambivalence toward classical rhetoric. As a
speaker he was without peer, the greatest preacher and biblical commentator
of the Greek church. He was trained by one of the most prominent rhetoricians of the age, Libanius. Yet he rebuked his audiences when they applauded
his sermons and insisted that preachers should be trained to be indifferent to
praise. Such training he believed to be essential in a rhetorical culture like his
own with its "passion for oratory." As a priest and later as Archbishop of Constantinople, Chrysostom steadfastly pursued holiness but instead found controversy. From his pulpit he passionately rebuked private and public immoral-
ity. His outspoken asceticism was more than the empress could tolerate, and
he died in his second exile. In contrast to the Alexandrian school of allegorical
interpretation, Chrysostom subjected his classical training to the authority of
the historical, literal text. With moral and psychological insight, he re-created
the "world" of the text with such realism that the contemporary reader may
still be moved by the sermons of this, "the patron saint of preachers." He also
addressed many of his sermons to political issues; his famous series *On the
Statues* was preached after mobs overturned statues of the royal family in protest against new taxes. In the *Paradiso* Dante places Chrysostom between Nathan, who rebuked a king, and Anselm, who endured exile for his convictions.

John Chrysostom, *Six Books on the Priesthood,* Book V, 1-8, trans. Graham Neville
(Crestwood, NY: St. Vladimir's Seminary Press, 1977), pp. 127-35.

I have given sufficient proof of the experience needed by the teacher in contending for the truth. I have one thing more to add to this, a cause of untold dangers: or rather, I will not blame the thing itself so much as those who do not know how to use it properly; in itself it conduces to salvation and to many benefits, when it happens to be handled by earnest, good men. And what is it? It is the great toil expended upon sermons delivered publicly to the congregation.

In the first place, most of those who are under authority refuse to treat preachers as their instructors. They rise above the status of disciples and assume that of spectators sitting in judgment on secular speech-making. In their case the audience is divided, and some side with one speaker and others side with another. So in church they divide and become partisans, some of this preacher and some of that, listening to their words with favor or dislike.

And this is not the only difficulty; there is another, no less serious. If it happens that a preacher weaves among his own words a proportion of other men's flowers, he falls into worse disgrace than a common thief. And often when he has borrowed nothing at all, he suffers on bare suspicion the fate of a convicted felon. But why mention the work of others? He is not allowed to repeat his own compositions too soon. For most people usually listen to a preacher for pleasure, not profit, like adjudicators of a play or concert. The power of eloquence, which we rejected just now, is more requisite in a church than when professors of rhetoric are made to contend against each other!

Here, too, a man needs a loftiness of mind far beyond my own littleness of spirit, if he is to correct this disorderly and unprofitable delight of ordinary people, and to divert their attention to something more useful, so that church people will follow and defer to him and not that he will be governed by their desires. It is impossible to acquire this power except by these two qualities: contempt of praise and the force of eloquence. If either is lacking, the one left is made useless through divorce from the other. If a preacher despises praise, yet does not produce the kind of teaching which is "with grace, seasoned with salt," he is despised by the people and gets no advantage from his sublimity. And if he manages this side of things perfectly well, but is a slave to the sound of applause, again an equal damage threatens both him and the people, because through his passion for praise he aims to speak more for the pleasure than the profit of his hearers. The man who is unaffected by acclamation, yet unskilled in preaching, does not truckle to the people's pleasure; but no more can he confer any real benefit upon them, because he has nothing to say. And equally, the man who is carried away with the desire for eulogies may have the ability to improve the people, but chooses instead to provide nothing but entertainment. That is the price he pays for thunders of applause.

The perfect ruler, then, must be strong in both points, to stop one being nullified by the other. When he stands up in the congregation and says things capable of stinging the careless, the good done by what he has said leaks away quickly if he then stumbles and stops and has to blush for want of words. Those who stand rebuked, being nettled by his words and unable to retaliate on him in any other way, jeer at him for his lack of skill, thinking to mask their shame by doing so. So, like a good charioteer, the preacher should have reached perfection in both these qualities, in order to be able to handle both of them as need requires. For only when he is himself beyond reproach in everyone's eyes will he be able, with all the authority he desires, to punish or pardon all who are in his charge. But until then it will not be easy to do.

But this sublimity must not only be displayed in contempt for applause; it must go further, if its benefit is not in turn to be wasted. What else, then, must he despise? Slander and envy. The right course is neither to show disproportionate fear and anxiety over ill-directed abuse (for the president will have to put up with unfounded criticism), nor simply to ignore it. We should try to extinguish criticisms at once, even if they are false and are leveled at us by quite ordinary people. For nothing will magnify a good or evil report as much as an undisciplined crowd. Being accustomed to hear and speak uncritically, they give hasty utterance to whatever occurs to them, without any regard for the truth. So we must not disregard the multitude, but rather nip their evil suspicions in the bud by convincing our accusers, however unreasonable they may be. We should leave nothing untried that might destroy an evil report. But if, when we have done all, our critics will not be convinced, then at last we must resort to contempt. For anyone who goes halfway to meet humiliation by things like this will never be able to achieve anything fine or admirable. For despondency and constant anxieties have a terrible power to numb the soul and reduce it to utter impotence.

The priest should treat those whom he rules as a father treats very young children. We are not disturbed by children's insults or blows or tears; nor do we think much of their laughter and approval. And so with these people, we should not be much elated by their praise nor much dejected by their censure, when we get these things from them out of season. This is not easy, my friend, and I think it may be impossible. I do not know whether anyone has ever succeeded in not enjoying praise. If he enjoys it, he naturally wants to receive it. And if he wants to receive it, he cannot help being pained and distraught at losing it. People who enjoy being wealthy take it hard when they fall into poverty, and those who are used to luxury cannot bear to live frugally. So, too, men who are in love with applause have their spirits starved not only when they are blamed offhand, but even when they fail to be constantly praised. Especially is this so when they have been brought up on applause, or when they hear others being praised.

What troubles and vexations do you suppose a man endures if he enters the lists of preaching with this ambition for applause? The sea can never be free from waves; no more can his soul be free from cares and sorrow. For though a man may have great force as a speaker (which you will rarely find), still he is not excused continual effort. For the art of speaking comes, not by nature, but by instruction, and therefore even if a man reaches the acme of perfection in it, still it may forsake him unless he cultivates its force by constant application and exercise. So the gifted have even harder work than the unskillful. For the penalty for neglect is not the same for both, but varies in proportion to their attainments. No one would blame the unskillful for turning out nothing remarkable. But gifted speakers are pursued by frequent complaints from all and sundry, unless they continually surpass the expectation which everyone has of them. Besides this, the unskillful can win great praise for small successes, but as for the others, unless their efforts are very startling and stupendous, they not only forfeit all praise but have a host of carping critics.

For the congregation does not sit in judgment on the sermon as much as on the reputation of the preacher, so that when someone excels everyone else at speaking, then he above all needs painstaking care. He is not allowed sometimes not to succeed — the common experience of all the rest of humanity. On the contrary, unless his sermons always match the great expectations formed of him, he will leave the pulpit the victim of countless jeers and complaints. No one ever takes it into consideration that a fit of depression, pain, anxiety, or in many cases anger, may cloud the clarity of his mind and prevent his productions from coming forth unalloyed; and that in short, being a man, he cannot invariably reach the same standard or always be successful, but will naturally make many mistakes and obviously fall below the standard of his real ability. People are unwilling to allow for any of these factors, as I said, but criticize him as if they were sitting in judgment on an angel. And anyhow men are so made that they overlook their neighbor's successes, however many or great; yet if a defect comes to light, however commonplace and however long since it last occurred, it is quickly noticed, fastened on at once, and never forgotten. So a trifling and unimportant fault has often curtailed the glory of many fine achievements.

You see . . . the ablest speaker has all the more need for careful application, and not application only, but greater tolerance than any of those I have so far mentioned. For plenty of people keep attacking him without rhyme or reason. They hate him without having anything against him except his universal popularity. And he must put up with their acrimonious envy with composure. For since they do not cover up and hide this accursed hatred which they entertain without reason, they shower him with abuse and complaints and secret slander and open malice. And the soul which begins by feeling pain and annoyance about each of these things cannot avoid being desolated with grief. For they not only attack him by their own efforts, but they set about doing so through others as well. They often choose someone who has no speaking ability and cry him up with their praises and admire him quite beyond his deserts. Some do this through sheer ignorance and others through ignorance and envy combined, to ruin the good speaker's reputation, not to win admiration for one who does not deserve it.

And that high-minded man has to contend, not just against this kind of opponent, but often against the ignorance of a whole community. For it is impossible for a whole congregation to be made up of men of distinction; and it generally happens that the greater part of the church consists of ignorant people. The rest are perhaps superior to these, but fall short of men of critical ability by a wider margin than the great majority fall short of them. Scarcely one or two present have acquired real discrimination. And so it is inevitable that the more capable speaker receives less applause and sometimes even goes away without any mark of approval. He must face these ups and downs in a noble spirit, pardoning those whose opinion is due to ignorance, grieving over those who maintain an attitude out of envy, as miserable, pitiable creatures, and letting neither make him think the less of his powers. For if a painter of first rank who excelled all others in skill saw the picture he had painted with great care scoffed at by men ignorant of art, he ought not to be dejected or to regard his painting as poor because of the judgment of the ignorant; just as little should he regard a really poor work as wonderful and charming because the unlearned admired it.

Let the best craftsman be the judge of his own handiwork too, and let us rate his productions as beautiful or poor when that is the verdict of the mind which contrived them. But as for the erratic and unskilled opinion of outsiders, we should not so much as consider it. So too the man who has accepted the task of teaching should pay no attention to the commendation of outsiders, any more than he should let them cause him dejection. When he has composed his sermons to please God (and let this alone be his rule and standard of good oratory in sermons, not applause or commendation), then if he should be approved by men too, let him not spurn their praise. But if his hearers do not accord it, let him neither seek it nor sorrow for it. It will be sufficient encouragement for his efforts, and one much better than anything else, if his conscience tells him that he is organizing and regulating his teaching to please God. For in fact, if he has already been overtaken by the desire for unmerited praise, neither his great efforts nor his powers of speech will be any use. His soul, being unable to bear the senseless criticisms of the multitude, grows slack and loses all earnestness about preaching. So a preacher must train himself above all else to despise praise. For without this addition, knowledge of the technique of speaking is not enough to ensure powerful speech.

And even if you choose to investigate carefully the type of man who lacks this gift of eloquence, you will find he needs to despise praise just as much as the other type. For he will inevitably make many mistakes if he lets himself be dominated by popular opinion. Being incapable of matching popular preachers in point of eloquence, he will not hesitate to plot against them, to envy them, to criticize them idly, and to do a lot of other disgraceful things. He will dare anything, if it costs him his very soul, to bring their reputation down to the level of his own insignificance. Besides this, he will give up the sweat of hard work because a kind of numbness has stolen over his spirit. For it is enough to dispirit a man who cannot disdain praise and reduce him to a deep lethargy, when he toils hard but earns all the less approbation. When a farmer labors on poor land and is forced to farm a rocky plot, he soon gives up his toil, unless he is full of enthusiasm for his work, or is driven on by fear of starvation.

If those who can preach with great force need such constant practice to preserve their gift, what about someone who has absolutely no reserves in hand, but needs to get preaching practice by actually preaching? How much difficulty and mental turmoil and trouble must he put up with, to be able to build up his resources just a little by a lot of labor! And if any of his colleagues of inferior rank can excel him in this particular work, he really needs to be divinely inspired to avoid being seized with envy or thrown into dejection. It requires no ordinary character (and certainly not one like mine) but one of steel for a man who holds a superior position to be excelled by his inferiors and to bear it with dignity. If the man who outstrips him in reputation is unassuming and very modest, the experience is just tolerable. But if he is impudent and boastful and vainglorious, his superior may as well pray daily to die, so unpleasant will the other man make his life by flouting him to his face and mocking him behind his back, by detracting frequently from his authority and aiming to be everything himself. And his rival will have derived great assurance in all this from the license people grant him to say what he likes, the warm interest of the majority in him, and the affection of those under his charge. Or do you not know what a passion for oratory has recently infatuated Christians? Do you not know that its exponents are respected above everyone else, not just by outsiders, but by those of the household of faith? How, then, can anyone endure the deep disgrace of having his sermon received with blank silence and feelings of boredom, and his listeners waiting for the end of the sermon as if it were a relief after fatigue; whereas they listen to someone else's sermon, however long, with eagerness, and are annoyed when he is about to finish and quite exasperated when he decides to say no more?

Perhaps this seems to you a trifling, negligible matter, because you have no experience of it. Yet it is enough to kill enthusiasm and paralyze spiritual energy, unless a man dispossesses himself of all human passions and studies to live like the disembodied spirits who are not hounded by envy or vainglory or any other disease of that sort. If there actually is anyone capable of subduing this elusive, invincible, savage monster (I mean popular esteem) and cutting off its many heads, or rather, preventing their growth altogether, he will be able to repulse all these attacks easily and enjoy a quiet haven of rest. But if he has not shaken himself free of it, he involves his soul in an intricate struggle, in unrelieved turmoil, and in the hurly-burly of desperation and every other passion. Why should I catalogue all the other troubles, which no one can describe or realize without personal experience?

GEORGE HERBERT

The Parson Preaching

Seventeenth-century Anglican spirituality is exemplified in the life of George Herbert (1593-1633), one-term member of Parliament, country rector, and England's greatest religious poet. The true center of Herbert's universe was neither the political world of London nor his obscure village of Bemerton, near Salisbury, but the church and its ministry. Herbert's spirituality strikes a perfect balance between the ascetic and the mundane service of God and between the soul's inner devotion and the community's corporate worship. The church's calling to ordinary, daily holiness is the central message of his prose classic, *The Country Parson,* written not to memorialize his own brief ministry but, as Herbert put it, "that I may have a mark to aim at." The treatise consists of thirty-seven brief chapters with such titles as "The Parson as a Father," "The Parson Comforting," "The Parson in His House," and "The Parson Arguing." In it he reminds his listeners that "sermons are dangerous things; that none goes out of church as he came in. . . ." The church's liturgy, calendar, and architecture form the organizing principle of his classic collection of poems, *The Temple.* Testimonies to Herbert's saintliness abound but perhaps none so eloquent as the poet's own description of every preacher's calling in "The Windows":

> Lord, how can man preach thy eternal word?
>   He is a brittle crazy glass:
> Yet in thy temple thou dost him afford
>   This glorious and transcendent place,
>   To be a window, through thy grace.
>
> But when thou dost anneal in glass thy story,
>   Making thy life to shine within
> The holy preachers; then the light and glory
>   More rev'rend grows, and more doth win, —
>   Which else shews wat'rish, bleak and thin.

The Parson Preaching

Doctrine and life, colors and light, in one
    When they combine and mingle, bring
A strong regard and awe: but speech alone
    Doth vanish like a flaring thing;
    And in the ear, not conscience, ring.

George Herbert, *The Temple* and *The Country Parson* (Boston: James B. Dow, 1842 [1652]), pp. 296-300, 368-69.

The country parson preacheth constantly. The pulpit is his joy and his throne. If he at any time intermit [is absent], it is either for want of health; or against some festival, that he may the better celebrate it; or for the variety of the hearers, that he may be heard at his return more attentively. When he intermits, he is ever very well supplied by some able man; who treads in his steps, and will not throw down what he hath built; whom also he entreats to press some point that he himself hath often urged with no great success, that "so in the mouth of two or three witnesses the truth may be more established."

When he preacheth, he procures attention by all possible art: both by earnestness of speech; it being natural to men to think that where is much earnestness, there is somewhat worth hearing: and by a diligent and busy cast of his eye on his auditors, with letting them know that he marks who observes, and who not: and with particularizing of his speech now to the younger sort, then to the elder, now to the poor, and now to the rich — "This is for you, and this is for you"; — for particulars ever touch, and awake, more than generals. Herein also he serves himself of the judgments of God: as of those of ancient times, so especially of the late ones; and those most, which are nearest to his parish; for people are very attentive at such discourses, and think it behooves them to be so, when God is so near them, and even over their heads. Sometimes he tells them stories and sayings of others, according as his text invites him: for them also men heed, and remember better than exhortations; which, though earnest, yet often die with the sermon, especially with country people; which are thick, and heavy, and hard to raise to a point of zeal and fervency, and need a mountain of fire to kindle them; but stories and sayings they will well remember. He often tells them that sermons are dangerous things; that none goes out of church as he came in, but either better or worse; that none is careless before his Judge; and that the word of God shall judge us.

By these and other means the parson procures attention; but the character of his sermon is *holiness*. He is not witty, or learned, or eloquent, but *holy:* — a character that Hermogenes never dreamed of, and therefore he could give no precepts thereof. But it is gained, — First, by choosing texts of devotion, not controversy; moving and ravishing texts, whereof the Scriptures are full. — Secondly, by dipping and seasoning all our words and sentences in our hearts before they come into our mouths; truly affecting, and cordially expressing, all that we say: so that the auditors may plainly perceive that every word is heart-deep. — Thirdly, by turning often, and making many apostrophes to God; as, "O Lord! bless my people, and teach them this point!" or, "O my Master, on whose errand I come, let me hold my peace, and do thou speak thyself; for thou art love; and when thou teachest, all are scholars." Some such irradiations scatteringly in the sermon, carry great holiness in them. The prophets are admirable in this. So Isaiah 64; "Oh, thou that wouldest rend the heavens, that thou wouldest come down," etc. And Jeremy (chapter 10), after he had complained of the desolation of Israel, turns to God suddenly, "O Lord! I know that the way of man is not in himself," etc. — Fourthly, by frequent wishes of the people's good, and joying therein; though he himself were, with St. Paul, "even sacrificed upon the service of their faith." For there is no greater sign of holiness than the procuring and rejoicing in another's good. And herein St. Paul excelled, in all his epistles. How did he put the Romans "in all his prayers" (Rom. 1:9); and "ceased not to give thanks" for the Ephesians (Eph. 1:16); and for the Corinthians (1 Cor. 1:4); and for the Philippians "made request with joy" (Phil. 1:4); and is in contention for them whether to live or die, be with them or Christ (v. 23); which, setting aside his care of his flock, were a madness to doubt of. What an admirable epistle is the second to the Corinthians! How full of affections! He joys, and he is sorry; he grieves, and he glories! Never was there such a care of a flock expressed, save in the great Shepherd of the fold, who first shed tears over Jerusalem, and afterward blood. Therefore this care may be learned there, and then woven into sermons; which will make them appear exceeding reverend and holy. — Lastly, by an often urging of the presence and majesty of God; by these, or such like speeches — "Oh, let us take heed what we do! God sees us; he sees whether I speak as I ought, or you hear as you ought; he sees hearts, as we see faces. He is among us; for if we be here, he must be here; since we are here by him, and without him could not be here." Then, turning the discourse to his majesty, — "and he is a great God, and terrible; as great in mercy, so great in judgment! There are but two devouring elements, fire and water; he hath both in him. 'His voice is as the sound of many waters,' (Rev. 1); and he himself is 'a consuming fire.'" (Heb. 12) — Such discourses show very holy.

The parson's method in the handling of a text consists of two parts: — First, a plain and evident declaration of the meaning of the text; — and secondly, some choice observations, drawn out of the whole text, as it lies entire and unbroken in the Scripture itself. This he thinks natural, and sweet, and grave. Whereas the other way, of crumbling a text into small parts, (as, the person speaking or spoken to, the subject, and object, and the like), hath neither in it sweetness, nor gravity, nor variety; since the words apart are not Scripture, but a dictionary, and may be considered alike in all the Scripture.

The parson exceeds not an hour in preaching, because all ages have thought that a competency: and he that profits not in that time, will less afterward; the same affection which made him not profit before, making him then weary; and so he grows from not relishing, to loathing.

A Prayer after Sermon

Blessed be God, and the Father of all mercy, who continueth to pour his benefits upon us. Thou hast elected us, thou hast called us, thou hast justified us, sanctified, and glorified us. Thou wast born for us, and thou livedst and diedst for us. Thou hast given us the blessings of this life, and of a better. O Lord! thy blessings hang in clusters; they come trooping upon us; they break forth like mighty waters on every side. And now, Lord, thou hast fed us with the bread of life. "So man did eat angel's food." O Lord, bless it! O Lord, make it health and strength to us! — still striving and prospering so long within us, until our obedience reach the measure of thy love, who hast done for us as much as may be. Grant this, dear Father, for thy Son's sake, our only Savior: to whom, with thee and the Holy Ghost, — three persons, but one most glorious, incomprehensible God, — be ascribed all honor, and glory, and praise, ever. Amen.

RICHARD BAXTER

On the Making of the Preacher

The Reformed Pastor by Richard Baxter (1615-1691) appeared only four years after Herbert's *The Country Parson* and immediately established itself as a trustworthy guide to pastoral theology and spirituality. Baxter's is a larger work and less introspective than Herbert's. It conveys the sense of emergency born of chaotic conditions in the churches and among the clergy during the interregnum. Baxter developed the book out of the famous Worcester *Agreement* signed by more than fifty ministers in Worcester. The Worcester clerics pledged to redress the "sins of the ministry" and to promote the restoration of holiness in the churches, with special attention given to the personal instruction of lapsed Christians and the spiritual renewal of preaching. In the following selection Baxter voices the need of a regenerated clergy. He predicts that if his proposals for the education of clergy were adopted, we might not have ministers who "read divinity like philosophers" but rather clerics who read "philosophy like divines." He makes a strenuous argument against the familiar two-step approach to clergy formation — first the liberal arts, then theology — arguing that future clergy should instead be inculcated with a theological habit of thinking from the very beginning of their education, which he calls practical divinity, so that their knowledge of science and the humanities might be suffused and shaped by the things of God. The influence of *The Reformed Pastor* has extended through the centuries, touching established and nonconforming Christians alike, including Philip Jacob Spener, Philip Doddridge, the Wesleys, Thomas Chalmers, C. H. Spurgeon, and countless others.

Richard Baxter, *The Reformed Pastor* (New York: T. Mason and G. Lane, 1837 [1656]), pp. 169-80.

See that the work of saving grace be thoroughly wrought on your own souls. It is a fearful case to be an unsanctified professor, but more to be an unsanctified preacher. Does it not make you tremble when you open the Bible, lest you should there read the sentence of your own condemnation? When you pen your sermons, little do you think that you are drawing up indictments against your own souls! . . . What can you do in persuading men to Christ, in drawing them from the world, in urging them to a life of faith and holiness, but conscience, if it were but awake, might tell you that you speak all this to your own confusion? . . . A graceless, unexperienced preacher is one of the most unhappy creatures upon earth; yet is he ordinarily most insensible of his unhappiness; for he hath so many counterfeits that seem like the gold of saving grace, and so many splendid stones that seem like the Christian's jewel, that he is seldom troubled with the thoughts of his poverty; but thinks he is rich and wanteth nothing, when he is poor and miserable and blind and naked. . . . O that while we hold the looking glass of the gospel to others, to show them the true face of the state of their souls, we should either look on the back of it ourselves where we can see nothing, or turn it aside, that it may misrepresent us to ourselves! . . .

It is the common danger and calamity of the church to have unregenerate and inexperienced pastors; and to have men become preachers before they are Christians; to be sanctified by dedication to the altar, as God's priests, before they are sanctified by hearty dedication to Christ as his disciples; and so to worship an unknown God, and to preach an unknown Christ, an unknown Spirit, an unknown state of holiness and communion with God, and a glory that is unknown, and likely to be unknown to them for ever.

He is likely to be but a heartless preacher who has not the Christ and grace that he preaches in his heart. O that all our students in the university would well consider this! What a poor business it is to themselves to spend their time in knowing some little of the works of God, and some of those names that the divided tongues of the nations have imposed on them, and not to know the Lord himself, exalt him in their hearts, nor to be acquainted with that one renewing work that should make them happy. They do but walk in a vain show, and spend their lives like dreaming men, while they busy their wits and tongues about abundance of names and notions, and are strangers to God and the life of saints. If ever God awaken them by his grace, they will have cogitations and employments so much more serious than their unsanctified studies and disputations were, that they will confess they did but dream before. A world of business they make themselves about *nothing*, while they are willful strangers to the primitive, independent, necessary Being, who is all in all. Nothing can be rightly known, if God be not known; nor is any study well managed, nor to any great purpose, where God is not studied.

We know but little of the creature, till we know it as it stands in its order and respect to God: single letters and syllables unconnected are nonsense. He who overlooks the Alpha and Omega, and sees not the beginning and end, and him in all, who is the *all* of all, sees nothing at all. All creatures are, as such, broken syllables: they signify nothing as separated from God. Were they separated *actually*, they would cease to be, and the separation would be an annihilation; and when we separate them in our *fancies*, we make *nothing* of them to ourselves. It is one thing to know the creatures as Aristotle, and another thing to know them as a Christian. None but a Christian can read one line of his physics so as to understand it rightly. . . . I hope you perceive what I aim at in all this, viz., that to see God in his creatures, to love him, and converse with him, was the employment of man in his upright state; that this is so far from ceasing to be our duty, that it is the work of Christ to bring us back to it: and, therefore, the most holy men are the most excellent students of God's works, and none but the holy can rightly study or know them. His works are great, sought out of all them that have pleasure therein; but not for themselves, but for him that made them.

Your study of physics and other sciences is not worth a rush if it be not God . . . that you seek after [in them]. To see and admire, to reverence and adore, to love and delight in God appearing to us in his works, and purposely to peruse them for the knowledge of God, this is the true and only philosophy, and the contrary is mere folly, and is called so again and again by God himself. This is the sanctification of your studies, when they are devoted to God, and when he is the life of them all, and they are directed to him as their end and principal object.

Therefore, I shall presume to tell you by the way, that it is a grand error, and of dangerous consequence in the Christian academies, (pardon the censure from one so unfit for it, seeing the necessity of the case commands it), that they study the creature before the Redeemer, and set themselves to physics, and metaphysics, and mathematics before they set themselves to theology; whereas no man who has not the vitals of theology is capable of going beyond a fool in philosophy; and all that such do is but doting about questions and opposition of sciences, falsely so called. And as by affecting a separated creature-knowledge Adam fell from God, so they who mind these profane, empty babblings, and oppositions of science, falsely so called, miss the end of all right study; they err concerning the faith; while they will needs prefer these, they miss that faith which they pretend to aim at. Their pretense is, that theology, being the end, and the most perfect branch, must be the last, and all the subservient sciences must go before it. . . .

It is evident therefore that theology must lay the ground and lead the way in all our studies, when we are once so far acquainted with words and things as is needful to our understanding the sense of its principles. If God must be searched after in our search of the creatures, and we must affect no separated knowledge of them, then tutors must read God to their pupils in all; and divinity must be the beginning, the middle, the end, the life, the all of their studies; and our physics and metaphysics must be reduced to theology, and nature must be read as one of God's books, which is purposely written for the revelation of himself.

The Holy Scripture is the easiest book. When you have first learned God and his will there, in the necessary things, address yourselves cheerfully to the study of his works, that you may see there the creature itself as your alphabet, and their order as the connection of syllables, words, and sentences, and God as the subject matter of all, and their respect to him as the sense or signification; and then carry on both together, and never more play the mere scriveners; stick no more in your letters and words, but read every creature as a Christian or a divine.

If you see not yourselves and all things as living, and moving, and having being in God, you see nothing, whatever you think you see. If you perceive not in your perusals of the creatures, that God is all, and in all, you may think perhaps that you know something, but you know nothing as you ought to know. He who sees and loves God in the creature, the same is known and loved of him. Think not so basely of the works of God and your physics as that they are only preparatory studies for boys. It is a most high and noble part of holiness to search after, behold, admire, and love the great Creator in all his works. How much have the saints of God been employed in it! The beginning of Genesis, the books of Job and the Psalms, may acquaint us that our physics are not so little akin to theology as some suppose. I do therefore, in zeal to the good of the church, and their own success in their most necessary labors, propound it to the consideration of all pious tutors, whether they should not as early and as diligently read to their pupils, or cause them to read, the chief parts of practical divinity (and there is no other) as any of the sciences; and whether they should not go together from the very first?

It is well that they hear sermons; but that is not enough. If they have need of private help in philosophy besides public lectures, how much more in theology! If tutors would make it their principal business to acquaint their pupils with the doctrine of life, and labor to set it home upon their hearts, that all might be received according to its weight, and read to their hearts as well as to their heads, and so carry on the rest of their instructions, that it might appear they made them but subservient to this, and that their pupils may feel what they drive at in all, and so that they would teach all their philosophy *in habitu theologico,* this might be a happy means to make happy souls, a happy church and commonwealth.

The same I mean also respecting schoolmasters to their scholars. But when languages and philosophy have almost all their time and diligence, and instead of reading philosophy like divines, they read divinity like philosophers, as if it were a thing of no more moment than a lesson of music or arithmetic, and not the doctrine of everlasting life; this is what blasts so many in the bud, and pesters the church with unsanctified teachers. Hence it is that we have so many worldlings to preach of the invisible felicity, and so many carnal men to declare the mysteries of the Spirit; and I would I had not cause to say, so many infidels to preach Christ, or so many atheists to preach the living God; and when they are taught philosophy before or without religion, what wonder if their philosophy be all, or most, of their religion; if they grow up into admirations of their unprofitable fancies, and deify their own deluded brains, when they know no other God; and if they reduce all their theology to their philosophy, as some have done.

Again: I address myself to all those who have the education of youth, especially in order to prepare them for the ministry. You who are schoolmasters and tutors, begin and end with the things of God. Speak daily to the hearts of your scholars those things which must be wrought into their hearts, or else they will be undone. Let some piercing words fall frequently from your mouths, of God, the state of their souls, and the life to come. Do not say they are too young to understand and entertain them. You little know what impressions they may make which you discern not. Not only the soul of that boy, but a congregation, or many souls therein, may have cause to bless God for your zeal and diligence, yea, for one such seasonable word. You have a great advantage above others to do them good. You have them before they are grown to the worst, and they will hear you when they will not hear another. If they are destined to the ministry, you are preparing them for the special service of God; and should they not first have the knowledge of him whom they must serve? O think with yourselves what a sad thing it will be to their own souls, and what a wrong to the church of God, if they come out from you with carnal hearts to so holy, spiritual, and great a work! Of a hundred students that are in one of your colleges, how many may there be who are serious, experienced, godly men: some talk of too small a number. If you should send one half of them on a work that they are unfit for, what bloody work will they make in the church! Whereas if you be the means of their thorough sanctification, how many souls may bless you, and what greater good can you possibly do the church! When their hearts are once savingly affected with the doctrine which they study and preach, they will study it heartily, and preach it heartily. . . .

Content not yourselves to have the main work of grace; but be also very careful . . . that you preach to yourselves the sermons you study before you preach them to others. . . . When I let my heart grow cold, my preaching is cold; and when it is confused my preaching is so too: and I can observe the same frequently in the best of my hearers, that, when I have a while grown cold in preaching, they have cooled accordingly; and the next prayers that I have heard from them have been too much like my preaching. We are the nurses of Christ's little ones. If we forbear our food we shall famish them; they will quickly find it in the want of milk, and we may quickly see it again in them in the cold and dull discharge of their several duties. If we let our love go down, we are not likely to raise theirs up. If we abate our holy care and fear, it will appear in our doctrine. If the matter show it not, the manner will. If we feed on unwholesome food, either errors or fruitless controversies, our hearers are likely to fare the worse for it. Whereas if we abound in faith, love, and zeal, how will it overflow to the refreshing of our congregations, and how will it appear in the increase of the same graces in others.

JARENA LEE

My Call to Preach the Gospel

"The Savior died for the woman as well as the man," wrote Jarena Lee (1783–ca. 1850) in defense of her evangelistic ministry at a time when a black woman was an unexpected and often unwelcome pulpit presence. Lee's personal call to preach came five years after she experienced a dramatic conversion under the influence of Richard Allen in the mother church of African Methodism, Bethel Chapel in Philadelphia. Although Allen at first refused Lee's request to preach, he later relented after seeing her in action, and Lee became the first female evangelist in the African Methodist Episcopal Church. Her itinerant ministry took her into homes, schools, and public meetinghouses across the northeastern United States in the decades that followed. But Lee often met with resistance since neither black nor white churches ordained women at that time. Her marriage interrupted her itinerancy and brought her great "debility" of spirit. After the death of her husband she once again, this time with the blessing of Bishop Allen, embarked on an evangelistic ministry of exhortation, depending on the support of friends in the rearing of her two small children. Like Phoebe Palmer, she drew her authority for preaching from the Holy Spirit, who inspired her words and blessed her labors with conversions among her black and white listeners. Lee's pathbreaking struggles opened the way for other African-American women, such as Amanda Smith, Sarah Hughes, and, in the next century, Martha Jayne Keys, to follow in her footsteps. The AME Church did not officially ordain women as itinerant elders until 1971. It appointed its first female bishop in 2000.

The Life and Religious Experience and Journal of Jarena Lee, A Coloured Lady, Giving an Account of Her Call to Preach the Gospel (Philadelphia: Printed and Published for the Author, 1836), pp. 12-15, 18-24.

B etween four and five years after my sanctification, on a certain time, an impressive silence fell upon me, and I stood as if someone was about to speak to me, yet I had no such thought in my heart. But to my utter surprise there seemed to sound a voice which I thought I distinctly heard, and most certainly understood, which said to me, "Go preach the gospel!" I immediately replied aloud, "No one will believe me." Again I listened, and again the same voice seemed to say, "Preach the gospel; I will put words in your mouth, and will turn your enemies to become your friends."

At first I supposed that Satan had spoken to me, for I had read that he could transform himself into an angel of light, for the purpose of deception. Immediately I went into a secret place, and called upon the Lord to know if he had called me to preach, and whether I was deceived or not; when there appeared to my view the form and figure of a pulpit, with a Bible lying thereon, the back of which was presented to me as plainly as if it had been a literal fact.

In consequence of this, my mind became so exercised that during the night following, I took a text, and preached in my sleep. I thought there stood before me a great multitude, while I expounded to them the things of religion. So violent were my exertions, and so loud were my exclamations, that I awoke from the sound of my own voice, which also awoke the family of the house where I resided. Two days after, I went to see the preacher in charge of the African Society, who was the Rev. Richard Allen, the same before named in these pages, to tell him that I felt it my duty to preach the gospel. But as I drew near the street in which his house was, which was in the city of Philadelphia, my courage began to fail me; so terrible did the cross appear, it seemed that I should not be able to bear it. Previous to my setting out to go to see him, so agitated was my mind that my appetite for my daily food failed me entirely. Several times on my way there, I turned back again; but as often I felt my strength again renewed, and I soon found that the nearer I approached to the house of the minister, the less was my fear. Accordingly, as soon as I came to the door, my fears subsided, the cross was removed, all things appeared pleasant — I was tranquil.

I now told him that the Lord had revealed it to me that I must preach the gospel. He replied by asking, in what sphere I wished to move in? I said, among the Methodists. He then replied that a Mrs. Cook, a Methodist lady, had also some time before requested the same privilege; who it was believed, had done much good in the way of exhortation, and holding prayer meetings; and who had been permitted to do so by the verbal license of the preacher in charge at the time. But as to women preaching, he said that our Discipline knew nothing at all about it — that it did not call for women preachers. This I was glad to hear, because it removed the fear of the cross — but no sooner did this feeling cross my mind, than I found that a love of souls had in a measure departed from me; that holy energy which burned within me, as a fire, began to be smothered. This I soon perceived.

O how careful ought we to be, lest through our bylaws of church government and discipline, we bring into disrepute even the word of life. For as unseemly as it may appear nowadays for a woman to preach, it should be remembered that nothing is impossible with God. And why should it be thought impossible, heterodox, or improper, for a woman to preach, seeing the Savior died for the woman as well as for the man?

If the man may preach, because the Savior died for him, why not the woman, seeing he died for her also? Is he not a whole Savior, instead of a half one, as those who hold it wrong for a woman to preach would seem to make it appear?

Did not Mary *first* preach the risen Savior, and is not the doctrine of the resurrection the very climax of Christianity — hangs not all our hope on this, as argued by St. Paul? Then did not Mary, a woman, preach the gospel? For she preached the resurrection of the crucified Son of God.

But some will say that Mary did not expound the Scripture, therefore she did not preach, in the proper sense of the term. To this I reply, it may be that the term *preach,* in those primitive times, did not mean exactly what it is now *made* to mean; perhaps it was a great deal more simple then than it is now — if it were not, the unlearned fishermen could not have preached the gospel at all, as they had no learning.

To this it may be replied, by those who are determined not to believe that it is right for a woman to preach, that the disciples, though they were fishermen, and ignorant of letters too, were inspired so to do. To which I would reply, that though they were inspired, yet that inspiration did not save them from showing their ignorance of letters, and of man's wisdom; this the multitude soon found out, by listening to the remarks of the envious Jewish priests. If then, to preach the gospel, by the gift of heaven, comes by inspiration solely, is God straitened; must he take the man exclusively? May he not, did he not, and can he not inspire a female to preach the simple story of the birth, life, death, and resurrection of our Lord, and accompany it too with power to the sinner's heart? As for me, I am fully persuaded that the Lord called me to labor according to what I have received in his vineyard. If he has not, how could he consistently bear testimony in favor of my poor labors, in awakening and converting sinners?

In my wanderings up and down among men, preaching according to my ability, I have frequently found families who told me that they had not for several years been to a meeting, and yet, while listening to hear what God would say by his poor colored female instrument, have believed with trembling — tears rolling down their cheeks, the signs of contrition and repentance toward

God. I firmly believe that I have sown seed, in the name of the Lord, which shall appear with its increase at the great day of accounts, when Christ shall come to make up his jewels.

At a certain time, I was beset with the idea that soon or late I should fall from grace, and lose my soul at last. I was frequently called to the throne of grace about this matter, but found no relief; the temptation pursued me still. Being more and more afflicted with it, till at a certain time when the spirit strongly impressed it on my mind to enter into my closet, and carry my case once more to the Lord, the Lord enabled me to draw nigh to him, and to his mercy seat, at this time, in an extraordinary manner; for while I wrested with him for the victory over this disposition to doubt whether I should persevere, there appeared a form of fire, about the size of a man's hand, as I was on my knees; at the same moment, there appeared to the eye of faith a man robed in a white garment, from the shoulders down to the feet; from him a voice proceeded, saying: "Thou shalt never return from the cross." Since that time I have never doubted, but believe that God will keep me until the day of redemption. Now I could adopt the very language of St. Paul, and say that nothing could have separated my soul from the love of God, which is in Christ Jesus [Rom. 8:35-39]. From that time, 1807, until the present, 1833, I have not ever doubted the power and goodness of God to keep me from falling, through the sanctification of the spirit and belief of the truth. . . .

The Subject of My Call to Preach Renewed

It was now eight years since I had made application to be permitted to preach the gospel, during which time I had only been allowed to exhort, and even this privilege but seldom. This subject now was renewed afresh in my mind; it was as a fire shut up in my bones. About thirteen months passed on while under this renewed impression. During this time, I had solicited of the Rev. Bishop Richard Allen, who at this time had become Bishop of the African Episcopal Methodists in America, to be permitted the liberty of holding prayer meetings in my own hired house, and of exhorting as I found liberty, which was granted me.

[Lee continues with a long digression recounting her role in the deathbed conversion of a young man.]

But to return to the subject of my call to preach. Soon after this, as above related, the Rev. Richard Williams was to preach at Bethel Church, where I with others were assembled. He entered the pulpit, gave out the hymn, which was sung, and then addressed the throne of grace; took his text, passed through the exordium, and commenced to expound it. The text he took is in Jonah, second chapter, ninth verse — "Salvation is of the Lord." But as he proceeded to explain, he seemed to have lost the spirit; when in the same instant, I sprang, as by an altogether supernatural impulse, to my feet, when I was aided from above to give an exhortation on the very text which my brother Williams had taken.

I told them that I was like Jonah; for it had been then nearly eight years since the Lord had called me to preach his gospel to the fallen sons and daughters of Adam's race, but that I had lingered like him, and delayed to go at the bidding of the Lord, and warn those who are as deeply guilty as were the people of Nineveh.

During the exhortation, God made manifest his power in a manner sufficient to show the world that I was called to labor according to my ability, and the grace given unto me, in the vineyard of the good husbandman.

I now sat down, scarcely knowing what I had done, being frightened. I imagined that for this indecorum, as I feared it might be called, I should be expelled from the church. But instead of this, the Bishop rose up in the assembly, and related that I had called upon him eight years before, asking to be permitted to preach, and that he had put me off; but that he now as much believed that I was called to that work, as any of the preachers present. These remarks greatly strengthened me, so that my fears of having given an offence, and made myself liable as an offender, subsided, giving place to a sweet serenity, a holy joy of a peculiar kind, untasted in my bosom until then.

The next Sabbath day, while sitting under the word of the gospel, I felt moved to attempt to speak to the people in a public manner, but I could not bring my mind to attempt it in the church. I said, Lord, anywhere but here. Accordingly, there was a house not far off which was pointed out to me, to this I went. It was the house of a sister belonging to the same society with myself. Her name was Anderson. I told her I had come to hold a meeting in her house, if she would call in her neighbors. With this request she immediately complied. My congregation consisted of but five persons. I commenced by reading and singing a hymn, when I dropped to my knees by the side of a table to pray. When I arose I found my hand resting on the Bible, which I had not noticed till that moment. It now occurred to me to take a text. I opened the Scripture, as it happened, at the 141st psalm, fixing my eye on the third verse, which reads: "Set a watch, O Lord, before my mouth, keep the door of my lips."

My sermon, such as it was, I applied wholly to myself, and added an exhortation. Two of my congregation wept much, as the fruit of my labor this time. In closing I said to the few, that if anyone would open a door, I would hold a meeting the next sixth-day evening; when one answered that her house was at my service. Accordingly I went, and God made manifest his power among the people. Some wept, while others shouted for joy. One whole seat of females, by the power of God, as the rushing of a wind, were all bowed to the floor at once, and screamed out. Also a sick man and woman in one house, the Lord convicted them both; one lived, and the other died. God wrought a judgment — some were well at night, and died in the morning. At this place I continued to hold meetings about six months. During that time I kept house with my little son, who was very sickly.

About this time I had a call to preach at a place about thirty miles distant, among the Methodists, with whom I remained one week, and during the whole time, not a thought of my little son came into my mind; it was hid from me, lest I should have been diverted from the work I had to, to look after my son. Here by the instrumentality of a poor colored woman, the Lord poured forth his spirit among the people. Though, as I was told, there were lawyers, doctors, and magistrates present, to hear me speak, yet there was mourning and crying among sinners, for the Lord scattered fire among them of his own kindling. The Lord gave his handmaiden power to speak for his great name, for he arrested the hearts of the people, and caused a shaking amongst the multitude, for God was in the midst.

I now returned home, found all well; no harm had come to my child, although I left it very sick. Friends had taken care of it which was of the Lord. I now began to think seriously of breaking up housekeeping and forsaking all to preach the everlasting gospel. I felt a strong desire to return to the place of my nativity, at Cape May, [New Jersey,] after an absence of about fourteen years.

To this place, where the heaviest cross was to be met with, the Lord sent me, as Saul of Tarsus was sent to Jerusalem, to preach the same gospel which he had neglected and despised before his conversion. I went by water, and on my passage was much distressed by seasickness, so much so that I expected to have died, but such was not the will of the Lord respecting me. After I had disembarked, I proceeded on as opportunities offered, toward where my mother lived. When within ten miles of that place, I appointed an evening meeting. There were a goodly number came out to hear. The Lord was pleased to give me light and liberty among the people. After meeting, there came an elderly lady to me and said, she believed the Lord had sent me among them; she then appointed me another meeting there two weeks from that night.

The next day I hastened forward to the place of my mother, who was happy to see me, and the happiness was mutual between us. With her I left my poor sickly boy, while I departed to do my Master's will. In this neighborhood I had an uncle, who was a Methodist, and who gladly threw open his door for meetings to be held there. At the first meeting which I held at my uncle's house, there was, with others who had come from curiosity to hear the colored woman preacher, an old man, who was a Deist, and who said he did not believe the colored people had any souls — he was sure they had none. He took a seat very near where I was standing, and boldly tried to look me out of countenance. But as I labored on in the best manner I was able, looking to God all the while, though it seemed to me I had but little liberty, yet there went an arrow from the bent bow of the gospel, and fastened in his still then obdurate heart. After I had done speaking, he went out, and called the people around him, said that my preaching might seem a small thing, yet he believed I had the worth of souls at heart. This language was different from what it was a little time before, as he now seemed to admit that colored people had souls, as it was to these I was chiefly speaking; and unless they had souls whose good I had in view, his remark must have been without meaning. He now came into the house, and in the most friendly manner shook hands with me, saying, he hoped God had spared him to some good purpose. This man was a great slaveholder, and had been very cruel; thinking nothing of knocking down a slave with a fence stake, or whatever might come to hand. From this time it was said of him that he became greatly altered in his ways for the better. At that time he was about seventy years old, his head as white as snow; but whether he became a converted man or not, I never heard.

The week following, I had an invitation to speak at the Court House of the County, when I spoke from the fifty-third chapter of Isaiah, third verse. It was a solemn time, and the Lord attended the word; I had life and liberty, though there were people there of various denominations. Here again I saw the aged slaveholder, who notwithstanding his age, walked about three miles to hear me. This day I spoke twice, and walked six miles to the place appointed. There was a magistrate present, who showed his friendship by saying in a friendly manner that he had heard of me: he handed me a hymn book, pointing to a hymn which he had selected. When the meeting was over, he invited me to preach in a schoolhouse in his neighborhood, about three miles distant from where I then was. During this meeting one backslider was reclaimed. This day I walked six miles, and preached twice to large congregations, both in the morning and evening. The Lord was with me, glory be to his holy name.

I next went six miles and held a meeting in a colored friend's house, at eleven o'clock in the morning, and preached to a well-behaved congregation of both colored and white. After service I again walked back, which was in all twelve miles in the same day. This was on Sabbath, or as I sometimes call it, seventh-day; for after my conversion I preferred the plain language of the Friends.

On fourth-day, after this, in compliance with an invitation received by note, from the same magistrate who had heard me at the above place, I preached to a large congregation, where we had a precious time: much weeping was heard among the people. The same gentleman, now at the close of the meeting, gave out another appointment at the same place, that day week. Here again I had liberty, there was a move among the people. Ten years from that time, in the neighborhood of Cape May, I held a prayer meeting in a school house, which was then the regular place of preaching of the Episcopal Methodists; after service, there came a white lady of the first distinction, a member of the Methodist Society, and told me that at the same school house, ten years before, under my preaching, the Lord first awakened her. She rejoiced much to see me, and invited me home with her, where I stayed till the next day. This was bread cast on the waters, seen after many days.

From this place I next went to Dennis Creek meetinghouse, where at the invitation of an elder, I spoke to a large congregation of various and conflicting sentiments, when a wonderful shock of God's power was felt, shown everywhere by groans, by sighs, and loud and happy amens. I felt as if aided from above. My tongue was cut loose, the stammerer spoke freely; the love of God, and of his service, burned with a vehement flame within me — his name was glorified among the people.

But here I feel myself constrained to give over, as from the smallness of this pamphlet I cannot go through with the whole of my journal, as it would probably make a volume of two hundred pages; which, if the Lord be willing, may at some future day be published. But for the satisfaction of such as may follow after me, when I am no more, I have recorded how the Lord called me to his work, and how he has kept me from falling from grace, as I feared I should. In all things he has proved himself a God of truth to me; and in his service I am now as much determined to spend and be spent, as at the very first. My ardor for the progress of his cause abates not a whit, so far as I am able to judge, though I am now something more than fifty years of age.

As to the nature of uncommon impressions, which the reader cannot but have noticed, and possibly sneered at in the course of these pages, they may be accounted for in this way: It is known that the blind have the sense of hearing in a manner much more acute than those who can see: also their sense of feeling is exceedingly fine, and is found to detect any roughness on the smoothest surface, where those who can see can find none. So it may be with such as I am, who has never had more than three months schooling; and wishing to know much of the way and law of God, have therefore watched more closely the operations of the Spirit, and have in consequence been led thereby. But let it be remarked that I have never found that Spirit to lead me contrary to the Scriptures of truth, as I understand them. "For as many as are led by the Spirit of God are the sons of God." — Romans 8:14.

I have only now to say, May the blessing of the Father, and of the Son, and of the Holy Ghost, accompany the reading of this poor effort to speak well of his name, wherever it may be read. AMEN.

HORACE BUSHNELL

Pulpit Talent

Often called the father of modern liberal theology in America, Horace Bushnell (1802-1876) was one of the most significant American theologians of the nineteenth century. Born in Connecticut, he attended Yale College where he studied journalism and law. After a conversion experience during a college revival, Bushnell entered Yale Divinity School and was eventually ordained a Congregational pastor. Strongly influenced, like so many others of his era, by Samuel Taylor Coleridge's *Aids to Reflection,* Bushnell imbibed much of the Romantic fervor stirred up in America by such thinkers as Friedrich Schleiermacher and the Boston transcendentalist Ralph Waldo Emerson. His creative revision of Christian doctrine provoked fierce opposition and even heresy charges from fellow clergy in New England. But his views on conversion, spiritual growth, the nature of language and doctrine, and the organic character of community life have had a lasting impact on modern Protestant thinking and preaching. *Christian Nurture* (1861), in which he argued that a child nurtured by Christian parents can grow into a Christian adult without ever experiencing a conversion, deeply influenced the Christian education movement in America. Bushnell's understanding of language as essentially tensive and indeterminate has its echoes in contemporary homiletical theory. His views on language caused him to resist absolute dogmatic constructions, especially in relation to the atonement. Bushnell's career as a religious thinker was closely bound to his life as the minister of a single congregation, North Church in Hartford, Connecticut, where he served from 1833 until poor health forced him to leave the pastorate in 1859. In the following lecture delivered at Andover Seminary in 1866, Bushnell addresses the question, "What does it take to be a great preacher?"

Horace Bushnell, "Pulpit Talent" in *Building Eras in Religion,* vol. 3 of Literary Varieties (New York: Charles Scribner's Sons, 1910 [1881]), pp. 182-92.

There was never a time, I think, when so much was made of talented preaching, and talents for preaching, as now. I wish we understood a good deal better what we mean by it. Every young candidate wants the talents of course, and everybody is very decided in the opinion that he must have them. Even the little new hamlets crowded under the woods, and the third-rate water-power villages sprinkled along the brooks, have made up their minds that they too must have a talented preacher; only they are not always quite clear as to what may be necessary to make one. Indeed, they are not as much baffled commonly in the matter of salvation itself as in finding just the minister that is worthy of them. The general refrain is: "Do not our people want as good a preacher as anybody?" And the real wonder often felt and sometimes expressed is that our schools, finding how much a larger supply of Beechers is wanted, do not turn out the number demanded. Nay, there is, I fear, a silent scolding of Providence that so few of them are born, when the world is overstocked by such myriads of men propagated in the common figure. The result is, that the young men, looking out on the field and preparing for it, are either prodigiously elated in the confidence that they have just the talents required, as perhaps they have been told by their admiring comrades; or else that they are miserably crushed by the discouraging prospect before them, because nobody has told them that they have any talent at all, and their modesty if not their real lack has withheld them from the consciousness of any.

Most wretched and pitiful are the hallucinations here encountered. These forty hundred or forty thousand churches, looking every one after a talented preacher, will certainly not get one; and the few that are boasting their success will be discovering almost certainly, after a while, that they have been a little mistaken. Almost as certainly the young men, going out with so great expectations, will find, a great part of them, that they do not catch the popular approval after all; or, if they do, will shortly be obliged to discover that they are much closer down to mediocrity than they supposed. Meantime, of those who go out in a tremor of weakness and discouragement, some at least will begin to be set on powerfully by a hidden force they were unconscious of and which did not enter into the computations of their friends. And so it will be shown, both by cases of unexpected failure and of equally surprising success, that factors are concerned in preaching not commonly included in our computations. What I propose, therefore, at the present time, is to discover, if I can, these hidden factors, and by that means right our conceptions where they seem to falter. And I have a considerable hope that, by a certain process, it may be done.

Attempts are often made in this direction that are much more distinctively Christian than what I now propose, and so far more genuine; but which, partly for that reason, do not succeed according to their merit. They undertake to show, and do really show, that preaching is not grounded in mere talent, but is and must forever be a divine gift. No man, they insist, ever becomes a prophet or a powerful Christian preacher in whom this divine gift is wanting. And here is the reason, they allege, why so many talented preachers come to nothing, and why so many that seemed to have little promise at first finally obtain so great power and conquer a degree of success so unexpected.

We generally assent to this kind of argument, because it is honorable to religion, and what is more, because it coincides with some very plain teachings of Scripture.

But the difficulty is that the truth asserted is too particularly spiritual, and requires too much faith to hold us up to it; therefore, we fall away from it shortly and, forgetting ourselves, begin again to base our calculations of promise on mere judgments of natural force; that is, on the talents as forces. What I propose therefore on the present occasion, is to follow the bad method myself; to subside into just this plane of unbelief or nonbelief, and show that, resting, as we so perversely do, all promise for the pulpit on mere computations of personal talent, we still need a complete revision commonly of our judgments, because of the very insufficient conceptions we have of the pulpit talents themselves. I shall make out, if I am successful, a larger inventory of the talents, and one that more sufficiently measures the personal momenta necessary to success.

As we commonly speak, it takes just four talents to make a great preacher; namely, — a talent of high scholarship; a metaphysical and theologic thinking talent; style or a talent for expression; and a talent of manner and voice for speaking. In these four talents the young men of the schools commonly settle their comparisons, and graduate their prognostications of success. The people too, so far as they think anything definitely in the matter, have no doubt that these four things will make up the man they are to seek. We may therefore call these four the canonical talents, for they certainly have that kind of preeminence.

Now, about the real importance of these four there is little room to doubt, and the high opinion held of them already makes it unnecessary to raise an argument for them. Our seminaries of learning lay their stress on these, and exist in no small degree for the culture of these; for these four, it happens, are the specially cultivatable talents. And so much being expended on them naturally induces a comparative over-valuation, which makes it necessary to pass them under review, if we are to get the scale of our inventory settled to a right adjustment.

It is very clear then, first of all, that a dolt in scholarship is not likely to become a great preacher. And it is about equally clear that one may be an easy, rapid learner, in the sense of acquisition, and be really nobody. Sometimes it will be found that a scholar preacher, who is partly somebody, will even kill a tolerable sermon by letting his scholarship into it. And then again it will sometimes be found that a preacher who is only not a scholar because he has never had the opportunity to be, will unfold the very highest preaching power in the field of mere practice, as we see by some noble examples among the great preachers of Methodism. Still even such, if we cannot speak of their scholarship, will be as far as possible from the state of ignorance.

Meantime, if it be not true, as it certainly is not, that the preachers from a given school will be graduated in their preaching merit and power by the amount of their learning, it must not be understood that we have in such a fact any derogation from the value of learning. In such an age as this, we must have a proportion at least of learned men in the cause of religion. Indeed, every preacher wants in a certain view, if it could be so, to know very nearly everything. And yet let him not mistake. Books are not everything by a great deal. It is even one of the sad things about book-learning that it so easily becomes a limitation upon souls, and a kind of dry rot in their vigor. The receptive faculty absorbs the generative, and the scholarhood sucks up the manhood. An oak that should undertake to be a sponge would not long be much of an oak. I know not how to put this matter of scholarship better than to say that it needs to be universal; to be out in God's universe, that is, to see, and study, and know everything, books and men and the whole work of God from the stars downward; to have a sharp observation of war, and peace, and trade, — of animals, and trees, and atoms, — of the weather, and the evanescent smells of the creations; to have bored into society in all its grades and meanings, its manners, passions, prejudices, and times; so that, as the study goes on, the soul will be getting full of laws, images, analogies, and facts, and drawing out all subtlest threads of import to be its interpreters when the preaching work requires. Of what use is it to know the German when we do not know the human? Or to know the Hebrew points when we do not know at all the points of our wonderfully punctuated humanity? A preacher wants a full storehouse of such learning, and then he wants the contents all shut in, so that they can never one of them get out, only as they leap out unbidden to help him and be a language for him. It should even be as if he had a sky-full of helpers thronging to his aid when they are not sent for, and endowing him with ministrations of power when they do not show their faces. As far as the preacher is concerned, this large, free kind of scholarship is the only kind that will do him much good.

The metaphysical and theologic thinking talent has a deeper and more positive vigor. There cannot be much preaching worthy of the name where there is no thinking. Preaching is nothing but the bursting out of light, which has first burst in or up from where God is, among the soul's foundations. And to this end, great and heavy discipline is wanted, that the soul may be drilled into orderly right working. And yet a merely cold, scientific thinking is vicious. The method of preaching is not the scientific method. The true thinking here is the original insight of premises or first things, and not the building of cob-house structures round them. An immense overdoing in the way of analysis often kills a sermon, if it does not quite kill the preacher. Death itself is a great analyzer, and nothing ever comes out of the analyzing process fully alive. There is a great deal of anatomizing thought, but it is the weakest, cheapest kind of thought that flesh is heir to.

The formulizing kind of thought is but a little better. True preaching struggles right away from formula, back into fact, and life, and the revelation of God and heaven. It is a flaming out from God; it reproves, testifies, calls, promises; thinking always of the angels going up to report progress, not of the answers formulated for a catechism. I make no objection to formulas; they are good enough in their place, and a certain instinct of our nature is comforted in having some articulations of results thought out to which our minds may refer. Formulas are the jerked meat of salvation, — if not always the strong meat, as many try to think, — dry and portable and good to keep, and when duly seethed and softened, and served with needful condiments, just possible to be eaten; but for the matter of living, we really want something fresher and more nutritious. On the whole, the kind of thinking talent wanted for a great preacher is that which piercingly loves; that which looks into things and through them, plowing up pearls and ores, and now and then a diamond. It will not seem to go on metaphysically, or scientifically, but with a certain round-about sense and vigor. And the people will be gathered to it because there is a gospel fire burning in it that warms them to a glow. This is power.

The rhetorical talent or talent of style is a very great gift, and one that can be largely cultivated. But the ambition of style, or the consciousness of it, does not always need to be. Neither is it always any great sign for a preacher that he shows a considerable luxury in this kind of excellence. About the weakest, falsest kind of merit, and most opposite to good preaching, is the studied, commonplace book-style. A great many preachers die of style, that is, of trying to soar; when, if they would only consent to go afoot as their ideas do, they might succeed and live. Sophist and rhetorician were very nearly synonymous in the classic days; for they had the same trade then of taking men by a seeming, or a pretentious lie, as now. The preacher wants of course to know his mother tongue, and have a clear, correct, and forcible way of expression in it. And then, if he has really something strong enough to say to call in angels of imagery that excel in strength to help him say it, there is no kind of symbol observed by him, in heaven above, or in the earth beneath, that will not be at hand to lend him wings and lift him into the necessary heights of expression. But the moment these aerial creatures begin to see that they are wanted for garnish, and not for a truth's sake, they will hide like partridges in the bush. To get up grand expressions in the manner of some, and then go a hunting after only weak ideas to put into them, is the very absurdest and wickedest violation possible of the second commandment. No man has a right to say any beautiful or powerful thing till he gets some thoughts beautiful and powerful enough to require it. Only good and great matter makes a good and great style. It is not difficult for power to be strong, or for any real fire to burn. But mere rhetorical fire will neither shake nor burn anything. And just here it is that the prodigious promise of so many young men is overestimated. Could they only understand how great a thing in style is honesty, simple, self-forgetting honesty, their would-be fine, or fanciful, or sublime would fall away, and they would finally rise just as much higher, even in style, as the cast-off trumpery of their affectations and laborious inanities permits them to rise. Simple modesty, earnest conviction, — what a lifting of the doom of impotence would they be to many!

What is called the speaking talent is often misconceived in the same way. It is mostly a natural talent, though it can be modulated and chastened by criticism. But the difficulty is, that such kind of discipline has to be commonly dispensed before the subject is sufficiently advanced in age and maturity of perception to have anything on hand that is at all worthy of a manner, or indeed even possible for it. How can he fitly speak sentiments before he has them and knows the weight of them? If he takes the boards in a declamation, astonishing everybody by the wondrous figure he makes, and compelling his auditors to imagine what a preacher he is destined to be, it is more likely by far that he is destined to be a very indifferent speaker in the humblest type of mediocrity. I have never known a great college declaimer that became a remarkable preacher; but I have known them that could only stammer and saw, and tilt up their rising inflections to the general pity of their audience, who became natural at once when they began to speak their own sentiments, and obtained great power in delivery. Meantime, this special fact in preaching is not always remembered, that the artistic air kills everything. The discovery of art is very nearly fatal everywhere, and is never in fit place save when it garnishes temptation, — to make the devil weaker than he would be. The absurdest thing ever believed by mankind is the story of Demosthenes and his pebbles; first, because it made such a hard time for his mouth; and second, because it made such a hard time for the pebbles; and third, because it made even a harder time for the sea that was obliged to hear such mouthings. All the worse if a speaker so trained gets to be absolutely faultless; for that is about the greatest fault possible. I have heard preaching more than once that became first wearisome, then shortly disgusting, for the simple reason that the manner was so perfectly shaped by skill and self-regulation. After such an exhibition, it is even refreshing to imagine the great "babbler" at Athens, jerking out his grand periods, and stammering his thunder in a way so uncouth as to be even a little contemptible to himself. He at least meant what he said, and because he did, was able to bring himself out in respect at the close. In just the same way, there are many young men who are thought to have no speaking talent, and are greatly depressed themselves because they have none, some of whom may yet become preachers of Christ in the highest rank of power and genuine eloquence.

PHOEBE PALMER

The Great Army of Preaching Women

"Do not be startled, dear reader. We do not intend to discuss the question of 'Women's Rights.' . . ." So begins *The Promise of the Father* by Phoebe Palmer (1807-1874), American Methodist evangelist and spiritual leader. True to her word, Palmer did not devote her books to the feminist cause, but her uncompromising pursuit of holiness or, in Wesleyan terms, "perfect love," led her to radical positions such as abolition, temperance, and the encouragement of women to the preaching office. Behind her stood not only the perfectionism of Wesley but also the pietism of Spener and others who wished to purify and sanctify the church. Before her lay the endless controversies concerning the second and third blessings which would eventually splinter one wing of American Methodism into an array of Holiness and Pentecostal groups. Phoebe Palmer's belief in the perfectibility of the Christian well accorded with the optimistic spirit of mid-nineteenth-century America. The "Tuesday Meetings for the Promotion of Holiness" held in her New York home drew visitors from around the world and continued even after her death. With her husband Walter C. Palmer she led evangelistic meetings in America and Europe. Her detractors questioned whether her emphasis on personal faith effectively excluded the work of the Holy Spirit, but her influence among American Methodists and Holiness groups remained strong into the 1880s. In this chapter Palmer offers a closely reasoned argument from Scripture on behalf of women's right to preach. To this she appends "A Life Picture" which graphically depicts the exclusion of women from the pulpit as a waste of resources and an offense to Jesus Christ.

Phoebe Palmer, *The Promise of the Father* (New York: W. C. Palmer Jr., 1872), pp. 21-33.

D id the tongue of fire descend alike upon God's daughters as upon his sons, and was the effect similar in each?

And did all these waiting disciples, who thus, with one accord, continued in prayer, receive the grace for which they supplicated? It was, as we observe, the gift of the Holy Ghost that had been promised. And was this promise of the Father as truly made to the daughters of the Lord Almighty as to his sons? See Joel 2:28-29: "And it shall come to pass afterward, that I will pour out my Spirit upon all flesh; and your sons and your daughters shall prophesy, your old men shall dream dreams, your young men shall see visions. And also upon the servants and upon the handmaids in those days will I pour out my Spirit." When the Spirit was poured out in answer to the united prayers of God's sons and daughters, did the tongue of fire descend alike upon the women as upon the men? How emphatic is the answer to this question! "And there appeared unto them cloven tongues, like as of fire, and it sat upon *each of them.*" Was the effect similar upon God's daughters as upon his sons? Mark it, O ye who have restrained the workings of this gift of power in the church. "And they were *all* filled with the Holy Ghost, and began to speak as the Spirit gave them utterance." Doubtless it was a well nigh impelling power, which was thus poured out upon these sons and daughters of the Lord Almighty, moving their lips to most earnest, persuasive, convincing utterances. Not alone only did Peter proclaim a crucified risen Savior, but each one, as the Spirit gave utterance, assisted in spreading the good news; and the result of these united ministrations of the Spirit, through human agency, was that three thousand were in one day pricked to the heart. Unquestionably, the whole of this newly baptized company of one hundred and twenty disciples, male and female, hastened in every direction, under the mighty constrainings of that perfect love that casteth out fear, and great was the company of them that believed.

And now, in the name of the Head of the church, let us ask, Was it designed that these demonstrations of power should cease with the day of Pentecost? If the Spirit of prophecy fell upon God's daughters, alike as upon his sons in that day, and they spake in the midst of that assembled multitude, as the Spirit gave utterance, on what authority do the angels of the churches restrain the use of that gift now? Has the minister of Christ, now reading these lines, never encouraged upon female testimony, in the charge which he represents? Let us ask, What account will you render to the Head of the church, for restricting the use of this endowment of power? Who can tell how wonderful the achievements of the cross might have been, if this gift of prophecy, in woman, had continued in use, as in apostolic days? Who can tell but long since the gospel might have been preached to every creature? Evidently this was a *speciality* of the last days, as set forth by the prophecy of Joel. Under the old dispensation, though there was a Miriam, a Deborah, a Huldah, and an Anna, who were prophetesses, the special outpouring of the Spirit upon God's daughters as upon his sons seems to have been reserved as a characteristic of the last days. This, says Peter, as the wondering multitude beheld these extraordinary endowments of the Spirit, falling alike on all the disciples, — this is that which was spoken by the prophet Joel, "And also upon my servants and upon my handmaidens will I pour out my Spirit."

And this gift of prophecy, bestowed upon all, was continued and recognized in all the early ages of Christianity. The ministry of the word was not confined to the apostles. No, they had a laity for the times. When, by the cruel persecutions of Saul, all the infant church were driven away from Jerusalem, except the apostles, these scattered men and women of the laity "went everywhere *preaching the word*," that is, proclaiming a crucified, risen Savior. And the effect was that the enemies of the cross, by scattering these men and women, who had been saved by its virtues, were made subservient to the yet more extensive proclamation of saving grace.

Impelled by the indwelling power within, these Spirit-baptized men and women, driven by the fury of the enemy in cruel haste from place to place, made all their scatterings the occasion of preaching the gospel everywhere, and believers were everywhere multiplied, and daily were there added to the church such as should be saved.

Says the Rev. Dr. Taft, "If the nature of society, its good and prosperity, in which women are jointly and equally concerned with men, if in *many cases,* their fitness and capacity for instructors being admitted to be equal to the other sex, be not reasons sufficient to convince the candid reader of woman's teaching and preaching, because of two texts in Paul's epistles (1 Cor. 14:34; 1 Tim. 2:12) let him consult the paraphrase of Locke, where he has proved to a demonstration that the apostle, in these texts, never intended to prohibit women from praying and preaching in the church, provided they were dressed as became women professing godliness, and were qualified for the sacred office. Nor is it likely that he would, in one part of his epistle, give directions how a woman, as well as a man, should pray and prophesy in public, and presently after, in the very same epistle, forbid women, endowed with the gifts of prayer and prophecy, from speaking in the church, when, according to his own explication of prophecy, it is 'speaking unto others for edification, exhortation, and comfort.' Besides, the apostle, in the epistle to the church at Corinth, says, 'Follow after charity, and desire spiritual gifts, but rather that ye may prophesy.' Again, 'I would that ye all spake with tongues, but rather that ye prophesied.' Here the apostle speaks to the church in general; and the word *all* must comprehend every individual member; and since he had just before given directions about a woman's praying and prophesying, we conclude that his desire extended to women as well as to men. Certainly the word *all* includes both men and women; otherwise the mind of Paul, 'who was made a minister of the Spirit,' would have been more narrow than that of Moses, who was only a minister of the law; for when Joshua came and told Moses that Eldad and Medad prophesied in the camp, and desired him to forbid them, Moses said unto him, 'Enviest thou for my sake? Would God that all the Lord's people were prophets, and that he would put his Spirit upon them.' Now all the Lord's people must certainly comprehend the Miriams and Deborahs in the camp, as well as the Eldads and Medads."

Dr. Clarke says (Rom. 16:12), "'Salute Tryphena and Tryphosa, who labored in the Lord. Salute the beloved Persis, who labored much in the Lord' — two holy women, who, it seems, were assistants to the apostle in his work, probably by exhorting, visiting the sick, etc. Persis was another woman who, it seems, excelled the preceding; for of her it is said, she *labored much in the Lord*. We learn from this, that Christian *women*, as well as *men*, labored in the ministry of the word. In those times of simplicity all persons, whether men or women, who had received the knowledge of the truth, believed it to be their duty to propagate it to the utmost of their power.

"Many have spent much useless labor in endeavoring to prove that these women did not *preach*. That there were some *prophetesses*, as well as *prophets*, in the Christian church, we learn; and that *woman* might pray or prophesy, provided she had her head covered, we know; and that whoever prophesied spoke unto others to edification, exhortation, and comfort, St. Paul declares, 1 Corinthians 14:3. That no preacher can do more, every person must acknowledge, because to edify, exhort, and comfort, are the prime ends of the gospel ministry. If women thus prophesied, then women preached."

Chrysostom and Theophylact take great notice of Junia, mentioned in the apostle's salutations. In our translation (Rom. 16:7) it is, "Salute Andronicus and Junia, my kinsmen, and my fellow prisoners, who are of note among the apostles." By the word *kinsmen* one would take Junia not to have been a woman, but a man. But Chrysostom and Theophylact were both Greeks; consequently, they knew their mother tongue better than our translators, and they say it was a woman. It should, therefore, have been translated, "Salute Andronicus and Junia, my kinsfolk." The apostle salutes other *women* who were of note among them, particularly Tryphena and Tryphosa, who labored in the Lord, and Persis, who labored much in the Lord.

Again, if we look into ecclesiastical history, we shall find women very eminent in the church long after the days of the apostles; I say women who were distinguished for their piety, their usefulness, and their sufferings. Witness the story of Perpetua and Felicitas, martyrs for the Christian faith, which contains traits that touch the most insensible, and cannot be read without a tear. Eusebius speaks of Potominia Ammias, a prophetess in Philadelphia, and others, who were equally distinguished by their zeal for the love which they bore to Jesus Christ.

Justin Martyr, who lived till about A.D. 150, says in his *Dialogue* with Trypho, the Jew, "that both *women* and *men* were seen among them who had the gifts of the Spirit of God, according as Joel the prophet had foretold, by which he endeavored to convince the Jew that the *latter days* were come; for by that expression, Manassah Ben Israel tells us, all their wise men understood the times of Messias."

Dodwell, in his *Dissertations on Irenaeus,* says "that the extraordinary gift of the spirit of prophecy was given to others besides the apostles, and that not only in the *first* and *second,* but in the *third* century, even to the time of Constantine, men of all sorts and ranks had these gifts — yea, and *women* too." Therefore we may certainly conclude that the prophetic saying of the Psalmist 68:11 was verified — . . . "The Lord shall give the word, that is, plentiful matter of speaking; so that he would call those which follow the great army of preaching women, viz., victories, or female conquerors."

A Supposition

Suppose one of the brethren who had received the baptism of fire on the day of Pentecost, now numbered among those who were scattered everywhere preaching the word, had met a female disciple who had also received the same endowment of power. He finds her proclaiming Jesus to an astonished company of male and female listeners. And now imagine he interferes and withstands her testimony by questioning whether women have a right to testify of Christ before a mixed assembly. Would not such an interference look worse than unmanly? And were her testimony, through this interference, restrained, or rendered less effectual, would it not, in the eye of the Head of the church, involve guilt? Yet we do not say but a person may err after the same similitude and be sincere, on the same principle that Saul was sincere when he withstood the proclamation of the gospel, and made such cruel havoc of the church. He verily thought he was doing God service. But when his mind was enlightened to see that, in persecuting these men and women, he was withstanding God, and rejecting the divinely ordained instrumentalities by which the world was to be saved, he could no longer have been sincere unless he had taken every possible pains to make his refutal of error as far-reaching as had been his wrong. And how the heart of that beloved disciple of the Savior would have been grieved, and her hands weakened, by one whom she would have a right to look to for aid against the common enemy, and for sympathy in her work!

A large proportion of the most intelligent, courageous, and self-sacrificing disciples of Christ are females. "Many women followed the Savior" when on earth; and, compared with the fewness of male disciples, many women follow him still. Were the women who followed the incarnate Savior earnest, intelligently pious, and intrepid, willing to sacrifice that which cost them something, in ministering to him of their substance? In like manner, there are many women in the present day, earnest, intelligent, intrepid, and self-sacrificing, who, were they permitted or encouraged to open their lips in the assemblies of the pious in prayer, or speaking as the Spirit gives utterance, might be instrumental in winning many an erring one to Christ. We say, were they permitted and encouraged; yes, encouragement may now be needful. So long has this endowment of power been withheld from use by the dissuasive sentiments of the pulpit, press, and church officials, that it will now need the combined aid of these to give the public mind a proper direction, and undo a wrong introduced by the man of sin centuries ago.

But more especially do we look to the ministry for the correction of this wrong. Few, perhaps, have really intended to do wrong; but little do they know the embarrassment to which they have subjected a large portion of the church of Christ by their unscriptural position in relation to this matter. The Lord our God is one Lord. The same indwelling spirit of might which fell upon Mary and the other women on the glorious day that ushered in the present dispensation still falls upon God's daughters. Not a few of the daughters of the Lord Almighty have, in obedience to the command of the Savior, tarried at Jerusalem; and, the endowment from on high having fallen upon them, the same impelling power which constrained Mary and the other women to speak as the Spirit gave utterance impels them to testify of Christ.

"The testimony of Jesus is the spirit of prophecy." And how do these divinely baptized disciples stand ready to obey these impelling influences? Answer, ye thousands of heaven-touched lips, whose testimonies have so long been repressed in the assemblies of the pious! Yes, answer, ye thousands of female disciples, of every Christian land, whose pent-up voices have so long, under the pressure of these manmade restraints, been uttered in groanings before God.

But let us conceive what would have been the effect, had either of the male disciples interfered with the utterances of the Spirit through Mary or any of those many women who received the baptism of fire on the day of Pentecost. Suppose Peter, James, or John had questioned their right to speak as the Spirit gave utterance before the assembly, asserting that it were unseemly, and out of the sphere of woman, to proclaim a risen Jesus, in view of the fact that there were *men* commingling in that multitude. How do you think that he who gave woman her commission on the morning of the resurrection, saying, "Go, tell my brethren," would have been pleased with an interference of this sort?

But are there not doings singularly similar to these being transacted now? We know that it is even so. However unseemly on the part of brethren, and revolting to our finer sensibilities, such occurrences may appear, we have occasion to know that they are not at all unusual in religious circles. We will refer to a Christian lady of more than ordinary intellectual endowments, of refined sensibilities, and whose literary culture and tastes were calculated to constitute her a star in the galaxy of this world.

A Life Picture

I have seen a lovely female turn her eye away from the things of time, and fix it on the world to come. Jesus, the altogether lovely, had revealed himself to her, and the vision of her mind was absorbingly entranced with his infinite loveliness, and she longed to reveal him to others. She went to the assembly of the pious. Out of the abundance of her heart she would fain have spoken, so greatly did her heart desire to win others over to love the object of her adoration. Had she been in a worldly assembly, and wished to attract others with an object of admiration, she would not have hesitated to have brought out the theme in conversation, and attracted listeners would have taken her more closely to their hearts, and been won with the object of her love. But she is now in the assembly of the pious. It is true many of them are her brothers and sisters, but cruel custom sealed her lips. Again and again she goes to the assembly for social prayer and the conference meeting, feeling the presence and power of an indwelling Savior enthroned uppermost in her heart, and assured that he would have her testify of him. At last she ventures to obey God rather than man. And what is the result? A committee is appointed to wait on her, and assure her that she must do so no more. Whisperings are heard in every direction that she has lost her senses; and, instead of sympathizing looks of love, she meets averted glances and heart repulses. This is not a fancy sketch; no, it is a life picture. Ye who have aided in bringing about this state of things, how does this life picture strike you?

Who Was Rejected?

Think of the feeling of the Christian lady, who has thrown herself in the bosom of your church community in order that she may enjoy the sympathies of Christian love and fellowship. Has grace divested her of refined sensibilities? No! grace has only turned those refined sensibils into a sanctified channel, and given her a yet more refined perception of everything pure, and lovely, and of good report. What must be the sufferings of that richly endowed, gentle, loving heart? But was it not her loving, gentle, indwelling Savior that would fain have had her testify for *him?* And in rejecting her testimony for Jesus, did not Jesus, the Head of the church, take it as done unto himself?

P. T. FORSYTH

The Authority of the Preacher

The word "prophetic" is often associated with the message of the great Scottish Congregationalist Peter Taylor Forsyth (1848-1921). His "positive" theology resisted orthodox biblicism and opposed the shallow liberalism of culture-Christianity decades before Barth and the later crisis-theology (a term coined by Forsyth). He focused on the kerygma as the principle of unity in the New Testament long before Dodd brought such thinking into vogue. Before Dibelius and Bultmann introduced the academy to Gospel criticism, the evangelical Forsyth made this startling observation: "The New Testament (the Gospels even), is a direct transcript, not of Christ, but of the preaching of Christ." No one since Luther had so firm a grasp of the kerygmatic nature of the New Testament, and no one in the twentieth century translated that insight into homiletical theology with greater passion than P. T. Forsyth. Toward the end of his twenty-five-year pastorate, before becoming principal of Hackney College in London, Forsyth apparently underwent a spiritual reconversion that completely reoriented his life and thought. His theology was now governed by the holiness of God and the centrality of the cross, which are mediated to humanity in a moral relationship with God. He elaborated his new vision in his famous sermon "Holy Father" and later in many books, including *The Person and the Place of Jesus Christ, The Work of Christ,* and in his 1907 Beecher Lectures at Yale, *Positive Preaching and the Modern Mind.* Forsyth was known as a "preacher's theologian," and his theology has undergirded the work of preaching for generations.

P. T. Forsyth, *Positive Preaching and the Modern Mind* (New York: A. C. Armstrong, 1907), pp. 3-5, 41-50.

It is, perhaps, an overbold beginning, but I will venture to say that with its preaching Christianity stands or falls. That is surely so, at least in those sections of Christendom which rest less upon the church than upon the Bible. Wherever the Bible has the primacy which is given it in Protestantism, there preaching is the most distinctive feature of worship. . . .

Preaching (I have said) is the most distinctive institution in Christianity. It is quite different from oratory. The pulpit is another place, and another kind of place, from the platform. Many succeed in the one, and yet are failures on the other. The Christian preacher is not the successor of the Greek orator, but of the Hebrew prophet. The orator comes with but an inspiration, the prophet comes with a revelation. In so far as the preacher and prophet had an analogue in Greece it was the dramatist, with his urgent sense of life's guilty tragedy, its inevitable ethic, its unseen moral powers, and their atoning purifying note. Moreover, where you have the passion for oratory you are not unlikely to have an impaired style and standard of preaching. Where your object is to secure your audience, rather than your gospel, preaching is sure to suffer. I will not speak of the oratory which is but rhetoric, tickling the audience. I will take both at their best. It is one thing to have to rouse or persuade people to do something, to put themselves into something; it is another to have to induce them to trust somebody and renounce themselves for him. The one is the political region of work, the other is the religious region of faith. And wherever a people is swallowed up in politics, the preacher is apt to be neglected; unless he imperil his preaching by adjusting himself to political or social methods of address. The orator, speaking generally, has for his business to make real and urgent the present world and its crises, the preacher a world unseen, and the whole crisis of the two worlds. The present world of the orator may be the world of action, or of art. He may speak of affairs, of nature, or of imagination. In the pulpit he may be what is called a practical preacher, or a poet-preacher. But the only business of the apostolic preacher is to make men practically realize a world unseen and spiritual; he has to rouse them not against a common enemy but against their common selves; not against natural obstacles but against spiritual foes; and he has to call out not natural resources but supernatural aids. Indeed, he has to tell men that their natural resources are so inadequate for the last purposes of life and its worst foes that they need from the supernatural much more than aid. They need deliverance, not a helper merely but a Savior. The note of the preacher is the gospel of a Savior. The orator stirs men to rally, the preacher invites them to be redeemed. . . . With preaching Christianity stands or falls because it is the declaration of a gospel. Nay more — far more — it is the gospel prolonging and declaring itself. . . .

I venture here to state at once what I will go on to explain, that the preacher is the organ of the only real and final authority for mankind. He is its organ, and even its steward; but he is not its vicar, except at Rome.

The question of the ultimate authority for mankind is the greatest of all the questions which meet the West, since the Catholic Church lost its place in the sixteenth century, and since criticism no longer allows the Bible to occupy that place. Yet the gospel of the future must come with the note of authority. Every challenge of authority but develops the need of it. And that note must sound in whatever is the supreme utterance of the church, in polity, pulpit, or creed. It seems clear, indeed, unless the whole modern movement is to be simply undone, that the church must draw in the range of its authority, and even Catholicism must be modified if it is to survive. But the church can never part with the tone of authority, nor with the claim that, however it may be defined, the authority of its message is supreme.

That is the very genius of an evangelical religion; for it declares that that which saves the world shall also judge the world, and it preaches the absolute right over us of the Christ who bought us — the active supremacy in conscience of our moral redemption. It is the absence of the note of authority that is the central weakness of so many of the churches; and it is the source of their failure to impress society with their message for the practical ends of the kingdom of God. It is useless to preach the kingdom when we do not carry into the center of life the control of a King. The first duty of every soul is to find not its freedom but its Master. And the first charge of every church is to offer, nay to mediate, him.

The authority of the preacher was once supreme. He bearded kings, and bent senates to his word. He determined policies, ruled fashions, and prescribed thought. And yet he has proved unable to maintain the position he was so able to take. He could not insure against the reaction which has now set in as severely as his authority once did. That reaction has long been in force; and today, however great may be his vogue as a personality, his opinion has so little authority that it is not only ignored but ridiculed. In that respect the pulpit resembles the press, whose circulation may be enormous, while elections, and such like events, show that the influence of its opinions is almost nil.

But between the press and the pulpit there is this mighty difference. The pulpit has a Word, the press has none. The pulpit has a common message and, on the strength of it, a claim, while the press has no claim to anything but external freedom of opinion and expression. The one has a gospel which is the source of its liberty, the other has no gospel but liberty, which in itself is no gospel at all. Liberty is only opportunity for a gospel. The true Gospels not only claim it, they create it. But, in itself, it is either the product of a gospel, or a means thereto; it is not an end. It is no more an end than evolution is, which is only the process of working out an end that the mere process itself does not give. Liberty in itself is not an end; and it has only the worth of its end. The chief object of the liberty of the press is facts. It must be free to publish facts. But the pulpit has not merely a fact but a Word. The press is there for information, or for suggestion at most, it is not there for authority; but the pulpit is there with authority; and the news it brings is brought for the sake of the authority. The press may offer an opinion as to how the public should act, but the pulpit is there with a message as to whom the acting public must obey and trust. The press is an adviser, but the pulpit is a prophet; the press may have a thought, the pulpit must have a gospel, nay a command. . . .

Therefore, the pulpit has an authority. If it have not, it is but a chair and not a pulpit. It may discourse, but it does not preach. But preach it must. It speaks with authority. Yet the authority is not that of the preacher's person; it is not mere authoritativeness. For us that goes without saying. What does not go unsaid, what needs saying, is that the preacher's authority is not the authority even of his truth. In the region of mere truth there is no authority. Mere truth is intellectual, and authority is a moral idea bearing not upon belief but upon will and faith, decision and committal. It is not statements that the preacher calls on us to believe. It is no scheme of statements. It is not views. It is not a creed or a theology. It is a religion, it is a gospel, it is an urgent God. In the region of mere theology we may be bold to say there is no authority; the authority is all in the region of religion. The creed of the church catholic should have great prestige, but not authority in the proper sense. Belief, in the region of theology, is a matter of truth or truths; it is science, simple or complex. And science knows no authority. But in the region of religion belief is faith. It is a personal relation. It is belief in a person by a person. It is self-committal to him. With the heart man believeth unto salvation. It is a personal act toward a person. It is trust in that person, and response to the power of his act. . . . It is a moral relation of obedience and authority.

The authority of the pulpit is thus a personal authority. Yet it is not the authority of the preacher's person, or even of his office. His office may demand much more respect than the fanatics of freedom allow, but it cannot claim authority in the strict sense. The personal authority of the pulpit is the authority of the divine person who is its burthen. It is an external authority, but it is the authority of an inward, objective, living, saving God, before whose visitation the prophet fades like an ebbing voice, and the soul of the martyr cries invisible from under the altar of the cross. . . .

For the soul, and conscience, the words higher or lower mean authority or they mean nothing. Even in the celestial time when the soul shall be in complete harmony with God the relation must always be worship, and therefore authority and obedience. The supreme thing is not a weight that lies on us but a crown that governs us and lifts us up forever. Unless we frankly adopt the positivist position, where humanity is to itself not only a law but an object of worship, there must be an authority both for man and men. And as for the externality of it — surely if there be an authority it must be external. It must come to us, and not rise out of us. It must come down on man and not proceed from him. It is a word to our race, not from it. The content of our conscience descends on us, it is no projection of ours. It were less than conscience if it were; for the law that we made we could unmake and the order we issued we could recall. Treat the autonomy of conscience as you will, but do not remove the accent from the *nomos* to the *autos*. If it be a *nomos* it is a product of more than ourselves, more than man — it is of God. Otherwise it would be but a self-imposed condition, from which at any time we might be self-released. And it could bind none, even while it remained binding, but him who had imposed it on himself. And then it would not be conscience but earnest whim.

But then, it is asked, is it not one of the greatest and surest results of modern progress that, if there be an authority, it must be inward, it must be in the soul, it must be by consent? Yes, indeed, that is one of the greatest and best blessings of the modern time. But do you realize what that means? Surely the more inward it is the more it is external. The more we retire to our inner castle the more we feel the pressure of the not-ourselves, and the presence of our Overlord. The more spiritual we are the more we are under law to another. To internalize the authority is to subtilize it, and therefore to emphasize it; for it is the subtler realities that bear upon us with the most persistent, ubiquitous, and effective pressure. The more inward we go the more external the authority becomes, just because it becomes more of an authority, and more unmistakably, irresistibly so.

If we were not so Philistine that the most accurate words seem pedantic, the proper word would not be external but objective. Because external has come, for the man in the street, to mean outside his own body, or his own family, or his own self-will, his own individuality; while what we are really concerned with is outside our own soul, our own personality. What we are suffering from is not mere externality but unconquered inwardness, subjectivism, individualism, ending in egotism. It is our subjectivism which gives externals their enslaving power over us. If within us we find nothing over us we succumb to what is around us. It is a cure for our subjectivism that we need, a cure for our egotism. And that is to be found in nothing physically external, nothing institutionally so, but only in an objective, moral and spiritual, congenial yet antithetic, in an objective to the ego, yea to the race, which objective alone gives morality any meaning. . . .

By all means then the divine authority must be inward — if we are sure what we mean, if we do not come to mean that we are our own authority — which I am afraid is the popular version with which the preacher has to contend. The authority must be inward, it is true. The modern preacher must accept that principle, and correct all its risks of perversion and debasement. His message must be more and more inward. But it must be *searchingly* inward. That is to say, it must be inward with the right of search, as an authority; and not simply as a servant, a suppliant, an influence, an impression, a sensibility. It must be above all else a moral authority, having right and not mere influence or prestige, demanding action, obedience, and sacrifice, and not merely echo, appreciation, stirrings, and thrills.

Thus when we move the authority from an external church or book to the forum of the conscience, when in the face of humanity or society we claim to call our soul our own, we have not ended the strife; we have but begun one more serious on another plane. And, in many cases, we have but opened the gates of confusion, and let loose the floods of inner tumult. The recognition of the inwardness, in many cases, seems to destroy the authority. Perhaps it does so in most cases at first. We are too full of ourselves to desire another to rule over us. And even when we desire it there are few who are so familiar with their inner selves as to be able to distinguish with any certainty the shepherd's voice, amid the gusts or sighings of their own fitful selves.

GARDNER C. TAYLOR

Portrait of a Prophet

Gardner C. Taylor has been described as the "dean of black preachers," but the title does not do justice to the breadth of his influence on preachers of every race and tradition in America. After serving congregations in Ohio and his native Louisiana, in 1948 he assumed the pastorate of the Concord Baptist Church of Christ in Brooklyn, where he remained until his retirement in 1990. He continues to preach regularly and travel the world as an ambassador of American Baptist churches. His national prominence was symbolized by his reception of the Presidential Medal of Freedom, awarded in 2000. Taylor's ministry, with its advocacy of civil rights and engagement with urban problems, proved to be a progressive force in Brooklyn and an inspiration to generations of pastors, including Martin Luther King Jr. In the pulpit he combines the influential homiletical voices of F. W. Robertson, Phillips Brooks, Harry Emerson Fosdick, and Paul Scherer with those of his mentors in the African-American tradition and his own distinctive experience as a black man in America. Although at his best when recollecting the lore of his childhood, Taylor is not so much a storyteller as an incisive and exciting performer of the text and a commentator on the state of the human soul. Stylistically, he has mastered the inventory of African-American pulpit rhetoric — understatement, the ponderous ingratiation, parallelism, antithesis, the prophetic stutter, peroration, and the adroit manipulation of thematic set pieces — all delivered in a voice like a pipe organ and without a hint of artificiality or self-conscious artistry. The following selection is taken from his 1975 Beecher Lectures. (See "Taylor, Gardner C.," in *Concise Encyclopedia of Preaching*, ed. William Willimon and Richard Lischer [Louisville: Westminster John Knox Press, 1995].)

Gardner C. Taylor, *How Shall They Preach* (Elgin, Ill.: Progressive Baptist Publishing House, 1977), pp. 77-93.

How we approach our preaching responsibility depends upon whether we consider proclamation of the gospel to be a matter of life or death. If we who preach go up into pulpits in order to pass on some interesting observations or to deliver some practical, beneficial homilies, or to issue some bulletins about the society's latest crisis, that is one thing. If we look upon ourselves as heralds of the great King, bearers, minus foolish and immodest preening, to the hearts of human beings of that upon which turns the eternal health or the fatal sickness of people in their private and corporate lives, then we shall see our work as preachers as something else again.

The whole sweep of biblical revelation asserts that the spokesperson for God stands in a grandly perilous post of responsibility. As an instance, to read the opening passages of the thirty-third chapter of Ezekiel is almost to tremble, if one feels called to preach. The word of the Lord is presented as addressing Ezekiel about the cruciality of the prophet's calling as an interpreter of God to men. The passage speaks of how a people, bracing themselves for invasion, choose as watchman "a man of their own coasts." What an apt phrase, "a man of their own coasts," since the preacher is not an alien among those to whom he or she speaks the word of God; he or she is, indeed, in geography and in condition one of those to whom the word is borne, "One of their own coasts."

It is this watchman's job to watch. Such a person is expected to scan the hills and to peer toward the valleys with the eye straining to see the rim of the horizon. One who is chosen to watch is freed from the regular occupational responsibilities of those who select him or her to be watchman. Those who have chosen the watchman agree to till the fields, to draw the water and all of that. They will bring to the watchman his or her needs. All that the people ask is that the watchman will be faithful in what he or she does in the time made free by the work and care of the rest of the community; that is, watch carefully and constantly the hills and valleys surrounding the community, lest an enemy come upon the people unawares. The community requires the watchman to look and squint carefully to see whether an enemy lurks on the far edges of the horizon where the sky seems to meet the earth. The watchman is to determine if some danger rolls on toward the entranceways of the dwellings and commercial places of the city.

It is the watchman's job to see, since for this cause came he or she to the appointed lookout tower. The watchman has been given the vantage point of an elevated position in order to see. The watchman has, likewise, no right to claim indifference or indolence or sleepiness, for he or she is spared many of the irksome annoyances of the work-a-day world. The sentry has no right to claim poor vision, since the capacity to see, to see clearly and accurately, is one of the principal requirements of a watchman. If the watchman cannot see or lacks clear vision, then the responsibility should not be accepted, since it is relatively safer for a people to know that they have no one standing sentry rather than to be lulled into a false security by the notion that a qualified watchman stands to the job, when in fact the watchman cannot see, or is asleep, or has been influenced by other considerations to close the eyes and turn the back to any hazard which may be gathering in the distance, though the danger at first sight seems scarcely more than a speck, "a little cloud out of the sea, like a man's hand." The sentry is chosen to watch and to see.

The watchman has the second responsibility of sounding the warning when an enemy is sighted approaching the city. A person so stationed to stand sentry dare not plead the excuse that he or she does not want to disturb fellow citizens (since they are people who do not like to be disturbed) or that he or she has their own affairs to which they must attend. The watchman's job is to sound the trumpet of warning. The watchman's own sense of urgency ought to take away any tentative, uncertain sound, for the sentry is no detached observer or mere mercenary, but a citizen of the city which must be alerted. His holdings are there, too.

In the early days of my ministry, Benjamin Perkins was one of the best known of the black preachers. He used to say that if a family's house is on fire, a neighbor worth being called such does not tiptoe to the burning house in the most proper fashion, timidly knock, and then say to the neighbor, "Apparently your house is on fire, for I see great billows of smoke coming up through the roof and fire is beginning to show in some of the lower windows. It would seem that you might seriously consider waking your children, and at your convenience, you might want to come out of the house." Not on your life! The cry rings through the air, "Fire!" The neighbor rushes to alert the family.

There is little place for ranting by the preacher, but there is a very large place, indeed, for urgency and for an earnest, honest passion. The stakes are high! The watchman is involved; the community under threat is his or her community; the people facing peril are bone of his bone and flesh of his flesh in the family of man. What is of greater and more critical import is that the watchman is liable for failure to warn the city. He does not get off, is not excused if he fails. . . .

The analogy of the preacher and the watchman will not walk on all fours, but then no analogy is meant to do that. The watchman is placed by the people, but the preacher is called by God, though appointed by the people of some other earthly instrumentality. There will not always be an approaching enemy for the watchman to see in guarding earthly settlements, but always humankind is imperiled by some invader whose siege threatens the souls of people. The analogy is apt surely in that the preacher, like the watchman, must watch and must see and must warn.

The person called of God is summoned to look at humanity under the light of God, *sub specie aeternitatis.* What will the preacher see? He or she will see people who are solitary-social animals. They are beings who never become quite social, an essential solitariness forever belonging to each of us. At the same time, people are never purely solitary, for they find their identity in participation and in drawing comparisons and contrasts between themselves and their fellows. Many a parent has come to understand that much of a teenager's recalcitrance is not merely of the devil, not merely, but is an attempt to sculpt and measure and to define his or her identity by defiance and challenge. In addition to people's inward turn, their solitariness, and their outward turn, their social contract, humans are lured upward. They have dealings with God, or better still, God has dealings with them. These three aspects of the human situation must ever be kept to the fore in the preacher's thinking — studying, praying, and observing.

Since each person finds his individuality partly in the give and take of the group of which he or she is a part, the preacher must never forget that one's gospel speaks as surely to people in community as it does to people in their solitariness.

How desperately do we need to be addressed in our communal ties! James Fowler reflects upon some of the radical sins of our society in an appreciative assessment he makes of the monumental work of H. Richard Niebuhr at Yale. He speaks of the theological-ethical legacy of Niebuhr as being "most helpful at the points of generating and renewing moral vision and perspective; in revealing the distortions and perversions of objectivity that result from self-serving loyalties; and in pointing to the relativity of human notions of justice when seen against the context of the righteousness of a sovereign and finally inscrutable God."

Our nation's loss of faith in itself is really consequent upon its absence of faith in "the righteousness of a sovereign and finally inscrutable God." Our national shame is a civil religion which sanctifies "distortions and perversions of objectivity that result from self-serving loyalties." Our chief national peril arises from our failure in "generating and renewing moral vision and perspective."

Now, it is the task of preaching to confront these maladies and by that I most assuredly do not mean a pulpit that is forever badgering and assaulting and attacking and belittling and berating the people in the pews of this country. The preacher, coming at the fearful, destructive sins of our society, surely must speak to them with a divine pity which weeps, so to speak, at the same time in which it challenges the community's delinquencies and derelictions.

This is not to say that the terms of judgment must be reduced; they cannot be reduced since they are of God and are not subject to public opinion nor the next referendum. The great corporate issues of our society — poverty, pollution, the international violence of war, anarchy, race, and the national priorities — are not primarily political matters; they are rooted profoundly in our attitude toward the God whose retainer the preacher is honored to be. That people will usually accept condemnation of their individual sins more graciously than they will accept condemnation of their society's sins may well say that the idolatry associated with tribal loyalties is greater than the idolatry of self; unless, of course, these communal groupings are really seen by people to be extensions of themselves.

At any rate, the preacher has no warrant to speak to our social ills save in the light of God's judgment and God's grace. For instance, racism is not merely an oppression by one people of another with all of its resultant group guilt, group degradation, and social disorder. Racism is set against the "one blood" tie which God ordained in our creation. Racism, whether it be the rapacity of a majority position or the reactionary toughness and terrorism of an outraged minority, assaults the mandate of our creation that we human beings are to have dominion over the "fish in the sea, the birds of the air, and every living creature that crawls on the earth," not over each other.

It will be well to remember that it was the sin of racism which first brought Jesus into conflict with his own people, as Dr. George Buttrick pointed out in his Beecher Lectures and as one of the ablest of the black preachers, Vernon Johns, dealt with in his unique, trenchant style. When Jesus returned home to Nazareth from his mighty victory over the Tempter in the wilderness, he was apparently received warmly. As he read the Scripture in his hometown synagogue, many a heart must have pounded at hearing the old, gracious words from the prophet Isaiah, "The Spirit of the Lord is upon me, because he hath anointed me to preach to the poor; he hath sent me to heal the brokenhearted, to preach deliverance to the captives, and recovering of sight to the blind, to set at liberty them that are bruised, to preach the acceptable year of the Lord." The sheer music of that passage, the hallowed memories of the nation's long and honored past which it evoked, the presence of the young carpenter, one of their own, sent a pleasant murmur through the assembly that day in the Nazareth synagogue.

Then the trouble began. Jesus dared to remind these proud Jews, with all of their twisted notions of what it meant to be God's chosen people, that there had been many widows in Israel at the time of Elijah and the great famine. The prophet Elijah rather had been sent of God to be sustained and lodged by a Gentile widow of a heathen coastal city, the ancient glassware center of Zarephath. As if this was not enough, he reminded these sons and daughters of the covenant that in the time of Elisha there had been many lepers in Israel. None of them was healed, but Namaan, the Syrian, the Arab, was made whole.

It was at this point, when Jesus struck at the racial arrogance and the presumptuous pride of his own people, that an angry stirring was heard in the same synagogue which but a moment earlier had known only the approving sighs and murmurs of the people. A riot ensued. The erstwhile worshipers, now in a purple rage and possessed of a terrible, insane anger, stormed the young prophet and would have lynched him that very hour had he not escaped in the midst of their blind fury and wild lunges. It was the racism of a people which brought this terrible scene to pass. Significantly, we hear no more of Nazareth ever as a place where Jesus did mighty works.

As in the matter of race, so the profoundly religious issues of poverty, war, crime, including the street and public office and corporate varieties, and pollution must be addressed by the preacher with the gospel of One who condemns and challenges and converts. It is the purpose of God not to stamp out and obliterate the kingdoms of this world; they are to be redeemed and are to "become the kingdoms of our Lord and of his Christ" in which "he shall reign forever and ever."

Along this line, in my own beloved and rambling Borough of Brooklyn there is in our civic center, in the heart of it, a monument to a tremendous life. The monument shows the likeness of a stocky, barrel-chested man with a broad face and great shoulders. The figure wears a cape and at the base of the statue are the figures of young girls whose facial features suggest that they are black children. The large likeness is that of Henry Ward Beecher, first lecturer in this series, whose far-sounding voice rose from Brooklyn Heights and echoed around the world in the cause of human freedom and in opposition to the foul institution of slavery, whose stench still sickens the nation a hundred years after the Emancipation Proclamation. Significantly, the monument faces Borough Hall, the seat of government, with Beecher's hand outstretched as if delivering to the majesty of government the will of the higher majesty of God. To be relevant to that moment in time and to that point in history in which each preacher speaks, he must throw the searchlight of his gospel of judgment and mercy upon the corporate arrangements of the society which are wrought by individuals and which in turn affect so vitally the quality of life available to each individual.

There may be a sense in which these massive institutional arrangements of a society have a life of their own and in which they exist independent of the attention and ministrations of persons. In another sense these corporate entities are the creations of individual men and women and the preacher must never forget that. There is endless interplay here. Once, years ago, I lectured at Gettysburg Seminary with one of the best known of the university preachers of America. Dealing one day with the worth of the individual, the preacher used the parables of the lost in Luke 15. He struck tellingly again and again on the note of the cruciality of "one," of the individual. He spoke of the importance of the one lost sheep, the one lost coin, and the one lost son. Appropriate enough, to be sure, but that evening we talked over coffee and I reminded him as gently as I knew how, and much to his delight, of the fact that in each case the one which was lost was presumably returned to the many, the group. The one lost sheep presumably was restored to the fold. The one lost coin was presumably restored to the family budget. Surely the lost son was returned to the family circle, the group.

A wise preacher then will remember that we can never separate individuals from their community nor the community from the individuals who comprise it. The most radical changes in community flow from the vision and consecration of individuals. Dr. Martin Luther King Jr., who may be the only authentic spiritual genius America has produced, tells of a deeply personal, interior, private experience which he had and which inspired him toward that destiny which made him one of history's truly great liberators, and not alone of black people, either. The liberation which he gave to white people can be seen in the sense of relief one seems to detect among many southern whites that now they no longer feel it necessary to practice the crudities and barbarities of segregation and incivility toward other human beings which too often characterized that region of America. Dr. King tells of how during the Montgomery bus boycott, the fountainhead of the Civil Rights struggles of the sixties, he came almost to the breaking point. He had been falsely accused and arrested, his home bombed, his wife's and little baby's lives endangered, hate mail threatening his life and loaded with obscenities came regularly to his home. He said that mornings he would look at his wife and baby and say to himself, "They can be taken away from me at any moment; I can be taken away from them at any moment."

One night in January of 1956, Dr. King went to bed after a long and trying day, but he could not fall asleep. A threatening telephone call came and it brought him to the saturation point of fear and anxiety. He reports that he got a pot of coffee and sat alone at the kitchen table. "In this state of exhaustion, when my courage had all but gone," he says, "I decided to take my problem to God. With my head in my hands I bowed over the kitchen table and prayed aloud. The words I spoke to God that midnight are still vivid in my memory. 'I am taking a stand for what I believe is right. But now I am afraid. The people are looking to me for leadership, and if I stand before them without strength and courage, they, too, will falter. I am at the end of my powers. I have nothing left. I've come to the point where I can't face it alone.'" At that moment Dr. King reports that he experienced the presence of the Divine as he had never experienced him before. "It seems," he writes, "as though I could hear the quiet assurances of an inner voice saying: 'Stand up for righteousness, stand up for truth;

and God will be at your side forever.' Almost at once my fears began to go. My uncertainty disappeared. I was ready to face anything." The most public issues are affected by personal, private, interior dealings deep within the hearts and minds of individuals.

Thus, every preacher ought never to forget in his preaching that one preaches to people who are initially and finally solitary animals with their own fears and courage, grief and guilt, joy and sorrow, anxiety and anger, and with that deep age-old hunger which the bread of this world cannot satisfy and a thirst which the waters of this life cannot quench. Jesus asserted this of which I now speak when he said, "Man shall not live by bread alone." This wistful yearning for spiritual reality and experience is expressed in a song my elders sang in the long ago, "I woke up this morning with my mind stayed on Jesus."

This strange, poignant wistfulness in each person which the preacher must sense and find and channel is to be explained partly, but not entirely, by the solitariness which occurs at both ends of our moral journey. We arrive here one by one. At the other end, as someone has put it, the way by which we leave, death, is a narrow passage and, no matter our loves, we cannot go out arm in arm. We must edge our way out one by one and sometimes sidewise, so to speak, with the jagged edges of the rocks of the narrow passage scratching and paining us. My own people sang of this:

> You got to stand your test in judgment
> You got to stand it for yourself
> There's nobody else can stand it for you
> You got to stand it for yourself.

Men and women are up against these things for themselves and, what may be even more poignant and touching, for those whom God has given them to love.

Above all, there is in each of us a dis-ease, a sense of unfulfillment of some high destiny unmet, of some lofty vow broken and shattered. We are sinners! We long for some word of forgiveness which will make us whole. We sense we have a homeland, but we are exiles. We perceive that we are of royal lineage, but our lives are being spent cheaply and shabbily and our purposes and ends are too narrow and parochial. We would be restored to our true estate. The old cry is in our literature, on our television screens, in the shame and shambles of public corruption as people seek security in money or influence. It is in the flight of our young into themselves and out toward some nirvana of drug-induced ecstasy. Paul has stated the case for so many of us, "for the good that I would I do not; but the evil which I would not, that I do. . . . O wretched man that I am! Who shall deliver me from the body of this death?"

With what awe and bated breath and how on tiptoe ought a preacher move with his or her gospel among these central sanctities! How shall a preacher know how to deal with these things? One of the great, sustaining strengths of the preacher is to be found in the fact that he or she is part of the human condition, seeing and experiencing ecstatic joys and knowing the cold chill of the floods of sorrow. Here again is the redeeming aspect of the scandal and the risk, if I may put it that way, which God took in putting the gospel of everlasting life upon sinful and mortal lips. . . .

We are surrogates of a gospel which has explored the secret places of the human heart, which has sounded the depths of the human predicament. The gospel of the Son of God, the word that the creation is built on the lines of a cruciform and which was once, once and for all, historicized at Calvary, is the answer to the questions that haunt and plague the human spirit. It is a gospel relevant to human experience; rather all human experience is relevant to that sovereign gospel. It says to those ages which deify the individual, the personal, that we are all of one blood, members of the family of man, all bound in the bundle of life. This gospel says to those ages which obscure the individual in some tribalism or other that the hairs of our heads are all numbered and that the Good Shepherd "calleth his own sheep by name."

· III ·

PROCLAIMING THE WORD

MARTIN LUTHER

Proclamation versus Moralism

Preaching is an event in which one person engages others with the gospel of God by means of a text from Scripture. The event of preaching is sponsored by the church. The sermon accomplishes its mission when it is articulated in an ecclesial or missionary setting and received by its listeners as the word of God. In preaching, the message, its articulation, and its reception are fused into a single transaction. Perhaps no one better understood the eventfulness of both the written gospel and the preached word than Martin Luther (1483-1546), who once said, "Faith is an acoustical affair." In a clear and irenic preface to a collection of his sermons, Luther reminds his readers that there is one gospel found in many forms in both the Old and New Testaments. Luther well understood the oral, sermonic basis of the New Testament and regularly used "gospel," "word," "kerygma," and "preaching" interchangeably. By these terms he meant an oral proclamation of the good news of God in Jesus Christ by which Christ himself is made available *pro nobis* (for us). "For the preaching of the gospel is nothing else than Christ coming to us, or we being brought to him." In the following selection Luther contrasts preaching that offers Christ as a gift with moralism, or the preaching of Christ-as-example. The saving benefit of Christ, he says, is not his example but his grace. The one who receives that grace, in turn, becomes a gift and example or, as Luther says elsewhere, a "little Christ" to the neighbor. (On the relation of Luther's preaching to his pastoral theology see Richard Lischer, preface to *Faith and Freedom: An Invitation to the Writings of Martin Luther,* ed. John F. Thornton and Susan Varenne, Vintage Spiritual Classics [New York: Vintage Books, 2002].)

Martin Luther, *A Brief Instruction on What to Look for and Expect in the Gospels,* trans. E. Theodore Bachmann, *Luther's Works* 35, ed. E. Theodore Bachmann and Helmut Lehmann (Philadelphia: Fortress, 1960 [1521]), pp. 117-23.

One should thus realize that there is only one gospel, but that it is described by many apostles. Every single epistle of Paul and of Peter, as well as the Acts of the Apostles by Luke, is a gospel, even though they do not record all the works and words of Christ, but one is shorter and includes less than another. There is not one of the four major Gospels anyway that includes all the words and works of Christ; nor is this necessary. Gospel is and should be nothing else than a discourse or story about Christ, just as happens among men when one writes a book about a king or a prince, telling what he did, said, and suffered in his day. Such a story can be told in various ways; one spins it out, and the other is a brief. Thus the gospel is and should be nothing else than a chronicle, a story, a narrative about Christ, telling who he is, what he did, said, and suffered — a subject which one describes briefly, another more fully, one this way, another that way.

For at its briefest, the gospel is a discourse about Christ, that he is the Son of God and became man for us, that he died and was raised, that he has been established as a Lord over all things. This much St. Paul takes in hand and spins out in his epistles. He bypasses all the miracles and incidents [in Christ's ministry] which are set forth in the four Gospels, yet he includes the whole gospel adequately and abundantly. This may be seen clearly and well in his greeting to the Romans, where he says what the gospel is, and declares, "Paul, a servant of Jesus Christ, called to be an apostle, set apart for the gospel of God which he promised beforehand through his prophets in the Holy Scriptures, the gospel concerning his Son, who was descended from David according to the flesh and designated Son of God in power according to the Spirit of holiness by his resurrection from the dead, Jesus Christ our Lord," etc.

There you have it. The gospel is a story about Christ, God's and David's Son, who died and was raised and is established as Lord. This is the gospel in a nutshell. Just as there is no more than one Christ, so there is and may be no more than one gospel. Since Paul and Peter too teach nothing but Christ, in the way we have just described, so their epistles can be nothing but the gospel.

Yes, even the teaching of the prophets, in those places where they speak of Christ, is nothing but the true, pure, and proper gospel — just as if Luke or Matthew had described it. For the prophets have proclaimed the gospel and spoken of Christ, as St. Paul here reports and as everyone indeed knows. Thus when Isaiah in chapter fifty-three says how Christ should die for us and bear our sins, he has written the pure gospel. And I assure you, if a person fails to grasp this understanding of the gospel, he will never be able to be illuminated in the Scripture nor will he receive the right foundation.

Be sure, moreover, that you do not make Christ into a Moses, as if Christ did nothing more than teach and provide examples as the other saints do, as if the gospel were simply a textbook of teachings or laws. Therefore you should grasp Christ, his words, works, and sufferings, in a twofold manner. First as an example that is presented to you, which you should follow and imitate. As St. Peter says in 1 Peter 4, "Christ suffered for us, thereby leaving us an example." Thus when you see how he prays, fasts, helps people, and shows them love, so also you should do, both for yourself and for your neighbor. However, this is the smallest part of the gospel, on the basis of which it cannot yet even be called gospel. For on this level Christ is of no more help to you than some other saint. His life remains his own and does not as yet contribute anything to you. In short this mode [of understanding Christ as simply an example] does not make Christians but only hypocrites. You must grasp Christ at a much higher level. Even though this higher level has for a long time been the very best, the preaching of it has been something rare. The chief article and foundation of the gospel is that before you take Christ as an example, you accept and recognize him as a gift, as a present that God has given you and that is your own.

This means that when you see or hear of Christ doing or suffering something, you do not doubt that Christ himself, with his deeds and suffering, belongs to you. On this you may depend as surely as if you had done it yourself; indeed as if you were Christ himself. See, this is what it means to have a proper grasp of the gospel, that is, of the overwhelming goodness of God, which neither prophet, nor apostle, nor angel was ever able fully to express, and which no heart could adequately fathom or marvel at. This is the great fire of the love of God for us, whereby the heart and conscience become happy, secure, and content. This is what preaching the Christian faith means. This is why such preaching is called gospel, which in German means a joyful, good, and comforting "message"; and this is why the apostles are called the "twelve messengers."

Concerning this Isaiah 9[:6] says, "To us a child is born, to us a son is given." If he is given to us, then he must be ours; and so we must also receive him as belonging to us. And Romans 8[:32], "How should [God] not give us all things with his Son?" See, when you lay hold of Christ as a gift which is given you for your very own and have no doubt about it, you are a Christian. Faith redeems you from sin, death, and hell and enables you to overcome all things. O no one can speak enough about this. It is a pity that this kind of preaching has been silenced in the world, and yet boast is made daily of the gospel.

Now when you have Christ as the foundation and chief blessing of your salvation, then the other part follows: that you take him as your example, giving yourself in service to your neighbor just as you see that Christ has given himself for you. See, there faith and love move forward, God's commandment is fulfilled, and a person is happy and fearless to do and suffer all things. Therefore make note of this, that Christ as a gift nourishes your faith and makes you a

Christian. But Christ as an example exercises your works. These do not make you a Christian. Actually they come forth from you because you have already been made a Christian. As widely as a gift differs from an example, so widely does faith differ from works, for faith possesses nothing of its own, only the deeds and life of Christ. Works have something of your own in them, yet they should not belong to you but to your neighbor. . . .

When you open the book containing the Gospels and read or hear how Christ comes here or there, or how someone is brought to him, you should therein perceive the sermon or the gospel through which he is coming to you, or you are being brought to him. For the preaching of the gospel is nothing else than Christ coming to us, or we being brought to him. When you see how he works, however, and how he helps everyone to whom he comes or who is brought to him, then rest assured that faith is accomplishing this in you and that he is offering your soul exactly the same sort of help and favor through the gospel. If you pause here and let him do you good, that is, if you believe that he benefits and helps you, then you really have it. Then Christ is yours, presented to you as a gift.

After that it is necessary that you turn this into an example and deal with your neighbor in the very same way, be given also to him as a gift and an example. . . .

What a sin and shame it is that we Christians have come to be so neglectful of the gospel that we not only fail to understand it, but even have to be shown by other books and commentaries what to look for and what to expect in it. Now the Gospels and Epistles of the apostles were written for this very purpose. They want themselves to be our guides, to direct us to the writings of the prophets and of Moses in the Old Testament so that we might there read and see for ourselves how Christ is wrapped in swaddling cloths and laid in the manger [Luke 2:7], that is, how he is comprehended [*Vorfassett*] in the writings of the prophets. It is there that people like us should read and study, drill ourselves, and see what Christ is, for what purpose he has been given, how he was promised, and how all Scripture tends toward him. For he himself says in John 5[:46], "If you believed Moses, you would also believe me, for he wrote of me." Again [John 5:39], "Search and look up the Scriptures, for it is they that bear witness to me." . . .

Therefore also Luke, in his last chapter [24:27], says that Christ opened the minds of the apostles to understand the Scriptures. And Christ, in John 10[:3, 9], declares that he is the door by which one must enter, and whoever enters by him, to him the gatekeeper (the Holy Spirit) opens in order that he might find pasture and blessedness. Thus it is ultimately true that the gospel itself is our guide and instructor in the Scriptures, just as with this foreword I would gladly give instruction and point you to the gospel.

But what a fine lot of tender and pious children we are! In order that we might not have to study in the Scriptures and learn Christ there, we simply regard the entire Old Testament as of no account, as done for and no longer valid. Yet it alone bears the name of Holy Scripture. And the gospel should really not be something written, but a spoken word which brought forth the Scriptures, as Christ and the apostles have done. This is why Christ himself did not write anything but only spoke. He called his teaching not Scripture but gospel, meaning good news or a proclamation that is spread not by pen but by word of mouth. So we go on and make the gospel into a law book, a teaching of commandments, changing Christ into a Moses, the one who would help us into simply an instructor.

What punishment ought God to inflict upon such stupid and perverse people! Since we abandoned his Scriptures, it is not surprising that he has abandoned us to the teaching of the pope and to the lies of men. Instead of Holy Scripture we have had to learn the *Decretales* [papal and conciliar decrees] of a deceitful fool and an evil rogue. O would to God that among Christians the pure gospel were known and that most speedily there would be neither use nor need for this work of mine. Then there would surely be hope that the Holy Scriptures too would come forth again in their worthiness. Let this suffice as a very brief foreword and instruction.

JONATHAN EDWARDS

Preaching the Terrors

Jonathan Edwards (1703-1758) was colonial America's foremost theologian, revivalist, philosopher, and psychologist. After graduating from Yale College and serving as a junior tutor there for three years, Edwards became the assistant to his grandfather, Solomon Stoddard, in the Congregational church in North-ampton, Massachusetts. During the 1730s and 40s he found himself under constant obligation to defend the spiritual authenticity of the waves of revival sweeping New England and his own parish, where in a six-month period three hundred people joined his church. Edwards buttressed his defense of revival with the new psychology of John Locke. The groanings and distress of those "under awakenings," i.e., whose consciences had been aroused, are to be understood as empirical manifestations of God's intervention and not as self-generated impulses. Theologically, such terrors to "the affections" are necessary in order to prepare the listeners to embrace the gospel. Only God can change the heart and redirect the affections, but the preacher can help the listener know God, especially, as in most of Edwards's sermons, the *love* of God. When the preacher is compelled to display the judgment of God, he is not unlike the surgeon who thrusts his lance to the "core of the wound" in order to effect complete healing, an image, incidentally, by which Martin Luther King Jr. would later justify the extreme social measures of his own ministry to America. Edwards's observations on suicide as a potential consequence of the preaching of the law give the modern reader some inkling of the deadly seriousness with which the Puritan mind approached the Sunday sermon. Edwards was not so much a preacher of hellfire as a remorseless clinician of the predicament of the human race, which in his most famous sermon he likened to a spider dangling perilously above a flame.

Jonathan Edwards, *Thoughts on the Revival of Religion in New England, 1740, to which is prefixed A Narrative of the Surprising Work of God in Northampton, Mass., 1735* (New York: American Tract Society, n.d.), pp. 244-52.

Another thing that some ministers have been greatly blamed for, and I think unjustly, is *speaking terror to them that are already under great terrors*, instead of comforting them. Indeed if ministers in such a case go about to terrify persons with that which is not true, or to affright them by representing their case worse than it is, or in any respect otherwise than it is, they are to be condemned; but if they terrify them only by still holding forth more light to them, and giving them to understand more of the truth of their case, they are altogether to be justified. When sinners' consciences are greatly awakened by the Spirit of God, it is by light imparted to the conscience, enabling them to see their case to be, in some measure, as it is; and if more light be let in, it will terrify them still more: but ministers are not therefore to be blamed because they endeavor to hold forth more light to the conscience, and do not rather alleviate the pain they are under, by intercepting and obstructing that light that shines already.

To say anything to those who have never believed in the Lord Jesus Christ, which represents their case any otherwise than exceeding terrible, is not to preach the word of God to them; for the word of God reveals nothing but truth, but this is to delude them. Why should we be afraid to let persons that are in an infinitely miserable condition know the truth, or to bring them into the light for fear it should terrify them? It is light that must convert them, if ever they are converted. The more we bring sinners into the light while they are miserable and the light is terrible to them, the more likely it is that by and by the light will be joyful to them. The ease, peace, and comfort that natural men enjoy have their foundation in darkness and blindness; therefore as that darkness vanishes and light comes in, their peace vanishes and they are terrified: but that is no good argument why we should endeavor to bring back their darkness that we may promote their present comfort.

The truth is, that as long as men reject Christ and do not savingly believe in him, however they may be awakened, and however strict and conscientious and laborious they may be in religion, they have the wrath of God abiding on them, they are his enemies and the children of the devil (as the Scripture calls all that be not savingly converted, Matt. 13:38; 1 John 3:10), and it is uncertain whether they shall ever obtain mercy. God is under no obligation to show them mercy, nor will he be if they fast and pray and cry never so much; and they are then especially provoking God under those terrors, in that they stand it out against Christ, and will not accept of an offered Savior, though they see so much need of him; and seeing this is the truth, they should be told so, that they may be sensible what their case indeed be.

To blame a minister for thus declaring the truth to those who are under awakenings, and not immediately administering comfort to them, is like blaming a surgeon because, when he has begun to thrust in his lance, whereby he has already put his patient to great pain, and he shrieks and cries out with anguish, he is so cruel that he will not stay his hand, but goes on to thrust it in further, until he comes to the core of the wound. Such a compassionate physician, who, as soon as his patient began to flinch, should withdraw his hand and go about immediately to apply a plaster to skin over the wound and leave the core untouched, would be one that would heal the hurt slightly, crying "peace, peace," when there is no peace.

Indeed something else besides terror is to be preached to them whose consciences are awakened. The *gospel* is to be preached to them: they are to be told that there is a Savior provided, that is excellent and glorious, who has shed his precious blood for sinners, and is every way sufficient to save them; that stands ready to receive them, if they will heartily embrace him; for this is also the truth, as well as that they now are in an infinitely dreadful condition: this is the word of God. Sinners, at the same time that they are told how miserable their case is, should be earnestly invited to come and accept of a Savior, and yield their hearts to him, with all the winning, encouraging arguments for them so to do that the gospel affords. But this is to induce them to *escape* from the misery of the condition that they are now in; but not to make them think their present condition less miserable than it is, or at all to abate their uneasiness and distress while they are in it. That would be the way to quiet them and fasten them in it, and not to excite them to fly from it.

Comfort, in one sense, is to be held forth to sinners under awakenings of conscience, that is, comfort is to be offered to them in Christ, on condition of their flying *from their present miserable state* to him: but comfort is not to be administered to them *in their present state,* as anything that they have now any title to while out of Christ. No comfort is to be administered to them from anything *in them,* any of their qualifications, prayers, or other performances, past, present, or future; but ministers should, in such cases, strive to their utmost to take all such comforts from them, though it greatly increases their terror. A person that sees himself ready to sink into hell is ready to strive, some way or other, to lay God under some obligation to him; but he is to be beat off from everything of that nature, though it greatly increases his terror to see himself wholly destitute, on every side, of any refuge, or anything of his own to lay hold of; as a man that sees himself in danger of drowning is in terror and endeavors to catch hold on every twig within his reach, and he that pulls away those twigs from him increases his terror; yet if they are insufficient to save him, and by being in his way prevent his looking to that which will save him, to pull them away is necessary to save his life. . . .

I am not afraid to tell sinners that are most sensible of their misery, that their case is indeed as miserable as they think it to be, and a thousand times more so; for this is the truth. Some may be ready to say that though it be the truth, yet the truth is not to be spoken at all times, and seems not to be seasonable then; but, it seems to me, such truth is never more seasonable than at such a time, when Christ is beginning to open the eyes of conscience. Ministers ought to act as co-workers with him: to take that opportunity, and to the utmost to improve that advantage and strike while the iron is hot; and when the light has begun to shine, then to remove all obstacles, and use all proper means that it may come in more fully, and the work be done thoroughly then. And experience abundantly shows that to take this course is not of a hurtful tendency, but very much the contrary. I have seen, in very many instances, the happy effects of it, and oftentimes a very speedy happy issue, and never knew any ill consequence in case of real conviction, and when distress has been only from thence.

I know of but one case wherein the truth ought to be withheld from sinners in distress of conscience, and that is the case of *melancholy:* and it is not to be withheld from them then because the truth tends to do them hurt, but because if we speak the truth to them, sometimes they will be deceived and led into error by it through the strange disposition there is in them to take things wrong; so that that which as it is spoken is truth, as it is heard, and received, and applied by them is falsehood; and the truth will be thus misapplied by them, unless it be spoken with abundance of caution and prudence, and consideration of their disposition and circumstances.

But the most awful truths of God's word ought not to be withheld from a *public congregation* because it may happen that some such melancholic persons may be in it, any more than the Bible is to be withheld from the Christian world because it is manifest that there are a great many melancholic persons in Christendom that exceedingly abuse the awful things contained in Scripture to their own wounding.

Nor do I think that to be of weight which is made use of by some as a great and dreadful objection against the terrifying preaching that has of late been in New England, namely, that there have been some instances of melancholic persons that have so abused it that the issue has been the murder of themselves. The objection from hence is no stronger against awakening preaching than it is against the Bible itself; hundreds, and probably thousands, of instances might be produced of persons that have murdered themselves under religious melancholy; and these murders probably never would have been if it had not been for the Bible, or if the world had remained in a state of heathenish darkness. The Bible has not only been the occasion of these sad effects, but of thousands and I suppose millions of other cruel murders that have been committed, in the persecutions that have been raised, that never would have been if it had not been for the Bible: many whole countries have been, as it were, deluged with innocent blood, which would not have been if the gospel never had been preached in the world. It is not a good objection against any kind of preaching, that some men abuse it greatly to their hurt.

It has been acknowledged by all divines as a thing common in all ages and all Christian countries, that a very great part of those that sit under the gospel do so abuse it that it only proves an occasion of their far more aggravated damnation, and so of men's eternally murdering their souls, which is an effect infinitely more terrible than the murder of their bodies. It is as unjust to lay the blame of these self-murders to those ministers who have declared the awful truths of God's word in the most lively and affecting manner they were capable of, as it would be to lay the blame of hardening men's hearts and blinding their eyes, and their more dreadful eternal damnation, to the prophet Isaiah, or Jesus Christ, because this was the consequence of their preaching with respect to many of their hearers (Isa. 6:10; John 9:39; Matt. 13:14). Though a very few have abused the late awakening preaching to so sad an effect as to be the cause of their own temporal death, yet it may be, to one such instance there have been hundreds, yea, thousands that have been saved by this means from eternal death.

What has more especially given offense to many, and raised a loud cry against some preachers, as though their conduct were intolerable, is their *frighting poor innocent children* with talk of hellfire and eternal damnation. But if those that complain so loudly of this really believe, what is the general profession of the country, that all are by nature the children of wrath and heirs of hell; and that everyone that has not been born again, whether he be young or old, is exposed every moment to eternal destruction under the wrath of Almighty God; I say, if they really believe this, then such a complaint and cry as this betrays a great deal of weakness and inconsideration. As innocent as children seem to us to be, yet if they are out of Christ they are not so in God's sight, but are in a most miserable condition as well as grown persons; they are naturally very senseless and stupid, being *born as the wild ass's colt,* and need much to awaken them. Why should we conceal the truth from them?

Will those children that have been dealt so tenderly with as to hide from them their sin, and that have lived and died insensible of their misery until they come to feel it in hell, ever thank parents and others for their tenderness in not letting them know what they were in danger of? If parents' love toward their children was not blind, it would affect them much more to see their children every day exposed to eternal burnings, and yet senseless, than to see them suffer the distress of that awakening that is necessary in order to their escape from them, and that tends to their being eternally happy as the children of God. A child that has a dangerous wound may need the painful lance as well as grown persons; and that would be a foolish pity, in such a case, that should hold back the lance and throw away the life. I have seen the happy effects of dealing plainly and thoroughly with children in the concerns of their souls, without sparing them at all in many instances, and never knew any ill consequences of it in any one instance.

JOHN WESLEY

Mixing Law and Gospel

When accused of being a "legal preacher," John Wesley (1703-1791) answered his critic with a stern letter in which he justified his homiletical method, including his use of the law in Christian assemblies. He worried about the future of the Methodist societies should the "old way" of preaching be replaced with "sweetmeats" and soft words. For Wesley, as for Luther and Edwards, the authentic practice of preaching depends upon the theological understanding of the relationship of law and gospel. Wesley advocates the "mixing" of law and gospel, but not their confusion in the order of salvation. Unlike Luther, who contraposed law and gospel as implacable foes, Wesley situates them on a continuum of God's good will toward humanity and is thus able to speak of the "comfort" of the law. Whereas Luther dwelt upon the convicting authority of the law over the sinner, Wesley expands the law's uses to the enlightenment and sustenance of the believing soul on its quest for holiness. In this letter he alludes to two uses of the law in preaching, one to prod the recalcitrant sinner, the other to encourage the believing saint. Thus the law plays a key role in the building up of one who has received Christ. Karl Barth's later formula — "the law is nothing else than the necessary form of the gospel, whose content is grace" — is congruent with Wesley's use of the law in service of the gospel. In another place Wesley offers his famous "general method of preaching," which is "to invite, to convince, to offer Christ, to build up — and to do this in some measure in every sermon." This Wesley did for more than fifty years in a ministry that spanned the hemispheres. (See Richard Heitzenrater, "Spirit and Life: John Wesley's Preaching," in *Mirror and Memory: Reflections on Early Methodism* [Nashville: Kingswood Books, 1989].)

John Wesley, "Letter on Preaching Christ," December 20, 1751, *The Works of the Rev. John Wesley, A.M.*, vol. 11, third ed. (London: John Mason, 1830), pp. 480-86.

The point you speak of in your letter of September 21, [1751], is of a very important nature. I have had many serious thoughts concerning it, particularly for some months last past; therefore, I was not willing to speak hastily or slightly of it, but rather delayed till I could consider it thoroughly.

I mean by *preaching the gospel*, preaching the love of God to sinners, preaching the life, death, resurrection, and intercession of Christ, with all the blessings which, in consequence thereof, are freely given to true believers.

By *preaching the law*, I mean, explaining and enforcing the commands of Christ, briefly comprised in the Sermon on the Mount.

Now, it is certain, preaching the gospel to penitent sinners "begets faith"; that it "sustains and increases spiritual life in true believers."

Nay, sometimes it "teaches and guides" them that believe; yea, and "convinces them that believe not."

So far all are agreed. But what is the stated means of feeding and comforting believers? What is the means, as of begetting spiritual life where it is not, so of sustaining and increasing it where it is?

Here they divide. Some think, preaching the law only; others, preaching the gospel only. I think, neither the one nor the other; but duly mixing both, in every place, if not in every sermon.

I think the right method of preaching is this: At our first beginning to preach at any place, after a general declaration of the love of God to sinners, and his willingness that they should be saved, to preach the law, in the strongest, the closest, and most searching manner possible; only intermixing the gospel here and there, and showing it, as it were, afar off.

After more and more persons are convinced of sin, we may mix more and more of the gospel, in order to "beget faith," to raise into spiritual life those whom the law hath slain: but this is not to be done too hastily neither. Therefore, it is not expedient wholly to omit the law; not only because we may well suppose that many of our hearers are still unconvinced; but because otherwise there is danger that many who are convinced will heal their own wounds slightly; therefore, it is only in private converse with a thoroughly convinced sinner that we should preach nothing but the gospel.

If, indeed, we could suppose a whole congregation to be thus convinced, we should need to preach only the gospel: And the same we might do, if our whole congregation were supposed to be newly justified. But when these grow in grace, and in the knowledge of Christ, a wise builder would preach the law to them again; only taking particular care to place every part of it in a gospel light, as not only a command, but a privilege also, as a branch of the glorious liberty of the sons of God. He would take equal care to remind them that this is not the cause, but the fruit, of their acceptance with God; that other cause, "other foundation can no man lay, than that which is laid, even Jesus Christ;" that we are still forgiven and accepted, only for the sake of what he hath done and suffered for us; and that all true obedience springs from love to him, grounded on his first loving us. He would labor, therefore, in preaching any part of the law, to keep the love of Christ continually before their eyes; that thence they might draw fresh life, vigor, and strength, to run the way of his commandments.

Thus would he preach the law even to those who were pressing on to the mark. But to those who were careless, or drawing back, he would preach it in another manner, nearly as he did before they were convinced of sin. To those, meanwhile, who were earnest, but feebleminded, he would preach the gospel chiefly; yet variously intermixing more or less of the law, according to their various necessities.

By preaching the law in the manner above described, he would teach them how to walk in him whom they had received. Yea, and the same means (the main point wherein, it seems, your mistake lies) would both sustain and increase their spiritual life. For the commands are food, as well as the promises; food equally wholesome, equally substantial. These, also, duly applied, not only direct, but likewise nourish and strengthen, the soul.

Of this you appear not to have the least conception; therefore, I will endeavor to explain it. I ask, then, Do not all the children of God experience, that when God gives them to see deeper into his blessed law, whenever he gives a new degree of light, he gives, likewise, a new degree of strength? Now I see, he that loves me, bids me do this; and now I feel I can do it, through Christ strengthening me.

Thus light and strength are given by the same means, and frequently in the same moment; although sometimes there is a space between. For instance: I hear the command, "Let your communication be always in grace, meet to minister grace to the hearers." God gives me more light into this command. I see the exceeding height and depth of it. At the same time I see (by the same light from above) how far I have fallen short. I am ashamed; I am humbled before God. I earnestly desire to keep it better; I pray to him that hath loved me for more strength, and I have the petition I ask of him. Thus the law not only convicts the unbeliever, and enlightens the believing soul, but also conveys food to a believer; sustains and increases his spiritual life and strength.

And if it increases his spiritual life and strength, it cannot but increase his comfort also. For, doubtless, the more we are alive to God, the more we shall rejoice in him; the greater measure of his strength we receive, the greater will be our consolation also.

And all this, I conceive, is clearly declared in one single passage of Scripture: —

"The law of the Lord is perfect, converting the soul; the testimony of the Lord is sure, making wise the simple; the statutes of the Lord are right, rejoicing the heart; the commandment of the Lord is pure, enlightening the eyes. More to be desired are they than gold, yea, than much fine gold; sweeter also than honey, and the honeycomb." They are both food and medicine; they both refresh, strengthen, and nourish the soul.

Not that I would advise to preach the law without the gospel, any more than the gospel without the law. Undoubtedly, both should be preached in their turns; yea, both at once, or both in one: All the conditional promises are instances of this. They are law and gospel mixed together.

According to this model, I should advise every preacher continually to preach the law; the law grafted upon, tempered by, and animated with, the spirit of the gospel. I advise him to declare, explain, and enforce every command of God; but, meantime, to declare, in every sermon (and the more explicitly the better), that the first and great command to a Christian is, "Believe in the Lord Jesus Christ;" that Christ is all in all, our "wisdom, righteousness, sanctification, and redemption;" that all life, love, strength, are from him alone, and all freely given to us through faith. And it will ever be found, that the law thus preached both enlightens and strengthens the soul; that it both nourishes and teaches; that it is the guide, "food, medicine, and stay," of the believing soul. . . .

In this manner John Downes, John Bennet, John Haughton, and all the other Methodists, preached, till James Wheatly came among them, who never was clear, perhaps not sound, in the faith. According to his understanding was his preaching; an unconnected rhapsody of unmeaning words, like Sir John Suckling's — verses, smooth and soft as cream,/in which was neither depth nor stream.

Yet (to the utter reproach of the Methodist congregations) this man became a most popular preacher. He was admired more and more wherever he went, till he went over the second time into Ireland, and conversed more intimately than before with some of the Moravian preachers.

The consequence was that he leaned more and more both to their doctrine and manner of preaching. At first, several of our preachers complained of this; but, in the space of a few months (so incredible is the force of soft words), he, by slow and imperceptible degrees, brought almost all of the preachers then in the kingdom to think and speak like himself.

These, returning to England, spread the contagion to some others of their brethren. But still the far greater part of the Methodist preachers thought and spoke as they had done from the beginning.

This is the plain fact. As to the fruit of this new manner of preaching, (entirely new to the Methodists), speaking much of the promises, little of the commands; (even to unbelievers, and still less to believers); you think it has done great good; I think it has done great harm.

I think it has done great harm to the preachers; not only to James Wheatly himself, but to those who have learned of him, — David Trathen, Thomas Webb, Robert Swindells, and John Maddern: I fear to others also; all of whom are but shadows of what they were; most of them have exalted themselves above measure, as if they only "preached Christ, preached the gospel." And as highly as they have exalted themselves, so deeply have they despised their brethren; calling them, "legal preachers, legal wretches;" and (by a cant name) "Doctors," or "Doctors of Divinity." They have not a little despised their ministers also, for "countenancing the Doctors," as they termed them. They have made their faults (real or supposed) common topics of conversation; hereby cherishing in themselves the very spirit of Ham; yea, of Korah, Dathan, and Abiram.

I think it has likewise done great harm to their hearers; diffusing among them their own prejudice against the other preachers; against their ministers, me in particular, (of which you have been an undeniable instance), against the scriptural, Methodist manner of preaching Christ, so that they could no longer bear sound doctrine; they could no longer hear the plain old truth with profit or pleasure, nay, hardly with patience.

After hearing such preachers for a time, you yourself (need we further witnesses?) could find in my preaching no food for your soul; nothing to strengthen you in the way; no inward experience of a believer; it was all barren and dry; that is, you had no taste for mine or John Nelson's preaching; it neither refreshed nor nourished you.

Why, this is the very thing I assert: That the gospel preachers, so called, corrupt their hearers; they vitiate their taste, so that they cannot relish sound doctrine; and spoil their appetite, so that they cannot turn it into nourishment; they, as it were, feed them with sweetmeats, till the genuine wine of the kingdom seems quite insipid to them. They give them cordial upon cordial, which make them all life and spirit for the present; but, meantime, their appetite is destroyed, so that they can neither retain nor digest the pure milk of the word.

Hence it is, that (according to the constant observation I have made, in all parts both of England and Ireland) preachers of this kind (though quite the contrary appears at first) spread death, not life, among their hearers. As soon as that flow of spirits goes off, they are without life, without power, without any strength or vigor of soul; and it is extremely difficult to recover them, because they still cry out, "Cordials! Cordials!" of which they have had too much already, and have no taste for the food which is convenient for them. Nay, they have an utter aversion to it, and that confirmed by principle, having been taught to call it husks, if not poison: How much more to those bitters which are previously needful to restore their decayed appetite!

This was the very case when I went last into the north. For some time before my coming, John Downes had scarce been able to preach at all; the three others in the round were such as styled themselves gospel preachers. When I came to review the societies, with great expectation of finding a vast increase, I found most of them lessened by one-third; one entirely broken up. That of Newcastle itself was less by a hundred members than when I visited it before. And of those that remained, the far greater number in every place were cold, weary, heartless, dead. Such were the blessed effects of this gospel preaching! of this new method of preaching Christ!

On the other hand, when, in my return, I took an account of the societies in Yorkshire, chiefly under the care of John Nelson, one of the old way, in whose preaching you could find no life, no food, I found them all alive, strong, and vigorous of soul, believing, loving, and praising God their Savior; and increased in number from eighteen or nineteen hundred, to upward of three thousand. These had been continually fed with that wholesome food which you could neither relish nor digest. From the beginning they had been taught both the law and the gospel. "God loves you; therefore, love and obey him. Christ died for you; therefore, die to sin. Christ is risen; therefore, rise in the image of God. Christ liveth evermore; therefore live to God, till you live with him in glory."

So we preached; and so you believed. This is the scriptural way, the Methodist way, the true way. God grant we may never turn therefrom, to the right hand or to the left!

CHARLES GRANDISON FINNEY

Preaching for Conversion

Charles G. Finney (1792-1875) is known as the father of modern revivalism. After his conversion, he left his law practice in Adams, New York, and, without formal theological training, sparked a series of revivals that helped prolong the Second Great Awakening in America. Finney brought to his preaching the rhetoric of the courtroom and the drama of the stage. Representatives of established churches regularly accused him of "demeaning the pulpit." In his *Memoirs,* the description of his own preaching helps the modern reader understand his critics: "The Lord let me loose upon them in a wonderful manner" and "the congregation began to fall from their seats in every direction and cry for mercy. . . ." Under his leadership revivalism became a pragmatic science of mass persuasion with the *Lectures on Revivals of Religion* being its textbook. One hundred years after Edwards waited mightily on the Holy Spirit to work repentance in the hearts of unbelievers in Northampton, Massachusetts, Finney wrote, "[Revival] is not a miracle, or dependent on a miracle, in any sense. It is a purely philosophical [i.e., technical] result of the right use of the constituted means. . . ." "Religion is something to *do,* not something to wait for." In the following selection, Finney has borrowed the story about Niagara Falls from his sermon, "Sinners Bound to Change Their Own Hearts." It was this sermon that exposed his Arminianism, that is, the position that allows for the operation of human decision in accepting or resisting God's offer of grace. Thus one dimension of Finney's role in the Second Great Awakening was to further dilute the Calvinist orthodoxy of Jonathan Edwards.

Charles G. Finney, "How to Preach the Gospel" in *Lectures on Revivals of Religion* (New York: Fleming H. Revell, 1868), pp. 186-210.

The Scriptures ascribe the conversion of a sinner to four different agencies — to *men,* to *God,* to the *truth,* and to the *sinner himself.* The passages which ascribe it to the truth are the largest class. That men should ever have overlooked this distinction, and should have regarded conversion as a work performed exclusively by God, is surprising. . . .

In the conversion of a sinner, it is true that God gives the truth efficiency to turn the sinner to God. He is an active, voluntary, powerful agent in changing the mind. But he is not the only agent. The one that brings the truth to his notice is also an agent. We are apt to speak of ministers and other men as only *instruments* in converting sinners. This is not exactly correct. Man is something more than an instrument. Truth is the mere unconscious instrument. But man is more, he is a voluntary, responsible agent in the business. In my printed sermon, No. 1, which some of you may have seen, I have illustrated this idea by the case of an individual standing on the banks of Niagara.

"Suppose yourself to be standing on the banks of the falls of Niagara. As you stand upon the verge of the precipice, you behold a man lost in deep reverie, approaching its verge unconscious of his danger. He approaches nearer and nearer, until he actually lifts his foot to take the final step that shall plunge him in destruction. At this moment you lift your warning voice above the roar of the foaming waters, and cry out, *Stop.* The voice pierces his ear, and breaks the charm that binds him; he turns instantly upon his heel; all pale and aghast he retires, quivering, from the verge of death. He reels and almost swoons with horror; turns and walks slowly to the public house; you follow him; the manifest agitation in his countenance calls numbers around him; and on *your* approach, he points to you, and says, That man saved my life. Here he ascribes the work to you; and certainly there is a sense in which you had saved him. But, on being further questioned, he says, *Stop!* How that word rings in my ears. Oh, that was to me the word of life! Here he ascribes it to the word that aroused him, and caused him to turn. But, on conversing still further, he says, Had I not turned at that instant, I should have been a dead man. Here he speaks of it, and truly, as his own act; but directly you hear him say, Oh the mercy of God! if God had not interposed, I should have been lost. Now the only defect in this illustration is this: In the case supposed, the only interference on the part of God was a *providential* one; and the only sense in which the saving of the man's life is ascribed to him is in a providential sense. But in the conversion of a sinner, there is something more than the providence of God employed; for here not only does the providence of God so order it that the preacher cries, *Stop,* but the Spirit of God urges the truth home upon him with such tremendous power as to induce him to turn."

Not only does the preacher cry, *Stop,* but through the living voice of the preacher the Spirit cries, *Stop.* The preacher cries, "Turn ye, why will ye die." The Spirit pours the expostulation home with such power that the sinner turns. Now in speaking of this change, it is perfectly proper to say that the Spirit turned him, just as you would say of a man, who had persuaded another to change his mind on the subject of politics, that he had converted him, and brought him over. It is also proper to say that the truth converted him; as in a case when the political sentiments of a man were changed by a certain argument, we should say that argument brought him over. So also with perfect propriety may we ascribe the change to the living preacher, or to him who had presented the motives; just as we should say of a lawyer who had prevailed in his argument with a jury; he has got his case, he has converted the jury. It is also with the same propriety ascribed to the individual himself whose heart is changed; we should say he had changed his mind, he has come over, he has repented.

Now it is strictly true, and true in the most absolute and highest sense; the act is his own act, the turning is his own turning, while God by the truth has induced him to turn; still it is strictly true that he has turned and has done it himself. Thus you see the sense in which it is the work of God, and also the sense in which it is the sinner's own work. The Spirit of God, by the truth, influences the sinner to change, and in this sense is the efficient cause of the change. But the sinner actually changes, and is therefore himself, in the most proper sense, the author of the change.

There are some who, on reading their Bibles, fasten their eyes upon those passages that ascribe the work to the Spirit of God, and seem to overlook those that ascribe it to man, and speak of it as the sinner's own act. When they have quoted Scripture to prove it is the work of God, they seem to think they have proved that it is that in which man is passive, and that it can in no sense be the work of man. Some months since a tract was written, the title of which was, "Regeneration, the effect of Divine Power." The writer goes on to prove that the work is wrought by the Spirit of God, and there stops. Now it had been just as true, just as philosophical, and just as scriptural, if he had said that conversion was the work of man. It was easy to prove that it was the work of God, in the sense in which I have explained it.

The writer, therefore, tells the truth, so far as he goes; but he has told only half the truth. For while there is a sense in which it is the work of God, as he has shown, there is also a sense in which it is the work of man, as we have just seen. The very title to this tract is a stumbling block. It tells the truth, but it does not tell the whole truth. And a tract might be written upon this proposition, that *"Conversion or regeneration is the work of man"*; which would be just as true, just as scriptural, and just as philosophical, as the one to which I have alluded.

Thus the writer, in his zeal to recognize and honor God as concerned in this work, by leaving out the fact that a change of heart is the sinner's *own act,* has left the sinner strongly entrenched, with his weapons in his rebellious hands, stoutly resisting the claims of his Maker, and waiting passively for God to make him a new heart. Thus you see the consistency between the requirement of the text, and the declared fact that God is the author of the new heart. God commands you to make you a new heart, expects you to do it, and if it ever is done, you must do it. . . .

Preaching should be *direct.* The gospel should be preached *to* men, and not *about* them. The minister must address his hearers. He must preach *to* them *about themselves,* and not leave the impression that he is preaching to them about others. He will never do them any good, farther than he succeeds in convincing each individual that he means him. Many preachers seem very much afraid of making the impression that they mean anybody in particular. They are preaching against certain *sins,* not that have anything to do with the *sinner.* It is the *sin,* and not the *sinner,* that they are rebuking; and they would by no means speak as if they supposed any of *their hearers* were guilty of these abominable practices. Now this is anything but preaching the gospel. Thus did not the prophets, nor Christ, nor the apostles. Nor do those ministers do this who are successful in winning souls to Christ. . . .

Another important thing to observe is, that a minister should dwell most on those particular points which are most needed. I will explain what I mean.

Sometimes he may find a people who have been led to place great reliance on their own resolutions. They think they can consult their own convenience, and by and by they will repent, when they get ready, without any concern about the Spirit of God. Let him take up these notions, and show that they are entirely contrary to the Scriptures. Let him show that if the Spirit of God is grieved away, *however able* he may be, it is *certain he never will* repent, and that by and by, when it shall be convenient for him to do it, he will have no inclination. The minister who finds these errors prevailing, should expose them. He should hunt them out, and understand just how they are held, and then preach the class of truths which will show the fallacy, the folly, and the danger of these notions.

So on the other hand. He may find a people who have got such views of election and sovereignty, as to think they have nothing to do but to wait for the moving of the waters. Let him go right over against them, and crowd upon them their ability to obey God, and show their obligation and duty, and press them with that until he brings them to submit and be saved. They have got behind a perverted view of these doctrines, and there is no way to drive them out of the hiding place but to set them right on these points. Whenever a sinner is entrenched, unless you pour light upon him *there*, you will never move him. It is of no use to press him with those truths which he admits, however plainly they may in fact contradict his wrong notions. *He supposes* them to be perfectly consistent, and does not see the inconsistency, and therefore it will not move him, or bring him to repentance.

I have been informed of a minister in New England, who was settled in a congregation which had long enjoyed little else than Arminian preaching, and the congregation themselves were chiefly Arminians. Well, this minister, in his preaching, strongly insisted on the opposite points, the doctrine of election, divine sovereignty, predestination, etc. The consequence was, as might have been expected where this was done with ability, there was a powerful revival. Some time afterward this same minister was called to labor in another field, in this state, where the people were all on the other side, and strongly tinctured with Antinomianism. They had got such perverted views of election, and divine sovereignty, that they were continually saying they had no power to do anything, but must wait God's time. Now, what does this minister do but immediately go to preaching the doctrine of election. And when he was asked, how he could think of preaching the doctrine of election so much to that people, when it was the very thing that lulled them to a deeper slumber, he replied, "Why, that's the very class of truths by which I had such a great revival in ———"; not considering the difference in the views of the people. And if I am correctly informed, there he is to this day, preaching away at the doctrine of election, and wondering that it does not produce as powerful a revival as it did in the other place. Probably those sinners never will be converted. You must take things as they are, find out where sinners lie, and pour in truth upon them *there*, and START THEM OUT from their refuges of lies. It is of vast importance that a minister should find out where the congregation are, and preach accordingly. . . .

When I entered the ministry, there had been so much said about the doctrine of election and sovereignty, that I found it was the universal hiding place, both of sinners and of the church, that they could not do anything, or could not obey the gospel. And wherever I went, I found it indispensable to demolish these refuges of lies. And a revival would in no way be produced or carried on, but by dwelling on that class of truths which holds up man's ability, and obligation, and responsibility. This was the only class of truths that would bring sinners to submission.

It was not so in the days when President Edwards and Whitefield labored. Then the churches in New England had enjoyed little else than Arminian preaching, and were all resting in themselves and their own strength. These bold and devoted servants of God came out and declared those particular doctrines of grace, divine sovereignty, and election, and they were greatly blessed.

They did not dwell on these doctrines exclusively, but they preached them very fully. The consequence was, that because *in those circumstances* revivals followed from such preaching, the ministers who followed *continued to preach these doctrines almost exclusively.* And they dwelt on them so long, that the church and the world got entrenched behind them, waiting for God to come and do what he required *them* to do, and so revivals ceased for many years.

Now, and for years past, ministers have been engaged in hunting them out from these refuges. And here it is all-important for the ministers of this day to bear in mind, that if they dwell exclusively on ability and obligation, they will get their hearers back on the old Arminian ground, and then they will cease to promote revivals. Here are a body of ministers who have preached a great deal of truth, and have had great revivals, under God. Now let it be known and remarked, that the reason is, they have hunted sinners out from their hiding places. But if they continue to dwell on the same class of truths till sinners hide themselves behind their preaching, another class of truths must be preached. And then if they do not change their mode, another pall will hang over the church, until another class of ministers shall arise and hunt sinners out of those new retreats. . . .

It is of great importance that the sinner should be made to *feel his guilt,* and not left to the impression that he is *unfortunate.* I think this is a very prevailing fault, particularly with printed books on the subject. They are calculated to make the sinner think more of his sorrows than of his sins, and feel that his state is rather unfortunate than criminal. Perhaps most of you have seen a very lovely little book recently published, entitled "Todd's Lectures to Children." It is very fine, exquisitely fine, and happy in some of its illustrations of truths. But it has one very serious fault. Many of its illustrations, I may say most of them, are not calculated to make a correct impression respecting the guilt of sinners, or to make them feel how much they have been to blame. This is very unfortunate. If the writer had guarded his illustrations on this point, so as to make them impress sinners with a sense of their guilt, I do not see how a child could read through that book and not be converted. . . .

Sinners ought to be made to feel that they have something to do, and that is to repent; that is something which no other being can do for them, neither God nor man, and something which they can do, and do now. Religion is something to *do,* not something to wait for. And they must do now, or they are in danger of eternal death.

Ministers should never rest satisfied, until they have ANNIHILATED every excuse of sinners. The plea of "inability" is the worst of all excuses. It slanders God so, charging him with infinite tyranny, in commanding men to do that which they have no power to do. Make the sinner see and feel that this is the very nature of his excuse. Make the sinner see that all pleas in excuse for not submitting to God, are an act of rebellion against him. Tear away the last LIE which he grasps in his hand, and make him feel that he is absolutely condemned before God. . . .

I wish now, secondly, to make a few remarks on the manner of preaching.

It should be conversational. Preaching, to be understood, should be colloquial in its style. A minister must preach just as he would talk, if he wishes to be fully understood. Nothing is more calculated to make a sinner feel that religion is some mysterious thing that he cannot understand than this mouthing, formal, lofty style of speaking, so generally employed in the pulpit. The minister ought to do as the lawyer does when he wants to make a jury understand him perfectly. He uses a style perfectly colloquial. This lofty, swelling style will do no good. The gospel will never produce any great effects, until ministers talk to their hearers, in the pulpit, as they talk in private conversation. . . .

Preaching should be parabolical. That is, illustrations should be constantly used, drawn from incidents, real or supposed. Jesus Christ constantly illustrated his instructions in this way. He would either advance a principle and then illustrate it by a parable, that is, a short story of some event real or imaginary, or else he would bring out the principle in the parable. There are millions of facts that can be used to advantage, and yet very few ministers dare to use them, for fear somebody will reproach them. "Oh," says somebody, "he tells stories." Tells stories! Why, that is the way Jesus Christ preached. And it is the only way to preach. Facts, real or supposed, should be used to show the truth. Truths not illustrated are generally just as well calculated to convert sinners as a mathematical demonstration. Is it always to be so? Shall it always be a matter of reproach that ministers follow the example of Jesus Christ in illustrating truths by facts? Let them do it, and let fools reproach them as storytelling ministers. They have Jesus Christ and common sense on their side. . . .

Preaching should be repetitious. If a minister wishes to preach with effect, he must not be afraid of repeating whatever he sees is not perfectly understood by his hearers. Here is the evil of using notes. The preacher preaches right along just as he has it written down, and cannot observe whether he is understood or not. If he interrupts his reading, and attempts to catch the countenances of his audience, and to explain where he sees they do not understand, he gets lost and confused, and gives it up. If a minister has his eyes on the people he is preaching to, he can commonly tell by their looks whether they understand him. And if he sees they do not understand any particular point, let him stop and illustrate it. If they do not understand one illustration, let him give another, and make it all clear to their minds, before he goes on. But those who write their sermons go right on, in a regular consecutive train, just as in an essay or a book, and do not repeat their thoughts till the audience fully comprehend them.

I was conversing with one of the first advocates in this country. He said the difficulty which preachers find in making themselves understood is that they do not repeat enough. Says he, "In addressing a jury, I always expect that whatever I wish to impress upon their minds, I shall have to repeat at least twice, and often I repeat it three or four times, and even as many times as there are jurymen before me. Otherwise, I do not carry their minds along with me, so that they can feel the force of what comes afterward." If a jury under oath, called to decide on the common affairs of this world, cannot apprehend an argument unless there is so much repetition, how is it to be expected that men will understand the preaching of the gospel without it. . . ?

A minister should aim to convert his congregation. But you will ask, Does not all preaching aim at this? No. A minister always has some aim in preaching, but most sermons were never aimed at converting sinners. And if sinners were converted under them, the preacher himself would be amazed. I once heard a fact on this point. There were two young ministers who had entered the ministry at the same time. One of them had great success in converting sinners, the other none. The latter inquired of the other, one day, what was the reason of this difference. "Why," replied the other, "the reason is, that I aim at a different end from you, in preaching. My object is to convert sinners, but you aim at no such thing. And then you go and lay it to sovereignty in God, that you do not produce the same effect, when you never aim at it. Here, take one of my sermons, and preach it to your people, and see what the effect will be." The man did so and preached the sermon, and it did produce effect. He was frightened when sinners began to weep; and when one came to him after the meeting to ask what he should do, the minister apologized to him, and said, "I did not aim to wound you, I'm sorry if I have hurt your feelings." Oh, horrible! . . .

It is impossible for a man who writes his sermons to arrange his matter, and turn and choose his thoughts, so as to produce the same effect as when he addresses the people directly, and makes them feel that he means them. Writing sermons had its origin in times of political difficulty. The practice was unknown in the apostles' days. No doubt written sermons have done a great deal of good, but they can never give to the gospel its great power. Perhaps many ministers have been so long trained in the use of notes, that they had better not throw them away. Perhaps they would make bad work without them. The difficulty would not be for the want of mind, but from wrong training. The bad habit is begun with the schoolboy, who is called to "speak his piece." Instead of being set to express his own thoughts and feelings in his own language, and with his own natural manner, such as nature herself prompts, he is made to commit another person's writing to memory, and then mouths it out in a stiff and formal way. And so when he goes to college, and to the seminary, instead of being trained to *extempore* speaking, he is set to writing his piece, and commit it to memory. I would pursue the opposite course from the beginning. I would give him a subject, and let him first think, and then speak his thoughts. Perhaps he will make mistakes. Very well, that is to be expected — in a beginner. But he will learn. Suppose he is not eloquent, at first. Very well, he can improve. And he is in the very way to improve. This kind of training alone will ever raise up a class of ministers who can convert the world. . . .

All ministers should be revival ministers, and all preaching should be revival preaching; that is, it should be calculated to promote holiness. People say, "It is very well to have some men in the church who are revival preachers and who can go about and promote revivals; but then you must have others to *indoctrinate* the church." Strange! Do they not know that a revival indoctrinates the church faster than anything else? And a minister will never produce a revival, if he does not indoctrinate his hearers. The preaching I have described is full of doctrine, but it is doctrine to be practiced. And that is revival preaching.

There are two objections sometimes brought against the kind of preaching which I have recommended:

That it is letting down the dignity of the pulpit to preach in this colloquial, lawyer-like style [is the first objection]. They are shocked at it. But it is only on account of its novelty, and not for any impropriety there is in the thing itself. I heard a remark made by a leading layman in the center of this state in regard to the preaching of a certain minister. He said it was the first preaching he ever heard that he understood, and the first minister he ever heard that spoke as if he believed his own doctrine, or meant what he said. And when he first heard him preach as if he was saying something that he meant, he thought he was crazy. But eventually, he was made to see that it was all true, and he submitted to the truth, as the power of God for the salvation of his soul.

What is the dignity of the pulpit? To see a minister go into the pulpit to sustain its dignity! Alas, alas! During my foreign tour, I heard an English missionary preach exactly in that way. I believe he was a good man, and out of the pulpit he would talk like a man that meant what he said. But no sooner was he in the pulpit, than he appeared like a perfect automaton — swelling, mouthing, and singing, enough to put all the people to sleep. And the difficulty seemed to be that he wanted to maintain the dignity of the pulpit.

It is objected that this preaching is theatrical. The bishop of London once asked Garrick, the celebrated play-actor, why it was that actors in representing a mere fiction, should move an assembly, even to tears, while ministers, in representing the most solemn realities, could scarcely obtain a hearing. The philosophical Garrick well replied, "It is because we represent fiction as reality, and you represent reality as a fiction." This is telling the whole story. Now what is the design of the actor in a theatrical representation? It is so to throw himself into the spirit and meaning of the writer, as to adopt his sentiments, make them his own, feel them, embody them, throw them out upon the audience as living reality. And now, what is the objection to all this in preaching? The actor suits the action to the word, and the word to the action. His looks, his hands, his attitudes, and everything are designed to express the full meaning of the writer. Now this should be the aim of the preacher. And if by "theatrical" be meant the strongest possible representation of the sentiments expressed, then the more theatrical a sermon is, the better. And if ministers are too stiff, and the people too fastidious, to learn even from an actor, or from the stage, the best method of swaying mind, of enforcing sentiment, and diffusing the warmth of burning thought over a congregation, then they must go on with their prosing, and reading, and sanctimonious starch. But let them remember that while they are thus turning away and decrying the art of the actor, and attempting to support "the dignity of the pulpit," the theaters can be thronged every night. The commonsense people will be entertained with that manner of speaking, and sinners will go down to hell.

H. H. FARMER

The I-Thou Encounter

Whether Luther, Wesley, Finney, or Brooks, most great preachers have sensed the eventfulness or immediacy of preaching as a form of encounter. Something happens when the word is spoken. In the Warrack Lectures for 1940, systematic theologian and Presbyterian minister Herbert Farmer (1892-1981) gave lucid homiletical expression to the widely held view of divine truth as God's encounter with humanity. Deeply influenced by Martin Buber and the Christian personalism of his teacher at Cambridge, John Oman, Farmer asserts that God, whom he occasionally calls "the infinite Person," "never enters into *personal* relationship with a man apart from other human persons." When this personal encounter takes the form of preaching, three elements are invariably present: the exercise of *will*, an articulated *claim*, and *shared meaning*. By "will" he means an experience in which one self-directing will relates itself to another in such a way that the latter remains free. By "claim" he does not mean a compulsion but an offer that can be rejected. The speaker first lays claim to the attention of the other. By "shared meaning" he describes a claim that can be accepted only if it is mutually understood by the speaker and the hearer. As a *reasoned* claim, it can be held at arm's length and considered. Farmer proposed his theology of the incarnation and the Christian person in his earlier works *The World and God* and *Towards Belief in God,* and subsequently in his Beecher Lectures at Yale, *God and Men* (1946). In 1949 he succeeded C. H. Dodd as Norris-Hulse Professor of Divinity at Cambridge.

H. H. Farmer, *The Servant of the Word* (Philadelphia: Fortress, 1964 [1942]), pp. 21-36.

I propose now to develop further the thought that preaching is only to be rightly understood and conducted when it is seen in the context of a Christian understanding of persons and their relationships with one another. It is first, last, and all the time a function of the personal world. . . .

I begin with the proposition that God's purpose is such, and he has so made humanity in accordance with that purpose, that he never enters into *personal* relationship with a man apart from other human persons. When he confronts me in the specifically personal I-thou relationship, to use the phraseology referred to in the last lecture, it is always closely bound up with the personal I-thou relationship I have with my fellows. I am related to the personal God in the neighbor, to the neighbor as personal in God. . . .

We might express it by saying that when God created man he *eo facto* [by this fact] created an order or structure of persons in relationship with himself and with one another. This is the ultimate secret of finite personal nature, of specifically human nature. Only as a man is part of, held in, that structure is he distinctively man. If, *per impossibile,* you could lift a man out of it, he would cease to exist as man. It is not that God creates a man and then pops him into the world of persons as a housewife makes a dumpling and pops it into the saucepan, both dumpling and saucepan being capable of existing apart from one another. To come into existence as a man is to be incorporated in this world of the personal, to be in relation to persons — the divine person and human persons — and existence as a man is not possible on any other terms.

It would be easy to interpret what has so far been said to mean that a man stands at one and the same time in *two* relationships which can in principle be separated from one another. On the one hand there is his relationship to the divine person, God, and on the other hand there is his relationship to finite persons, his fellows. Christian thought has not infrequently expressed itself in terms which give countenance to such an idea. The great commandment itself lends color to it — thou shalt love the Lord thy God *and* thy neighbor as thyself. We speak of duties to God *and* of duties to the neighbor. There is Augustine's oft-quoted saying, "Thou hast made us for thyself and our hearts are restless until they find rest in thee." There is the whole mystical tradition, of which Augustine's words are probably in some measure an echo, that man finds God by withdrawing from the world, including the world of persons. Yet the true Christian understanding is that these two relationships cannot ever be separated from one another. Indeed it would perhaps be better to say that there are not two relationships but only one relationship which is twofold; or, better still, there is one personal continuum with two poles, the infinite personal on the one hand, the finite personal on the other. The individual is related all the time to his neighbor in God and to God in his neighbor, even when he is not aware of it, even when he denies it, and in that relationship his distinctive quality as a human person resides. So that Augustine's saying should be rewritten, "Thou hast made us for thyself and for one another and our hearts are restless until they find rest in Thee in one another and in one another in Thee." . . .

If now I am asked to say more precisely what is meant by a personal relationship, by an I-thou relationship, to use Buber's terminology, I am in a difficulty just because we are here dealing with an ultimate in the world of being. An ultimate cannot be expressed in terms of anything else; if it could it would not be an ultimate. But seeking to describe what must primarily be identified by each one in the immediacy of experience, it may be said that the heart of the matter is in the relationship of self-conscious, self-directing wills to one another in a situation which is important and significant for both. If you ask me what I mean by a "self-conscious, self-directing will," I cannot say. I can only refer to your own immediate self-awareness. But it is possible to say something about the relationship between such wills which constitutes the specifically "I-thou" world. It is a relationship wherein the activity of one self-conscious, self-directing will is conditioned by that of another in such wise that each remains free. . . .

How then can your will condition mine so that my will remains free? It can do so only by confronting me as an inescapable claim. Both words are important. I am free to reject it — that is why it is claim; if I were not so free, it would be compulsion — but I am not free to escape it, for my rejection of it at once enters into the structure of history, your history, and in varying degree universal history. If the claim be a right claim, that is, one rooted in the essential nature of the personal world as this has been created by God, the rejection of it can have the most disastrous consequences. Herein, in part, lies the problem of atonement. The problem of atonement is the problem of setting right in a world of inaccessible, "non-manipulatable" wills the rejection of claims which is already part of history and at work in history. It is the restoration of the fabric of the I-thou world when it has been torn.

The idea of a claim, in the sense in which we are here using the term, is, I think, another indefinable. Its impact has to be felt to be known, and it is not analyzable into other notions. It is the basis of the ethical concept of "ought," which is also for that reason unanalyzable, as Sidgwick insists. The ethical is the personal world, the world of history. One thing, however, we can say, and that is that a claim only conditions my will by being understood. I am free to accept or reject it, but I can only accept or reject it by first understanding it. I have not dealt with your claim at all if I have not understood it, if I have not grasped in some measure your world, your point of view, your meaning, and made it my own. This presupposes that though we see things from a different point of view

— it is the differences of points of view that make claims possible — yet we are both in the same world and can speak and act in terms of it. This is but to say that reason and self-conscious, self-directing personality go together. By the same argument reasoning *together,* the possibility of, nay the necessity for, a community of insight and understanding, for shared meaning, is an essential part of the personal, the I-thou world.

In the light of these remarks it is possible to see how and why *speech* is so absolutely central and indispensable in the world of personal relationships. In view of what we have to say later about preaching, it is necessary to dwell on this for a little.

What a strange and potent thing speech is! And how the familiarity of it hides from us its strangeness and potency! We sometimes hear debated whether we would rather lose sight or hearing, if we were shut up to such a frightful option. The immediate reaction as a rule is to choose to retain the faculty of sight; the thought of a permanently dark and colorless world affrights us. But I am not sure but what the wiser part would be to choose to retain hearing, for whereas the loss of sight would cut you off from all the loveliness and interest of the world of objects, the loss of hearing would cut you off from the world of persons, and there is no question which is the graver loss, which is the heavier blow at the innermost citadel of our being. The spoken word is right within the core of the I-thou relationship, and the written or printed word is always a poor substitute for it. Mankind seems to have instinctively known this from earliest times. Primitive peoples have a sense of the power of the spoken word which is exaggerated to the point of superstition, but which like many primitive ideas is founded on reality. We used to say in our childhood,

> Sticks and stones may break my bones
> But words will never hurt me!

Nothing could be more false. Words can and do hurt much more penetratingly and destructively than sticks and stones. Perhaps it was because deep down we knew that words can hurt most frightfully that we were so anxious to protest that they did not. The New Testament has a better understanding on the matter: "The tongue is a little member and boasteth great things. Behold how great a matter a little fire kindleth. And the tongue is a fire, a world of iniquity. So is the tongue among our members that it defileth the whole body, and setteth on fire the course of nature, and it is set on fire of hell." The absolute centrality of speech in the world of personal relationships is brought home to you when you are in a foreign country and know nothing of the language and nobody there knows anything of yours. Here you have in effect the frightful situation of both persons being deaf. The sense of utter frustration and loneliness, of alienation and unreality, has to be experienced to be known.

The reason why the spoken word is thus at the very heart of the world of persons in relationship of the I-thou relationship, is that it is supremely that medium of communication wherein the three elements mentioned above, will and claim and shared meaning, are, or can be, at a maximum together in a single, fused unity.

Thus, first, in the spoken word my will objectifies itself for you with such force and immediacy that it and its objectification are one and indissoluble, almost indistinguishable. The word is my will, and my will is the word. This is clumsily and therefore inaccurately expressed, but a single consideration will show what I mean. Precisely at the moment when my will is withdrawn the word ceases as absolutely as annihilation. And it comes into being again just where and when my will ordains it. This is perhaps the nearest we get to the divine activity of creation out of nothing, and of preservation — pure creative and sustaining will. It is this immediate dependence of the spoken word on the will that gives it its superiority over the printed word as a medium of personal relationship. What seems, what indeed from one point of view is, the advantage of the printed word, is that it can be listened to again and again whenever *I* choose — I have only to take the book down from my shelves and read it, and it can stay on my shelves a score or more years and not perish. This is precisely its disadvantage from the point of view of personal relationship; for the essence of the personal relationship is in the activity of *your* will bringing the word into being and giving it the only being it possesses, not in the activity of my will. . . .

Second, and to be taken inseparably with what has just been said, in the spoken word you have in a maximal form the element of claim. When I speak to you my will claims yours. Speech is full of claim.

To begin with, I claim your attention. I should not speak if I did not want you to listen. By speech I ask you to listen. If you will not listen, I waste my breath, as the saying is. Sometimes when I have had occasion to rebuke one of my children, he stuffs his fingers into his ears. The result is a feeling of frustration and impotence in me which is not merely injured parental dignity and *amour propre*. It is as though the child had temporarily vanished, as though a thick wall, infinitely thicker than his puny little fingers, had come down between us. It is not that he has gone deaf, though that would be bad enough. He has *willed* to go deaf. He has repudiated my claim. That stopping of the ears symbolizes, as nothing else can, the awful fact of freedom which lies at the heart of the personal world. And dare we speculate that God gave us no lids for our ears as he did for our eyes, precisely that we might always be open to one another and to the word?

Then, further, by my speech I claim your answer. My word, containing my will, is addressed to your will, and asks your answer containing yours, even if it be only the answer of a nod or a shake of the head. I want response. It is a knock on the door — a call for attention which is also a call for an answer.

Then, again, there is implicit in my speech the claim of truth. Thus there is within it, as there is in all personal dealings, the germ at least of the ethical. Even when I speak to deceive you I rest upon the claim of truth to your allegiance; my lies must have verisimilitude. If neither of us acknowledges the claim of truth, personal intercourse is in so far forth as impossible as if we were both stone deaf. Yet the fact that lies and deception are possible at all shows that we are in the region of claim and not of mechanical necessitation.

This, however, has already involved us in the third point, not to be separated from the other two, that the distinctive *raison d'être* of speech is to convey reasoned meaning, or meaning to reason and understanding. It is the supreme and distinctive vehicle of ideas, propositions, judgments, of truth in a form in which it can be, so to say, held at arm's length and considered. It may include other things in its intention as well, of course. Speech may be designed to excite feeling, or to create an aesthetic impression, or even, as in an advertising slogan, to affect, by repetition and sheer suggestive force, a man's actions almost without his knowing it, but in none of these things does its unique quality appear. Music can evoke feeling, a landscape or a flower can make an aesthetic impression, a forceful gesture or example can act as a powerful suggestion, without speech entering in at all. Speech is nonessential to these things.

The unique function of speech is that of conveying in the most explicit way possible the judgment of one self-conscious awareness to another in such wise that both are brought directly and inescapably under the claim of truth. If it does, or seeks to do, any of these other things that we have mentioned — to stimulate feeling, to create aesthetic impression, to influence the will by force of suggestion — *without* doing this, it has not fulfilled its distinctive and noblest function, which, I repeat, is to convey truth in the form of an appeal from one personal insight to another under a common obligation to the truth. . . .

It is perhaps not superfluous to insist that I am not wishing to suggest that speech is the only medium for the conveying of truth from one personality to another. There are other symbols besides words and sentences, as, for example, those of music, art, ritual, and so on. Nor would I wish to restrict the category of truth only to those matters which can be expressed in propositional form. There is truth of feeling and valuation, and it is precisely this kind of truth that transcends verbal expression and requires other symbols. This is not the occasion to go into these matters, though I shall make incidental reference to them again later. But I do maintain that speech is superior to all other means of communication in that it unites, or can unite, in a maximal form that we have called will, claim, and reasoned meaning, and so can be as nothing else can the medium of personal relationship.

HENRY H. MITCHELL

Preaching as Celebration

One of the most insightful contemporary interpreters of African-American preaching is the Baptist minister and lecturer, Henry H. Mitchell. In several books and articles he has explored the genius of black preaching in light of its African heritage and the political, cultural, and religious experience of black people in America. He combines his appreciation of the freedom and cathartic drama of black preaching with a vigorous critique of the white, middle-class pulpit, which he characterizes as "cerebral" and lifeless. He would agree with theologian James Cone that the African-American preacher's evocation of life across the Jordan does not merely offer an otherworldly escape to oppressed people but also serves as a critique of the racist conditions and policies that continue to make this world hard to endure. In the following selection, which supplements his Beecher Lectures given in 1974, he explains how celebration or the "climax" in the black sermon lifts both preacher and congregation to the joyous, self-affirming, yet self-forgetting enjoyment of God. By his reference to "the transconscious," a term borrowed from the historian of religions, Mircea Eliade, Mitchell means to describe (in Eliade's words) the "result of immemorial existential situations" now embedded in the black tradition of worship and preaching.

Henry H. Mitchell, *The Recovery of Preaching* (San Francisco: Harper and Row, 1977), pp. 54-62.

The best of gospel preaching is at once proclamation and celebration. Let us agree then as to what we mean by the term *celebration*. For our purposes celebration is both the literal and the symbolic or ritual expression of praise or joy. It may be in regard to an event or a person, historical or legendary, past or present; or it may relate to an object or a belief. A part of the genius of Black preaching has been its capacity to generate this very kind of celebration, despite the hardest of circumstances. This genius for celebration is partly responsible for the fact that enslaved and otherwise oppressed Blacks have survived the seemingly unbearable. When the oppressor thought they were too ignorant or insensitive to pain to know the depth of their plight, they were in fact well aware of it, but also involved in a vital tradition which literally sustained them by engaging them in praise of God — the dramatic expression of a worldview affirming creation and Creator and the ineradicable value of the gift of life.

Preaching *without* celebration is a de facto denial of the good news, in *any* culture. Stated positively, what I propose is that preaching *with* celebration greatly enhances the transconscious retention and the true understanding and application of the gospel. It is my purpose here to spell out the meaning and the supporting rationale of these perhaps sweeping statements.

As I have already indicated in the second chapter, the African folk/oral tradition was so accurately communicated from generation unto generation because of rites which were celebrative. The massive corpus was inculcated in the minds of the young under circumstances which were joyous for the most part. That is to say, most of the folk gatherings were around the happy themes of birth, marriage, planting, harvest, and the advancement of the young through the stages of life. Even the feasts about death were not without joy. The result was a well-remembered corpus of proverbs and rites, with many ordinary folk capable of meticulous recall. More importantly, this tradition was so impressed upon the total transconscious that the life decisions of folk were heavily conditioned if not absolutely controlled by traditional belief. The importance of celebration in this cultural forebear of the Black religious tradition is inescapable. The joy and celebration which characterize Black worship even now are very important in the explanation of miraculous survival of this beauty and richness under the shadows of the oppressed ghetto.

Lest somebody get the notion that this is just the tenacity of a traditional "trip" of Black folks, let us look at the role or function of joy, fun, ecstasy, or celebration in worship, particularly preaching. In the first place, that which is joyously given, received, and celebrated is well nigh unforgettable. The emotional/intellectual tape or script is well cut by the etching agent of ecstasy. The transconsious data bank of the soul can much more readily be depended upon to recall that which was recorded in the midst of such pleasant associations.

And when in the dark night of the soul it seems impossible to recapture the joy of the celebration, there is a higher signal which may draw it forth from the data pool even so. The first function of celebration in preaching is reinforcement for retention and availability.

The very title of George Leonard's book, *Education and Ecstasy,* indicates how important joy is to real learning even in the public schools. That importance is still greater in the learning of spiritual values and foundations. In a volume entitled *How Churches Teach* I once declared:

Shouting may, at times, be put on or manipulated. But at its best it *teaches* "Aunt Jane" and all the rest that the presence of God is sheer ecstasy — that before God we can be absolutely free and uninhibited — and that God freely accepts and loves the real person that we have to hide almost everywhere else. The ecstasy of being somebody-to-the-hilt for even five minutes, *teaches* enough faith to keep an oppressed and despised Black man courageous and creative for another week. Ecstasy teaches *and* reinforces teaching. It does not always express itself in shouting in the Black tradition, but it does always involve deep feelings. Such feelings generate deep trust levels and inscribe the faith indelibly on the transconscious.

A second function of celebration is its fulfillment and affirmation of personhood and identity by means of free expression, which is accepted in the religiocultural context. This has been mentioned already in the quote above, where the shouting Christian is accepted by God while expressing his or her real feelings. This acceptance by God is mediated by the congregation, whose cultural expectations place high value on the shouting [as] evidence of the presence of the Holy Spirit. If the congregation were to view shouting in a different light, it would be hard to sense the acceptance of God counterculturally. Celebration, therefore, provides a supportive structure in which persons are free to pour forth their deepest feelings and to celebrate their own personhood in the midst of celebrating the goodness of God.

Some time ago I was crushed in an Amanuel Day crowd of thousands, stretched as far as eye could see in all directions from Amanuel Church in Addis Ababa. They were celebrating Ethiopian Orthodox Christmas Eve. As the procession bearing the symbolic Ark of the Covenant passed round and round the church, shouts of great joy arose from wave after wave in a sea of literally happy faces. They were a terribly poverty-stricken lot for the most part, and Marx would have called this joy an opiate of the people. But I know that the religious forefathers of these same folk have survived the onslaughts of European and Arab invasion time and again. In the barren wastes to which they have had to retreat to live, they have survived more by an abundance of spiritual feast days than [by an abundance] of physical food. Amanuel Day is only one of the nine *minor* feasts, but those thousands were gathered because their chants and cheers, their waving and dancing, had meaning there which gave *them* meaning and fulfillment also. The owners of those voices and hands and feet were affirmed as persons while praising God, despite the vastness of their numbers and their great physical need by American standards.

This vast crowd also illustrates a third function of celebration, that of drawing people into community. Celebration is best achieved in the group relationship. It is good, of course, to praise God in solitude, but the enjoyment of God's goodness is multiplied by the sharing of the news. It binds together the host of those who affirm the goodness of God, who are affirmed in his praise, and who joyously affirm others as recipients of that same goodness. The celebrating community may not be personally acquainted, but the group tradition nevertheless provides a supportive context for the expression of the most personal feelings. In turn, the free expression binds the ritual congregation into a warm and emotionally permissive symbolic community.

A fourth facet or function of celebration is that of defining a habitable "living space" — the establishment of a celebrative island of consciousness in an ocean of oppression and deprivation. It might be thought of as roughly equivalent to the Western concept of the power of positive thinking. But it is far more than a wishful and naive attempt to exercise some fancied power of mind over matter. Rather, it couples a realistic facing of the hardest aspects of existence with a firm determination to fix consciousness on whatsoever things exist for which there can be praise to God. The spiritual puts it, "Nobody knows the trouble I see, Glory Hallelujah!"

Preaching which authentically celebrates the goodness of God and of life provides not only ideas but total experiences for the recall of the hearer. The celebration event as event and not just as comforting thought may then be "rerun" by the person in the oppressed audience, as a means of transcending the discouragement of later circumstances. In so doing one elects to live amidst and to focus consciousness on the joyous elements in past experience, as opposed to the perhaps vast majority of painful elements — the horror story of which one is the chief character and which one is, for the time, powerless to change. A spiritual expressed the process of focus of consciousness thus: "Woke up this mornin' with my mind stayed on Jesus, Hallelu, Hallelu, Hallelujah!" Preaching which celebrates the goodness of God equips hearers to stay their minds and focus their consciousness, choosing their living space and transcending the tragedies of oppressed existence.

The final role of celebration is that fitting climax to a balanced proclamation which has already included exegesis, exposition, explanation, application, and deeply meaningful illustration. The gospel should have been proclaimed throughout with joy. But the best reinforcement and the greatest expression of joy must naturally occur when, so to speak, the lesson is completed and summarized, and thanks and celebration are offered for it at the end. All else leads up to this climactic moment, and whatever follows is inevitably anticlimax. Like a symphony, the theme is stated majestically and powerfully, with prior elaborations now taken for granted. Fresh spiritual insight and illumination, joyous recall, and persons fulfilled in community are celebrated together.

To take all these blessings for granted to the extent of a bland and unenthusiastic response would be to give evidence of having failed to appreciate and benefit from it in the first place. No blessing is ever enjoyed fully unless and until it is carried from the stage of mere mention to the stage of grateful praise and celebration. The intensity of the celebration is the accurate index to the depth of the response. If in fact the gospel is what we have been saying it is — the power of God unto the very salvation of persons — how can preacher or people respond other than in celebration?

The question that haunts all of us is simply how one goes about the task of preaching in such a way as to make possible the gift of authentic celebration from time to time, especially as we near the close of the proclamation.

The first and most penetrating answer to this hard question is that great celebration is only generated by the treatment of great themes. It should be obvious enough that clever intellectual technicalities do not beget great joy among any save their inventors. And even they can't live by their own noodle nuggets in the storms and crises of life. Black Americans have come through trials and tribulations of suicidal proportions, and they have kept on living when others would have given up long since, simply because they have been fed on the great themes of the culture. These would include the goodness of life in the context of a good creation, and the justice, mercy, goodness, and providence of the Creator. These have generated celebration by building a worldview among churched and unchurched which upheld a hazardous existence by means of a transconscious trust. Without such high trust and meaning levels, life would have been squandered in a struggle for a security which is otherwise impossible for Blacks in this country and within the gift of God alone. With the embrace of the affirmations of the faith and culture, life is free to be abundant, enjoyed, and therefore celebrated, no matter how brutally beset. Great themes and affirmations beget celebration.

It should be equally obvious that celebration is generated by the satisfaction of deep-seated human needs. Gratitude begets celebration, and gratitude flows naturally when the cry of persons has been heard answered from the word of God. This may sound trite or old-fashioned, but it is no small thing when a saintly sister says to the preacher, "Son, you lifted my burden this morning." Such a response is heard all too seldom, because it is so infrequently deserved. The comforts of an automated age have not spread to the *souls* of our parishes. Indeed, the saints we serve are more and more isolated and alienated in the midst of their earthly toys. The suburban people-trap also breeds great spiritual needs. With physical existence so well cared for, there is less and less to divert attention from the pressing claims of the ultimate concerns. Persons are more restless than ever until they gratefully find their rest in the God of the great gospel. It is then altogether appropriate that they should celebrate.

Thirdly, celebration is generated by the fulfillment of persons. In the culture of the Black masses this is joyously accomplished in the dialogic character of the preaching tradition. When a Black preacher says, "Surely, this was the Son of God," or "Surely goodness and mercy shall follow me all the days of my life," he pauses after the "Surely." At that point, all who wish may lend a hand in the proclamation of the certitude by offering their own "Surely's." Or when the preacher cries "Have mercy!" in prayer or sermon, he waits for whosoever will to echo the plaintive and ubiquitous petition. Early morning has ancient importance in Black culture, and when the preacher says that Mary went early or "soon" Easter morning, to the tomb, he places the "early" first in the sentence. Then he pauses for the response — the joyous and predictable participation of persons caught up in a story which they literally help to tell. . . .

My final suggestions as to how to foster authentic celebration in preaching have to do with the sensitive timing of the truths presented, coupled with an adequate medium for summation and celebration. For many this may seem an altogether new consideration in organizing a sermon, but timing seriously affects sequence toward celebration. We usually think of sequence in logical, theological, or even chronological terms, but we seldom think of the timing of impact. What is this timing all about? What has it to do with cogency and power?

By timing we really mean emotional pace. To consider timing is to apply and to take seriously the fact that the gospel must be communicated to the whole person, or transconsciously. This takes time, as we have already seen, but time for truth to "sink in" and reach the deeper, slower-moving emotions may not be used indiscriminately. Concern for timing involves the weighing of emotional impact. This input, in turn, is used alongside the various other logics possible in the final determination of the sequence of material. It is, of course, understood that the gospel must make a certain kind of sense, but it must do it transconsciously. Like such other art forms as the symphony, the sermon must avoid erratic movement, emotionally speaking, and it must build up to the final statement/celebration and coda.

There are two obvious extremes in this regard. One is the common practice of utter unawareness of emotional impact. It is the sin of being both overly intellectual and inadequately sensitive to the movements of the feelings of the audience. The other extreme is that of the so-called emotional preacher, whose solid content is conveyed unaware of it at all. His chief conscious concern is to move people; and his sole criterion for the little organization he does of his material is that of how it will "slay" the congregation.

In between there is a synthesis which teaches as it moves persons, and moves persons as it teaches. It is my deep conviction that God in his providence will never place his messenger in the predicament of having to choose between the two. In fact, I *know* that he calls on us at all times both to illumine and to inspire. There can never be true learning and growth without deep involvement of the feelings, nor can there be depth of Christian emotion without real growth. Our challenge as preachers is to be as aware of the one factor as of the other, and to build up to a celebration which is, at one and the same time, appropriately summary and reinforcing, as well as unforgettably satisfying emotionally.

WALTER BRUEGGEMANN

Prophetic Energizing

One of the best-known Old Testament scholars today and an ordained minister in the United Church of Christ, Walter Brueggemann has a career that has spanned the academy and the church and narrowed the gap between ancient biblical texts and postmodern culture. Brueggemann taught at Eden Seminary in St. Louis for twenty-five years before joining the faculty of Columbia Theological Seminary in Decatur, Georgia. His fifty books include *Texts Under Negotiation: The Bible and Postmodern Imagination,* and his award-winning *Theology of the Old Testament: Testimony, Dispute, Advocacy.* Brueggemann's family background is German Evangelical, and he calls his father, who was a pastor, "my first and best teacher, who taught me the artistry as well as the authority of Scripture." His commitment to the church's ministry is indicative of one of his abiding scholarly interests: the relation of the Old Testament to Christian preaching. In one of his best-known books, *The Prophetic Imagination,* Brueggemann outlines the prophetic protest against what he calls the "royal consciousness," which represents established religion as a cultural and political power. Employing vivid and poetic language, the prophet exposes the corruption of this dominant paradigm. The prophet then helps the people tap into an alternative source of energy by announcing a new reality and articulating a hopeful message. This is what the Hebrew prophets did, and, says Brueggemann, this is what the preacher does in a supposedly Christian nation. The preacher exposes the extent to which Christianity is bound up with the dominant paradigm of consumerism and militarism and, like the prophet, energizes those who sit in darkness with the announcement of an alternative reality. In *Finally Comes the Poet: Daring Speech for Proclamation* (his 1989 Beecher Lectures), Brueggemann argues that preachers must become "poets that speak against a prose world."

Walter Brueggemann, *The Prophetic Imagination* (Philadelphia: Fortress, 1978), pp. 62-75.

M y governing hypothesis is that the alternative prophetic community is concerned both with criticizing and energizing. On the one hand, it is to show that the dominant consciousness (which I have termed "royal") will indeed end and that it has no final claim upon us. On the other hand, it is the task of the alternative prophetic community to present an alternative consciousness that can energize the community to fresh forms of faithfulness and vitality. Having considered the first of these tasks in the tradition of Jeremiah, I now turn to the second function of prophecy, to energize. I propose this hypothesis: *The royal consciousness leads people to despair about the power to new life. It is the task of prophetic imagination and ministry to bring people to engage the promise of newness that is at work in our history with God.*

Numb people do not discern or fear death. Conversely, despairing people do not anticipate or receive newness.

(1) As a beginning point it may be affirmed that the royal consciousness militates against hope. For those who are denied entry into prosperity there is a kind of hopelessness because there is little or no prospect for change. In Israel there was no doubt that since the Solomonic achievement the royal prosperity was increasingly closed to large numbers of the citizens. That indeed is a key point in the polemics of Amos. And so in that time as in our own, the royal arrangement surely and properly evokes despair among those who are shut out.

It is equally important to perceive that those who have entry to power and prosperity are also victims of hopelessness, or, as we are wont to say in our time, have a sense of powerlessness. The royal consciousness means to overcome history and therefore by design the future loses its vitality and authority. The present ordering, and by derivation the present regime, claims to be the full and final ordering. That claim means there can be no future that either calls the present into question or promises a way out of it. Thus the fulsome claim of the present arrangement is premised on hopelessness. This insidious form of realized eschatology requires persons to live without hope. The present is unending in its projection, uncompromising in its claim of loyalty, and unaccommodating in having its own way. In the words of a recent beer commercial, you can be totalitarian when "you believe in what you're doing" and you conclude that one way is the "right way." I believe the Solomonic regime created such a situation of despair. Inevitably it had to hold on desperately and despairingly to the present, for if the present slipped away there would be nothing. The future had already been annulled. I do not find it farfetched to imagine the lack of promise in Ecclesiastes 1:9-10 to be pertinent to the royal consciousness:

> What has been is what will be,
> and what has been done is what will be done;

and there is nothing new under the sun.
Is there a thing of which it is said,
    "See, this is new"?
It has been already,
    in the ages before us.

There is nothing new, partly because nothing seemed to be happening but also because the regime had ordered and decreed it that way. The need to annul the future must lead to a situation in which hope is also denied.

(2) More specifically, the termination of the present in the fall of 587, just as Jeremiah had anticipated, created a situation in which the royal consciousness found itself without resource. The very kings who could not cope with the thought that an end might come could also not imagine a new beginning. Those who had worked so hard to deny the future and banish hope could not all of a sudden permit hope to happen. It is unthinkable for the king to imagine or experience a really new beginning that is underived or unextrapolated from what went before. Kings were accustomed to new arrangements and new configurations of the same pieces, but the yearning to manage and control means that new intrusions are not regarded as desirable. Neither are they regarded as possible or discerned when they happen. And thus the same royal consciousness that could not imagine endings and so settled for numb denial is the one that could not imagine beginnings and so settled for hopeless despair and a grim endurance of the way things now are. Beginnings are no more thinkable or acceptable to kings than endings are, for both announce an inscrutable sovereignty that kings cannot entertain. . . .

The inability to imagine or even tolerate a new intrusion is predictable, given the characteristic royal capacity to manage all the pieces. It is so even in our personal lives, in which we conclude that the given dimensions we have frequently rearranged are the only dimensions that exist. To imagine a new gift given from the outside violates our reason. We are able to believe no more in the graciousness of God than we are in the judgment of God.

We are largely confined to reflections on the given pieces and our modest expectations are confined by our reason, our language, and our epistemology. We have no public arenas in which serious hopefulness can be brought to articulation. What is most needed is what is most unacceptable — an articulation that redefines the situation and that makes way for new gifts about to be given. Without a public arena for the articulation of gifts that fall outside our conventional rationality we are fated to despair. We know full well there are not among these present pieces the makings of genuine newness. And short of genuine newness life becomes a dissatisfied coping, a grudging trust, and a managing that dares never ask too much.

My judgment is that such a state of affairs not only is evident in the exile of Judah but is characteristic of most situations of ministry. When we try to face the holding action that defines the sickness, the aging, the marriages, and the jobs of very many people, we find that we have been nurtured away from hope, for it is too scary. Such hope is an enemy of the very royal consciousness with which most of us have secured a working arrangement. The question facing ministry is whether there is anything to be said, done, or acted in the face of the ideology of hopefulness.

(3) The task of prophetic imagination and ministry, especially as we see it in sixth-century Judah, is to cut through the despair and to penetrate the dissatisfied coping that seems to have no end or resolution. There is not much a prophet can do in such a situation of hopelessness, so I suggest a quite basic and modest task. It includes three actions:

(a) *The offering of symbols* that are adequate to contradict a situation of hopelessness in which newness is unthinkable. The prophet has only the means of word, spoken word and acted word, to contradict the presumed reality of his or her community. The prophet is to provide the wherewithal whereby hope becomes possible again to a community of kings who now despair of their royalty. After a time kings become illiterate in the language of hope. Hope requires a very careful symbolization. It must not be expressed too fully in the present tense because hope one can touch and handle is not likely to retain its promissory call to a new future. Hope expressed only in the present tense will no doubt be co-opted by the managers of this age.

What a commission it is to express a future that none think imaginable! Of course this cannot be done by inventing new symbols, for that is wishful thinking. Rather, it means to move back into the deepest memories of this community and activate those very symbols that have always been the basis for contradicting the regnant consciousness. Therefore the symbols of hope cannot be general and universal but must be those that have been known concretely in this particular history. And when the prophet returns, with the community, to those deep symbols, they will discern that hope is not a late, tacked-on hypothesis to serve a crisis but rather the primal dimension of every memory of this community. The memory of this community begins in God's promissory address to the darkness of chaos, to barren Sarah, and to oppressed Egyptian slaves. The speech of God is first about an alternative future.

In offering symbols the prophet has two tasks. One is to mine the memory of this people and educate them to use the tools of hope. The other is to recognize how singularly words, speech, language, and phrase shape consciousness and define reality. The prophet is the one who, by use of these tools of hope, contradicts the presumed world of the kings, showing both that that presumed world does not square with the facts and that we have been taught a lie and have believed it because the people with the hardware and the printing press told us it was that way. And so the offering of symbols is a job not for a timid clerk who simply shares the inventory but for people who know something different and are prepared, out of their own anguish and amazement, to know that the closed world of managed reality is false. The prophetic imagination knows that the real world is the one that has its beginning and dynamic in the promising speech of God and that this is true even in a world where kings have tried to banish all speech but their own.

(b) The task of prophetic imagination and ministry is to *bring to public expression those very hopes and yearnings* that have been denied so long and suppressed so deeply that we no longer know they are there. Hope, on the one hand, is an absurdity too embarrassing to speak about, for it flies in the face of all those claims we have been told are facts. Hope is the refusal to accept the reading of reality which is the majority opinion; and one does that only at great political and existential risk. On the other hand, hope is subversive, for it limits the grandiose pretension of the present, daring to announce that the present to which we have all made commitments is now called into question. Thus the exilic community lacked the tools of hope. The language of hope and the ethos of amazement have been partly forfeited because they are an embarrassment. The language of hope and the ethos of amazement have been partly squelched because they are a threat.

It is mind-boggling to think of the public expression of hope as a way of subverting the dominant royal embrace of despair. I am not talking about optimism or development or evolutionary advances but rather about promises made by one who stands distant from us and over against us but remarkably *for us*. Speech about hope cannot be explanatory and scientifically argumentative; rather, it must be lyrical in the sense that it touches the hopeless person at many different points. More than that, however, speech about hope must be primally theological, which is to say that it must be in the language of covenant between a personal God and a community. Promise belongs to the world of trusting speech and faithful listening. It will not be reduced to the "cool" language of philosophy or the private discourse of psychology. It will finally be about God and us, about his faithfulness that vetoes our faithlessness. Those who would be prophetic will need to embrace that absurd practice and that subversive activity.

This urging to bring hope to public expression is based on a conviction about believing folks. It is premised on the capacity to evoke and bring to expression the hope that is within us (see 1 Peter 3:15). It is there within and among us, for we are ordained of God to be people of hope. It is there by virtue of our being in the image of the promissory God. It is sealed there in the sacrament of baptism. It is dramatized in the Eucharist — "until he comes." It is the structure of every creed that ends by trusting in God's promises. Hope is the decision to which God invites Israel, a decision against despair, against permanent consignment to chaos (Isa. 45:18), oppression, barrenness, and exile.

Hope is the primary prophetic idiom not because of the general dynamic of history or because of the signs of the times but because the prophet speaks to a people who, willy-nilly, are God's people. Hope is what this community must do because it is God's community invited to be in God's pilgrimage. And as Israel is invited to grieve God's grief over the ending, so Israel is now invited to hope in God's promises. That very act of hope is the confession that we are not children of the royal consciousness.

Of course prophetic hope easily lends itself to distortion. It can be made so grandiose that it does not touch reality; it can be trivialized so that it does not impact reality; it can be "bread and circuses" so that it only supports and abets the general despair. But a prophet has another purpose in bringing hope to public expression, and that is to return the community to its single referent, the sovereign faithfulness of God. It is only that return which enables a rejection of the closed world of royal definition. Only a move from a managed world to a world of spoken and heard faithfulness permits hope. It is that overriding focus which places Israel in a new situation and which reshapes exile, not as an eternal fate but as the place where hope can most amazingly appear. There is no objective norm that can prevent a prophet of hope from being too grandiose or too trivial or simply a speaker for bread and circuses. It is likely that the only measure of faithfulness is that hope always comes after grief and that the speaker of this public expression must know and be a part of the anguish which permits hope. Hope expressed without knowledge of and participation in grief is likely to be false hope that does not reach despair. Thus, as Thomas Raitt has shown, it is precisely those who know the death most painfully who can speak the hope most vigorously.

(c) The prophet must *speak metaphorically about hope but concretely about the real newness that comes to us and redefines our situation.* The prophet must speak not only about the abandonment of Israel by its God but about the specificity of Babylon. Talk about newness in exile comes not from a happy piety or from a hatred of Babylon but from the enduring jealousy of Yahweh for his people. This jealousy, so alien to our perceptual world, includes rejection of his people, which sends them and even Yahweh himself into exile. It is a jealousy that stays with his people, making their anguish his anguish and his future

161

their future. The hope that must be spoken is hope rooted in the assurance that God does not quit even when the evidence warrants his quitting. The hope is rooted in God's ability to utilize even the folly of Israel. The memory of this community-about-to-hope revolves around such hope-filled events as that of Cain, the murderer of a brother, being marked protectively; of the chaos of royal disarray resolved in praise; of rejected Joseph observing to his brothers that in all things God works for good; of Solomon, very Solomon, born in love to this shabby royal couple — and out of that comes a word that contradicts the exile.

(4) The hope-filled language of prophecy, in cutting through the royal despair and hopelessness, is the language of amazement. It is a language that engages the community in new discernments and celebrations just when it had nearly given up and had nothing to celebrate. The language of amazement is against the despair just as the language of grief is against the numbness. I believe that rightly embraced there is no more subversive or prophetic idiom than the practice of doxology which sets us before the reality of God, of God right at the center of a scene from which we presumed he had fled. Indeed, the language of amazement is the ultimate energizer in Israel, and the prophets of God are called to practice that most energizing language.

Second Isaiah serves as the peculiar paradigm for a prophet of hope to kings in despair. This great poet of the exile understood that speech which arranges the pieces and which echoes the management mentality of its contemporaries is not worth the bother. Second Isaiah presumably lived through and knew about the pathos of Lamentations and the rage of Job. Nevertheless, he goes beyond pathos and rage to speeches of hope and doxology.

I believe Thomas Raitt has made it clear that Second Isaiah has indispensable precursors in Jeremiah and Ezekiel. But more than these or any other, it is Second Isaiah who announces to exiled Israel a genuine *novum*. His announcement depends first of all on the audacity of his person and his poetry. He must have been a remarkable person to say things that violated the entire perceptual field of his community. Second, his speaking depends on the reality that his time was indeed a newness of time in which all the old certitudes were becoming unglued. Babylon was going and Persia was coming and this poet knew precisely what time it was. Third, and most important, his speaking depends on the reality and confession of God's radical freedom, freedom not only from the conceptions and expectations of his people but from God's own past actions as well. God, much like Reinhold Niebuhr, does have courage to change. His freedom is not some pious or spiritual event, for God's freedom is visible in the public place. . . . God is operating under a new plan. This is Second Isaiah's first word to the exiles, a word of forgiveness:

Comfort, comfort my people, says your God.
Speak tenderly to Jerusalem,
   and cry to her
that her warfare is ended,
    that her iniquity is pardoned.   (Isa. 40:1-2)

The discomforted are comforted. This is not a word in a vacuum or general theory about a gracious God. The poet responds precisely and concretely. He responds to Jeremiah's Rachel who refuses to be comforted (31:15). He speaks directly to and against the poems of Lamentations that found "none to comfort"
(Lam. 1:2, 16, 17, 21). To find comfort in exile is not thinkable, but in this remarkable beginning the poet refuses all that. The free God is ending that whole
situation and now there is an amnesty that was unthinkable before the speech.
That speech let Israel know what she did not know before he spoke. Hope is
created by speech and before that speech Israel is always hopeless. Indeed, are
we not all? Before we are addressed we know no future and no possible newness. Where there is no speech we must live in despair. And exile is first of all
where our speech has been silenced and God's speech has been banished. But
the prophetic poet asserts hope precisely in exile.

    The hope announced is not a nice feeling or a new inner spiritual state.
Rather, it is grounded in a radical discernment of Israel's worldly situation. The
poet employs a radical *political* announcement twice. First he instructs the
watchman to announce a new reality:

Get you up to the high mountain,
   O Zion, herald of good tidings;
Lift up your voice with strength,
   O Jerusalem, herald of good tidings,
    lift it up, fear not;
Say to the cities of Judah,
   "Behold your God!"
Behold, the Lord God comes with might. . . .   (Isa. 40:9-10)

Note that the prophet may have been afraid to say such an absurd and subversive word, but he is not to fear; he is to make this exile-transforming announcement. The new reality is that the One who seemed to be dismissed as useless
and impotent has claimed his throne. And he has done so right in exile; right
under the nose of the Babylonians. The poet brings Israel to an enthronement
festival, even as Jeremiah had brought Israel to a funeral. Whereas that scenario
left Israel in consuming grief, Second Isaiah brought Israel to new buoyancy.

Whereas Jeremiah tried to penetrate the *numbness,* Second Isaiah had to deal with *despair.* Both had to speak out of Moses' liberating tradition against the royal mentality that would not let people grieve or hope.

We should hold to the metaphor of enthronement and not leave it too soon or reduce it too concretely. The poet is not changing external politics but is reclaiming Israel's imagination. He asserts a newness that is so old Israel had forgotten, but it is there in memory. The energizing song of Moses ended with enthronement: "The Lord will reign for ever and ever" (Exod. 15:18). It is as though Second Isaiah means to bring Israel back to the doxology of Moses, but it is not only a memory recalled. It is a seizure of power in this moment that carries with it the delegitimizing of all other claimants and definers of reality. The other claimants to power and definers of reality are, in this act of language, like the ancient Egyptians, dead upon the seashore. This public act of poetic articulation reshapes Israel's destiny. Exile with the crowned sovereign is very different from kingless exile because it means the grimness is resolvable.

And what a God has now claimed his rule! He is as terrifyingly masculine as a warrior with sleeves rolled up for battle and as gently maternal as a carrier of a lamb. It is all there — for exiles. There is the comfort of enormous power, with stress on *fort* [strengthen]; there is the comfort of nurture, with stress on *com* [along with]. Israel is in a new situation where singing is possible again. Have you ever been in a situation where because of anger, depression, preoccupation, or exhaustion you could not sing? And then you could? What changed things was to be addressed, called by a name, cared for, recognized, and assured. The prophet makes it possible to sing and the empire knows that people who can boldly sing have not accepted the royal definition of reality. If the lack of singing is an index of exile, then we are in it, for we are a people who scarcely can sing. The prophet makes the hopefulness of singing happen again. The second enthronement formula is even more familiar:

> How beautiful upon the mountains
>   are the feet of him who brings good tidings . . .
> who publishes salvation,
> who says to Zion, "Your God reigns."   (Isa. 52:7)

The very one who seems to have lost charge is in charge now. The one who seemed to end in grief and bankruptcy in Jeremiah is the one who now will invert history. And the poet knows well that the inversion to real power happens only by suffering (49:14-15). The rejoicing belongs to those who know about the abandonment and the pathos. It is a curious route to kingship, but that is how it comes in Israel's history.

The effect of Second Isaiah is to energize Israel to fresh faith. But notice the radical, bold, even revolutionary form energizing takes. Here there are no psychological gimmicks and no easy meditative steps because the issues are not private, personal, spiritual, or internal. The only serious energizing needed or offered is the discernment of God in all his freedom, the dismantling of the structures of weariness, and the dethronement of the powers of fatigue. (Jesus, in his talk about weariness and rest and changing yokes [Matt. 11:28-30], is faithful to Second Isaiah.) Lament is the loss of true kingship, whereas doxology is the faithful embrace of the true king and the rejection of all the phony ones. . . .

The contrast of the gods and the ridicule of the Babylonian gods is brought closer by a parallel ridicule of Madam Babylon. What kind of madam is Dame Babylon? A grand dame with courtly manner? A tyrannical old lady? A lady with a house like such a lady keeps? That is all over, for the new history of Israel with Yahweh means the end of this imperial history:

> Come down and sit in the dust,
>   O virgin daughter of Babylon;
> Sit on the ground without a throne,
>   O daughter of the Chaldeans!
> For you shall no more be called
>   tender and delicate.
> Take the millstones and grind meal,
>   put off your veil,
> strip off your robe, uncover your legs,
>   pass through the rivers.
> Your nakedness shall be uncovered,
>   and your shame shall be seen.   (47:1-3)

The poet engages in the kind of guerilla warfare that is always necessary on behalf of oppressed people. First, the hated one must be ridiculed and made reachable, for then she may be disobeyed and seen as a nobody who claims no allegiance and keeps no promises. The big house yields no real life, need not be feared, cannot be trusted, and must not be honored.

When the Babylonian gods have been mocked, when the Babylonian culture has been ridiculed, and when the dethroned king is reenthroned, then history is inverted. Funeral becomes festival, grief becomes doxology, and despair turns into amazement. Perhaps it is no more than a cultic event, but don't sell it short, because cult kept close to historical experience can indeed energize people. For example, witness the black churches and civil rights movements or the liberation resistance in Latin America. The cult may be a staging for the inversion that the kings think is not possible. It is the inversion that the grim royal middle class among us does not believe in and it is the inversion that surprises people who are powerless. Inversions are not easy, not without cost, and never neat and clear. But we ought not underestimate the power of the poet.

· IV ·

BIBLICAL INTERPRETATION

AUGUSTINE

Literal and Figurative Interpretation

Jesus began his public ministry by preaching on a text from Isaiah, which he interpreted as a witness to his own messianic office. He parried a lawyer's question about eternal life with the counterquestions, "What is written in the law? How do you read?" (Luke 10:26) Since the time of Jesus his followers have been people of a book, and his preachers have honored the Scriptures as the source and norm of their proclamation. Already in the patristic period the rules and methods of discovering the meaning of the sacred text were crucial to preaching, so much so that when Augustine of Hippo (354-430) produced the first textbook on homiletics, *On Christian Doctrine* (or *Teaching Christianity*), he conceived it as a manual for biblical interpretation. The first three books deal with the relation of *things,* or essential realities such as the Trinity, and *signs,* or language that points beyond itself toward things. Although the abundance of the Bible's figurative signs may pose a problem for the interpreter, Augustine saw amidst the complexity of linguistic forms a discernible simplicity: all Scripture unfolds the essence of God's love. Where the essential teaching *(doctrina)* is veiled, as it is in much of the Old Testament, the interpreter must either penetrate the veil by means of related, clearer passages or elevate the letter by means of allegorical interpretation. Allegorical or figurative interpretation serves a number of functions. It defends the divine authority of the whole Bible; it pursues central theological themes such as grace and love even where they are not apparent; it reinforces the ecclesial provenance of the Bible; and it develops the spirituality of the interpreter, to whom direct knowledge of God has been lost in the Fall.

Augustine, *Teaching Christianity* [*On Christian Doctrine,* trans. Edmund Hill, OP, ed. John E. Rotelle, OSA, in *The Works of Saint Augustine,* vol. 11, bk. 3, selected paragraphs (Hyde Park, N.Y.: New City Press, 1990-97), pp. 169-87.

But when ambiguities arise in Scripture about the meaning of words used in their proper sense, the first thing we must do is see whether we have phrased or pronounced them wrongly. So when, on paying closer attention, you still see that it is uncertain how something is to phrased, or how to be pronounced, you should refer it to the rule of faith, which you have received from the plainer passages of Scripture and from the authority of the church, about which we dealt sufficiently when we were talking in the first book about *things*. But if both possibilities, or all of them, if it is a multiple ambiguity, are consonant with the faith, it remains to refer to the whole context, to the sections that precede and that follow the ambiguous passage, holding it in the middle between them, so that we may see which of the several meanings that present themselves the context will vote for and allow to fit in with itself. . . .

But ambiguities arising from metaphorical language, about which we have to talk from now on, call for no ordinary care and attention. For in the first place, you have to beware of taking a figurative expression literally. And this is where the apostle's words are relevant, *The letter kills, but the spirit gives life* (2 Cor. 3:6). When something that is said figuratively, you see, is taken as though it were meant in its proper literal sense, we are being carnal in our way of thinking. Nor can anything more suitably be called the death of the soul than when that in it too, which surpasses the brute beasts, that is to say its intelligence, subjects itself to the flesh by following the letter.

When you follow the letter, you see, you take in their proper literal sense words that are being used metaphorically, and fail to refer what is signified in this proper sense to the signification of something else; but if, for example, you hear the word "sabbath," and all you understand by it is this one of the seven days which recurs week by week; and when you hear the word "sacrifice," your thoughts do not go beyond what is usually done with victims from the flock and the fruits of the earth. This, precisely, is the wretched slavery of the spirit, treating signs as things, and thus being unable to lift up the eyes of the mind above bodily creatures, to drink in the eternal light.

Such slavery, however, in the Jewish people was something different by far from the deadness of the other nations, seeing that the Jews were subjected to temporal things in such a way that in all of them the one God was being brought to their attention. And although they observed the signs of spiritual things as things in their own right, quite unaware of what they should be referred to, it was still second nature to them to suppose that by such a slavery they were pleasing the one God of the universe, whom they could not see. This, the apostle writes, was like being in the custody of a minder of children. And that is why those who clung so stubbornly to such signs could not tolerate the Lord, who made light of them when the time had already come for unveiling their real meaning, and why their leaders piled up charges against him that he cured people on the sabbath, and why the people, in bondage to those signs as though they were the ultimate realities, could not believe that one who refused to take any notice of them, in the way they were observed by the Jews, could be God or could have come from God.

But those of them who came to believe, who formed the first church in Jerusalem, showed well enough how very useful it had been for them to be kept under that child-minder; it meant that the signs which had been imposed on them as slaves for a time had tied the ideas of those who observed them to the worship of the one God *who made heaven and earth* (Ps. 121:2).

Thus because they had been close to spiritual things already (for in those actual temporal and carnal signs and votive offerings, although they were unaware of how they were meant to be understood spiritually, they had at least learned that only the one eternal God was to be honored), they turned out to be so ready for the Holy Spirit that they sold all their possessions, and *laid the price at the feet of the apostles* (Acts 4:35), to be distributed to the poor; and in this way they dedicated themselves totally to God as a new temple, the earthly image of which, that is the old temple, they used to be enslaved to. . . .

Those, you see, who practice or venerate some kind of thing which is a significant sign, unaware of what it signifies, are enslaved under signs, while those who either carry out or venerate useful signs established by God, fully understanding their force and significance, are not in fact venerating what can be seen and passes away, but rather that reality to which all such things are to be referred. Such people are spiritual and free even during the time of slavery, in which it is not yet opportune for carnal spirits to have those signs openly explained to them, because they still need to be broken in under their yoke. Such spiritual people, however, were the patriarchs and prophets, and all those in the people of Israel through whose ministry the Holy Spirit has provided us with the help and the consolation of the Scriptures themselves.

In this time, though, after the clearest indication of our freedom has shone upon us in the resurrection of our Lord, we are no longer burdened with the heavy duty of carrying out even those signs whose meaning we now understand. But the Lord himself and the discipline of the apostles has handed down to us just a few signs instead of many, and these so easy to perform, and so awesome to understand, and so pure and chaste to celebrate, such as the sacrament of baptism, and the celebration of the Lord's body and blood. When people receive these, they have been so instructed that they can recognize to what sublime realities they are to be referred, and so they venerate them in a spirit not of carnal slavery, but rather of spiritual freedom.

But just as following the letter and taking signs for the things signified by them is a matter of slavish weakness, so too interpreting signs in a useless way is a matter of error going badly astray. Those, however, who do not understand what a sign signifies, and still understand that it is a sign, are also not being oppressed by the yoke of slavery. But it is better even to be oppressed by signs that are useful though not understood than by interpreting them in a useless manner to withdraw one's neck from the yoke of slavery, only to insert it in the noose of error.

Rules for Telling What Are
Figurative Expressions and What Are Not

To this warning against treating figurative expressions, that is metaphorical ones, as though they were meant in the literal, proper sense, we also have to add this one, to beware of wanting to treat literal, proper statements as though they were figurative. So first of all we must point out the method for discovering if an expression is proper or figurative. And here, quite simply, is the one and only method: anything in the divine writings that cannot be referred either to good, honest morals or to the truth of the faith, you must know is said figuratively. Good honest morals belong to loving God and one's neighbor, the truth of the faith to knowing God and one's neighbor. As for hope, that lies in everybody's own conscience, to the extent that you perceive yourself to be making progress in the love of God and neighbor, and in the knowledge of them. All this formed the subject of the first book.

The human race, however, is inclined to judge sins, not according to the gravity of the evil desire involved, but rather with reference to the importance attached to their own customs. So people frequently reckon that only those acts are to be blamed which in their own part of the world and their own time have been customarily treated as vicious and condemned, and only those acts to be approved of and praised which are acceptable to those among whom they live. Thus it can happen that if Scripture either commands something which does not accord with the customs of the hearers, or censures something which does fit in with them, they assume they are dealing with a figurative mode of speech — if, that is, their minds are bound by the authority of God's word. Scripture, though, commands nothing but charity, or love, and censures nothing but cupidity, or greed, and that is the way it gives shape and form to human morals.

Again, if people's minds are already in thrall to some erroneous opinion, whatever Scripture may assert that differs from it will be reckoned by them to be said in a figurative way. The only thing, though, it ever asserts is Catholic faith, with reference to things in the past and in the future and in the present. It tells the story of things past, foretells things future, points out things present; but all these things are of value for nourishing and fortifying charity or love, and overcoming and extinguishing cupidity or greed.

What I mean by charity or love is any urge of the spirit to find joy in God for his own sake, and in oneself and one's neighbor for God's sake; by cupidity or greed any impulse of the spirit to find joy in oneself and one's neighbor, and in any kind of bodily thing at all, not for God's sake. Now what unrestrained greed does by way of corrupting the human spirit and its body can be called infamous, while whatever it does to harm someone else can be called criminal. And all sins fall into these two categories, but infamous deeds come first. When these have drained the spirit dry and reduced it to a kind of want, it bursts out into criminal acts in order to eliminate obstacles to its infamous behavior, or to secure assistance in it.

Again, what charity does, or love, to profit self is usefulness, while whatever it does to profit the neighbor is called kindness. And here usefulness comes first, because one cannot profit one's neighbor with what one does not have oneself. For the more the kingdom of greed is whittled away, so much the more is that of love increased.

So then anything we read of in the Scriptures as coming from the person of God or his saints that sounds harsh and almost savage in deed and word is of value for whittling away the kingdom of greed. And if its meaning is crystal-clear, it is not to be referred to something else, as though it were said figuratively, like this from the apostle: *He is storing up for himself wrath on the day of wrath and of the revelation of the just judgment of God, who will pay back each and all according to their works; to those indeed who by patient endurance in doing good are seeking glory and honor and imperishability, eternal life; to those however who are given to quarrels and who distrust the truth while they trust iniquity, wrath and indignation. Tribulation and distress upon every human soul that works evil, Jew first and also Greek* (Rom. 2:5-9). But this is being addressed to those who are being overthrown together with their greed, because they have been unwilling to overcome it.

But when the kingdom of greed is being undermined in those people it used to dominate, we have this plain statement: *But those who are Jesus Christ's have crucified their flesh, with its passions and lusts* (Gal. 5:24), except that in these instances too some words are to be treated as metaphorical, such as "the wrath of God" and "have crucified"; but they are not so many, or so placed, as to obscure the plain sense and make it all into an allegory or a riddle, which is what I properly call a figurative expression. But coming to what Jeremiah was told, *Behold, I have set you today over nations and kingdoms, to pull down and to destroy, and to scatter and to rout* (Jer. 1:10), it is undoubtedly all a figurative utterance, to be referred to that end which we have mentioned.

Those things, however, that strike the ignorant as infamous, whether they are only said, or also done, whether attributed to God or to men whose holiness is being commended to us, they are all to be taken as figurative, and their secret meanings have to be winkled out for the nourishment of charity. Anyone, though, who makes use of passing things more sparingly than is customary with those among whom he lives, is either temperate or superstitious, while anyone who makes use of them in a way that exceeds the bounds that are acceptable to the good people among whom he spends his time is either signifying something, or is behaving infamously. In all such cases it is not the use of things, but the caprice of the user that is at fault.

Nor will any in their right mind even begin to believe that the Lord's feet were anointed by the woman with precious ointment in the same sort of way as wantonly extravagant and worthless people are familiar with, in those orgies of theirs which we abominate. The good odor, after all, stands for the good reputation which those of good life will have from their works, while they follow in Christ's footsteps, and as it were shed over his feet the most precious fragrance. Thus what is generally infamous in other persons is, in the person of God or a prophet, the sign of some important reality. Certainly, association with a harlot is one thing in men of abandoned morals, another in the prophetic activity of Hosea; nor, if it is infamous conduct to strip off your clothes in drunken and licentious parties, does that mean that it is equally infamous to be naked in the baths.

So we have to pay careful attention to what befits places and times and persons, in order not to judge behavior rashly as infamous. It can happen, after all, that a wise person will make use of the most expensive food without a hint of the vice of self-indulgence or greediness, while a fool will be disgustingly on fire with gluttony for the cheapest stuff imaginable. And sane people would much rather eat fish as the Lord did than lentils in the way Esau, Abraham's grandson, did, or oats the way horses do. Just because most wild animals, after all, live on less refined kinds of food than we do, this does not mean that they are more self-restrained than we are. For in all matters of this kind it is not the nature of the things we make use of, but our reason for making use of them and the manner in which we set about getting them, that decides whether what we do deserves approval or disapproval.

The just men of old in the earthly kingdom pictured the heavenly kingdom to themselves, and foretold it. Provision of offspring was the reason for the blameless custom of one man having several wives at once; and that is why it was not also decent for one woman to have many husbands, because that does not make her any the more fruitful. To seek either gain or children by sleeping around is simply the disgraceful style of the prostitute. In this sphere of morals Scripture does not find fault with whatever the holy men of those times did without lustfulness, although they did what today can only be done out of lust or lechery. And all such stories as are told there are not only to be interpreted literally as historical accounts, but also to be taken figuratively as prophetic in some way, pointing to that end of the love of God or of neighbor, or of both.

Thus it was a matter of infamy among the ancient Romans to wear ankle-long, long-sleeved tunics, whereas now it is infamous for those born to high station not to wear them, even when they are informally dressed. In the same sort of way we have to observe that such lustful inclinations should be banished from every other kind of use we make of things; for not only do they vilely abuse the very customs of the people among whom one is living, but they will even exceed all bounds and erupt, very often, in the most infamous display of their ugliness, which was previously lurking concealed behind the enclosure walls of conventional morals.

But anything that fits in with the customs of those among whom this life has to be spent, and is either imposed on one by necessity or undertaken out of duty, is to be seen as directed by good and important people to the end of usefulness and of kindness, either literally, which is how we too should do it, or even figuratively, as befits the prophets.

When unlearned people who have other customs come across such deeds in their reading, they think, unless checked by authority, that they are acts of infamy, and they are quite unable to appreciate that the whole of their own way of life, in their marriages, or their parties, or their clothing, and in all other aspects of human life and culture, would seem infamous to other nations and other times. Some people, moved by the variety of innumerable customs, and half asleep, if I may so put it, being neither sunk in the deep slumber of folly, nor able to wake up fully to the light of wisdom, have supposed that there is no such thing as justice in itself, but that each nation takes it for granted that its own customs are just; as these differ from nation to nation, while justice ought to remain immutable, it becomes obvious, they conclude, that there is no justice anywhere.

They have not understood, to mention just one point, that *What you do not wish done to you, do not do to another* (Tobit 4:15) can suffer no variation through any diversity of national customs. When this maxim is referred to love of God, all infamous conduct dies; when to love of neighbor, all crimes. We none of us, after all, like our dwellings ruined; so we ought not to ruin God's dwelling, namely ourselves. And we none of us wish to be harmed by anyone else; therefore let us not harm anyone else ourselves.

The tyranny of cupidity or greed being thus overthrown, charity or love reigns supreme with its just laws of loving God for God's sake, and oneself and one's neighbor for God's sake. So this rule will be observed in dealing with figurative expressions, that you should take pains to turn over and over in your mind what you read, until your interpretation of it is led right through to the kingdom of charity. But if this is already happening with the literal meaning, do not suppose the expression is in any way a figurative one.

If it is an expression of command, either forbidding infamy or crime, or ordering usefulness or kindness, it is not figurative. But if it seems to command infamy or crime, or to forbid usefulness or kindness, then it is figurative. *Unless you eat*, he says, *the flesh of the Son of man and drink his blood, you shall not have life in you* (John 6:53). He seems to be commanding a crime or an act of infamy; so it is said figuratively, instructing us that we must share in the Lord's passion, and store away in our minds the sweet and useful memory that his flesh was crucified and wounded for our sakes.

Scripture says, *If your enemy is hungry, feed him; if he is thirsty, give him a drink.* Here there can be no doubt that it is enjoining a kindness upon us. But with what follows: *For in doing this you will be heaping coals of fire upon his head* (Rom. 12:20; Prov. 25:21-22), you might suppose a spiteful crime is being commanded. So you must have no doubt that it is said figuratively; and while it can be interpreted in two ways, in one for doing harm, in the other for giving support, let charity rather call you back to kindness, and to understanding by coals of fire the red hot pangs of repentance, which heal the pride of the man, who is grieved at having been the enemy of the person he is being helped by in his plight.

Again, when the Lord says, *Whoever loves his life, let him throw it away* (John 12:25), he must not be supposed to be forbidding those useful acts by which we all ought to preserve our lives. But "let him throw away his life" is said figuratively; that is, let him do away with and lose that use he now makes of it, namely a perverse and topsy-turvy use, so taken up with temporal things that he gives no thought to eternity.

It is written, *Give to the kindhearted person, and do not support the sinner* (Sir. 12:4). The second part of this maxim seems to be forbidding a kindness, in saying *do not support the sinner*. So you should understand that "sinner" is put figuratively for sin, and thus it means you must not support him in his sin.

Various Other Rules and Considerations

But it often happens that those who have reached a higher stage of the spiritual life, or think they have, consider that instructions meant for the lower stages are said figuratively; for example, those who have embraced the celibate life, and *have castrated themselves for the sake of the kingdom of heaven* (Matt. 19:12), will argue that whatever the holy books enjoin about loving and ruling wives must be taken metaphorically and not properly; and anyone who has decided to keep his virgin unmarried will attempt to give a figurative interpretation of the text, *Give your daughter in marriage, and you have accomplished a great work* (Sir. 7:25).

Among points, therefore, to be observed in trying to understand the Scriptures there will also be this one, that we should realize that some things are enjoined universally upon everybody, others upon this or that particular class of person; thus medicine is provided not only to ensure a general state of good health, but also to cope with each member's own peculiar weakness. What cannot be raised up to a higher class is of course to be cured in its own lower one.

Again one has to be on one's guard against supposing that whatever in the Old Testament, with respect to the condition of those times, is not an infamy nor a crime either, even when understood literally and not figuratively, can be transferred also to these times and put into practice in life today. Not unless cupidity or greed is lording it over you, and seeking the support of the very Scriptures which are meant to undermine it, will you do such a thing. If you do, you are miserably failing to understand the value of such things being set down there; it is to help persons of good hope to come to the salutary realization both that a custom which they abhor can have a good use, and that one they favor can be condemned, if they look in the first case to the love and in the second to the greed of those who observe it.

The fact is, if one person, given the time he lived in, could be chaste in his association with many wives, another can be lustful in his association with one. I have more respect, you see, for the man who makes use of the fertility of many wives for the sake of something else than for the one who finds enjoyment in the flesh of one for its own sake. In the first instance an advantage is being sought suitable to the needs of the times, in the second an appetite wrapped up in passing pleasures is being satisfied. And those men to whom the apostle allows carnal congress, each with his own one wife, by way of concession on account of their lack of self-restraint, were at a lower stage in their progress toward God than those who, though they each had several wives, were only looking in their sexual relations with them to the procreation of children, like the wise man whose only consideration in food and drink is bodily health. And so if they had still been found alive when the Lord came, when it was no longer *a time to throw away stones, but a time to gather stones together* (Eccl. 3:5), they would straightaway have castrated themselves for the sake of the kingdom of heaven; you only find it difficult, after all, to go without something, when you are greedy to possess it. . . .

So then, all the doings, or practically all of them, which are contained in the books of the Old Testament, are to be taken not only in their literal sense, but also as having a figurative sense. All the same, when the people in the narratives, which the reader takes in the proper literal sense, were praised for doing things that are abhorrent to the manners of good men and women who keep God's commandments after the Lord's coming, the reader should not take the actual deeds as models for moral behavior, but should try to understand their figurative meaning. There are many things, after all, which at that time were done out of duty that now can only be done out of lust.

If, however, you read about any signs of great men, and yet are able to notice and explore them in some figurative representations of future realities, you should still turn the proper literal meaning of the thing done to this good use: that as a result of seeing the tempests such men were in danger from and the shipwrecks they had to bewail, you should never even think of congratulating yourself on what you have done rightly, or of looking down upon other people as sinners from the vantage point of your own justice. The recording even of these men's sins, you see, had this purpose, to make that judgment of the apostle's strike terror on all sides, *Therefore let anyone who seems to stand see to it that he does not fall* (1 Cor. 10:12). There is, in fact, almost no page of the holy books in which the lesson is not echoed, that *God withstands the proud, but gives grace to the humble* (Prov. 3:34; James 4:6; 1 Peter 5:5).

Some Further, More Technical Rules of Interpretation

And so the thing that has to be ascertained above all else is whether the passage we are trying to understand is intended to be taken literally or figuratively. For on being assured of its figurative nature, it is easy, by applying the rules we set out in the first book, to turn the passage over this way and that until we arrive at its true meaning, especially when our use of these rules is reinforced by being exercised devoutly and reverently. But we discover whether the passage is to be taken literally or figuratively by considering all that has been said above. When this becomes clear, the words employed in the expression will be found to be drawn from similar things or from things approximating more or less closely.

But because there are many ways in which things are seen to be like other things, we should not think it is *de rigueur* for us to assume that a thing always has to signify what it happens to signify in one passage by its resemblance to something else. Thus the Lord talked of yeast in a negative sense when he said, *The kingdom of heaven is like a woman who hid some yeast in three measures of flour, until it was all leavened* (Luke 13:21).

Observation, therefore, will show that this variety takes two forms: thus things can signify this as well as that in such a way that they signify either contraries or merely diverse realities. Contraries, that is to say, when the same thing is put as a simile for something good in one place, something bad in another, like what I have just said about yeast. Such too is the case with the lion, which signifies Christ where it says, *The lion from the tribe of Judah has conquered* (Rev. 5:5); and also signifies the devil where it is written, *Your adversary the devil goes about roaring like a lion, seeking whom he may devour* (1 Peter 5:8). In the same way we have the serpent in a good sense: *As cunning as serpents* (Matt. 10:16); while in a bad sense, *The serpent seduced Eve by his cunning* (2 Cor. 11:3). Bread in a good sense: *I am the living bread, who have come down from heaven;* in a bad sense: *Eat hidden loaves of bread with pleasure* (Prov. 9:17). And these instances I have mentioned, of course, leave no doubts about their meaning, because to illustrate the point it was necessary to mention only clear cases.

There are others, however, where it is uncertain in what sense, good or bad, they should be taken, like: *A goblet of pure wine in the hand of the Lord is full and mixed.* It is uncertain whether it signifies the wrath of God, but not down to the final punishments, that is down to the dregs, or whether it rather signifies the grace of the Scriptures passing from the Jews to the nations, because *he turned it this way and that,* while there remained with the Jews the observances which they understand in a carnal, literal sense, *because its dregs have not been emptied out* (Ps. 75:8). But as an example of a thing put to signify, not contraries, but simply diverse realities, we have water signifying the people, as we read in the Apocalypse, and the Holy Spirit in the text, *Rivers of living water shall flow from his belly* (John 7:38), and anything else that water can be taken to signify in other places where it is mentioned.

In the same way there are other things which, considered not in their general use, but in any particular instance, signify not only two different things but sometimes even several, depending on the place the sentence occurs in.

But wherever their meaning is clear, there we must learn how they are to be understood in obscurer places. After all, there is no better way of understanding what was said to God in the verse, *Take up arms and shield, and arise to help me* (Ps. 35:2), than from that other place where we read, *Lord, you have crowned us as with the shield of your good will* (Ps. 5:12). This does not mean, however, that wherever we read of a shield as some kind of defense we should only take it to mean God's good will; it says elsewhere, after all, *And the shield of faith, with which you can quench all the fiery arrows of the wicked one* (Eph. 6:16). Nor again, in spiritual equipment of this sort, should we confine faith only to the shield, since another place also talks of the breastplate of faith: *Putting on,* he says, *the breastplate of faith and love* (1 Thess. 5:8).

But when from the same words of Scripture not just one, but two or more meanings may be extracted, even if you cannot tell which of them the writer intended, there is no risk if they can all be shown from other places of the Holy Scriptures to correspond with the truth. However, those who are engaged in searching the divine utterances must make every effort to arrive at the intention of the author through whom the Holy Spirit produced that portion of Scripture. But as I say, there is nothing risky about it, whether they do get at this, or whether they carve out another meaning from those words which does not clash with right faith, and is supported by any other passage of the divine utterances. That author, in fact, possibly even saw this very meaning in the same words which we wish to understand; and certainly the Spirit of God who produced these texts through him foresaw without a shadow of a doubt that it would occur to some reader or listener; or rather he actually provided that it should occur to them, because it is upheld by the truth. How, after all, could the divine Scriptures make more abundant and generous provision, than by ensuring that the same words could be understood in several ways, which are underwritten by other no less divine testimonies?

But where a possible meaning emerges which cannot be made entirely clear by other certain testimonies of the Holy Scriptures, it remains to elucidate it with arguments from reason, even if the writer whose words we are trying to understand did not perhaps intend that meaning. But this habit is risky; it is really much safer to walk along with the divine Scriptures; when we wish to examine passages rendered obscure with words used metaphorically, either let something emerge from our scrutiny that is not controversial, or else if it is so, let the matter be settled from the same Scripture by finding and applying testimonies from anywhere else in the sacred books.

Educated readers, however, should know that our authors used all the figures of speech, to which grammarians give the Greek name of tropes, much more freely and abundantly than people who are unfamiliar with them, and who have learned about these things in other writings, could possibly guess or believe. Still, those who know these tropes will recognize them in the holy texts, and will to some extent be helped by this knowledge in understanding them. But this is not the right place for handing them on to those who are ignorant of them; else I might seem to be teaching the art of grammar. My advice certainly is that this should be learned elsewhere. . . .

Not only, though, are there examples in the divine books of all these tropes, but even the names of some of them can be read there, like allegory, enigma, parable. As a matter of fact, though, practically all these tropes, which are said to be learned in the liberal art of grammar, are also to be found in the speech of people who have never taken any courses in grammar, and are quite happy with the speech of common people. Is there anybody, after all, who never says, "May you blossom like that," which is the trope called metaphor? Or who does not call any pool a fish pond, even though it has no fish in it, and was not even made for fish? And yet it got its name from fish; this trope is called catachresis.

It would take too long to run through the rest of the tropes in this way; after all, common speech gets as far as using those which are all the more surprising, because they signify the opposite of what is said, such as the one called irony or antiphrasis. But irony indicates by the tone of voice what is intended to be understood, as when we say to a person behaving badly, "You *are* behaving well," whereas antiphrasis manages to signify the opposite of what it says, not by the tone of voice, but either by having its own words, which derive from the opposite meaning, like calling a grove a *lucus*, though it is almost devoid of *lucis*, light, or by saying something in that way, although it can also be said without meaning the opposite, as when we ask for something which is not there, and are told, "There's plenty," or when we show by the context of our other words that what we say is to be understood in the opposite sense, as if we were to say, "Beware of that fellow, because he's a good man."

And are there any uneducated people who do not use such expressions, though they do not have the slightest idea of what tropes are, or what they are called? The reason knowledge of them is necessary for unraveling the ambiguities of the Scriptures is that when the sense of the words, if they are taken literally, is absurd, we have of course to inquire whether the passage we do not understand was said according to this or that trope; and in this way, often enough, the meaning of what was obscure is laid bare.

JOHN CASSIAN

The Fourfold Reading

Much of the life of John Cassian (ca. 360–ca. 430) is veiled in obscurity, including his nationality (though there is evidence he was born in the region of present-day Romania). He received a classical education, and when he was a young man he joined a monastery in Bethlehem, traveling often to Egypt where he visited the great ascetics. He became a deacon of the church in Constantinople and was sent by John Chrysostom to Rome bearing letters to Pope Innocent I. While in Rome he made the acquaintance of the future Leo the Great, who later asked him to write a refutation of Nestorian christology *(On the Incarnation of Christ against Nestorius)*. In 415 Cassian founded two monasteries in Marseilles, one for men and one for women. Cassian's *Institutes*, setting forth his rules for monastic life derived largely from his experiences with the Egyptian ascetics, was held in high esteem by St. Benedict and had a lasting impact on monasticism both in the East and in the West. His greatest work was *The Conferences*, a collection of dialogues supposedly reconstructed from conversations held with Egyptian abbots and dealing with various aspects of the spiritual life such as discretion, love, and prayer. One conference addressed the issue of free will, which Cassian defended against the extreme Augustinian emphasis on prevenient grace and predestination; his position was later called "Semi-Pelagianism." The following excerpt from the Fourteenth Conference shows the great importance Cassian placed upon memorization of and meditation on Scripture. His explanation of the four senses of Scripture (historical, tropological, allegorical, and anagogical), derived from Origen's three senses, was the basis for the standard fourfold method of biblical interpretation in the West until the Enlightenment. (See Owen Chadwick, *John Cassian: A Study in Primitive Monasticism* [Cambridge: Cambridge University Press, 1950].)

John Cassian: The Conferences, trans. Boniface Ramsey, OP, in Ancient Christian Writers, ed. Walter J. Burghardt, John Dillon, and Dennis D. McManus, vol. 57 (New York: Paulist, 1997), VIII–XI.1, pp. 509-15.

"But let us return to discussing the knowledge that was spoken of at the beginning. As we said previously, the *praktike* [practical knowledge] is dispersed among many professions and pursuits. The *theoretike* [theoretical knowledge], on the other hand, is divided into two parts — that is, into historical interpretation and spiritual understanding. Hence, when Solomon had enumerated the different forms of grace in the church, he added: 'All who are with her are doubly clothed.' Now, there are three kinds of spiritual knowledge — tropology, allegory, and anagogy — about which it is said in Proverbs: 'But you describe those things for yourself in threefold fashion according to the largeness of your heart.'

"And so history embraces the knowledge of past and visible things, which is repeated by the Apostle thus: 'It is written that Abraham had two sons, one from a slave and the other from a free woman. The one from the slave was born according to the flesh, but the one from the free woman by promise.' The things that follow belong to allegory, however, because what really occurred is said to have prefigured the form of another mystery. 'For these,' it says, 'are two covenants, one from Mount Sinai, begetting unto slavery, which is Hagar. For Sinai is a mountain in Arabia, which is compared to the Jerusalem that now is, and which is enslaved with her children.'

"But anagogy, which mounts from spiritual mysteries to certain more sublime and sacred heavenly secrets, is added by the Apostle: 'But the Jerusalem from above, which is our mother, is free. For it is written: Rejoice, you barren one who do not bear, break out and shout, you who are not in labor, for the children of the desolate one are many more than of her who has a husband.'

"Tropology is moral explanation pertaining to correction of life and to practical instruction, as if we understood these same two covenants as *praktike* and as theoretical discipline, or at least as if we wished to take Jerusalem or Zion as the soul of the human being, according to the words: 'Praise the Lord, O Jerusalem; praise your God, O Zion.'

"The four figures that have been mentioned converge in such a way that, if we want, one and the same Jerusalem can be understood in a fourfold manner. According to history it is the city of the Jews. According to allegory it is the church of Christ. According to anagogy it is that heavenly city of God 'which is the mother of us all.' According to tropology it is the soul of the human being, which under this name is frequently either reproached or praised by the Lord. Of these four kinds of interpretation the blessed Apostle says thus: 'Now, brothers, if I come to you speaking in tongues, what use will it be to you unless I speak to you by revelation or by knowledge or by prophecy or by instruction?'

"Now, revelation pertains to allegory, by which the things that the historical narrative conceals are laid bare by a spiritual understanding and explanation. Suppose, for example, that we tried to make clear how 'all our fathers were under the cloud, and all were baptized in Moses in the cloud and in the sea, and [how] all ate the same spiritual food and drank the same spiritual drink from the rock that followed them. But the rock was Christ.' This explanation, which refers to the prefiguration of the body and blood of Christ that we daily receive, comprises an allegorical approach.

"But knowledge, which is also mentioned by the Apostle, is tropology, by which we discern by a prudent examination everything that pertains to practical discretion, in order to see whether it is useful and good, as when we are ordered to judge for ourselves 'whether it befits a woman to pray to God with unveiled head.' This approach, as has been said, comprises a moral understanding.

"Likewise, prophecy, which the Apostle introduced in the third place, bespeaks anagogy, by which words are directed to the invisible and to what lies in the future, as in this case: 'We do not want you to be ignorant, brothers, about those who are asleep, so that you may not be saddened like others who have no hope. For if we believe that Christ has died and has arisen, so also God will bring those who have fallen asleep in Jesus with him. For we say this to you by the word of the Lord, that we who are alive at the coming of the Lord shall not anticipate those who have fallen asleep in Christ, for the Lord himself shall descend from heaven with a command, with the voice of an angel and with the trumpet of God, and the dead who are in Christ shall arise first.' The figure of anagogy appears in this kind of exhortation.

"But instruction lays open the simple sequence of a historical exposition in which there is no more hidden meaning than what is comprised in the sound of the words, as in this case: 'I delivered to you first what I also received, that Christ died for our sins according to the Scriptures, that he was buried, that he rose on the third day, and that he was seen by Cephas.' And: 'God sent his Son, made of woman, made under the law, to save those who were under the law.' And this: 'Hear, O Israel: The Lord your God is one Lord.'

"Therefore, if you are concerned to attain to the light of spiritual knowledge not by the vice of empty boastfulness but by the grace of correction, you are first inflamed with desire for that blessedness about which it is said: 'Blessed are the pure of heart, for they shall see God,' so that you may also attain to that about which the angel said to Daniel: 'Those who are learned shall shine like the splendor of the firmament, and those who instruct many in righteousness like the stars forever.' And in another prophet: 'Enlighten yourselves with the light of knowledge while there is time.'

"Maintaining the diligence in reading that I think you have, then, make every effort to get a complete grasp of practical — that is, ethical — discipline as soon as possible. For without this the theoretical purity that we have spoken of cannot be acquired. The only people who attain to it, possessing it as a reward after the expenditure of much toil and labor, are those who have found perfection not in the words of other teachers but in the virtuousness of their own acts. Obtaining this understanding not from meditating on the law but as a result of their toil, they sing with the psalmist: 'From your commandments I have understood.' And after all their passions have been purified they say with confidence: 'I will sing and I will understand in the undefiled way.' For the one who is singing the psalm, who is moving forward in the undefiled way with the stride of a pure heart, will understand what is sung.

"Therefore, if you wish to prepare a sacred tabernacle of spiritual knowledge in your heart, cleanse yourselves from the contagion of every vice and strip yourselves of the cares of the present world. For it is impossible for the soul which is even slightly taken up with worldly distractions to deserve the gift of knowledge or to beget spiritual understanding or to remember the sacred readings.

"Take care first of all, then . . . that your lips maintain strict silence, lest your pursuit of reading and the intensity of your desire come to naught because of empty pride. This is the first beginning of practical discipline — that with attentive heart and as it were silent tongue you receive the institutes and words of all the elders, preserve them carefully in your breast, and strive to fulfill them rather than to teach them. For from the latter the dangerous presumption of a vainglory will spring, but from the former the fruit of spiritual knowledge. Consequently, do not dare to put anything forward during a conference of the elders unless either a harmful ignorance or the need to know something compels you to ask a question, since some people who are puffed up with the love of vainglory make up questions about things that they know very well in order to show off their learning. For it is impossible for a person who pursues reading persistently with the intention of winning human praise to deserve the gift of true knowledge. Whoever has been overcome by this passion is invariably entangled in other vices too, and especially in pride. Thus, having come to ruin with the practical and ethical, he will not acquire the spiritual knowledge that springs from it. Be in every respect, therefore, 'quick to hear, but slow to speak,' lest there befall you what Solomon mentions: 'If you see a man who is quick with words, know that a fool has more hope than he.'

"Nor should anyone presume to teach in words what he has not previously done in deed. Our Lord taught us by his own example that we should follow this order, as it is said: 'Which Jesus began to do and teach.' Be careful, therefore, that you not jump to teaching before you have acted and be counted among those of whom the Lord speaks to his disciples in the Gospel: 'Observe and do what they say, but do not do according to their works. For they bind heavy burdens, hard to carry, and place them on people's shoulders, but they themselves do not move them with their finger.' For if the person 'who breaks the least commandment and teaches people so shall be called least in the kingdom of heaven,' it follows that whoever neglects many great things and dares to teach is certainly not merely least in the kingdom of heaven but should be considered greatest in the punishment of Gehenna.

"Therefore you should be careful lest you be stirred to teach by the example of those who have acquired skill in speaking and a fluent tongue and who are believed by those who are unable to discern its power and character to possess spiritual knowledge because they can say whatever they want elaborately and at length. For it is one thing to speak with ease and beauty and another to enter deeply into heavenly sayings and to contemplate profound and hidden mysteries with the most pure eye of the heart, because certainly neither human teaching nor worldly learning but only purity of mind will possess this, through the enlightenment of the Holy Spirit.

"If you wish to attain to a true knowledge of Scripture, then, you must first hasten to acquire a steadfast humility of heart which will, by the perfection of love, bring you not to the knowledge which puffs up but to that which enlightens. For it is impossible for the impure mind to receive the gift of spiritual knowledge. Therefore, avoid this very carefully, lest by zealous reading there arise in you, out of arrogant vanity, not the light of knowledge or the everlasting glory that is promised by the enlightenment of teaching but rather the means of your own destruction.

"Then, once all worldly cares and preoccupations have been cast out, you must strive in every respect to give yourself assiduously and even constantly to sacred reading. Do this until continual meditation fills your mind and as it were forms it in its likeness, making of it a kind of ark of the covenant, containing in itself two stone tablets — that is, constant steadfastness under the aspect of a twofold Testament; a golden jar, too — that is, a pure and sincere memory, which preserves safely and lastingly the manna that is contained in it — namely, the enduring and heavenly sweetness of spiritual understandings and of the angelic bread; and also the rod of Aaron — that is, the banner of salvation of our true high priest Jesus Christ, ever green with undying remembrance, for this is the rod which had been cut from the root of Jesse and which, having died, flourishes again with still greater life. All of these are guarded by two cherubim — that is, by the fullness of historical and spiritual knowledge, for the cherubim are interpreted as the breadth of knowledge. They constantly guard the propitiatory of God — that is, your interior calm — and protect it from every assault of the evil spirits. Thus your mind, having advanced not only as far as the ark of the divine covenant but even as far as the priestly kingdom, and by

186

its unshakable love of purity being as it were absorbed in spiritual discipline, will fulfill the priestly command that is laid down in this way by the Lawgiver: 'He shall not go forth from the holy places, lest he pollute the sanctuary of God' — that is, his own heart, in which the Lord promises that he will always dwell when he says: 'I will dwell in them and walk among them.'

"Hence the successive books of Holy Scripture must be diligently committed to memory and ceaselessly reviewed. This continual meditation will bestow on us double fruit. First, inasmuch as the mind's attention is occupied with reading and with preparing to read, it cannot be taken captive in the entrapments of harmful thoughts. Then, the things that we have not been able to understand because our mind was busy at the time, things that we have gone through repeatedly and are laboring to memorize, we shall see more clearly afterward when we are free from every seductive deed and sight, and especially when we are silently meditating at night. Thus, while we are at rest and as it were immersed in the stupor of sleep, there will be revealed an understanding of hidden meanings that we did not grasp even slightly when we were awake.

"But as our mind is increasingly renewed by this study, the face of Scripture will also begin to be renewed, and the beauty of a more sacred understanding will somehow grow with the person who is making progress. For its form is also adapted to the capacity of the human intelligence, and it will appear as earthly to carnal persons and as divine to spiritual persons, such that those to whom it previously seemed wrapped in thick clouds will be unable to grasp its subtlety or endure its splendor. . . ."

MARTIN LUTHER

The Letter and the Spirit

Martin Luther (1483-1546) was not the first to exalt the authority of Scripture over tradition, but he was clearest in his understanding of the symbiotic relationship of church traditions and the allegorical interpretation of the Bible. He therefore repudiated the fourfold interpretation, seeking in its stead the "literal, ordinary, natural sense" of Scripture. He particularly objected to those, such as Origen, who found warrant for a spiritual hermeneutic in 2 Corinthians 3, a passage Luther interpreted *theologically* in terms of the ministry of law and gospel. What is killing about the Old Testament, said Luther, is not its native, literal sense, but rather the revelation of God's law and wrath. Hence his extra measure of abuse for the "superspiritual" Jerome Emser against whom Luther waged a protracted pamphlet war. Despite his protestations, Luther did not abandon spiritual interpretation. He acknowledged the "hidden sense" or "mysteries" but insisted that any meaning deeper than the ordinary must be signaled by Scripture itself. Luther eventually advanced the "historical" interpretation of Scripture by which he retrojected the history of Christ and the church into the Old Testament's domain of allegory. To use Augustine's terms, Luther's Christ becomes the one essential "thing" amidst an array of biblical "signs." His hermeneutic thus prefigures two radical approaches to biblical interpretation: nineteenth-century historicism and twentieth-century theological existentialism.

Martin Luther, ". . . Answer to the Superchristian, Superspiritual, and Superlearned Book of Goat Emser of Leipzig," trans. A. Steimle, in *Works of Martin Luther*, vol. 3 (Philadelphia: Muhlenberg Press, 1930), pp. 346-60.

St. Paul says, 2 Corinthians 4 [3:6]: "The letter killeth, but the spirit giveth life." This my Emser explains to mean that the Scriptures have a twofold meaning, an external sense and a secret sense, which he calls the literal and the spiritual. The literal sense is supposed to kill and the spiritual to give life. In this he builds on the teaching of Origen, Dionysius, and some others, and thinks he has hit the mark squarely and does not need even to look at the clear Scriptures, since he has the teachings of men. He would like me to imitate him, to abandon the Scriptures and likewise accept the teachings of men. That is something I will not do, although I, too, labored under that error for a time, and I desire to take this opportunity to show clearly how Origen, Jerome, Dionysius, and some others were in the wrong, and how Emser builds his house on the sand, and that it is always necessary to compare the writings of the fathers with the Scripture, and to judge them according to its light.

In the first place, if their opinion were right, that the spiritual sense giveth life and the literal sense killeth, we should be obliged to confess that all sinners are holy and all the saints are sinners; nay, Christ himself with all the angels must at the same time be both living and dead. This we shall make so clear that even Emser with all his ability to lie shall not be able to contradict it. We will take the passage from St. Paul in Galatians 4, where according to the literal sense, the letter, it is stated that Abraham had two sons, Isaac and Ishmael, by two wives, Sarah and Hagar. This is the sense accepted by Christ, God the Holy Spirit, and all the angels and saints. They hold that what the literal sense conveys here is true. And it is indeed true. Well, Emser, where is your Origen now? If you are really the man who fights not with the scabbard but strikes with the blade, speak up now and say that the letter and the literal sense kill Christ and the Holy Spirit together with all the angels and saints. Can a man say anything more blasphemous than Emser does in his madness, that all the truth in the Scripture kills and destroys?

Again, that Abraham signifies Christ, the two women the two Testaments, the two sons the people of the two Testaments, as St. Paul interprets, this is, as you say, the spiritual meaning. But this meaning is held not only by the saints but also by the worst sinners, yea even by the devils in hell. Come right out into the open, my Emser, strike away with the blade and say that all the devils and knaves are holy and have the life which the spirit giveth. Now be honest and confess that when you take this trick away from Origen, Dionysius, Jerome, and many others there is nothing left of them. Are not the Scriptures clearer on this point than all the fathers? . . .

In this way we must interpret all the Scriptures, even the ancient types. For instance, the Jews were forbidden to eat swine or hare because neither swine nor hare cheweth the cud. This is the literal sense. Thus it was understood by David, all the holy prophets, and by Christ himself, together with his disciples, and if they had not thus understood and observed it, they would have set themselves against God. Why did the letter not kill them? Again, that the swine signify the carnal teachings or whatever other spiritual sense one wishes to apply can be understood even by those who live in mortal sin, and by the devils even more easily. Why does not the spirit give life to them? Where are you, O knight with the mighty Leipzig sword? . . . Truly, you must now see and yourself admit what I have told you, that you do not have an inkling of the meaning of "spirit" and "letter" in the Scriptures. You had better tend to your business and let the Scriptures alone. See how little it helps to quote many writers and to build on what they say.

Furthermore, St. Paul says, Romans 7: "The divine law is spiritual, but I am carnal." He cites one of the ten commandments, namely, the *Non concupisces,* Thou shalt not covet, and in an extended and skillful argument shows how that same spiritual law killeth. What will you do here, my Emser? Where are you, O man of the spear and of the dagger and of the edged sword? St. Paul here says that the spiritual law killeth, but you say that the spiritual sense giveth life. Come, pipe up, show your skill: what is the literal, and what the spiritual sense in this commandment, *Non concupisces?* Surely you cannot deny that no other sense can be taken out of these words than that given by their literal meaning. Paul here speaks of the evil lusts of the flesh and yet he calls this law spiritual and maintains that it killeth. And you say, it were better to read a poet's tale than the literal sense of the Scriptures. This is St. Paul's opinion, and he who finds in this commandment any other sense than this literal sense concerning evil lusts finds no meaning in it at all. How well Emser accords with St. Paul: like a donkey singing a duet with a nightingale. All the commandments of God must be treated in the same way, whether they refer to ceremonies or other matters, small or great. It is plain how pitifully Emser has erred in this thing and has shown that he knows less about the Scriptures than a child.

Besides, his mistaken and wrong interpretation is a dishonor to the entire sacred Scriptures and a disgrace to himself. All the labor and diligence of the teachers have no other object than to find the literal sense which alone they regard as valid, so that Augustine declares: *Figura Nihil probat,* that is, Emser's "spiritual sense" is not valid, but the other sense is the highest, best, strongest; in short, it is the whole substance, essence, and foundation of Scripture, so that if the literal sense were taken away, all the Scriptures would be nothing. The spiritual sense, which Emser magnifies, is not valid in any controversy. It does not hold water, nor would it matter if no one knew anything about it, as I proved in my book *On the Papacy.* For even if no one knew that Aaron is a type of Christ, it would not matter, neither can it be proven. We must let Aaron be simply Aaron in the ordinary sense, except where the Spirit himself gives a new interpretation, which is then a new literal sense, as St. Paul, for instance, in the Epistle to the Hebrews makes Aaron to be Christ.

How can you be so bold, Emser, as to make the assertion that this literal sense killeth? You are floundering about in ignorance of the import of your own words, when you prate that it is better to read one of Virgil's poems than to read the literal sense of the Scriptures. Thereby you condemn the entire Scripture and give preference to the lies and fictions of the devil over the holy Word of God, which has no other valid meaning than the one you call deadly and teach men to shun. But this is smiting with the blade and a correct Emserian spiritual interpretation; thus must the heretic Luther be struck! Turn the tables, Emser, and you will find that the sense which you call spiritual and life-giving, is the very one — if you cling only to it and let the literal sense go — for which it would be better to exchange the poets' tales, for the spiritual sense is unsafe, and the Scriptures exist without it, but they cannot exist without the literal sense. They were right aforetimes who prohibited the books of Origen, for he paid too much attention to this spiritual sense, which was unnecessary, and he neglected the necessary literal sense. For that means the destruction of Scripture and will never make sound theologians. Such are developed only by the one, true, original, and native sense of the words.

The Holy Spirit is the plainest writer and speaker in heaven and earth, and therefore his words cannot have more than one, and that the very simplest, sense, which we call the literal, ordinary, natural sense. That the things indicated by the simple sense of his simple words should signify something further and different, and therefore one thing should always signify another, is more than a question of words or of language. For the same is true of all other things outside of the Scriptures, since all of God's works and creatures are living signs and words of God, as St. Augustine and all the teachers declare. But we are not on that account to say that the Scriptures or the Word of God have more than one meaning.

A painted picture of a living man signifies a person, without need of a word of explanation. But that does not cause you to say that the word "picture" has a twofold sense, a literal sense, meaning the picture, and a spiritual sense, meaning the living person. Now, although the things described in the Scriptures have a further significance, the Scriptures do not on that account have a twofold sense, but only the one which the words give. Beyond that we can give permission to speculative minds to seek and chase after the various significations of the things mentioned, provided they take care not to go too far or too high, as sometimes happens to the chamois hunters and did happen to Origen.

It is much surer and safer to abide by the words in their simple sense; they furnish the real pasture and right dwelling-places for all minds. . . .

Many sensible men have made the mistake of calling the "letter" a figure of speech, Augustine among them. As if I were to say, Emser is a stupid ass, and a simple-minded man hearing these words would understand that Emser were actually an ass with long ears and four legs. The man would have been deceived by the letter, whereas I wanted to convey, through the figure of speech, what a blockhead Emser is. Figures of speech are a subject of study in the schools and are called in Greek *schemata,* and in Latin *figurae,* because they are a decking out of speech, even as you adorn the body with jewels. The Scriptures are full of such figures of speech, particularly the books of the prophets. John and Christ in Luke 3 call the Jews *genimina viperarum,* generation of vipers. St. Paul in Colossians 2 [Phil. 3:2] calls them dogs. Psalm 109 [110:3] says: "The dew of thy children shall come out of the womb of the morning." Again: "God shall send the rod of thy strength out of Zion." That means the children of Christ are born, not physically from a mother's womb, but without the work of man, like the dew from heaven, out of the morning of the Christian Church. Further, Christ says, Matthew 5: "Ye are the salt of the earth and the light of the world." But this is not what St. Paul means by the word "letter." This belongs to the study of grammar in the schools.

If you can humble yourself and not despise me altogether, I will do what out of Christian duty I owe to my enemy, and not withhold from you God's gift to me. I will give you better instruction in this matter — I say this without boasting — than any you have received heretofore from any teacher except St. Augustine, if perchance you have read his *De Spiritu et Litera.* None of the others will teach you aright. You will not find a single letter in the whole Bible that agrees with what you, together with Origen and Jerome, call the spiritual sense. St. Paul calls it a mystery, a secret, hidden sense, wherefore the earliest of the fathers called it an anagogical, that is, a more remote sense, a meaning by itself, and sometimes also an allegory, St. Paul himself using the latter term in Galatians 4. But that is not yet the "spirit," although the Spirit has given it as well as the letter and all the gifts, as we see from 1 Corinthians 14: "The Spirit speaketh mysteries." Some, however, because they did not understand this matter, ascribed a fourfold sense to Scripture, the literal, the allegorical, the anagogical, and the tropological, for which there is no foundation whatever.

It is, therefore, not well named the literal sense, for by letter Paul means something quite different. They do much better who call it the grammatical, historical sense. It would be well to call it the speaking or language sense as St. Paul does in 1 Corinthians 14, because it is understood by everybody in the sense of the spoken language. He who hears the words that Abraham had two sons by two wives receives them in that sense and has no further thoughts than those indicated by the language, until the Spirit goes farther and reveals the hidden sense concerning Christ and the two covenants and peoples. Such hidden meanings are then called mysteries, just as St. Paul in Ephesians 5 calls the union of Christ and the church in one body a mystery, although the letter of the Scriptures in Genesis 2 speaks of man and wife. Great care is necessary, however, that not everyone shall of himself invent mysteries, as some have done and still do. The Spirit must do it himself or one must prove them by Scripture, as I said in the treatise *On the Papacy.*

Therefore, the text of St. Paul in 2 Corinthians 4 [3:6], "The letter killeth but the spirit giveth life," squares with this twofold sense, the spiritual and the literal, as perfectly as Emser's head squares with philosophy and theology. How and why Origen, Jerome, and some other fathers also turned and twisted this text in the same manner I will not discuss now. It is generally known and can easily be proved that they treated other passages in the same way in order to refute the Jews and the heretics. But we ought to excuse them for that and not follow them here like unclean animals who gulp down everything they find and make no distinctions in the work and teaching of the fathers, until at last we follow them only in those things wherein the beloved fathers — as human beings — erred, and depart from them in the things they did well. I could prove this easily from the teachings and the lives of all who now are considered the very worthiest among them.

Let us now consider the text concerning the letter and the spirit. In that passage St. Paul does not write one iota about these two senses, but declares that there are two kinds of preaching or ministries. One is that of the Old Testament, the other that of the New Testament. The Old Testament preaches the letter, the New Testament the spirit. . . .

We see clearly that St. Paul speaks of two tables and two kinds of preaching. The tables of Moses were of stone, on which the law was inscribed by God's finger, Exodus 20. The tables of Christ, or the epistles of Christ, as he calls them here, are the hearts of Christians, in which are written, not letters as on Moses' tables, but the spirit of God, through the preaching of the gospel and the ministry of the apostles. Now, just what does this mean? The letter is naught else but the divine law and commandment which is given in the Old Testament, through Moses, and is taught and proclaimed through Aaron's priesthood. It is called "letter" because it is written with letters on the tables of stone and in books. A letter it must ever remain; it never gives anything except its command. For no man is made better by the law, but only worse, for the law does not give help or grace; it merely commands and demands that a man do what a man never willingly does, and indeed, cannot do. But the spirit, which is divine

193

grace, gives strength and power to the heart, yea, creates a new man who grows to love God's commandments and does with joy all that he ought to do.

This spirit cannot be contained in any letter, it cannot be written with ink, on stone, or in books, as the law can be, but is written only in the heart, a living writing of the Holy Spirit who uses no means at all. Therefore, St. Paul calls it Christ's epistle, not Moses' tables; it is written not with ink, but with the Spirit of God. By this spirit or grace a man does what the law commands and satisfies it. In this manner he becomes free from the letter that kills him and lives through the grace of the Spirit. Everyone that does not have this grace of the living Spirit is dead, although he make a fine show in the outward keeping of the whole law. For this reason the apostle says of the law that it kills, that it makes no one alive and would keep one eternally in bondage to death unless grace come to set him free and to give him life.

These, then, are the two ministries. The priests, preachers, and ministries of the Old Testament deal with naught else but the law of God; they have as yet no open proclamation of the spirit and of grace. But in the New Testament all the preaching is of grace and the spirit given to us through Christ. For the preaching of the New Testament is naught else but an offering and presentation of Christ to all men out of the pure mercy of God, in such wise that all who believe in him receive God's grace and the Holy Spirit, by which all sin is forgiven, all law is fulfilled, they become God's children, and have eternal salvation. Therefore St. Paul here calls the New Testament proclamation *ministerium spiritus*, a ministry of the spirit, i.e., a ministry by which the spirit and grace of God are presented and offered to all who by the law have been burdened, killed, and made to long for grace. The law he calls *ministerium literae*, a ministry of the letter, i.e., a ministry which offers nothing but the letter or the law, that produces no life nor a fulfillment of the law whose demands no man can satisfy. Therefore it must needs remain a letter, and as a letter it can accomplish nothing more than to kill a man, i.e., it shows him what he ought to do and yet cannot do; this makes him realize that he is in disgrace and dead before God, whose commandments he does not keep and yet must keep. . . .

Here we see how excellently St. Paul teaches us to understand aright, Christ, God's grace, and the New Testament. It is all comprised in the fact that Christ came unto our sin, bore it in his body on the cross, and blotted it out, so that all who believed on him were rid of their sin and received grace henceforth to satisfy God's law and the letter that killeth, and thus were made partakers of eternal life. See, that is what is meant by *ministerium spiritus, non literae*, the preaching of the spirit, the preaching of grace, the preaching of a right indulgence, the preaching of Christ, i.e., the New Testament, of which much could be said if the evil spirit had not blinded the world through the pope, and by man-teaching had led it into the abyss of outermost darkness.

Now we see that all commandments lead unto death, since even divine commandments mean death, for everything that is not spirit or grace means death. It is, therefore, monstrous ignorance to call allegories, tropologies, and the like, spirit. They can all be encompassed in language and do not give life, but grace has no receptacle save the heart. . . .

It is indeed true that where only the law is preached and the letter insisted on, as in the Old Testament, and this is not followed by the preaching of the Spirit, there can be only death without life, sin without grace, anguish without comfort. Such preaching produces wretched and captive consciences, and makes men finally despair and die in their sins, and, through this preaching, be eternally damned. This has been done in our day and still is done by the murderous sophists in their *summa* and *confessionalia,* in which they drive and torment the people with contrition, confession, penance and satisfaction. Then they teach good works and preach good doctrine as they say, but not once do they hold up the Spirit and Christ to the afflicted consciences; so that now Christ is unknown to all the world, the gospel lies in a corner, and the whole ministry of the New Testament is suppressed. . . .

To preach the letter and the spirit gives us more to do than we are equal to, even if we began at the beginning of the world and kept on until doomsday.

RUDOLF BULTMANN

Is Exegesis without Presuppositions Possible?

Between Reformation exegesis and the modern era lies a revolution in biblical interpretation. Modern hermeneutics expanded the function of the traditional rules of interpretation to include theological and philosophical questions of *understanding*. Hermeneutics asks how the preacher or interpreter can assist twenty-first-century people to enter into the world of an ancient text in such a way that the modern reader appropriates what is alien. Rudolf Bultmann (1884-1976) posed this question to New Testament interpreters and devoted his scholarly life to answering it. In 1941 his essay "The New Testament and Mythology" outlined his famous program of demythologizing, which has continued to shadow contemporary biblical and theological debates. Bultmann's intention was not to abolish New Testament teaching, as his critics insisted, but by means of philological, literary, and existentialist criticism to isolate its authentic kernel and to reinterpret it for a new age. In this enterprise he used Heidegger's philosophy to establish a preunderstanding of the problematic nature of human existence. Only the kerygma, or proclaimed summons, of the Crucified One, however, has the power to rescue humanity from inauthentic existence. Bultmann worked out his existentialist hermeneutic in the hope that it would make modern preaching more intelligible. He had learned from Schleiermacher that absolute objectivity in interpretation is impossible and from Luther that the interpreter is finally justified by faith and not historical proof.

Rudolf Bultmann, "Is Exegesis Without Presuppositions Possible?" in *Existence and Faith: Shorter Writings of Rudolf Bultmann* (New York: Meridian, 1960), pp. 289-96. (*Existence and Faith* has more recently been published under the title *New Testament and Mythology*.)

The question whether exegesis without presuppositions is possible must be answered affirmatively if "without presuppositions" means "without presupposing the results of the exegesis." In this sense, exegesis without presuppositions is not only possible but demanded. In another sense, however, *no* exegesis is without presuppositions, inasmuch as the exegete is not a *tabula rasa,* but on the contrary, approaches the text with specific questions or with a specific way of raising questions and thus has a certain idea of the subject matter with which the text is concerned.

The demand that exegesis must be without presuppositions, in the sense that it must not presuppose its results (we can also say that it must be without prejudice), may be clarified only briefly. This demand means, first of all, the rejection of all allegorical interpretation. When Philo finds the Stoic idea of the apathetic wise man in the prescription of the law that the sacrificial animal must be without blemish (*Spec. Neg.* I, 260), then it is clear that he does not hear what the text actually says, but only lets it say what he already knows. And the same thing is true of Paul's exegesis of Deuteronomy 25:4 as a prescription that the preachers of the gospel are to be supported by the congregations (1 Cor. 9:9) and of the interpretation in the Letter of Barnabas (9:7f.) of the 318 servants of Abraham (Gen. 14:14) as a prophecy of the cross of Christ.

However, even where allegorical interpretation is renounced, exegesis is frequently guided by prejudices. This is so, for example, when it is presupposed that the evangelists Matthew and John were Jesus' personal disciples and that therefore the narratives and sayings of Jesus that they hand down must be historically true reports. In this case, it must be affirmed, for instance, that the cleansing of the temple, which in Matthew is placed during Jesus' last days just before his passion, but in John stands at the beginning of his ministry, took place twice. The question of an unprejudiced exegesis becomes especially urgent when the problem of Jesus' Messianic consciousness is concerned. May exegesis of the Gospels be guided by the dogmatic presupposition that Jesus was the Messiah and was conscious of being so? Or must it rather leave this question open? The answer should be clear. Any such Messianic consciousness would be a historical fact and could only be exhibited as such by historical research. Were the latter able to make it probable that Jesus knew himself to be the Messiah, this result would have only relative certainty; for historical research can never endow it with absolute validity. All knowledge of a historical kind is subject to discussion, and therefore, the question as to whether Jesus knew himself as Messiah remains open. Every exegesis that is guided by dogmatic prejudices does not hear what the text says, but only lets the latter say what it wants to hear.

The question of exegesis without presuppositions in the sense of unprejudiced exegesis must be distinguished from this same question in the other sense in which it can be raised. And in this second sense, we must say that *there cannot be any such thing as presuppositionless exegesis.* That there is no such exegesis in fact, because every exegete is determined by his own individuality, in the sense of his special biases and habits, his gifts and his weaknesses, has no significance in principle. For in this sense of the word, it is precisely his "individuality" that the exegete ought to eliminate by educating himself to the kind of hearing that is interested in nothing other than the subject matter of which the text speaks. However, the one presupposition that cannot be dismissed is *the historical method* of interrogating the text. Indeed, exegesis as the interpretation of historical texts is a part of the science of history.

It belongs to the historical method, of course, that a text is interpreted in accordance with the rules of grammar and of the meaning of words. And closely connected with this, historical exegesis also has to inquire about the individual style of the text. The sayings of Jesus in the Synoptics, for example, have a different style from the Johannine ones. But with this there is also given another problem with which exegesis is required to deal. Paying attention to the meaning of words, to grammar, and to style soon leads to the observation that every text speaks in the language of its time and of its historical setting. This the exegete must know; therefore, he must know the historical conditions of the language of the period out of which the text that he is to interpret has arisen. This means that for an understanding of the language of the New Testament the acute question is, "Where and to what extent is its Greek determined by the Semitic use of language?" Out of this question grows the demand to study apocalypticism, the rabbinic literature, and the Qumran texts, as well as the history of Hellenistic religion.

Examples at this point are hardly necessary, and I cite only one. The New Testament word *pneuma* is translated in German as "Geist." Thus it is understandable that the exegesis of the nineteenth century (e.g., in the Tübingen school) interpreted the New Testament on the basis of the idealism that goes back to ancient Greece, until Hermann Gunkel pointed out in 1888 that the New Testament *pneuma* meant something entirely different — namely, God's miraculous power and manner of action.

The historical method includes the presupposition that history is a unity in the sense of a closed continuum of effects in which individual events are connected by the succession of cause and effect. This does not mean that the process of history is determined by the causal law and that there are no free decisions of men whose actions determine the course of historical happenings. But even a free decision does not happen without a cause, without a motive, and the task of the historian is to come to know the motives of actions. All decisions and all deeds have their causes and consequences; and the historical method presupposes that it is possible in principle to exhibit these and their connection and thus to understand the whole historical process as a closed unity.

This closedness means that the continuum of historical happenings cannot be rent by the interference of supernatural, transcendent powers and that therefore there is no "miracle" in this sense of the word. Such a miracle would be an event whose cause did not lie within history. While, for example, the Old Testament narrative speaks of an interference by God in history, historical science cannot demonstrate such an act of God, but merely perceives that there are those who believe in it. To be sure, as historical science, it may not assert that such a faith is an illusion and that God has not acted in history. But it itself as science cannot perceive such an act and reckon on the basis of it; it can only leave every man free to determine whether he wants to see an act of God in a historical event that it itself understands in terms of that event's immanent historical causes.

It is in accordance with such a method as this that the science of history goes to work on all historical documents. And there cannot be any exceptions in the case of biblical texts if the latter are at all to be understood historically. Nor can one object that the biblical writings do not intend to be historical documents, but rather affirmations of faith and proclamation. For however certain this may be, if they are ever to be understood as such, they must first of all be interpreted historically, inasmuch as they speak in a strange language in concepts of a faraway time, of a world-picture that is alien to us. Put quite simply, they must be *translated,* and translation is the task of historical science.

If we speak of translation, however, then the hermeneutical problem at once presents itself. To translate means to make understandable, and this in turn presupposes an understanding. The understanding of history as a continuum of effects presupposes an understanding of the efficient forces that connect the individual historical phenomena. Such forces are economic needs, social exigencies, the political struggle for power, human passions, ideas, and ideals. In the assessment of such factors historians differ; and in every effort to achieve a unified point of view the individual historian is guided by some specific way of raising questions, some specific perspective.

This does not mean a falsification of the historical picture, provided that the perspective that is presupposed is not a prejudice, but a way of raising questions, and that the historian is self-conscious about the fact that his way of asking questions is one-sided and only comes at the phenomenon or the text from the standpoint of a particular perspective. The historical picture is falsified only when a specific way of raising questions is put forward as the only one — when, for example, all history is reduced to economic history. Historical phenomena are many-sided. Events like the Reformation can be observed from the standpoint of church history as well as political history, of economic history as well as the history of philosophy. Mysticism can be viewed from the standpoint of its significance for the history of art, etc. However, some specific way of raising questions is always presupposed if history is at all to be understood.

But even more, the forces that are effective in connecting phenomena are understandable only if the phenomena themselves that are thereby connected are also understood! This means that an understanding of the subject matter itself belongs to historical understanding. For can one understand political history without having a concept of the state and of justice, which by their very nature are not historical products but ideas? Can one understand economic history without having a concept of what economy and society in general mean? Can one understand the history of religion and philosophy without knowing what religion and philosophy are? One cannot understand Luther's posting of the ninety-five theses, for instance, without understanding the actual meaning of protest against the Catholicism of his time. One cannot understand the Communist Manifesto of 1848 without understanding the principles of capitalism and socialism. One cannot understand the decisions of persons who act in history if one does not understand man and his possibilities for action. In short, historical understanding presupposes an understanding of the subject matter of history itself and of the men who act in history.

This is also to say, however, that historical understanding always presupposes a relation of the interpreter to the subject matter that is (directly or indirectly) expressed in the texts. This relation is grounded in the actual life-context in which the interpreter stands. Only he who lives in a state and in a society can understand the political and social phenomena of the past and their history, just as only he who has a relation to music can understand a text that deals with music, etc.

Therefore, a specific understanding of the subject matter of the text, on the basis of a "life-relation" to it, is always presupposed by exegesis; and insofar as this is so no exegesis is without presuppositions. I speak of this understanding as a "preunderstanding." It as little involves prejudices as does the choice of a perspective. For the historical picture is falsified only when the exegete takes his preunderstanding as a definitive understanding. The "life-relation" is a genuine one, however, only when it is vital, i.e., when the subject matter with which the text is concerned also concerns us and is a problem for us. If we approach history alive with our own problems, then it really begins to speak to us. Through discussion the past becomes alive, and in learning to know history we learn to know our own present; historical knowledge is at the same time knowledge of ourselves. To understand history is possible only for one who does not stand over against it as a neutral, nonparticipating spectator, but himself stands in history and shares in responsibility for it. We speak of this encounter with history that grows out of one's own historicity as the *existentiell* encounter. The historian participates in it with his whole existence.

This *existentiell* relation to history is the fundamental presupposition for understanding history. This does not mean that the understanding of history is a "subjective" one in the sense that it depends on the individual pleasure of the historian and thereby loses all objective significance. On the contrary, it means that history precisely in its objective content can only be understood by a subject who is *existentiell* moved and alive. It means that, for historical understanding, the schema of subject and object that has validity for natural science is invalid.

Now what has just been said includes an important insight — namely, that historical knowledge is never a closed or definitive knowledge — any more than is the preunderstanding with which the historian approaches historical phenomena. For if the phenomena of history are not facts that can be neutrally observed, but rather open themselves in their meaning only to one who approaches them alive with questions, then they are always only understandable now in that they actually speak in the present situation. Indeed, the questioning itself grows out of the historical situation, out of the claim of the now, out of the problem that is given in the now. For this reason, historical research is never closed, but rather must always be carried further. Naturally, there are certain items of historical knowledge that can be regarded as definitively known — namely, such items as concern only dates that can be fixed chronologically and locally, as, for example, the assassination of Caesar or Luther's posting of the ninety-five theses. But what these events that can thus be dated mean as historical events cannot be definitively fixed. Hence one must say that a historical event is always first knowable for what it is — precisely as a historical event — in the future. And therefore one can also say that the future of a historical event belongs to that event.

Naturally, items of historical knowledge can be passed on, not as definitively known, but in such a way as to clarify and expand the following generation's preunderstanding. But even so, they are subject to the criticism of that generation. Can we today surmise the meaning of the two world wars? No; for it holds good that what a historical event means always first becomes clear in the future. It can definitively disclose itself only when history has come to an end.

What are the consequences of this analysis for exegesis of the biblical writings? They may be formulated in the following theses:

(1) The exegesis of the biblical writings, like every other interpretation of a text, must be unprejudiced.

(2) However, the exegesis is not without presuppositions, because as historical interpretation it presupposes the method of historical-critical research.

(3) Furthermore, there is presupposed a "life-relation" of the exegete to the
subject matter with which the Bible is concerned and, together with this
relation, a preunderstanding.

(4) This preunderstanding is not a closed one, but rather is open, so that
there can be an *existentiell* encounter with the text and an *existentiell* decision.

(5) The understanding of the text is never a definitive one, but rather remains
open because the meaning of the Scriptures discloses itself anew in every
future.

In the light of what has already been said, nothing further is required in
the way of comment on the first and second theses.

As regards the third thesis, however, we may note that the preunderstanding has its basis in the question concerning God that is alive in human life. Thus
it does not mean that the exegete must know everything possible about God,
but rather that he is moved by the *existentiell* question for God — regardless of
the form that this question actually takes in his consciousness (say, for example,
as the question concerning "salvation," or escape from death, or certainty in the
face of a constantly shifting destiny, or truth in the midst of a world that is a
riddle to him).

With regard to the fourth thesis, we may note that the *existentiell* encounter with the text can lead to a yes as well as to a no, to confessing faith as well as
to express unfaith, because in the text the exegete encounters a claim, i.e., is
there offered a self-understanding that he can accept (permit to be given to
him) or reject, and therefore is faced with the demand for decision. Even in the
case of a no, however, the understanding is a legitimate one, i.e., is a genuine
answer to the question of the text, which is not to be refuted by argument because it is an *existentiell* decision.

So far as the fifth thesis is concerned, we note simply that because the text
speaks to existence it is never understood in a definitive way. The *existentiell* decision out of which the interpretation emerges cannot be passed on, but must
always be realized anew. This does not mean, of course, that there cannot be
continuity in the exegesis of Scripture. It goes without saying that the results of
methodical historical-critical research can be passed on, even if they can only
be taken over by constant critical testing. But even with respect to the exegesis
that is based *existentiell* there is also continuity, insofar as it provides guidance
for the next generation — as has been done, for example, by Luther's under-

standing of the Pauline doctrine of justification by faith alone. Just as this understanding must constantly be achieved anew in the discussion with Catholic exegesis, so every genuine exegesis that offers itself as a guide is at the same time a question that must always be answered anew and independently. Since the exegete exists historically and must hear the word of Scripture as spoken in his special historical situation, he will always understand the old word anew. Always anew it will tell him who he, man, is and who God is, and he will always have to express this word in a new conceptuality. Thus it is true also of Scripture that it only is what it is with its history and its future.

GERHARD EBELING

Word of God and Hermeneutics

The hermeneutical thought of Gerhard Ebeling (1912-2001), for many years professor of theology at the University of Zürich, owes much to the influence of his teacher, Rudolf Bultmann, as well as to Bonhoeffer and Luther. Like Bultmann, Ebeling's concern with hermeneutics is directly tied to preaching. Following Bonhoeffer (as well as colleague Ernst Fuchs), he seeks to "translate" biblical language into a nonreligious idiom. With Luther, he is preoccupied with the effectiveness of the word of God to illumine, address, and transform human beings. The term "New Hermeneutic" is often associated with Ebeling's school of thought. Traditional interpretation sought to get control of the object under investigation, namely, the scriptural text. Ebeling understands the word of God as a dynamic act of transmission. It is not a passive or static entity to be brought under the interpreter's control but is "living and active, sharper than any two-edged sword, . . . discerning the thoughts and intentions of the heart" (Heb. 4:12). The essence of the word is interpretive. The interpreter, then, does not seek to understand the word but to understand human existence *by means of* the word, a process Paul Ricoeur terms the "archaeology of the subject." Preaching will not content itself with excavating the past and drawing contemporary applications. The traditional sequence of exegesis, exposition, and application is taken up by the new and broadened science of hermeneutics with the result that the interpreter/preacher "executes" the text. The written word is set free and allowed to become what it originally was — a spoken word of address.

Gerhard Ebeling, *Word and Faith* (Philadelphia: Fortress, 1963), pp. 311-18, 327-31.

Whatever precise theological definition may be given to the concept of the word of God, at all events it points us to something that happens, viz. to the movement which leads from the text of Holy Scripture to the sermon ("sermon" of course taken in the pregnant sense of proclamation in general). As a first definition of the concept of the word of God the reference to this movement from text to proclamation may suffice. For this is in fact according to Christian tradition the primary place of the concept of the word of God. We here set aside questions that probe behind that — why the Holy Scripture that presses for proclamation or the proclamation that takes its stand on Holy Scripture should be marked out in particular above other things as word of God; or what form of the word of God to some extent precedes Scripture; and whether the word of God is not found also outside the relation of text and sermon. For according to Christian conviction the answers to all these questions can be truly known only in connection with that movement from the text to the sermon. But it is of decisive importance to choose this movement as the starting point for the definition of the concept of the word of God. . . .

Now if in the word of God we have a case of the word-event that leads from the text of Holy Scripture to the proclamation, then the question is, whether hermeneutics can be expected to help toward that happening rightly. Here doubts arise at once. Can the event of the word of God be served at all by scientific methods? Must the hermeneutic approach as such not at once have a destructive effect on the concept of the word of God, as also on the corresponding concept of the Holy Spirit? But doubts, too, of a less radical kind also call in question the service of hermeneutics here. Can hermeneutics not deal only with an exposition which is subject to scientific criteria? Even then there are, as is well known, already great methodological difficulties. Now in so far as the sermon is preceded by a scientific exposition of the text, hermeneutics may also have significance for it. But then the question remains what the scientific exposition contributes to the sermon and what distinguishes it from the exposition that takes place in the sermon itself; whether it is appropriate to contrast the latter as "practical" exposition with the scientific kind and so withdraw it from the strict standpoint of hermeneutics, or to distinguish it as *applicatio* from the *explicatio* and thereby deny that the sermon in its essential nature is exposition at all, however much it may contain textual exposition. Yet is it not bringing the event of the word of God into dangerous isolation from word-events in general, if we withdraw it from the reach of hermeneutics? Indeed, is it not the case that the concept of the word of God can be used at all only when hermeneutic justification can be given for it? But what does "hermeneutics" then mean? Let us therefore attempt first of all a more precise clarification of the concept hermeneutics.

According to the common view there is a sharp distinction between exegesis as the process of exposition itself and hermeneutics as the theory of exposition. And here indeed it is assumed that verbal statements are the object of exposition, i.e., the thing requiring exposition. According to the several kinds of verbal statement, general hermeneutics may be differentiated into various special hermeneutics, though of course without departing from the comprehensive framework of general hermeneutics.

This customary view of hermeneutics requires correction in various respects.

On the threshold of the Enlightenment the "distinction of general and special hermeneutics" had taken the place of the very differently articulated Orthodox distinction of *hermeneutica sacra* and *hermeneutica profana*. The basic proposition that Holy Scripture is not to be differently interpreted from other books seemed, it is true, now to allow of only one single science of hermeneutics and to relieve theology of any special discussion of the hermeneutic problem, indeed even to forbid it. But owing to the colorlessness and abstractness of the proposition of a general hermeneutics, it did not exclude the introduction of various special hermeneutics applied and related to concrete subjects, as long as these various special hermeneutics remained subject to and derived from general hermeneutic criteria. Indeed, modern hermeneutics developed at first almost entirely in the form of special hermeneutics of such kinds, in the construction of which theology played an outstanding part along with classical philology and jurisprudence. It can even be said that the principle of a single science of hermeneutics worked itself out in practice as the principle of an increasing hermeneutic specialization.

For theology this meant in the first instance that, although specifically theological hermeneutics disappeared, there arose within theology various hermeneutics in different degrees of specialization, such as biblical, Old Testament, or New Testament hermeneutics, or (the demand for this at all events has already been made) in such a way that each biblical book requires a special hermeneutics. We must not let ourselves be deceived about the real nature of this state of affairs by, say, the fact that such extreme specialization was never realized, and that biblical or Old or New Testament hermeneutics owing to the theological dignity of these books at once gives the impression of theological hermeneutics. Strictly, however, the basic conception is, that there is no such thing as theological hermeneutics. For the differentiation in hermeneutics is held to be justified indeed from the standpoint of different literary complexes, but not on the basis of particular, nonuniversal epistemological principles such as those of theology. Thus hermeneutics in theology became the methodology of definite individual disciplines — viz. the biblical ones — and therewith at once the boundary separating them from dogmatics, which as such had nothing to do with hermeneutics.

The fact that in contrast to this, historical and systematic theology today join hands in the hermeneutic problem and hermeneutics has expanded to become the methodology no longer merely of individual theological disciplines but of theology as a whole, is to a great extent a distant result of Schleiermacher. For his pioneer view of hermeneutics as the theory of the conditions on which understanding is possible modified the relation of general and special hermeneutics in a twofold way.

First: a special hermeneutics must now take strict account of what can here be *differentia specifica*. The view which Schleiermacher himself here put forward in detail is doubtless obsolete. His basic demand, however, is still valid. The view emphatically advanced today by Bultmann that the difference as to what one is after in the interrogation has differentiating character in the hermeneutic sphere is a first step toward further clarification of this side of the hermeneutic problem — a step that is capable of being developed and certainly also stands in need of further development. This provides, without relapsing into an alleged *hermeneutica sacra*, the possibility of speaking of a hermeneutics related to theology as a whole, which on the basis of the specifically theological approach works out structures and criteria of theological understanding that apply in theology not only to the exegetical but also to the dogmatic understanding. It is absolutely necessary that this should then be done in demonstrable connection with a general theory of understanding. The nature of the connection, however, raises difficult problems.

The other impulse which Schleiermacher gave to the further history of hermeneutics is today discernible above all in a surprisingly extended use of the word "hermeneutics." It is not only that hermeneutics can now be spoken of in sciences in which it was not possible before and which do not have to do with texts at all but with phenomena — for example psychology. Rather, the development from Schleiermacher via Dilthey to Heidegger shows that the idea of a theory of understanding is on the move toward laying the foundation of the humanities, indeed even becomes the essence of philosophy, that hermeneutics now takes the place of the classical epistemological theory, and indeed that fundamental ontology appears as hermeneutics.

Thus outside of theology, too, hermeneutics today is breaking through the old, narrow bounds of philological or historiographical hermeneutics, or is plumbing their depths. For theology the hermeneutic problem is therefore today becoming the place of meeting with philosophy. And that always involves at the same time both community and contrast. This confirms once again that in an approach so radical as this there is point in speaking of theological hermeneutics without in any way refurbishing the division into *hermeneutica sacra* and *profana*.

The customary view that hermeneutics is the theory of the exposition of texts already seemed a moment ago to have undergone correction in that phenomena can also be objects of exposition. If we followed that further, then we should doubtless have to limit it to phenomena in so far as they have to do with the linguisticality of existence, and are thus "texts" in the wider sense. Hermeneutics would then also remain related to the word-event. But what is now to be held against the usual view is something other than that.

It is usually taken for granted that the reason why hermeneutics has to do with the word-event is that verbal statements pose the problem of understanding. Now however much the need for hermeneutics does in fact arise primarily from difficulties of understanding in the word-event, it is nevertheless completely false to take this situation as the point of orientation for one's basic grasp of the relation between word and understanding and of what is ultimately constitutive for hermeneutics. The superficial view of understanding turns matters upside down and must therefore be completely reversed. The primary phenomenon in the realm of understanding is not understanding *of* language, but understanding *through* language. The word is not really the object of understanding, and thus the thing that poses the problem of understanding, the solution of which requires exposition and therefore also hermeneutics as the theory of understanding. Rather, the word is what opens up and mediates understanding, i.e., brings something to understanding. The word itself has a hermeneutic function.

This opens up a deeper insight into the nature of the word-event. As communication word is promise. It is most purely promise when it refers to something that is not present but absent — and that, too, in such a way that in the promise the absent thing so to speak presents itself; that is, when in word the speaker pledges and imparts himself to the other and opens a future to him by awakening faith within him. The conjunction of God, word, faith, future as the prime necessity for the good of man's human nature requires to be understood as a single vast coherent complex and not as some sort of chance conglomeration to be accepted on positivist terms.

This word-event takes place, Christians confess, in the gospel. It is savingly related to the word-event which always proceeds from God and strikes the foolish man as the law which kills. But for that reason, too, it is only in the light of the gospel that we can grasp what God's word really means and how far the law is God's word. For God's word must not on any account be reduced to a formal concept which would be indifferent toward any intrinsic definition of the word of God. For God's word is not various things, but one single thing —

the word that makes man human by making him a believer, i.e., a man who confesses to God as his future and therefore does not fail his fellowmen in the one absolutely necessary and salutary thing, viz. true word.

There is no need to state here the reasons why the proclamation of the word of God appeals to Scripture, and Scripture thus becomes the text of the sermon. I would merely go on to add in conclusion an explanation of how that happens, in what sense Scripture is the text of the sermon, and thus how text and sermon are related to each other.

We begin with the question: What is the aim of the text? It aims at all events to be preserved, real and handed on — and that, too, in the service of the proclamation. Here of course we should at once have to make differentiations, not only between Old and New Testament texts, but also in both cases between different degrees of explicitness with which the aim is proclamation. The question of the aim of the text could indeed be shifted from the individual text to the biblical canon as such. It would of course be a question whether the original intention of the canon would be done justice to by asserting that it aims at being a collection of sermon texts. But above all in face of the individual text it would be a doubtful proceeding to ignore that text itself where this basic question is concerned. It should not be supposed that any and every text in Holy Scripture is in itself a sermon text. What is claimed to be a sermon text must at all events seek to serve the proclamation of the word of God. Yet it would not be right to say: the text seeks to be proclaimed. Apart from the fact that such a direct, authoritative aim is present in relatively few texts, that way of putting it would also be fundamentally wrong. For it is not texts that are to be proclaimed. Rather, it is God's word that is to be proclaimed, and that is one single word, but not words of God, not a variety of different texts.

Indeed, we must put a still sharper point on it: if the word-character of God's word is taken strictly, then it is absurd to designate a transmitted text as God's word. Not out of contempt for its content or for its being written, but rather precisely out of respect for both. It is of course entirely true of sermon texts by and large that they are concerned with proclamation that has taken place, and to that extent — if it was right proclamation — with past occurrence of the word of God. Naturally the form of direct speech on God's part cannot here rank as criterion. It is significant that with Jesus (apart from Christian imitations of the prophets) the stylistic form "Thus saith the Lord" ceases — a fact well worth bearing in mind for the doctrine of the word of God. But if it is a case of proclamation that has taken place, then we shall have to say of the sermon text: its aim is, that there should be further proclamation — and that, too, with an ear open toward the text, in agreement with it and under appeal to it.

The process from text to sermon can therefore be characterized by saying:

proclamation that has taken place is to become proclamation that takes place. This transition from text to sermon is a transition from Scripture to the spoken word. Thus the task prescribed here consists in making what is written into spoken word or, as we can now also say, in letting the text become God's word again. That that does not normally happen through recitation should surely be clear. If the concept of exposition can now be applied to this process, then we should have to say it is a question of interpreting the text *as word*.

But is the application of the concept "exposition" here not questionable? This misgiving is in fact justified. Yet we must be very careful in giving place to it. For it is manifestly true all the same that the movement from the text to the sermon is a hermeneutic process in which, indeed to an eminent degree, it is a case of understanding and bringing to understanding. It would undoubtedly be wrong to assert that this movement from the text to the sermon does not come within the scope of the hermeneutic problem as posed by that text. For if its aim is that what it has proclaimed should be further proclaimed, then the hermeneutic task prescribed by the text in question is not only not left behind when we turn to the sermon, but is precisely then for the first time brought to its fullest explication. The problem of theological hermeneutics would not be grasped without the inclusion of the task of proclamation; it is not until then that it is brought decisively to a head at all. And that, too, because the biblical texts would not be rightly heard unless they were seen to present us with the task of proclamation. . . .

The sermon as such is in point of fact not *exposition* of the text — whereby exposition here means the concentration of the historical task of understanding. For to understand this text as a text means to understand it in its historical givenness as proclamation that has taken place. Now of course the sermon certainly does presuppose intensive efforts toward such understanding of the text. How could it otherwise appeal to it? And it contains also according to the particular circumstances a greater or lesser degree of explicit interpretation of the text. But the sermon as a sermon is not exposition of the text as past proclamation, but is itself proclamation in the present — and that means, then, that the sermon is *execution* of the text. It carries into execution the aim of the text. It is proclamation of what the text has proclaimed. And with that the hermeneutic sense of direction is so to speak reversed. The text which has attained understanding in the exposition now helps to bring to understanding what is to attain understanding by means of the sermon — which is (we can here state it briefly) the present reality *coram Deo,* and that means, in its radical futurity. Thus the text by means of the sermon becomes a hermeneutic aid in the understanding of present experience. Where that happens radically, there true word is uttered, and that in fact means God's word.

PAUL RICOEUR

The Hermeneutic Question

The thought of Paul Ricoeur has enriched homiletical theory in many ways. His seminal work on metaphor has helped preachers to gain a clearer understanding of the difference between the derivative nature of illustration and the creative power of metaphor. His work in narrative and structuralism has undergirded the pulpit's renewed appreciation of story as a powerful instrument of proclamation. His theory of symbol as that which is rooted in the cosmos has encouraged thoughtful preachers to seek expression of the archetypal truth that lies beneath the surface of both doctrine and experience. It is in the field of hermeneutics, however, that Ricoeur's work has entered into direct dialogue with homiletical theology. No summary can do justice to the complexities of his hermeneutical philosophy. Like Bultmann, Ricoeur's investigations in hermeneutics include an analysis of the relation of the interpreter to the thing interpreted. As in Bultmann, hermeneutics is nothing less than the science of human understanding, the equivalent of philosophy itself. Both men reject the nineteenth century's notion of hermeneutics as a quest for the original author's psyche or life-experience. In the final analysis, both Bultmann and Ricoeur subject themselves to the disclosive power and revelatory authority of *texts*. Ricoeur writes, "The sense of the text is not behind the text, but in front of it. It is not something hidden but something disclosed. What has to be understood is not the initial situation of discourse, but what points toward a possible world" (*Interpretation Theory,* p. 87). The following selection is from Ricoeur's "Preface to Bultmann," in which he outlines three dimensions of Christianity's concern with hermeneutics.

Paul Ricoeur, *The Conflict of Interpretations,* ed. Don Ihde (Evanston: Northwestern University Press, 1974), pp. 381-88.

Although there has always been a hermeneutic problem in Christianity, the hermeneutic question today seems to us a new one. What does this situation mean, and why does it seem marked with this initial paradox?

There has always been a hermeneutic problem in Christianity because Christianity proceeds from a proclamation. It begins with a fundamental preaching that maintains that in Jesus Christ the kingdom has approached us in decisive fashion. But this fundamental preaching, this word, comes to us through writings, through the Scriptures, and these must constantly be restored as the living word if the primitive word that witnessed to the fundamental and founding event is to remain contemporary. If hermeneutics in general is, in Dilthey's phrase, the interpretation of expressions of life fixed in written texts, then Christian hermeneutics deals with the unique relation between the Scriptures and what they refer to, the *kerygma* (the proclamation).

This relation between writing and the word and between the word and the event and its meaning is the crux of the hermeneutic problem. But this relation itself appears only through a series of interpretations. These interpretations constitute the history of the hermeneutic problem and even the history of Christianity itself, to the degree that Christianity is dependent upon its successive readings of Scripture and on its capacity to reconvert this Scripture into the living word. Certain characteristics of what can be called the hermeneutic situation of Christianity have not even been perceived until our time. These traits are what makes the hermeneutic problem a modern problem.

Let us try to chart this hermeneutic situation, in a more systematic than historical way. Three moments can be distinguished here which have developed successively, even though implicitly they are contemporaneous.

The hermeneutic problem first arose from a question which occupied the first Christian generations and which held the fore even to the time of the Reformation. This question is: what is the relation between the two Testaments or between the two Covenants? Here the problem of allegory in the Christian sense was constituted. Indeed, the Christ-event is hermeneutically related to all of Judaic Scripture in the sense that it interprets this Scripture. Hence, before it can be interpreted itself — and there is our hermeneutic problem — the Christ-event is already an interpretation of a preexisting Scripture.

Let us understand this situation well. Originally, there were not, properly speaking, two Testaments, two Scriptures; there was one Scripture and one event. And it is this event that makes the entire Jewish economy appear ancient, like an old letter. But there is a hermeneutic problem because this novelty is not purely and simply substituted for the ancient letter; rather, it remains ambiguously related to it. The novelty abolishes the Scripture and fulfills it. It changes its letter into spirit like water into wine. Hence the Christian fact is itself understood by effecting a mutation of meaning inside the ancient Scripture. The first Christian hermeneutics is this mutation itself. It is entirely contained in the relation between the letter, the history (these words are synonyms), of the old Covenant and the spiritual meaning which the gospel reveals after the event. Hence this relation can be expressed quite well in allegorical terms. It can resemble the allegorizing of the Stoics or that of Philo, or it can adopt the quasi-Platonic language of the opposition between flesh and spirit, between shadow and true reality. But what is at issue here is basically something else. It is a question of the typological value of the events, things, persons, and institutions of the old economy in relation to those of the new. Saint Paul creates this Christian allegory. Everyone knows the interpretation of Hagar and Sarah, the two wives of Abraham, and of their lineage. In their regard the Epistle to the Galatians says: "These things are said allegorically." The word "allegory" here has only a literary resemblance to the allegory of the grammarians, which, Cicero tells us, "consists in saying one thing to make something else understood." Pagan allegory served to reconcile myths with philosophy and consequently to reduce them as myths. But Pauline allegory, together with that of Tertullian and Origen, which depend on it, is inseparable from the mystery of Christ. Stoicism and Platonism will furnish only a language, indeed a compromising and misleading surplus.

Hence there is hermeneutics in the Christian order because the kerygma is the rereading of an ancient Scripture. It is noteworthy that orthodoxy has resisted with all its force the currents, from Marcion to Gnosticism, which wanted to cut the gospel from its hermeneutic bond to the Old Testament. Why? Would it not have been simpler to proclaim the event in its unity and thus to deliver it from the ambiguities of the Old Testament interpretation? Why has Christian preaching chosen to be hermeneutic by binding itself to the rereading of the Old Testament? Essentially to make the event itself appear, not as an irrational irruption, but as the fulfillment of an antecedent meaning which remained in suspense. The event itself receives a temporal density by being inscribed in a signifying relation of "promise" to "fulfillment." By entering in this way into a historical connection, the event enters also into an intelligible liaison. A contrast is set up between the two Testaments, a contrast which at the same time is a harmony by means of a transfer. This signifying relation attests that the kerygma, by this detour through the reinterpretation of an ancient Scripture, enters into a network of intelligibility. The event becomes advent. In taking on time, it takes on meaning. By understanding itself indirectly, in terms of the transfer from the old to the new, the event presents itself as an understanding of relations. Jesus Christ himself, exegesis and exegete of Scripture, is manifested as logos in opening the understanding of the Scriptures.

Such is the fundamental hermeneutics of Christianity. It coincides with the spiritual understanding of the Old Testament. Of course, the spiritual meaning is the New Testament itself; but because of this detour through a deciphering of the Old Testament, "faith is not a cry" but an understanding.

The second root of the hermeneutic problem is also Pauline. This is so even though it did not reach its full growth until very recently and, in certain respects, only with the moderns, specifically with Bultmann. This idea is that the interpretation of the Book and the interpretation of life correspond and are mutually adjusted. Saint Paul creates this second modality of Christian hermeneutics when he invites the hearer of the word to decipher the movement of his own existence in the light of the passion and resurrection of Christ. Hence, the death of the old man and the birth of the new creature are understood under the sign of the cross and the paschal victory. But their hermeneutic relation has a double meaning. Death and resurrection receive a new interpretation through the detour of this exegesis of human existence. The "hermeneutic circle" is already there, between the meaning of Christ and the meaning of existence which mutually decipher each other.

Thanks to the admirable work of de Lubac on the "four meanings" of Scripture — historical, allegorical, moral, anagogical — the breadth of this mutual interpretation of Scripture and existence is known. Beyond this simple reinterpretation of the old Covenant and the typological correlation between the two Testaments, medieval hermeneutics pursued the coincidence between the understanding of the faith in the *lectio divina* and the understanding of reality as a whole, divine and human, historical and physical. The hermeneutic task, then, is to broaden the comprehension of the text on the side of doctrine, of practice, of meditation on the mysteries. And consequently it is to equate the understanding of meaning with a total interpretation of existence and of reality in the system of Christianity. In short, hermeneutics understood this way is coextensive with the entire economy of Christian existence. Scripture appears here as an inexhaustible treasure which stimulates thought about everything, which conceals a total interpretation of the world. It is hermeneutics because the letter serves as foundation, because exegesis is its instrument, and also because the other meanings are related to the first in the way that the hidden is related to the manifest. In this way the understanding of Scripture somehow enrolls all the instruments of culture — literary and rhetorical, philosophical and mystical. To interpret Scripture is at the same time to amplify its meaning as sacred meaning and to incorporate the remains of secular culture in this understanding. It is at this price that Scripture ceases to be a limited cultural object: explication of texts and exploration of mysteries coincide. This is the aim of hermeneutics in this second sense: to make the global sense of mystery coincide with a differentiated and articulated discipline of meaning. It is to equate the *multiplex intellectus* with the *intellectus de mysterio Christi*.

Now, among the "four meanings" of Scripture, the Middle Ages made a place for the "moral meaning," which marks the application of the allegorical meaning to ourselves and our morals. The "moral meaning" shows that hermeneutics is much more than exegesis in the narrow sense. Hermeneutics is the very deciphering of life in the mirror of the text. Although the function of allegory is to manifest the newness of the gospel in the oldness of the letter, this newness vanishes if it is not a daily newness, if it is not new *hic et nunc*. Actually, the function of the moral sense is not to draw morals from Scripture at all, to moralize history, but to assure the correspondence between the Christ-event and the inner man. It is a matter of interiorizing the spiritual meaning, of actualizing it, as Saint Bernard says, of showing that it extends *hodie usque ad nos*, "even to us today." That is why the true role of moral meaning comes after allegory. This correspondence between allegorical meaning and our existence is well expressed by the metaphor of the mirror. It is a matter of deciphering our existence according to its conformity with Christ. We can still speak of interpretation because, on the one hand, the mystery contained in the book is made explicit in our experience and its actuality is confirmed here, and because, on the other hand, we understand ourselves in the mirror of the word. The relation between the text and the mirror — *liber et speculum* — is basic to hermeneutics.

This is the second dimension of Christian hermeneutics.

The third root of the hermeneutic problem in Christianity was not fully recognized and understood until the moderns — until the critical methods borrowed from the secular sciences of history and philology had been applied to the Bible as a whole. Here we return to our initial question: how is it that the hermeneutic problem is so old and so modern? Actually this third root of our problem relates to what can be called the hermeneutic situation itself of Christianity, that is, it is related to the primitive constitution of the Christian kerygma. We must return, in fact, to the witness character of the gospel. The kerygma is not first of all the interpretation of a text; it is the announcement of a person. In this sense, the word of God is, not the Bible, but Jesus Christ. But a problem arises continually from the fact that this kerygma is itself expressed in a witness, in the stories, and soon after in the texts that contain the very first confession of faith of the community. These texts conceal a first level of interpretation. We ourselves are no longer those witnesses who have seen. We are the hearers who listen to the witnesses: *fides ex auditu*. Hence, we can believe only by listening and by interpreting a text which is itself already an interpretation. In short, our relation, not only to the Old Testament, but also to the New Testament itself, is a hermeneutic relation.

This hermeneutic situation is as primitive as the two others because the gospel is presented from the time of the second generation as a writing, as a new letter, a new Scripture, added to the old in the form of a collection of writings which will one day be gathered up and enclosed in a canon, the "Canon of Scriptures." The source of our modern hermeneutic problem, then, is this: the kerygma is also a Testament. To be sure, it is new, as we said above; but it is a Testament, that is, a new Scripture. Hence the New Testament must also be interpreted. It is not simply an interpreting with regard to the Old Testament, and an interpreting for life and for reality as a whole; it is itself a text to be interpreted.

But this third root of the hermeneutic problem, the hermeneutic situation itself, has somehow been masked by the two other functions of hermeneutics in Christianity. So long as the New Testament served to decipher the Old, it was taken as an absolute norm. And it remains an absolute norm as long as its literal meaning serves as an indisputable basis on which all the other levels of meaning — the allegorical, moral, and anagogical — are constructed. But the fact is that the literal meaning is itself a text to be understood, a letter to be interpreted.

Let us reflect on this discovery. At first glance it may seem to be a product of our modernity, that is, something which could have been discovered only recently. This is true, for reasons which will be mentioned later. But these reasons themselves refer us back to a fundamental structure which, despite its having been recently discovered, nonetheless was present from the beginning. This discovery is a product of our modernity in the sense that it expresses the backlash of the critical disciplines — philology and history — on the sacred texts. As soon as the whole Bible is treated like the *Iliad* or the Presocratics, the letter is desacralized and the Bible is made to appear as the word of humans. In the same way, the relation "human word/word of God" is placed, no longer between the New Testament and the rest of the Bible, no longer even between the New Testament and the rest of culture, but at the very heart of the New Testament. For the believer, the New Testament itself conceals a relation that needs deciphering. This relation is between what can be understood and received as word of God and what is heard as human speaking.

This insight is the fruit of the scientific spirit, and in this sense it is a recent acquisition. But reflection brings us to discover in the first hermeneutic situation of the gospel the ancient reason for this later discovery. This situation, we have said, is that the gospel itself has become a text, a letter. As a text, it expresses a difference and a distance, however minimal, from the event that it proclaims. This distance, always increasing with time, is what separates the first witness from the entire line of those who hear the witness. Our modernity means only that the distance is now considerable between the place I myself oc-cupy at the center of a culture and the original site of the first witness. This dis-tance, of course, is not only spatial; it is above all a temporal one. But the dis-tance is given at the beginning. It is the very distance between the hearer and the witness of the event.

Thus the somehow accidental distance of a twentieth-century man, situ-ated in another, a scientific and historical, culture, reveals an original distance which remained concealed because it was so short; yet it was already constitu-tive of primitive faith itself. This distance has only become more manifest, par-ticularly since the work of the *Formgeschichte* school. This school has made us conscious of the fact that the witnesses gathered in the New Testament are not only individual witnesses — free witnesses, one might say; they are already situ-ated in a believing community, in its cult, its preaching, and the expression of its faith. To decipher Scripture is to decipher the witness of the apostolic com-munity. We are related to the object of its faith through the confession of its faith. Hence, by understanding its witness, I receive equally, in its witness, what is summons, kerygma, "the good news."

I hope this reflection has shown that hermeneutics has for us moderns a sense that it did not have for the Greek or Latin Fathers, for the Middle Ages, or even for the Reformers, that the very development of the word "hermeneutics" indicates a "modern" sense of hermeneutics. This modern meaning of herme-neutics is only the discovery, the manifestation, of the hermeneutic situation which was present from the beginning of the gospel but hidden. It is not para-doxical to defend the thesis that the two ancient forms of hermeneutics we have described have contributed to concealing what was radical in the Christian her-meneutic situation. The meaning and function of our modernity is to unveil, by means of the distance which today separates our culture from ancient cul-ture, what has been unique and extraordinary in this hermeneutic situation since the beginning.

JAMES A. SANDERS

Contextual Hermeneutics

Recent studies in hermeneutics have reminded preachers of the philosophical, political, ideological, or gendered lens through which the Bible may be interpreted for preaching. James A. Sanders does not minimize the importance of the external context of interpretation but, like Ricoeur, encourages preachers to recover the internal hermeneutic at work within the canon itself. Sanders, who taught intertestamental and biblical studies at the School of Theology in Claremont, California, calls attention to the layers of interpretation and reinterpretation in the Bible and cites these as warrant for the church's continuing interpretive activity. When a preacher applies a text to a contemporary situation, he or she is often engaging in a process not unlike the original author's handling of the received tradition. The contemporary interpreter's continuity with the Bible lies in his or her participation in the ongoing conversation of readers and listeners that extends from biblical times to our own day. According to Sanders, the Bible is not a casket of gems, or timeless truths, but a paradigm for faith, life, and interpretation. Two theological principles guide the preacher's interpretation of texts. The first is prophetic critique, which dwells on God's creative freedom, a freedom to be God above all people and institutions. The second he calls constitutive hermeneutics, or the principle of covenantal love, by which God binds himself to a particular people. Although Sanders believes that contemporary culture requires prophetic critique, he makes it clear that both principles are necessary to a faithful explication of God's word. Sanders's terms recall Luther's vocabulary of judgment and promise and underscore the necessity of a theological framework for preaching from the Bible. The following selection is a part of the author's introduction to a collection of his sermons.

James A. Sanders, *God Has a Story Too* (Philadelphia: Fortress, 1979), pp. 7-17, 20-25.

Hermeneutics is of two main sorts. One involves the exegetic tools which have been developed by biblical scholars over the past two centuries in order to recover points originally scored in Bible times by the biblical authors and theologians themselves. These are the "principles, rules, and techniques whereby the interpreter of a text attempts to understand it in its original context." These include all the biblical "criticisms" — text criticism, source criticism, form criticism, tradition criticism, redaction criticism, and canonical criticism — as well as philology and archaeology. These tools have been developed and honed over the past two hundred years and continue to develop. They are focused on both the ancient text and the ancient context.

That meaning, however, is not the one most people have in mind when they speak today of hermeneutics. When one hears the term today, outside of such strictly defined Old Testament or New Testament exegetical settings as a seminary class or a meeting of Bible scholars, it usually refers to the second main sort of hermeneutics: those means used to translate a thought or event from one cultural context (from an ancient text) to another (our modern times). This is a sane and sage recognition of the fact that both the ancient writer and the modern interpreter are conditioned by the cultures in which they lived or live. There has to be some kind of conversion key, as it were, to bring the one over into the other if the integrity of the text is to be honored and somehow preserved, and if that text is to be heard at all by the modern listener.

First, then, we try to understand the text in its original context; that requires scientific, exegetical tools of the first sort of hermeneutics. Then we try to understand it in our own context; that is the second sort. The number of people with the expertise to do the former is somewhat limited. But the fruit of their labors is available in books and commentaries published by denominational and secular publishing houses. Part of the reason the churches are asked to support their seminaries in modern times is to support the trained scholars who often teach in those seminaries so that they can do the research and publishing necessary to make that expertise available to the pastors, teachers, and layfolk in the churches.

There are not many people abroad who can engage equally well in both sorts of hermeneutics. Indeed, there is a widespread attitude of dichotomy among both scholars and interpreters which causes people to assume that no one person can do both. . . .

In part because of such dichotomy of thinking Bible scholars have sometimes left the second sort of hermeneutics to folk outside their professional guild. A notable exception has been Rudolf Bultmann, a great New Testament scholar who has spent a great deal of his professional life developing the second sort of hermeneutics. A good many of his students and grand-students have continued his work, agreeing with him and disagreeing with him, trying to work out valid modern enlightenment modes of hermeneutics whereby to render the New Testament messages potent and pertinent today. But aside from such efforts on the part of some Bible scholars most work of the second sort has been done by philosophers and theologians. And all of them tend to import their hermeneutics to the Bible from modern thought forms. There has been some confusion therefore, between hermeneutics — the means of converting ancient thoughts to contemporary thought forms — and those contemporary thought forms which receive the ancient.

Just as linguists speak of modern "receptor languages" into which ancient texts are translated, so we can speak of modern "receptor thought forms" into which ancient thought forms are rendered by hermeneutics. It is in part the thesis of this book that a valid hermeneutic we might use in interpreting the Bible today can be derived from the biblical experience itself, and not imported from the outside.

The first sort of hermeneutics of which we have spoken, the scholarly tools developed over the past two hundred years which help us recover the points originally scored back in biblical times, has now reached the point in its own development that we are able, to a greater or lesser degree, depending on the passage involved, to recover not only the original points scored but in many cases to recover the hermeneutics used by the biblical thinkers and authors! This was not possible until the development of modern biblical criticism, and even then has become feasible only in very recent times as biblical criticism has improved its tools. Those tools continue to need experimentation and improvement. And at times they fail us. They especially fail us when they become ends in themselves. But they provide us now with the possibility of recovering, in many passages, the hermeneutics used in antiquity when still more ancient traditions were contemporized.

One of the most fruitful newer emphases in biblical study is to begin work on a biblical passage by locating in it citations from or allusions to older traditions which the author called on in advancing his own argument or theme. Sometimes in a New Testament passage there are rather full citations of an Old Testament passage, but often the text has been modified and altered by the New Testament author to suit his or her argument. Sometimes the New Testament author simply used a text of the Old Testament different from those we have, but more often than not the later author actually adapted the older text to the new purposes. Sometimes the later author simply wove Old Testament traditions into the argument by using familiar Old Testament phrases or themes or ideas. Once such references have been identified, then one begins work on *how* the later author adapted them and made the Old Testament tradition relevant to problems in the early churches. Such re-presentation of older traditions begins of course way back in Old Testament times. Most Jewish literature dating from after the middle of the sixth century B.C.E. was composed in the terms and accents of older traditions. To recover the hermeneutics employed by the biblical author on the tradition cited or alluded to we need to know as much as possible about the ancient context for which the author was writing so as to reconstruct as nearly as possible the concerns of the congregation or community among whom or for whom the author wrote. This is not always possible, and where possible is rarely precise. But there are tools for doing so and they are improving.

The Bible is full of such unrecorded hermeneutics because it is itself so full of re-presented tradition. New Testament study has until recently tended to pay minimal attention to the Old Testament in the New. For some students there seemed to be regret over the amount of good New Testament space taken up and lost in quoting the Old. It was part of the centuries-long Christian conviction in many quarters that the New Testament had superseded the Old. Now we realize what a mine of information can be gained by focusing attention, initially, on the hermeneutic question of an ancient text. A question some of us are asking is whether such unrecorded biblical hermeneutics may not be as important for the churches and synagogues today as anything expressly stated in the Bible. The answer to that question depends in part on one's view of the ontology of the Bible, its nature. If one views the Bible primarily as a source of wisdom, a casket of ancient gems still negotiable today, then the answer is likely to be no. But if one views the Bible primarily as a paradigm to be applied dynamically to modern idioms and verbs, then the answer is quite likely to be yes, for then we want to learn how they back there, right in the canonical literature itself, dynamically applied their own prior traditions to their day.

The question might arise at this point as to why we should go to all the trouble of recovering the points they scored back then. Is it not the nature of canon, as we say, to be adaptable, and if so why can we not just read it directly for ourselves without bothering to find out how it functioned or what it said specifically back then? There are some very wise and sane people who are saying this today. There is a new group of biblical interpreters who call themselves structuralists. They disdain the use of biblical criticism and focus on the overall structure of a biblical passage no matter when or how it was first composed, or for what purpose. One might rightly point out that the biblical authors themselves did not rehash the original meaning of the traditions or Scripture they cited; usually they simply interpreted the tradition quite directly for their own time. There are interesting exceptions, but for the most part the biblical authors sought value in the tradition directly rather than recovering the points it first scored and then applying those points to their time.

It is generally a trait of our post-Enlightenment era to seek original points of traditional material. In fact, it is quite possible to think that biblical criticism has gone too far in its tendency to find authority only in the most primitive meaning of a passage; in this respect it has been a bit antiquarian. Canonical criticism has opened the way to understand the pluralism of how a single tradition may have as many different meanings as there are allusions to it or citations of it in the Bible itself — and how the most primitive is not the only authoritative one.

But neither is the meaning we may discern out of our immediate modern contexts the only authoritative one. On the contrary, unless there are firm exegetic controls applied in reading a text, it is possible that we might never hear what Jeremiah or Jesus said, or what their first hearers understood them to say. The points originally scored by the biblical thinkers and authors gave rise to the very process of preservation of the biblical materials we inherit. No one started out to write a biblical book with such authority that it would be accepted by the several early believing communities. What the original thinker said must have been valuable enough to be remembered and then passed on. We are sophisticated enough to know that what a person intended to communicate and what was heard and understood even by those immediately present may be two quite different things. Then of course the reasons for preserving the material and the reasons the first subsequent generation also found it valuable may have been quite different. What Baruch understood Jeremiah to say in Jerusalem before the Temple fell and what the exiles understood a repetition of his message to mean for them a decade or two later may have been quite different. The factor of context in understanding a text is very important indeed. In fact, recognition of the factor of modern context in reading an ancient text is important if we want to recover the points originally scored. We need to be aware of our own needs and what they do to us when we formulate our questions to pose to an ancient text.

Even scholars, or especially scholars, need to be aware of their own limitations in this regard. A cursory review of the history of biblical criticism in the past two hundred years is informative in this regard. We can now see how the questions which interested scholars in the eighteenth century, or in the nineteenth century, or early in the twentieth, influenced the way they saw a text. Knowledge of such a history of shifting interest and method in scholarly work raises our own consciousness as to what questions we are now asking and makes us aware of the methods we are using. We have only recently been released from the almost unconscious hermeneutic of evolutionism. Interest in this sort of self-criticism has arisen only recently, parallel to the new discipline called the sociology of knowledge. One observation which results from such a review of the past two hundred years is that modern scholarship has lines of continuity with earlier pre-Enlightenment scholarship: We are all human and subject to the Zeitgeist of our times. Another observation such a review affords is that each generation in one way or another felt that it had a special claim on truth, that history was to some degree culminating in its work. With the new sociology of knowledge, and in part because of it, we are in danger of thinking that we are liberated from the earlier tendencies and that we truly have a corner on truth! That is the Catch-22 aspect of intellectual endeavor.

We can all read into a text what we need to find there. Biblical criticism at its best, employed circumspectly, is the best means of avoiding abuse of the Bible. For all our observations that we are all human, scholarship has developed tools over the past two hundred years that can help us recover, to a good degree of probability, the thoughts and understandings of ancient folk. And there is perhaps no field of literary scholarship that is more scrupulously circumspect than biblical criticism. Most folk engaged in it have their identity in some modern denominational form of its traditions (Jewish, Muslim, or Christian), and most of us are extra careful in this regard, more so perhaps than when we work on Ugaritic literature or Homer or Herodotus. Indeed, the reaction of some people in the churches and in theology is that we have been too scrupulous: with our methods and tools we have tended to lock the Bible into the past, we have become antiquarian.

Even so the tools developed are very valuable and can now be employed to recover the points originally scored within the biblical orbit (that is, the understandings of a "text" not only when first spoken or written but also in the generations and contexts immediately following, within the range of biblical history). It is only by so doing that we can also recover the hermeneutics of the biblical authors and thinkers themselves. Anytime they contemporized a tradition in their time, they used hermeneutics. The time has now arrived in biblical scholarship to work on those hermeneutics; and we can do so only by using all the tools of biblical scholarship to gauge how the most ancient texts functioned in the less ancient contexts. That requires discerning the ancient contexts and the needs of the earliest believing communities who heard the actual biblical thinkers as much as it requires discerning the ancient texts. We must work not only on biblical literary criticism (source criticism, form criticism, tradition criticism, redaction criticism) but also on biblical historical criticism (philology, archaeology, history of religions, anthropology, secular historiography). We must work not only on text but on context. And if we do so we can then begin to discern these unrecorded hermeneutics latent throughout the Bible. The literature available on internal biblical hermeneutics is not yet very large, but it is growing.

Hermeneutics is theology and theology is hermeneutics. The wisdom of this very old observation is almost immediately and directly applicable to study of biblical or canonical hermeneutics. That is, the deciding light in which one reads a passage is determined by the reader's operative view of God or, to use Dietrich Bonhoeffer's term, of reality, or if one prefers, of truth. And one's view of God tends to emphasize either God's freedom or God's commitment to promises made in a covenantal pact issuing from and out of some great redemptive act (such as the Exodus event or the Christ event). The latter is called divine grace.

On the one hand tradition has always maintained that God is God and hence free to create new factors in the human situation and pull surprises even on his own elect people. John Calvin called this aspect of God's work *opera aliena* (from Isa. 28:21): God is free to follow his own agenda which may surprise even his most faithful adherents. God's freedom is inherent in his role as Creator, which is an ongoing role and was not abandoned after Creation. On the other hand God's function as Redeemer emphasizes God's faithfulness to promises made either to the elect-redeemed or to all creation or to both. God's grace then stresses his reliability and long-suffering.

The hermeneutic of God's freedom as Creator of all the world and of all humankind may be called the hermeneutic of prophetic critique. The hermeneutic of God's grace and commitment to the promises made as the peculiar and particular Redeemer of one ongoing community or group may be called constitutive hermeneutics. The one hermeneutic stresses God's role as Creator of all and the other tends to emphasize God's role as Redeemer of a particular group; the one focuses on the doctrine of creation and the other on the doctrine of redemption. Other doctrines or views tend to be colored by which of these two one stresses, and the history of Christian thought seems to alternate between stress on the one and emphasis on the other. The doctrines of election, ecclesiology, providence, and eschatology may be colored by whether one focuses on God as universal Sovereign of all or on God as Redeemer of a particular group. The one hermeneutic is theocentric, the other christocentric.

Actually, part of the Bible's pluralism is seen in its ability to hold these two emphases in tension. One may employ the most sophisticated tools of biblical criticism to see how Genesis 1 came from one ancient source and Genesis 2 from another. Such an observation helps to understand the apparent contradictions between the two chapters — how, for instance, humanity was created last according to Genesis 1 but was created first according to Genesis 2. So far so good. But it is also very important to observe that some good editor wisely put the two chapters, despite such obvious discrepancies, back to back. And he was supported in that juxtaposition by subsequent believing communities who accepted his work and passed it along as valuable. (This last is a canonical-critical observation.) What then do the two chapters say back to back? They say that God is both majestically transcendent and humbly immanent: neither view of God excludes the other. Traditionally, holding two such opposing views at the same time is called a paradox. But it is very important to observe that the Bible presents these two pictures of God — majestically creating the world by divine fiat *and* calling on Adam and Eve like a pastor — rather constantly throughout. In fact one could say they keep reappearing in alternating cadences.

All efforts to combine the two and mix them so as to view God as a sort of majestic pastor seem to fail. On the contrary the canon as a whole consists of literary units, small and large, some of which almost exclusively stress the one (Ecclesiastes, say) or the other (the Gospel of John). That is the reason the word *paradox* has been used. Other efforts to stress one to the exclusion of the other also fail. To press an exclusivistic christocentric or redemptional view of God runs the danger of denominational hermeneutics: God is our God because he did such and such for us and made us promises he made nobody else, so everybody had best join our church. Or it runs the danger of so stressing divine forgiveness and grace that ethics loses ground altogether. Blessed assurance is absolutely right in Christian doctrine (and Jewish, for that matter); but if it stands alone, out of tension with God's freedom to judge his own people, it becomes cheap grace, or what a student once called sloppy agape. On the other hand to press an inclusivistic theocentric view of God as universal sovereign of all peoples, unfettered by any expectation of how he might act, runs the danger of the view that God is but whimsical and unreliable; ethics loses ground here also.

Holding the two in tension, not attempting either to opt absolutely and always for the one or the other, or to mix them into a neat fifty-fifty formula, seems to be what the Bible does. The reason is that in some contexts or situations in which the believing communities found themselves they needed to hear the challenge of God's freedom, and in other contexts they needed to hear the comfort of God's grace. This is what is meant by the ancient assertion that God's word comforts the afflicted and afflicts the comfortable. Falsehood enters in when a biblical passage or ancient tradition is brought to bear upon a context where it could either comfort cruel people (by stressing God's grace when they needed to hear a challenge) or quench a dimly burning wick (by stressing God's freedom when they needed to hear of comfort and support). Any passage, actually, can be interpreted either way according to the hermeneutic employed — either the hermeneutic of prophetic critique stressing for that context and for that reading God's freedom, or the hermeneutic of constitutive support stressing for that context and for that reading God's grace. . . .

So one of the first hermeneutic techniques we can use to employ prophetic critique in application of a text is dynamic analogy. We should look for the persons and figures in it who might represent different folk today dynamically. Dynamic analogy means we can read a text in different ways by identifying with different people in it. For example if we always identify with Jesus in the passage in Luke 4, his sermon at Nazareth, then we will read the last verse of the pericope (Luke 4:30) wondering how Jesus managed to escape that awful crowd. How marvelous! But if we read the passage again, identifying with the good folk in the synagogue, Jesus' relatives and friends of his hometown, and see how he so sorely offended them that they tried to lynch him, then by the time we get to verse 30 we ask an entirely different question: How did the scoundrel get away?

That is far from blasphemy. In much of his gospel Luke tries to get us to see why Jesus was crucified — because his sermons and messages were often offensive to the good responsible Presbyterians, I mean Pharisees, of his day. The challenge is then ours. We hear it for ourselves dynamically. We in our day, like them in theirs, presume too much and assume too much of God. We have perhaps domesticated God, made God a sort of guarantor of our agendas, of what we know best. Prophetic critique is full of surprises of this sort (Isa. 28:21). It stresses that besides being the particular Redeemer of Israel, and the God present in Christ, God is the Creator of the whole world and of all peoples, and as such is free to follow his own agenda.

Closely related to the technique of dynamic analogy in reading and interpreting a text for today is the ancient principle from which it comes, that of "memory." In biblical terms the concept of remembering is the concept of recalling traditions about Israel's past in such a way as to identify with those in the story who were our ancestors in the faith. Judaism's annual reading of the complete Torah in the synagogue, parashah by parashah (paragraph) each week, enables Jews to remember who they are. In the opening scene of *Fiddler on the Roof* Tevya sings of the function of tradition in the life of a Jew: by reciting the traditions, especially the basic tradition, Torah, Jews are reminded — no matter where they may be in the world, whether in times of crisis or when tempted to assimilate to the dominant culture, in times of ease when identity so easily slips away — that they are Jews. The Torah story reminds Jews constantly that they are the "people come out of Egypt" (Exod. 1:1); they are the slaves-freed-from-Egypt folk (Exod. 12 and Josh. 24). Down through the centuries it has been the same. The Passover Haggadah stresses it. Memory shapes identity.

In effect, therefore, to remember God's mercies or deeds is to recite the basic Torah story. It is to tell the story of what God has done and said: Creation, election, redemption from Egyptian slavery, guidance in the wilderness, suggestions as to how to shape life and society at Sinai, entrance into the land. The remembrance of God's works tells the faithful who they are, even when the contexts in which they live change, whether they live in or out of Palestine, in this or that culture, under whatever threat, whether in pain or at ease.

So also to remember Christ is to tell what for Christians is the climax of the Torah story, what God did in Christ according to the New Testament. To "do this in remembrance" of him, as Christ commanded the followers at the Last Supper, is to tell the story along with the partaking of the bread and the cup. To do so means a sort of breaking down of the barriers of time and space. Just as the Jew experiences time transcended in remembering freedom from slavery and identifies with that first generation of redeemed slaves so that the ancient event is contemporized, so the Christian at the communion table experiences the presence of Christ and the disciples — and indeed of all the saints and martyrs of the church triumphant through the centuries. Not only is time transcended so that the church through the centuries once more knows who it is in the presence of "so great a cloud of witnesses" (Heb. 12:1), but space is also transcended. The present church militant can experience the transcending of the walls of their meeting houses and cathedrals, and have a contemporary sense of the ecumenical nature of the living body of Christ now. Debates in church history about whether such re-presentation in the Eucharist was effected by transubstantiation (Catholic), "real" presence (Lutheran), or by an immediate act of the Holy Spirit dependent on the faith and intentionality of the participants (left-wing Reformation) all stem from this ancient concept.

In a context of worship and retelling the story remembrance is a powerful tradition, whether at Passover or in the Eucharist. To remember the work of God in Israel and in Christ is to have a renewed sense of who we are, no matter the context into which circumstances have moved us, no matter "where we are." . . .

And this may be done by reading the story not as though it were of events way back there about ancient folk but by reading it dynamically, identifying with those who provide us the best mirrors for our identity. The Bible, except in its Wisdom Literature and traditions, provides very few models of morality. An honest reading of the Bible indicates how many biblical characters were just as limited and full of shortcomings as we today. It would seem that about seventy-five percent of the Bible celebrates the theologem *errore hominum providentia divina:* God's providence works in and through human error and sin. The Bible offers no great or infallible models, no saints in the meaning that word has taken on since biblical times — nearly perfect people. None! It offers indeed very few models to follow at all except the work of God in Creation and in Israel in the Old Testament and the work of God in Christ in the New. Biblical people were just like us! Abraham and Sarah lied when they were scared (Gen. 12:13;

18:15) and laughed (Gen. 17:17; 18:12) when they could not believe their own ears or God either. Jacob, our father, was a liar and supplanter (Gen. 27:19). Joseph was an obnoxious imp (Gen. 37:10). Moses was a murderer and fugitive from justice (Exod. 5:12-15).

The presentation of the disciples in all three Synoptic Gospels follows the same theologem: they appear to be incredulous and even rather stupid. Judas's betrayal of Jesus is told in the same scenes as Peter's denial of Jesus and the bickering, sleep, and flight of all the disciples (Luke 22:3-62). When one has come to realize that God can take the selling of our brother Joseph into slavery and turn our evil into our later salvation (Gen. 50:20), then one has also realized that God has taken our selling of Christ to Caesar and made it our salvation. Then one also comes to thank God that Judas too was at the table at the Last Supper and that he also received the bread and the wine, because if he had not been there I could not now come to that table myself. God's greatest grace was manifest in the midst of the drama of betrayal. He gave us the broken bread on the very night we betrayed him.

We need to read the Bible honestly, recognizing that much of it celebrates God's willingness to take our humanity, our frailty, and our limitations and weave them into his purposes. God's grace is not stumped by our limitations, indeed not even by Ramses' need of slave labor nor by Herod's fear of losing his position of power. Did Pharaoh's army pursue the fleeing slaves? Did Herod send troops to kill baby boys in Bethlehem? The answer to such questions lies not in "history," but in the theologem that God is not offended by either Pharaoh's chariots or Herod's swords. And that is reality. That meets us where we are in history, at whatever point of action, or of reaction to power shifting or threatening to shift from one base to another — and that is on every page of history. What could possibly thwart God's grace at this late date? What can a modern Ramses or Nebuchadnezzar or Herod or Pilate do, qualitatively, that could outreach such freedom or such grace? . . .

Finally, the best way to understand the Bible as the churches' book today is to think of it primarily as a paradigm, not as a box or casket of gems and jewels to be mined. A paradigm is a pattern of function of a noun or verb in any language. The Bible comes to us from a twelve- to fifteen-hundred-year time span covering five different culture eras and reflecting the idioms and metaphors of all those cultures. But as a whole it should be viewed in large part as a paradigm in its function in the believing communities today. A paradigm, first, of the verbs and nouns of God's activities and speech, and then, thereupon, a putative paradigm of the verbs and nouns of our activities and speech, in our time and in our contexts. Just as verbs have finite forms and inflections, tenses, modes, and various functions, so the Bible as canon indicates the verbs of God's works, and hence ours in the light thereof. The ontology of the Bible as canon is that of paradigm addressing the faithful in context when they seriously ask the questions, who are we and what are we to do? The answers come in paradigms of faith (identity) and of obedience (lifestyle) appropriate to the contexts in which the questions seek them. There are a number of ways to recite the paradigm in our day and in our contexts — in liturgy, in drama, in dance, in sermons, and most of all by living thoughtfully in its reflection.

NICHOLAS LASH

Performing the Scriptures

Born in India in 1934, British theologian Nicholas Lash was educated at Oscott
College and Cambridge. He was ordained a priest in the Roman Catholic
Church in 1963 and became a fellow of St. Edmund's House, Cambridge, in
1969, and dean in 1971. After serving for several years as an assistant lecturer,
Lash was named Norris Hulse Professor of Divinity at Cambridge in 1978, becoming the first Roman Catholic professor of divinity at Cambridge since the
sixteenth century. He held this post until he retired in 1999. He has also served
as a member of the theological committee of the Roman Catholic Episcopal
Conference of England and Wales. A significant figure in post–Vatican II Roman Catholic theology, Lash has written on doctrinal development, the Eucharist, ecclesiastical authority, and theological method in the postmodern world.
His publications include *Theology on Dover Beach, Easter in Ordinary,* and *The
Beginning and the End of 'Religion'.* His work has explored the knowledge of
God through ordinary human experiences and events. In the following influential essay from his collection *Theology on the Way to Emmaus* (1986), Lash addresses the perennial separation of the interpreting subject and the investi-
gated object in hermeneutics. Like George Lindbeck, whose programmatic *The
Nature of Doctrine* appeared in 1985, Lash not only proposes the church's worship as the most appropriate *site* for biblical interpretation but designates the
church as the true interpreter of Scripture. He draws an analogy between the
interpretation of Scripture and the interpretation of a musical score or a dramatic script. Like great works of art, Scripture delivers its full, fresh meaning
only as it is "brought into play" in the life of the believing community.
Preaching, too, by extension, participates in the church's performance of the
word.

Nicholas Lash, "Performing the Scriptures," in *Theology on the Way to Emmaus* (London:
SCM Press, 1986), pp. 37-46.

Open a copy of the New Testament, leaf through its pages. What do we see? A letter from Paul to his friends in Corinth? Matthew's account of the passion of Jesus? John's reflections on the significance of this one man whose words and fate, whose particular flesh, "speak" from beyond all time and circumstance? No, we don't see anything of the kind. All that we *see* is a set of black marks on white paper.

What does one do with a set of black marks on white paper? One could decide that they make so pleasing a pattern that their best use would be to frame them and hang them on the wall. (That is not a completely far-fetched suggestion: a friend of mine, an expert in Hebrew calligraphy, once wrote a letter in Hebrew to my wife; it hangs in the hall, not for its message, but for its appearance. Family Bibles are sometimes like that, decorative rather than functional.) But, confronted with a pattern of black marks that we recognize as a form of notation, what we usually do is to try to make sense of it, to read it, to interpret it.

How does one "read" or interpret a text? The activity is so familiar that the question may seem foolish. And yet a moment's reflection suggests that, for different kinds of text, different kinds of activity count as what we might call the primary or fundamental form of their interpretation.

Two random examples. A group of people tramping across the hills, bits of paper in one hand, compasses in the other. What are they doing? They are engaged in what the army calls a "map-reading exercise." Another group, in a pub, one speaking, the others listening, are taking part in a poetry reading. (Notice that all of them, not just the speaker, are "taking part" in the reading.)

There are some texts the interpretation of which seems to be a matter of, first, "digging" the meaning out of the text and then, subsequently, putting the meaning to use, applying it in practice. That might be a plausible description of what someone was doing who, armed with a circuit diagram, tried to mend his television set. But it would be a most misleading description of what a judge is doing when, in the particular case before him, he interprets the law. In this case, interpretation is a creative act that could not have been predicted by a computer because it is the judge's business to "make" the law by his interpretation of precedent. What the law means is decided by his application of it.

What it means to read or interpret a text depends in part, then, on the kind of text that is being used. Different kinds of text call for different kinds of reading. And the reader must take responsibility for the reading, for deciding what kind of text it is with which he or she is dealing. This does not mean that it is simply "up to me" arbitrarily to decide what to do with a text. (It would be silly to sing railway timetables, rather than use them to catch trains.) What it does mean is that it is the *reading* of the text, rather than merely the text itself, the material object, the black marks on white paper, which embodies decisions as to what kinds of reading are appropriate. And the richer the text, the more complex its relationship to the culture which reads and remembers it, the more varied the range of more or less appropriate readings which it evokes.

Thus (briefly to anticipate the discussion of the New Testament which I shall get round to eventually) it is possible, at least in some versions, to read the Scriptures for the beauty of their language; it is possible to read them because they speak to our condition; it is possible to read them because they speak of Jesus; it is possible to read them because they speak the mystery of God. And however we decide to take them, the decision to take them one way rather than another is *ours,* at each reading. We cannot pass the buck. It is, therefore, incumbent upon us to read as competently and responsibly as we can.

This raises another set of problems, because not just anybody can read just any text. I am useless at reading circuit diagrams, and I can't read Polish. Confronted by such texts, I have to pass the buck to the appropriate expert.

Open a copy of the New Testament, leaf through its pages. If it happens to be a copy of the Greek text, most of us would be stuck from the start. We would need the help of the expert. But do we also need his help in the case of texts that were written in, or have been translated into, a language with which we are familiar? And, if the answer is "Yes," what is the relationship between the expert's contribution to the task of interpretation, and that of the "general reader"?

At the time of the Reformation, the attempt was made to rescue the New Testament from the clutches of the ecclesiastical authorities, who claimed that they alone were competent to interpret the text, and to place it once again in the hands of those for whom it was written. But a lot has happened since the invention of the printing press helped to bring about that particular revolution in the reading of the New Testament. We have become very conscious of the fact that there is no such thing as what any text "obviously" means. What a text obviously *seems* to mean, at first sight, on examination may turn out to have little or nothing to do with what it meant to those who produced it or to those for whom it was originally produced. (What did *they* make of the story of Christmas, or the Sermon on the Mount, or the trial before Pilate? And how do we know, without trying to find out?) This is by no means only true of ancient texts, produced in cultural contexts whose patterns of thought and argument, illustration and imagery, memory and expectation, were very different from our own. But it undoubtedly *is* true of such texts. And so, between the New Testament and the ordinary Christian, who seeks so to read these texts as to hear in them the Word of Life, there seem to be set up thickets of expertise, insurmountable barriers of scholarship. And as everybody knows, there is not a line in the New Testament concerning the interpretation of which the experts are not deeply divided. If the New Testament once needed rescuing from the ecclesiastical authorities (some of whom have still perhaps too tight a grip on it) does it now need rescuing from the professors of theology?

So far, I have only tried to make four simple points. In the first place, "reading" is always a matter of interpreting a text, of putting it to appropriate use. In the second place, what counts as an appropriate strategy of use or interpretation will depend upon the kind of text with which we are dealing. In the third place, the reader cannot avoid taking personal responsibility for the interpretative strategy which he or she employs. In the fourth place, there are difficulties concerning the relationship between our use of the New Testament, as ordinary Christians, and the responsibilities of "authoritative" interpreters, whether ecclesiastical authorities or academic experts.

I suggested earlier that, for different kinds of text, different kinds of activity count as the fundamental form of their interpretation. I would now like to illustrate this suggestion and to indicate, at the same time, something of the relationships that exist between such fundamental interpretative activity and the interpretative tasks of the scholar and critic.

There is a set of black marks on white paper which are recognizable as the score of one of Beethoven's late string quartets. Consider four people playing the quartet. What are they doing? They are interpreting the text. Even if the performance is technically faultless (and is, in that sense, a "correct" interpretation) we might judge it to be lifeless, unimaginative. There is a creativity in interpretation which, far from being arbitrary (the players cannot do whatever they like with the score) is connected in some way with the fidelity, the "truthfulness" of their performance.

There is, undoubtedly, an expertise which the musicians need. Behind any great performance lie years of disciplined experience. But the particular expertise necessary for good performance is neither the same as, nor in competition with, the academic skills of the textual critics who make the score available through scholarly research and the critics and musicologists who have their own contribution to make to the continuing history of Beethoven interpretation. The fundamental form of the interpretation of Beethoven consists in the performance of his texts. The academics have an indispensable but subordinate part to play in contributing to the quality and appreciation of the performance.

Since the differences between a Beethoven score and the text of the Gospel according to Matthew are more obvious than the similarities, consider another example: a company of actors and an audience performing *King Lear*. Once again, the activity upon which they are engaged is that of interpreting a text. And, once again, the quality of the interpretation depends partly upon an element of creativity that is essential to the interpretative task. We look to the actors and the producer to enable us in some measure freshly to experience and understand the play.

But, at the end of an outstanding performance of *King Lear,* is it only the *play* that we feel ourselves newly to have understood? If we say, after the performance, "I'd never *seen* that before," are we referring only to something which we had never previously seen in the text? Or are we also referring to an element of self-discovery which the performance had helped us to achieve? And what is the relationship between these two discoveries? Might it be that, in the performance of a great work of art, a "classic," self-discovery and the discovery of fresh meaning in the text converge? Might it be that the "greatness" of a text lies in its inexhaustible capacity to express, to dramatize, fundamental features of the human drama?

Leaving such questions on one side for the time being, *King Lear* does seem to be another example of a text the fundamental form of the interpretation of which consists in its performance. As in the case of the musical analogy, the expertise required by actors and producer in order to perform well is of a different order from that required of the indispensable but subordinate academic interpreters: the textual critics, historians of Elizabethan drama, literary critics, and philosophers.

What both these examples suggest is that there are at least some texts that only begin to deliver their meaning in so far as they are "brought into play" through interpretative performance. This is also true, I suggest, of such other "works of art" as the poem, the novel, and the story.

Now, at last, we are getting to the point. Not all the texts of the New Testament are stories but, taken together, they "tell the story" of Jesus and the first Christian communities. I want to suggest, first, that, although the texts of the New Testament may be read, and read with profit, by anyone interested in Western culture and concerned for the human predicament, the fundamental form of the *Christian* interpretation of Scripture is the life, activity, and organization of the believing community. Secondly, that Christian practice, as interpretative action, consists in the *performance* of texts which are construed as "rendering," bearing witness to, one whose words and deeds, discourse and suffering, "rendered" the truth of God in human history. The performance of the New Testament enacts the conviction that these texts are most appropriately read as the story of Jesus, the story of everyone else, and the story of God.

In comparison with some other "models" of the relationship between interpretation and discipleship, Bible and theology, Scripture and tradition, this suggestion does at least have the merit of reminding us that the *poles* of Christian interpretation are not, in the last analysis, written texts (the text of the New Testament on the one hand and, on the other, whatever appears today in manuals of theology and catechetics, papal encyclicals, pastoral letters, etc.) but patterns of human action: what was said and done and suffered, then, by Jesus and his disciples, and what is said and done and suffered, now, by those who seek to share his obedience and his hope. We talk of "Holy" Scripture, and for good reason. And yet it is not, in fact, the *script* that is "holy," but the people: the company who perform the script.

Moreover, as my musical and dramatic analogies were intended to indicate, the model has the further advantage of keeping the experts firmly in their place while acknowledging their skills to be indispensable. To say that the fundamental form of the Christian interpretation of Scripture is the performance of the biblical text affords no license to that "fundamentalism" which is still a depressingly widespread feature of popular preaching and catechesis. In order to do the job properly, Christian discipleship, the performative interpretation of Scripture, needs (just as much as does the interpretation of Beethoven and Shakespeare) the services of scholarship and critical reflection.

I have been at pains to emphasize that those who engage in the activity of reading a text bear personal responsibility for their reading. But to say that the responsibility is personal is not to say that it is executed by isolated individuals. Personal responsibility is not the same thing as "private judgment." Christian living, construed as the interpretative performance of Scripture, is, for two reasons, necessarily a collaborative enterprise.

This is so, first, because (as I have pointed out already) the performers need the help of the "experts." The second reason arises from the nature of the texts: it takes two to tango and rather more to perform *King Lear.*

For even the most dedicated musician or actor, the interpretation of Beethoven or Shakespeare is a part-time activity. Offstage, the performers relax, go shopping, dig the garden. But there are some texts the fundamental form of the interpretation of which is a full-time affair because it consists in their enactment as the social existence of an entire human community. The Scriptures, I suggest, are such texts. This is what is meant by saying that the fundamental form of the Christian interpretation of Scripture is the life, activity, and organization of the believing community. The performance of Scripture *is* the life of the church. It is no more possible for an isolated individual to perform *these* texts than it is for him to perform a Beethoven quartet or a Shakespeare tragedy.

Another analogy may help. The fundamental form of the political interpretation of the American Constitution is the life, activity, and organization of American society. That society exists (not without change, conflict, and confusion) as the *enactment* of its Constitution. Similarly, we might say that the Scriptures are the "constitution" of the church.

Even in the case of societies that have a written constitution, the interpretation of that constitution is an unending enterprise. Times change, circumstances change. The "meaning" of the constitution is never definitively "captured"; it is, ever and again, sought and constructed. Similarly, each new performance of Beethoven or Shakespeare is a new event in the history of the meaning of the text. There is no such thing as an interpretation that is "final" and "definitive" in the sense of bringing that history to an end.

But how can this be true of the New Testament? How can we square the recognition that the history of the meaning of the text continues indefinitely with the ascription of *finality* to God's work of revelation in Jesus the Christ? This is a large question; all I can do is offer a couple of clues.

In the first place, the range of appropriate interpretations of a dramatic or literary text is constrained by what the text "originally meant." This is what keeps the historians and textual critics in business. Good Shakespearean production, for example, presupposes an effective and abiding interest in what was originally meant. The author retains his authority if it is *his* text, and not some other, that we seek to interpret.

In the second place, in order to understand a text we have to understand the question to which it is an answer. We may give up the enterprise: there are texts that we no longer bother to read, or which we feel ourselves unable to make sense of. But so long as the enterprise continues, so long as we continue to seek to perform *these* texts, we are continuing to endorse that which we take the texts to have originally meant.

And if the question to which the text sought originally to provide an answer was a question concerning the ultimate and definitive character, outcome, and significance of human history: and if the answer (expressed in the text) consisted in the ascription of ultimate, unsurpassable, effective significance to the words and work and death of one man, then, to continue appropriately to perform this text is to continue to ascribe such significance to this man.

To put it very simply: as the history of the meaning of the text continues, we can and must tell the story differently. But we do so under constraint: what we may *not* do, if it is *this* text which we are to continue to perform, is to tell a different story.

There is another objection to the model I am proposing which needs briefly to be considered. *King Lear* is fiction; the Gospels are, in some sense, historical. They therefore carry a built-in reference to particular, completed past events which renders them resistant to the interpretative relativism to which fictional constructions are subject.

Once again, all I can do here is to offer some clues to the resolution of the dilemma. In the first place, we would not bother to continue performing *King Lear* (except as a museum piece) if we no longer believed in it, if we no longer found it "true to life." Some people, I think, give up the practice of Christianity for a similar reason.

In the second place, however, the New Testament texts do not simply give symbolic, narrative expression to certain fundamental and pervasive features of the human drama (although Christians are apt to overlook the extent to which the fact that they *do* do this is part of their enduring power and attractiveness). They also express their authors' confidence in one man in whom the mystery of divine action is seen to have been embodied and disclosed.

We can perform *King Lear* even if the central character in the text had no particular prototype. But if we were to read the New Testament on this supposition, or on the supposition that the accuracy of the portrait did not matter, we should have excised a central element from what the text originally meant. We would be telling a different story.

Moreover, the texts of the New Testament not only purport to express the fact and significance of one man but, in doing so, they refer both fact and significance to the mystery of divine action. It follows that, for the practice of Christianity, the performance of the biblical text, to be true, it must be not only "true to life," but "true to *his* life"; and not only "true to his life," but "true to God." That it is so, and may be made so, is at once our responsibility, our hope, and our prayer.

I have been suggesting that the fundamental form of the Christian interpretation of Scripture is the life, activity, and organization of the Christian community, construed as performance of the biblical text. The best illustration of what this might mean is, of course, the celebration of the eucharist. Here, that interpretative performance in which all our life consists — all our suffering and care, compassion, celebration, struggle, and obedience — is dramatically distilled, focused, concentrated, rendered explicit. In this context, the principal forms of discourse are "practical": in praise, confession, petition, they seek to *enact* the meanings which they embody. And if, in the liturgy of the Word, the story is told, it is told not so that it may merely be relished or remembered, but that it may be *performed,* in the following of Christ.

At the end of a performance of *Lear,* the actors leave the stage, remove their costumes, "return to life." But, for each Christian actor, the performance of the biblical text ends only at death. The stage on which we enact our performance is that wider human history in which the church exists as the "sacrament," or dramatic enactment, of history's ultimate meaning and hope. If the texts of the New Testament are to express that which Christian faith declares them capable of expressing, the quality of our *humanity* will be the criterion of the adequacy of the performance. And yet this criterion is, in the last resort, hidden from us in the mystery of God whose meaning for man we are bidden to enact.

KATHARINE DOOB SAKENFELD

Feminist Uses of Biblical Materials

Katharine Doob Sakenfeld is William Albright Eisenberger Professor of Old Testament Literature and Exegesis at Princeton Theological Seminary. As a member of the RSV Bible Committee and co-editor of the Oxford Study Bible, she has devoted considerable energy to questions of biblical translation and interpretation. Her chief scholarly interest is women in the Old Testament and women as interpreters of the Bible. In the following article Sakenfeld outlines three feminist strategies for reading the Old Testament: (1) The interpreter can employ texts about women to counteract famous texts used against women. Although the Old Testament reflects a patriarchal culture, it also contains a counterliterature or submerged witness to the importance of selected women in the tradition and to the feminine characteristics of God, though the latter have been obscured by many translations of the Bible. (2) The interpreter may discover in the Bible a general theological principle — what the Bible is "all about" — with which to combat patriarchy. Such a principle may rest on the prophetic critique of all oppression or, as in the New Testament, the example of Jesus or the radical equality of all who are baptized into Christ. (3) By uncovering the true condition of women in ancient Israel or the church, the interpreter may derive lessons from the stories of women. Such an approach does not seek to rehabilitate the text, but by means of literary analysis (e.g., Phyllis Trible) or historical reconstruction (Elisabeth Schüssler Fiorenza), the interpreter helps the reader encounter and identify with the struggles of women in the Bible. Sakenfeld's options place new and greater demands on the preacher, whose gender or social position may obstruct the message of the text.

Katharine Doob Sakenfeld, "Feminist Uses of Biblical Materials," in *Feminist Interpretation of the Bible,* ed. Letty M. Russell (Philadelphia: Westminster, 1985), pp. 55-64.

As a Christian who teaches the Bible and who also calls herself a feminist, I am often asked, "How can feminists use the Bible, if at all? What approach to the Bible is appropriate for feminists who locate themselves within the Christian community? How does the Bible serve as a resource for Christian feminists?" These are not easy questions to answer, but it is possible to identify several different ways in which contemporary Christian feminists approach the biblical material. This chapter describes some of these ways of listening to the Bible.

Feminism may be viewed as a contemporary prophetic movement that announces judgment on the patriarchy of contemporary culture and calls for repentance and change. How does such a prophetic movement relate itself to its religious heritage? The prophets of the Hebrew Scriptures sometimes highlighted forgotten traditions of ancient Israel; on other occasions, they found it necessary to reinterpret traditions that had been skewed or misunderstood; at times they even had to reject time-honored traditions as false in their understanding of God's way. Christian feminists who intend and hope, like the biblical prophets, to work within their religious heritage must address themselves to the authority of the Bible in the life of their community of faith. They must seek faithful ways of recovering, reinterpreting, and discerning God's way in the tradition handed on in the Bible.

Their beginning point, shared in common with all feminists studying the Bible, is appropriately a stance of radical suspicion. . . . Feminists recognize in common that patriarchy was one of the most stable features of ancient biblical society over the thousand-plus years of the Bible's composition and redaction. Thus, in studying any biblical texts, feminists need to be alert not only for explicit patriarchal bias but also for evidence of more subtle androcentrism in the worldview of the biblical authors. Only such a frank and often painful assessment of the depth of patriarchal perspective in the text provides an honest starting point for considering how the tradition can be meaningful today. If in studying a text feminists discover that some suspicions are unfounded, then there is cause for rejoicing, but in the meantime they have not fooled themselves by refusing to face the problem.

Recognizing the patriarchy of biblical materials, Christian feminists approach the text with at least three different emphases:

1. Looking to texts about women to counteract famous texts used "against" women.
2. Looking to the Bible generally (not particularly to texts about women) for a theological perspective offering a critique of patriarchy (some may call this a "liberation perspective").

3. Looking to texts about women to learn from the intersection of history and stories of ancient and modern women living in patriarchal cultures.

These emphases are not presented as the only possibilities but rather as major categories identifiable in current feminist biblical interpretation. Before I describe them, two important points should be noted about their interrelationship.

First, these three approaches represent options. They do not necessarily occur as a series of stages in the life of a feminist struggling with the biblical text, nor do they represent a chronological history of feminist biblical interpretation generally. One may move from one approach to another in the order described here, but one may also enter into feminist dialogue with the Bible beginning with any one of these approaches. Feminist interpretation moves back and forth among these options.

Second, these three options are not actually mutually exclusive. Many general essays on feminism and the Bible incorporate some combination of them. Some interpreters use different approaches on different occasions, depending on the purpose and the audience. Thus it is important not to associate individual feminists simplistically with just one of these options. . . .

Option 1: Looking to Texts about Women
to Counteract Famous Texts Used "Against" Women

The various ways in which the Bible has been and is still used to justify women's traditional place in Western culture have been recounted many times over. Texts and traditions used to bolster the cultural status quo include (among many others) the themes that woman was created second (Gen. 2) and sinned first (Gen. 3 and the reinforcement of this view in 1 Tim. 2:13-14); that women must keep silent in church (1 Cor. 14; 1 Tim. 2); and that they should be submissive to their husbands (Eph. 5). Feminism as a prophetic movement identifies such texts, or the traditional interpretation of them, as "against" women. Within option 1, feminists offer a twofold response: on the one hand, there is an effort to reinterpret some of these well-known texts; on the other hand, "forgotten" texts that present women in a different light are brought into the discussion.

So, for example, a number of studies of Genesis 2–3 have suggested fresh interpretations that are not so negative toward women. The creation of woman at the end of chapter 2 may in fact mean that she is equal to the man; in the encounter with the serpent, the woman and the man should be viewed as "mutually responsible," united in disobedience. In a similar vein, New Testament specialists point out that Paul's instruction for women to keep silent (1 Cor. 14) is advice peculiar to a disruptive situation in the church at Corinth. The discussion of marriage in Ephesians 5 is often treated by emphasizing the theme of mutual subjection of verse 21, which introduces the section.

Complementary to such reinterpretation of negatively viewed passages is a new emphasis on those texts which seem to speak positively of women. Galatians 3:28 is surely the parade example: "There is neither Jew nor Greek, there is neither slave nor free, there is neither male nor female; for you are all one in Christ Jesus." Many Christian feminists ground their view of women's place in family, society, and church on this text, which for them points beyond the generally restrictive practice of the early church and applies to actual living in the world, not simply to personal salvation.

Feminists have also turned to the many stories of Jesus' relationship to women as recorded in the Gospels and to the scattered indications of women in leadership roles that are treated with approval in Scripture. The role and actions of biblical characters such as Miriam, Deborah, the women at Jesus' tomb, Priscilla, and many others are treated paradigmatically to suggest that women may assume leadership and authority in their communities. Jesus' attitude toward women (speaking with them, taking them seriously) is regarded as exceptional and even revolutionary for his time — an attitude which then informs a critique of patriarchy both in the early church and today. The story of Jesus' encounter with the Samaritan woman at the well (John 4) is often drawn upon: Jesus first announces his messiahship to this symbolic outcast of society — a woman of questionable repute who is also a Samaritan.

This first option — using reinterpreted or forgotten texts about women to counteract texts used "against" women — has its own strengths and limitations. Some of these will be described briefly. Readers are encouraged to reflect on the implications of these for the passages just mentioned or for other texts about women in which they have special interest.

A great strength of this approach, in my view, lies in drawing our attention to the diversity of biblical testimony concerning women by its recovery of forgotten positive texts and traditions. The very existence of such potentially positive material suggests that the Bible is not necessarily to be rejected out of hand as an instrument of patriarchy. At the same time, the reinterpretation of allegedly negative texts serves as reminder of the ongoing power of patriarchy in biblical interpretation. The reinterpretations, by their very existence, challenge the claim that exegesis is scientifically factual and value-neutral. The prophetic tasks of recovery and reinterpretation work together to suggest that some parts of the traditional Christian view of women may be false.

But in this strength lurks also a potential limitation. The assumptions which sometimes underlie this option are that the Bible has some clear and explicit teaching concerning the status and role of women, that the locus of this teaching is in texts specifically concerning women, and that it may be (re-)discovered by careful exegetical study. Yet the reinterpretations of texts used against women certainly have not gained universal acceptance. A single agreed-upon methodology yields radically different conclusions in the hands of different exegetes. How is a feminist to deal with the absence of exegetical agreement concerning many, if not all, of the critical passages under discussion? Given the assumption that careful exegesis of texts about women will yield a sure answer about women's proper role in church and culture, the lack of interpretive consensus undermines the very purpose for which many feminists use this approach.

Furthermore, if there remain some negative texts concerning women for which no reinterpretation seems possible (and surely such do remain), what principle of discernment decides which set of texts is authoritative? How does one choose between texts that uphold the status quo and texts that challenge it? Although most careful studies try to suggest some principle (such as New Testament over Hebrew Scriptures; Jesus over Paul; eternally valid statements over culture-bound statements), the person struggling with the issue often perceives the situation simply as one in which competing proof texts are at work. Galatians 3:28 is tossed into the ring to compete with 1 Timothy 2, and no real headway is made. And of course any of the principles of discernment just mentioned raise other serious problems, in suggesting that some parts of the Bible are more trustworthy than others or in implying that some biblical material may not be culture-bound.

Each of these two main areas of limitation — exegetical uncertainty and competing proof-texting — points to basic questions about the meaning of biblical authority and the usefulness of the Bible for Christian faith. These questions will be addressed briefly at the conclusion of this chapter.

Option 2: Looking to the Bible Generally for a Theological Perspective Offering a Critique of Patriarchy

This approach does not set out to avoid texts mentioning women but, unlike the first option, it does not focus upon such texts as the sole or even primary basis for developing a Christian perspective on the role and status of women. It approaches the Bible in the hope of recognizing what the gospel is really all about and then works from that recognition toward a specificity about women.

At the most general level, this option is illustrated by the understanding of the Bible as words that bear witness to the incarnate Word of God, Jesus Christ. This view of Scripture suggests that the Bible is not an instruction book but that the test of any situation would be an understanding of God's way with the world made known in Jesus of Nazareth. The problem, of course, within this option is to discern some central witness of Scripture that can be identified as what Christianity is all about. Feminist efforts in this direction tend to set their reflection within the larger context of liberation theology.

Letty Russell, for example, emphasizes the theme of *koinonia* as partnership and the many ways in which people are partners together in God's liberating action. To live out this partnership, she suggests, Christians need to develop the "art of anticipation" so that they may think from the context of God's future, discern the signs of liberation, and act on the basis of that hope. It is by such theological anticipation that feminists see "both male and female in community as God's intention for New Creation." This New Creation perspective is grounded in Jesus Christ as Prince of Shalom and witnessed to in the biblical traditions of unexpected deliverance from oppression and unexpected establishment of a new covenant. God's horizon is always out ahead of people, challenging them to transform their worldview.

Rosemary Ruether's chapter entitled "Biblical Resources for Feminism: The Prophetic Principles" in her book *Sexism and God Talk* provides a second illustration of this approach. For Ruether, the prophetic principles "imply a rejection of every elevation of one social group against others as image and agent of God, every use of God to justify social domination and subjugation." In Ruether's view the application of this prophetic message of liberation must be pressed beyond the content of the Bible itself in order to apply it to women. Old Testament Israel, imbued with patriarchy, simply never noticed that women were among those oppressed and in need of liberation. And despite first-century Christian glimpses of a transformed relationship between women and men, the early church quashed nascent change in this direction. Ruether's approach involves regarding the "egalitarian, countercultural vision" (which must be read between the lines of the New Testament) as the "true norm of Christianity [so that] the authority of the official canonical framework is overturned."

In common, Ruether and Russell look to the biblical message overall, not in the first place to texts about women. The range of biblical texts appropriate to the task thus conceived is wide indeed. Possibilities range from the exodus, to the jubilee year, to Zacchaeus, to the abundant life, to Paul on freedom.

One great strength of this approach is that it can look beyond the reactive side of feminism as anti-patriarchalism and move to (even start from) the more positive and constructive side of feminist emphasis on *shalom,* wholeness or salvation in the broadest and deepest sense of the term. Because this *shalom* encompasses all people, both women and men, in all conditions of life (race, ethnicity, class), this option puts feminist use of biblical materials concretely in touch with the concerns and quests of other oppressed groups. It provides a basis for affirming the solidarity of the whole human community and for questioning any arbitrary prioritizing of the needs of one group over another. The attempt to start from an understanding of "what the Christian thing is all about" (gospel as humanization; prophetic critique of oppression) also has the advantage of reminding us that each particular biblical passage takes on meaning in the light of many others. The range of texts offering good news for women is vastly expanded by comparison to option 1.

But as with option 1, so here also strength is at the same time limitation. "The gospel" is very general, and for many people encounter with the general message of Christianity is vague and diffuse by comparison to encounter with specific texts. And when this option turns to consider specific texts, the encounter with the liberation theme in general may still be experienced as diffuse despite its application to the condition of women.

Elisabeth Schüssler Fiorenza has pointed to two other potential limitations of this option. While they are not in my view inherent in the approach, they do represent concerns that should be considered by those focusing on this option.

First, this approach runs the risk of concealing patriarchy in the biblical witness itself. Those who use this option are quick to agree that radical suspicion is necessary and that the whole Bible is infused with patriarchy. In fact, they use this option in part because they do see patriarchal bias even in the many texts about women that can be remembered or reinterpreted to challenge the status quo. And yet there is a danger that the patriarchal character of the liberation texts as they were written will be forgotten. Ruether's radicalizing of the biblical critique of oppression to include women would then be lost, and one would fall into the false assumption that biblical authors speaking against oppression had in mind women as well as other oppressed groups.

A second limitation lies in the possible claim that there is some timeless or eternal truth to be identified in Scripture, while all the actual writers and texts fall short of that truth. Indeed, for many people this is precisely the assumption underlying this second option, so that their goal in using this approach is to shuck off the culturally conditioned parts of the Bible and find that timeless truth. But many who work from this assumption discover that seeking for something free of historical conditioning is like peeling an onion: There is no core. I do not find that either Russell or Ruether, carefully read, succumbs to this peeling-the-onion approach, although I appreciate Fiorenza's concern. To identify key elements of a tradition is not necessarily to remove the tradition from the context in which it was hammered out, but avoiding this consequence requires deliberate attention to the problem.

Again, as with option 1, the limitations of option 2 call into question the ultimate usefulness of the biblical materials and direct our attention to issues of authority.

Option 3: Looking to Texts about Women to Learn from the History and Stories of Ancient and Modern Women Living in Patriarchal Cultures

I have tried to state this third option to open up in principle any biblical text dealing with women as one that can have meaning for modern feminists. In contrast to option 1, in which texts about women are categorized as for or against women, in this third option all these texts are taken to address the condition of women as persons oppressed because of their sex and as persons yearning to be free. Within this option it does not ultimately matter whether a given text can be proved exegetically to support feminist concerns. It does not matter because here the Bible is not (in contrast to option 1) looked to as a source of direct and specific rules for living. Rather, the Bible is viewed as an instrument by which God shows women their true condition as people who are oppressed and yet who are given a vision of a different heaven and earth and a variety of models for how to live toward that vision. The work of two biblical specialists who make use of very different exegetical styles and skills also illustrates this option.

Phyllis Trible's *Texts of Terror* gives close literary attention to narratives portraying women as victims, some of whom nonetheless find ways to declare their personhood. Trible describes this task as retelling biblical stories of terror *in memoriam.* She interprets the story of the rape, murder, and dismemberment of an unnamed woman (Judges 19), the story of a daughter offered as human sacrifice because of her father's foolish vow (Judges 11), and other stories "on behalf of their female victims in order to recover a neglected history, to remember a past that the present embodies, and to pray that these terrors shall not come to pass again."

A historical rather than literary focus characterizes Elisabeth Schüssler Fiorenza's contribution within the scope of this third option. As a historian of earliest Christianity, she seeks to reconstruct the life and practice of Christians and congregations in the earliest church. In this task she examines New Testament texts against women not in order to rehabilitate them (as in option 1) but rather to reconstruct the practices that the New Testament authors were rejecting so as to clarify our picture of church life in the New Testament period and to describe women's role in that church life. Recognizing that the Bible is thoroughly androcentric, recorded and canonized by men, Fiorenza moves the locus of revelation beyond the text itself to the reconstructed ministry of Jesus and the life of the early church, in which at every stage the picture is one of "struggle for equality and against patriarchal domination."

Despite significant differences in critical method and in presupposition about the place of the biblical text in the life of the church, both Trible and Fiorenza are focusing on the "intersection of history and stories of ancient and modern women living in patriarchal cultures." One strength common to their work is the possibility of facing the pervasive androcentrism of the biblical material head on, without excuse or evasion. Women may appropriate the tradition by identifying with biblical women both in their oppression and in their exercise of freedom.

Yet, like the other options, this one too has its limitation as it brings its user up against the question of authority. How does one know that, insofar as a text perpetuates violence and oppression against women (or against anyone), it is in that respect not authoritative? The problem is that, for option 3, the discernment of what is authoritative must come from somewhere outside the option itself, whether from biblical reflection done from the perspective of option 2, or from the personal and communal experience of the person approaching the text, or perhaps most fruitfully from some combination of these.

To Give Up on the Bible — or to Understand Its Authority in a New Way?

Whichever option they find most congenial, Christian feminists sometimes assume that if they use the Bible in that particular way, patriarchy will be undone in their own lives; and that if enough others follow their use of the Bible, patriarchy will disappear. But if and when they find that the systemic pervasiveness of patriarchy is such that patriarchy will not disappear in their lifetime or even in the next generation, then attention to the Bible begins to seem futile, for the Bible is no longer seen as the key to "solving the problem" of patriarchy. Indeed, the continuing power of the Bible to support the patriarchal status quo underlines its seeming uselessness. With the question "Why would God let such a book become the church's book?" these women and men begin to give up on Christian faith as well.

In addition to this general reason for giving up on the Bible, each of the three options may lead in its own way to rejection of the Bible as not authoritative or not useful in any positive way for the feminist struggle.

The person who comes to see option 1 as merely a proof-texting game may well conclude that the Bible cannot function normatively if it disagrees with itself. The recognition that expert scholars cannot agree on the meaning or significance of given texts will serve only to reinforce this conclusion. To make the Bible worth using, some new conception of authority would need to be offered that could replace the old assumptions about the function of the Bible in the life of faith.

Similarly, with option 2, the Bible's minimal and marginal critique of patriarchy itself may become a stumbling block. What warrant is there, someone will ask, for extending the Bible's general critique of oppression to a critique of patriarchy that is not in the text and seems even to be counterindicated by much of the text? Or the Bible's general attitude toward women may appear so incongruous in light of the central gospel witness to Jesus Christ that the very usefulness of the Bible is thereby called into question.

Finally, option 3 may also lead to abandonment of the Bible as not useful. In this option, the explicit emphasis on the depth and continuity of patriarchy simply highlights the many painful oppressive portions of biblical material and makes clear that the church has often perpetuated precisely those oppressive emphases. The undercurrent of women living freed and freeing lives within the context of patriarchy has always remained just that — only an undercurrent. In the face of such overwhelming patriarchy, how can one say that this undercurrent should rightly be viewed as the mainstream of the good news of God? Unless feminists find some understanding of how women's rejected history and untold story can be regarded as authoritative, even those using this third approach may in the end give up on the Bible.

Thus no feminist use of biblical material is finally immune to the risk of finding the Bible hurtful, unhelpful, not revealing of God, and not worth the effort to come to grips with it. Regardless of approach, feminists may find that the Bible seems to drive them away from itself (and sometimes from God), rather than drawing them closer. At the heart of the problem, [finally], lies the issue of biblical authority. . . .

JUSTO L. GONZÁLEZ AND CATHERINE G. GONZÁLEZ

The Neglected Interpreters

Justo L. González, born in Cuba and educated at Yale University, is considered by many to be the foremost Protestant Hispanic theologian in the United States. A prolific writer of over sixty books and a prominent scholar in the field of historical theology, he has long been respected for his three-volume *History of Christian Thought* (1970-1975). In the last decade, with such publications as the groundbreaking *Mañana: Christian Theology from a Hispanic Perspective* (1990), he has turned his attention to the development of a Hispanic/Latino theology that arises from the experience of an oppressed and marginalized people. González calls this "reading the Bible in Spanish" — that is, from a Hispanic viewpoint. He is the founder and editor of *Apuntes,* the first Hispanic/Latino theological journal, and currently directs the Hispanic Theological Initiative. His wife, Catherine Gunsalus González, is an ordained Presbyterian pastor and professor of church history at Columbia Theological Seminary in Decatur, Georgia. She specializes in the history of liturgy. Justo and Catherine González have co-authored numerous works, including *Liberation Preaching, In Accord: Let Us Worship, The Liberating Pulpit,* and *Revelation.* The work of the Gonzálezes significantly enlarges the hermeneutical circle beyond the psychology of Schleiermacher and the philosophical preunderstanding identified by Bultmann to include the political, economic, and ideological environment in which the text is read. The poor read the Bible differently than do the rich — an assertion dramatically documented by Ernesto Cardenal in *The Gospel in Solentiname.* On the basis of this reality, the interpreter must ask a new set of questions: What are the cultural biases of European and American historical criticism? To what extent do our sermons reflect the cultural values of those in power? What groups are silenced by our sermons?

Justo L. González and Catherine G. González, *The Liberating Pulpit* (Nashville: Abingdon, 1994), pp. 47-65.

For too long there has been in Protestant circles an excessive emphasis on private Bible study. There is no doubt that such study is necessary. It does not take ten people working together to look up a word in a Hebrew lexicon. When one adds to this the devotional dimension, there is also no doubt that there is an important place in the Christian life for private devotions, and that these ought to be centered on the study of the Bible. But the problem comes when we seem to say that private Bible study is somehow better or deeper or more meaningful than corporate study — when we forget that the Bible comes out of a community and is addressed to a community. As a result of this individualistic approach to the Bible, there are some in our culture for whom private reading of Scripture and prayer are the ultimate forms of Christian worship, and for whom, therefore, the church is a dispensable item. One does not need the community of faith for the reading or understanding of Scripture. One's own interpretation is quite sufficient. Radio and TV religious programs give an illusion of community, but actually increase the individualism of the listener, who tunes in or out readily. . . .

The impact of a purely individualistic reading of Scripture goes far beyond what immediately comes to mind — a loss of the sense of being a community. It also obscures from us some of the dimensions of what Scripture may be saying. Take for instance the very much debated passages in Ephesians and elsewhere about wives and husbands, masters and slaves. The early church was a very mixed group. It is one thing for this to be read out loud to a mixed group in the early church, where the husbands and the masters receive their share of very sobering instruction which the wives and the slaves are privileged to overhear, and quite another for a woman today to read it in private trying to determine how a good wife ought to behave. The author of Ephesians intended for the wives to overhear the word addressed to their husbands, "be subject to one another out of reverence for Christ," "husbands should love their wives as their own bodies"; and for slaves to overhear the masters being addressed: "masters, do the same to them, and forbear threatening." Granted, such public reading does not solve all the problems posed by these passages; but purely private reading does exacerbate the problems.

Scripture is addressed to a community, and to individuals as part of that gathering. Even read privately, there is the need to see that the Word comes to us as those who are called to or are already part of the People of God. Scripture itself often calls the community of faith to remember their ancestors — either their sinfulness so that the current People would not be so tempted, or their faith which should be continued. But that is not the way it is usually read in our culture. Even the way we tell Bible stories to our children shows a strong individualistic bias. We have the heroes who are to be models, but the stories about the community of faith may be ignored, even when the hero would not have been understood individualistically by the writers or the hearers of Scripture in past centuries.

Things were very different in the early church. The printing press was yet to appear, so copies of Scripture were not available for all to have at home, and therefore when the congregation gathered, a great deal of time was spent reading the Scripture — at first the Old Testament, to which soon were added the "memoirs of the apostles" (Gospels) and the Epistles. The sermon was expected to be an exposition of Scripture. Lay people learned many passages by heart and had a sense that they knew and understood what the Bible was saying. They listened to the readings eagerly, even coming early to the worship service so that they could hear more Scripture read aloud before the service began.

It may be argued that the invention of the printing press, and the resultant fact that Christians can read their Bibles at home, has changed this situation, and that therefore there is little or no need for that sort of corporate Bible study. But the problem is that most of the Bible was written to be read, not in private, but in public, often within the context of corporate worship. Just as it is not the same to read a sermon as it is to hear it preached, it is not the same to read the Bible in private as it is to read and hear it being read in the midst of the People of God. The Lone-Ranger student of the Bible loses a great deal that cannot be regained by any amount of study or private devotion.

To make matters worse, in the services of some of our churches — often those that pride themselves on being most "biblical" — very little attention is paid to the Bible. In some cases, even the sermon, rather than attempting to put us under the scrutiny and the mercy of the Word of God, uses the biblical text as a pretext, as a jumping off point from which to go far afield.

Unfortunately, there are too many examples of this kind of preaching. Yet, we have encountered none worse than a sermon we heard a few years ago. The text was from the Book of Revelation: "And the sea was no more." "Why will the sea be no more?" asked the preacher. "Because in the sea there are monsters. There are sharks, like Jaws. . . . But the worst of all the monsters of the sea is the octopus. The octopus has eight tentacles, and it grabs you, and it squeezes you, and it crushes you. And so is the octopus of sin. It too has eight tentacles. First, there is the tentacle of pride. . . . Then there is the tentacle of lust." And so he went, on and on, finally to come to his conclusion: "Therefore, let us come out of the tentacles of the octopus of sin and into the arms of Jesus!"

The obvious shortcoming of this sort of preaching is that it ultimately ignores or circumvents the authority of Scripture, which is made to say whatever the preacher wishes. But a further, and often unrecognized, consequence of this proceeding is that people are discouraged from the study of Scripture. Even if they are enlightened and strengthened in their Christian lives by such a sermon, they see no way that they could have learned from the biblical text what the preacher claims to find in it. Rather than encouraging their hearers to delve further into the Bible, such preachers actually are discouraging them. The Bible becomes an esoteric book that only those with specialized education or gifts can possibly be able to understand. It is not a book for the lay Christian, but only for the "professional." This is hardly an attitude that should be encouraged in the church.

But the Lone Ranger himself did not roam the West alone. He had Tonto with him. Tonto, whose name means "dimwit," as any Hispanic in the Southwest would know. Tonto, who hardly ever spoke, except for an occasional either enigmatic or meaningless "kemo sabe." And in spite of this the white hero was called "lone," because his Indian companion, who repeatedly saved his life, simply did not count. He did not count for two reasons: first, he was seen as a projection of his white leader; second, the Lone Ranger never seemed to take the time to listen to him.

There is then a type of "Lone-Ranger" Bible study which, although not necessarily done in private, is done in the same sort of almost meaningless company which Tonto provided for the hero. This happens when our biblical interpretation fails to be challenged by others, either because they share our own perspective, or because, since they differ from us, we classify them as "Tontos" whose perspectives we need not take into account.

The ideologically suspicious preacher soon comes to the realization that, given the social structure of our denominations and of our housing patterns, it is very difficult to avoid the Lone-Ranger Bible study. We may try to have more corporate study of the Bible, and certainly something is gained from doing so; but it is still difficult to provide for the various perspectives which would allow us to see the Bible in a different light.

Even within the social uniformity and racial monochrome of most of our churches, a degree of diversity could be helpful. People of different ages and genders, for instance, are present. And yet, even here church leaders segregate our Bible study by age and by gender! Of course we expect a place for a graded Sunday school and for women's circles of Bible study, but do we not lose something of the enrichment that we could be to each other when most or all our study of the Bible is done in such settings? If it is true that God has "hidden these things from the wise and understanding and revealed them to babes" (Luke 10:21), do not adults cheat themselves out of the opportunity for deeper insight into the will of God when they fail to provide for Bible study that cuts across age groups? And, if it is true that those who are oppressed and whom society counts as nothing go first into the Reign of God, do not young adults miss an opportunity to see the work of God when they put the aged "out to pasture" and do not give them an opportunity to show them, through constant interaction in love, what the Bible says from the perspective of those who once were powerful and respected, but now often find themselves merely tolerated?

Something similar is true in the case of women. The difference between their experience and that of men should be a significant factor in the study of the Bible, especially since traditionally most biblical commentary and exegesis has been done from a male perspective. It is common for male preachers to try to guess what women will find significant, or how they will react to a certain text. And usually they fail miserably! An easy experiment, which may serve to show this, is to ask a group of men to list the five passages in the Bible that they believe will be most significant for women, and then to ask a group of women to list the five passages that they themselves have found most significant in their Christian lives. Chances are that there will be very little overlapping between the two lists. Men will usually choose those passages that speak about women, whereas women will list those that speak of strength in the midst of difficulty or of confidence when there is cause for despair. What this shows is that, quite unconsciously, men tend to believe that the Bible is addressed to them, for they are the typical, normative human beings, and that only those passages which speak of females will be of significance to women. It often comes as a shock to discover, not only that these are not the passages that the women list, but also that their interpretations of the passages that they do choose show valuable insights derived from their experience as females.

When it comes to questions of class, race, and culture, the average North American white church finds it much more difficult to overcome the Lone-Ranger syndrome. Many members of our congregations are willing to see their sisters and brothers of other groups as fellow travelers in the Christian life, and are even willing to help them along. But they still will tend to see them as "Tontos" whose contribution to the understanding of the Christian message will be no more than a grunt or an occasional "kemo sabe." Even where there is an interest in hearing what these people have to say, the social and racial composition of most white churches makes it very difficult. In order to be able to listen to what the supposed "Tontos" are saying and to the way they experience and interpret the message of the Bible, it is necessary to have a close association with them, to share in their experience, in a way and to a degree that very few in the white community are willing to risk.

What then of the sincere, white, male preacher who believes that there are valuable insights in these communities and wishes to pursue them to make them his own and to lead his congregation in hearing them? For such a person, there is only one way: the pain and struggle of the hermeneutic circle. He cannot live out of another's experience of oppression. He must discover how the system that oppresses the African American, the Hispanic, the Native American, and the woman also oppresses him. He must come to see for himself how much of the theology he has been taught serves to bolster that system of oppression. He must develop the ideological suspicion without which there is no liberating theology. He must begin to work for his own emancipation, and do his theology out of that struggle. And then he will really be able to look at the theology of other groups, and to learn from it.

Resources from Christian Tradition

It may seem odd to begin a discussion on a liberating reading of Scripture and of theology by speaking of the resources of Christian tradition. Indeed, many of those who are involved in various struggles for liberation feel that Christian tradition has been so oppressive that it must be discarded altogether. Others, mostly those who come out of a background of liberal theology, have been taught that the past is a burden of which they must rid themselves, and that what must be done is to interpret Christianity in a "modern" way, more adapted to our present circumstances.

It is true that a great deal of Christian tradition has been oppressive. It is also true that, if the Word of God is to be relevant, it must be relevant *today,* and that the very notion of history, so central to the gospel itself, implies that today's preaching will not be the same as yesterday's. In fact, preaching would not be necessary if there were no need to relate the gospel message to a contemporary situation. In spite of all this, there is still a great deal of Christian tradition that must be recovered.

That recovery is a difficult task, for from a very early date the process began by which those elements of the tradition that could not be assimilated into the status quo were suppressed or ignored. We have already referred to Eusebius' attempt to show that the persecutions were little more than a grave misunderstanding on the part of the Roman Empire. More recent historians have also read history in a similar manner. For instance, treatises on the ethics of the early church deal almost exclusively with sexual mores, lying, homicide, and so forth, but fail to take into account the astonishing teachings of early Christian writers regarding property, the use and distribution of wealth, and the like. The reason for this is that the definition of what are "ethical" questions has been narrowed in our capitalist society, precisely so as not to include issues such as whether private property is morally correct, or what are the rights of the poor. On the basis of such a definition, historians of Christian ethics tend to ignore the very radical things that have been said in earlier centuries of Christian history, and thus give us the impression that today's radical questioning of the rights of property, for instance, is a new phenomenon, about which Christian tradition has little to say.

The ideologically suspicious preacher is not quick to accept such a verdict, but rather asks a further question: Is the history of Christian ethics a faithful rendering of what ancient Christians actually taught, or is it rather one more case in which the interests of the powerful are being served by what seems to be impartial scholarship? Even before examining the evidence, such an ideologically suspicious person will remember that the early church was not generally composed of rich and powerful people, and will therefore expect to find a different perspective than that which seems to pervade Christian teaching in later times.

Although this is not the only issue of concern to liberation theologies, let us for the moment center our attention on economic matters, and we may be surprised by what we shall find in early Christian writing. On this score, the picture that most of us have is that of a primitive church that had all things in common, discovered that such a system did not work, and promptly forgot it, together with any attempt to reorder or critique the existing economic system. But, although it is true that soon the church began having some rich folk in its midst, and therefore began to mollify some of Jesus' strictures against the rich, it is also true that for centuries it kept alive an understanding of God's will that there should be neither rich nor needy, but that all should have that which was necessary for their sustenance, and that some of its leaders had very harsh words to say about the prevailing economic system and those who profited from it.

Ignatius of Antioch, who wrote seven letters early in the second century while on his way to martyrdom, has been correctly depicted as a zealous defender of orthodoxy. But what most scholars have failed to note is that to him orthodoxy was not only a matter of proper doctrine, but also a matter of right relationship to those in need:

> As to those who profess teachings that have nothing to do with the grace of Jesus Christ . . . you must come to a full realization that those doctrines are completely opposed to the mind of God, for they care nothing about love, they care not for the widow and the orphan, they care not for the hard pressed, nor do they care who is in chains or free, or who is hungry or thirsty.

And a few decades later, Hermas wrote that those who are in need live anxious and tormented lives to the point that some of them are driven to commit homicide, and therefore any Christian who knows of a person in dire need and fails to respond to that situation may be guilty of homicide.

On the other hand, already at the time of Hermas, the rich were joining the church in increasing numbers, and there were those who sought to make it easier for them. Thus, for instance, Clement of Alexandria, in his treatise, *Who Is the Rich to be Saved?* turned what Jesus had to say to the rich ruler into an allegory and said that what mattered was not the riches themselves, but one's attachment to them. If one had riches, but one loved God above them, they would be no obstacle to salvation, but rather a help, for one could then perform greater works of charity.

The question of property and its use, however, became crucial after the conversion of Constantine. Many who flocked to the church were rich. Most church leaders simply accepted such people and were all too glad to have them add part of their wealth and prestige to the church. But there were many others who, while not absolutely refusing to receive the rich, felt that they must insist on the old Christian teachings regarding riches and the responsibility of those who had more than they needed toward those others who were in want. Most of the great "fathers" of the church held economic views which would be considered quite radical in our day.

Ambrose of Milan, for instance, says that "the earth has been created in common for all, rich and poor. Why do you [the rich] claim for yourselves the right to own the land?" And in another place he says that "God created all things to be the common food, and the land to be the common possession of all. Thus, nature begat the common right, and usurpation begat the private." The result of this is that, when you give to the needy, "you do not give to the poor what is yours, but rather return what is theirs." The reason why the birds of the air do not go hungry is that they do not claim anything in particular for each of them, but rather share equally the bounty of God. But a few rich claim everything for themselves, "not only the land, but the sky, the air, the sea," — and here one is reminded of today's quip that solar energy will be developed when someone invents a way to hang a meter on the sun — with the result that "every day are the needy murdered."

These views were shared by many of the great Christian leaders of the fourth and fifth centuries. Among them, Basil the Great says to the rich: "The bread that you hoard belongs to the hungry. The cloak that you keep in your chests belongs to the naked. The shoes that rot in your house belong to the unshod." And therefore, anyone who can do something for the needy and refuses to do so is justly condemned as a homicide. But Basil goes even farther than Ambrose in attacking the wanton growth of capital: "The beasts become fertile when they are young, but quickly cease to be so. But capital produces interest from the very beginning, and this in turn multiplies unto infinity. All that grows ceases to do so when it reaches its normal size. But the money of the greedy never stops growing." . . .

Following the long established tradition to which we have already referred, Chrysostom agrees that iniquity is the only possible source of great riches, for if it is not the very person who is opulent that has committed the necessary iniquities, it must have been that person's ancestors. Since the earth is the Lord's, and the fullness thereof, nothing is to be held by any as privately owned. The rich are not really such, for what they have belongs to others. Anything that one might have, even though legitimately earned, in truth belongs to the poor. And the unjust distribution of wealth increases as time goes by, for all are drawn into the whirlwind of greed, with each trying to outdo those who have gone on before. The rich try to glorify themselves by building opulent palaces, but after their death passersby who never knew them say, "How many tears must that house have cost! How many widows must have suffered injustice, and laborers cheated out of their wages!" Therefore, the result of the vain glory of the rich is exactly the opposite of what they had sought, for even after their death they are cursed, and even by those who never knew them. Finally, it is significant that, commenting on Matthew 25, Chrysostom points out that the judge does not condemn those on his left "because you fornicated, because you committed adultery, because you stole, because you gave false witness or committed perjury. All of these sins are obviously evil, but not as great as callousness and lack of humanity."

Such were the teachings of the first centuries regarding property, riches, and the economic order. And although never again as prevalent as at that time, such teachings were never entirely abandoned.

So far we have dealt only with the question of riches and of the existing economic order. But it is well known that, on such matters as slavery, the church remained silent for centuries. At least, so we have been led to believe. However, when we begin studying the tradition on our own, without the filtering process that has become so common, we find startling cases of opposition to slavery, such as the following words of Gregory of Nyssa, addressed to a slaveowner:

> "I have bought slaves, male and female." Pray tell, at what price? What have you found among all the creatures that is worth as much as human nature? How much money is the mind worth? How many staters did you pay in order to walk away with this creature of God? "Let us make man in our own image and likeness," said God. Tell me, then, who dares buy, who dares sell, one who is the image of God, who is to rule over the earth, who received

from God as an heir all that there is upon the earth? Such power belongs only to God. And I am inclined to say that not even to God.

And yet, we were told that it took Christians centuries to come to the conclusion that slavery was against the divine will, when what in fact did happen was that voices such as that of Gregory and Chrysostom were drowned by those in the church who catered to the powerful.

Surely when it comes to the issues of women and their place in society the situation must be different. And indeed it is, for most of the writings that we have come from males — many of them male ascetics who felt threatened by the very existence of women. But even in this case one occasionally finds surprising words, such as the following, addressed by Cyprian to a consecrated virgin in the church:

> "I will multiply," says God to the woman, "thy sorrows and thy groanings, and in sorrow thou shalt bring forth children, and thy desire shall be to thy husband, and he shall rule over thee." You are free from this sentence. You do not fear the sorrows and the groans of women. You have no fear of child-bearing; nor is your husband lord over you; but your Lord and Head is Christ, after the likeness and in place of man; with that of men your lot and your condition is equal. . . .

In conclusion, although there is no doubt that a great deal of Christian tradition has been oppressive, it is also true that there has been a filtering of the tradition, a selective forgetfulness, so that what we now perceive is a distorted view of the past of the church. Thus, the preacher will carry the principle of ideological suspicion a step further and refuse to take truisms for granted when we are told that there is nothing useful in the church's past. It may well be that the seemingly sympathetic statement is simply an expression of the way tradition appears after it has been filtered by the interests of the powerful. It may well be that a rereading of the documents from the Christian past, particularly those produced by people who were persecuted, maligned, or otherwise opposed by the powerful, will yield fresh insights into the meaning of Scripture when read, so to speak, "from below." We need to remember that early monasticism was a protest against the way the church changed once it became dominated by the concerns of the powerful. Therefore, theology written by those who have taken vows of voluntary poverty often reflects the views of the poor. Ambrose, Augustine, Basil the Great, Gregory the Great, and many of the others quoted above were part of that company, as well as bishops in the church. Their writings can be very rewarding. As a more immediate measure, whenever one is working with a specific biblical text it can also be helpful to check the Scripture reference index that is usually included in the standard translations of these works.

Contemporary Resources

In order to avoid the Lone-Ranger syndrome, the preacher may begin to establish a dialogue with earlier Christian tradition. But this is a lifelong task, and cannot replace the face-to-face contact with living dialogue partners. There can be study groups set up within a ministerial alliance in a local community — or simply by neighboring pastors. This is particularly useful where pastors use *The Revised Common Lectionary.* Then the study can focus on the preaching for a specific day. Because this lectionary is used with adaptation by many denominations, including Protestants and Catholics, such study can challenge the different traditional interpretations we all bring to a text.

The past several years have seen many more minorities and women in this country publish commentaries — including lectionary commentaries — as well as sermons. In addition, there is increasing availability of such resources from around the world — from Asia and Africa, from Latin America and Eastern Europe. Each of these can be very helpful.

African Americans, Hispanics, women, and others who already know and study the writings of representatives of their own groups do not need to be encouraged to do so, for the major figures will already be familiar and helpful to them. However, all may need to be encouraged to read the writings of other groups, as well as interpretations coming from the Third World. This is important, for these various groups will necessarily clash. African Americans resent white women, Hispanics, or Asian Americans entering the labor market and taking the lower paying jobs that previously were theirs. African Americans understandably might resent the growing attention which the Hispanic and Asian minorities are receiving in the media. All oppressed groups in the United States will find their situation worsened by any international economic changes that lessen the flow of wealth to the United States. Furthermore, those who are in power will foster such conflicts between various oppressed groups, so that the conflict is deflected from their communities. The result is a tendency for each group to look after itself — and in a certain way they must, for no one else will.

In particular, English-speaking persons must be very careful in not imposing on other languages English solutions regarding gender. Most languages reflect the culture which gave them shape; and, since such cultures are often sexist, languages also tend to be sexist. Yet, they do this in different ways, and therefore solutions that work in one language do not work in another. Much significant work has been done in English, in order to find ways to make the language more inclusive in terms of gender. It is necessary for those who speak other languages to work in the same direction with reference to their own languages. However, when English-speakers seek to impose on those other languages solutions that work in English, they often project an imperialistic attitude, and a lack of sensitivity to the structure of languages, that is justly resented by others.

In order to minimize such clashes, we must remember that we are not struggling only against a particular person or group that oppresses us. We are struggling against systems that prevent the fulfillment of God's purposes for all creation. There is a connection between racism, classism, colonialism, and sexism. Each of our groups may be attacking the apocalyptic beast from a different angle, and the beast may defend itself by setting us against each other. But we know that the beast is only one, and that the victory won by the Lamb and promised to us is also one.

For these reasons, preachers who are related to one group ought not eschew those resources which reflect other backgrounds. From these they will come to a deeper understanding of the nature of the oppression against which we must all struggle, and will also gain insight into the meaning of the gospel message which they could not have gained from their own group.

Furthermore, as has already been pointed out, we stand at more than one place in the oppressor-oppressed continuum. A Hispanic male may be part of the oppressed minority, but as a male he must also become aware of the oppression of women, both in his culture and in others. A white North American woman may well be aware of the difficulties of her own situation, but from the point of view of those in poor countries, she is part of the society of over-consumption which so oppresses the Third World. In addition, women of every racial and national group need to encounter the views of other women — and there are now writings in translation that make that possible for English-speaking readers. Therefore, as each of us approaches the resources available from other groups, we must use our own hermeneutical circle to understand what these resources have to say.

Obviously, we cannot offer here an exhaustive introduction to all such resources. We shall attempt simply to offer some examples, to show what words of biblical and theological insight are coming from those whom the Lone Rangers take to be no more than dimwitted Tontos.

Unfortunately, the insights of the poor seldom reach printed form directly. We have a startling exception in Ernesto Cardenal's *The Gospel in Solentiname* [Maryknoll, N.Y.: Orbis, 1976-82]. Cardenal is a mystic and a poet, a priest and a political activist, who founded the lay monastery of Our Lady of

Solentiname on an island in a lake in Nicaragua. This was during the time of Somoza, before the Sandanistas came to power. In fact, after the events that we are describing here, but still during the war that led to the downfall of Somoza, the settlement was attacked by the military, and many were killed.

On Sundays, after the reading of the Gospel, Cardenal encouraged the people of the islands — mostly fishermen and their wives, with an occasional student back home for the weekend — to discuss the gospel lesson for the day. The book is simply the transcribed tapes of those conversations. The North American reader may be surprised — perhaps even shocked — by the radical political views of the group and by the way these views are related to the gospel. This alone may serve as a corrective to our tendency to read the Bible in purely "religious" terms. But there is also in the comments of many of these uneducated people an insight into the meaning of various texts, an ability to see what scholarly commentators hardly ever note, which seems to prove the contention that the poor and the oppressed have an edge when it comes to understanding the meaning of the Bible.

In discussing the annunciation, for instance (Luke 1:26-36), these poor people seem to be much more aware of what is going on than are most of our better-educated congregations:

> Someone said: "That angel was being subversive just by announcing that. It's as though someone in Somoza's Nicaragua was announcing a liberator." . . . And another added: "And Mary joins the ranks of the subversives, too, just by receiving that message. I suppose that by doing that she probably felt herself entering into a kind of underground. The birth of the liberator had to be kept secret. It would be known only by the most trusted and a few of the poor people around there, villagers." [pp. 15-16]

And at the end of the conversation a certain Alejandro shows a profound understanding of the relationship between obedience, love, and risk: "It seems to me that here we should admire above all her [Mary's] obedience. And so we should be ready to obey too. This obedience is revolutionary, because it's obedience to love. Obedience to love is very revolutionary, because it commands us to disobey everything else" [p. 18].

There may be much here that an average North American reader will find strange, and even offensive. Yet, the insight remains valuable, that what is taking place in the annunciation is very risky business. Mary is not risking only her good name, as those of us who have been brought up in a middle-class mores will readily understand. She is also risking her very life, by consenting to bear a child who will challenge the existing order.

Let us look at another example from the same book. We have already referred to the political blunder of the magi as they asked around in Jerusalem where was the new king of the Jews that had been born. This point, usually missed by commentators, did not escape the sagacity of these poor and uneducated Nicaraguans, and one of them remarked that "it would be like someone going to Somoza now to ask him where's the man who's going to liberate Nicaragua" [p. 62].

A final example comes from a discussion of the Wedding at Cana (John 2:1-12). We are so used to reading the Bible as a religious document, and so sure of what is proper within the field of religion and what is not, that we miss a great deal of what the Bible has to say against sanctimonious religiosity. But these fisherfolk do not react in the same way. They realize that what is going on is a big party. One of them observes, "isn't it interesting that Jesus gets himself involved for a party? His hour will come sooner because he gave wine at a party. It wasn't for anything more serious." But the most surprising comment is made by a participant who does not speak too often: "If all the water they had for purifying themselves turned into wine on them, now how were they going to perform their ceremonies? I'm sure some of them must have asked him: 'Master, and now how do I purify myself?' And he must have answered them: 'The orders are to have a drink'" [pp. 154, 152].

To our minds, trained to believe about Jesus only that which is proper, this seems sacrilegious. But, does it not come closer than most of our interpretations to the spirit of the Master's teachings and to his repeated disapproval of the religious folk of his time?

The same sort of insight comes from feminist interpretations. Joanna Dewey, after asserting that we must "read the Bible afresh," proceeds to a study of the beginning of the book of Exodus from which she draws unexpected but well substantiated conclusions:

> Certainly in both the story about the midwives and the story of the women's rescue of the baby, the women are acting independently and not as adjuncts of men.
>
> In both stories the actions of the women are actions of disobedience to the authority of Pharaoh. . . . And in both stories the disobedience results in deliverance: The disobedience of the midwives saves the Hebrew people; the disobedience of the mother, sister, and Pharaoh's daughter saves Moses. . . .
>
> And if God was later acting through Moses to deliver the people, then God first of all acted through these women to deliver the people. Women as well as men are God's agents of salvation and, in the story of the exodus,

God's first agents. [Letty M. Russell, ed. *The Liberating Word* (Philadelphia: Westminster, 1976), p. 65]

When one reads the biblical account, one is driven to conclude that she is right. And yet, how many of us have heard sermons stating this fact? By bringing their own experience to bear on the reading of the texts, Dewey and other women are offering the entire church new insights into the biblical message.

Some of these insights have to do with the impact of Jesus' teaching on the commonly accepted views regarding women. Those women who have become conscious of the manner in which they are usually stereotyped object to the prevalent view that a woman is to be defined above all else in her roles as mother and wife. They do not object to those options, nor do they seek to demean their value, just as no male would object to the options and the value of being a husband and a father. What they reject is the notion that, while such roles are not all that a man is expected to be, women are often seen only as real, potential, or frustrated wives and mothers. This obviously serves to keep women at home in their subservient roles, and to prevent them from competing with men in other fields of endeavor. As in other such cases, the traditional interpretation of the Bible leads one to believe that the women who object to such stereotyping will find no support in Scripture. But exactly the opposite is shown by women such as Rachel Conrad Wahlberg, who focuses her attention on two well-known passages.

The first of these is Luke 11:27-28: "While he [Jesus] was saying this, a woman in the crowd raised her voice and said to him, 'Blessed is the womb that bore you, and the breasts that nursed you!' But he said, 'Blessed rather are those who hear the word of God and obey it!'" (NRSV).

Most traditional interpretation centers on the fact that Jesus corrected the woman. Others use this text as an argument against the excessive veneration of Mary. But Rachel Conrad Wahlberg points out here that Jesus is rejecting the stereotype of woman as first of all a reproductive being:

Subsequent centuries have been so accepting of the stereotyped woman that they have not noticed what Jesus said. Religious interpreters have not known what to do with this radical rejection by Jesus of the uterus image. Does he mean to put down the idea of woman as child-bearer? Is he demeaning her function as a fetus-carrier and a baby-suckler?

Remember that only if a woman had children, and preferably boys, was she honored. If she were "barren" she was regarded as one to be pitied. Actually her status in that society was based on the uterus image. Her worth *was* in her procreativeness.

It is mind-blowing to realize that Jesus was actually rejecting this commonly accepted justification for the existence of woman. If not a child-bearer, what was woman? Jesus is saying, *She is one who can hear the will of God and do it.* [*Jesus According to a Woman* (New York: Paulist, 1975), p. 44]

The same author deals with the woman-as-wife stereotype when discussing Mark 12:18-25 and its parallel texts in Matthew and Luke. That is the familiar story of the Sadducees who posed to Jesus the question of the man who died and left a wife, but no children. She was then married in succession to six brothers of her late husband, all of whom died leaving no issue. The question that the Sadducees posed was, whose wife will she be in the resurrection? And Jesus' answer is well known: "When they rise from the dead, they neither marry nor are given in marriage, but are like angels in heaven."

This text is usually interpreted in the sense that in heaven there will be no sexuality. Some males have even understood it to mean that in heaven women will be unnecessary! But when a woman reads this text, she sees much more in it. The question posed by the Sadducees was based on the view of a woman as primarily a wife and someone's possession. It is significant that the question does not start by referring to "a woman who was widowed," but to "seven brothers." The important question is not what will happen to the woman herself. The question is rather that she *belongs* to seven different brothers in this life, and that therefore in the next it will be difficult to decide to which of the seven brothers she belongs. For all intents and purposes, the story could have been about seven brothers who successively inherited a cow from each other. A woman who knows that society stereotypes a woman as "someone's wife" will see in this text much more than will a man.

A woman hears about a durable woman who outlived seven husbands.

A woman hears that this person was someone's property — *seven someones.*

A woman hears that this someone was passed from brother to brother perhaps without her approval, because it was the Deuteronomic law and custom.

A woman understands that not having children would have placed an added stigma on the woman.

A woman hears that Jesus, although he says nothing about levirate marriage, disclaims the dependency of the marriage bond in the resurrection.

A woman hears Jesus declaring that she is not someone's property, that she has equal status in the resurrection, that she has a position not relative to anyone else. She is a spiritual being. At least in heaven she will not achieve her identity through someone else. [*Jesus According to a Woman,* p. 65]

. . . For too long the theological and ecclesiastical establishment of the North Atlantic has been doing theology as if the rest of the world did not exist or had only the secondary sort of existence of the Lone Ranger's Tonto. Tonto has finally decided to speak up. And he is making much more sense than the Lone Ranger ever did! The Lone Ranger, with his mask, his white horse, and his flashy gear, thought that he knew all about doing justice. But Tonto is telling him that one can only know injustice when one suffers it. The only way one can have real access to the resources mentioned in this chapter, and to others like them, is to join the Tontos of our day in the struggle against injustice, and to join them in such a way as to be deprived of white horses and flashy gear. Do-gooder preaching is out. Cries of "hi-ho, Silver" will no longer do. The word of the gospel today, as in the times of Jesus, as ever, comes to us most clearly in the painful groans of the oppressed. We must listen to those groans. We must join the struggle to the point where we too must groan. Or we may choose the other alternative, which is not to hear the gospel at all.

RICHARD B. HAYS

A Hermeneutic of Trust

Richard B. Hays is George Washington Ivey Professor of New Testament at Duke Divinity School. He is a leader in the field of New Testament studies, internationally recognized for his work on the letters of Paul and on New Testament ethics. His scholarly work has bridged the disciplines of biblical criticism and literary studies, exploring the traditional and innovative ways in which early Christian writers interpreted Scripture. Hays is the author of six books, including *Echoes of Scripture in the Letters of Paul, First Corinthians* (a commentary), and *The Moral Vision of the New Testament: Community, Cross, New Creation*. Trained at Yale and Emory universities, Hays follows the "Yale School" led by Hans Frei and George Lindbeck (as well as Nicholas Lash) in his understanding of the ecclesial nature of Scripture and the church's authority in its interpretation. Like few biblical scholars, Hays moves easily (and sometimes controversially) between the church and the academy. He has gone against the grain of much modern biblical criticism by recognizing the theological integrity of the New Testament. There is something *prior* and larger in the New Testament than isolated texts, namely, the self-revelation of God in Jesus Christ. In the essay below — originally given as an address before the Society of Biblical Literature and later adapted for publication — he argues that the interpreter must submit himself or herself to the Bible and begin, hermeneutically, from the trustworthiness of the revealed God and not from various cultural or ideological "suspicions." Although Hays has written relatively little on homiletics, his biblical and theological work brims with implications for Christian preaching.

Richard B. Hays, "Salvation by Trust? Reading the Bible Faithfully," *The Christian Century* 114, no. 7 (26 February 1997): 218-23.

The Protestant Reformers of the sixteenth century proclaimed that God's word in Scripture must serve as the final judge of all human tradition and experience. Left to our own devices we are capable of infinite self-deception, confusion, and evil. We therefore must turn to Scripture and submit ourselves to it, the Reformers insisted, in order to find our disorders rightly diagnosed and healed. Only through the biblical writers' testimony do we encounter the message of God's grace; only the revelation of Jesus Christ, disclosed uniquely and irreplaceably through the testimony of the evangelists and apostles, tells us the truth about the merciful God and our relationship to that God. Without this word which comes to us from outside ourselves, we are lost.

Clearly, the climate in which we read the Bible has changed drastically since Luther and Calvin put pen to paper. Living as we do on this side of the Enlightenment, we cannot escape the intellectual impact of the great "masters of suspicion": Nietzsche, Marx, and more recently Foucault, along with other purveyors of "critical theory." These thinkers have sought to demystify language and to expose the ways in which our linguistic and cultural systems are constructed by ideologies that further the interests of those who hold power.

The Bible has not been exempt from such suspicious scrutiny. One need only consider the book display at the annual American Academy of Religion convention. Anyone who spends time browsing there will find the stalls flooded with books that apply a hermeneutic of suspicion to biblical texts. Some portray the apostolic witnesses less as revelatory witnesses to God's mercy than as oppressive promulgators of abusive images of God. Elisabeth Schüssler Fiorenza, for example, writes that "a feminist critical hermeneutics of suspicion places a warning label on all biblical texts: *Caution! Could be dangerous to your health and survival*" (in *Feminist Interpretation of the Bible*, edited by Letty Russell).

I'm not suggesting that suspicious interpreters categorically reject the Bible; most of them believe it can contain both liberating and oppressive messages. They insist, nonetheless, that the Bible be subjected to ideological critique. Elsewhere, Schüssler Fiorenza explains:

> No biblical patriarchal text that perpetuates violence against women, children, or "slaves" should be accorded the status of divine revelation if we do not want to turn the God of the Bible into a God of violence. That does not mean that we cannot preach . . . on the household code texts of the New Testament. It only means that we must preach them critically in order to unmask them as texts promoting patriarchal violence *(Bread Not Stone: The Challenge of Feminist Biblical Interpretation).*

I welcome the moral passion of statements like Schüssler Fiorenza's. Sadly, our common history is marked by epidemic violence, including violence against women, children, and the powerless. Certainly this violence is to be condemned, and interpreters of the Bible have good grounds for proclaiming such condemnation. The difficulty in which we find ourselves, however, is this: If the Bible itself, the revelatory identity-defining text of the Christian community, is portrayed as oppressive, on what basis do we know God or relate to God? A corollary question has crucial implications for biblical interpretation: If the Bible is dangerous, on what ground do we stand in conducting a critique of Scripture that will render it less harmful?

For Schüssler Fiorenza the answer to the latter question is clear: a feminist critical hermeneutic "does not appeal to the Bible as its primary source but begins with women's own experience and vision of liberation." Experience (of a certain sort) is treated as unambiguously revelatory, and the Bible is critically scrutinized in its light. Regrettably, many practitioners of the hermeneutics of suspicion, and by no means only feminist interpreters, are remarkably credulous about the claims of experience. As a result, they endlessly critique the biblical texts but rarely get around to hearing Scripture's critique of us or hearing its message of grace.

While the hermeneutics of suspicion — rightly employed — occupies a proper place in any attempt to interpret the Bible for our time, I want to argue that a hermeneutics of trust is also both necessary and primary. In order to get our bearings on the question of our fundamental attitude toward Scripture, I propose that we take our cue from the Reformers and return to Scripture itself.

If we attend carefully to Paul's treatment of trust and distrust in his Letter to the Romans, the apostle may lead us to suspect our own suspicions. We can gain a purchase on Paul's thinking about trust and distrust by examining how in Romans he uses the words *faith* (in Greek, *pistis*) and its opposite, literally *unfaith (apistia)*. According to Paul, those who stand in right relation to God are those who hear and trust what God has spoken. He laments Israel's tragic failure to do this, and the name he gives that failure is *apistia*. The term refers both to the failure of the people of Israel to obey God's Torah and to their failure to trust God's covenant promises — and the two things are bound closely together. Their *apistia* has been brought into stark focus for Paul through their negative response to the proclaimed gospel of Jesus Christ. He addresses the problem explicitly in Romans 3:1-4:

> Then what advantage has the Jew? Or what is the value of circumcision? Much in every way. For in the first place they were entrusted with the ora-

cles of God. What if some were unfaithful *(epistesan)?* Their *apistia* doesn't nullify the *pistis* of God, does it? By no means!

Paul's wordplay highlights the contrast between human infidelity and God's fidelity. God's faithfulness *(pistis)* to Israel is declared to Israel through the word of promise. But Israel, failing to trust that word, is guilty of unfaithfulness — *apistia.* We might well translate the word here as "distrust" or "suspicion." Rather than trusting the scriptural oracles of God (which, in Paul's view, point to Christ and the church), they have slid away into unfaithfulness just like the Gentiles. Nonetheless, their unfaithfulness cannot negate the faithfulness of the God who has embraced them through the covenant promise spoken to them.

The paradoxical relation between Israel's unfaithfulness and the divine faithfulness creates the problem that Paul wrestles with throughout the letter. His reflections on these issues culminate in chapter 11, where the theme of Israel's *apistia* arises once again in Paul's metaphor about the olive branches broken off the tree: "They were broken off because of their *apistia,* but you [Gentiles] stand only through *pistis.* . . . But even these, if they do not persist in *apistia,* will be grafted in, for God has the power to graft them in again."

Earlier in the letter, Paul has depicted Abraham, in contrast to unfaithful Israel, as the figural type of trust in God:

> Hoping against hope, he trusted that he would become "the father of many nations," according to what was said, "So numerous shall your descendants be" [Gen. 15:5]. He did not weaken in trust *(pistis)* when he considered his own body, which was already as good as dead (for he was about a hundred years old), or when he considered the barrenness of Sarah's womb. No *apistia* made him waver concerning the promise of God, but he grew strong in trust *(pistis)* as he gave glory to God, being fully convinced that God was able to do what he had promised (4:18-21).

This passage is particularly interesting because Abraham's *pistis* is interpreted explicitly as his trust in God's promise despite the promise's incongruity with Abraham's own experience of sterility and frustration. Abraham might have had good reason to exercise a hermeneutic of suspicion toward the divine word that had promised him numerous descendants; all the empirical evidence — his experience — seemed to disprove God's word.

Nonetheless, according to Paul, Abraham wrestled with his doubts, discounted his own experience, rejected skepticism, and clung to the promise of God: "No *apistia,* no suspicion, made him waver. . . ." Thus, Abraham becomes the prototype of the community of faith, which interprets all human experience through trust in God's word. In short, Abraham exemplifies a hermeneutic of consent, a hermeneutic of trust.

A trusting hermeneutic is essential for all who believe the word of the resurrection but do not yet see death made subject to God. The hermeneutics of trust turns out to be, on closer inspection, a hermeneutics of death and resurrection — a way of seeing the whole word through the lens of the kerygma. Our reliance on God entails a death to common sense, and our trust is validated only by the resurrection.

For Paul the theme of trust — *pistis* — is also intimately related to the formation of right relations between God and humans. Another way of saying this is that for Paul the themes of trust and atonement are inseparable. But I must sound an important caveat here. We must not suppose that we can place ourselves in right relation to God through our own act of trust, as though faith were a meritorious work. Rather, Paul's argument is that covenant relationship is restored by God's initiative "through the faithfulness of Jesus Christ." Thus, for Paul, trust and atonement are inextricably linked, but they are linked in the person of Jesus Christ.

Paul's view of the relationship between trust and atonement is most compactly articulated in Romans 3. The argument goes like this:

1. Israel's *apistia* cannot nullify the *pistis* of God (3:3-6a).
2. Jews and Greeks alike are under the power of sin (3:9-18).
3. The Law holds the whole world accountable to God but has no power to justify those who are under the power of sin — to set them in right relation to God (3:19-20).
4. Therefore God's justice has been manifested apart from the Law through the faithfulness of Jesus Christ (3:21-22) — through his obedient, self-sacrificial death on the cross.

Thus, according to Paul, God has overcome our *apistia* through a dramatic new act of *pistis* — the *pistis* of Jesus Christ whom God "put forward" as a definitive demonstration of God's own covenant-faithfulness (3:25). That is the meaning of "the righteousness of God" (3:21). Our relationship of trust with God is restored through the faith of Jesus Christ.

Those who receive this good news respond to it in turn with trust. Their *pistis,* which is prefigured in the Old Testament story of Abraham, becomes shaped by the pattern of Jesus' own faith-obedience. That is part of what Paul means when he says that those whom God calls are to be "conformed to the image of his Son" (Rom. 8:29), and when he calls on his readers to model themselves upon Christ Jesus who emptied himself and became obedient even unto death on a cross (Phil. 2:5-13).

Thus, atonement for Paul is not merely the forgiveness of sins through a vicarious blood sacrifice. Atonement also entails the transformation of God's people into the image of Jesus Christ, who is the embodiment of trust in God. Because Jesus trusted, we are both called and enabled to trust.

Paul's understanding of trust not only shapes his view of atonement; it also informs the apostle's own hermeneutical theory and practice. Israel, he says, failed to trust the oracles of God (Rom. 3:2-3), but he is determined that this error not be repeated in the interpretative practices of the new community of faith constituted by the trust of Jesus. With his mind remade by the gospel, Paul goes back to Scripture and reads it anew through a hermeneutic of trust.

Rereading Scripture from a new perspective was as challenging a task for Paul as trusting God's promise was for Abraham. The actual experience of Paul's missionary preaching had created a serious difficulty for both Paul and the new community. As the scholar Paula Fredriksen has expressed it, among those who believed the gospel, there were "too many Gentiles, too few Jews, and no end in sight." If God's purpose was to overcome Israel's *apistia,* what had gone wrong? Why did Israel persist in *apistia* even when it heard the good news proclaimed?

The Jews' rejection and the Gentiles' acceptance of the gospel drove Paul back to Scripture. The promises of God to Israel must be true, he reasoned, because "the gifts and the call of God are irrevocable" (Rom. 11:29). But how can this be true in light of his own experience? Jews refused to accept the good news, and God apparently had conferred grace upon those who had not even been seeking righteousness at all — the Gentiles. Scripture must be true, but how can this situation be understood?

The problem comes to a head in Romans 9–11. "I say then, has God abandoned his people?" (11:1). Paul's answer is a ringing "By no means!" Trusting that God had not abandoned Israel, he wrestled with Scripture and found his way to a powerful new reading of God's promises.

Romans 9–11 is a powerful example of the hermeneutics of trust in action. In these chapters Paul achieves a transformative rereading of Scripture through the lens of the conviction he articulated earlier in Romans 5:8: "God shows his love for us in that while we were yet sinners Christ died for us." This conviction, applied to the problem of Israel's *apistia,* leads Paul to discover in Scripture both the prefiguring of God's calling of the Gentiles ("Those who were not my people, I will call 'my people'" — 9:25, quoting Hosea 2:23) and the prefiguring of God's ultimate mercy on Israel ("God has not abandoned his people, 'whom he foreknew'" — 11:2, quoting Psalm 94:14).

In Paul's fresh reading of Scripture the whole mysterious drama of God's election of Israel — Israel's hardening, the incorporation of Gentiles into the people of God, and Israel's ultimate restoration — is displayed as foretold in Scripture itself, but this foretelling can be recognized only when Scripture is read through the hermeneutics of trust. God's oracles and promises are interpreted anew, in ways that no one could have foreseen, in light of the experience of grace through the death and resurrection of Jesus. At the same time, the church's experience in Paul's own historical moment is interpreted in light of Scripture, which leads Paul to warn Gentile believers against being wise in their own conceits. Events are in God's hands. Gentiles have no reason to boast. The process through which experience is positively correlated with Scripture is possible only through the hermeneutics of trust.

What consequences follow from this analysis of Paul's hermeneutic of trust for our own work as interpreters of the word? At least three things can be said. First, in order to read Scripture rightly, we must trust the God who speaks through Scripture. As Schüssler Fiorenza rightly insists, this God is not a God of violence, not an abuser, not a deceiver. This God so passionately desires our safety and wholeness that he has given his own Son to die for us. "The one who did not spare his own Son but gave him up for us all, how will he not also graciously give us all things, along with him?" (Rom. 8:32). Like Abraham, like Mary, like Jesus, like Paul, we stand before God with empty and open hands. That is the posture in which the reading of Scripture is rightly performed. The German New Testament scholar Peter Stuhlmacher says something similar when he speaks of a "hermeneutics of consent" — a readiness to receive trustingly what a loving God desires to give us through the testimony of those who have preceded us in the faith.

Second, if we adopt a hermeneutics of trust, what becomes of the hermeneutics of suspicion? Is all questioning to be excluded, all critical reading banished? By no means. Asking necessary and difficult questions is not to be equated with *apistia*. When we read Scripture through the hermeneutics of trust in God we discover that we should indeed be suspicious — suspicious first of ourselves, because our own minds have been corrupted and shaped by the present evil age. Our minds must be transformed by grace, and that happens nowhere more powerfully than through reading Scripture receptively and trustingly with the aid of the Holy Spirit.

Reading receptively and trustingly does not mean accepting everything in the text at face value, as Paul's own critical sifting of the Torah demonstrates. Cases may arise in which we must acknowledge internal tensions within Scripture that require us to choose guidance from one biblical witness and to reject another. Because the witness of Scripture itself is neither simple nor univocal, the hermeneutics of trust is necessarily a matter of faithful struggle to hear and discern. Consequently, we welcome the readings offered by feminists and other interpreters whose experience enables them to hear the biblical texts in new and challenging ways.

At the same time, we should be suspicious of the institutions that govern and shape interpretation. That means not only ecclesiastical but also academic institutions. If our critical readings lead us away from trusting the grace of God in Jesus Christ, then something is amiss, and we would do well to interrogate the methods and presuppositions that have taught us to distance ourselves arrogantly or fearfully from the text and to miss Scripture's gracious word of promise.

My concern that distrust may impede our reading of the Bible leads me to my final point. The real work of interpretation is to hear the text. We must consider how to read and preach Scripture in a way that opens up its message and both models and fosters trust in God. So much of the ideological critique that currently dominates the academy fails to foster these qualities. Scripture is critiqued but never interpreted. The critic exposes but never exposits. Thus the word itself recedes into the background, and we are left talking only about the politics of interpretation, having lost the capacity to perform interpretations.

Most of us in the academy are weary of these tactics of critical evasion. And perhaps the tide is beginning to turn. This past fall, Frank Lentricchia, who teaches English at Duke University, published a remarkable public recantation of his prior complicity with an approach to literary criticism that concentrates on theory and ignores literature. The piece, which appeared in *Lingua Franca,* is titled "Last Will and Testament of an Ex-Literary Critic."

Lentricchia, whose earlier work earned him the epithet "the Dirty Harry of literary theory," is the author of *Criticism and Social Change* (1983), which urges us to regard all literature as "the most devious of rhetorical discourses (writing with political designs upon us all), either in opposition to or in complicity with the power in place." But Lentricchia has grown impatient with having his own critical perspective parroted by graduate students who have no love of literature, no appreciation for the themes and content of great literature — indeed, who rarely read it at all because they are so enamored of "critical theory." So now Lentricchia repents publicly:

> Over the last ten years, I've pretty much stopped reading literary criticism, because most of it isn't literary. But criticism it is of a sort — the sort that stems from the sense that one is morally superior to the writers that one is supposedly describing. This posture is assumed when those writers represent the major islands of Western literary tradition, the central cultural en-

gine — so it goes — of racism, poverty, sexism, homophobia, and imperialism: a cesspool that literary critics would expose for mankind's benefit. . . . It is impossible, this much is clear, to exaggerate the heroic self-inflation of academic literary criticism. . . . The fundamental, if only implied, message of much literary criticism is self-righteous, and it takes this form: "T. S. Eliot is a homophobe and I am not. Therefore, I am a better person than Eliot. Imitate me, not Eliot." To which the proper response is: "But T. S. Eliot could really write, and you can't. Tell us truly, is there no filth in your soul?" (*Lingua Franca*, Sept.-Oct. 1996, p. 60)

Lentricchia's question, "Tell us truly, is there no filth in your soul?" reaches back, perhaps unwittingly, to the deeper roots from which the Western literary imagination springs — an imaginative tradition that owes much to Paul's hermeneutic of trust in God and suspicion of ourselves. Precisely because there is filth in our own souls we come to the texts of Scripture expecting to find the hidden things of our hearts laid bare and expecting to encounter there the God who loves us.

When I was an undergraduate at Yale University, students flocked to Alvin Kernan's lecture courses on Shakespeare. Kernan's work predated the academy's current infatuation with ideological criticism. Even though it was the late 1960s and we were all living in an atmosphere charged with political suspicion and protest, none of this overtly impinged on Kernan's lectures. Kernan was not a flashy lecturer. What, then, was the draw?

He loved the texts. His teaching method, as I remember it, was simply to engage in reflective close readings of the Shakespeare tragedies and comedies, delineating their rich texture of image and metaphor and opening up their complex central themes — moral, philosophical, and religious. Often, Kernan would devote a significant part of his lecture time to reading the text aloud, not in a highly dramatic manner, but with sensitivity to the texts' rhythms and semantic nuances. I would often sit in class thinking, "Oh, I hadn't *heard* that in the text before." And I would leave the class pondering the problems that Shakespeare addressed: love, betrayal, fidelity, sacrifice, death, and hope.

In Shakespeare's *Measure for Measure,* the self-righteous villain Angelo pronounces a death sentence on Claudio, who is guilty of committing fornication. Claudio's sister Isabella comes to Angelo to plead for the life of her brother, but Angelo, who is trying to manipulate Isabella into bed with him, spurns her suit, saying,

Your brother is a forfeit of the law,
And you but waste your words.

Isabella's reply alludes to the great theme of Romans and calls upon the hypocritical judge Angelo to see his life anew in light of God's judgment and grace:

> Why, all the souls that were were forfeit once;
> And He that might the vantage best have took
> Found out the remedy. How would you be
> If He, which is the top of judgment, should
> But judge you as you are? O, think on that;
> And mercy then will breathe within your lips,
> Like man new made.

Isabella resists the oppressor by applying a hermeneutic of suspicion to his pose of righteousness and by appealing to a hermeneutic of trust in the biblical story of God's mercy. Isabella is a profound interpreter of Scripture. We should follow her example.

· V ·

RHETORIC

AUGUSTINE

The Uses of Rhetoric

Rhetoric is the theory and practice of persuasive discourse. An ancient art, it encompasses the written and the spoken word. Many of the church's greatest preachers and bishops were trained as rhetoricians. Before he became a priest and a bishop, Augustine (354-430) occupied the imperial chair of rhetoric in Milan. Nevertheless, the church agonized over its use of rhetorical strategies and forms, encumbered as the classical tradition was with pagan associations. Where was the Holy Spirit in the rhetoric of preaching? The contemporary debate over rhetoric has centered on the use of communications theory and media techniques in service of the gospel. Theologians such as Amos Wilder have questioned the classical focus on *persuasion* as the end of all speech, celebrating instead the rich diversity of biblical forms of expression. Augustine helped relieve the church's problem for well over a millennium by codifying a Christian approach to the rhetoric of preaching. He asked why the sophists should brandish their rhetorical artillery while Christians stand unarmed. His principle of the church's ownership of all truth and beauty, wherever they are found, helped lay the foundations of Christian culture. In Book 4 of *On Christian Doctrine* Augustine restates broad Ciceronian principles and transposes them into homiletical theory. He addresses standard considerations of audience, diction, rhythm, and style, but subjects them all to the authority of the Bible, which, in Augustine's treatment, is not only a source of doctrine but also a handbook of style. Thus the preacher not only exegetes the text but also uses it as a stylistic model for his sermon. Augustine profusely illustrates his comments on the subdued, the temperate, and the majestic styles with detailed rhetorical analyses of New Testament texts. In both his preaching and his homiletics, he steered the Western church between the casualness of the simple homily and the excesses of the grand oration. He joined his discriminating love of rhetoric to the prior claims of Christian truth and in so doing produced the church's first and most influential rhetoric of preaching.

Augustine, *Teaching Christianity* [*On Christian Doctrine*], trans. Edmund Hill, OP, ed. John E. Rotelle, OSA, in *The Works of Saint Augustine*, Vol. 11, bk. 4, par. 2-64 *passim* (Hyde Park, N.Y.: New City Press), pp. 201-6, 212-22, 233-41.

A nd so first of all I must preface my remarks by dashing the expectations of any readers, who may think perhaps that I am going to give them the rules of rhetoric which I myself learned and taught in the secular schools. I hereby warn them not to expect such things from me, not because they are of no use at all, but because even if they are of some use, they are to be learned elsewhere, if any good man should chance to have the leisure to study this subject too. Only they should not be looked for from me, either in this work or in any other.

Rhetoric, after all, being the art of persuading people to accept something, whether it is true or false, would anyone dare to maintain that truth should stand there without any weapons in the hands of its defenders against falsehood; that those speakers, that is to say, who are trying to convince their hearers of what is untrue, should know how to get them on their side, to gain their attention and have them eating out of their hands by their opening remarks, while these who are defending the truth should not? That those should utter their lies briefly, clearly, plausibly, and these should state their truths in a manner too boring to listen to, too obscure to understand, and finally too repellent to believe? That those should attack the truth with specious arguments, and assert falsehoods, while these should be incapable of either defending the truth or refuting falsehood? That those, to move and force the minds of their hearers into error, should be able by their style to terrify them, move them to tears, make them laugh, give them rousing encouragement, while these on behalf of truth stumble along slow, cold and half asleep?

Could anyone be so silly as to suppose such a thing? So since facilities are available for learning to speak well, which is of the greatest value in leading people either along straight or along crooked ways, why should good men not study to acquire the art, so that it may fight for the truth, if bad men can prostitute it to the winning of their vain and misguided cases in the service of iniquity and error?

But be that as it may, whatever the rules whose observance makes for what is called fluency and eloquence, when habitually applied by a skillful tongue in its choice of a wide and colorful vocabulary, they should be learned apart from what I am writing here, in the proper time and place set aside for such work, and at the most suitable age, by those who can learn them quickly. For even the leading lights of Roman eloquence did not hesitate to say that unless you can master this art quickly, you can never master it at all. Whether this is true or not, what need is there for us to decide? For even if they could eventually be mastered by the slower spirits, we do not consider them of such importance that we would wish to impose the learning of them upon men of mature or even venerable age. It is enough that this subject should be the concern of the young, and not even of all of those whom we desire to have educated for the service of the church, but only of those who are not yet busy with more urgent requirements, which undoubtedly take precedence over this one.

The fact is that, given a bright and eager disposition, eloquence will come more readily to those who read and listen to eloquent speakers than to those who pore over the rules of eloquence. Nor is there any lack of ecclesiastical writers, over and above the canon of Scripture that has been set for our salvation at the summit of authority, by whose style a capable man will be influenced when he reads them, even if that is not his concern, but he is only interested in what they have to say; and he will put this to good use when he has occasion to write, or dictate, or finally even to preach what he has in mind that accords with piety and the rule of faith.

But if such a disposition is lacking, then these rules of rhetoric cannot be grasped; or even if they can be to some extent and with great effort impressed on a person and understood, they will not be of any use, seeing that those who have learned them and are fluent and attractive speakers cannot all think about them, in order to speak in accordance with them, while they are speaking, unless they are actually discussing them. Indeed I imagine that there are scarcely any of them who can do both at the same time, that is speak well, and in order to do this think about those rules for public speaking while they are speaking. You would have to take care, after all, not to let what you had to say escape your mind, while you were giving all your attention to saying it artistically. And yet in the speeches and the style of eloquent speakers you will find that the rules of eloquence have been implemented, which they were not thinking about either in order to speak, or while they were speaking, and this whether they had learned them formally, or never even encountered them. They implement them because they are eloquent, they do not apply them in order to be eloquent.

So then, infants only become speakers by learning the speech and pronunciation of speakers; why cannot people become eloquent without any formal training in the art of public speaking, but simply by reading and hearing the speeches of the eloquent and, as far as they have the chance to follow this up, by imitating them? Why, we have surely all experienced examples of this, have we not? I mean, we know a great many people, quite innocent of the rules of rhetoric, who are much more eloquent than a great many people that have learned them; but we don't know anybody like this who has not read and heard the debates and the style of eloquent speakers.

Even the art of grammar, after all, in which we learn about correctness of speech, would not need to be taught to boys, if they had the good fortune to grow up and live among people who spoke correctly. That is to say, without knowing any of the names of grammatical faults, their own sound habits of speech would enable them to point out and avoid faulty grammar on the lips of any speaker, in the way townspeople, even though illiterate, will find fault with the speech of rustics.

The interpreter and teacher of the divine Scriptures, therefore, the defender of right faith and the hammer of error, has the duty of both teaching what is good and unteaching what is bad; and in this task of speaking it is his duty to win over the hostile, to stir up the slack, to point out to the ignorant what is at stake and what they ought to be looking for. When, though, he finds them friendly, attentive, willing to learn, or renders them so himself, further tactics have to be employed, as the case requires. If the listeners need to be instructed, this calls for the narrative style, provided, at least, that they need to be informed about the subject being dealt with, while for the clearing up of doubts and the establishment of certainty, reasoned arguments and documentary proofs are needed.

But if the listeners are to be moved rather than instructed, so as not to become sluggish in acting upon what they know, and so as to give a real assent to things they admit are true, more forceful kinds of speaking are called for. Here what is necessary is words that implore, that rebuke, that stir, that check, and whatever other styles may avail to move the audience's minds and spirits. And in fact practically nobody, when it comes to public speaking, neglects doing the things I have said.

Some people, of course, do it all in a dull, unattractive, and cold sort of way, while others do it with wit, elegance, and feeling. In any case, those who can speak and discuss things wisely, even though they cannot do so eloquently, must now undertake the task we are concerned with in such a way as to benefit their listeners, even though less than they would have benefited them if they could also speak eloquently. Beware, on the other hand, of those whose unwisdom has a flood of eloquence at its command, and all the more so, the more their audience takes pleasure in things it is profitless to hear, and assumes that because they hear them speaking fluently, they are also speaking the truth. This consideration did not even escape those who thought the art of rhetoric was worth teaching; for they admitted that "wisdom without eloquence is of little use to society, while eloquence without wisdom is frequently extremely prejudicial to it, never of any use." If those therefore who have propounded the rules of eloquence have been obliged, in the very books in which they have done this, to make such a confession at the instigation of truth, even though they were ignorant of the true, that is to say the heavenly, wisdom which *comes down from the Father of lights* (James 1:17); how much more ought we to have no other opinion, seeing that we are sons and ministers of this wisdom?

Now a person is all the more or the less able to speak wisely, the more or less progress he has made in the Holy Scriptures. I don't mean just in reading them frequently and committing them to memory, but in understanding them well and diligently exploring their senses. There are people, after all, who read them and neglect them — read them in order to have them all at their fingertips, neglect trying to understand them. Unquestionably far and away to be preferred to these are people who do not have their words at their fingertips, but can see into the heart of them with the eyes of their own hearts. But better than either is the man who can both quote them at will and understand them as they deserve.

For the man, therefore, who has the duty of saying wisely even what he cannot say eloquently, it is supremely necessary that he should have the words of the Scriptures at his fingertips. For the poorer he perceives himself to be in his own words, the richer it behooves him to be in those of Scripture. In this way he can prove what he says in his own words from the words of Scripture, and what carried less weight said in his own words can somehow or other grow weightier with the support of that greater testimony. For though he may not be so good at pleasing his audience by the way he states his point, he will please them by proving it.

There is the man, on the other hand, who wishes to speak not only wisely but eloquently, since he will surely be of more use if he can do both. Him I much prefer to send off to read or listen to eloquent speakers and to practice imitating them, rather than instructing him to devote his time to teachers of the art of rhetoric, provided, that is, that those whom he reads or listens to are genuinely and reliably renowned for having spoken, or for speaking, wisely as well as eloquently. Those, you see, who speak eloquently are listened to with pleasure, those who speak wisely, with wholesome profit. That is why Scripture does not say, "A multitude of eloquent men" but *A multitude of wise men is the health of the world* (Wisd. Sol. 6:24). Now just as bitter but wholesome things often have to be taken, so pernicious sweet things have to be shunned. But what could be better than the pleasantly wholesome, or the wholesomely pleasant? The more eagerly, after all, what pleases is sought here, the easier it is for what is wholesome to be imparted. There are, then, churchmen who have commented on the divine utterances not only wisely but also eloquently; it is more a matter of there not being time enough to read them than of their not being available to those who have the will and the leisure to do so.

Examples of Eloquent Wisdom
from Biblical Authors: Saint Paul

Here, no doubt, someone may ask whether our authors, whose divinely inspired writings have provided us with a canon of the most salutary authority, are only to be called wise, or also eloquent. This is indeed a question that it is the easiest thing in the world for me to answer, and for those who agree with what I say in this matter. The fact is that where I understand these authors, it seems to me that not only could there be nothing wiser, but also nothing more eloquent. And I make bold to say that all who rightly understand what these authors are saying also thereby understand that they could not and should not have said it in the least differently. For just as one sort of eloquence goes with youth, while another suits riper years — and it should not in fact be called eloquence if it does not match the person of the speaker — so too there is a kind that becomes men thought worthy of the highest authority and in fact of being called divine. This is the style in which they spoke, and no other becomes them, nor does this one become any other persons. With them it accords perfectly, whereas the more lowly it appears, the higher does it soar above other writers, not by any kind of windiness, but by its very solidity.

Where, however, I do not understand them, their eloquence is indeed less apparent to me, but I do not doubt that it is of the same quality as where I do understand. It was also right for this obscurity of the divine and saving utterances to be mixed in with such clear eloquence, because in order for us to make progress in our understanding we need the mental exercise of wrestling with the text as well as the intellectual satisfaction of discovering what it means.

Here are these people, rating their style above the style of our authors because it is more inflated, not because it is grander; well, I could show them all the strengths and graces of eloquence, on which they so preen themselves, in the sacred writings of those authors, whom divine providence has provided us with, to instruct us and transfer us from this crooked age into one of blessedness. But it is not what these men have in common with the orators or poets of the Gentiles that delights me more than I can say in their style of eloquence. What really amazes and astonishes me is that through another kind of eloquence of their own they employed this eloquence of ours in such a way that it was neither lacking nor obtrusive in their writings, because it was important that it should be neither rejected nor paraded by them. The first would be true if they avoided it altogether, the second could be thought to be the case, if it was too easily recognized in their writings. And in those passages where it can perhaps be detected by the learned, such things are being said that the words they are said with seem to spring spontaneously from the subject matter, rather than to be contributed by the writer, so that you could almost imagine wisdom stepping out from her own house, that is from the breast of the wise man, followed by eloquence as her inseparable, even if uninvited, lady in waiting.

Could anybody fail to see, for example, what the apostle was wishing to say here, and how wisely he said it: *We glory in tribulations, knowing that tribu-*

lation results in patience, patience in approbation, approbation in hope, while hope does not confound, because the love of God has been poured out in our hearts through the Holy Spirit which has been given to us (Rom. 5:3-5)? Were any inexpert expert, if I may so put it, to maintain that here the apostle was observing the rules of the art of rhetoric, would he not be laughed out of court by Christians both learned and unlearned? And yet one can here observe the figure of speech which in Greek is called *klimax,* while in Latin some people called it *gradatio,* because they were unwilling to say "ladder"; when words or meanings are linked together, one being spun from another, as here we can see patience spun from tribulation, approbation from patience, hope from approbation.

There is also another embellishment to be observed, that after some phrases, each terminated by a pause, which our people call "clauses" or just "phrases," while the Greeks call them *kolons* and *kommas,* there follows a round or circuit, which they call a *periodos,* whose clauses are held in suspense by the voice of the speaker, until it ends with the last of them. Thus the first of the clauses that precede the period is *that tribulation results in patience,* the second is *patience in approbation,* the third *approbation in hope.* Then the period is joined on, consisting of three clauses, of which the first is *while hope does not confound,* the second *because the love of God has been poured out in our hearts,* the third *through the Holy Spirit which has been given to us.* Now this is the sort of thing that is taught in courses on the art of eloquence. So while we are not saying that the apostle deliberately observed the rules of eloquence, we are still not denying that eloquence waited upon his wisdom. . . .

Precisely this is eloquence, then, in the matter of teaching: to ensure, not that what was thought repellent should be found to be pleasing, or that something disliked should still be done, but that a point that was obscure or simply missed should be indicated and cleared up. If this is done, however, in a disagreeable way, only a few listeners will get any profit from it, and those the most serious, who are eager to know what there is to be learned, however dismally and crudely it is expressed. When they have attained this object, they feed enjoyably on truth itself; it is indeed the characteristic trait of good minds and dispositions to love in words what is true, not the words themselves.

What, after all, is the use of a golden key if it cannot open what we want, or what is wrong with a wooden key if it can, since all we are looking for is that closed doors should be opened to us? But yes, there is a certain similarity between feeding and learning; so because so many people are fussy and fastidious, even those foodstuffs without which life cannot be supported need their pickles and spices.

Three Functions of Eloquence:
To Teach, to Delight, to Sway

An eloquent man once said, you see, and what he said was true, that to be eloquent you should speak "so as to teach, to delight, to sway." Then he added,
"Teaching your audience is a matter of necessity, delighting them a matter of
being agreeable, swaying them a matter of victory." Of these three, the one put
first, that is the necessity of teaching, is to be found in the things we are saying,
the remaining two in the way we say it. Therefore the person who is saying
something with the intention of teaching should not consider he has yet said
anything of what he wants to the person he wishes to teach, so long as he is not
understood. Because even if he has said something he understands himself, he
is not to be regarded as having said it to the person he is not understood by,
while if he has been understood, he has said it, whatever his way of saying it
may have been.

If on the other hand he also wishes to delight the person he is saying it to,
or to sway him, he will not succeed in doing so whatever his way of saying it
may have been; but in order to do so, it makes all the difference how he says it.
Now just as the listener needs to be delighted if you are to hold his attention
and keep him listening, so he needs to be swayed, if you are to move him to act.
And just as he is delighted if you speak agreeably, so in the same way he is
swayed if he loves what you promise him, fears what you threaten him with,
hates what you find fault with, embraces what you commend to him, deplores
what you strongly insist is deplorable; if he rejoices over what you declare to be
a matter for gladness, feels intense pity for those whom your words present to
his very eyes as objects of pity, shuns those whom in terrifying tones you proclaim are to be avoided; and anything else that can be done by eloquence in the
grand manner to move the spirits of the listeners, not to know what is to be
done, but to do what they already know is to be done.

But if they still do not know, they must, of course, be taught before being
moved. And perhaps when they are simply informed of the matters in hand,
they will be moved in such a way that there is no need for them to be moved any
more by greater eloquence of a more forceful kind. When there is a need of this,
however, it must be done; and the need arises precisely then, when they know
what should be done, and do not do it. And thus teaching is a matter of necessity. People, after all, are able both to act and not to act upon what they know;
who though would ever say that they should act upon what they do not know?
And that is why swaying an audience is not a matter of necessity, because it is
not always needed, if the listener gives his full assent to the person who is teaching, or also delighting him. The reason, though, why it is a matter of victory is

that an audience can be taught and delighted, and still not give their full assent to the speaker. And what use will those two be if this third thing is lacking?

But neither is delighting an audience a matter of necessity, seeing that when things that are true are being pointed out in a speech, which is what the function of teaching is about, it is not the concern of the speaker, nor is it expected of him, that either his manner or his speech should give delight; but his manner by itself, being true, delights simply by being shown to be so. Which is why it frequently happens that even falsehoods give delight when they are convincingly laid bare and revealed to an audience. It is not because they are false, you see, that they delight, but because it is true that they are false, the speech by which this is shown to be true also gives delight.

There are, however, fastidious people who do not take pleasure in the truth if it is presented in any old fashion, but only if it is presented in such a way that the speaker's style too is pleasing; and that is why no slight place in the art of eloquence is also allotted to the function of giving delight. Adding it, all the same, is not enough for the hardened cases who do not profit either from having understood or from having been delighted by the style of the person teaching them. What good, after all, do these two things do the man, who both admits that what has been said is true, and has high praise for the speech it has been said in, and still does not yield that full assent, which is the only thing the speaker is concentrating his attention on, when he is trying by what he says to persuade to a particular course of action?

For if the things that are being taught are of the kind which it is sufficient to believe or know, consenting to them simply means admitting that they are true. When, however, something is being taught that has to be done, and is precisely being taught so that it may be done, in vain does the way and style in which it is said give pleasure, if it is not put across in such a way that action follows. It is the duty, therefore, of the eloquent churchman, when he is trying to persuade the people about something that has to be done, not only to teach, in order to instruct them; not only to delight, in order to hold them; but also to sway, in order to conquer and win them. There still remains, in fact, that type to be swayed by eloquence in the grand manner to give his full assent, in whom that result has not been produced by his admitting the truth of what has been demonstrated, even when this has been done in the most agreeable style. . . .

More Advice from Cicero

The man, therefore, who is striving by speaking to persuade people to do what is good, bearing in mind each of those three things, namely that he is meant to be teaching, delighting, and swaying them, should pray, and take pains to ensure, as we said above, that he is listened to with understanding, with enjoyment, and with obedience. When he does this in a fitting and suitable manner, he cannot be undeservedly called eloquent, even if he does not win the assent of his audience. For to these three things, that is teaching, delighting, and swaying, that other trio seems to have been attached, according to the mind of the great founder of Roman eloquence himself, when he said in similar vein, "That man therefore will be eloquent who can talk about minor matters calmly, about middling ones moderately, about great matters grandly." It's as if, were he to add those other three as well, he could set it all out in one and the same judgment by saying, "That man therefore will be eloquent who, in order to teach, can talk about minor matters calmly; in order to delight, about middling matters moderately; in order to sway, about great matters grandly."

Now he could have illustrated these three modes, as stated by him, with instances taken from the law courts, but not from ecclesiastical occasions, which this man whom we wish to instruct will be concerned with in his public speaking. There, you see, those are minor matters in which a judgment is being sought in questions about money; great matters are those in which the welfare, even the life of persons is at stake, while occasions on which no such judgment has to be given, and nothing is done to get the listener to act or to make a decision, but only to delight him, they put in between the two, so to say, and thus called them middling.

But in our sphere we have to refer everything we say, above all what we say from our higher position to our congregations, to the welfare of persons, to their eternal, not merely temporal, welfare what's more, which also means warning them to beware of eternal perdition. So here everything we say is a great matter, to the extent that not even what the ecclesiastical teacher has to say about money and acquiring or losing it should be regarded as a minor matter, whether it's a minor or major sum of money involved. Justice, after all, is not a minor matter, and this of course we must maintain even where trifling sums are at stake, seeing that the Lord says, *Anyone who is faithful in a minimal amount is also faithful in a great amount* (Luke 16:10). So a minimal amount is certainly minimal, but being faithful in a minimal amount is a great thing. The essence of roundness, that is where the lines from the center to the edge are all equal, is the same in a large dish as in a tiny coin; in the same way, where minor matters are dealt with justly, this does not diminish the greatness of justice.

In any case, when the apostle was talking about secular judgments and lawsuits (what kind, to be sure, if not ones to do with money?), he said, *Does any of you dare, when he has a case against another, to seek a judgment from the wicked, and not have recourse to the saints? Or do you not know that the saints will judge the world? And if the world is being judged by you, are you unfit to pass judgment on trifling matters? Do you not know that we shall judge angels, let alone secular matters? If therefore you have secular lawsuits, set those who are contemptible in the Church, yes set them to judge them. I say it to your shame. So, is there really nobody among you wise enough to be able to judge between his brothers? But brother goes for judgment against brother, and this before unbelievers. It is already indeed a serious fault that you have lawsuits among yourselves at all. Why not rather put up with injustice? Why not rather let yourselves be cheated? You, though, act unjustly and cheat, and your own brothers at that. Or do you not know that the unjust will not inherit the kingdom of God?* (1 Cor. 6:1-9).

Why is it that the apostle is waxing so indignant, so censorious, so vehemently reproachful, so threatening? Why is it that he shows the intensity of his feelings by such frequent and such harsh changes of tone? Why is it, finally, that he speaks so grandly about minimal matters? Did secular lawsuits merit such treatment from him? Surely not. But he is taking this line on account of justice, of charity, of mutual respect, which nobody of sound and sober mind will doubt are great things, however trifling and minimal the matters they are concerned with.

Certainly, if we were advising people how they should conduct their secular business, whether on their own account or that of their clients, before ecclesiastical judges, we would rightly advise them to present it calmly, as a minor matter. But when we are discussing the proper style of speaking for the man whom we wish to be a teacher of the truths by which we are delivered from eternal evils and conducted to eternal good things, wherever these are being presented, whether to the people, or privately to one person or several, whether to friends or enemies, whether in unbroken discourse or in conversation, whether in treatises or in books, whether in letters either lengthy or brief — they are great matters.

Unless, of course, because a cup of cold water is a trifling thing, and worth practically nothing, this means that the Lord was saying something trifling and worthless, when he said that whoever gives one to a disciple of his *shall not lose his reward* (Matt. 10:42); or that when this teacher gives a sermon on this point in church, he should reckon he is talking about a minor matter, and therefore should not speak either in the grand manner or even moderately, but only calmly. Is it not the case that when we have happened to speak to the people on this point, and God has helped us to say something suitable, it's as though a flame has leapt up out of that cold water, and fired even people with the coldest of hearts to perform works of mercy out of hope of a heavenly reward?

And yet, while this teacher ought always to be setting forth great matters, he does not always have to say them in the grand manner. But he should do it calmly when he is teaching, moderately when he has something to blame or praise. But when it is something to be done, and we are addressing people who ought to do it, and yet are not willing to, that is when great matters are to be uttered in the grand manner, and in a way suited to swaying minds and hearts. And sometimes one and the same great matter is spoken of calmly if it is being taught, moderately if it is being proclaimed and preached, and grandly if spirits that have turned away from it are being urged to turn back and be converted.

What, after all, could be greater than God himself? Does that mean that we cannot learn about him? Or that someone who is teaching the unity of the Trinity ought to discuss the matter other than calmly, so that a subject involving such difficult distinctions may as far as God may grant be understood? Is it rhetorical flourishes that are required here, and not rather instructive models? Does the hearer have to be persuaded and swayed to do something, and not rather assisted to learn something? But when God is being praised, either in himself or in his works, what a vast prospect of beautiful and glowing language will occur to the speaker, in order to praise as best he can the one whom nobody can praise as befits him, nobody can fail to praise somehow or other!

[Here follow lengthy examples from Paul's letters of the three styles of speaking: low (to teach), moderate (to delight), and grand (to sway).]

More General Remarks on the Three Styles: An Experience of His Own

Nor should anybody suppose that it is against the rules to mix these three styles: on the contrary, to the extent that it can reasonably be done, a speech should be given variety by the use of all of them, because when it continues too long in one vein, it ceases to hold the listener's attention. But when a transition is made from one to another, a discourse proceeds more acceptably, even if it goes on rather too long, although each style has its own variations in the mouths of eloquent speakers, which prevent it from growing cold or stale in the ears of those who are listening. Nonetheless, it is easier to endure the plain style alone for any length of time than the grand manner alone. The fact is that the more profoundly the listeners' emotions need to be stirred if we are to win their assent, the shorter the time they can be held at that pitch, once they have been sufficiently aroused. And that is why we must beware lest, while we are wishing to stir to a still higher pitch feelings that are already running high, they should in fact fall away from the level to which our rousing oratory has brought them. But after introducing some things that can be said more calmly and plainly, you can then profitably return to what has to be said in the grand manner, thus letting the force of your speech alternate like the waves of the sea. From all this it follows that the grand manner of speaking, if you have to speak for any length of time, should not be offered neat, but should be varied by the inclusion of other styles; but the whole speech, all the same, is to be attributed to that style which predominates.

For it makes a difference what style is introduced into which in particular and necessary places. Thus it is correct always, or nearly always, to begin a speech that is to be in the grand manner with a moderate opening. And an eloquent speaker is quite capable of saying some things calmly and plainly which could be delivered in the grand manner, so that what he does actually say in the grand manner is rendered grander still in comparison, its brilliance highlighted by what you could call the shadows of the other passages. But if in a speech where any style predominates there are knotty problems to be solved, what is called for is acumen, and this claims the calm, plain style as its own. And thus this style is to be employed even in the other two kinds, when such points occur.

In the same way, when something is to be praised or faulted, but where neither a person's life nor liberty is at stake, and no kind of assent to some action is being sought, the moderate style should be applied and introduced, in whatever other kind of speech the point arises. Thus in a speech in the grand manner the other two styles can also find a place, and the same is true for a discourse in the calm, plain style. The moderate kind of speech, however, sometimes though not always requires the plain style if, as I said, a knotty problem crops up that needs to be solved, or when some matters that could be are deliberately not embellished, but are expressed in plain, unadorned words, in order to throw into relief some more decorative and nicely turned embellishments. But a speech in the moderate style never calls for the grand manner, since it is delivered in order to delight the spirits of the audience, not to stir them to action.

Certainly it is not to be assumed that if a speaker is applauded rather frequently and warmly he must therefore be speaking in the grand manner; shrewd arguments in the plain style and embellishments in the moderate can elicit the same response, after all. The grand manner, however, by its very weight frequently makes the voices hush, makes the tears gush. Well anyway, I was once in Caesarea of Mauritania, trying to dissuade the people from their local civil war, or rather something more than civil, which they called "the mob" — for it is not only citizens but also neighbors, brothers, indeed parents and sons, divided into two parties, ritually fighting each other with stones at a certain time of the year, and each of them killing anyone he could; and I did indeed speak and act in the grand manner, to the best of my ability, in order to root out such a cruel and inveterate evil from their hearts and habits and rid them of it by my speaking. But still I did not consider I had achieved anything when I heard them applauding me, but only when I saw them weeping. Their applause only showed they were being instructed and delighted, while their tears indicated that they were being swayed. When I observed these, I was confident, even before the outcome confirmed it, that I had beaten that monstrous custom, handed down from their fathers and grandfathers and their remote ancestors, which was laying hostile siege to their breasts, or rather was in full possession of them. I soon finished the sermon, and turned their hearts and tongues to giving thanks to God. And here we are, something like eight years or more later, and by the good favor of Christ nothing of the sort has since been attempted. There are many other experiences which have taught me that people have shown by their groans rather than their shouts, sometimes also by their tears, and finally by the change in their lives, what the grandeur of a wise man's speech has achieved in them.

People have also frequently been changed by the calm and plain kind of speaking — but so as to know what they were ignorant of, or to believe what used to strike them as incredible; not, however, to do what they already knew should be done and were reluctant to do. For swaying that kind of stubbornness, after all, hard-hitting talk in the grand manner is needed. Again, when praise and blame are being eloquently distributed, while this belongs to the moderate style, some people are so affected that not only are they delighted by the eloquence displayed in praising and blaming, but they themselves also start trying to live in a praiseworthy way and to give up a blameworthy kind of life. But do all who are delighted by this style also imitate the examples given, as all who are swayed by the grand manner proceed to act? And do all who are being taught in the plain style *ipso facto* know or believe to be true what they were ignorant of?

From all this one concludes that those two kinds of speaking which are intended to achieve something are supremely necessary for the person who wishes to speak both wisely and eloquently. But the one which engages in the moderate style, that is in order to delight the hearer by its very eloquence, is not to be made use of for its own sake, but in order that matters which are being usefully and properly talked about, even though they do not call for a style that either instructs or moves, because an audience is being addressed which is both knowledgeable and favorable, might the more readily win that audience's assent and stick in its memory.

After all, the universal task of eloquence, in whichever of these three styles, is to speak in a way that is geared to persuasion. The aim, what you intend, is to persuade by speaking. In any of these three styles, indeed, the eloquent man speaks in a way that is geared to persuasion, but if he doesn't actually persuade, he doesn't achieve the aim of eloquence. . . .

Conclusion: Those Who Cannot Compose Their Own Sermons Should Learn by Heart and Preach Those of Acknowledged Masters

There are, of course, some people who can declaim and enunciate well, but cannot think up and compose anything to say and declaim. But if they take things that have been written eloquently and wisely by others, and proffer them to the people, provided they have that role to play, they are not acting improperly. For in this way too we get the useful result of there being many preachers of the truth without there being many masters, if all say the same thing, taught by the one true master, and there are no schisms among them. Nor should such men be deterred by the words of the prophet Jeremiah, through whom God reproves those *who steal his words, each one from his neighbor* (Jer. 23:30). Those who steal, after all, are purloining what does not belong to them; but God's word does belong to those who do what he tells them. In fact, it's the man who speaks well and lives badly that really speaks words that do not belong to him. For any good things that he says seem to be the product of his own wits, but do not go along at all with his morals. And so the ones who God said are stealing his words are those who want to give the appearance of being good by speaking what belongs to God, when in fact they are bad by doing what belongs to themselves.

Nor, in fact, is it they who are saying the good things they do say, if you pay careful attention. How, after all, can they be saying in words what they are contradicting in deeds? It was not for nothing, you see, that the apostle said about such people: *They claim that they know God, but contradict it with their deeds* (Titus 1:16). So in one way it is they who are saying it, and again in another way it is not they who are saying it, since each thing is true that Truth has said. Speaking of such people, *What they say,* he said, *do, but what they do, do not do,* that is, do what you hear from their mouths; do not do what you see in their works; *for they say,* he went on, *and do not do* (Matt. 23:3). Therefore, although they do not do, they still say. But in another place where he is chiding such people, *Hypocrites,* he says, *how can you say good things, since you are bad?* (Matt. 12:34). And consequently it is not they who say even the things they do say, when they say good things, inasmuch as by will and work they contradict what they say.

Thus it can come about that a learned but bad man may compose a sermon in which the truth is proclaimed, to be spoken by another man who is not learned, but is good; when this happens, he is himself handing over from himself what does not belong to him, while the other man is receiving what is in fact his own from someone it does not belong to. But when good men who are believers do this service for good men who are believers, both parties are saying what is their own, because God too is theirs and the things they are saying are his. And those who are unable to compose these good sermons make them their own, when they compose themselves to live according to what they contain.

But whether you are at this very moment about to preach to a congregation, or give a talk to any kind of group, or whether you are on the point of dictating something that is to be preached to a congregation, or to be read by anyone who wishes and is able to, you should pray that God may put good words into your mouth. After all, if Queen Esther prayed, when she was going to speak in the king's presence for the temporal salvation of her people, that God might put suitable words into her mouth, how much more should you pray to receive such a favor, when you are toiling in word and teaching for the people's eternal salvation?

Those, however, who are going to say something that they have received from others, should pray for those they receive it from even before they do so, that they may be given what they hope to receive from them; and when they have received it, they should pray both that they themselves may give it out well, and that those they give it out to may take it well; and on the successful conclusion of the talk they must give thanks to the same God from whom they cannot doubt that they have received it, so that he that boasts may boast in the one *in whose hand are both we and our words* (Wisd. Sol. 7:16).

This book has turned out longer than I wished, and than I expected. But for the reader or listener to whom it is acceptable it will not be too long, while anyone who does find it too long, and who wants to know what it contains, should read it piecemeal. As for those who are not interested in knowing what is in it, they should not complain about its length. I, for my part, give thanks to our God that in these four books I have set out to the best of my poor ability, not what sort of pastor I am myself, lacking many of the necessary qualities as I do, but what sort the pastor should be who is eager to toil away, not only for his own sake but for others, in the teaching of sound, that is of Christian, doctrine.

ROBERT OF BASEVORN

Ornamentation

Nothing is known of Robert of Basevorn except that in 1322 he wrote an influential treatise, *The Form of Preaching*. We know Robert's name only because he reveals it in an acrostic combination of letters from the chapter headings of the book. In his treatise he speaks knowledgeably of preaching styles in Paris and Oxford. Robert's work is representative of a highly developed medieval genre, the *ars praedicandi*, a handbook of sermon design and construction. Such manuals appeared in profusion in the thirteenth and fourteenth centuries. They describe the "thematic" or "university" sermon whose complex arrangement was probably more directly influenced by scholastic (Aristotelian) logic than by Augustinian (Ciceronian) rhetoric. The typical manual prescribes a sermon in six parts: (1) theme: a scriptural quotation; (2) protheme: introduction of the theme followed by a prayer; (3) repetition of theme with explanation of the sermon's purpose; (4) division or partition of theme (usually into threes) with "authorities" of various sorts to "prove" each division; (5) subdivision of theme; (6) amplification of each division. The rigorous division of theme was a medieval commonplace. Although it was modified by Renaissance classicism and repudiated by the Reformation, the three-point outline has survived as a staple for many preachers. In the following selection we see intimations of the growing division between dialectical reasoning (or logic) and rhetoric, with the latter eventually reduced to and equated with *style*. We also glimpse the medieval origins of the many uses and abuses of the sermon illustration!

Robert of Basevorn, *The Form of Preaching*, trans. Leopold Krul, O.S.B., in *Three Medieval Rhetorical Arts*, ed. James J. Murphy (Berkeley: University of California Press, 1971), pp. 132-33, 138-39, 145-48.

W e must come now to our proposal to discuss the ornamentation which is used in sermons by certain of the careful craftsmen. It must be realized that in the most carefully contrived sermons twenty-two ornaments are especially employed. These are: Invention of the Theme, Winning-over of the Audience, Prayer, Introduction, Division, Statement of the Parts, Proof of the Parts, Amplification, Digression, which is properly called "Transition," Correspondence, Agreement of the Correspondence, Circuitous Development, Convolution, Unification, Conclusion, Coloration, Modulation of Voice, Appropriate Gesture, Timely Humor, Allusion, Firm Impression, Weighing of Subject Matter. The first fifteen of these are inserted into their proper places once, or at any rate into a few places; the remaining three, and generally Allusion and Firm Impression, can be placed almost anywhere. The element that follows after these, Humor, ought to be used in a few places and very sparingly. The last must be observed in all places. All these, when concurring, embellish a sermon elegantly, and so can be called the ornaments of a sermon. And if perhaps there are more elements than have been enumerated, they can be reduced to these.

For a good Invention of the Theme the following are required: that it concur with the feast, that it beget full understanding, that it be on a Bible text which is not changed or corrupted, that it contain not more than three statements or convertible to three, that sufficient concordances can be found on these three ideas, even vowel concordances, and that the theme itself can serve in place of the antetheme or protheme. For example, concerning the first, suppose that someone has to preach about Advent and he takes as his theme: *Come, Lord Jesus,* from the Nativity: *the Grace of God has appeared,* from the Epiphany: *A great sign has appeared;* thus he will find the above-mentioned conditions concurrent.

Likewise concerning the saints. He should consider what or which things about the saints or saint about whom he preaches he especially wishes to commend. For example, as I consider St. Andrew, I see much that is especially commendable in him: that he hung on the cross for so long and did not waver, that in spirit he seemed rather affixed to Christ than corporally to the cross. And thus the saying of his fellow Apostle is seen in his own person: *with Christ I am nailed to the cross* (Gal. 2:20). . . .

Further, in this method of preaching only three statements, or the equivalent of three, are used in the theme — either from respect to the Trinity, or because a threefold cord is not easily broken, or because this method is mostly followed by Bernard, or, as I think more likely, because it is more convenient for the set time of the sermon. A preacher can follow up just so many members without tiring his hearers; and if he should mention fewer, he would occupy too little time.

The reason why a theme may be the equivalent of three statements is that it can happen that some words which cannot be divided and should not be may fall into a theme. Of such kind are prepositions and conjunctions, and also a general word which is included in every other word. Hence, if the theme were: *the just is delivered out of distress,* no division would fall upon *out of* nor upon *is.* . . .

No matter how many statements there may be, as long as I can divide them into three, I have a sufficient proposition. Posit that the theme on the annunciation, on the vigil of nativity, or on the day, and on the first Sunday within the octave of the nativity, and on the day of circumcision: *God sent his Son made of a woman, made under the law, that he might redeem them who were under the law.* Here are seventeen words; yet the whole can be divided into three so that it may be said that in these words three things are touched upon: (1) There is noted in the doctor a generously-expended sublimity because it says *God sent his Son.* (2) There is shown how virtuously-shown humility heals because it says *made of a woman, made under the law.* (3) There is shown how fruitfully-extended utility is derived, because it says *that he might redeem them who were under the law.*

But when the theme is thus divided, one must see that the dividing parts correspond with the parts of that which is divided. For example, here is said that in the doctor is noted a sublimity, etc. when is said *God sent* etc. Notice the correspondence, because *God:* sublimity; because *he sent:* expended; because *his Son:* generously. And thus about the rest. There is no lack of artistry if these three things can be confirmed by one authority in which verbally there are the three: God, sent, and Son, and that in the sentence such great nobility is communicated to us. But because such authorities are difficult to find, themes of so many words are not commonly accepted. . . .

Now that we have treated in general the first ornament of preaching, to wit, the Invention of the Theme, the second ornament follows, namely the Winning-over of the Audience. The preacher, as far as he can do so according to God, ought to attract the mind of the listeners in such a way as to render them willing to hear and retain. This can be done in many ways. One way is to place at the beginning something subtle and interesting, some authentic marvel which can be fittingly drawn in for the purpose of the theme. For instance, suppose that the theme is concerned with the ascension or the assumption: *a spring rose from the earth.* One could adduce that marvel which Gerald narrates in his book, *De mirabilibus Hiberniae* about the spring in Sicilia: if anyone approaches it dressed in red clothing, immediately water gushes from the place of the spring though none appeared there before, while it remains unmoved in the presence of all other colors. That spring is Christ, about whom it is written in Eccles[iasticus] 1: *the word of God is the fountain of wisdom,* to whom he "approaches dressed in red" who, devoutly suffering with him and as it were incarnadined [reddened] with the blood of his Passion, intently and inwardly revolves the thought (of him), and considers the saying of Isaiah: *why is thy apparel red?* Such a one approaching finds living water, viz, graces, because his blood was of such virtue that, when it was shed, the earth quaked and the rocks were torn asunder. Much more ought our hearts to quake and be torn by the cry of God's word, unless they be drier than the earth and harder than rocks.

Likewise if an unknown cause of some saying is used, it is reducible to the same category, for example if a cause is given to explain why the eye does not have a determined color; because if it did have a definite color, it would perceive only that color and there would have to be as many senses as there are colors; and this may be applied to sinners, especially the avaricious and clever ones who do not perceive the word of God or its effect because they are totally determined by its opposite.

Another way is to frighten them by some terrifying tale or example, in the way that Jacques de Vitry [a compiler of popular sermon illustrations] talks about someone who never willingly wanted to hear the word of God; finally when he died and was brought to the church, and the priest in the presence of the parish began the eulogy which is wont to be spoken over the body of the dead, the image of Christ standing between the choir and the church tore away and pulled his hands from the nails piercing them and from the wood to which they were fixed, and plugged his ears, as if to intimate that he did not wish to hear the prayer for him who once spurned to listen to him in his preachers.

Likewise, pertinent to the same topic are the different stories which teach how Christ appeared to some hardened sinners, extending his palm full of blood taken from his side, saying: This blood which you do obdurately contemn will bear witness against you on the day of judgment. After they lived awhile it was frequently disclosed that the blood could not be washed away and they were buried with it. Some repented and confessed and then easily enough, as it were, it disappeared.

This second example I myself have come upon, in connection with an infamous woman hardened to all sermons. Christ appeared to her and took the woman's hand, putting it into the wound in his side, saying, as she herself had said: the blood which you reject will adhere to you for evil, unless you correct yourself. It is well known that she confessed; still it adhered to her and could not be washed away till finally in some way she confessed a great hidden sin and immediately after that it disappeared. Such terrifying stories have great value in the beginning of a sermon.

The third way is to show by an example or story that the devil always tries to hinder the word of God and the hearing of it.

The fourth way is to show that to hear the word of God is a great sign of predestination. To this are reduced those ways which show that other benefits, earthly or heavenly, such as the fertility of the earth, the disposition to penitence, and the like, accrue to those who listen willingly.

The fifth way is to show that the preacher intends only to convert them, and not immediately after that to start begging. He should draw them to the love of God, to the fear of evil, to the honor of God, lest, if it is a principal feast, it may lack due honor. Then he should put the hearers into the right disposition for the indulgence, which is granted to those who listen to the word of God, and preach like things by which he rightly deems to win over the hearers according to their condition.

WILLIAM PERKINS

The Art of Prophesying

William Perkins (1558-1602) was a Puritan theologian whose writings on the task and method of the preacher shaped Protestant homiletics for more than one hundred years. Educated at Christ's College, Cambridge, where he was a fellow from 1584 to 1594, Perkins never repudiated the Church of England. He was not, however, as interested in questions of polity as with practices of piety, wishing to reform the church rather than break away from it. Though he denied the label "puritan" applied to him by others, he shared with the Puritans common concerns about inadequately trained clergy, overly intellectual preaching, and the need for spiritual renewal. He became well known through his lectures, sermons, and writings as a staunch anti-Catholic and supporter of Calvinist principles, and his treatise in defense of predestination (De Praedestinationis Modo et Ordine) evoked an almost immediate reply by Jacobus Arminius. Perkins' most lasting contribution, however, was as a practical theologian whose example of Christian piety and pastoral ministry enjoyed enormous popular appeal. Troubled by the lack of formal theological training among the clergy (in 1583 only one-sixth of the English clergy were officially licensed to preach), he set about to remedy this deficiency by writing instructive manuals. His Cases of Conscience examined specific theological and practical issues faced in pastoral care. The Arte of Prophecying was Perkins' textbook on homiletical method. It was based on his belief that correct interpretation of the revealed word of God — in a way that was both logically sound and practically applicable — was central to the preacher's task. That his work is here included in the section on Rhetoric indicates his lasting influence on the Puritan "plain style" of preaching. (See Ian Breward, introduction, The Works of William Perkins [Abingdon, England: Sutton Courtenay Press, 1970].)

William Perkins, The Arte of Prophecying, or A Treatise Concerning the Sacred and Onely True Manner and Methode of Preaching, trans. Thomas Tuke (London: Felix Kyngston, 1607), pp. 90-148.

Of the Right Dividing of the Word

Hitherto we have spoken of interpreting the word. We are now come to speak of the right cutting, or the right dividing of it. Right cutting of the word is that whereby the word is made fit to edify the people of God (2 Tim. 3:15). . . . The parts thereof are two — resolution, or partition, and application. Resolution is that whereby the place propounded is, as a weaver's web, resolved (or untwisted or unloosed) into sundry doctrines (Acts 18:28). Resolution is either notation or collection. Notation is when the doctrine is expressed in the place propounded (Rom. 3:9-11; Acts 2:24-27). Collection is when the doctrine not expressed is soundly gathered out of the text. This is done by the help of the nine arguments, that is of the causes, effects, subjects, adjuncts, dissentaries [opposites], comparatives, names, distribution and definition. . . .

In gathering of doctrines we must specially remember that an example in his own kind (that is an ethical, economical, political, ordinary, and extraordinary example) hath the virtue of a general rule in ethical, economical, political, ordinary, and extraordinary matters. The examples of the fathers are patterns for us (1 Cor. 10:11). And it is a principle in logic that the genus is actually in all the species and a rule in the optics that the general species of things are perceived before the particular. . . . That also I add, that collections ought to be right and sound; that is to say, derived from the genuine and proper meaning of the Scripture. If otherwise, we shall draw any doctrine from any place. . . .

It shall be lawful also to gather allegories: for they are arguments taken from things that are like and Paul in his teaching useth them often (1 Cor. 9:9). But they are to be used with these caveats: let them be used sparingly and soberly; let them not be far-fetched, but fitting to the matter in hand; they must be quickly dispatched; they are to be used for the instruction of the life and not to prove any point of faith.

Any point of doctrine collected by just consequence is simply of itself to be believed and doth demonstrate (Acts 18:24, 28). From hence it followeth: first, that human testimonies, whether of the philosophers or of the fathers, are not to be alleged. Yet with this exception — unless they convince the conscience of the hearer. Thus Paul alleged the testimony of Aratus (Acts 17:28-29). . . . And then also it must be done sparingly and with leaving out the name of the profane writer. Secondly, that a few testimonies of Scripture are to be used for the proof of the doctrine and that sometimes there is need of none. Lastly, hence it follows that the prophets delivering their doctrines thus are not to be reproved of other prophets (1 Cor. 14:32, 37).

Of the Ways How to Use and Apply Doctrines

Application is that whereby the doctrine rightly collected is diversely fitted according as place, time, and person do require (Ezek. 34:15-16; Jude 22-23). The foundation of application is to know whether the place propounded be a sentence of the law or of the gospel. For when the word is preached, there is one operation of the law and another of the gospel. For the law is thus far effectual as to declare unto us the disease of sin and by accident to exasperate and stir it up, but it affords no remedy. Now the gospel, as it teacheth what is to be done, so it hath also the efficacy of the Holy Ghost adjoined with it, by whom being regenerated we have strength both to believe the gospel and to perform those things which it commandeth. The law therefore is first in order of teaching and the gospel second.

It is a sentence of the law which speaketh of perfect inherent righteousness, of eternal life given through the works of the law, of the contrary sins and of the curse which is due unto them (Gal. 3:10; Matt. 3:7, 10). A sentence of the gospel is that which speaketh of Christ and his benefits and of faith being fruitful in good works (John 3:16). Hence it is that any sentences which seem to belong to the law are by reason of Christ to be understood not legally, but with the qualification of the gospel (Luke 11:28; Deut. 30:11, 14). The sentence which is legal in Moses is evangelical in Paul (Rom. 10:8; Ps. 119:1-2; John 14:21, 23; Gen. 6:9, 17:1).

The ways of application are chiefly seven, according to the divers condition of men and people, which is sevenfold.

    I. Unbelievers who are both ignorant and unteachable . . .
   II. Some are teachable, but yet ignorant . . .
 III. Some have knowledge, but are not as yet humbled . . .
 IV. Some are humbled . . .
  V. Some do believe . . .
 VI. Some are fallen . . .
VII. There is a mingled people . . . .

Of the Kinds of Application

Application is either mental or practical. Mental is that which respecteth the mind and it is either doctrine or redargution (2 Tim. 3:16-17). Doctrine is that whereby doctrine or teaching is used for the information of the mind to a right judgment concerning things to be believed. Redargution [refutation, disproving] is that whereby teaching is used for the reformation of the mind from error. In confutations which are made publicly before the assembly these cautions must be used. The thing that is determined, or the state of the question that is to be discussed, must be thoroughly understood. Let those errors only be reproved which trouble the church in which we live: all other being altogether let alone which do either lie dead, or are external, unless some danger be ready to ensue of them (Matt. 16:6). If the error be out of the foundation of faith, the confutation must not only be Christian-like, as it should be ever, but also a friendly, a gentle and brotherly dissension.

Practical application is that which respecteth the life and behavior: and it is instruction and correction. Instruction is what whereby doctrine is applied to frame a man to live well in the family, commonwealth, and church. To this place belong consolation and exhortation (Rom. 15:4). Correction is that whereby the doctrine is applied to reform the life from ungodliness and unrighteous dealing. Hitherto belongs admonition. This must be done first generally, the circumstances of the persons being omitted (2 Sam. 12; Acts 19:26, 35-37). Afterward, if the former reproof prevail not, it must be urged after a more special manner (1 Tim. 5:20). But always in the very hatred of sin, let the love of the person appear in the speeches and let the minister include himself (if he may) in his reprehension, that it may be more mild and gentle (Dan. 4:16-19; Gal. 2:15; 1 Cor. 4:6). Now these four kinds of application do offer themselves in every sentence of the Scripture. . . .

Hitherto hath been spoken of the preparation or provision of the sermon. The promulgation or uttering of it followeth. In the promulgation two things are required: the hiding of human wisdom and the demonstration or showing of the Spirit. Human wisdom must be concealed, whether it be in the matter of the sermon or in the setting forth of the words, because the preaching of the word is the testimony of God and the profession of the knowledge of Christ and not of human skill: and again, because the hearers ought not to ascribe their faith to the gifts of man, but to the power of God's word (1 Cor. 2:1-2, 5).

If any man think that by this means barbarism should be brought into pulpits, he must understand that the minister may, yea and must, privately use at his liberty the arts, philosophy, and variety of reading while he is framing his sermon, but he ought in public to conceal all these from the people and not to make the least ostentation. *Artis etiam celare artem:* it is also a point of art to conceal art.

The demonstration of the Spirit is when as the minister of the word doth in the time of preaching so behave himself that all, even ignorant persons and unbelievers, may judge that it is not so much he that speaketh, as the Spirit of

God in him and by him (1 Cor. 2:4; 4:19-20; 14:24-25; Mic. 3:8). This makes the ministry to be lively and powerful (Luke 11:27).

This demonstration is either in speech or in gesture. The speech must be spiritual and gracious. That speech is spiritual which the Holy Spirit doth teach and it is a speech both simple and perspicuous, fit both for the people's understanding and to express the majesty of the Spirit (1 Cor. 2:13; Acts 17:2-3; Gal. 3:1; 2 Cor. 4:2-4). Wherefore neither the words of arts, nor Greek and Latin phrases and quirks must be intermingled in the sermon. They disturb the mind of the auditors, that they cannot fit those things that went afore with those that follow. A strange word hindereth the understanding of those things that are spoken. It draws the mind away from the purpose to some other matter. Here also the telling of tales and all profane and ridiculous speeches must be omitted.

The speech is gracious wherein the grace of the heart is expressed (Luke 4:22; John 7:46). Grace is either of the person, or of the ministry. Grace of the person is the holiness of the heart and an unblamable life, which however it makes not a minister, yet it is very necessary. Because the doctrine of the word is hard both to be understood and to be practiced, therefore the minister ought to express that by his example which he teacheth, as it were by a type (1 Peter 5:3; 1 Tim. 4:12; Phil. 4:8-9). He that is not godly, howsoever he may understand the Scriptures, yet doth he not perceive the inward sense and experience of the word in his heart (Ps. 25:8-9; Amos 3:7; Gen. 18:17-19). It is a thing execrable in the sight of God that godly speech should be conjoined with an ungodly life (Ps. 50:16-17). . . . It is an ecclesiastical secret that the minister ought to cover his infirmities, that they be not seen, for the simple people behold not the ministry, but the person of the minister (Mark 6:20). . . . For words make not such an impression in the soul as works do. A minister that is wicked, either openly or secretly, is not worthy to stand before the face of the most holy and the almighty God (Jer. 15:19; Isa. 6:6-8; Lev. 10:3). And hence it is that the judgments of God remain for wicked ministers to tremble at (1 Sam. 2:17, 25).

The parts of sanctity are especially:

1. A good conscience (2 Cor. 1:12; 1 Tim. 1:19; Acts 24:16). If this be wanting, the mouth of the speaker is shut (Isa. 56:10).
2. An inward feeling of the doctrine to be delivered. Wood that is capable of fire doth not burn unless fire be put to it: and he must first be godly affected himself who would stir up godly affections in other men. Therefore what motions a sermon doth require, such a preacher shall stir up privately in his own mind, that he may kindle the same in his hearers.
3. The fear of God, whereby being thoroughly stricken with a reverent regard of God's majesty, he speaketh soberly and moderately.

4. The love of the people (1 Thess. 2:7). And that affection may appear, the minister's duty is to pray seriously and fervently for the people of God (1 Sam. 12:23).

5. The minister must also be venerable, that is such an one as is to be reverenced for constancy, integrity, gravity, and truth-speaking, who also knoweth how to perform reverence to others, either privately or publicly, as is befitting the persons of all his hearers.

6. He must be temperate, who restraineth inwardly his over-vehement affections and hath his outward fashions and gestures moderate and plain, by the which dignity and authority may be procured and preserved. Therefore he must be neither covetous, a lover of silver, a follower of wine, nor litigious, nor a striker, nor wrathful: and let the young men exercise themselves to godliness and fly the lusts of youth (1 Tim. 4:7).

The grace of the ministry is:

1. To be apt to teach (1 Tim. 3:2). Now Paul's meaning is that it is not only decent and laudable if this gift be had, but also that it is so necessary, as that may not be wanting. . . .

2. Authority, whereby he speaketh as the ambassador of the great Jehovah (Titus 2:15; 1 Peter 4:11).

3. Zeal, whereby being most desirous of God's glory he doth endeavor to fulfill and execute the degree of election concerning the salvation of men by his ministry (Job 32:18-19; Col. 1:28-29; 2 Tim. 2:25).

Gesture is either in the action of the voice or of the body. The voice ought to be so high that all may hear (Isa. 58:1; John 7:37; Acts 2:14). In the doctrine he ought to be more moderate, in the exhortation more fervent and vehement. Let there be that gravity in the gesture of the body which may grace the messenger of God. It is fit, therefore, that the trunk or stalk of the body being erect and quiet, all the other parts, as the arm, the hand, the face, and eyes, have such motions as may express and (as it were) utter the godly affections of the heart. The lifting up of the eye and the hand signifieth confidence, the casting down of the eyes signifieth sorrow and heaviness (2 Chron. 6:13; Luke 18:13). Concerning the gesture, other precepts cannot be delivered: only let the example of the gravest ministers in this kind be instead of a rule. . . .

The Order and Sum of the Sacred and Only Method of Preaching

1. To read the text distinctly out of the canonical Scriptures.
2. To give the sense and understanding of it being read, by the Scripture it-self.
3. To collect a few and profitable points of doctrine out of the natural sense.
4. To apply, if he have the gift, the doctrines rightly collected to the life and manners of men in a simple and plain speech.

The Sum of the Sum

Preach one Christ by Christ to the praise of Christ.

The writers which lent their help to the framing of this *Arte of Prophecying* are: Augustine, Hemmingius, Hyperius, Erasmus, Illyricus, Wigandus, Jacobus Matthias, Theodorus Beza, Franciscus Junius.

Soli Deo Gloria.

FRANÇOIS FÉNELON

Natural Communication

Augustine's *On Christian Doctrine* was said by Charles Baldwin to "begin rhetoric anew," but the *Dialogues* of François Fénelon (1651-1715) constitute the first modern rhetoric. Following the model of Plato and Cicero, Fénelon, who was later Archbishop of Cambrai, allows his position on preaching to emerge dialectically through a conversation of characters designated A, B, and C. Character A expresses Fénelon's opposition to the neo-scholasticism of Peter Ramus. One hundred years earlier Ramus had assigned rhetoric's traditional tasks of *invention* (research) and *disposition* (presentation or arrangement) to dialectic and had restricted rhetoric to ornamental eloquence (see "Ornamentation" by Robert of Basevorn). Fénelon described the effects of Ramism on the French pulpit of the seventeenth century. Mere ingenuity of speech was of no help to preachers like Fénelon, who were concerned with a persuasive, missionary apostolate to the Huguenots. In an effort to restore the integrity of rhetoric (and preaching with it), he advocated a plain style of discourse and encouraged preachers to interpret and apply the Scriptures according to the way in which the hearer most naturally appropriates the truth. The purposes of the gospel, he said, are not served by the artificially divided and tiered scholastic sermon. According to Fénelon's method, the message is logically unfolded rather than displayed. Although his proposal stops short of modern "inductive preaching," it is clearly influenced by the growing pressures of seventeenth-century experimental science. Fénelon's rhetoric was part of a comprehensive revolution in the relations of experience, thought, and discourse. Reliance on the predetermined structures of reason or on any other "authorities" would no longer do.

François Fénelon, *Three Dialogues on Pulpit Eloquence*, trans. Samuel J. Eales (London: Thomas Baker, 1901 [1717]), pp. 1-9, 95-102.

A: Good morning, sir! Have you then been to hear one of the sermons to which you have so often been desirous to take me? For my part, I am contented with the preacher of our parish.

B: I was charmed with mine; you have lost much, sir, by not having been present to hear him. I have rented a seat, so as to not lose one of the sermons for Lent. He is an admirable preacher; if you had once heard him you would be dissatisfied with every other.

A: I shall be careful, then, not to hear him, for I do not at all wish that one preacher should give me a distaste for all others; on the contrary, I wish for a man who will give me such a taste for and delight in the word of God, that I shall be the more disposed to listen to it whenever I can. But since I have, as you say, lost so much by not hearing this fine sermon, and you are full of it, you can make up to me for part of that loss if you will be so kind as to repeat to me something of what you remember of it.

B: My account would do injustice to the sermon. There were a hundred beauties in it which I fail to remember. It would require a preacher to give you an account. . . .

A: But still; his plan, his demonstrations, his practical lessons, the chief truths which made up the body of his discourse — do none of these remain in your mind? Or were you not attentive?

B: Far from it! I never listened with more attention and pleasure.

A: What then! Do you wish me to beg and entreat you? . . .

B: Listen, then! I will repeat to you what I am able to remember. This was the text: "I have eaten ashes as it were bread" (Ps. 102:9). How could you find a more ingenious text for Ash Wednesday? He showed how, according to this passage, ashes ought to be on this day the food of our souls; then he interwove in his introduction, in the most ingenious way in the world, the story of Artemisia and the ashes of her husband. His transition to the "Ave Maria" was full of art. Then his division of his subject was happy; you shall judge of it. "These ashes," he said, "although they are a sign of penitence, are a principle of happiness: although they seem to humble us they are, in reality, a source of glory: although an emblem of death they are a remedy which leads to immortality." This division he repeated in various forms, and each time gave it a new luster by his antitheses. The rest of the discourse was no less polished and brilliant. . . .

A: I am rather afraid to tell you my opinion of that sermon, or to lower the high estimate which you have of it. . . .

B: Do not be afraid of that in the present instance. It is not at all from curiosity that I ask this of you. I have need to have correct ideas upon this matter. I wish to obtain solid information, not only for my own sake, but for that of others, since I too am, by my profession, under the obligation to preach. Speak to me, then, without reserve; do not hesitate to contradict me, nor fear that I shall be shocked.

A: As you wish it I will do so, and even from your report of that sermon I judge that it was exceedingly faulty.

B: In what respect?

A: You will see. Can a sermon be considered good in which the applications of Scripture are false, in which a story out of secular history is related in a puerile and unedifying manner, in which a false affectation of brilliancy is predominant everywhere?

B: Doubtless it cannot, but the sermon of which I have been telling you does not seem to me to be at all of that character.

A: Wait a little, and you will agree with what I say. When a preacher has chosen for his text these words, "I have eaten ashes as it were bread," ought he to have contented himself with tracing out a mere connection of words between the text and the ceremony of this day? Ought he not to have begun by explaining the true sense of his text before applying himself to his subject?

B: No doubt.

A: Would it not also have been desirable to look thoroughly into the circumstances and take the trouble to understand the whole occasion and design of the Psalm? Would it not have been proper to examine if the interpretation about which he was occupied was in accordance with the true sense of the words before giving it to the people as the word of God?

B: Most truly; but in what respect was it otherwise?

A: David, or whoever was the author of Psalm 102, is speaking in that passage of his own misfortune. He says that his enemies cruelly taunted him, seeing him beaten down into the dust, lying at their feet, and reduced (he uses here a poetic metaphor) to feed upon bread made of ashes, and water mixed with tears. What resemblance is there between the complaints of David, when he was driven from his throne and persecuted by his son Absalom, and the humiliation of a Christian who puts ashes upon his head in order to bring himself to think of death, and to withdraw from the pleasure of the world? Was there no other text in the Scripture that he could have taken? Had Jesus Christ, the apostles, the prophets never spoken of death and of the ashes of the tomb to which God brings down our human weakness? Are not the Scriptures full of a thousand touching phrases about this truth? . . .

B: You are growing too warm on this subject, sir. It is true, however, that this text is not used in a literal sense, but the preacher's explication of it may, nevertheless, have been very fine.

A: For my part I like to know if a saying be true before I find any beauty in it. But what as to the remainder?

C: The remainder of the sermon was of the same kind as the text. But what was the advantage of saying pretty things upon a subject so terrible, and of amusing the hearer by the secular story of the grief of Artemisia, when he was bound to speak gravely and solemnly, and to give only terrible ideas of death?

B: I see that you do not love flashes of wit on such occasions. But unless these are allowed, what would become of eloquence? Would you reduce all preachers to the simplicity of missionaries? That is needful for the unlearned people of course, but those who are cultivated have more delicate ears, and it is necessary to adapt our discourses to their taste.

A: Now you are leading me to another subject, but I was endeavoring to show you how ill-conceived this sermon was, and I was just about to speak of the division of it, but I think that you understand what it is that I am obliged to disapprove of. Here is a man who divides the whole subject of his discourse into three points. Now, when a division is made, it ought to be simple and natural; it should be a division which is found ready made in the subject itself, which clears up the details and arranges them in order, which is itself easily remembered, and which helps the hearer to remember other things: finally, a division which displays the greatness of a subject and of its parts. But here, on the contrary, you see a man who endeavors in the first place to dazzle you, who displays before you three epigrams, or three riddles, which he turns round and round with a practiced hand until you think you are looking at the passes of a juggler. Is that such a serious and grave manner of address as is calculated to make you hope for something useful and important? . . .

B: You have already frequently mentioned that *order:* do you mean anything else than a division? Have you upon that subject also some peculiar opinion?

A: You are, as you think, speaking in jest: but the fact is, that I am not less singular in my opinion on that subject than on the others.

B: Are you really serious?

A: Be assured that I am: and since we are on the subject, I am going to show you how defective is the *order* adopted by the greater number of orators.

B: Since you love order so much, *divisions* ought not to displease you.

A: But I am far from approving of them.

B: Why? Do they not render a discourse orderly and methodical?

A: Frequently, and indeed generally, they are put where they should not properly be, and thus they hinder a discourse, and render it uninteresting. They cut it up into two or three parts, which interrupts the action of the orator, and hinders the effect which it ought to produce. There is no longer a true unity in the discourse: it is divided into two or three different discourses, which are united only by an arbitrary bond. The sermon of the day before yesterday, that of yesterday, and that of today, provided that they are according to a plan strictly followed out, like the plans of sermons for Advent, make up just as much the body of a single discourse as the three points of one of those sermons make up together one sermon.

B: But what is order then, according to your views? What confusion there would be in a discourse which was not divided at all!

A: Do you suppose that there was much more confusion in the harangues of Demosthenes and of Cicero, than in the sermons of the preacher of your parish?

B: I do not know: I suppose not.

A: Do not be afraid to concede too much: the harangues of those great men are not divided as are the sermons of the present time. Not only they, but also Isocrates, of whom we have said so much, and the other ancient orators never adopted that method of division at all. The Fathers of the church did not even know of it. S. Bernard, the last of them, often marks divisions; but he does not follow them, nor does he formally divide his sermons at all. Preaching existed for a long while without sermons having been divided; and it is a very modern invention which comes to us from the scholastic divines.

B: I allow that the schoolmen are but a faulty model for eloquence; but what form was there then anciently given to a discourse?

A: I am about to tell you that. A discourse was not formally divided at all: but all the subjects which it was necessary to distinguish from each other were carefully taken in succession, its own place was assigned to each, and each subject was arranged in proper order, so that it should follow where it would be most likely to make an impression upon the hearer. Often a consideration which, if put forth at first, would have appeared of little importance, becomes decisive when it is reserved for the time when the hearer shall have been prepared by other reasonings to appreciate all the power of it. Often a single word, happily employed in the place to which it belongs and which suits it, brings out an entire truth in all its clearness.

Sometimes it is needful to leave a truth veiled and disguised till the very end of the speech: it is Cicero who asserts this. In every case there ought to be an orderly succession of proofs; the first should prepare the way for the second, and the second should strengthen the first.

It is needful to give a general view of the whole subject to begin with, and to dispose the mind of the hearer favorably toward it, by a modest and winning opening, by order of probity and candor. Then the preacher should go on to lay down *his general principles,* after that to state the *facts* he is engaged upon in a simple, clear, and telling manner, laying special stress upon those of which he means to make use afterward. First *principles,* then *facts;* and from these draw the *conclusions* which you desire to reach; taking care to arrange the reasoning in such a manner as that the proofs will admit of being borne in mind easily.

All this ought to be done in such a manner that the discourse should be continually growing; and that the hearer should feel more and more the growing weight of truth. Then is the time to throw out vivid and striking metaphors, and transitions of rhetoric calculated to excite the feelings. For that purpose it is needful to be acquainted with the interconnections of the feelings; to know which of them may be aroused most easily at first, and may then serve to arouse the others; and finally, which of them are able to produce the greatest effects; for with these latter the discourse should be brought to a close. It is often useful to make at the end a recapitulation or summary, which gathers up in a few sentences all the power of the orator, and sets anew before the hearers all that he has said which is most winning and persuasive. At the same time, it is not absolutely necessary always to follow that order in a uniform manner; each subject has its fitnesses and its exceptions. But even in this order a variety may be found almost infinite. This method, which is almost marked out for us by Cicero, cannot, as you see, be followed in a discourse which is cut invariably into three parts, nor observed absolutely in every point. An order is needful, but not an order that is expressly stated and shown from the commencement of the discourse. Cicero says that the best course, almost always, is to conceal it; and to lead on the hearer without his perceiving it. He goes so far as to state distinctly (I remember it well) that a speaker ought to conceal even the number of his arguments, so that they may not be counted, although they may be distinct in themselves, and in his own mind: and that a discourse ought not to have any clearly marked divisions. But the lack of discernment of late has gone so far that people do not recognize at all the order of a discourse, unless the speaker warns them of it at the commencement, and makes a pause at each point.

C: But do not divisions serve as an assistance to the mind and memory of the hearer? It is for this practical purpose they are made.

A: Divisions help the memory of the *speaker.* But the observance of a natural and consecutive order in subjects would effect that object still better, and that without being specially marked: since the true connection of subjects best guides the mind. But as for divisions, the only people whom they help are those who have studied it, and whom their course of instruction has rendered familiar with that method; and if the great body of hearers remember the divisions better than the rest of the discourse, it is because they have been repeated more frequently. Generally speaking, things which are plain and practical will be best remembered.

JOHN BROADUS

Rhetoric and Homiletics

John Broadus (1827-1895) was at various times in his life a Baptist preacher, Confederate army chaplain, church leader, and seminary professor. He was born in Culpepper County, Virginia. After a teenage conversion experience during a "protracted meeting," he entered the University of Virginia for the purpose of becoming a schoolteacher, but after graduation he became the pastor of a Baptist church in Charlottesville. In 1859 he joined the small faculty of the new Baptist Seminary in Greenville, South Carolina (the school moved to Louisville in 1877), as professor of New Testament and homiletics. During the Civil War the seminary closed and Broadus served for a time as a chaplain to Lee's army in Virginia. After the war he helped restore the seminary and from 1889 until his death served as its president. Broadus was well respected both as a preacher and a scholar; he published several books including a *Commentary on the Gospel of Matthew* and a *Harmony of the Gospels*. It was his textbook on homiletics, however, that became his legacy. Based on lectures given to one blind student during the difficult years after the war, *A Treatise on the Preparation and Delivery of Sermons* first appeared in print in 1870 and remained the authoritative work for more than fifty years. (By 1889 the book was in its fourteenth edition.) In 1889 Broadus became the first Southern Baptist to give the Lyman Beecher Lectures in Preaching at Yale. Although he warned against "the dangers of rhetoric," his own homiletic was informed by Aristotle, Longinus, Cicero, and Horace. One of his maxims helped perpetuate the durable misconception: "homiletics may be called a branch of rhetoric, or a kindred art." Such a view reflected Peter Ramus's restriction of rhetoric to style and delivery, and inadvertently prolonged the separation of homiletics from biblical studies, theology, and liturgics.

John Broadus, *A Treatise on the Preparation and Delivery of Sermons* (New York: A. C. Armstrong & Son, 1889 [1880]), pp. 25-31.

The difference between skill and the lack of it in speaking, is almost as great as in handling tools, those, for example, of the carpenter or the blacksmith. And while no real skill can be acquired without practice — according to the true saying, "The only way to learn to preach is to preach" — yet mere practice will never ring the highest skill; it must be heedful, thoughtful practice, with close observation of others and sharp watching of ourselves, and controlled by good sense and good taste.

Now in respect of skill, preaching is an *art;* and while art cannot create the requisite powers of mind or body, nor supply their place if really absent, it can develop and improve them, and aid in using them to the best advantage. To gain skill, then, is the object of rhetorical studies, skill in the construction and in the delivery of discourse.

Origin of the Rules of Rhetoric

The rules of rhetoric are properly the result of induction. They are sometimes spoken of as if they had been drawn up by would-be wise men, who undertook to tell, on general principles, how one *ought* to speak. But they simply result from much thoughtful observation of the way in which men *do* speak, when they speak really well. Everyone will sometimes see occasion to depart from these rules; but he ought to understand that in disregarding the "rules of rhetoric," he is not nobly spurning artificial fetters and barriers, but simply turning aside, for the time, and for good reason, from the path in which it is usually found best to walk. And to do this will be wise or not wise, according as there is real occasion for it, and it is well managed. So too, we notice, men of sense often exactly conform to these rules, without knowing anything about them; for this is only saying that they speak exactly as men of sense usually do.

What we call rules are but the convenient expression of a principle. They put the principle into a compact form, so as to be easily remembered and readily applied. But the rule, however judiciously framed, can never be as flexible as the principle it represents. There will therefore be cases, and as regards some rules many cases, in which one *may violate the rule and yet be really conforming to the principle,* these being cases in which the principle would bend, and adapt itself to peculiar conditions, while the rule cannot bend. This consideration explains many of the instances in which a speaker produces a powerful effect though utterly violating the rules of rhetoric. Other such instances are explained by the sort of shock produced by a departure from what is usual, as the sleeping miller will wake when the mill stops. And in still other cases, the effect is produced by a man's power in other respects, *in spite of* the particular violation of rule.

Dangers of Rhetorical Studies

(1) *Thinking more of the form than the matter.* Rhetoric has to do with the use we make of material, the choice, adaptation, arrangement, expression. But after all, the material itself is more important. We hold that Demosthenes did not mean to contradict this, when he said (if he ever did in fact say it), that the first thing, second thing, third thing, in speaking is delivery. He took the other for granted. No man has ever surpassed Demosthenes in thorough mastery of the subjects upon which he spoke. But delivery had been with him a matter of peculiar difficulty, his deficiencies in that respect had defeated his early attempts, and his subsequent excellence had been gained only by enormous labor; it was natural that he should lay stress upon its importance, supposing that no man of sense could overlook the necessity of being fully acquainted with his subject. Now the things which ought *most* to be thought of by the preacher, are piety and knowledge, and the blessing of God. Skill, however valuable, is far less important than these; and there is danger that rhetorical studies will cause men to forget that such is the case. It is lamentable to see how often the remarks upon preaching made by preachers themselves, in conversation and in newspaper critiques, are confined to a discussion of the performance and the performer. Unsympathizing listeners or readers have, in such cases, too much ground for concluding that preachers are anxious only to display skill and gain oratorical reputation.

(2) *Imitation.* All are aware that there is both a conscious and an unconscious imitation. That which is unconscious is of course not so blameworthy, but it cannot fail to be injurious, and it is a subtle evil which should be guarded against with the sharpest self-inspection. Everyone observes, too, that imitators are especially apt to imitate a man's faults. The reason is easily seen. The excellencies of a good speaker are apt to be symmetrical, while his faults are salient, prominent. The latter, therefore, will most readily attract unconscious imitation. As to the conscious imitator, he is sure to be a superficial observer, who will think that what he notices most in some admired speaker is the secret of his power, and will go to imitating that. Besides, it is *easier* to ape the single, salient fault than the symmetrical combination of many excellencies.

Is the danger of imitation increased by attendance upon institutions of learning? Hardly. He who is so susceptible on the one hand, or on the other hand, so silly, as to fall readily into it, will find someone to imitate, wherever he may be. Every country district has some favorite preacher, whom others around may be seen to imitate. When many of these imitators are gathered at a public institution, the men they imitate are fewer and more generally known, and therefore the fact attracts more attention. On the other hand, they are more likely to have pointed out to them the danger and the evils of imitation, so as utterly to eschew that which is conscious, and promptly to correct the unconscious, when made aware of it. Nor is there any greater danger of such imitation at a theological institution than at a college or university. Still, some men are very liable to this fault, and when about to hear the same speaker several times a week for many months, all ought to be on their guard against imitating his peculiarities.

(3) *Artificiality.* There is much artificiality which ought not to be called by the odious name of affectation. The speaker's motives are good; he merely errs in judgment and taste. But a great error it is. In all speaking, especially in preaching, naturalness, genuineness, even though awkward, is really more effective for all the highest ends, than the most elegant artificiality. "But it is the highest art to conceal art." Nay, no art *can* conceal art. We may not perceive it, but we dimly, instinctively feel that there is something the matter, and perhaps wonder what it is; somehow, the preacher's well-meant efforts are failing to reach their aim. The danger of artificiality in speaking is very great. When one begins, he is apt to feel awkward in the new and strange situation. As one unaccustomed to riding on horseback must *learn* to sit naturally, and feel at ease, in the saddle, so very many speakers, perhaps all, have to *learn to be natural*. It follows that a preacher ought never to preach merely for practice; this will inevitably tend to encourage artificiality. The first few efforts of a young man — which will often go much farther than he is at the time aware to form his habits for life — ought to be genuine, *bona fide* preaching. If he ever preaches in the presence of none but his fellow students, and instructors, it ought to be only upon a subject thoroughly suited to *their* religious wants, and with a most earnest and prayerful effort to do them good. It is believed that the plan of causing students to preach before the class results, upon the whole, in more harm than good, and that it ought to be avoided. Let them preach where it can be real preaching, or not at all. Even the debating society proposes a present end to be gained, and awakens some living interest.

As regards all that pertains to preaching, and especially delivery, our efforts at rhetorical improvement must be *mainly negative*. We endeavor to gain correct general principles, and some idea of the errors and faults to which speakers are generally liable. We then speak, aiming to be guided by these principles, and to correct our faults as they may arise. It is unwise to set up at the outset some standard of excellence, and aim to conform to that. If one should take a fancy that cedar trees are more beautiful than oaks and attempt to trim his oaks into the shape, and color them into the hue, of cedars, the result could only be ridiculous. Let the young cedar grow as a cedar, and the young oak as an oak, but straighten, prune, improve each of them into the best possible tree of its kind. And so as to speaking, be always yourself, your actual, natural self, but yourself developed, corrected, improved into the very best you are by nature capable of becoming.

Relation of Homiletics to Rhetoric

The Greek word *homilia* signifies conversation, mutual talk, and so familiar discourse. The Greek writer Photius (9th cent.) says of Chrysostom's expository sermons on Genesis, that he finds the book bearing the name of discourses, but that they are much more like homilies (talks), because he so often speaks as if seeing the hearers before him, asks questions, and answers, and makes promises, etc., and because they have not the formal arrangement of discourses. The Latin word *sermo* (from which we get *sermon*) has the same sense, of conversation, talk, discussion, etc. It is instructive to observe that the early Christians did not apply to their public teachings the names given to the orations of Demosthenes and Cicero, but called them *talks,* familiar discourses. From the word *homily* has been derived the term *homiletics,* as denoting the science or art of Christian discourse, or a treatise on that subject, embracing all that pertains to the preparation and delivery of sermons. Homiletics may be called a branch of rhetoric, or a kindred art. Those fundamental principles, which have their basis in human nature, are of course the same in both cases, and this being so, it seems clear that we must regard homiletics as rhetoric applied to this particular kind of speaking. Still, preaching is properly very different from secular discourse, as to the primary source of its materials, as to the directness and simplicity of style which become the preacher, and the unworldly motives by which he ought to be influenced. And while these and other peculiarities do not render it proper to treat homiletics as entirely distinct from rhetoric, they ought to be constantly borne in mind by the student of homiletics and by the working preacher.

CHARLES HADDON SPURGEON

Illustrations in Preaching

For more than thirty years the self-educated Baptist preacher Charles Haddon Spurgeon (1834-1892) captivated a weekly congregation of six thousand people in his Metropolitan Tabernacle in South London. He was the foremost of the "princes of the pulpit" in what has been called the Age of Preaching; everywhere he appeared Spurgeon drew huge crowds. On October 7, 1857, 23,654 people packed the Crystal Palace to hear him. At the Surrey Gardens Music Hall he drew more than twelve thousand attendees. In his heyday his "penny pulpit" series sold at London newsstands and in railway stations at the rate of twenty-five thousand per week. Spurgeon combined oratorical prowess and evangelistic fervor with a deep concern for social issues such as slavery, alcoholism, and urban poverty. He published multitudes of books of helps for preachers, including his seven-volume *Treasury of David,* and founded a Pastors' College that continues as Spurgeon's College. His regular classes on preaching were incorporated into his *Lectures to My Students,* which include practical advice on "The Minister's Fainting Fits" and "To Workers with Slender Apparatus." His own sermons teemed with stories, anecdotes, news events, analogies, and, most successfully, illustrations from nature. Despite both his fame and his larger-than-life talent, Spurgeon retained a sense of reverence for the responsibility and act of preaching. He is one of the few great preachers in whose printed sermons one can still hear something of the man. In the following lecture, Spurgeon uses his own gift of metaphor-making — the image of a window — to explain the function of illustrations in the sermon. He suggests a limit of eight metaphors per sermon, a rule he broke with great exuberance. (See Craig Skinner, "Charles Haddon Spurgeon," in the *Concise Encyclopedia of Preaching,* ed. William Willimon and Richard Lischer.)

Charles Haddon Spurgeon, *Lectures to My Students* (Grand Rapids: Baker Book House, 1977 [1894]), Third Series, Lecture 1, pp. 1-13.

The topic now before us is the use of illustrations in our sermons. Perhaps we shall best subserve our purpose by working out an illustration in the present address; for there is no better way of teaching the art of pottery than by making a pot. Quaint Thomas Fuller says, "reasons are the pillars of the fabric of a sermon; but similitudes are the windows which give the best lights." The comparison is happy and suggestive, and we will build up our discourse under its direction.

The chief reason for the construction of windows in a house is, as Fuller says, *to let in light*. Parables, similes, and metaphors have that effect; and hence we use them to *illustrate* our subject, or, in other words, to *"brighten it with light,"* for that is Dr. Johnson's literal rendering of the word *illustrate*. Often when didactic speech fails to enlighten our hearers we may make them see our meaning by opening a window and letting in the pleasant light of analogy. Our Savior, who is the light of the world, took care to fill his speech with similitudes, so that the common people heard him gladly: his example stamps with high authority the practice of illuminating heavenly instruction with comparisons and similes. To every preacher of righteousness as well as to Noah, wisdom gives the command, "A window shalt thou make in the ark." You may build up laborious definitions and explanations and yet leave your hearers in the dark as to your meaning; but a thoroughly suitable metaphor will wonderfully clear the sense. The pictures in *The Illustrated London News* give us a far better idea of the scenery which they represent than could be conveyed to us by the best descriptive letter-press; and it is much the same with scriptural teaching: abstract truth comes before us so much more vividly when a concrete example is given, or the doctrine itself is clothed in figurative language. There should, if possible, be at least one good metaphor in the shortest address; as Ezekiel, in his vision of the temple, saw that even to the little chambers there were windows suitable to their size. If we are faithful to the spirit of the gospel we labor to make things plain; it is our study to be simple and to be understood by the most illiterate of our hearers; let us, then, set forth many a metaphor and parable before the people. . . .

Windows greatly add to the pleasure and agreeableness of a habitation, and so do *illustrations make a sermon pleasurable and interesting*. A building without windows would be a prison rather than a house, for it would be quite dark, and no one would care to take it upon lease; and, in the same way, a discourse without a parable is prosy and dull, and involves a grievous weariness of the flesh. The preacher in Solomon's Ecclesiastes "sought to find out acceptable words," or, as the Hebrew has it, "words of delight": surely, figures and comparisons are delectable to our hearers. Let us not deny them the salt of parable with the meat of doctrine. Our congregations hear us with pleasure when we give them a fair measure of imagery: when an anecdote is being told they rest, take breath, and give play to their imaginations, and thus prepare themselves for the sterner work which lies before them in listening to our profounder expositions.

Riding in a third-class carriage some years ago in the eastern counties, we had been for a long time without a lamp; and when a traveller lighted a candle, it was pleasant to see how all eyes turned that way, and rejoiced in the light; such is frequently the effect of an apt simile in the midst of a sermon, it lights up the whole matter, and gladdens every heart. Even the little children open their eyes and ears, and a smile brightens up their faces as we tell a story; for they, too, rejoice in the light which streams in through our windows. We dare say they often wish that the sermon were all illustrations, even as the boy desired to have a cake made all of plums; but that must not be: there is a happy medium, and we must keep to it by making our discourse pleasant hearing, but not a mere pastime.

No reason exists why the preaching of the gospel should be a miserable operation either to the speaker or to the hearer. Pleasantly profitable let all our sermons be. A house must not have thick walls without openings, neither must a discourse be all made up of solid slabs of doctrine without a window of comparison or a lattice of poetry; if so, our hearers will gradually forsake us, and prefer to stay at home and read their favorite authors whose lively tropes and vivid images afford more pleasure to their minds.

Every architect will tell you that he looks upon his windows as *an opportunity for introducing ornament into his design.* A pile may be massive, but it cannot be pleasing if it is not broken up with windows and other details. The palace of the popes at Avignon is an immense structure; but the external windows are so few that it has all the aspect of a colossal prison, and suggests nothing of what a palace should be. Sermons need to be broken up, varied, decorated, and enlivened; and nothing can do this so well as the introduction of types, emblems, and instances. Of course, ornament is not the main point to be considered; but still, many little excellences go to make up perfection, and this is one of the many, and therefore it should not be overlooked. When wisdom built her house she hewed out her seven pillars, for glory and for beauty, as well as for the support of the structure; and shall we think that any rough hovel is good enough for the beauty of holiness to dwell in? Certainly a gracious discourse is none the better for being bereft of every grace of language. Meretricious ornament we deprecate, but an appropriate beauty of speech we cultivate. Truth is a king's daughter, and her raiment should be of wrought gold; her house is a palace, and it should be adorned with "windows of agate and gates of carbuncle."

Illustrations tend to enliven an audience and quicken attention. Windows, when they will open, which, alas, is not often the case in our places of worship, are a great blessing by refreshing and reviving the audience with a little pure air, and arousing the poor mortals who are rendered sleepy by the stagnant atmosphere. A window should, according to its name, be a wind-door, through which a breath of air may visit the audience; even so, an original figure, a noble image, a quaint comparison, a rich allegory, should open upon our hearers a breeze of happy thought, which will pass over them like life-giving breath, arousing them from their apathy, and quickening their faculties to receive the truth.

Those who are accustomed to the soporific sermonizings of certain dignified divines would marvel greatly if they could see the enthusiasm and lively delight with which congregations listen to speech through which there flows a quiet current of happy, natural illustration. Arid as a desert are many volumes of discourses which are to be met with upon the booksellers' dust-covered shelves; but if in the course of a thousand paragraphs they contain a single simile, it is an oasis in the Sahara, and serves to keep the reader's soul alive. In fashioning a discourse think little of the bookworm, which will be sure of its portion of meat however dry your doctrine, but have pity upon those hungering ones immediately around you who must find life through your sermon or they will never find it at all. If some of your hearers sleep on they will of necessity wake up in eternal perdition, for they hear no other helpful voice.

While we thus commend illustrations for necessary uses, it must be remembered that they are not the strength of a sermon any more than a window is the strength of a house; and for this reason, among others, *they should not be too numerous.* Too many openings for light may seriously detract from the stability of a building. We have known sermons so full of metaphors that they became weak, and we had almost said *crazy,* structures. Sermons must not be nosegays of flowers, but sheaves of wheat. Very beautiful sermons are generally very useless ones. To aim at elegance is to court failure. It is possible to have too much of a good thing: a glass house is not the most comfortable of abodes, and besides other objectionable qualities it has the great fault of being sadly tempting to stone throwers. When a critical adversary attacks our metaphors he generally makes short work of them. To friendly minds images are arguments, but to opponents they are opportunities for attack; the enemy climbs up by the window. . . .

Illustrate, by all means, but do not let the sermon be all illustrations, or it will be only suitable for an assembly of simpletons. A volume is all the better for engravings, but a scrapbook which is all woodcuts is usually intended for the use of little children. Our house should be built up with the substantial masonry of doctrine, upon the deep foundation of inspiration; its pillars should be of solid scriptural argument, and every stone of truth should be carefully laid in its place; and then the windows should be ranged in due order, "three rows," if we will: "light against light," like the house of the forest of Lebanon. But a house is not erected for the sake of the windows, nor may a sermon be arranged with the view of fitting in a favorite apologue. A window is merely a convenience subordinate to the entire design, and so is the best illustration. We shall be foolish indeed if we compose a discourse to display a metaphor; as foolish as if an architect should build a cathedral with the view of exhibiting a stained-glass window. We are not sent into the world to build a Crystal Palace in which to set out works of art and elegancies of fashion; but as wise master-builders we are to edify a spiritual house for the divine inhabiting. Our building is intended to last, and is meant for everyday use, and hence it must not be all crystal and color. We miss our way altogether, as gospel ministers, if we aim at flash and finery.

It is impossible to lay down a rule as to how much adornment shall be found in each discourse: every preacher must judge for himself in that matter. True taste in dress could not be readily defined, yet everyone knows what it is; and there is a literary and spiritual taste which should be displayed in the measuring out of tropes and figures in very public speech. "*Ne quid nimis*" is a good caution: do not be too eager to garnish and adorn. Some seem never to have enough of metaphors: each one of their sentences must be a flower. They compass sea and land to find a fresh piece of colored glass for their windows, and they break down the walls of their discourses to let in superfluous ornaments, till their productions rather resemble a fantastic grotto than a house to dwell in. They are grievously in error if they think that thus they manifest their own wisdom, or benefit their hearers. I could almost wish for a return of the window-tax if it would check these poetical brethren.

The law, I believe, allowed eight windows free from duty, and we might also exempt "a few, that is eight" metaphors from criticism; but more than that ought to pay heavily. Flowers upon the table at a banquet are well enough; but as nobody can live upon bouquets, they will become objects of contempt if they are set before us in lieu of substantial viands. The difference between a little salt with your meat and being compelled to empty the salt-cellar is clear to all; and we could wish that those who pour out so many symbols, emblems, figures, and devices would remember that nausea in oratory is not more agreeable than in food. Enough is as good a feast; and too many pretty things may be a greater evil than none at all. . . .

Illustrations should really cast light upon the subject in hand, otherwise they are sham windows, and all shams are an abomination. When the window-tax was still in force many people in country houses closed half their lights by plastering them up, and then they had the plaster painted to look like panes; so that there was still the appearance of a window, though no sunlight could enter. Well do I remember the dark rooms in my grandfather's parsonage, and my wonder that men should have to pay for the light of the sun. Blind windows are fit emblems of illustrations which illustrate nothing, and need themselves to be explained. Grandiloquence is never more characteristic than in its figures; there it disports itself in a very carnival of bombast. . . .

It may be well to note that *illustrations should not be too prominent,* or, to pursue our figure, they should not be painted windows, attracting attention to themselves rather than letting in the clear light of day. I am not pronouncing any judgment upon windows adorned with "glass of various colors which shine like meadows decked in the flowers of spring"; I am looking only to my illustration. Our figures are meant not so much to be seen as to be seen through. If you take the hearer's mind away from the subject by exciting his admiration of your own skill in imagery, you are doing evil rather than good. I saw in one of our exhibitions a portrait of a king; but the artist had surrounded his majesty with a bower of flowers so exquisitely painted that everyone's eye was taken away from the royal figure. All the resources of the painter's art had been lavished upon the accessories, and the result was that the portrait, which should have been all in all, had fallen into a secondary place. This was surely an error in portrait-painting, even though it might be a success in art. We have to set forth Christ before the people, "evidently crucified among them," and the loveliest emblem or the most charming image which calls the mind away from our divine subject is to be conscientiously foresworn. Jesus must be all in all; his gospel must be the beginning and end of all our discoursing; parable and poesy must be under his feet, and eloquence must wait upon him as his servant. Never by any possibility must the minister's speech become a rival to his subject; that were to dishonor Christ, and not to glorify him. Hence the caution that the illustrations be not too conspicuous.

Out of this last observation comes the further remark that *illustrations are best when they are natural, and grow out of the subject.* They should be like those well-arranged windows which are evidently part of the plan of a structure, and not inserted as an afterthought, or for mere adornment. The cathedral of Milan inspires my mind with extreme admiration; it always appears to me as if it must have grown out of the earth like a colossal tree or rather like a forest of marble. From its base to its loftiest pinnacle every detail is a natural outgrowth, a portion of a well developed whole, essential to the main idea; indeed, part and parcel of it. Such should a sermon be; its exordium, divisions, arguments, appeals, and metaphors should all spring out of itself; nothing should be out of living relation to the rest; it should seem as if nothing could be added without being an excrescence, and nothing taken away without inflicting damage. There should be flowers in a sermon, but the bulk of them should be the flowers of the soil; not dainty exotics, evidently imported with much care from a distant land, but the natural upspringing of a life natural to the holy ground on which the preacher stands. Figures of speech should be congruous with the matter of the discourse; a rose upon an oak would be out of place, and a lily springing from a poplar would be unnatural; everything should be of a piece and have a manifest relationship to the rest. . . .

Elaboration into minute points is not commendable when we are using figures. The best light comes in through the clearest glass: too much paint keeps out the sun. God's altar of old was to be made of earth, or of unhewn stone, "for," said the word, "if thou lift up thy tool upon it, thou hast polluted it." A labored, artificial style, upon which the graver's tool has left abundant marks, is more consistent with human pleadings in courts of law, or in the forum, or in the senate, than with prophetic utterances delivered in the name of God and for the promotion of his glory. Our Lord's parables were as simple as tales for children, and as naturally beautiful as the lilies which sprang up in the valleys where he taught the people. He borrowed no legend from the Talmud, nor fairy tale from Persia, neither fetched he his emblems from beyond the sea; but he dwelt among his own people, and talked of common things in homely style, as never man spake before, and yet as any observant man should speak. His parables were like himself and his surroundings; and were never strained, fantastic, pedantic, or artificial. Let us imitate him, for we shall never find a model more complete, or more suitable for the present age. . . .

There will be little need to borrow from the recondite mysteries of human art, nor to go deep into the theories of science; for in nature golden illustrations lie upon the surface, and the purest is that which is uppermost and most readily discerned. Of natural history in all its branches we may well say, "the gold of that land is good": the illustrations furnished by everyday phenomena seen by the ploughman and the waggoner are the very best which earth can yield. An illustration is not like a prophet, for it has most honor in its own country; and those who have oftenest seen the object are those who are most gratified by the figure drawn from it.

I trust that it is scarcely necessary to add that *illustrations must never be low or mean.* They may not be high-flown, but they should always be in good taste. They may be homely, and yet chastely beautiful; but rough and coarse they should never be. A house is dishonored by having dirty windows, cobwebbed and begrimed, patched with brown paper, or stuffed up with rags: such windows are the insignia of a hovel rather than a house. About our illustrations there must never be even the slightest trace of anything that would shock the most delicate modesty. We like not that window out of which Jezebel is looking. Like the bells upon the horses, our lightest expressions must be holiness unto the Lord. Of that which suggests the grovelling and the base we may say with the apostle, "Let it not be once named among you, as becometh saints."

All our windows should open toward Jerusalem, and none toward Sodom. We will gather our flowers always and only from Emmanuel's land; and Jesus himself shall be their savor and sweetness, so that when he lingers at the lattice to hear us speak of himself he may say, "Thy lips, O my spouse, drop as the honeycomb: honey and milk are under thy tongue." That which grows beyond the border of purity and good repute must never be bound up in our garlands, nor placed among the decorations of our discourses. That which would be exceedingly clever and telling in a stump orator's speech, or in a cheap-jack's harangue, would be disgusting from a minister of the gospel. Time was when we could have found far too many specimens of censurable coarseness, but it would be ungenerous to mention them now that such things are on all hands condemned.

AMOS N. WILDER

The New Utterance

The contribution of Amos N. Wilder (1895-1993) to homiletics is indirect but seminal. Wilder, who until his retirement in 1963 was Hollis Professor of Divinity at the Harvard Divinity School, is best known for his studies in ethics, eschatology, and aesthetics, and for his poetry, including the volume *Grace Confounding*. He was the brother of playwright Thornton Wilder, and famous at the time of his death for being the oldest living person to have played center court at Wimbledon! At age ninety-five he published *The Bible and the Literary Critic* (1991). His studies in Christianity and rhetoric transcend the older Bible-as-literature approaches by demonstrating the indissoluble connection between the content of the Christian message and its literary form. Wilder taught New Testament scholars (and preachers) that the question of *how* is as important to understanding a text as *what*. In many ways his work is most suggestive for preaching. Preaching does not require an esoteric or otherworldly vocabulary. The New Testament language, he says, is common, ordinary, *Kleinliteratur* — a kind of folk art — and at the same time uncommonly tilted toward the eschatological future. One of the marks of the literary Gospels is their brevity, a concision born of apocalyptic urgency. Focusing on the dialogue, story, and poem in the New Testament, Wilder reminds preachers of the oral-aural basis of the gospel and challenges the church to recover the potency of its best language and its earliest preaching.

Amos N. Wilder, *Early Christian Rhetoric: The Language of the Gospel* (Cambridge, Mass.: Harvard University Press, 1964; reissue, 1971), pp. 1-2, 9-15.

Men of our time have inevitably had their attention called to the problem of language, and in various aspects. As modern devices make the world smaller and smaller, and throw us ever closer to peoples we had thought of as alien and remote, we find ourselves under the necessity of mastering more foreign tongues. But it is not only a matter of diverse languages. We are now more conscious of the problem of communication itself even in our own language. Familiar words have lost their meaning for many; or the same word means different things to different people. Jargon and clichés usurp the place of discriminating speech in many areas of life. It is not only in the modern arts that we wrestle with the problem of meaning. It is not surprising that philosophy is today occupied above all with language, or that social science interests itself in the rhetoric of propaganda, or the church with the task of communication. In a situation like ours any use of language that aspires to a wide audience, as with mass entertainment or advertising, has perforce to sink to a very low common denominator of what is not so much language as elementary stimuli by verbal gags, pictures, and rhythms.

No doubt we are going through a period of the death and birth of language, one of the primordial features of human nature and culture. We have to become dumb before we can learn to use names and words faithfully again. It is in modern poetry that one sees this struggle most revealingly. In view of all this it is again not surprising that a main concern of the Christian church today is that of communication. The preacher, we are told, is like a man speaking into a dead microphone. We hear on all sides about the need for the modernization of the Christian message, translation of the ancient ideas and images, rediscovery of effective media of discourse. It has seemed worthwhile, therefore, to study the speech-forms and utterance of the early church and see what we can learn from it.

We are concerned first of all, therefore, not so much with what the early Christians said as how they said it. Yet this is a false distinction. The two cannot really be separated, but they can be looked at separately. We are interested here in all that has to do with the form and style of the New Testament writings. In this sense we are taking a literary approach. One could call it a study of the literary forms and genres of the early church. However, we must deal here not only with the writings as such but with the oral speech that lies behind them. It is not only a question of how the first Christians wrote but how they spoke and talked. It is better, therefore, to call our topic "early Christian rhetoric." It is true that the term "rhetoric" has unfortunate connotations. But it has the advantage of covering both written and oral discourse. . . .

Jesus of Nazareth and his first followers broke into the world of speech and writing of their time, and, indeed, into its silence, with a novel and powerful utterance, that is, with a "word," and the word of a layman. Ignatius of Antioch states the matter in his own surrealist style: "Jesus Christ, his son, who is his word proceeding from silence" (Ignatius's *Letter to the Magnesians* 8:2); "he is the mouth which cannot lie, by which the Father has spoken truly" (Ignatius's *Letter to the Romans* 8:2).

Just on the secular level note how significant this was and has been. At least there was here a new dynamics in human speech. One thinks of what John Keats said about "the indescribable gusto of the Elizabethan voice." But one searches for more significant analogies. It is a question of a word from the depths, with power. One analogy would be that of the man who stands up when a panic is spreading in a theater or a riot in the streets and recalls men to their true selves by a compelling word of authority. But this new word in Israel initiated a new world of meaning that went on spreading through ancient society. Here an analogy would be that of the impact of Dante's use of his vernacular dialect rather than Latin upon the spiritual culture of Europe. One can think also of the train of consequences that ensued upon the writing by the teenager Arthur Rimbaud of his *Bateau ivre*. This new spring of symbolist incantation determined much of the history of modern poetic utterance.

Thus we can understand the sense in which Ernst Fuchs has called the rise of the gospel a "speech-event" *(Sprachereignis)*. By this he means a new departure, not just in the sense of a new religious teaching, but rather the opening up of a new dimension of man's awareness, a new breakthrough in language and symbolization. He can also say that the gospel represented a renewal of myth in Israel and the ancient world. The new enlargement of language took on ever new articulation in the course of the apostolic age.

To quote Professor Fuchs further: "Primitive Christianity is itself a speech-phenomenon. It is for that very reason that it established a monument in the new style-form which we call a 'gospel.' The Johannine apocalypse and, indeed, in the first instance the apostolic epistle-literature, these are creations of a new utterance which changes everything that it touches" [*Zur Frage nach dem historischen Jesus* (Tübingen, 1960), p. 261].

He adds that it is only on the margin of the New Testament that one can observe direct assimilation of pagan rhetoric, as for example in the Pastoral Epistles and in post-canonical writings; at a time, that is, when ecclesiastical patterns had begun to solidify.

Early Christianity, of course, brought forth new forms not only in language but in life itself, not only in writing but in ritual. One could say the same thing about other religions. But the spoken and written word have a basic role in the Christian faith. We note the background for this in the Old Testament. The religion of Israel is very much a matter of hearing rather than of seeing. Even

God's actions are spoken of by the prophets as his word. No man can see God and live, but he is known in his speaking. By contrast it is the gods of the nations that are mute, and their visible images are dumb. As we read in Psalm 115:7, "They do not make a sound in their throat." Throughout Scripture, revelation is identified above all with speaking and hearing, with writing and reading, with colloquies and recitals, with tablets and scrolls and parchments, rather than with the imagery of the visual arts. Even visions are converted into writing: "Write the vision," we read in Habakkuk 2:2; and "write what you see in a book" in Revelation 1:11. The seer, indeed, seems to confuse the senses when he speaks of seeing the voice or of the "little scroll" which he was bidden to eat which was "as sweet as honey" in his mouth (10:10). Of course, like all religions Christianity has its sacred actions and spectacles, sacred places and times, sacred arts and objects, but it is in connection with God speaking that they are sacred.

It is intriguing to classify religions or even Christian groups according as they assign priority to auditory or visual images. On the one hand we have religion identified with word and answer; on the other with vision and ecstasy or metamorphosis. The New Testament speaks of the divine apprehension in terms of all the senses, not only hearing and sight but touch and smell (this last in the form of incense and fragrant odors). Yet the hearing mode is primary. The spirit may be rapt in vision, but it is with the heart that the man hears the word of faith and with his mouth that he confesses and is saved (Rom. 10:8-10). Language, then, is more fundamental than graphic representation, except where the latter is itself a transcript in some sense of the word of God. . . .

In this light it is significant that the emotional dynamics of the gospel were always controlled by the meaningfulness of speech. To this, visionary and psychic phenomena were subordinated. And the language in question was not only the spoken word but personal address; it was not only in the indicative mode but in the imperative; it was not only in the third person but in the second and the first; it was not only a matter of declaration but a dialogue.

We can, therefore, appreciate the special incentives to the literary arts that Christianity has always provided, just as other faiths have provided special incentives to the visual arts or to music and dancing. Christianity is a religion of the Book and this has had its corollaries for its total cultural thrust. It is true that when the church took over the heritage of classical culture — ancient rhetoric, architecture, painting, and sculpture — it related itself to all the arts and has exploited them all ever since in changing situations. But the thesis still holds that the faith identifies itself fundamentally with the arts of hearing as against those of sight and touch. Even when the Christian paints or carves or dances or sings he does so to a text, and identifies himself with an archetypal dialogue between God and man.

Even so far as the literary arts themselves are in view — arts which have, of course, come to consummate expression in many religious traditions — one could argue that particular genres are at home both in the church and in particular Christian cultures of different periods. Erich Auerbach has studied the peculiar forms and styles of biblical and post-biblical Christian narrative forms as compared with classical. Martin Jarrett-Kerr has presented illustrations in different periods of Western literature of the special morphology of writings of Christian inspiration. One can also say that the novel as it has evolved in the modern period is a form which is only possible in a world whose view of man and society has been shaped by Christian presupposition.

Throughout our analysis we shall find ourselves recurring to one feature of the *earliest* Christian speech including that of Jesus. It is naïve, it is not studied; it is *extempore* and directed to the occasion, it is not calculated to serve some future hour. This utterance is dynamic, actual, immediate, reckless of posterity; not coded for catechists or repeaters. It is only one aspect of this that it is oral and not written. We find ourselves at first and for a rather long time in the presence of oral and live face-to-face communication. The gospel meant freedom of speech in this deeper sense. One did not hoard its formulas, since when occasion arose the Spirit would teach one what to say and how to witness and what defense to make. The earliest Christians lived on the free bounty of God in this sense also. The speech of the gospel was thus fresh and its forms novel and fluid; it came and went, as Ernst Fuchs says, with the freedom of sunshine, wind, and rain.

Even the writing forms of the early church are better understood if we keep in mind the primal role of oral speech in the beginning. *Viva voce* communication is more malleable, more personal, and more searching. These qualities were to distinguish Christian discourse even when it was obliged to take on written form. So far as we know Jesus never wrote a word, except on that occasion when, in the presence of the woman taken in adultery, "he bent down and wrote with his finger on the ground." In secular terms we could say that Jesus spoke as the birds sing, oblivious of any concern for transcription. Less romantically we can say that Jesus' use of the spoken word alone has its own theological significance. For one thing speaking is more direct than writing, and we would expect this in him through whom God openly staged his greatest controversy with his people. This transaction in which Jesus was involved was neither more nor less than a trial, and the parties in a trial confront each other in direct confrontation, as in Jesus' parables of the talents and the sheep and the goats. Jesus was a voice not a penman, a herald not a scribe, a watchman with his call in the marketplace and the Temple, and not a cry of alarm in the wilderness like John the Baptist. This deportment of Jesus is a sign. We are reminded of the

acted parables of certain of the prophets of earlier times: one of whom was eloquently dumb for a period. In Israel's tradition God's servants the prophets did
not write unless they were ordered to, however it might be with the scribes.

That Jesus confined himself to the spoken and precarious words is of a
piece with his renunciation of all cultural bonds such as home and trade and
property; and with his instruction to his disciples to "take nothing for their
journey except a staff; no bread, no bag, no money in their belts; but to wear
sandals and not to put on two tunics" (Mark 6:8-9). This deportment had its
true significance in the crisis with which Jesus was identified. For him and his
generation history was fractured, time's course was in dissolution, continuities
were broken. The act of writing presupposes continuities and a future. Jesus'
word was for the present, the last hour. Indeed, his whole manifestation was a
presence. This observation agrees with Günther Bornkamm's thesis in his *Jesus
of Nazareth*. The Judaism of the time looked back to the Lawgiver and the covenants, and forward to the time of salvation. In so doing, the contemporaries of
Jesus forfeited the present. Jesus brought both the will of God and the promises
of God into the present with inexorable sharpness and actuality. Only the living
voice can serve such an occasion.

Professor Fuchs makes this observation that Jesus wrote nothing and
adds that even Paul wrote reluctantly. When he and other authors of our New
Testament writings *did* write or dictate, their speech still has a special character,
since the new depth and freedom of speech perpetuated itself even in the written productions. The voice of the writer is the voice of the speaker to a remarkable degree.

Paul wrote reluctantly and in any case without an extended historical perspective. He saw himself in the situation of harvester of the last days (Rom.
10:18), and as vocal herald of a world-crisis, as is suggested in the passage he
cites from Psalm 19: "Their voice has gone out to all the earth, and their words
to the ends of the world."

Paul writes always as one thwarted by absence and eagerly anticipating
meeting or reunion. He is distressed by circumstances which prevent face-to-
face address: "I could wish to be present with you now," he writes to the
Galatians, "and change my tone, for I am perplexed about you" (4:20). Even in
writing he falls into the style of direct oral plea and challenge. The very nature
of the gospel imposes upon him ways of expression that suggest dramatic immediacy: devices and rhythms of the speaker rather than the writer; imagined
dialogue; the situation of a court hearing or church trial with its accusations
and defenses; the use of direct discourse; challenges not so much to understand
the written words but to listen and behold; queries, exclamations, and oaths.

To return to the sayings of Jesus. It is true that we do have evidence that his words and deeds were carried in memory and reported. We find such statements in the Gospels as the following: "At that time Herod the tetrarch heard about the fame of Jesus" (Matt. 14:1); or, "so his fame spread throughout all Syria" (Matt. 4:24). But we should make a distinction between an inevitable live diffusion of Jesus' words, on the one hand, and formal memorization or writing down of what he said, on the other. Some scholars hold that Jesus taught much as the scribes did with a view to the learning by heart of his words and deeds as though for catechetical use among his disciples. They have a plausible argument in the poetic and formal structure of much of his utterance. They even speak of mnemonic devices employed: parallelism, assonance, chiasmus, and various scribal patterns of pronouncement. But all this ignores the radical difference between Jesus and the Jewish teachers, the eschatological outlook of Jesus, who was not schooling his followers in a learned mode for new generations to come, and the intense urging with which he spoke to the immediate crisis and the face-to-face hearer. The incomparable felicity and patterning of his sayings is indeed evident, but this formal perfection is not a matter of mnemonics; it is the countersign of the most effective communication of the moment. Naturally his words and parables were remembered and retold, often with great accuracy, so lucid and inevitable was his phrasing. But here as always the new speech of the gospel was not a matter of words on a tablet but a word in the heart, not a copybook for recitation but winged words for life.

JOSEPH SITTLER

Imagining a Sermon

One of the most neglected dimensions of preaching, that of the imagination, is addressed by Joseph Sittler (1904-1987) in his Beecher Lectures of 1959. For Sittler the imagination is much more than a twister of texts or a turner of phrases. One of its functions is to fuse the theological *what* and the rhetorical *how* of each text; indeed, to show the inevitability of the *how*. Sittler's work on the rhetoric of preaching reflects the concerns of Amos Wilder, though Sittler approaches his task from a theological rather than a biblical and literary perspective. Theologically, he pioneered this generation's passion for the created order and ecology. Because humanity lives fully in the overlap of nature and grace, the religious imagination must be true to both, even if that fidelity means the loss of symmetry and polished assurance. He cautions preachers who have a penchant for the touch of inspiration or the happy ending, "What God has riven asunder let no preacher too suavely join together." Sittler offers preachers a succinct definition of the imagination: "Imagination is the process by which there is reenacted in the reader the salvatory immediacy of the word of God as this word is witnessed to by the speaker." Speaking from the vantage of hermeneutics, Ebeling makes a similar point when he says that the preacher "executes the text" — allows it to work its original will on the hearer. By using Paul as a *rhetorical* as well as a theological paradigm, Sittler models an approach to preaching begun by Augustine. But instead of enjoining us to *imitate* Paul's *style* as it is revealed in selected passages, Sittler would have the preacher *imagine* Paul's *faith* as it is given shape, tonality, and style in language.

Joseph Sittler, *The Ecology of Faith* (Philadelphia: Fortress, 1961), pp. 46-48, 53-59.

I magination is not used here to designate that mere vivacity of the mind whereby unlikely juxtaposition of things or notions imparts startling cleverness to discourse; it is not a quality produced by the accidental endowment of the temperament with whimsicality. Contemporary preaching is full of dramatic and piquant turnings of the text, irresponsible arbitrariness in strained if ever so personable interpretations of biblical figures, events, and statements. That these practices are indulged in does not define imagination; one might be so unkind as to suggest that they define the preacher.

Imagination in its proper meaning is never an addition, it is an evocation. It is perception, not piquancy. Its work is not cosmetical or decorative; it is a function of percipiency. It is exercised not only in the perception of new qualities in things, but also in the discovery of hitherto unseen relationships between things. . . .

We move even closer to the definition of the role of imagination in preaching when we proceed from that judicious statement about general religious discourse to affirm that specifically Christian discourse is intrinsically needful of the same thing. For the central revelation of God in an incarnation of grace in a world of nature inwardly requires that all discourse inclusive of these two magnitudes is of necessity dialectical. And imagination is the name for that category-transcending and fusing vision and speech which is proper to the given character of God's self-disclosure. The problem of proper Christian statement may be put in another way.

The "power and the truth" of the Christian gospel is in the level and the dimensions of its assault upon the hurt God-man relationship. When once it is acknowledged that man is a creature of nature who nevertheless cannot settle for the natural and that he is an object of grace who nevertheless must celebrate grace *in* the natural — it is at the same time settled that any adequate theological explication must forever be two-sided; that is, dialectical. Its statements will always have to walk the knife-edge at the frontier or fuse together the magnitudes of nature and grace.

This double character of Christian communication, if lost or blurred by oversimplification, banalization, or moralization, can perhaps achieve a hearing — but usually at the cost of the truth. Every simple term of the faith must be set forth in such a way that the multiple dimensions of its own content are exposed. . . .

Suppose that the substance of the sermon is a section from one of the epistles of St. Paul. The substance and the style are here so wedded that the full-blooded personal substance of what the man is saying cannot be apprehended if the imagination has not been quickened and informed by the style of the utterance. There are ways of saying this, but we shall be better instructed if we test

[Richard] Kroner's statement that "Imagination maintains the original unity of elements separated by abstract thought" by testing it against a concrete instance of the Pauline style.

In the whole of Scripture there is perhaps no passage in which is so tightly compressed and interwoven a various company of massive ideas as in the eighth chapter of Romans. To make a unity out of that complexity, a symphony out of that baffling polyphony of powerful voices, is a task before which the dissecting intelligence feels its incompetence. And yet one has to know little of Paul to know that he, who wrote this, was in no confusion. His mind, though intricate in its matter and process, was no chaotic jumble of high epigrams. The task then is to seek from the inside of that passage its vital motif, its invisible cohesive element. And it is in this task that the imagination, if it has been informed by acquaintanceship with the ways of men as immemorially they have uttered in speech their turgid and passionate hearts, may silently and in strange ways come to an apprehension of what otherwise eludes the mind.

With the character of that passage in Romans in your memory, consider this: That there is here exhibited a quality of the mind in its working which is not permeable to the merely analytical intelligence. Here is a quality that inheres as much in the *how* of a man's speech as in the *what* of it. The prose is forward leaning, eager, exuberant — a manifestation of that end-over-end precipitousness that Deissmann remarked in Paul's writing, and caught in the phrase, "his words come as water jets in uneven spurts from a bottle held upside down!" By imaginative association of this peculiarity of Paul's prose with other evidences of this quality in experience we can come closer to knowing what it was that made him write so. And when we know that, we shall perceive in this particular instance the value claimed for the imagination in our first proposition — perceptive clarity. For is not this exuberance precisely what nature regularly exhibits at every moment of arriving at something? A horse runs with a new rhythmic vitality when he turns the last curve and straightens out on the home stretch. This vitality is due not only to the drive to win but arises out of something elemental — the combination of joy and release, the sudden realization of a long and burdening task almost done. An intricate piece of music draws its diffuse parts together in its last pages and in a muscular and positive *coda* resolves its far-wandering voices. Mighty Burke, when he "arrives" at the end of his persuasive paragraphs, gathers together his powers of thought and language for coalescence into final words of authoritative eloquence.

To have "gotten through," to have come to the end, to sense the laborious process of "working toward" about to break through into an "end achieved," is a feeling we all know. I once worked in a shop where it was my job to operate an electric drill, boring holes at marked intervals in four-by-four timbers. For the first three and a half inches, it goes its way with a steady, dull growl. And then the sound becomes more open, the machine gains speed, small splinters fly as the bit bites through the last solid stuff and spins and whines with singing ease. All "arriving," all completion has this quality, whether it be a four-inch timber, a symphony, a running horse, or a work of the mind. Can you, I wonder, have failed to observe that our minds have this quality in their working? — or can we fail to catch the tempo of "arriving" in these paragraphs of the apostle? For thirty verses Paul's powerful mind twists and turns and torments with as mighty a complex of ideas, actions, heavenly wonders as ever lived together in a sane man's mind. His language, like thought, is muscular, contorted, and tense — but always leaning forward . . . boring . . . boring into the hard deeps of his great subject. And then, at the thirty-first verse, "at last he beats his music out" in the amazing march of affirmations: "What shall we say to these things? . . . If God be for us, who shall be against us? . . ." And passes into that song of intolerable joy that ends the chapter.

Here is imagination operating exegetically to do for a passage what studious mastery of its individual parts could never accomplish. For the imagination understands that this chapter is not only argument but adoration, not a series but a sequence, not an order but an organism. Meanings "by the way" are only to be understood from the peak of spiritual song which is the brave conclusion. The ideas here are not unrelated equals pitched into a rhetorical concatenation by enthusiasm; here is, rather, the sovereignty of grace battering its way to victory through all the torments and doubts and opacities of this man's embattled soul. . . .

It is possible to state how the imagination, immersed in the Pauline substance and peculiar style, works to prepare the preacher for more lively and fuller utterance of the writer's intention. The proposition is this: Imagination is the process by which there is reenacted in the reader the salvatory immediacy of the word of God as this word is witnessed to by the speaker.

The peculiarity of the style mirrors the fierce dialectic set up in the psyche by the invasive word. The strange jump, the quick, unselfconscious corrections, the contradictions — these, which bring pain to the teacher of composition, bring theological light to the preacher. The natural-religious man can make a clean explication of his case; and the beatified child of grace could, presumably, write untroubled prose descriptive of his life in God. But the epistles of Paul stand at the intersection of nature and grace. They are the utterances of a man drawn taut between the huge repose of "a man in Christ" and the huge realism of a man of flesh and earth. It's the same man at the same time bearing witness to an inseparable movement of faith who can say: "Wretched man that I am. . . . There is therefore now no condemnation." "I don't care what you think of me. . . . I am troubled about what you think of me." Work out your own salvation in fear and trembling because no man can work out his own salvation and does not have to, for God is at work in you!

Preaching dare not put into unbroken propositions what the tormented peace of simultaneous existence in nature and grace can utter only in broken sentences. What God has riven asunder let no preacher too suavely join together. When we find, as we regularly do, that Paul stops the forward rush of active-voice statements to crack the integral structure of the affirmation with a joyous and devout regrounding of everything he is saying in the ultimacy of the passive voice, then we are obliged to stop with him. The salvatory power of the word of God is eloquent precisely at the embarrassed halt. Where grammar cracks, grace erupts.

"I know," says Paul. And then he reflects upon what he knows, how he came to know it, and what kind of a religious confidence it was within which such knowledge occurred. The reflection stops the assertion cold, and he writes, "I mean, rather, that I have been known."

"I love," says Paul. And then he reflects upon how he came to the point where he can say that, by virtue of what startling and reconstitutive convulsion it has been made possible, and he stops the active voice in the remembrance of ". . . this Son of God who loved me, and gave himself. . . ."

"I accept," says Paul. And then the reflection! And in the course of it the remembrance of the forgiving madness of the Holy which is the creator of all sanity, the huge and obliterating acceptance by God which powers all acceptances among men. The passive both destroys and recreates the active in its own image; and the Christian life is spun on the axis of this holy freedom whose one end is sunk in the accepting mercy of God, its other end in the need of man for an ultimate acceptance.

This transformation of the realm of the active by the power of the passive is a key not only to isolated fragments of Paul's witness, but also to an understanding of the man's total bearing within the world of nature and history. A peculiarly illuminating instance of this transformation is the memorable passage near the end of the Philippian letter. "Finally, brethren, whatever is true, whatever is honorable, whatever is just, whatever is pure, whatever is lovely, whatever is gracious, if there is any excellence, if there is anything worthy of praise, think about these things."

This paragraph, occurring as the summary of the argument of the entire epistle, is strange. It's almost as if Paul had forgotten what he had written, or taken back what he had so passionately affirmed, or suddenly replaced his intense and consecrated gaze by a genial and relaxed smile. For three chapters he has hacked away at the adequacy of all the confidences and solidities of religion, morality, culture. I count everything as loss . . . even as refuse, he says — and drills through to the "surpassing worth of knowing Christ Jesus my Lord. . . . That I may know him and the power of his resurrection, and may share his sufferings, becoming like him in his death, that if possible I may attain the resurrection from the dead."

And then the shift. From the packed and intense inwardness of that statement, which locates the dynamics of the faith-full life of the Christian within the enacted morphology of the incarnation and resurrection, he passes, after sundry personal and admonitory asides, to the blithe and humane: "Finally, brethren, whatever is true, whatever is honorable, whatever is just, whatever is pure, whatever is lovely. . . ."

This change in tone is not a shift in center. It is, in fact, not a shift at all. It is simply the language of a man who raises his eyes from the center to the circumference. It is the maturation of centered faith into a kind of evangelical humanism. It is rhetorical celebration of a basic Christian paradox: The way to breadth is by the road of narrow concentration; the road to beauty, graciousness, justice is a road that begins with the beauty of holiness, the graciousness of grace, the justice of judgment. The really humane is a function of the fully human; the fully human is beheld and bestowed in the new man who is the second Adam who, obedient in Gethsemane, restores to God and to himself the first Adam, faithless in Eden.

These too brief samplings of the Pauline style, while sufficient perhaps to make our formal point, suggests further and more subtle things to be learned from the apostle to the Gentiles. To these we shall give some attention in the next. But these do suffice to bring under question the venerable practice of preaching from isolated texts, or even brief pericopes. This practice, perilous enough when exercised upon the Gospels, is intrinsically disastrous when applied to the epistles of Paul. For to a degree unmatched in the world's literature, anything the man wrote has to be made luminous in the glow of everything he wrote. The apparent unsystematic of his language must be inwardly controlled and ordered by the central systematic of his passion. And he is the first to protest that this passion is a passive; that it is God's before it is his, and that it is his only because God's passion became a historical fact in a locatable garden.

DAVID BUTTRICK

Designing Moves

David Buttrick taught homiletics and worship at Vanderbilt Divinity School for many years. In his long career he combined interests in theological and technical homiletics. He demonstrated the homiletical significance of biblical materials in several books, including *Preaching Jesus Christ: An Exercise in Homiletic Theology; The Mystery and the Passion: A Homiletic Reading of the Gospel Traditions;* and *Speaking Parables: A Homiletic Guide.* His best-known book, however, *Homiletic: Moves and Structures* (1987), is a work of technical homiletics in which he immerses the reader in the rhetorical strategies of sermon construction. *Homiletic* is well suited to the postmodern era, for its raison d'être is the transcending of the subject/object split in preaching — the notion that there is an objective truth "out there" independent of the subject's participation in it. The sermon must create "consciousness" in the hearer via the images and patterns of the sermon. Through the proper use of language, the preacher builds a "faith-world" in the consciousness, a new linguistic reality in which the hearer can live with integrity. Buttrick's rhetoric of "moves" in the sermon appears to be his homiletical correlative to the modern loss of objective truth. A sermon usually contains five or six "moves," or sections. The moves are neither anchored to nor limited by a static thesis or traditional structure. They do not witness to some other reality but create a new reality. Buttrick's is perhaps the first homiletic geared to our culture of images, for in his system the sermon proceeds televisually by scenes and not by "points." With so much riding on language, Buttrick develops an exhaustive guide to its right deployment in the sermon. In what follows he outlines the rationale for and technical details of speaking in "moves."

David Buttrick, *Homiletic: Moves and Structures* (Philadelphia: Fortress, 1987), pp. 37-53.

While preaching is not an art, it is artful. There is craft connected with the shaping of sermons. The odd idea that preachers whose hearts have been strangely warmed will spill out sermons, instantly compelling and exquisitely formed, is, of course, nonsense. Just as a carpenter must learn to use tools in order to make a box, so preachers must acquire basic skills to preach. Though some preachers may be unusually gifted, preachers are *not* born, they are *trained.* We learn our homiletic skills.

Designing moves is a skill we can learn. Every move in a sermon must be shaped, and each shaped differently. Though moves will be quite differently designed, there are *basic* skills which we can study. All moves have an opening "Statement" and some sort of "Closure." In between, moves have some kind of developmental pattern. So, we shall study the components of moves — openings, closings, and in between.

The Statement

Where do silences occur in speaking? Talks are made out of words and pauses; where do the pauses usually happen? Answer: pauses happen between moves. While there may be other pregnant pauses within a sermon, often for effect, generally when we shift from one developed subject to another, we pause. There is a silence almost as if we were pausing in the midst of a journey to catch our breath before we launch forth again. Studies indicate that, after a pause, audiences are alert; their attention level is high, they hear well. Such heightened attention will last for a few sentences after the pause before, gradually, attention will relax. Thus, wise speakers know that they have only a few sentences — perhaps three — in which to focus audience attention and to establish what it is they will be speaking. Therefore, the statement of a move may not be delayed without good reason lest, unfocused, an audience hear but not hear. So, as a matter of craft, the first few sentences of a move are crucial and demand careful consideration.

Lately, an odd homiletic convention seems to have developed, namely, a preference for what might be described as "oblique" starts to moves, the indirect discourse of a cautious speaker. For example:

> There's an old-fashioned word. A word we are hesitant to use. You will still find the word in Bibles, or hymnbooks, or prayers we say in church. The word is almost forgotten in daily conversation. Yet, the word is crucial, the word "sin." The fact is, *we are all sinners. . . .*

In the example, we do not get to the nub of our conversation until five preliminary sentences have passed. By then, of course, attention has been relaxed. Apparently preachers suppose that oblique starts are kinder, or perhaps build suspense, or are easier for congregations to handle. Not so. Actually such starts are apt to irritate an audience. Moreover, the word "sin" enters the move in a subordinate clause which means it will enter consciousness peripherally. A congregation hearing the move will be forced to make an adjustment. The preacher began by speaking of "a word." Leading the congregation to suppose some discussion of "the word" would follow. Instead, with the sixth sentence the preacher turns to focus on the subject of sin. Maybe a congregation will adjust, and maybe not. While, on occasion, a delayed start may be used to build up suspense, as a general practice the convention of the oblique start is devastating. We are given only a few sentences after a pause in which to focus consciousness and we must not waste the opportunity.

We must use *all* the sentences we are given. It will require at least three sentences, and often more, to establish initial focus in consciousness. Some older homiletic works mentioned "key sentences" and suggested that when moving into a subject matter, all that was needed was *one* clear, strong "topical sentence," after which developmental material — examples, illustrations, forms of argumentation — could occur. No, a single sentence carries little weight in group consciousness, particularly when followed by vivid developmental material. While we can switch subject matters rapidly in one-to-one conversation, with a gathered audience the process will require several sentences. In effect, a speaker is turning an audience from one focus to another, and such a turn must be made strongly. Thus, starts to moves that travel through a series of statements simply will not register in communal consciousness.

> We are all sinners. Nowadays the word isn't in style. We talk instead of psychological problems — phobias, complexes, neuroses. We aren't much into "sin." . . .

In the example there is only one "key sentence" before a contrapuntal theme is introduced. As a result, group consciousness will be confused at the outset; the move statement has not been firmly established before being countered. Probably, a congregation would simply go blank and have to catch up with the subject matter later in the move. We must realize that with group consciousness about three sentences will function with the strength of one in intimate conversation. In other words, at the start of a move when focus is crucial, we shall have to wield a block of sentences as if they were one.

> We are sinners. Sinners — the word may sound old-fashioned, but it's true. We are all of us sinners.

339

Preachers may feel unnatural using reiterative sentences to establish focus at the start of a move; the language will seem artificial and scarcely conversational in style. It must be remembered, though, that speaking to group consciousness is very different from one-to-one chats. If you watch an actor close at hand, gestures will seem too large and quite abnormal; but to an audience, the actor's movements will seem natural. By analogy, though a block of sentences at the start of a move will seem positively strained to a speaker, to a congregation the language may well register as a single sentence. Being natural is not the purpose of homiletics; serving our neighbors in the gospel is.

Actually, the block of sentences used to focus consciousness at the start of a move may have to be extended, if subsequent developmental material is unusually vivid. If, for example, we plan to follow the start with a highly visual illustration or with a strong contrapuntal, we will have to develop the start by exploring the subject matter more fully in order to fix focus before refocusing to any extent. When congregations drift off into wanderings of mind, it is *always* the fault of the speaker. Most often such drifting is caused by the weak starts of moves, by a failure to establish focus firmly. If we do not enter a move with strength, the entire move may fail to form in consciousness and may simply delete from the overall structure of a sermon. Human consciousness is like a camera lens. At the starts of moves, we who speak are turning the "lens" of congregational consciousness in a particular direction and establishing focus. Therefore, the opening statement of a move is all-important.

The first few sentences of a move are exceedingly difficult to prepare. For not only do the first sentences establish focus, they must accomplish a number of other things. In addition to focus, the statement of a move must show *connective logic,* the logic by which one move follows another; it must indicate the *perspective* (or "point-of-view") of the move, and it must set the "mood" of the move. Suppose, for example, that in a sermon we have two moves in sequence, one which celebrates human virtue — how neat and nice and smart we human beings can be — followed by another which admits our sin. Imagine what the conjunction of moves might be:

> . . . So we are not unkind, are we? All in all, we are decent human beings. Well, time to "fess up." Time to get down on our knees and admit we are sinners. "Sinners," the word is full of anguish. We are sinners all. . . .

In the example above, we see the ending of one move and the start of another. The logic of connection is dialectical — statement and counterstatement. . . .

Move Development

A Basic Rhetoric of Moves

Between the opening statement of a move and its closure, some idea is developed. The problem for preachers is deciding *how* to develop material. A preacher must determine what material is to be used and how the material is to be arranged. Once upon a time, ministers were trained in rhetoric. Therefore, they had at hand different rhetorical logics, strategies, tropes, and so forth. While rhetorical training could lead to insubstantial ornamentation or verbal pyrotechnics, for the most part rhetorical wisdom assisted preaching. After all, rhetoric is an ancient wisdom that undergirds all human conversation. Thus, older works on homiletics could assume rhetorical training and concentrate on matters specific to preaching. We cannot. What we can do is offer some general comments about rhetoric before providing examples of move development.

Often homiletics is based on some sort of understanding of congregation. What exactly is a "congregation"? If we assume that a congregation is made up of believers, people who share common faith, then we will tend to view preaching as an explication of common faith — faith seeking understanding. On the other hand, if congregations are regarded as representatives of the world-age, preaching may be understood as conversion and forms of development as persuasion or even argumentation — switching people from unfaith to faith. The trouble is that neither of these paradigms is appropriate and, therefore, neither gets at the true quality of homiletic language. Every congregation must be regarded as being-saved in the world; thus congregations have a peculiar double consciousness.

On a Sunday morning congregations are constituted in liturgy as "people of God" and, in fact, within the symbolic structures of liturgy understand themselves as so constituted. At the same time, we know we are "in the world" and share worldly ways of understanding. Thus, because we are "*in* but not *of* the world," preaching will have to speak to a double consciousness. Theological reality is primary, thus preaching will be explication, a "bringing into view" of our common faith. At the same time, because awareness of being-saved involves a distinguishing of Christian faith from understandings of the world-age in which we live, the language of preaching will wrestle with ideas, assumptions, social attitudes which we bring to church. If preaching does involve conversion, it is the constant conversion of Christian formation. In a worldly language, preaching shapes the faith-consciousness of the church.

In view of the peculiar character of congregations, we must try to describe a basic Christian rhetoric. Christian preaching involves a "bringing out" or a "bringing into view" of convictional understandings — understandings of God, of God's mysterious purposes, and of unseen wonders of grace in human lives. Christians understand God *through* symbols of revelation; therefore, Christian rhetoric "brings out" by exploring symbols. Most of the time, we live with day-to-day immediacies in consciousness, and with convictions (matters of faith) in the background. Thus, by exploring symbols, preaching will be bringing into view our often unspoken faith. Likewise, preaching will be bringing out the reality of our being-saved, which is often mediated through ritual symbols — praise, baptism, Eucharist. "Bringing out and into view" will be accomplished by many different rhetorical means — depiction, analogy, metaphor, explanation, analysis, and credal explorations.

Thus we have deliberately bypassed the rationalistic definitions of preaching found in didactic homiletics. Preachers do not explicate teachings; they explore symbols. Faith does have content, but not a content that can be spelled out in propositional statements for instruction. So, Christian rhetoric involves a bringing out through language.

Christian rhetoric also *associates*. In preaching, we put together Christian understandings with images of lived experience. In so doing, preaching demonstrates that our Christian convictions are true to life. Preaching does not trade in formal proofs or argued syllogisms. If, in sermons, we turn to rational proofs, we will elevate reason to a position of ultimacy instead of faith-consciousness. Moreover, though rational proofs may well have a proper role in arbitrating some kinds of "truth," they cannot displace faith's appeal to lived truth. Thus, Christian preaching does not dabble in pragmatic justifications or argued tautologies; it merely interfaces Christian understandings with depictions of lived experience. In particular, preaching brings together the gospel and portrayals of being-saved new life in the world. The rhetoric of association is a language of imagery, illustration, example, testimony, and the like. In congregational consciousness, we bring out Christian meanings and associate them with fields of lived experience. In so doing, the truth of the gospel will be evident.

Of course, Christian preaching will also *disassociate*. We are being-saved-in-the-world and, therefore, possess a peculiar double consciousness — a consciousness of being-saved and a consciousness of being-in-the-world. Being-saved is aware of itself, not only in relation to Christian symbols, but as it experiences tension with worldly styles, strategies, and modes of thinking. Thus, again and again, preaching will distinguish Christian understandings from our common social attitudes — the "isms," "ologies," popular slogans, and tacit assumptions which may be fashionable. Likewise, preaching will demark Christian lifestyles from the conventional ethos of human communities; presumably, the ways and means of Christian love will be different. For example, if the gospel anticipates reconciled "peace on earth," it is bound to disassociate itself from forms of jingoism and superpatriotic nonsense. Preaching will speak tenderly, but, nonetheless, critically of being-in-the-world. Preaching will discriminate. Disassociation employs familiar rhetorical systems, such as dialectic, antithesis, opposition, and, at times, perhaps even a charitable giggling.

Basic Christian rhetoric, then, involves "bringing out," "associating," and "disassociating." Moves in a sermon will develop from these basic rhetorical intentions. For example, in the sample move "We are all sinners," all three intentions are present: an understanding of human nature under sin, a disassociation of sin from popular psychological orientations, and an association of sin with images of social and personal lived experience. Of course, the move, following the same structural pattern, could have drawn on different types of material — quoting a particular psychiatrist, or using an illustration of someone's self-discovery of sin, or citing statistics of crime. Though types of evidence could change, the basic rhetorical intentions would still be present — bringing out, associating, and disassociating. Moves will always contain one or more of these forms of basic rhetoric.

In addition to basic rhetorical intentions, we can isolate different languages, related to particular modes of consciousness. These languages may be labeled *temporal, spatial, social,* and *personal.* As we develop moves, we can think historically, calling on memory, or we can survey the world in which we live; we can turn in on ourselves to chase down motives, fantasies, and impulses, or we can express types of social awareness. For example, if we are attempting to probe the nature of sin, we could scan pages of history, tracing human lovelessness since time began. On the other hand, we could study the world in which we live for evidence of sin, a world of wars and grinding deprivations. We could explore our own psyches, tracking down our split motives and our chronic self-interests. Or, we could examine our shared social prejudices, our strident nationalisms, and the like. Human experience is appropriated temporally (diachronic thinking), spatially (synchronic thinking), socially (corporate consciousness), and personally (self-awareness). Each of these orientations will produce a different language.

Books on preaching will often list different things to do when developing ideas — examples, illustrations, descriptions, explanations, appeals to authority, analogies, confessions, proofs, and so on. Instead, we are suggesting that all these different rhetorical strategies may be catalogued according to basic intentions — bringing out, associating, disassociating — within which there may be different orientations: spatial, temporal, personal, and social. We turn now to see how to develop moves in actual practice.

Move Designs

Between an opening statement and closure, a move is developed. Beginning with a simple sentence (e.g., "God is a mystery" or "We are all sinners"), preachers will think through theological meanings, cultural and religious oppositions, forms of lived experience, as well as optional strategies. From such initial thinking through, ideas of development will come. Modes of development will be chosen rhetorically, however, not only to fit congregational consciousness, but to relate to other moves within a sermon scenario. In order to describe the process of move development, imagine that we must develop a simple sentence, "Most Christians nowadays have grown up in a church." Even with what may appear to be a self-evident statement, we will still think through the move.

There are theological issues involved in the statement, "Most Christians nowadays have grown up in a church." Obviously, the notion of church is broader than some local steeple. Rightly, church is holy, catholic, and apostolic. Moreover, there are issues such as church "visible" and "invisible" to reckon with. In thinking over the statement we may be dismayed. From an evangelical standpoint, the statement may bear witness to the church's failure to reach out into the world with the word of the gospel. We may sense that theologically the statement could be positive or negative: a church built on childhood familiarity might be nothing more than Kierkegaard's "Sunday Twaddle," or perhaps the statement is positive in that the grip of the gospel does shape human self-understanding so that human beings stay in community by faith. Even with what appears to be a self-evident statement, there are theological dimensions to be considered.

An analysis of actual lived experience can involve many different kinds of study. We may read up on statistical research to support the claim, and in doing so discover that, though most Christians have grown up in church, they church-hop; they shop for churches as they shop for hamburgers in fast-food stores. We may also discover that, statistically, American Christian communities overall may well be dwindling as compared with African communities which are enlarging rapidly. Phenomenal analysis may plunge us into looking at the membership of some actual congregation, or into recall — a remembering of how it was to grow up in a church, from Sunday-morning church-pew wiggling, to Sunday-school chaos, to hymn sings in the evening, to the sweet disarray of family-night suppers.

Are there oppositions? Perhaps. The statement may be appalling to an anti-institutional Christianity. Or, the statement may simply seem to endorse a middle-class-value Christianity of a fairly thoughtless variety. In addition to reactions, the statement itself may not seem true when we view Asian, European, and African Christianity.

344

In thinking through this simple statement, we engage in the process of gathering all kinds of ideas, images, statistics, and theological questions. Probably, we will also read articles, look at books on the church, perhaps study surveys of church growth and the like. From a simple one-sentence statement we have gathered an astonishing amount of material that somehow must be shaped by *selection* and *organization* into a coherent move.

In preaching to a congregation in which virtually everyone present has in fact grown up in church, development of the statement will be relatively easy. All we will have to do is to put the statement together with congregational lived experience. Because the phrase "grown up" seems to imply memory, the mode of development will probably involve personal recall. For example:

> *Statement A:* Most Christians nowadays have grown up in church. Though some of us here may have been born in other cities, we share a common church background. We can hardly remember when we were not in church. Once little children, now grown adults, we've lived our lives within the church.

> *Development A:* Think back through the years. You won't recall your first day in church, the day when as a baby you were baptized — perhaps right here. But you do remember being a kid in church. Remember wiggling during sermons, or children's day pageants, or did you run around playing tag in the fellowship hall? Think back and recall your church-school teachers. Think of the stories you were told of Moses, and Paul, and above all stories of Jesus. Later, when you were older, do you remember how proud your parents were when, finally, you stood up in church and said, "I believe," and were counted as a adult member? We do share common memories, don't we?

> *Closure A:* We were baptized, we were instructed, we worshipped. We are church people. Most people nowadays have grown up in faith.

The system we have constructed as an example can be described as a simple system. Within the framework of the move, there is only *one* developmental system organized as a personal, *temporal* memory. Actually, such simple systems will seldom be used because congregations are rarely so unified or traditional in character, and theological understandings are normally much more complex.

Suppose, for example, that we are speaking to exactly the same congregation, but have decided that for theological reasons, we should not praise homogeneity or elevate local customs. We might wish to design a more complex move.

Statement A: Most Christians nowadays have grown up in church. Though some of us here may have been born in other cities, we share a common church background. We can hardly remember when we weren't in church.

Contrapuntal B: Of course, perhaps, we shouldn't be proud. Maybe churches in Africa which are drawing a hundred thousand converts a day are healthy. Perhaps they are more exciting than we are, and much more like the first-century Christians.

Development of Statement A: But, we are what we are. Most of us here have grown up in the church. Think back through the years . . . etc.

Closure for Statement A: We were baptized, we were instructed, . . . etc.

In the example, we have added to the simple structure a preliminary contrapuntal section looking at Third World Christian communities and suggesting that they may be healthier than American Christian churches. Notice that in the move there are two different systems, one disassociative (B) and one associative (A), one a spatial survey of a social phenomenon and the other a personal-temporal development.

But imagine that instead of speaking to a homegrown, homogeneous congregation, we are addressing a mission church that mostly draws non-Christians into faith. Obviously, if we intend to make the same statement, "Most Christians nowadays have grown up in church," we will have to devise a more complex system in which to develop the idea. Imagine what kind of a move we might shape:

Statement A: Surprise! Know it or not, most Christians in America have grown up in church. They were born in the church, baptized as babies, and brought up in church year after year. They are old-time Christians.

Contrapuntal B: How hard it is for us to imagine. Most of us stumbled newborn into our Christian faith. Here in church we learned ways of worship, heard the gospel, said our prayers for the first time. And, we're excited about our newfound faith.

Development C: In a way, we're like the first Christians back in the days of the apostles. For we have been drawn out of the world into faith. To us, as to the very first Christians, the gospel is new, a new good news for our lives.

Development of Statement A: But look around the U.S.A., most churches were built years ago in little frontier villages. They have housed generations of Christians — founders, and children, and children's children. So most people can say truthfully, "I don't even remember when I wasn't a Christian!" Most people in churches were born to church families. They were baptized as infants, attended church school — all their lives they've lived in church.

Closure for Statement A: Look, though it may be hard for us to imagine, don't forget most Christians in America are not newborn believers. Most Christians around us have grown up in the church.

The move still begins with the same sentence, "Most Christians in America have grown up in church." Even though the statement is untrue to the audience, we must still commence with the statement which we are going to establish, and with which we will close. If we were to start with the experience of our audience and then turn to look at the national norm, the move would split into two moves, each too brief to form in consciousness. No matter what the character of the congregation, the statement we intend must initiate the move. The point of view with which the move begins is quite different, however — "Surprise! Know it or not . . ." [but] [t]he move itself is a three-part system. . . .

Contrapuntals

Because there may be oppositions or exceptions to ideas we are presenting, we have suggested that contrapuntal systems may be necessary. And, because we preach between the ages, we suppose such systems may be more necessary now than in previous years. Contrapuntal parts to moves, however, must be handled with care. Obviously, if a contrapuntal becomes too strong we will end up with a move that splits consciousness, that preaches in two directions at the same time. After all, the move *statement* is what we are attempting to establish, not its opposition. Thus, we will keep contrapuntals under control. A contrapuntal may never exceed the time given to a development of the statement, may not have brighter imagery, or be illustrated. Basically, contrapuntal systems "let off steam" within a move and do not become major blocks of content. If a contrapuntal is crucial because oppositions are very strong, a separate contrapuntal *move* may be required. Normally, however, a contrapuntal acknowledges, but does not reinforce, an opposition. Therefore, it will occur within a move either shortly after the fixing of an initial statement or immediately prior to a strong reiterative closure. While many preachers may wish to exercise their own skepticisms, or to display their own modern doubts, contrapuntal sections acknowledge but do not preach oppositions. They must therefore be handled with restraint.

Variety

In general, every move within a sermon scenario ought to be shaped differently. Often we will hear a speaker who, though using vivid language and glittering imagery, is strangely tedious. Usually the cause of our boredom is a similarity in developmental systems — many of the ideas being presented come to us in the same rhetorical shape. So, unless a speaker is skilled enough to shape deliberately two different ideas in the same way so that they will overlap in consciousness, the general rule will be *different development for different ideas. . . .*

Variety in development may also be assured by keeping an eye on the kinds of rhetorical intentions involved — bringing out, associating, disassociating — as well as modes of developmental language: temporal, spatial, personal, social. Thus, for example, if many moves in a sermon feature appeals to personal recall, the sermon will inevitably be tedious no matter how interesting the content of personal memory may be. Likewise, if every move begins by making a statement and then follows with a disassociating contrapuntal system, boredom is bound to occur. Probably the most common form of repetitive development is caused by ministers who compulsively put an illustration in every move, so that moves, though different in content, sound the same because they all feature statement-illustration-closure. A mobile sequence of moves in a sermon will call for fewer illustrations, however, because a moving system will be intrinsically more exciting than types of categorical or deductive organization.

Unity

Above all, moves must be unified: They must make a single statement. Basically moves are an elaboration of an idea that can be expressed in a single clear sentence, e.g., "We are all sinners," "God is a mystery," "Most American Christians have grown up in church." A test of unity is to read a move and be sure that it can be summed up in a simple (noncompound) clear sentence. If, on rereading a move, you discover you are forced to summarize in a complex clausal sentence, the move may be pulling apart in consciousness. Still another test is to examine the opening statement and the closure to see if they are unified; if they do not match thematically, you may have constructed a split move or at least a traveling move.

What causes moves to fragment in consciousness? The causes are usually either an *alteration in focus* or a *traveling idea*. For example, it will be exceedingly difficult to hold a move together if it splits focus between a past-tense look at Scripture and a present-tense viewing of our world. The same sort of split may occur if a contrapuntal system grows too large so that the move ends up with two developed ideas in dialectical tension. In both cases, a preacher may have to frame two moves. When a move splits in consciousness, the result is that we are speaking two *brief* moves, neither of which will be strong enough or long enough to form in consciousness. Thus, the whole split move may not register at all, causing a congregational lapse — a wandering of mind. With a traveling idea, the statement and closure of the move will often be quite different; the preacher has produced a sequence of ideas moving from idea A to idea C. For example, suppose we have designed a move with the following component parts:

Statement A: Most Americans have grown up in church.

Development B: How different from Third World churches.

Development C: So perhaps we had better turn to evangelizing again.

It is almost impossible to return to our original statement — the move has traveled. The effect of such a construction is that a congregation will hear three different short ideas, none of which is developed sufficiently to form in consciousness. The rapidity of the movement of thought will almost certainly produce a blank in congregational understanding. The move has fragmented.

Preachers may discover that if they write out a sermon manuscript, it will be helpful to paragraph according to *move*. If we paragraph each section of a move's internal development, we will probably end up with a move that tends to fall apart. First sentences of paragraphs tend to be syntactically different; they break the flow of a forming idea. A sermon manuscript is above all a script for oral delivery, not an essay to be read. Therefore, rules drummed into us by grade-school grammarians do not apply. Each move in an oral sermon forms a single understanding, imaged and explored in consciousness. Though a move may take between three and four minutes to deliver, it must form as a *single* understanding in communal consciousness. Therefore, attention to unity is crucial.

Closure

Every move *must have closure.* By returning to an initial statement in some manner at the close of a move, we ensure that a single understanding will form in congregational consciousness. If strong opening statements to moves are essential, so also are firm closures. When, suddenly, in the midst of a sermon, a congregation drifts off into inattention and restlessness, it is often caused by failure to close a move before initiating a new move. Let us suppose that we have two moves in sequence, one saying, "Most Christians have grown up in church," and another beginning, "How different were the first Christians." Compare the following:

Example A:

. . . Later, when you were older, do you remember how proud your parents were when, finally, you stood up in church and said, "I believe," and were counted as an adult member?

How different were the first Christians. . . .

Example B:

. . . Later, when you were older, do you remember how proud your parents were when, finally, you stood up in church and said, "I believe," and were counted as an adult member? We do share common memories, don't we? We were baptized, we were instructed, we worshiped. We are church people. Most people, nowadays, have grown up in faith.

How different were the first Christians. . . .

In example A, there is no closure. As a result, we are still involved in remembering when a shift in focus is attempted. Congregational consciousness will be thrown into confusion and may or may not catch up with a new idea — "How different were the first Christians" — when it is presented. In example B, however, a closure has been made so that the shift to a new idea can be managed easily. As a rule, some sort of closure must be designed for every move.

Forming closure will always involve a return to the idea of the statement with which the move began. On occasion, the return may be accomplished by use of exactly the same sentence with which the move began. Of course, if every move in a sermon begins and ends with a similar sentence, the repetitious device may become intolerable. So, though some moves may well begin and conclude with the same sentence, others will end differently, but *always* with a return to the initiating *idea* of the move. What we may not do is to end with a different, new idea, or to end with what is a developmental part of a move. The originating statement of a move must be echoed in some fashion at the conclusion. Closure is *crucial.*

In general, the last sentence of a move ought to be simple; it should be a terse, final sentence. Compound sentences will not close. Sentences with many clauses will invariably sound as if an idea is being developed rather than stopped. For the same reason, sentences that conclude with a participle, implying a continuing action, will not work. The last sentence of a move should be a strong simple sentence, and preferably a sentence with a strong definite noun rather than sentences that begin with "It" or "This." . . .

The matter of closure is more important than we know. Moves must start strongly and end with equal strength; they must "round out" and conclude. Preachers should realize that they are in charge of focus. With language they focus congregational consciousness on some field of meaning. With closure they frame a field of meaning in consciousness so as to be able to shift focus in a different direction. Ideally, a sermon should involve a series of formed, framed ideas that move through congregational consciousness as *their* own thoughts, each module of language a designed "thought." Even quite impressionistic sermons must still be designed as a series of defined moves. While ministers may rankle — sharply defined starts and finishes will seem quite unnatural or possibly artificial — we are serving a people, not our own comfort in speaking. Fuzzy starts and finishes will produce an odd effect in the consciousness of a congregation. People will catch only occasional glimpses of meaning amid a flow of murky verbiage. They will fight to hold attention against involuntary wanderings of mind. Moves must begin and conclude with all-but-overstated strength. Internally, they must be developed with care, each differently, so as to form as natural understandings in communal consciousness.

· VI ·

THE HEARER

GREGORY THE GREAT

Catalogue of Hearers

The ancient rhetorical arts were not concerned with audience analysis. It was the occasion — forensic, political, or ceremonial — that determined the quality of the speech. Although Aristotle examined the stimulation of various emotions in the hearer in Book II of the *Rhetoric,* neither he nor Augustine after him addressed the problem of a mixed audience, which was the uniquely Christian problem created by the intellectual, social, and economic diversity represented at any given worship service. To this heterogeneity Gregory the Great (ca. 540-604) spoke as no one had before him. He wrote the *Pastoral Rule* in 591 shortly after his election to the episcopacy of Rome. Like Chrysostom's *On The Priesthood,* it deals with the responsibilities of the bishop, especially preaching and pastoral care. Rather than focusing on rhetorical theory, his treatise reflects the pragmatic, administrative concerns of a pastor for his huge flock. Under the rubric of "one doctrine — many exhortations" Gregory first enumerates thirty-six pairs of opposite characters and then proceeds with a sermonette appropriate to each pairing. Thus this section of the *Pastoral Rule* is a series of sermon helps designed, in Gregory's words, "to suit all and each for the several needs." Although his treatise reflects the diversity of Christian audiences, he does not wish to accommodate the gospel to the needs of the hearers. His concerns suggest, indirectly, how the sermon not only addresses an audience but by means of its own "world" of discourse implies or constructs a congregation of hearers.

Gregory the Great, *The Book of Pastoral Rule,* pt. III, 1-3, 8, trans. James Barmby, *A Select Library of Nicene and Post-Nicene Fathers of the Christian Church,* vol. XII (New York: The Christian Literature Company, 1894), pp. 24-29.

Since, then, we have shown what manner of man the pastor ought to be, let us now set forth after what manner he should teach. For, as long before us Gregory Nazianzen of reverend memory has taught, one and the same exhortation does not suit all, inasmuch as neither are all bound together by similarity of character. For the things that profit some often hurt others; seeing that also for the most part herbs which nourish some animals are fatal to others; and the gentle hissing that quiets horses incites whelps; and the medicine which abates one disease aggravates another; and the bread which invigorates the life of the strong kills little children. Therefore according to the quality of the hearers ought the discourse of teachers to be fashioned, so as to suit all and each for their several needs, and yet never deviate from the art of common edification. For what are the intent minds of hearers but, so to speak, a kind of tight tensions of strings in a harp, which the skillful player, that he may produce a tune not at variance with itself, strikes variously? And for this reason the strings render back a consonant modulation, that they are struck indeed with one quill, but not with one kind of stroke. Whence every teacher also, that he may edify all in the one virtue of charity, ought to touch the hearts of his hearers out of one doctrine, but not with one and the same exhortation.

What Diversity There Ought to Be in the Art of Preaching

Differently to be admonished are these that follow:

> Men and women.
> The poor and the rich.
> The joyful and the sad.
> Prelates and subordinates.
> Servants and masters.
> The wise of this world and the dull.
> The impudent and the bashful.
> The forward and the fainthearted.
> The impatient and the patient.
> The kindly disposed and the envious.
> The simple and the insincere.
> The whole and the sick.
> Those who fear scourges, and therefore live innocently; and those who have grown so hard in iniquity as not to be corrected even by scourges.
> The too silent, and those who spend time in much speaking.
> The slothful and the hasty.

The meek and the passionate.

The humble and the haughty.

The obstinate and the fickle.

The gluttonous and the abstinent.

Those who mercifully give of their own, and those who would fain seize what belongs to others.

Those who neither seize the things of others nor are bountiful with their own; and those who both give away the things they have, and yet cease not to seize the things of others.

Those that are at variance, and those that are at peace.

Lovers of strife, and peacemakers.

Those that understand not aright the words of sacred law; and those who understand them indeed aright, but speak them without humility.

Those who, though able to preach worthily, are afraid through excessive humility; and those whom imperfection or age debars from preaching, and yet rashness impels to it.

Those who prosper in what they desire in temporal matters; and those who covet indeed the things that are of the world, and yet are wearied with the toils of adversity.

Those who are bound by wedlock, and those who are free from the ties of wedlock.

Those who have had experience of carnal intercourse, and those who are ignorant of it.

Those who deplore sins of deed, and those who deplore sins of thought.

Those who bewail misdeeds, yet forsake them not; and those who forsake them, yet bewail them not.

Those who even praise the unlawful things they do; and those who censure what is wrong, yet avoid it not.

Those who are overcome by sudden passion, and those who are bound in guilt of set purpose.

Those who, though their unlawful deeds are trivial, yet do them frequently; and those who keep themselves from small sins, but are occasionally whelmed in graver ones.

Those who do not even begin what is good, and those who fail entirely to complete the good begun.

Those who do evil secretly and good publicly; and those who conceal the good they do, and yet in some things done publicly allow evil to be thought of them.

But of what profit is it for us to run through all these things collected together in a list, unless we also set forth, with all possible brevity, the modes of admonition for each?

Differently, then, to be admonished are men and women; because on the former heavier injunctions, on the latter lighter are to be laid, that those may be exercised by great things, but these winningly converted by light ones.

Differently to be admonished are young men and old; because for the most part severity of admonition directs the former to improvement, while kind remonstrance disposes the latter to better deeds. For it is written, "Rebuke not an elder, but entreat him as a father" (1 Tim. 5:1).

How the Poor and the Rich Should Be Admonished

Differently to be admonished are the poor and the rich: for to the former we ought to offer the solace of comfort against tribulation, but in the latter to induce fear as against elation. For to the poor one it is said by the Lord through the prophet, "Fear not, for thou shalt not be confounded" (Isa. 54:4). And not long after, soothing her, he says, "O thou poor little one, tossed with tempest." And again he comforts her, saying, "I have chosen thee in the furnace of poverty." But, on the other hand, Paul says to his disciple concerning the rich, "Charge the rich of this world, that they be not high-minded nor trust in the uncertainty of their riches" (1 Tim. 6:17); where it is to be particularly noted that the teacher of humility in making mention of the rich, says not "Entreat," but "Charge"; because, though pity is to be bestowed on infirmity, yet to elation no honor is due. To such, therefore, the right thing that is said is the more rightly commanded, according as they are puffed up with loftiness of thought in transitory things. Of them the Lord says in the Gospel, "Woe unto you that are rich, which have your consolation" (Luke 6:24). For, since they know not what eternal joys are, they are consoled out of the abundance of the present life. Therefore consolation is to be offered to those who are tried in the furnace of poverty; and fear is to be induced in those whom the consolation of temporal glory lifts up; that both those may learn that they possess riches which they see not, and these become aware that they can by no means keep the riches that they see. Yet for the most part the character of persons changes the order in which they stand; so that the rich man may be humble and the poor man proud. Hence the tongue of the preacher ought soon to be adapted to the life of the hearer so as to smite elation in a poor man all the more sharply as not even the poverty that has come upon him brings it down, and to cheer all the more gently the humility of the rich as even the abundance which elevates them does not elate them. . . .

But sometimes, when the powerful of this world are taken to task, they are first to be searched by certain similitudes, as on a matter not concerning them; and, when they have pronounced a right sentence as against another man, then in fitting ways they are to be smitten with regard to their own guilt; so that the mind puffed up with temporal power may in no wise lift itself up against the reprover, having by its own judgment trodden on the neck of pride, and may not try to defend itself, being bound by the sentence of its own mouth. For hence it was that Nathan the prophet, having come to take the king to task, asked his judgment as if concerning the cause of a poor man against a rich one (2 Sam. 12:4-5ff.), that the king might first pronounce sentence, and afterward hear of his own guilt, to the end that he might by no means contradict the righteous doom that he had uttered against himself. Thus the holy man, considering both the sinner and the king, studied in a wonderful order first to bind the daring culprit by confession, and afterward to cut him to the heart by rebuke. He concealed for a while whom he aimed at, but smote him suddenly when he had him. For the blow would perchance have fallen with less force had he purposed to smite the sin openly from the beginning of his discourse; but by first introducing the similitude he sharpened the rebuke which he concealed. He had come as a physician to a sick man; he saw that the sore must be cut; but he doubted of the sick man's patience. Therefore he hid the medicinal steel under his robe, which he suddenly drew out and plunged into the sore, that the patient might feel the cutting blade before he saw it, lest, seeing it first, he should refuse to feel it.

How the Joyful and the Sad Are to Be Admonished

Differently to be admonished are the joyful and the sad. That is, before the joyful are to be set the sad things that follow upon punishment; but before the sad the promised glad things of the kingdom. Let the joyful learn by the asperity of threatenings what to be afraid of; let the sad hear what joys of reward they may look forward to. For to the former it is said, "Woe unto you that laugh now! For ye shall weep" (Luke 6:25); but the latter hear from the teaching of the same Master, "I will see you again, and your heart shall rejoice, and your joy no man shall take from you" (John 16:22). But some are not made joyful or sad by circumstances, but are so by temperament. And to such it should be intimated that certain defects are connected with certain temperaments; that the joyful have lechery close at hand, and the sad wrath. Hence it is necessary for everyone to consider not only what he suffers from his peculiar temperament, but also what worse thing presses on him in connection with it; lest, while he fights not at all against that which he has, he succumb also to that from which he supposes himself free.

How Subjects and Prelates Are to Be Admonished

Differently to be admonished are subjects and prelates; the former that subjection crush them not, the latter that superior place elate them not; the former that they fail not to fulfill what is commanded them, the latter that they command not more to be fulfilled than is just; the former that they submit humbly, the latter that they preside temperately. For this, which may be understood also figuratively, is said to the former, "Children, obey your parents in the Lord": but to the latter it is enjoined, "And ye, fathers, provoke not your children to wrath" (Col. 3:20-21). Let the former learn how to order their inward thoughts before the eyes of the hidden judge; the latter how also to those that are committed to them to afford outwardly examples of good living.

For prelates ought to know that, if they ever perpetrate what is wrong, they are worthy of as many deaths as they transmit examples of perdition to their subjects. Wherefore it is necessary that they guard themselves so much the more cautiously from sin as by the bad things they do they die not alone, but are guilty of the souls of others, which by their bad example they have destroyed. Wherefore the former are to be admonished, lest they should be strictly punished, if merely on their own account they should be unable to stand acquitted; the latter, lest they should be judged for the errors of their subjects, even though on their own account they find themselves secure. Those are to be admonished that they live with all the more anxiety about themselves as they are not entangled by care for others; but these that they accomplish their charge of others in such wise as to not desist from charge of themselves, and so to be ardent in anxiety about themselves, as not to grow sluggish in the custody of those committed to them.

To the one, who is at leisure for his own concerns, it is said, "Go to the ant, thou sluggard, and consider her ways, and learn wisdom" (Prov. 6:6): but the other is terribly admonished, when it is said, "My son, if thou be surety for thy friend, thou hast stricken thy hand with a stranger, and art snared with the words of thy mouth, and art taken with thine own speeches." For to be surety for a friend is to take charge of the soul of another on the surety of one's own behavior. Whence also the hand is stricken with a stranger, because the mind is bound with the care of a responsibility which before was not. But he is snared with the words of his mouth, and taken with his own speeches, because, while he is compelled to speak good things to those who are committed to him, he must needs himself in the first place observe the things that he speaks. He is therefore snared with the words of his mouth, being constrained by the requirement of reason not to let his life be relaxed to what agrees not with his teaching. Hence before the strict judge he is compelled to accomplish as much in deed as it is plain he has enjoined on others with his voice. . . .

Wherefore those who are over others are to be admonished, that through earnestness of circumspection they have eyes watchful within and round about, and strive to become living creatures of heaven. For the living creatures of heaven are described as full of eyes round about and within. And so it is meet that those who are over others should have eyes within and round about, so as both in themselves to study to please the inward judge, and also, affording outwardly examples of life, to detect the things that should be corrected in others.

Subjects are to be admonished that they judge not rashly the lives of their superiors, if perchance they see them act blamably in anything, lest whence they rightly find fault with evil they thence be sunk by the impulse of elation to lower depths. They are to be admonished that, when they consider the faults of their superiors, they grow not too bold against them, but, if any of their deeds are exceedingly bad, so judge of them within themselves that, constrained by the fear of God, they still refuse not to bear the yoke of reverence under them. . . .

How the Forward and the Faint-Hearted Are to Be Admonished

Differently to be admonished are the forward and the faint-hearted. . . .

For we then best correct the forward, when what they believe themselves to have done well we show to have been ill done; that whence glory is believed to have been gained, thence wholesome confusion may ensue. But sometimes, when they are not at all aware of being guilty of the vice of forwardness, they more speedily come to correction if they are confounded by the infamy of some other person's more manifest guilt, sought out from a side quarter; that from that which they cannot defend, they may be made conscious of wrongly holding to what they do defend. . . .

But on the other hand we more fitly bring back the faint-hearted to the way of well-doing, if we search collaterally for some good points about them, so that, while some things in them we attack with our reproof, others we may embrace with our praise; to the end that the hearing of praise may nourish their tenderness, which the rebuking of their fault chastises. And for the most part we make more way with them for their profit, if we also make mention of their good deeds; and, in case of some wrong things having been done by them, if we find not fault with them as though they were already perpetrated, but, as it were, prohibit them as what ought not to be perpetrated; that so both the favor shown may increase the things which we approve, and our modest exhortation avail more with the faint-hearted against the things which we blame.

JOHN CALVIN

The Internal Testimony of the Spirit

Few have written extensively of the work of the Holy Spirit in preaching. The doctrine of inspiration affirms the Spirit's role in the production of the Scriptures, and preachers have long relied on the Spirit for both the "inspiration" and the delivery of their sermons. The mighty preacher, theologian, and renewer of the church John Calvin (1509-1564) stresses the importance of the Holy Spirit both in the interpretation of Scripture and in the "manner of receiving the grace of Christ." In the following selections from Books I and III of the *Institutes* Calvin describes the necessity of the Bible for knowledge of the true God. Using his famous figure of the spectacles, he portrays the revealed word as bringing the universal revelation of God into focus. Even though God is the author of the Bible and its words can be heard clearly, they do not "take" on the heart of the sinful human being. For the word to "print" on the heart, the Holy Spirit is needed first to "seal" the message, then to seal the heart against unbelief. The process is circular: the word teaches us about the Holy Spirit, and the Holy Spirit authenticates the word beyond all rational dispute. The Spirit causes some who hear to believe; others who hear the same word refuse to believe, but by their own will. Why this should be so, says Calvin, alluding to Augustine, is a "depth of the cross." For Calvin the tasks of biblical interpretation and preaching are closely linked. His description of the Spirit's testimony in both serves to set the whole cycle of sermon preparation, delivery, *and* reception into the context of the ongoing activity of God the Holy Spirit.

John Calvin, *Institutes of the Christian Religion,* ed. John T. McNeill, trans. Ford Lewis Battles (Philadelphia: Westminster, 1960 [1559 Latin]), The Library of Christian Classics, vol. 20, book I, vi, 1; I, vii, 4; I, vii, 5; Book III, ii, 33-36 (pp. 69-70; 78-81; 580-84).

God Bestows the Actual Knowledge of Himself upon Us Only in the Scriptures

That brightness which is borne in upon the eyes of all men both in heaven and on earth is more than enough to withdraw all support from men's ingratitude — just as God, to involve the human race in the same guilt, sets forth to all without exception his presence portrayed in his creatures. Despite this, it is needful that another and better help be added to direct us aright to the very Creator of the universe. It was not in vain, then, that he added the light of his word by which to become known unto salvation; and he regarded as worthy of this privilege those whom he pleased to gather more closely and intimately to himself. For because he saw the minds of all men tossed and agitated, after he chose the Jews as his very own flock, he fenced them about that they might not sink into oblivion as others had. With good reason he holds us by the same means in the pure knowledge of himself, since otherwise even those who seem to stand firm before all others would soon melt away. Just as old or bleary-eyed men and those with weak vision, if you thrust before them a most beautiful volume, even if they recognize it to be some sort of writing, yet can scarcely construe two words, but with the aid of spectacles will begin to read distinctly; so Scripture, gathering up the otherwise confused knowledge of God in our minds, having dispersed our dullness, clearly shows us the true God. This, therefore, is a special gift, where God, to instruct the church, not merely uses mute teachers but also opens his own most hallowed lips. Not only does he teach the elect to look upon a god, but also shows himself as the God upon whom they are to look. He has from the beginning maintained this plan for his church, so that besides these common proofs he also put forth his word, which is a more direct and more certain mark whereby he is to be recognized. . . .

The Witness of the Holy Spirit: This Is Stronger than All Proof

We ought to remember what I said a bit ago: credibility of doctrine is not established until we are persuaded beyond doubt that God is its Author. Thus, the highest proof of Scripture derives in general from the fact that God in person speaks in it. The prophets and apostles do not boast either of their keenness or of anything that obtains credit for them as they speak; nor do they dwell upon rational proofs. Rather, they bring forward God's holy name, that by it the whole world may be brought into obedience to him. Now we ought to see how apparent it is not only by plausible opinion but by clear truth that they do not call upon God's name heedlessly or falsely. If we desire to provide in the best way for our consciences — that they may not be perpetually beset by the instability of doubt or vacillation, and that they may not also boggle at the smallest quibbles — we ought to seek our conviction in a higher place than human reasons, judgments, or conjectures, that is, in the secret testimony of the Spirit.

True, if we wished to proceed by arguments, we might advance many things that would easily prove — if there is any god in heaven — that the law, the prophets, and the gospel come from him. Indeed, ever so learned men, endowed with the highest judgment, rise up in opposition and bring to bear and display all their mental powers in this debate. Yet, unless they become hardened to the point of hopeless impudence, this confession will be wrested from them: that they see manifest signs of God speaking Scripture. From this it is clear that the teaching of Scripture is from heaven.

And a little later we shall see that all the books of sacred Scripture far surpass all other writings. Yes, if we turn pure eyes and upright senses toward it, the majesty of God will immediately come to view, subdue our bold rejection, and compel us to obey. . . .

Since by unbelieving men religion seems to stand by opinion alone, they, in order not to believe anything foolishly or lightly, both wish and demand rational proof that Moses and the prophets spoke divinely. But I reply: the testimony of the Spirit is more excellent than all reason. For as God alone is a fit witness of himself in his word, so also the word will not find acceptance in men's hearts before it is sealed by the inward testimony of the Spirit. The same Spirit, therefore, who has spoken through the mouths of the prophets must penetrate into our hearts to persuade us that they faithfully proclaimed what had been divinely commanded. Isaiah very aptly expresses this connection in these words: "My Spirit which is in you, and the words that I have put in your mouth, and the mouths of your offspring, shall never fail" [Isa. 59:21].

Some good folk are annoyed that a clear proof is not ready at hand when the impious, unpunished, murmur against God's word. As if the Spirit were not called both "seal" and "guarantee" [2 Cor. 1:22] for confirming the faith of the godly; because until he illumines their minds, they ever waver among many doubts!

Scripture Bears Its Own Authentication

Let this point therefore stand: that those whom the Holy Spirit has inwardly taught truly rest upon Scripture, and that Scripture indeed is self-authenticated; hence, it is not right to subject it to proof and reasoning. And the certainty it deserves with us, it attains by the testimony of the Spirit. For even if it wins reverence for itself by its own majesty, it seriously affects us only when it is sealed upon our hearts through the Spirit. Therefore, illumined by his power, we believe neither by our own nor by anyone else's judgment that Scripture is from God; but above human judgment we affirm with utter certainty (just as if we were gazing upon the majesty of God himself) that it has flowed to us from the very mouth of God by the ministry of men.

We seek no proofs, no marks of genuineness upon which our judgment may lean; but we subject our judgment and wit to it as to a thing far beyond any guesswork! This we do, not as persons accustomed to seize upon some unknown thing, which, under closer scrutiny, displeases them, but fully conscious that we hold the unassailable truth! Nor do we do this as those miserable men who habitually bind over their minds to the thralldom of superstition; but we feel that the undoubted power of his divine majesty lives and breathes there. By this power we are drawn and inflamed, knowingly and willingly, to obey him, yet also more vitally and more effectively than by mere human willing or knowing!

God, therefore, very rightly proclaims through Isaiah that the prophets together with the whole people are witnesses to him; for they, instructed by prophecies, unhesitatingly held that God has spoken without deceit or ambiguity [Isa. 43:10]. Such, then, is a conviction that requires no reasons; such, a knowledge with which the best reason agrees — in which the mind truly reposes more securely and constantly than in any reasons; such, finally, a feeling that can be born only of heavenly revelation. I speak of nothing other than what each believer experiences within himself — though my words fall far beneath a just explanation of the matter.

I now refrain from saying more, since I shall have opportunity to discuss this matter elsewhere. Let us, then, know that the only true faith is that which the Spirit of God seals in our hearts.

✳   ✳   ✳

The Word Becomes Efficacious for Our Faith through the Holy Spirit

And this bare and external proof of the word of God should have been amply sufficient to engender faith, did not our blindness and perversity prevent it. But our mind has such an inclination to vanity that it can never cleave fast to the truth of God; and it has such a dullness that it is always blind to the light of God's truth.

Accordingly, without the illumination of the Holy Spirit, the word can do nothing. From this, also it is clear that faith is much higher than human understanding. And it will not be enough for the mind to be illumined by the Spirit of God unless the heart is also strengthened and supported by his power. In this matter the Schoolmen go completely astray, who in considering faith identify it with a bare and simple assent arising out of knowledge, and leave out confidence and assurance of heart. In both ways, therefore, faith is a singular gift of God, both in that the mind of man is purged so as to be able to taste the truth of God and in that his heart is established therein. For the Spirit is not only the initiator of faith, but increases it by degrees, until by it he leads us to the kingdom of heaven. "Let each one," says Paul, "guard the precious truth . . . entrusted by the Holy Spirit who dwells in us" [2 Tim. 1:14]. We can with no trouble explain how Paul teaches that the Spirit is given by the hearing of faith [Gal. 3:2]. If there had been only one gift of the Spirit, it would have been absurd of Paul to call the Spirit the "effect of faith," since he is its Author and cause. But because he proclaims the gifts with which God adorns his church and brings it to perfection by continual increase of faith, it is no wonder if he ascribes to faith those things which prepare us to receive them! This, indeed, is considered most paradoxical: when it is said that no one, unless faith be granted to him, can believe in Christ [John 6:65]. But this is partly because men do not consider either how secret and lofty the heavenly wisdom is, or how very dull men are to perceive the mysteries of God; partly because they do not have regard to that firm and steadfast constancy of heart which is the chief part of faith.

Only the Holy Spirit Leads Us to Christ

But if, as Paul preaches, no one "except the spirit of man which is in him" [1 Cor. 2:11] witnesses the human will, what man would be sure of God's will? And if the truth of God be untrustworthy among us also in those things which we at present behold with our eyes, how could it be firm and steadfast when the Lord promises such things as neither eye can see nor understanding can grasp [cf. 1 Cor. 2:9]? But here man's discernment is so overwhelmed and so fails that the first degree of advancement in the school of the Lord is to renounce it. For, like a veil cast over us, it hinders us from attaining the mysteries of God, "revealed to babes alone" [Matt. 11:25; Luke 10:21]. "For flesh and blood does not reveal this" [Matt. 16:17], "but the natural man does not perceive the things that are of the Spirit"; rather, God's teaching is "foolishness to him . . . because it must be spiritually discerned" [1 Cor. 2:14]. Therefore, the support of the Holy Spirit is necessary, or rather, his power alone thrives here. "There is no man who has known the mind of God, or has been his counselor" [Rom. 11:34]. But "the Spirit searches everything, even the depths of God" [1 Cor. 2:10]. It is through the Spirit that we come to grasp "the mind of Christ" [1 Cor. 2:16]. "No one can come to me," he says, "unless the Father who has sent me draw him" [John 6:44]. "Everyone who has heard from the Father and has learned, comes" [John 6:45]. Not that anyone has ever seen the Father but him who was sent by God [John 1:18; cf. John 5:37].

Therefore, as we cannot come to Christ unless we be drawn by the Spirit of God, so when we are drawn we are lifted up in mind and heart above our understanding. For the soul, illumined by him, takes on a new keenness, as it were, to contemplate the heavenly mysteries, whose splendor had previously blinded it. And man's understanding, thus beamed by the light of the Holy Spirit, then at last truly begins to taste those things which belong to the kingdom of God, having formerly been quite foolish and dull in tasting them. For this reason, Christ, in clearly interpreting the mysteries of his kingdom to two disciples [Luke 24:27], still makes no headway until "he opens their minds to understand the Scriptures" [Luke 24:45]. Although the apostles were so taught by his divine mouth, the Spirit of truth must nevertheless be sent to pour into their minds the same doctrine that they had perceived with their ears [John 16:13]. Indeed, the word of God is like the sun, shining upon all those to whom it is proclaimed, but with no effect among the blind. Now, all of us are blind by nature in this respect. Accordingly, it cannot penetrate into our minds unless the Spirit, as the inner teacher, through his illumination makes entry for it.

Without the Spirit Man Is Incapable of Faith

In another place, when we had to discuss the corruption of nature, we showed more fully how unfit men are to believe. Accordingly, I shall not weary my readers with repeating the same thing. Let it suffice that Paul calls faith itself, which the Spirit gives us but which we do not have by nature, "the spirit of faith" [2 Cor. 4:13]. He therefore prays that in the Thessalonians "God . . . may fulfill with power all his good pleasure . . . and work of faith" [2 Thess. 1:11]. Here Paul calls faith "the work of God," and instead of distinguishing it by an adjective, appropriately calls it "good pleasure." Thus he denies that man himself initiates faith, and, not satisfied with this, he adds that it is a manifestation of God's power. In the letter to the Corinthians he states that faith does not depend upon men's wisdom, but is founded upon the might of the Spirit [1 Cor. 2:4-5]. He is speaking, indeed, of outward miracles; but because the wicked, being blind, cannot see these, he includes also that inner seal which he mentions elsewhere

[Eph. 1:13; 4:30]. And God, to show forth his liberality more fully in such a glorious gift, does not bestow it upon all indiscriminately, but by a singular privilege gives it to those to whom he will. We have above cited testimonies of this. Augustine, the faithful interpreter of them, exclaims: "Our Savior, to teach us that belief comes as a gift and not from merit, says: 'No one comes to me, unless my Father . . . draw him' [John 6:44], and '. . . it be granted him by my Father' [John 6:65]. It is strange that two hear: one despises, the other rises up! Let him who despises impute it to himself; let him who rises up not arrogate it to himself." In another passage he says: "Why is it given to one and not to another? I am not ashamed to say: 'This is the depth of the cross.' Out of some depth or other of God's judgments, which we cannot fathom, . . . comes forth all that we can do. . . . I see what I can do; I do not see whence I can do it — except that I see this far: that . . . it is of God. But why one and not the other? This means much to me. It is an abyss, the depth of the cross. I can exclaim in wonder; I cannot demonstrate it through disputation." To sum up: Christ, when he illumines us into faith by the power of his Spirit, at the same time so engrafts us into his body that we become partakers of every good.

Faith as a Matter of the Heart

It now remains to pour into the heart itself what the mind has absorbed. For the word of God is not received by faith if it flits about in the top of the brain, but when it takes root in the depth of the heart that it may be an invincible defense to withstand and drive off all the stratagems of temptation. But if it is true that the mind's real understanding is illumination by the Spirit of God, then in such confirmation of the heart his power is much more clearly manifested, to the extent that the heart's distrust is greater than the mind's blindness. It is harder for the heart to be furnished with assurance than for the mind to be endowed with thought. The Spirit accordingly serves as a seal, to seal up in our hearts those very promises the certainty of which it has previously impressed upon our minds; and takes the place of a guarantee to confirm and establish them. After "you believed" (the apostle declares), "you were sealed with the Holy Spirit of promise, who is the guarantee of our inheritance" [Eph. 1:13-14]. Do you see how Paul teaches that the hearts of believers have, so to speak, been sealed with the Spirit; how, for this reason, Paul calls him the "Spirit of promise," because he makes firm the gospel among us?

PHILIP JACOB SPENER

Listening with the Heart

As supervisor of the ministerium in Frankfurt am Main Philip Jacob Spener (1635-1705) was moved to protest the formalism and bureaucracy of his church, the Lutheran church in Germany. Like George Herbert and Richard Baxter, Spener was painfully aware of the shortcomings of the clergy. But he added to their admonitions a systematic critique of the ecclesiastical structures and conventional worship practices that contributed to the ineffectiveness of the sermon. In his official capacity he strengthened the catechizing of the young, instituted home meetings for the cultivation of holiness (known as the *collegia pietatis*), encouraged lay participation in worship, and urged the reform of preaching and homiletical training. He objected to the aridity of orthodoxist scholasticism and its unedifying influence on preaching. In 1675 Spener published his best-known book, *Pia Desideria [Pious Wishes]*, in which he outlines the corruptions of the church and his hope for its renewal. Much of German Pietism has a familiar ring to contemporary Christians, especially Spener's criticism of the lectionary and the monologic sermon, as well as his advocacy of small-group discussion of Christian issues. In all his proposals Spener's concern was practical. In preaching, for example, he insisted "that *sermons* be so prepared by all that their purpose (faith and its fruits) may be achieved in the hearers to the greatest possible degree." The aim of his program for preaching was not a new homiletical technique, but the re-formation of the "inner man," a transformation which, if it is to be effected in the congregation, must begin in the soul of the preacher. (For another Pietist view of preaching see "A Letter to a Friend Concerning the Most Useful Way of Preaching" by August Hermann Francke in *Pietists*, ed. Peter C. Erb [New York: Paulist Press, 1983], pp. 117-27).

Philip Jacob Spener, *Pia Desideria*, trans. and ed. Theodore G. Tappert (Philadelphia: Fortress, 1964), pp. 87-91, 95-97, 115-17.

Thought should be given to a more extensive use of the word of God among us. We know that by nature we have no good in us. If there is to be any good in us, it must be brought about by God. To this end the word of God is the powerful means, since faith must be enkindled through the gospel, and the law provides the rules for good works and many wonderful impulses to attain them. The more at home the word of God is among us, the more we shall bring about faith and its fruits.

It may appear that the word of God has sufficiently free course among us inasmuch as at various places (as in this city) there is daily or frequent preaching from the pulpit. When we reflect further on the matter, however, we shall find that with respect to this first proposal, more is needed. I do not at all disapprove of the preaching of sermons in which a Christian congregation is instructed by the reading and exposition of a certain text, for I myself do this. But I find that this is not enough. In the first place, we know that "all Scripture is inspired by God and profitable for teaching, for reproof, for correction, and for training in righteousness" (2 Tim. 3:16). Accordingly *all* Scripture, without exception, should be known by the congregation if we are all to receive the necessary benefit. If we put together all the passages of the Bible which in the course of many years are read to a congregation in one place, they will comprise only a very small part of the Scriptures which have been given to us. The remainder is not heard by the congregation at all, or is heard only insofar as one or another verse is quoted or alluded to in sermons, without, however, offering any understanding of the entire context, which is nevertheless of the greatest importance.

In the second place, the people have little opportunity to grasp the meaning of the Scriptures except on the basis of those passages which may have been expounded to them, and even less do they have opportunity to become as practiced in them as edification requires. Meanwhile, although solitary reading of the Bible at home is in itself a splendid and praiseworthy thing, it does not accomplish enough for most people.

It should therefore be considered whether the church would not be well advised to introduce the people to Scripture in still other ways than through the customary sermons on the appointed lessons.

This might be done, first of all, by diligent reading of the Holy Scriptures, especially of the New Testament. It would not be difficult for every housefather to keep a Bible, or at least a New Testament, handy and read from it every day or, if he cannot read, to have somebody else read. . . .

Then a second thing would be desirable in order to encourage people to read privately, namely, that where the practice can be introduced the books of the Bible be read one after another, at specified times in the public service, without further comment (unless one wished to add brief summaries). This would be intended for the edification of all, but especially of those who cannot read at all, or cannot read easily or well, or of those who do not own a copy of the Bible.

For a third thing it would perhaps not be inexpedient (and I set this down for further and more mature reflection) to reintroduce the ancient and apostolic kind of church meetings. In addition to our customary services with preaching, other assemblies would also be held in the manner in which Paul describes them in 1 Corinthians 14:26-40. One person would not rise to preach (although this practice would be continued at other times), but others who have been blessed with gifts and knowledge would also speak and present their pious opinions on the proposed subject to the judgment of the rest, doing all this in such a way as to avoid disorder and strife. This might conveniently be done by having several ministers (in places where a number of them live in a town) meet together or by having several members of a congregation who have a fair knowledge of God or desire to increase their knowledge meet under the leadership of a minister, take up the Holy Scriptures, read aloud from them, and fraternally discuss each verse in order to discover its simple meaning and whatever may be useful for the edification of all. Anybody who is not satisfied with his understanding of a matter should be permitted to express his doubts and seek further explanation. On the other hand, those (including the ministers) who have made more progress should be allowed the freedom to state how they understand each passage. Then all that has been contributed, insofar as it accords with the sense of the Holy Spirit in the Scriptures, should be carefully considered by the rest, especially by the ordained ministers, and applied to the edification of the whole meeting. Everything should be arranged with an eye to the glory of God, to the spiritual growth of the participants, and therefore also to their limitations. Any threat of meddlesomeness, quarrelsomeness, self-seeking, or something else of this sort should be guarded against and tactfully cut off, especially by the preachers who retain leadership in these meetings.

Not a little benefit is to be hoped for from such an arrangement. Preachers would learn to know the members of their own congregations and their weakness or growth in doctrine and piety, and a bond of confidence would be established between preachers and people which would serve the best interests of both. At the same time the people would have a splendid opportunity to exercise their diligence with respect to the word of God and modestly to ask their questions (which they do not always have the courage to discuss with their minister in private) and get answers to them. In a short time they would experience personal growth and would also become capable of giving better religious instruction to their children and servants at home.

In the absence of such exercises, sermons which are delivered in continually flowing speech are not always fully and adequately comprehended because there is no time for reflection in between or because, when one does stop to reflect, much of what follows is missed (which does not happen in a discussion).

On the other hand, private reading of the Bible or reading in the household, where nobody is present who may from time to time help point out the meaning and purpose of each verse, cannot provide the reader with a sufficient explanation of all that he would like to know. What is lacking in both of these instances (in public preaching and private reading) would be supplied by the proposed exercises. It would not be a great burden either to the preachers or to the people, and much would be done to fulfill the admonition of Paul in Colossians 3:16, "Let the word of Christ dwell in you richly, as you teach and admonish one another in all wisdom, and as you sing psalms and hymns and spiritual songs." In fact, such songs may be used in the proposed meetings for the praise of God and the inspiration of the participants.

This much is certain: the diligent use of the word of God, which consists not only of listening to sermons but also of reading, meditating, and discussing (Ps. 1:2), must be the chief means for reforming something, whether this occurs in the proposed fashion or in some other appropriate way. The word of God remains the seed from which all that is good in us must grow. If we succeed in getting the people to seek eagerly and diligently in the book of life for their joy, their spiritual life will be wonderfully strengthened and they will become altogether different people. . . .

[T]he people must have impressed upon them and must accustom themselves to believing that it is by no means enough to have knowledge of the Christian faith, for Christianity consists rather of *practice*. Our dear Savior repeatedly enjoined love as the real mark of his disciples. . . . In his old age dear John (according to the testimony of Jerome in his letter to the Galatians) was accustomed to say hardly anything more to his disciples than "Children, love one another!" . . .

If we can therefore awaken a fervent love among our Christians, first toward one another and then toward all men (for these two, brotherly affection and general love, must supplement each other according to 2 Peter 1:7), and put this love into practice, practically all that we desire will be accomplished. For all the commandments are summed up in love (Rom. 13:9). Accordingly the people are not only to be told this incessantly, and they are not only to have the excellence of neighborly love and, on the other hand, the great danger and harm in the opposing self-love pictured impressively before their eyes . . . but they must also practice such love. They must become accustomed not to lose sight of any opportunity in which they can render their neighbor a service of love, and yet while performing it they must diligently search their hearts to discover whether they are acting in true love or out of other motives. . . .

For this purpose, as well as for the sake of Christian growth in general, it may be useful if those who have earnestly resolved to walk in the way of the Lord would enter into a confidential relationship with their confessor or some other judicious and enlightened Christian and would regularly report to him how they live, what opportunities they have had to practice Christian love, and how they have employed or neglected them. This should be done with the intention of discovering what is amiss and securing such an individual's counsel and instruction as to what ought now to be done. There should be firm resolution to follow such advice at all times unless something is expected that is quite clearly contrary to God's will. . . .

There are probably few places in our church in which there is such want that not enough sermons are preached. But many godly persons find that not a little is wanting in many sermons. There are preachers who fill most of their sermons with things that give the impression that the preachers are learned men, although the hearers understand nothing of this. Often many foreign languages are quoted, although probably not one person in the church understands a word of them. Many preachers are more concerned to have the introduction shape up well and the transitions be effective, to have an outline that is artful and yet sufficiently concealed, and to have all the parts handled precisely according to the rules of oratory and suitably embellished, than they are concerned that the materials be chosen and by God's grace be developed in such a way that the hearers may profit from the sermon in life and death. This ought not to be so. The pulpit is not the place for an ostentatious display of one's skill. It is rather the place to preach the word of the Lord plainly but powerfully. Preaching should be the divine means to save the people, and so it is proper that everything be directed to this end. Ordinary people, who make up the largest part of a congregation, are always to be kept in view more than the few learned people, insofar as such are present at all.

As the catechism contains the primary rudiments of Christianity, and all people have originally learned their faith from it, so it should continue to be used even more diligently (according to its meaning rather than its words) in the instruction of children, and also of adults if one can have these in attendance. A preacher should not grow weary of this. In fact, if he has opportunity, he would do well to tell the people again and again in his sermons what they once learned, and he should not be ashamed of so doing.

I shall here gladly pass over additional observations that might well be made about sermons, but I regard this as the principal thing: Our whole Christian religion consists of the inner man or the new man, whose soul is faith and whose expressions are the fruits of life, and all sermons should be aimed at this. On the one hand, the precious benefactions of God, which are directed toward this inner man, should be presented in such a way that faith, and hence the inner man, may ever be strengthened more and more. On the other hand, works should be so set in motion that we may by no means be content merely to have the people refrain from outward vices and practice outward virtues and thus be concerned only with the outward man, which the ethics of the heathen can also accomplish, but that we lay the right foundation in the heart, show that what does not proceed from this foundation is mere hypocrisy, and hence accustom the people first to work on what is inward (awaken love of God and neighbor through suitable means) and only then to act accordingly.

One should therefore emphasize that the divine means of word and sacrament are concerned with the inner man. Hence it is not enough that we hear the word with our outward ear, but we must let it penetrate to our heart, so that we may hear the Holy Spirit speak there, that is, with vibrant emotion and comfort feel the sealing of the Spirit and the power of the word. Nor is it enough to be baptized, but the inner man, where we have put on Christ in baptism, must also keep Christ on and bear witness to him in our outward life. Nor is it enough to have received the Lord's Supper externally, but the inner man must truly be fed with that blessed food. Nor is it enough to pray outwardly with our mouth, but true prayer, and the best prayer, occurs in the inner man, and it either breaks forth in words or remains in the soul, yet God will find and hit upon it. Nor, again, is it enough to worship God in an external temple, but the inner man worships God best in his own temple, whether or not he is in an external temple at the time. So one could go on.

Since the real power of all Christianity consists of this, it would be proper if sermons, on the whole, were pointed in such a direction. If this were to happen, much more edification would surely result than is presently the case.

The Inner Turmoil of the Awakened

Jonathan Edwards (1703-1758) wrote his *Narrative of the Surprising Work of God in Northampton, Mass., 1735,* to explain and defend the revival known as the Great Awakening. In the course of the narrative he draws a composite psychological portrait of the person "being wrought upon." His account includes the story of a woman who declared that it was pleasant to think of lying in the dust all the days of her life, mourning for sin, and the famous case study of four-year-old Phoebe Bartlett, who spent a part of each day in her closet contemplating hell. The narrative concludes with the "Gradual Withdrawing of the Spirit" instanced first by a townsman who slit his own throat. Edwards's psychology focused on the "affections" or emotions as the source of all behavior. In genuine cases of revival the affections were influenced and augmented by a supernatural sense given by the Holy Spirit. But because the affections are so crucial to religious behavior, they are also the workshop in which Satan creates false images and religious delusions. Although Edwards is aware of some "impure" elements in the Awakening, he judges it on the whole to be a "work of God." The question of the listener's emotional response and its validity as a measurement of conversion is one that has persisted in contemporary discussions of preaching. What is the most appropriate *form* — liturgical, psychological, or otherwise — of the listener's response to the word? While the *Narrative* does not answer the question, it says much about the inner turmoil and the pressures of the social environment that weighed upon those to whom Jonathan Edwards preached and ministered.

Jonathan Edwards, *Thoughts on the Revival of Religion in New England, 1740, to which is prefixed a Narrative of the Surprising Work of God in Northampton, Mass., 1735* (New York: American Tract Society, n.d.), pp. 28-34.

I therefore proceed to give an account of the manner of persons being wrought upon; and here there is a vast variety, perhaps as manifold as the subjects of the operation; but yet in many things there is a great analogy in all.

Persons are first awakened with a sense of their miserable condition by nature, the danger they are in of perishing eternally, and that it is of great importance to them that they speedily escape and get into a better state. Those that before were secure and senseless are made sensible how much they were in the way to ruin in their former courses. Some are more suddenly seized with convictions; it may be, by the news of others' conversion, or something they hear in public or in private conference, their consciences are suddenly smitten, as if their hearts were pierced through with a dart; others have awakenings that come upon them more gradually; they begin at first to be more thoughtful and considerate, so as to come to a conclusion in their minds that it is their best and wisest way to delay no longer, but to improve the present opportunity; and have accordingly set themselves seriously to meditate on those things that have the most awakening tendency, on purpose to obtain convictions; and so their awakenings have increased, till a sense of their misery, by God's Spirit setting in therewith, has had fast hold of them. Others that, before this wonderful time, had been something religious and concerned for their salvation, have been awakened in a new manner, and made sensible that their slack and dull way of seeking was never like to attain their purpose, and so have been roused up to a greater violence for the kingdom of heaven.

These awakenings, when they have first seized on persons, have had two effects: one was, that they have brought them immediately to quit their sinful practices, and the looser sort have been brought to forsake and dread their former vices and extravagancies. When once the Spirit of God began to be so wonderfully poured out in a general way through the town, people had soon done with their old quarrels, backbitings, and intermeddling with other men's matters; the tavern was soon left empty, and persons kept very much at home; none went abroad unless on necessary business, or on some religious account, and every day seemed, in many respects, like a Sabbath day. And the other effect was, that it put them on earnest application to the means of salvation, reading, prayer, meditation, the ordinances of God's house, and private conference; their cry was, "What shall we do to be saved?" The place of resort was now changed — it was no longer the tavern, but the minister's house; and that was thronged far more than ever the tavern had been wont to be.

There is a very great variety as to the degree of fear and trouble that persons are exercised with before they obtain any comfortable evidences of pardon and acceptance with God: some are from the beginning carried on with abundantly more encouragement and hope than others; some have had ten times less trouble of mind than others, in whom yet the issue seems to be the same. Some have had such a sense of the displeasure of God, and the great danger they were in of damnation, that they could not sleep at night; and many have said that when they have lain down, the thoughts of sleeping in such a condition have been frightful to them, and they have scarcely been free from terror while they have been asleep, and they have awaked with fear, heaviness, and distress still abiding on their spirits. It has been very common that the deep and fixed concern that has been on persons' minds, has had a painful influence on their bodies, and given disturbance to animal nature.

The awful apprehensions persons have had of their misery have, for the most part, been increasing the nearer they have approached to deliverance, though they often pass through many changes in the frame and circumstances of their minds. Sometimes they think themselves wholly senseless, and fear that the Spirit of God has left them, and that they are given up to judicial hardness; yet they appear very deeply exercised about that fear, and are in great earnest to obtain convictions again.

Together with those fears, and that exercise of mind which is rational, and which they have just ground for, they have often suffered many needless distresses of thought, in which Satan probably has a great hand to entangle them and block up their way; and sometimes the disease of melancholy has been evidently mixed; of which, when it happens, the tempter seems to make great advantage, and puts an unhappy bar in the way of any good effect. One knows not how to deal with such persons; they turn everything that is said to them the wrong way, and most to their own disadvantage. And there is nothing that the devil seems to make so great a handle of as a melancholy humor, unless it be the real corruption of the heart.

But it has been very remarkable that there has been far less of this mixture in this time of extraordinary blessing, than there was wont to be in persons under awakenings at other times; for it is evident that many that before had been exceedingly involved in such difficulties, seemed now strangely to be set at liberty. Some persons that had before for a long time been exceedingly entangled with peculiar temptations of one sort or other, and unprofitable and hurtful distresses, were soon helped over former stumbling blocks that hindered any progress toward saving good, and convictions have wrought more kindly, and they have been successfully carried on in the way to life. And thus Satan seemed to be restrained till toward the latter end of this wonderful time, when God's Spirit was about to withdraw.

Many times persons under great awakenings were concerned because they thought they were not awakened, but miserable, hard-hearted, senseless creatures still, and sleeping upon the brink of hell. The sense of the need they have to be awakened, and of their comparative hardness, grows upon them with their awakenings, so that they seem to themselves to be very senseless, when indeed most sensible. There have been some instances of persons that have had as great a sense of their danger and misery as their natures could well subsist under, so that a little more would probably have destroyed them; and yet they have expressed themselves much amazed at their own insensibility and dullness in such an extraordinary time as it then was.

Persons are sometimes brought to the borders of despair, and it looks as black as midnight to them a little before the day dawns in their souls. Some few instances there have been of persons who have had such a sense of God's wrath for sin, that they have been overborne and made to cry out under an astonishing sense of their guilt, wondering that God suffers such guilty wretches to live upon the earth, and that he doth not immediately send them to hell; and sometimes their guilt does so glare them in the face, that they are in exceeding terror for fear that God will instantly do it; but more commonly the distresses under legal awakenings have not been to such a degree. In some these terrors do not seem to be so sharp, when near comfort, as before; their convictions have not seemed to work so much that way, but they seem to be led further down into their own hearts to a further sense of their own universal depravity, and deadness in sin.

The corruption of the heart has discovered itself in various exercises in the time of legal convictions. Sometimes it appears in a great struggle like something roused by an enemy, and Satan, the old inhabitant, seems to exert himself like a serpent disturbed and enraged. Many, in such circumstances, have felt a great spirit of envy toward the godly, especially toward those that are thought to have been lately converted, and most of all toward acquaintances and companions when they are thought to be converted: indeed some have felt many heart-risings against God, and murmurings at his ways of dealing with mankind, and his dealings with themselves in particular. It has been much insisted on, both in public and private, that persons should have the utmost dread of such envious thoughts, which, if allowed, tend exceedingly to quench the Spirit of God, if not to provoke him finally to forsake them. And when such a spirit has much prevailed, and persons have not so earnestly strove against it as they ought to have done, it has seemed to be exceedingly to the hindrance of the good of their souls, but in some other instances where persons have been much terrified at the sight of such wickedness in their hearts, God has brought good to them out of evil, and made it a means of convincing them of their own desperate sinfulness, and bringing them off from all self-confidence. The drift of the Spirit of God in his legal strivings with persons, has seemed most evidently to be to make way for and to bring a conviction of, *their absolute* dependence on his sovereign power and grace, and the universal necessity of a mediator, by leading them more and more to a sense of their exceeding wickedness and guiltiness in his sight; the pollution and insufficiency of their own righteousness, that they can in no wise help themselves, and that God would be wholly just and righteous in rejecting them and all that they do, and in casting them off for ever, though there be a vast variety as to the manner and distinctness of persons' convictions of these things.

As they are gradually more and more convinced of the corruption and wickedness of their hearts, they seem to themselves to grow worse and worse, harder and blinder, and more desperately wicked, instead of growing better. They are ready to be discouraged by it, and oftentimes never think themselves so far off from the good, as when they are nearest. Under the sense which the Spirit of God gives them of their sinfulness, they often think that they differ from all others; their hearts are ready to sink with the thought, that they are the worst of all, and that none ever obtained mercy who were so wicked as they.

JOHN HENRY NEWMAN

University Preaching

John Henry Newman (1801-1890) was born in London to evangelical Anglican parents. After graduating from Oxford University, he became a fellow of Oriel College and vicar of the University Church of St. Mary the Virgin, where he proved to be an influential preacher. During his Oxford years he began to undertake close study of the Church Fathers and became a leading figure in the Oxford Movement, a group of scholars committed to the liturgical and doctrinal renewal of the Church of England. Newman's views grew more and more Roman Catholic in tone, and his *Tracts for the Times* were condemned by Anglicans after he argued that the Thirty-Nine Articles were compatible with Rome. He converted to Catholicism in 1845 and, after a year of theological study in Rome, was ordained a priest in 1847. In 1879 he was named a Cardinal of the Church. As theological works, Newman's *Essay on the Development of Doctrine* and *Essay in Aid of a Grammar of Assent* are venerated as classics. His *Apologia pro Vita Sua* is regarded as one of the finest autobiographies of the nineteenth century. Along with *The Idea of a University,* it is also essential to an understanding of Newman the preacher, for it was through the rich yet finely chiseled prose of his sermons that this eminent Victorian forged his distinctively Catholic theology. In his "Biglietto Speech," given in 1879 when he was made a Cardinal, Newman might have been prophesying of our own day when he criticized those who teach that revealed religion "is not a truth, but a sentiment and a taste; not an objective fact; not miraculous: and it is the right of each individual to make it say just what strikes his fancy." In the contested world of British religion, all Newman's works were concerned with audience — with friends to be sustained and opponents refuted. In the selection that follows, though he analyzes the rarefied audience of "University Preaching," his homiletical advice reflects the breadth of his motto, drawn from St. Francis de Sales: *Cor ad cor loquitur* (Heart speaks to heart).

John Henry Cardinal Newman, *The Idea of a University* (London: Longmans, Green, and Co., 1910 [1852]), pp. 405-20.

When I obtained from various distinguished persons the acceptable promise that they would give me the advantage of their countenance and assistance by appearing from time to time in the pulpit of our new university, some of them accompanied that promise with the natural request that I, who had asked for it, should offer them my own views of the mode and form in which the duty would be most satisfactorily accomplished. On the other hand, it was quite as natural that I on my part should be disinclined to take on myself an office which belongs to a higher station and authority in the church than my own; and the more so, because, on the definite subject about which the inquiry is made, I should have far less direct aid from the writings of holy men and great divines than I could desire. Were it indeed my sole business to put into shape the scattered precepts which saints and doctors have delivered upon it, I might have ventured on such a task with comparatively little misgiving. Under the shadow of the great teachers of the pastoral office I might have been content to speak, without looking out for any living authority to prompt me. But this unfortunately is not the case; such venerable guidance does not extend beyond the general principles and rules of preaching, and these require both expansion and adaptation when they are to be made to bear on compositions addressed in the name of a university to university men. They define the essence of Christian preaching, which is one and the same in all cases; but not the subject matter or the method, which vary according to circumstances. Still, after all, the points to which they do reach are more, and more important, than those which they fall short of. I therefore, though with a good deal of anxiety, have attempted to perform a task which seemed naturally to fall to me; and I am thankful to say that, though I must in some measure go beyond the range of the simple direction to which I have referred, the greater part of my remarks will lie within it.

So far is clear at once, that the preacher's object is the spiritual good of his hearers. . . . As a marksman aims at the target and its bull's-eye, and at nothing else, so the preacher must have a definite point before him, which he has to hit. So much is contained for his direction in this simple maxim, that duly to enter into it and use it is half the battle; and if he mastered nothing else, still if he really mastered as much as this, he would know all that was imperative for the due discharge of his office.

For what is the conduct of men who have one object definitely before them, and one only? Why, that, whatever be their skill, whatever be their resources, greater or less, to its attainment all their efforts are simply, spontaneously, visibly, directed. This cuts off a number of questions sometimes asked about preaching, and extinguishes a number of anxieties. . . . We ask questions perhaps about diction, elocution, rhetorical power; but does the commander of a besieging force dream of holiday displays, reviews, mock engagements, feats of strength, or trials of skill, such as would be graceful and suitable on a parade ground when a foreigner of rank was to be received and *feted;* or does he aim at one and one thing only, viz., to take the strong place? Display dissipates the energy, which for the object in view needs to be concentrated and condensed. We have no reason to suppose that the divine blessing follows the lead of human accomplishments. Indeed, St. Paul, writing to the Corinthians, who made much of such advantages of nature, contrasts the persuasive words of human wisdom "with the showing of the Spirit," and tells us that "the kingdom of God is not in speech, but in power."

But, not to go to the consideration of divine influences, which is beyond my subject, the very presence of simple earnestness is even in itself a powerful natural instrument to effect that toward which it is directed. Earnestness creates earnestness in others by sympathy; and the more a preacher loses and is lost to himself, the more does he gain his brethren. Nor is it without some logical force also; for what is powerful enough to absorb and possess a preacher has at least a *prima facie* claim of attention on the part of his hearers. On the other hand, anything which interferes with this earnestness, or which argues its absence, is still more certain to blunt the force of the most cogent argument conveyed in the most eloquent language. Hence it is that the great philosopher of antiquity, in speaking, in his Treatise on Rhetoric, of the various kinds of persuasives, which are available in the Art, considers the most authoritative of these to be that which is drawn from personal traits of an ethical nature evident in the orator; for such matters are cognizable by all men, and the common sense of the world decides that it is safer, where it is possible, to commit oneself to the judgment of men of character than to any considerations addressed merely to the feelings or to the reason.

On these grounds I would lay down a precept, which I trust is not extravagant, when allowance is made for the preciseness and the point which are unavoidable in all categorical statements upon matters of conduct. It is, that preachers should neglect everything whatever besides devotion to their one object, and earnestness in pursuing it, till they in some good measure attain to these requisites. Talent, logic, learning, words, manner, voice, action, all are required for the perfection of a preacher; but "one thing is necessary," — an intense perception and appreciation of the end for which he preaches, and that is, to be the minister of some definite spiritual good to those who hear him. Who could wish to be more eloquent, more powerful, more successful than the Teacher of the Nations? Yet who more earnest, who more natural, who more unstudied, who more self-forgetting than he?

And here, in order to prevent misconception, two remarks must be made, which will lead us further into the subject we are engaged upon. The first is, that, in what I have been saying, I do not mean that a preacher must aim at *earnestness,* but that he must aim at his *object,* which is to do some spiritual good to his hearers, and which will at once *make* him earnest. It is said that, when a man has to cross an abyss by a narrow plank thrown over it, it is his wisdom, not to look at the plank, along which lies his path, but to fix his eyes steadily on the point in the opposite precipice at which the plank ends. It is by gazing at the object which he must reach, and ruling himself by it, that he secures to himself the power of walking to it straight and steadily. The case is the same in moral matters, no one will become really earnest by aiming directly at earnestness; any one may become earnest by meditating on the motives, and by drinking at the sources, of earnestness. We may of course work ourselves up into a pretence, nay, into a paroxysm, of earnestness; as we may chafe our cold hands till they are warm. But when we cease chafing, we lose the warmth again; on the contrary, let the sun come out and strike us with his beams, and we need no artificial chafing to be warm. The hot words, then, and energetic gestures of a preacher, taken by themselves, are just as much signs of earnestness as rubbing the hands or flapping the arms together are signs of warmth; though they are natural where earnestness already exists, and pleasing as being its spontaneous concomitants. To sit down to compose for the pulpit with a resolution to be eloquent is one impediment to persuasion; but to be determined to be earnest is absolutely fatal to it.

He who has before his mental eye the Four Last Things will have the true earnestness, the horror or the rapture, of one who witnesses a conflagration, or discerns some rich and sublime prospect of natural scenery. His countenance, his voice, speak for him, in proportion as his view has been vivid and minute. . . .

It is this earnestness, in the supernatural order, which is the eloquence of saints; and not of saints only, but of all Christian preachers, according to the measure of their faith and love. As the case would be with one who has actually seen what he relates, the herald of tidings of the invisible world also will be, from the nature of the case, whether vehement or calm, sad or exulting, always simple, grave, emphatic, and peremptory; and all this, not because he has proposed to himself to be so, but because certain intellectual convictions involve certain external manifestations. . . .

My second remark is, that it is the preacher's duty to aim at imparting to others, not any fortuitous, unpremeditated benefit, but some *definite* spiritual good. It is here that design and study have their place; the more exact and precise is the subject which he treats, the more impressive and practical will he be; whereas no one will carry off much from a discourse which is on the general subject of virtue, or vaguely and feebly entertains the question of the desirable-ness of attaining heaven, or the rashness of incurring eternal ruin. As a distinct image before the mind makes the preacher earnest, so it will give him something which it is worthwhile to communicate to others. Mere sympathy, it is true, is able, as I have said, to transfer an emotion or sentiment from mind to mind, but it is not able to fix it there. He must aim at imprinting on the heart what will never leave it, and this he cannot do unless he employ himself on some definite subject, which he has to handle and weigh, and then, as it were, to hand over from himself to others.

Hence it is that the Saints insist so expressly on the necessity of his addressing himself to the intellect of men, and of convincing as well as persuading. . . . In St. Ignatius's Exercises, the act of the intellect precedes that of the affections. Father Lohner seems to me to be giving an instance in point when he tells of a court-preacher who delivered what would be commonly considered eloquent sermons, and attracted no one; and next took to simple explanations of the Mass and similar subjects, and then found the church thronged. So necessary is it to have something to say, if we desire any one to listen.

Nay, I would go the length of recommending a preacher to place a distinct categorical proposition before him, such as he can write down in a form of words, and to guide and limit his preparation by it, and to aim in all he says to bring it out, and nothing else. . . . Nay, is it not expressly conveyed in the Scripture phrase of "preaching the *word*"? For what is meant by "the word" but a proposition addressed to the intellect? Nor will a preacher's earnestness show itself in anything more unequivocally than in his rejecting, whatever be the temptation to admit it, every remark, however original, every period, however eloquent, which does not in some way or other tend to bring out this one distinct proposition which he has chosen. Nothing is so fatal to the effect of a sermon as the habit of preaching on three or four subjects at once. I acknowledge I am advancing a step beyond the practice of great Catholic preachers when I add that, even though we preach on only one at a time, finishing and dismissing the first before we go to the second, and the second before we go to the third, still, after all, a practice like this, though not open to the inconvenience which the confusing of one subject with another involves, is in matter of fact nothing short of the delivery of three sermons in succession without break between them.

Summing up, then, what I have been saying, I observe that, if I have understood the doctrine of St. Charles, St. Francis, and other saints aright, *definiteness of object* is in various ways the one virtue of the preacher; — and this means that he should set out with the intention of conveying to others some spiritual benefit; that, with a view to this, and as the only ordinary way to it, he should select some distinct fact or scene, some passage in history, some truth, simple or profound, some doctrine, some principle, or some sentiment, and should study it well and thoroughly, and first make it his own, or else have already dwelt on it and mastered it, so as to be able to use it for the occasion from a habitual understanding of it; and that then he should employ himself, as the one business of his discourse, to bring home to others, and to leave deep within them, what he has, before he began to speak to them, brought home to himself.

What he feels himself, and feels deeply, he has to make others feel deeply; and in proportion as he comprehends this, he will rise above the temptation of introducing collateral matters, and will have no taste, no heart, for going aside after flowers of oratory, fine figures, tuneful periods, which are worth nothing, unless they come to him spontaneously, and are spoken "out of the abundance of the heart." Our Lord said on one occasion: "I am come to send fire on the earth, and what will I but that it be kindled?" He had one work, and he accomplished it. "The words," he says, "which thou gavest me, I have *given* to them, and they have *received* them, . . . *and now* I come to thee." And the apostles, again, as they had received, so were they to give. "That which *we* have seen and heard," says one of them, "we declare unto *you*, that you may have *fellowship* with us." If, then, a preacher's subject only be some portion of the divine message, however elementary it may be, however trite, it will have a dignity such as to possess him, and a virtue to kindle him, and an influence to subdue and convert those to whom it goes forth from him, according to the words of the promise, "My word, which shall go forth from my mouth, shall not return to me void, but it shall do whatsoever I please, and shall prosper in the things for which I sent it."

And now having got as far as this, we shall see without difficulty what a university sermon ought to be just so far as it is distinct from other sermons; for, if all preaching is directed toward a hearer, such as is the hearer will be the preaching, and, as a university auditory differs from other auditories, so will a sermon addressed to it differ from other sermons. This, indeed, is a broad maxim which holy men lay down on the subject of preaching. Thus, St. Gregory says: "The self-same exhortation is not suitable for all hearers; for all have not the same disposition of mind, and what profits these is hurtful to those."

It is true, this is also one of the elementary principles of the art of rhetoric; but it is no scandal that a saintly bishop should in this matter borrow a maxim from secular, nay, from pagan schools. For divine grace does not overpower nor supersede the action of the human mind according to its proper nature; and if heathen writers have analyzed that nature well, so far let them be used to the greater glory of the author and source of all truth. Aristotle, then, in his celebrated treatise on rhetoric, makes the very essence of the art lie in the precise recognition of a hearer. It is a relative art, and in that respect differs from logic, which simply teaches the right use of reason, whereas rhetoric is the art of persuasion, which implies a person who is to be persuaded. As, then, the Christian preacher aims at the divine glory, not in any vague and general way, but definitely by the enunciation of some article or passage of the revealed word, so further, he enunciates it, not for the instruction of the whole world, but directly for the sake of those very persons who are before him. He is, when in the pulpit, instructing, enlightening, informing, advancing, sanctifying, not all nations, nor all classes, nor all callings, but those particular ranks, professions, states, ages, characters, which have gathered around him. Proof indeed is the same all over the earth, but he has not only to prove, but to persuade; — *Whom?* A hearer, then, is included in the very idea of preaching; and we cannot determine how in detail we ought to preach, till we know whom we are to address.

In all the most important respects, indeed, all hearers are the same, and what is suitable for one audience is suitable for another. All hearers are children of Adam; all, too, are children of the Christian adoption and of the Catholic church. The great topics which suit the multitude, which attract the poor, which sway the unlearned, which warn, arrest, recall, the wayward and wandering, are in place within the precincts of a university as elsewhere. A *Studium Generale* is not a cloister, or novitiate, or seminary, or boarding school; it is an assemblage of the young, the inexperienced, the lay, and the secular; and not even the simplest of religious truths, or the most elementary article of the Christian faith, can be unseasonable from its pulpit. A sermon on the divine omnipresence, on the future judgment, on the satisfaction of Christ, on the intercession of saints, will be not less, perhaps more, suitable there than if it were addressed to a parish congregation. . . .

However, after all, a university has a character of its own; it has some traits of human nature more prominently developed than others, and its members are brought together under circumstances which impart to the auditory a peculiar color and expression even where it does not substantially differ from another. . . .

And first as to his *matter* or subject. Here I would remark upon the circumstance, that courses of sermons upon theological points, polemical discussions, treatises *in extenso,* and the like, are often included in the idea of a university sermon, and are considered to be legitimately entitled to occupy the attention of a university audience; the object of such compositions being, not directly and mainly the edification of the hearers, but the defense or advantage of Catholicism at large, and the gradual formation of a volume suitable for publication. Without absolutely discountenancing such important works, it is not necessary to say more of them than that they rather belong to the divinity school, and fall under the idea of lectures, than have a claim to be viewed as university sermons. Anyhow, I do not feel called upon to speak of such discourses here. And I say the same of panegyrical orations, discourses on special occasions, funeral sermons, and the like.

Putting such exceptional compositions aside, I will confine myself to the consideration of what may be called sermons proper. And here, I repeat, any general subject will be seasonable in the university pulpit which would be seasonable elsewhere; but, if we look for subjects especially suitable, they will be of two kinds. The temptations which ordinarily assail the young and the intellectual are two: those which are directed against their virtue, and those which are directed against their faith. All divine gifts are exposed to misuse and perversion; youth and intellect are both of them goods, and involve in them certain duties respectively, and can be used to the glory of the Giver; but, as youth becomes the occasion of excess and sensuality, so does intellect give accidental opportunity to religious error, rash speculation, doubt, and infidelity. That these are in fact the peculiar evils to which large academical bodies are liable is shown from the history of universities; and if a preacher would have a subject which has especial significance in such a place, he must select one which bears upon one or other of these two classes of sin. I mean, he would be treating on some such subject with the same sort of appositeness as he would discourse upon almsgiving when addressing the rich, or on patience, resignation, and industry, when he was addressing the poor, or on forgiveness of injuries when he was addressing the oppressed or persecuted.

To this suggestion I append two cautions. First, I need hardly say, that a preacher should be quite sure that he understands the persons he is addressing before he ventures to aim at what he considers to be their ethical condition; for, if he mistakes, he will probably be doing harm rather than good. I have known consequences to occur very far from edifying, when strangers have fancied they knew an auditory when they did not, and have by implication imputed to them habits or motives which were not theirs. Better far would it be for a preacher to select one of those more general subjects which are safe than risk what is evidently ambitious, if it is not successful.

My other caution is this: that, even when he addresses himself to some special danger or probable deficiency or need of his hearers, he should do so covertly, not showing on the surface of his discourse what he is aiming at. I see no advantage in a preacher professing to treat of infidelity, orthodoxy, or virtue, or the pride of reason, or riot, or sensual indulgence. To say nothing else, commonplaces are but blunt weapons; whereas it is particular topics that penetrate and reach their mark. Such subjects rather are, for instance, the improvement of time, avoiding the occasions of sin, frequenting the sacraments, divine warnings, the inspirations of grace, the mysteries of the rosary, natural virtue, beauty of the rites of the church, consistency of the Catholic faith, relation of Scripture to the church, the philosophy of tradition, and any others which may touch the heart and conscience, or may suggest trains of thought to the intellect, without proclaiming the main reason why they have been chosen.

Next, as to the *mode of treating* its subject, which a university discourse requires. It is this respect, after all, I think, in which it especially differs from other kinds of preaching. As translations differ from each other, as expressing the same ideas in different languages, so in the case of sermons, each may undertake the same subject, yet treat it in its own way, as contemplating its own hearers. This is well exemplified in the speeches of St. Paul, as recorded in the book of Acts. To the Jews he quotes the Old Testament; on the Areopagus, addressing the philosopher of Athens, he insists, — not indeed upon any recondite doctrine, contrariwise, upon the most elementary, the being and unity of God; — but he treats it with a learning and depth of thought, which the presence of that celebrated city naturally suggested.

And in like manner, while the most simple subjects are apposite in a university pulpit, they certainly would there require a treatment more exact than is necessary in merely popular exhortations. It is not asking much to demand for academical discourses a more careful study beforehand, a more accurate conception of the idea which they are to enforce, a more cautious use of words, a more anxious consultation of writers of authority, and somewhat more of philosophical and theological knowledge.

But here again, as before, I would insist on the necessity of such compositions being unpretending. It is not necessary for a preacher to quote the holy Fathers, or to show erudition, or to construct an original argument, or to be ambitious in style and profuse of ornament, on the ground that the audience is a university; it is only necessary so to keep the character and necessities of his hearers before him as to avoid what may offend them, or mislead, or disappoint, or fail to profit.

PHILLIPS BROOKS

The Congregation

In several ways the homiletical theory of Phillips Brooks (1835-1893) exemplifies the liberal tradition in America, especially liberalism's optimistic view of human nature. Yale theologian Lewis Brastow, writing at the turn of the twentieth century, observes that "[Brooks] was the consummate flower of nine generations of cultured Puritan stock. . . . [O]n the one side he inherited the Puritan's high sense of the worth of humanity, his large estimate of its possibilities of development, his recognition of the sacredness of the individual soul, and his enthusiastic devotion to its highest welfare. This was the spring of that lofty idealism that passed into an optimism that was unmatched in his generation" (*Representative Modern Preachers* [New York: Macmillan, 1904], pp. 195-96). The loftiness of perspective in Brooks is always tempered by common sense and the working pastor's eye for reality. For example, after heralding the "ideal and heroic" qualities of the assembled congregation, Brooks adds soberly, "It may be a delusion." His view of the congregation as a microcosm of humanity adds balance and breadth to the parochialism of much preaching. His counter-insistence on the preacher's rootedness and sense of place derives ultimately from his liberal understanding of the incarnation: just as Jesus assumed human nature in order to lead it to its highest attainable level, so preaching strives to elevate its audience by helping it recognize and capitalize on its higher nature.

Phillips Brooks, *Lectures on Preaching* (New York: E. P. Dutton & Company, 1907 [1877]), pp. 180-90.

I have said what I had to say about the preacher and about the sermon. Today I want to speak to you about the congregation. There is something remarkable in the way in which a minister talks about "my congregation." They evidently come to seem to him different from the rest of humankind. There is the rest of our race, in Europe, Asia, Africa, and America, and the Islands of the Sea, and then there is "my congregation." A man begins the habit the moment he is settled in a parish. However young, however inexperienced he may be, he at once takes possession of that fraction of the human family and holds it with a sense of ownership. He immediately assumes certain fictions concerning them. He takes it for granted that they listen to his words with a deference quite irrespective of the value of the words themselves. He talks majestically about "what I tell my congregation," as if there were some basis upon which they received his teachings quite different from that upon which other intelligent men listen to one who takes his place before them as their teacher. He supposes them to be subject to emotions which he expects of no one else. He thinks that, in some mysterious way, their property as well as their intelligence is subject to his demand, to be handed over to him when he shall tell them that he has found a good use to which to put it. He imagines that, though they are as clear-sighted as other people, little devices of his which are perfectly plain to everybody else impose upon them perfectly. He talks about them so unnaturally that we are almost surprised when we ask their names and find that they are men and women whom we know, men and women who are leading ordinary lives and judging people and things by ordinary standards, with all the varieties of character and ways which any such group must have, whom he has separated from the rest of humanity and distinguished by their relation to himself and calls "my congregation."

I think that a good deal of the unreality of clerical life comes from this feeling of ministers about their congregations. I have known many ministers who were frank and simple and unreserved with other people for whom they did not feel a responsibility, but who threw around themselves a cloak of fictions and reserves the moment that they met a parishioner. They were willing to let the stranger clearly see that there were many things in religion and theology which they did not know at all, many other questions on which they were in doubt, points of their church's faith which they thought unimportant to salvation, methods of their church's policy which they thought injudicious. All this they would say freely as they talked with the wolf over the sheepfold wall, or with some sheep in the next flock; but in their own flock they held their peace, or said that everything was right, and never dreamed that their flock saw through their feeble cautiousness. The result of all this has sometimes been that parishioners have trusted other men more than their minister just because he was their minister, and have gone with their troublesome questions and dark experiences to someone who should speak of them freely because he should not feel that he was speaking to a member of his congregation.

It is easy to point out what are the causes of this feeling which we thus see has its dangers. The bad part in it is a love of power. The better part is an anxious sense of responsibility, made more anxious by the true affection which grows up in the preacher's heart. It is almost a parental feeling in its worse as in its better features, in its partialness and jealousy as well as in its devotion and love. But besides these there is another element in the view which the preacher takes of his congregation which I beg you to observe and think about. It is the way in which he assumes a difference in the character of people when they are massed together from any which they had when they were looked at separately. This is the real meaning of the tone which is in that phrase "my congregation." It is to the minister a unit of a wholly novel sort. There is something in the congregation which is not in the men and women as he knows them in their separate humanities, something in the aggregate which was not in the individuals, a character in the whole which was not in the parts. This is the reason why he can group them in his thought as a peculiar people, hold them in his hand as a new human unity, his congregation.

And no doubt he is partly right. There is a principle underneath the feeling by which he vaguely works. A multitude of people gathered for a special purpose and absorbed for the time into a common interest has a new character which is not in any of the individuals which compose it. If you are a speaker addressing a crowd you feel that. You say things to them without hesitation that would seem either too bold or too simple to say to any man among them if you talked with him face to face. If you are a spectator and watch a crowd while someone else is speaking to it, you can feel the same thing. You can see emotions run through the mass that no one man there would have deigned to show or submitted to feel if he could have helped it. The crowd will laugh at jokes which every man in the crowd would have despised, and be melted by mawkish pathos that would not have extorted a tear from the weakest of them by himself. Imagine Peter the Hermit sitting down alone with a man to fire him up for a crusade. Probably all this is less true for one of our New England audiences than of any other that is ever collected in our land. In it every man keeps guard over his individuality and does not easily let it sink in the character of the multitude. And yet we are men and women even here, and the universal laws of human nature do work even among us. And this is a law of nature which all men have observed. "It is a strange thing to say," says Arthur Helps in "Realmah," "but when the number of any public body exceeds that of forty or fifty, the whole assembly has an element of joyous childhood in it, and each member revives at times the glad, mischievous nature of his schoolboy days." Canning used to say that the House of Commons as a body had better taste than the man of the best taste in it, and Macaulay was much inclined to think that Canning was right.

What are the elements of this new character which belongs to a congregation, a company of men? Two of them have been suggested in the two instances which I have just quoted, — the spontaneousness and liberty, and the higher standard of thought and taste. It is not hard to see what some of the other elements are. There is no doubt greater receptivity than there is in the individual. Many of the sources of antagonism are removed. The tendency to irritation is put to rest. The pride of argument is not there; or is modified by the fact that no other man can hear the argument, because it cannot speak a word, but must go on in a man's own silent soul. It is easier to give way when you sit undistinguished in an audience, and your next neighbor cannot see the moment when you yield. The surrender loses half its hardness when you have no sword to surrender and no flag to run down. And besides this, we have all felt how the silent multitude in the midst of which we sit or stand becomes ideal and heroic to us. We feel as if it were listening without prejudice, and responding unselfishly and nobly. So we are lifted up to our best by the buoyancy of the mass in which we have been merged. It may be a delusion. Each of these silent men may be thinking and feeling meanly, but probably each of them has felt the elevation of the mass about him of which we are one particle, and so is lifting and lifted just as we are. Who can say which drops in the great sweep of the tide are borne, and which bear others toward the shore, on which they all rise together?

This, then, is the good quality in the character of the congregation. It produces what in general we call responsiveness. The compensating quality which takes away part of the value of this one is its irresponsibility. The audience is quick to feel, but slow to decide. The men who make up the audience, taken one by one, are slower to feel an argument or an appeal to their higher nature, but when they are convinced or touched, it is comparatively easy to waken the conscience, and make them see the necessity of action. . . .

The result of all this is that in the congregation you have something very near the general humanity. You have human nature as it appears in its largest contemplation. Personal peculiarities have disappeared and man simply as man is before you. This is a great advantage to the preacher. "It is more easy to know man in general than to know a man in particular," said La Rochefoucauld. If in the crowd to whom you preach you saw every man not merely in general but in particular, if each sat there with his idiosyncrasies bristling all over him, how could you preach? There are some preachers, I think, who are ineffective from a certain incapacity of this larger general sight of humanity which a congregation ought to inspire. . . .

I think that it is almost necessary for a man to preach sometimes to congregations which he does not know, in order to keep this impression of preaching to humanity, and so to keep the truth which he preaches as large as it ought to be. He who ministers to the same people always, knowing them minutely, is apt to let his preaching grow minute, to forget the world, and to make the same mistakes about the gospel that one would make about the force of gravitation if he came to consider it a special arrangement made for these few operations which it accomplishes within his own house. I think there are few inspirations, few tonics for a minister's life, better than, when he is fretted and disheartened with a hundred little worries, to go and preach to a congregation in which he does not know a face. As he stands up and looks across them before he begins his sermon, it is like looking the race in the face. All the nobleness and responsibility of his vocation comes to him. It is the feeling which one has had sometimes in traveling when he has passed through a great town whose name he did not even learn. There were men, but not one man he knew; houses, shops, churches, bank, post office, business and pleasure, but none of them individualized to him by any personal interest. It is human life in general, and often has a solemnity for him which the human lives which he knows in particular have lost. And this is what we often find in some strange pulpit, facing some congregation wholly made up of strangers.

But this should be occasional. A constant traveling among unknown towns would no doubt weaken and perhaps destroy our sense of humanity altogether. There can be no doubt that it is good for a man that his knowledge of a congregation should be primarily and principally the knowledge of his own congregation, certain dangers of a too exclusive relationship being obviated by preaching sometimes where the people are all strange. It is remarkable how many of the great preachers of the world are inseparably associated with the places where their work was done, where perhaps all their life was lived. In many cases their place has passed into their name as if it were a true part of themselves. Chrysostom of Constantinople, Augustine of Hippo, Savonarola of Florence, Baxter of Kidderminster, Arnold of Rugby, Robertson of Brighton, Chalmers of Glasgow, and in our New England a multitude of such associations which have become historic and compel us always to think of the man with the place and of the place with the man. Everywhere a man must have his place. The disciples are sometimes set before us as if our pastoral life of modern times were an entire departure from their methods; and yet they had their pastorates. Think of St. Paul at Ephesus. Think of St. John in the same city. Think of St. James at Jerusalem. The same necessity, may we not say, which required that the incarnation should bring divinity, not into humanity in general, but into some special human circle, into a nation, a tribe, a family, requires that he who would bear fruit everywhere for humanity should root himself into some special plot of human life and draw out the richness of the earth by which he is to live at some one special point. There is nothing better in a clergyman's life than to feel constantly that through his congregation he is getting at his race. Certainly the long pastorates of other days were rich in the knowledge of human nature, in a very intimate relation with humanity. These three rules seem to have in them the practical sum of the whole matter. I beg you to remember them and apply them with all the wisdom that God gives you. First, have as few congregations as you can. Second, know your congregation as thoroughly as you can. Third, know your congregation so largely and deeply that in knowing it you shall know humanity.

HARRY EMERSON FOSDICK

Preaching as Personal Counseling

Harry Emerson Fosdick (1878-1969) is recognized by many as the most influential American preacher of the twentieth century. He was pastor of Riverside Church in New York City from 1926 to 1946 and professor of practical theology at Union Seminary from 1915 to 1946. From his platform at Riverside and in more than twenty books he established himself as the popular voice of liberalism in America. As such, he served countless Christians as their theological guide from the ancient tradition into the modern world. Although he never wrote a book on preaching, a discernible method emerges from his several articles on homiletics and his many published sermons. Fosdick rejected both expository preaching and topical preaching. The former tends toward biblical antiquarianism, about which he famously remarked, "Only the preacher proceeds still upon the idea that folk come to church desperately anxious to discover what happened to the Jebusites." The latter, topical approach, leads to subjectivism. The individual preacher, not the church or Scripture, decides what theme or idea is of greatest importance for the sermon. Fosdick's alternative was the "project method" of preaching, by which he linked preaching to pastoral counseling. He writes, "A good sermon is an engineering operation by which a chasm is bridged so that spiritual goods on one side — the 'unsearchable riches of Christ' — are actually transported into personal lives upon the other." In the language of the Aristotelian triangle of speaker, message, and audience, Fosdick's method always begins with the experience and situation of the audience. Like Brooks, Fosdick imagines an audience of individuals whose trials are the "presenting problem" of each sermon. A sampling of his sermon titles suggests the practical orientation of his preaching: "Handicapped Lives," "Handling Life's Second Bests," "On Catching the Wrong Bus," "The Sacred and the Secular are Inseparable."

Harry Emerson Fosdick, "Personal Counseling and Preaching," *Pastoral Psychology* (March 1952), pp. 11-15. Reprinted in *Harry Emerson Fosdick's Art of Preaching*, ed. Lionel Crocker (Springfield, Ill.: Charles C. Thomas, 1971).

The relationship between personal counseling and preaching is a two-way street. Any preacher who in his sermons speaks to the real condition of his people, making evident that he knows what questions they are asking, and where their problems lie, is bound to be sought out by individuals wanting his intimate advice. And any pastor who, with intelligence and clairvoyance, practices such personal counseling, is bound to find his sermons, in content and form, insight and impact, profoundly affected. The right kind of preacher is coerced to become a personal counselor, and the right kind of personal counselor gains some of the most necessary ingredients of preaching.

One does not mean to say that a man cannot be an excellent preacher without being an excellent personal counselor, and vice versa. Gifts differ. Certainly there are expert counselors who cannot preach, and I suppose that there are powerful preachers who do little or no individual counseling — although how that latter thing can be true I only with difficulty see. Our statement about this relationship, however, is not negative but positive. For some of us, at least, the two functions of the ministry are mutually indispensable to each other.

The only way I see to make this statement vital is to make it autobiographical, and I may as well be frankly that. When I began my ministry I did not know how to preach. I had been trained to stand up and talk in public, so that, however little I had to say, I could at least say it, but how my first parishioners endured those early sermons I do not see. In reminiscence I can discern several factors which helped me out of that morass of homiletical frustration and bewilderment, but one factor is primary. Perhaps I now overemphasize my first victorious experience in personal counseling, but it certainly was crucial.

A young man from one of the church's finest families, falling victim to alcoholism, sought my help. I recall my desperate feeling that if the gospel of Christ did not have in it available power to save that youth, of what use was it? When months of conference and inward struggle ended in triumph, when that young man said to me, "If you ever find anyone who doesn't believe in God, send him to me — I know!" something happened to my preaching that courses in homiletics do not teach. *This* was the kind of effect that a *sermon* ought to have. It could deal with real problems, speak directly to individual needs, and because of it transforming consequences could happen to some person then and there. From that day on, the secret prayer which I have offered, as I stood up to preach, has run like this: Somewhere in this congregation is one person who desperately needs what I am going to say: O God, help me to get at him!

Personal counseling has its routine aspects, its drudgeries and boredoms, but ever and again it becomes thrilling. A real problem is presented and a real victory gained. The gospel works. One sees a miracle take place before one's eyes. A life is made over, a family is saved, a valuable youth turns about in his tracks and heads right, a potential suicide becomes a happy and useful member of society, a skeptic who had thought that life comes from nowhere, means nothing and goes nowhither, accepts the Christian faith and is "transformed by the renewing of his mind." Such experiences in the consultation room — indubitable experiences of sometimes almost incredible regeneration — must have a profound effect when the counselor steps into the pulpit.

For one thing, personal counseling deepens the preacher's clairvoyance. He learns a lot about human nature which otherwise he could not have known. Books on nervous disorders are useful, but now he has *seen* what the books talk about. Newspapers tell him the news, but now he has confronted at first hand what the news is doing to real people inside. He gains that elemental factor without which all preaching is futile — insight into what actually is going on in the lives of those he preaches to.

For another thing, personal counseling deepens the preacher's confidence in the gospel of Christ, and in the power which it makes available. He intimately faces frustration, despair about the world, abysmal sin, fear, and the endless disasters of egocentricity, and he actually watches the miracle of transformation wrought. *It can happen* — not just because the Bible says so, or because it is orthodox to think it, but because he has seen it, and has helped to mediate the truth and power that did it. Nothing so much as this experience, I suspect, can send a man into the pulpit, sure that preaching can be personal consultation on a group scale, and that someone's life that morning can be made all over.

For another thing, personal counseling tends to shift the preacher's mind from obsession with his sermon's subject to a purposeful concern about its object. A famous Scotch preacher was once greeted after service by an admiring friend who exclaimed, "That was a wonderful sermon"; and the preacher turned on him. "What did it *do?*" he said; "What did it *do?*" Far too many sermons are harmless discussions of a subject, intelligent as it may be, well thought out and well delivered but lacking any purposeful drive to achieve an object. I do not see how a pastor experienced in counseling can preach like that. When he goes into the pulpit he is after something with definite, deliberate intent. When he lifts a great truth, he intends, like a pile driver, to drop it on something. He has a subject, of course, but when he chose his subject, he had an object. He proposed that somebody that morning should face his Damascus Road.

We are not saying that personal counseling by itself can make a good preacher. Obviously it cannot. But it can give tone and direction and significance to preaching which our generation critically needs.

During a long ministry I have watched with interest two familiar types of sermon. The first is the expository model — elucidation of a scriptural text, its historic occasion, its logical meaning in the context, its setting in the theology and ethic of the ancient writer; and then, at long last, application to the auditors of the truth involved. That a vital preacher can use that model with excellent effect goes without saying; but is there not something the matter with the model? To start with a biblical passage, and spend nearly all the sermon on its historic explanation and exposition, presupposes the assumption that the congregation came to church that morning primarily concerned about the meaning of those venerable texts — which, in my experience, is a condition contrary to fact. Long ago I wrote petulantly: "Only the preacher proceeds still upon the idea that folk come to church desperately anxious to discover what happened to the Jebusites."

In revolt against the expository model the topical preachers arose. They searched contemporary life in general and the newspapers in particular for subjects. Instead of concentrating on textual analysis, they dealt with present-day themes about which everyone was thinking. I watched those topical preachers with a dubious mind. Week after week, turning their pulpits into platforms and their sermons into lectures, they strained after new intriguing subjects, and one knew that in private they were straining even more strenuously after new intriguing ideas about them. Instead of launching out from a great text, they started with their own opinions on some matter of current interest, often much farther away than a good biblical text would be from the congregation's vital concerns and needs. Indeed, the fact that history had thought it worthwhile to preserve the text for centuries would cause a wise gambler to venture confidently on the text's superior vitality. If people do not come to church to learn what happened to the Jebusites, neither do they come yearning to hear a lecturer express his personal opinion on themes which editors, columnists, and radio commentators have been discussing all the week.

Jesus dealt primarily with individuals, and after that he spoke to the multitude. Does that not indicate a third approach to preaching which our generation needs? At any rate, it has been a godsend to me. People come to church with every kind of difficulty and problem flesh is heir to. A sermon is meant to meet such needs — the sins and shames, the doubts and anxieties that fill the pews. This is the place to start, with the real problems of the people. This is a sermon's specialty, which makes it a sermon — not an essay, an exposition, a lecture. Every sermon should have for its main business the head-on, constructive meeting of some problem which is puzzling minds, burdening consciences, distracting lives, and no sermon which so meets real human difficulty, with light to throw on it and power to win victory over it, can possibly be futile. Any preacher who, with even moderate skill, is thus helping people, is functioning, delivering the goods which the community has a right to expect from him. Even when he addresses a multitude, he speaks to them as individuals and is still a personal counselor.

Of course, these three approaches to preaching are not mutually exclusive. When one tries to bring the truth of the gospel to bear on personal needs, the great texts of the Bible beg to be used, and their exposition can be the backbone of the sermon. And when one deals seriously with personal perplexities, one runs straight into social, economic, and international problems which loom in the background and penetrate the foreground of every life. Nevertheless, the orientation of a sermon is profoundly affected when one approaches the pulpit as though one were beginning a personal consultation.

To plead for such an approach without pointing out its dangers would be unfair. I once presented this approach in a group of experienced ministers and collected a galaxy of warnings about its possible perversions. They had endeavored so precisely to deal with a real problem that Mr. Smith woke up to the fact that they were talking about him; or they had been so practical in dealing with some definite problem that they had become trivial, failing to bring the eternal gospel to bear on the issue; or they had been so anxious to deal with felt needs in the congregation that they had forgotten still deeper needs, unfelt but real; or they had so limited the difficulties they preached about to private, psychological maladjustments that they became merely amateur pulpit psychiatrists; or they had been so concerned to help people that they had become soft nursemaids of sick souls and had omitted all the stern, thunderous, prophetic affirmations of God's truth which our generation ought to hear. Unskilled mishandling of any homiletical method can wreck it.

The most familiar and deplorable danger in attempting to make sermons personal consultations on a group scale is, I think, the limitation of the preacher's scope. If his field of private counseling is confined pretty much to neurotic disorders, his pulpit may all too easily reflect the fact. Every Sunday he will be telling people how to overcome anxiety and fear and achieve peace of mind. He rides a hobby, attracts an audience of nervous patients, and in the pulpit becomes a homiletical neurologist. This is a pathetic perversion of what we are trying to say. We are supposed to preach to "all sorts and conditions of men," and no minister's private consultations include them all. His insight must run beyond his individual experience in the consultation room. He has other ways of gaining clairvoyance into human need, and he should use them all. His scope, like the Bible's, should include all human life, personal and social, and the whole message of the gospel.

Nevertheless — while any approach to preaching can be misused — it is a great day in a minister's life when, having seen what miracles can be wrought by

Christ's truth and power brought to bear on individual souls, he mounts his pulpit sure that a sermon, too, can be thus a medium of creative and transforming effects. No longer on Sunday is he merely making a speech about religion; he is engaged in an engineering operation, building a bridge by which a chasm is spanned so that spiritual goods on one side — the "unsearchable riches of Christ" — are actually transported into personal lives on the other.

At this point the old preachers have much to teach us. At their best they did achieve results. Their sermons were appeals to the jury, and they got decisions. They knew where the powerful motives were and appealed to them with conclusive effect. While we modern preachers talk about psychology much more than our predecessors did, we commonly use it a good deal less ably.

As the experience involved in personal counseling can thus minister to a preacher's power, so preaching can open up to the pastor hitherto unguessed opportunities for individual usefulness. One of the best tests of a sermon is the number of people who afterward wish to see the preacher alone. It was a notable day in my own experience when, feeling that pastoral calling from house to house was not filling the bill, I announced a consultation hour for those who wished privately to talk with me. That first day I found myself facing a suicidal case, with fourteen others awaiting their turn. That was a generation ago, before the development of personal counseling clinics in Protestant churches had begun. Our churches are on their way now to meet that kind of need, which by many of our ministers had been long unguessed. Unfortunately some ministers who did not see that need were right; they did not evoke the need in their parishes; their sermons were not of a kind to make hungry and distracted souls want to see them alone. One of the most hopeful movements in Protestantism today is the growing tie-up between preaching and personal counseling — the first so directed that it leads inevitably to the second, and the second so used that it gives individual force and impact to the first.

John Wesley is known as a preacher who customarily addressed audiences of twenty thousand people. He certainly spoke to the multitude. But Wesley was always a tireless personal counselor, and his whole "Society" was organized with a view to the care and supervision of individuals. Surely this factor in Wesley's habit and experience is basic in any explanation of his preaching power. How else can one account for John Nelson's statement concerning the first sermon he heard Wesley preach, before a great audience at Moorfields? "When he did speak," wrote Nelson, "I thought his whole discourse was aimed at me."

FRED B. CRADDOCK

By Way of the Hearer

Until his retirement in 1993 Fred B. Craddock taught preaching and New Testament at Candler School of Theology in Atlanta, Georgia. One of the most influential of contemporary homileticians, Craddock was an early proponent of inductive, parabolic, and narrative preaching. His method incorporates the traditional concerns of rhetoric: subject matter, speech-design, and analysis of the hearer, which are usually taken up in that order. But in his Beecher Lectures for 1978, *Overhearing the Gospel*, as well as in his earlier book, *As One Without Authority*, he argued that the last element, the hearer, is the proper starting point for homiletics. The inductive approach to preaching does not prove a thesis but assembles the particulars of experience in a narrative order in such a way that they culminate in a coherent message. Induction works well in the sermon because it conforms to the ordinary, human dialectic of search and discovery. It mirrors the way we learn. The three-point deductive sermon violates the fundamental movement of thought and conversation. It tells too much too soon. Moreover, in a culture desensitized to the Christian message, urgent proclamation or the proving of propositions will alienate rather than communicate. Only the less-invasive, narrative genre offers listeners the aesthetic and religious distance they need. When the preacher crafts narratives that reflect the dynamic of the biblical story, his or her listeners *overhear* the good news. In the moment of overhearing, they re-experience and re-recognize a truth that, at some level, they already know. Intimations of Craddock's concerns are present in the rhetorician Fénelon, the pietist Spener, and the problem-solver Fosdick. But the most profound modern theorist of indirect discourse was Kierkegaard, whose comment Craddock takes as the epigraph to *Overhearing the Gospel*: "There is no lack of information in a Christian land; something else is lacking, and this is a something which the one man cannot directly communicate to the other."

Fred B. Craddock, *Overhearing the Gospel* (Nashville: Abingdon, 1978), pp. 120-23, 129-30, 134-40.

The modest proposal being offered here is that the listener's experience of overhearing is a natural, effective, and at times life-changing dynamic that belongs in the church's classroom and sanctuary. And since it is also appropriate to the study, the transition from desk to pulpit or lectern is made less awkward and difficult. The discussion began with the perspective of the listener, not with the speaker's preparation or with the format of the content to be communicated. The reason was simple: with the listener is the place to begin. This has not always been the case. As we have observed, in the community of critical scholarship, the fear of the loss of objectivity and historical honesty made it seem essential that research and the reporting of that research be done with no consciousness of the existence of listener or reader. Otherwise, the listener's own needs and circumstances would add a variable to the investigations and color the results. The point is, in a laboratory or in a library the gathering of listeners would be an intrusion, an interruption of the proper business conducted in those settings. But in a classroom or sanctuary, listeners are not intruders; they are as ingredient to the proper business of these settings as equipment and formulae in the laboratory or books in the library. And the proper business in classroom and sanctuary is communication. To that end the teacher or preacher is servant and instrument; to that end, the subject matter is shaped and aimed.

It is so vital to our task that we be aware that the experience of listening is not a secondary consideration after we have done our exegesis of the texts and theological exploration. The listener is present from the beginning. The Christian tradition, biblical and extrabiblical, came to us from those who *heard* it and we *hear* it and pass it on to other *hearers*. The stamp of listening and the listenability of the message is on it when we get it, and in telling it, we confirm that it is listenable. To give such attention to the listener is not a concession to "what they want to hear," playing to the balcony or to the groundlings, nor is it an introduction to how to succeed as a speaker; it is no more or less than to describe the shape of the subject matter (it came from listeners) and the nature of the occasion (to effect a hearing).

Having begun with the experience of listening as the governing consideration in a communicative event and as the preoccupation that harnesses the imaginative, emotive, and cognitive powers of the speaker, I characterized that posture of listening called overhearing as consisting of two elements: distance and participation. Because the term and idea of distance may need rehabilitation I have urged that we think of distance as that quality in a communicative event that preserves invaluable benefits for the message and for the listener. For the message, distance preserves its objectivity as history, its continuity as tradition, and its integrity as a word that has existence prior to and apart from me as a listener. In other words, the distance between the message and the listener conveys the sense of the substantive nature and independence of the message, qualities that add to rather than detract from the persuasive and attention-drawing power of the message. I am much more inclined toward a message that has its own intrinsic life and force and that was prepared with no *apparent* awareness of me than toward a message that obviously did not come into being until I as a listener appeared and then was hastily improvised with desire for relevance offered as reason for the sloppy form and shallow content. These didactic and hortatory pieces are usually offered by well-meaning speakers who so highly prize relevance that they prepare their messages during the delivery. I do not wish to be sarcastic. My students who resist the lectionary and advanced planning for preaching with the retort "Who can know in January what will be relevant in June?" have a point, a good point, but a point that has its value only when held in tension with the *extra nos* of the gospel: the word does not have its source in the listener. This I am calling distance, a necessary dimension of the experience of overhearing that says to the listener, "You are sitting in on something that is of such significance that it could have gone on without you."

As for the benefit distance provides the listener, we have talked of the room the listener has, room in which to reflect, accept, reject, decide. As a listener, I must have that freedom, all the more so if the matter before me is of ultimate importance. As a listener who is also a teacher and preacher, I am aware that being armed with Holy Writ and the word of God tempts the communicator to think the urgency and weight of the message call for pressing in and pressing down, leaving the hearer no room for lateral movement. But the listener worth his salt will soon, against this assault, launch a silent but effective counterattack: find flaws in the speaker's grammar or voice or logic or dress; raise questions about the speaker's real motives; wonder imaginatively if the speaker has a dark past or even at this moment is entangled in affairs illicit; make distracting body movements; count things, such as light bulbs, knots in wood, number of persons present wearing glasses, etc. I need go no further; your list of things to do when surrounded by such a speaker probably is longer than mine.

The other element in the experience of overhearing is participation: free participation on the part of the hearer in the issues, the crises, the decisions, the judgment, and the promise of the message. Participation means the listener overcomes the distance, not because the speaker "applied" everything, but because the listener identified with experiences and thoughts related in the message that were analogous to his own. The fundamental presupposition operative here is the general similarity of human experiences. It is this which makes communication possible, but it is surprising how many speakers do not trust this to be the case and feel it incumbent on themselves to supply descriptions of experiences as though they were foreign to the hearer. If both speaker and listener have observed an old man asleep in church, lengthy description is unnecessary; if not, lengthy description evokes nothing. The story the speaker is telling and the personal story of the hearer must intersect at points or the hearer will despair; however, if they are exactly the same, the hearer will be bored or suspicious or defensive. Of course, the speaker who wants the listeners to overhear will preserve distance in narration, but the vocabulary, idiom, imagery, and descriptive detail will be such as will allow points or moments in the process at which the listener can "enter," identify, be enrolled. Otherwise, the listener cannot overcome the distance, and the communication, if attended to, becomes nothing more than shared information or a speech on a certain topic. . . .

There is a way of presenting a message that can be "consumed by the listener," a desirable goal if one is convinced that the meaning for a listener is not a product at the end of the event but rather that meaning is coextensive with the process of listening. We may be helped in understanding by the distinction between rhetoric and dialectic in Plato.

Rhetoric satisfies the listener, and at the end of a rhetorical presentation, the listener says, "That was a good speech." As a speech it is an identifiable entity, it has form and substance and can be repeated as is or printed and published. Dialectic, however, disturbs a listener toward a kind of conversion of thought or values or life direction, but it proceeds *at its own expense.* As it effects an experience in the listener, the presentation itself is used up. The early part of it moves you on to the next part, which may cause you to lose interest in or abandon the earlier part. And so the entire presentation proceeds. If effectively done, the listener could hear the earlier portions of the message repeated and be uninterested or even reject them. Why? Because the words and sentences and images moved the listener along in changing views or values; as those words did their work, they died. They were not framed to carry a truth statement or a position on a doctrine, but they were in the service of the listeners, to the end that what remained after the occasion would not be "a good speech" but a listener modified or changed or at least beginning to experience anew old notions fast asleep in the soul. . . .

Among the aids for generating listener experience, perhaps none is more effective than the metaphor. A metaphor is not simply a way of prettifying what is already known but a "medium of riper fuller knowing" [Phillip Wheelwright]. "A metaphor after all is the verbal recognition of a similarity between the apparently dissimilar" [Brian Wicker, *The Story-Shaped World* (Notre Dame: University of Notre Dame Press, 1975), p. 15]. The metaphor thus sets up a tension that can give a fresh new vision of that which had become familiar. Of course, some object to metaphors as imprecise, dishonest, and self-indulgent. For instance, why not clearly and directly say "the clouds are gray" instead of describing the clouds as *sad?* "To use metaphors for example to speak of 'capricious' weather, 'majestic' mountains, or the 'merciless' sun, is to taint a mere object with illicitly anthropomorphic and moral meaning" [Wicker, p. 2]. The objection, however, presupposes that the only proper and valid use of language is positivistic, measured, and accurately descriptive, and forgets that a major function of language is to evoke, to draw the mind to the limits of the known, to hold the world before the eye at a new angle, to offer new configurations that shatter old calculations. The use of metaphor is for the communicator an act of creative imagination that has its completion in the equally creative and imaginative act of hearing the metaphor. At the heart of the parables of Jesus is the metaphor.

But imaginative language without a carefully chosen structure that it serves may be little more than teasing and dancing before the listeners. The shape of the communication is paramount in the business of effecting listener experience, and if the experience being sought is overhearing, the structure most congenial and with greatest potential for effectiveness is narrative. Before a narrative the hearer's posture is naturally that of the overhearer. A narrative is told with distance and sustains it in that the story unfolds on its own, seemingly only casually aware of the hearer, and yet all the while the narrative is inviting and beckoning the listener to participation in its anticipation, struggle, and resolution.

However, so much has been written and said in recent years about "narrative" and "story" in theological discourse that I feel it important to clarify what I do *not* mean and what I *do* mean by narrative structure for generating the dynamic of overhearing. First, I do not mean that narrative is to replace rational argument in Christian discourse. Rational argument serves to keep the communication self-critical, athletically trim, and free of a sloppy sentimentality that can take over in the absence of critical activity. We need always to be warned against the use of narratives and stories to avoid the issues of doctrine, history, and theological reflection. In the church we are doing more than telling anecdotes and sharing illustrations. Some readers of SK [Kierkegaard] become enamored of his stories and forget his insistence that Christianity can be conceptualized, and there are times and arenas in which that is the proper business. Nevertheless, it would be fatal for the cause of the gospel to allow logos (argument, proof) to discredit the story simply because "telling stories, even listening to stories, counts in our society as an unscientific occupation." Wherever the narrative is outlawed by theology as precritical, then theology becomes an exercise in trading symbols and terms, no longer nourished by experience. And if theology does not reflect critically upon human experiences with a view to changing or modifying them, what then does it do?

Second, I do not mean by proposing narrative form that the communicator is to do exegesis and interpretation in the texts of secular literature, ferreting out religious meanings that would justify using these pieces as the substance of Christian communications. There is, no doubt, great value in exploring the explicit and implicit dialogues between the Christian tradition and the secular literature of a given period, but there is something second-rate about combing through this literature for Christian meanings. It often represents a reaction against or an early abandoning of the texts of the Christian faith in favor of impoverishing and depleting the rich world of literature for "relevant" ideas. Many of us are weary of "meanings" and interpretation that tames art by reducing it to content and then applying the content. Just leave me alone with the narratives, to overhear them and to allow them and me room to maneuver. And this includes the narratives of the Bible.

Third, I do not mean by narrative structure that the lecture or sermon consists merely of reading or reciting long narrative portions of Scripture verbatim, as though the ancient texts can be thus simply and uncritically transferred from one language, land, culture, century, to another. The biblical text is always carried through history on the lap of the church, and it is her task, through the Holy Spirit, to keep the voice of Scripture a living voice through her teaching and preaching. But having said that, let me urge the irreplaceable value, for speaker and listener, of direct exposure to the text. Paul Ricoeur has written perceptively of the value of a naïve reading of the text, allowing the text to touch all our faculties and instincts. Such a reading should be followed by critical examination of the text without fear or reservation. Finally, the student returns to the text with a second naïveté, recovering again the narrative and discourse nature of the text. And even before Ricoeur, SK had urged a threefold method: spontaneity — reflection — spontaneity.

Finally, by narrative structure I am not proposing that the lecture or sermon be a long story or a series of stories or illustrations. While such may actually be the form used for a given message, it is not necessary in order to be narrative. Communication may be narrativelike and yet contain a rich variety of materials: poetry, polemic, anecdote, humor, exegetical analysis, commentary. To be narrativelike means to have the scope that ties it to the life of a larger community; it means the message has memory and hope; it means to be lifesize in the sense of touching all the keys on the board rather than only intellectual or emotional or volitional; it means conveying the sense of movement *from* one place *to* another; it means having this movement on its own, as though the presence of the listeners were not essential to its process; it means thinking alongside the hearers.

Narratives do not summarize events and relationships with commentary and application following. No listeners overhear that. Narratives reproduce and re-create events, with characters developing and events unfolding, and the teller reexperiencing while narrating. This reexperiencing is the source of the emotive and imaginative power in the telling. Emotion and imagination are not added as though options on the part of the speaker. In addition, narratives move from beginning to end, not vice versa for the benefit of lazy ears that want to be sure of the speaker's position, that want to be secure about "where he comes out," but that do not want to have to listen to the message to ascertain it. And finally, narratives move at a pace that most accurately re-creates the pace of that which is narrated, sometimes slow, sometimes fast, now meandering, now running.

I pause here to remind myself how difficult it is to do what I have described in the last few sentences. For example, it is not easy to share with listeners the story of Abraham's offering of Isaac without rushing to the part about the ram caught in the bush. SK often complained that preachers would hurry to the happy fact of the ram in the bush or begin with it to assure the anxious or interrupt themselves often to promise the hearers that there will be a ram in the bush soon! Of course we know the story thus ended, but if the ending is allowed to scatter its smile back over the long and tortuous path of Abraham, then his faith is no longer seen as faith; it has been robbed of fear and trembling and is far removed from the pilgrimage of the hearer. A narrative that reproduces the painful journey up Mount Moriah reexperiences all the churning chemistry of a faith that is absolute in its obedience. And those who overhear the story begin to wish for and to despair of, to want and to dread, to seek and to fear, finding such faith. These can then enter into Abraham's profound joy and gratitude when the ram appears in the story.

In the same fashion, Easter can abort genuine appreciation of the pilgrimage of Jesus or any real grasp of what it means to follow Jesus. Of course, Easter is there and from that experience early Christians remembered and anticipated. But introduced too soon into the narrative, and too easily, Easter can make Jesus' ministry a walk-through rehearsal, script in hand, and can make discipleship a real winner. I have heard pastors at funerals make the bereaved feel guilty for their tears. "Don't you believe in the resurrection?" Unfeeling chatter! Easter is *for* the tearful. The Christian faith insists the resurrection perpetuated the nail prints, it did not erase them. Easter has been put too soon in the story from many pulpits with the result that the tomb was not a cave, it was a short tunnel. In many churches Easter celebrations are empty of meaning because no one really was dead. The problem? The narrative is lost. In her wisdom the historic church insisted on the narrative: suffering, Good Friday, Easter, waiting, Pentecost. But what if Good Friday services are dropped because they are not successful, and Pentecost is dropped because it comes so late school is out and vacations have begun? I know; we can make up for it by having three services on Easter. No — the story has been lost. I go a-fishing.

Probably one reason people will overhear a story with more sustained attention than they will give to many lectures and sermons obviously prepared for them and addressed to them is that a narrative is of the nature of life itself. The form fits. "We dream in narrative, daydream in narrative, remember, anticipate, hope, despair, believe, doubt, plan, revise, criticize, construct, gossip, learn, hate, and love by narrative" [Wicker, p. 47]. All traditional societies have community stories in which the people live and by which they explain to themselves and to each other their social and metaphysical relationships. The chronology of a narrative locates the participants in time and place. Stories are read and heard because the experience of movement through time, common to the story and all its hearers, reassures that we are alive and can enlarge our living by identifying, participating, appropriating, the experiences of others. This is true even if the narrative disturbs and shocks. And if someone tells me a story large enough, with enough memory and enough hope to provide a context for my own personal narrative, then I am interested.

And this is the story Christians tell. It is very important that the structure of the message be a narrative. A narrative, by its structure, provides order and meaning, and therefore I cannot stress too heavily the indispensability of narrative shape and sequence. Change the shape, for instance, into a logical syllogism, and the question of whether the *content* of the message is altered is a moot one; the important point is the *function* of the message as narrative is now lost. The movement from chaos to order, from origin to destiny is broken, and in its place are some ideas, well argued.

Again, let the Scriptures provide some models. Treat yourself to the experience of reading Mark in a single sitting. Let the narrative form of the Gospel move you along through meaningful activity, to crisis, through death, into an open future. Or the book of Acts: its impact is not solely in its message but in the form of its message. Casting the message as history puts the reader in touch with purposeful struggle toward a future which is God's. In fact, a narrative tends to *do* what it *tells*, mediating suffering and healing and salvation. These values accrue, not in a discussion about the story outside the narrative process, but in the actual telling.

PREACHING AND THE CHURCH

P. T. FORSYTH

The One Great Preacher

Early in the twentieth century the Scottish theologian P. T. Forsyth (1848-1921) assessed the relation of preaching to the church by asserting the sacramental character of preaching. Too much preaching, he said, is concerned exclusively with the conversion of the world. Too many preachers position themselves over and against their congregations, as if they were not addressing and building up the congregation of Christ. Before the individual preacher gets at the world, he (or she) mediates Christ to the church and, in turn, articulates the faith of the church. The preacher functions as a sacrament to the church, conveying the real presence of the crucified Christ who dwells in the midst of his people. Preachers do not (or should not) articulate truths; they are conduits for the living One. As Bonhoeffer would have said, the only content of their sermons is Jesus Christ. All the rest is fluff. Since the congregation is the fullest embodiment of Christ, it is the church, rather than any individual, that is the one great preacher. It is the role of theology to help the church recognize this, its most profound vocation. It does so by eschewing the lesser truths and establishing the theological principle of grace as the substantive core of all preaching. The theological principle of grace gives the preacher his or her staying power. For Forsyth the principle of grace is the expression of a living and holy Christ by whose cross the world is changed forever. The objectivity of the atonement and the necessity of its proclamation lie at the center of Forsyth's "positive theology," by which he meant "evangelical theology." In his famous Beecher Lectures, Forsyth, the first great evangelical of the twentieth century, challenged preachers to discover their theological principle and the living Christ within it.

P. T. Forsyth, *Positive Preaching and the Modern Mind* (New York: A. C. Armstrong, 1907), pp. 71-83, 86-91.

The one great preacher in history, I would contend, is the church. And the first business of the individual preacher is to enable the church to preach. Yet so that he is not its echo but its living voice, not the echo of its consciousness but the organ of its gospel. Either he gives the church utterance, or he gives it insight into the gospel it utters. He is to preach to the church from the gospel so that with the church he may preach the gospel to the world. He is so to preach to the church that he shall also preach *from* the church. That is to say, he must be a sacrament to the church, that with the church he may become a missionary to the world.

You perceive what high ground I take. The preacher's place in the church is sacramental. It is not sacerdotal, but it is sacramental. He mediates the word to the church from faith to faith, from his faith to theirs, from one stage of their common faith to another. He does not there speak to un-faith. He is a living element in Christ's hands (broken, if need be) for the distribution and increment of grace. He is laid on the altar of the cross. He is not a mere reporter, nor a mere lecturer on sacred things. He is not merely illuminative, he is augmentive. His work is not to enlighten simply, but to empower and enhance.

Men as they leave him should be not only clearer but greater, not only surer but stronger, not only interested, nor only instructed, nor only affected, but fed and increased. He has not merely to show certain things but to get them home, and so home that they change life, either in direction or in scale. It is only an age like the present age of mere knowledge that tends to make preaching the statement of sound and simple truth, interesting but powerless. It is only an age which starves the idea of revelation, by its neglect of the sacramental idea, that reduces preaching to evangelizing alone. It is only an age engrossed with impressions and careless about realities that could regard the preacher's prime work as that of converting the world, to the neglect of transforming the church. It is only such an age that could think of preaching as something *said* with more or less force, instead of something *done* with more or less power.

We spend our polemic upon the Mass, and fitly enough in proper place. But the Catholic form of worship will always have a vast advantage over ours so long as people come away from its central act with the sense of something done in the spirit world, while they leave ours with the sense only of something said to this present world. In true preaching, as in a true sacrament, more is done than said. And much is well done which is poorly said. Let the preacher but have real doings with God and even with a stammering tongue and a loose syntax he will do much for life which has never yet been done by a finished style. The preacher may go "lame but lovely," to use Charles Lamb's fine phrase. His word may lack finish if it have hands and feet. He is a man of action. He is among the men who do things. That is why I call him a sacramental man, not merely an expository, declaratory man.

In a sacrament is there not something done, not merely shown, not merely recalled? It is no mere memorial. How can you have a mere memorial of one who is always living, always present, always more potent than our act of recall is, always the mover of it? What he once put there might be a memorial, but what he is always putting there is much more than that. It is at least his organ. It is, indeed, his act. It is something practical and not spectacular. A revelation may be but something exhibited, but in a sacrament there is something effected. And the one revelation in the strict sense is the sacrament of the cross, the cross as an effective act of redemption. A revelation of redemption is a revelation of something done; and it is only a deed that can reveal a deed. If the preacher reveal redemption he does it by a deed, by a deed in which the Redeemer is the chief actor, by some self-reproduction by Christ, some function of the work of the cross. He has to reproduce the word of the beginning, the word of the cross which is really the cross's own energy, the cross in action. No true preaching of the cross can be other than part of the action of the cross. If a man preach let him preach as the Oracle of God, let him preach as Christ did, whose true pulpit was his cross, whose cross made disciples apostles, in whose cross God first preached to the world, whose preaching from the cross has done for the world what all his discourses — even his discourses — failed to do.

The preacher, in reproducing this gospel word of God, prolongs Christ's sacramental work. The real presence of Christ crucified is what makes preaching. It is what makes of a speech a sermon, and of a sermon gospel. This is the work of God, this continues his work in Christ, that ye should believe in him whom he hath sent. We do not repeat or imitate that cross, on the one hand; and we do not merely state it, on the other. It re-enacts itself in us. God's living word reproduces itself as a living act. It is not inert truth, but quick power. All teaching about the truth as it is in Jesus culminates in the preaching of the truth which is Jesus, the self-reproduction of the word of reconciliation in the cross. Every true sermon, therefore, is a sacramental time and act. It is God's gospel act reasserting itself in detail. The preacher's word, when he preaches the gospel and not only delivers a sermon, is an effective deed, charged with blessing or with judgment. We eat and drink judgment to ourselves as we hear.

It is not an utterance, and not a feat, and not a treat. It is a sacramental act, done together with the community in the name and power of Christ's redeeming act and our common faith. It has the real presence of the active word whose creation it is. If Christ set up the sacrament, his gospel set up the sermon. And if he is real in our sacramental act still, no less is his deed real in our preached word which prolongs that deed. And it is known to be real by the insight of faith, however many counterfeits there are, with no insight but only zeal, and sometimes with nothing but stir. . . .

True preaching presupposes a church, and not merely a public. And wherever the church idea fades into that of a mere religious club or association you have a decay in preaching. Wherever the people are but a religious lecture society the pulpit sinks. When it is idolized it always sinks. It does not lose in interest, or in the sympathetic note, but it loses in power, which is the first thing in a gospel. If the preacher but hold the mirror up to our finer nature the people soon forget what manner of men they are.

But you point out to me that the preaching of the apostles was addressed to the public, that it was very largely of the gathering, of the missionary, kind. Yes, but even that began and worked from the faith it found. It began with the susceptible among the Jews. At first it was not so much converting for Gentiles as stirring for Jews. It was always with the local synagogue that Paul began when he could, with the votaries of the Old Testament word; and while he could he worked through them or their proselytes. Jesus himself began so. His relations beyond Israel grew out of his relations with Israel. It was his earnest dealings with Israel that provoked the cross, which alone universalized the gospel.

So the preacher has his starting point in the stated and solemn assemblies of the church, though he does not end there. Through these, he works also on his public who are present, though not of the church. Then in the end he goes to the world without. But his first duty, if he is a settled pastor, and not a preaching friar, is to his church. Nothing could be more misplaced, when a young preacher enters on a church, than a neglect or contempt of its corporate life and creed, or a sudden inversion of these in order that he may get at the world. He has no right to stop the building that he may start elsewhere. He has no right to use his church merely to provide himself with an outside pulpit. It is together that they must go to the world, he and his church. What Christ founded was not an order of preachers, nor the institution of preaching, but a community, a church, whose first charge his preaching should be. It is church and preacher together that reach the world.

The preaching even to the church, being in the presence of the public, has of course due regard to their presence. The sermon is not a mere homily to an inner circle. It is gospelling. The church is addressed in the presence of people who are not of the church. The preacher indeed renews for believers the reality of the gospel; but he does it in a large way that concerns also those who have not confessed their faith explicitly. He dwells for the most part on the large and broad features of the gospel rather than on individual and casuistic situations. He declares the whole counsel of God; that is, the counsel of God as a whole. If he handle individual cases, it is as illustrations of wider truth. He leaves cases of conscience to private intercourse. He is not in the pulpit a director of con-science so much as a shepherd or a seeker of souls. And he may give expression to his own private experiences only in so far as is seemly and useful for the more public aspects of his gospel. If he is ever beside himself, it must be privately to God; for the people's sake he is sober and sane. Preaching is not simply pastoral visitation on a large scale. Teaching from house to house meant for the apostles not visitation, but ministering to the church gathered in private houses, as it had then to be.

The first *vis-à-vis* of the preacher, then, is not the world, but the gospel community. The word is living only in a living community. Its spirit can act outward only as it grows inwardly and animates a body duly fed and cared for. The preacher has to do this tending. He has to declare the church's word, and to utter the church's faith, to itself, in order that he and the church together may declare them to the world. The church may use, but cannot rely upon, evange-lists who are evangelists and nothing else. When the preacher speaks to believ-ers it is to build them *up as* a Christian community; when he speaks to the world it is to build them *into* a Christian community. And the church is built up by taking sanctuary, by stopping to realize its own faith, by the repetition of its own old gospel, by turning aside to see its great sight, by standing still to see the salvation of the Lord.

Its own old gospel! It is not needful that the preacher should be original as a genius is, but only as a true believer is. What he brings to the church is not something unheard of, and imported from outside, to revolutionize it. He has to offer the church, in outer form, the word which is always within it, in order that the church, by that presentation, may become anew what by God's grace it already is. He must be original in the sense that his truth is his own, but not in the sense that it has been no one else's.

You must distinguish between novelty and freshness. The preacher is not to be original in the sense of being absolutely *new,* but in the sense of being *fresh,* of appropriating for his own personality, or his own age, what is the standing possession of the church, and its perennial trust from Christ. He makes discovery *in* the gospel, not *of* the gospel. Some preachers spoil their work by an incessant strain after novelty, and a morbid dread of the common-place. But it was one no less original than Goethe who said, the great artist is not afraid of the commonplace. To be unable to freshen the commonplace is to be either dull or bizarre. Yet to be nothing but new is like a raw and treeless house shouting its plaster novelty on a beautiful old brown moor.

The artist may treat revelation as discovery. He may create what he finds but as chaos. He finds but power, and he issues it in grace. But it is otherwise with the preacher. It is the converse. He finds revelation in all discovery. He finds to his hand the grace which he has to issue with power. His word is to send home a word which was articulate from the beginning, "What we have seen and heard of the word of life declare we to you." The artist's grace is not the preacher's. Nor is it true without modification that "all grace is the grace of God."

The preacher has often been compared with the actor, and often he has succumbed to the actor's temperament, or to his arts. But there is a point of real analogy. The actor creates a part, as the phrase is; but it is only by appropriating a personality which the dramatist really created and put into his hands. And that is what the preacher has to do. He has to work less with his own personality than with the personality provided him in Christ, through Christ's work in him. He has to interpret Christ. Moreover, the actor's is a voice which is forgotten, while the poet's is a voice that remains. So also the preacher's originality is limited. By the very Spirit that moves him he speaks not of himself. He must not expect the actor's vogue. Self-assertion or jealousy are more offensive in him than in the artist. It is enough if he be a living voice; he is not a creative word. He is not the light; he but bears witness to it. . . .

God forbid that I should say a word to seem to justify the dullness that infects the pulpit. Alas! If our sin crucify Christ afresh, our stupidity buries him again. But the cure for pulpit dullness is not brilliancy, as in literature. It is reality. It is directness and spontaneity of the common life. The preacher is not there to astonish people with the unheard of; he is there to revive in them what they have long heard. He discovers a mine on the estate. The church, by the preacher's aid, has to realize its own faith, and take home anew its own gospel. That which was from the beginning declare we unto you — that fresh old human nature and that fresh old grace of God.

FRANK BARTLEMAN

Power in a Pentecostal Congregation

Calvin, Edwards, and their successors identified a discrete role for the Holy Spirit in biblical interpretation, preaching, and conversion. It was Wesley's emphasis on spiritual perfection, however, that gave birth to holiness movements in Europe and America. The holiness groups stressed the "second blessing" of sanctification. A child of the holiness movement, American Pentecostalism insisted on glossolalia or "speaking in tongues" as the third and definitive mark of the true Christian. Modern American Pentecostalism was born in a three-year revival from 1906 to 1909 at the Azusa Street Mission in downtown Los Angeles. City newspapers gave the revival bad press under such headlines as "Weird Babel of Tongues," and many were offended by the Pentecostals' mixing of races. Yet "Azusa" became a lively shrine for holiness and Pentecostalist Christians from around the world. The Azusa Street revival was chronicled by Frank Bartleman (1871-1935), an itinerant holiness preacher and reporter for religious magazines. His eye-witness reports of the infectious power of the movement are among the classic documents of American religious history. Pentecostal preaching relies on the immediacy of the Holy Spirit in the assembly and, as the following reports indicate, provokes a variety of physical manifestations of the Spirit's power. (For a comprehensive background, see Grant Wacker, *Heaven Below: Early Pentecostals and American Culture* [Cambridge: Harvard University Press, 2001].)

Frank Bartleman, *How Pentecost Came to Los Angeles — As It Was in the Beginning* [1925], pp. 26-27, 48-49, 60, 71-73, 75-76, 121-22.

One evening [in Los Angeles] I went to Brother Manley's tent meeting, without a thought of taking part in the service. I sat in the rear. Soon the Spirit came mightily upon me. I rose and spoke and the power of God fell upon the congregation. The whole company fell on their faces. For three hours the whole tent was an altar service and prayer continued. A number were saved and everybody seemed to get help from God. It was a wonderful visitation of the Spirit. The people were not as rebellious in those days as they are now. They were more willing to have the program broken into, and there were not so many fanatical spirits to hinder. There was a real hunger for God. Almost every night found me taking part in some meeting. The Lord continued to pour out his Spirit. . . .

One evening at the Holiness camp the Lord told me he wanted me to preach. I went out in the woods and tried to pray for the meeting. But he said, I want you to preach. I told him they would not let me. They had a dozen of their own itching for the opportunity. Besides they were half afraid of me. I did not belong to their particular branch of religion. But he said preach! I told him if he would close every other mouth that night I would obey him. Throwing the responsibility thus on him I went to the meeting. It was time for the message. They looked at one another but every tongue was tied. No one looked at me. The Spirit came upon me and I sprang to my feet. God flooded my soul with power. The message came straight from him and went like an arrow to the mark. It shook the camp. . . .

I gave a message at my first meeting at "Azusa." Two of the saints spoke in "tongues." Much blessing seemed to attend the utterance. It was soon noised abroad that God was working at "Azusa." All classes began to flock to the meetings. Many were curious and unbelieving, but others were hungry for God. The newspapers began to ridicule and abuse the meetings, thus giving us much free advertising. This brought the crowds. The devil overdid himself again. Outside persecution never hurt the work. We had the most to fear from the working of evil spirits within. Even spiritualists and hypnotists came to investigate, and to try their influence. Then all the religious soreheads and crooks and cranks came, seeking a place in the work. We had the most to fear from these. But this is always the danger to every new work. They have no place elsewhere. This condition cast a fear over many which was hard to overcome. It hindered the Spirit much. Many were afraid to seek God, for fear the devil might get them.

We found early in the "Azusa" work that when we attempted to steady the Ark the Lord stopped working. We dared not call the attention of the people too much to the working of the devil. Fear would follow. We could only pray. Then God gave victory. There was a presence of God with us, through prayer, we could depend on. The leaders had a limited experience, and the wonder is the work survived at all against its powerful adversaries. But it was of God. That was the secret. . . .

[At the Azusa Street Mission] someone might be speaking. Suddenly the Spirit would fall upon the congregation. God himself would give the altar call. Men would fall all over the house, like the slain in battle, or rush for the altar *en masse,* to seek God. The scene often resembled a forest of fallen trees. Such a scene cannot be imitated. I never saw an altar call given in those early days. God himself would call them. And the preacher knew when to quit. When he spoke we all obeyed. It seemed a fearful thing to hinder or grieve the Spirit. The whole place was steeped in prayer. God was in his holy temple. It was for man to keep silent. The shekinah glory rested there. In fact some claim to have seen the glory by night over the building. I do not doubt it. I have stopped more than once within two blocks of the place and prayed for strength before I dared go on. The presence of the Lord was so real. . . .

On the afternoon of August 16, at Eighth and Maple, the Spirit manifested himself through me in "tongues." There were seven of us present at the time. It was a weekday. After a time of testimony and praise, with everything quiet, I was softly walking the floor, praising God in my spirit. All at once I seemed to hear in my soul (not with my natural ears), a rich voice speaking in a language I did not know. I have later heard something similar to it in India. It seemed to ravish and fully satisfy the pent up praises in my being. In a few moments I found myself, seemingly without volition on my part, enunciating the same sounds with my own vocal organs. It was an exact continuation of the same expressions that I had heard in my soul a few moments before. It seemed like a perfect language. I was almost like an outside listener. I was fully yielded to God, and simply carried by his will, as on a divine stream. I could have hindered the expression but would not have done so for worlds. A heaven of conscious bliss accompanied it. It is impossible to describe the experience accurately. It must be experienced to be appreciated. There was no effort made to speak on my part, and not the least possible struggle. The experience was most sacred, the Holy Spirit playing on my vocal cords, as on an Aeolian harp. The whole utterance was a complete surprise to me. I had never really been solicitous to speak in "tongues." Because I could not understand it with my natural mind I had rather feared it.

I had no desire at the time to even know what I was saying. It seemed a soul expression purely, outside the realm of the natural mind or understanding. I was truly "sealed in the forehead," ceasing from the works of my own natural mind fully. I wrote my experience for publication later, in the following words: "The Spirit had gradually prepared me for this culmination in my experience, both in prayer for myself, and others. I had thus drawn nigh to God, my spirit greatly subdued. A place of utter abandonment of will had been reached, in absolute consciousness of helplessness, purified from natural self-activity." . . .

In the experience of "speaking in tongues" I had reached the climax in abandonment. This opened the channel for a new ministry of the Spirit in service. From that time the Spirit began to flow through me in a new way. Messages would come, with anointings, in a way I had never known before, with a spontaneous inspiration and illumination that was truly wonderful. This was attended with convincing power. The Pentecostal baptism spells complete abandonment, possession by the Holy Ghost, of the whole man, with a spirit of instant obedience. I had known much of the power of God for service for many years before this, but I now realized a sensitiveness to the Spirit, a yieldedness, that made it possible for God to possess and work in new ways and channels, with far more powerful, direct results. I also received a new revelation of his sovereignty, both in purpose and action, such as I had never known before. I found I had often charged God with seeming lack of interest, or tardiness of action, when I should have yielded to him, in faith, that he might be able to work through me his sovereign mighty will. I went into the dust of humility at this revelation of my own stupidity, and his sovereign care and desire. I saw that the little bit of desire I possessed for his service was only the little bit that he had been able to get to me of his great desire and interest and purpose. His word declares it. All there was of good in me, in thought or action, had come from him. Like Hudson Taylor I now felt that he was asking me simply to go with him to help in that which he alone had purposed and desired. I felt very small at this revelation, and my past misunderstanding. He had existed, and had been working out his eternal purpose, long before I had ever been thought of, and would be long after I would be gone. . . .

The early church lived in this, as its normal atmosphere. Hence its abandonment to the working of the Spirit, its supernatural gifts, and its power. Our wiseacres cannot reach this. Oh, to become a fool, to know nothing in ourselves, that we might receive the mind of Christ fully, have the Holy Ghost teach and lead us only, and at all times. We do not mean to say we must talk in "tongues" continually. The "baptism" is not all "tongues." We can live in this place of illumination and abandonment and still speak in our own language. The Bible was not written in "tongues." But we may surely live in the Spirit at all times, though possibly few, if any, always do. Oh, the depth of abandonment, all self gone! Conscious of knowing nothing, of having nothing, except as the Spirit shall teach and impart to us. This is the true place of power, of God's power, in the ministry of service. There is nothing left but God, the pure Spirit. Every hope or sense of capability in the natural is gone. We live by his breath, as it were. The wind on the day of Pentecost was the breath of God — Acts 2:2. But what more can we say? It must be experienced to be understood. It cannot be explained. We have certainly had a measure of the Spirit before without this. To this fact all history testifies. The church has been abnormal since its fall. But we cannot have the Pentecostal baptism without it, as the early church had it. The apostles received it suddenly, and in full. Only simple faith and abandonment can receive it. Human reason can find all kinds of flaws and apparent foolishness in it.

I spoke in "tongues" possibly for about fifteen minutes on this first occasion. Then the immediate inspiration passed away, for the time. I have spoken at times since, also. But I never try to reproduce it. The act must be sovereign with God. It would be foolishness and sacrilege to try to imitate it. The experience left behind it the consciousness of utter God-control, and of his presence naturally in corresponding measure. It was a most sacred experience. Many have trifled most foolishly with this principle and possession. They have failed to continue in the Spirit and have stumbled many. This has wrought great harm. But the experience still remains a fact, both in history and present day realization. The greater part of most Christians' knowledge of God is and has always been, since the loss of the Spirit by the early church, an intellectual knowledge. Their knowledge of the word and principles of God is an intellectual one, through natural reasoning and understanding largely. They have little revelation, illumination, or inspiration direct from the Spirit of God. . . .

[Later, on tour in Indianapolis,] the Lord gave me a number of messages. We had a wonderful time. In fact I had not felt the power of God in such measure for a long time. There was tremendous opposition also, but God gave the victory. The work had been split into two factions. They came together in the meeting but were not reconciled. At one meeting the Spirit was so mightily on me in the message that the opposing faction held on to their seats and stiffened their backs to keep from yielding. I have seldom seen such resistance to the Spirit of God, and by Pentecostal saints, at that. It was simply awful. One night they had arranged for foot-washing. I gave the message that night and by the time I got through I think they had forgotten all about the foot-washing. They were too busy getting right with God, and with one another. Their souls needed washing more.

The Lord blessed me much at Indianapolis. I was so glad I had obeyed him and gone there. I was there by his invitation purely. But I seldom if ever had felt such a wonderful flow of the Spirit before. The message seemed to be fairly drawn out of me in preaching. I felt almost drawn off the platform by the hungry desire of the people. I could not talk as rapidly as the thoughts came to me and almost fell over myself trying to speak fast enough. At one meeting when I was through the slain of the Lord lay all over the floor. I looked for the preachers behind me and they lay stretched out on the floor too. One of them had his feet tangled up in a chair, so I knew they had gone down under the power of God. I stepped over near the piano, among the people. My body began to rock under the power of God and I fell over onto the piano and lay there. It was a cyclonic manifestation of the power of God. We left the convention with great victory. I had not received a penny since leaving home and the devil was tempting me much over the matter. But the Lord kept assuring me he would make it up to me later on. I had to take his word for it, for I could not understand the situation. It was a new one to me. But I knew God had spoken.

KARL BARTH

Preaching, Revelation, and the Church

For Karl Barth (1886-1968), preaching may not be restricted to a particular locus of Christian doctrine, be it Christology, pneumatology, or ecclesiology. According to the *Church Dogmatics,* preaching is "the attempt by someone called
thereto in the church, in the form of the exposition of some portion of the biblical witness to revelation, to express in his own words and to make intelligible
to the men of his own generation the promise of the revelation, reconciliation
and vocation of God as they are to be expected here and now" (I, 1, p. 56). The
greatest part of Barth's discussion of preaching occurs under the heading
"Word of God." That word is threefold: the revealed word made flesh, the written word of Scripture, and the preached word. The preached word and sacraments constitute the church's proclamation. It is not the task of dogmatic theology to provide the content of sermons. "This content must be found each
time in the middle space between the particular text in the context of the whole
Bible and the particular situation of the changing moment." Dogmatics can
only help the preacher choose what must be said in a given circumstance or
what must not be said under any circumstance (I, 1, p. 79). Ultimately, dogmatics helps to insure that the church's talk conforms to the church's being,
which is the richness of its life given to it by God. As in Forsyth, the centrality
of revelation in Barth's theology means that preaching is a divine activity. True
preaching does not add to or embellish the revelation with "vain images" or
"outpourings of sentimental eloquence." Preaching is a human activity that
becomes the word of God where and whenever it witnesses and attests to the
primary revelation of God in Jesus Christ. The following selection from Barth's
lectures on preaching is based on notes recorded by his students.

Karl Barth, *The Preaching of the Gospel,* trans. B. E. Hooke, English translation (Philadelphia:
Westminster, 1963), pp. 12-28.

The relation of preaching to revelation may be considered first in its negative aspect. It is not the function of the preacher to reveal God or to act as his intermediary. When the gospel is preached, God speaks: there is no question of the preacher revealing anything or of a revelation being conveyed through him. It is necessary, in all circumstances, to have regard to the fact that God has revealed himself (Epiphany) and will reveal himself (Parousia). Whatever happens by means of preaching — in the interval between the first and the second coming — is due to its divine subject. Revelation is a closed system in which God is the subject, the object, and the middle term.

The practical consequences of this are as follows:

Preaching cannot claim to convey the truth of God; neither can its aim be to provide a rational demonstration of the existence of God by expounding briefly or at length certain theoretical propositions. There is no proof that God exists except that which he himself provides. Nor are we required to display the truth of God in an artistic form by the use of vain images or by presenting Jesus Christ in outpourings of sentimental eloquence. When Paul told the Galatians that he had portrayed before their eyes Jesus Christ crucified, he was not referring to speeches in which he had used every device of artistry to capture the imagination of his hearers. For him, to portray Christ was to show him forth in plain truth without embellishments. We are under orders to "make no image or likeness." Since God wills to utter his own truth, his word, the preacher must not adulterate that truth by adding his own knowledge or art. From this point of view, the representation of the figure of Christ in art, the crucifix in churches, as well as symbolic images of God, may be of doubtful value.

Neither must the preacher seek to establish the reality of God. His task is to build God's kingdom and he must work toward a decision. His message must be authentic and alive; he must lay bare man's actual situation and confront him with God. But he is going too far if he thinks of this confrontation as "a sickness which leads to death" (Kierkegaard). This phrase no doubt presupposes things which are implicit in preaching, but it concerns the action of God and no man ought to intrude in what is not his province.

If it is maintained that a preacher ought to convert others and cause his hearers to share his own faith, this can only be understood in the sense that he should be aware of what is happening when he is bearing witness. The preacher who believes in Christ will never present himself to his congregation in such a way that they will suppose him able to bestow on them Christ and the Spirit, or think that the initiative in what is done is his. God is not a *Deus otiosus;* he is the author of what is done. We can act only in obedience to the task given to us; neither our aims nor our methods are of our own devising.

Our preaching does not differ in essence from that of the prophets and apostles who "saw and touched"; the difference is due to the different historical setting in which it takes place. The prophets and apostles lived during that moment of the historical revelation of which Scripture is the record. We, on the other hand, bear witness to the revelation.

But if God speaks through our words, then in fact the same situation is produced: the prophets and apostles are present even though the words are spoken by an ordinary minister. But we must not think of ourselves as uttering prophecies; if Christ deigns to be present when we are speaking, it is precisely because the action is God's, not ours. Since this is the way things happen, the preacher can make no claims for his own program.

Thus any independent undertaking that is attempted, whether with the intention of developing a theoretical subject or with the practical purpose of leading one's hearers into a certain frame of mind, can in fact be nothing else but a waiting on God, so that he may do with it what he will. If the preacher sets himself to expound a particular idea, in some form or another — even if the idea is derived from a serious and well-informed exegesis — then the Scripture is not allowed to speak for itself; the preacher is discoursing on it.

To put it more positively, preaching should be an explanation of Scripture; the preacher does not have to speak "on" but "from" *(ex)*, drawing from the Scriptures whatever he says. He does not have to invent, but rather to repeat something. No thesis, no purpose derived from his own resources, must be allowed to intervene: God alone must speak. Perhaps, afterward, he will have to ask himself whether he has allowed himself to be influenced by an idea of his own or has attempted to arrive at a unity which only God could create. He must follow the special trend of his text, and keep to it wherever it may lead him, not raising questions about a subject which may, as it seems to him, arise from the text.

In this connection it may be pointed out that the choice of a text may present dangers, in that one may choose a text because it bears on a subject one would like to discuss; one may even turn to the Bible in order to find in it something which fits in with one's own thoughts! To have to speak from a particular text to a particular congregation in an actual situation is in itself a dangerous undertaking. It may be that in that situation God will speak and work a miracle, but we must not build on that miracle in advance. Otherwise it would be easy for a preacher to become a sort of pope and indoctrinate his congregation with his own ideas by presenting them as the word of God.

The positive aspect of this matter must now be considered. The starting point is the fact that God wills to reveal himself; he himself bears witness to his revelation; he has effected it and will effect it. Thus preaching takes place in obedience, by listening to the will of God. This is the process in which the preacher is involved, which constitutes part of his life and controls the content as well as the form of his preaching. Preaching is not a neutral activity, nor yet a joint action by two collaborators. It is the exercise of sovereign power on the part of God and obedience on the part of man.

Only when preaching is controlled by this relationship can it be regarded as "kerygma," that is, as news proclaimed by a herald who thereby fulfills his function. Then the preacher is omnipotent, but only because of the omnipotence of the one who has commissioned him. The kerygma means therefore to start from the Epiphany of Christ in order to move toward the Day of the Lord. Thus New Testament preaching consists in a dual movement: God has revealed himself, God will reveal himself.

From these considerations certain consequences follow: The fixed point from which all preaching starts is the fact that God has revealed himself, and this means that the Word has become flesh; God has assumed human nature; in Christ he has taken on himself fallen man. Man, who is lost, is called back to his home. The death of Christ is the final term of the incarnation. In him our sin and our punishment are put away, they no longer exist; in him man has been redeemed once for all; in him God has been reconciled with us. To believe means to see and know and recognize that this is so.

If then preaching is dominated by this starting point, the preacher can adopt no attitude other than that of a man to whom everything is given. He knows, without any possible doubt, that everything has been restored by God himself. He is, however, constantly beset by the temptation to denounce man's sin or to attack his errors. Certainly it is necessary to speak of human sin and error, but only in order to show that sin is annihilated and error destroyed. For either it is true that man is forgiven or else there is no forgiveness whatever. Sin cannot be spoken of except as borne by the Lamb of God.

At the same time, to separate the gospel from the law in preaching is not Christian. How is it possible to proclaim the gospel without also hearing the law which says: "Thou shalt fear and love God"? This danger is particularly noticeable in Calvinism.

Moreover, from its first to its last word, preaching follows a movement. This has nothing to do with the preacher's convictions, or his earnestness, or his zeal. The movement starts from the fact that the word became flesh, and the preacher must abandon himself to its guidance. If this rule were observed, how many introductory remarks would become quite unnecessary! The movement does not consist so much in going toward men as in coming from Christ to meet them. Preaching therefore proceeds downward; it should never attempt to reach up to a summit. Has not everything been done already?

It has already been pointed out that preaching has one single point of departure, which is that God has revealed himself. It should also be recognized that it has one unique end: the fulfillment of the revelation, the redemption which awaits us.

From beginning to end the New Testament looks toward the achievement of salvation. This, however, is not to deny that all has been accomplished once for all. The Christ who has come is the one who will return. The life of faith is orientated toward the day of the Parousia. The point of departure and the point to which everything tends are summed up in the declaration: "Christ the same yesterday, today, and forever." And assuming that we await the whole Christ, christology and eschatology may be said to be one. Revelation, therefore, is before as well as behind us.

It follows, then, that preaching moves in an atmosphere of expectation. There is no settling down comfortably in faith and the assurance of salvation, as if divine grace manifested in the past allowed us now to take our rest in tranquility. Without doubt there is a profound and joyful assurance, but there is also the solemn and earnest concern of one who watches because the end is near. Preaching, like all Christian life, grows to its fullness between the first advent and the second.

We walk by faith, not by sight (2 Cor. 5:7). If in this present time we were living by sight, we should have nothing to wait for: there would be neither yesterday nor tomorrow. But we live by faith, that is to say, we come from Christ and are going to Christ. Peace and joy abound on either hand, but on this journey we go from riches to destitution and from destitution to new riches. The preacher must show the real nature of this journey in faith; that is to say, he must make it clear that confident assurance is not Christian unless it is shot through with longing for a salvation yet to be realized in its fullness in Christ. Christ has come, Christ will come again, and we await the day of his coming: this is the word of command. "The Word was made flesh" has as its response: "Amen, come quickly, Lord Jesus."

The Lutheran tendency is to confine itself to what is past, and for this reason its preaching is always liable to be biased toward dogmatism and religious experience. But Philippians 3 refers to Philippians 2; having described the Christian vocation, the apostle declares: "Not that I have already attained . . . but I press on." There is movement even in the tranquility of faith. The preacher must proclaim with conviction that "all has been done" but also that "all must be changed." We look for a new heaven and a new earth. We know, indeed, that we are reconciled with God, but we still await the fulfillment of the promise: "See, I make all things new." That is why preaching rests entirely on hope, for the Christian "now" is simply the passage from yesterday to tomorrow, from Epiphany to Parousia. From this point of view we are a people which walks in darkness, but we see a great light; "the night is far spent, the day is at hand." If the preacher's message is to conform to Revelation, these two fixed points must be kept in mind.

Preaching and the Church

Preaching has its place within the context of what is called the church; it is bound up with the church's existence and its mission. Precisely for this reason, preaching must conform to revelation. But it should be noted that revelation is set in the framework of the Old and New Testaments and is therefore a particular, concrete event taking place at a specific period in history; it is not an idea of general significance which could arise at any time or in any place. Consequently, preaching is not concerned with aspects of human existence in its natural state or with the progress of its history; it is not inspired by any philosophy or conceptual view of life and the world; its subject is solely that particular event, the gift of God in the context of history.

Again it must be emphasized that preaching is not man's attempt to add something to revelation; the movement which proceeds from the first to the second advent is not initiated by man but is due simply to the action of God's grace. God draws near to men; men cannot, by their own efforts, rise to win for themselves what God has appointed for them.

The task of the preacher can therefore be summed up thus: to reproduce in thought that one unique event, the gift of God's grace. If once he has recognized the impossibility of doing otherwise, then he will see clearly that no philosophical, political, or aesthetic considerations can influence his choice of a field for his activity. In the nature of things there can only be one — the church.

There a relationship exists which is prior to anything we know on earth — whether of family, society, nation, or race; and the nature of that relationship is entirely different from that of the created order. In the church, where the word of reconciliation rings out, all other relationships are seen to be stained with impurities, contaminated, submerged in a fallen world and, as such, lying under the stroke of judgment. But that same word also assures us that our sickness is healed and the whole burden of the consequence of sin is carried away. Moreover, in the word of reconciliation there is also the message of creation.

Preaching, when it is true to what God has revealed to us, effects reconciliation; and wherever men receive this Word, there is the church, the assembly of those who have been called by the Lord. Not general reflections on man and the cosmos but revelation is the only legitimate ground for preaching. Because this call is sounded and men are able to hear it, the church exists. Thus the bond which links preaching to the church results directly from its faithfulness to revelation.

The foregoing considerations will become clearer if two points are emphasized. The true church is characterized by the fact that *"Evangelium pure docetur et recta administrantur sacramenta"* [The gospel is taught in purity and the sacraments are rightly administered] (*Augsburg Confession*, VII). These two concepts, sacraments and preaching the gospel, throw light on the connection between the church and conformity to revelation.

The sacrament, with all its wealth of meaning, may first be considered, for it is impossible to understand what preaching is without understanding what the sacrament is. There is indeed no preaching, in the precise meaning of the term, except when it is accompanied and illuminated by the sacrament. What is the sacrament? Unlike preaching or any other ecclesiastical activity, the sacrament goes back to the action of the revelation which founded the church and constitutes her promise, for the sacrament is not merely a word but an action, physically and visibly performed.

Baptism confers on a man the seal of belonging to the church, for his life begins not with his birth but with his baptism. To be baptized means that a relationship between the revelation and a man has been established and is made actual in a specific situation (Rom. 6:3). If baptism represents the event which is the point of departure, the Lord's Supper, on the other hand, is the sign of the same event but turned toward the future which we all await (1 Cor. 11:26).

Preaching, then, is given within that church where the sacrament of grace and the sacrament of hope are operative, but each partakes at once of the character of grace and hope, for neither sacrament nor preaching has significance except within the church, where each is authenticated by its relation to the other. Preaching, in fact, derives its substance from the sacrament which itself refers to an action in the total event of revelation. Preaching is a commentary on and an interpretation of the sacrament, having the same meaning but in words. If this fact be recognized, it will be clear that preaching is impossible except within the territory of the church, in that setting where, in baptism and the Lord's Supper, man is chosen by God himself to belong to the body of Christ, to be nourished and protected during his journey to eternal life. And we should know that all those who hear are baptized and called to partake of grace, and what has been thus begun in them will be fulfilled.

In this way, by reference to baptism and the Lord's Supper, the origin and the aim of preaching, [as well as] the course it pursues, are more clearly defined, and the place of the messenger of the word is more plainly seen.

Having discussed these theoretical questions, let us consider what goes on in the evangelical church. At the outset something appears to be lacking. In those circles which embraced the Reformation, the sacramental Church of Rome was replaced by a Church of the Word. Very soon, preaching became the center of worship and the celebration of the sacrament came to occupy a more restricted place, so that today in the Roman church, the church of the sacrament, preaching has little significance, while in the Reformed church the sacrament, while it exists, does not form an integral and necessary element of worship. These two positions are in effect a destruction of the church. What meaning can there be in preaching which exalts itself at the expense of the sacrament, and does not look back to the sacrament which it should interpret? Our life does not depend on what the minister may be able to say, but on the fact that we are baptized, that God has called us. This lack has indeed been recognized, and attempts have been made to fill it by various means (reform of the liturgy, beautifying worship with music, etc.). But these palliative measures are bound to fail because they do not touch the real issue.

Those who advocate such methods of renewing the forms of worship take their stand — mistakenly — on Luther. But he, seeking to retain all that was of value in the Roman liturgy, gave first place to the Lord's Supper. Calvin, also, constantly emphasized the necessity for a service of Communion at every Sunday worship. And this is precisely what we lack today: the sacrament every Sunday. The order of worship should be as follows: at the beginning of the service, public baptism; at the end, the Lord's Supper; between the two sacraments, the sermon, which in this way would be given its full significance. This would indeed be *"recte administrare sacramentum et pure docere evangelium."* So long as the true significance of evangelical worship in its totality is not understood, no theological efforts or liturgical movements will be efficacious. Only when worship is rightly ordered, with preaching and sacrament, will the liturgy come into its own, for it is only in this way that it can fulfill its office, which is to lead to the sacrament. The administration of the sacraments must not be separated from the preaching of the gospel, because the church is a physical and historical organism, a real and visible body as well as the invisible, mystical body of Christ, and because she is both these at once.

There is no doubt that we should be better Protestants if we allowed ourselves to be instructed in this matter by Roman Catholicism; not to neglect preaching, as it so often does, but to restore the sacrament to its rightful place. It is open to question whether the motive for our liturgical efforts is anything more than a desire to approach nearer to the "beautiful services" of the Church of Rome. But what is rightly to be sought is not an elaboration of the liturgy but the true significance of the sacrament in the church. A good Protestant will allow himself to admit this, and at the same time will insist on good preaching.

In preaching, all that is necessary is to recount again what concerns the prior event of revelation. And in order to distinguish the two actions to which revelation refers, the preacher may point to the sacrament on the one hand and holy Scripture on the other; the one looks back to the act of revelation which God accomplished, the other refers to the nature of the revelation. It is idle to oppose sacrament to preaching; they cannot be separated, since they are two aspects of the same thing.

The divine act of revelation took place at the heart of human life and history. The church, however, cannot hand it on directly. In holy Scripture the truth and actuality of the revelation are preserved, for Scripture represents the testimony of chosen intermediaries, the prophets and apostles. The church rests on the foundation of witnesses individually called to be apostles. When witness is borne to the revelation, that is to say, when Scripture is read and expounded, the church should understand that she does not live for herself alone; her life is not her own, nor does it rest on its own foundation; but the church is founded on the sole and unique action of God accomplished in Israel and in Christ — those two centers of revelation: a people and a savior. On the one hand, that erring people who, through their inability to keep the law, so frequently lapsed into sin but were never abandoned by God; on the other, the overflowing of grace, the Savior of the people, the fulfillment of the law and, in consequence, the gospel.

It is clear that revelation is not to be thought of as a general principle regulating the relations between God and the world. On the contrary, it is one unique event. Scripture, therefore, has a concrete quality and is not an intellectual system. The fact of holding closely to Scripture bears witness to the unique character — unique in time and in method — of revelation.

In her relationship with God the church represents not humankind in general, but men gathered together by the work of revelation; for this reason she is based on the Scriptures. If, then, the church is constituted by the testimony of the apostles, the mediators of revelation, what, in this context, is the function of preaching? It is, simply, to make this witness understood.

This leads to a consideration of preaching from a text; the text will always be from the Bible and will relate at once to the sacrament and to the word of the prophets and apostles. No reasons can be given for preferring the Bible, nor is it necessary to justify the choice. The starting point is the fact that the church is the place where the Bible is open; there God has spoken and still speaks. There we are given our mission and our orders. By taking our stand on the Bible we dare to do what has to be done. These writings which lie before us are prior to our testimony, and our preaching must take into account what has already been given. We can no more liberate ourselves from the Bible than a child can liberate himself from his father.

In conclusion it may be said that the ecclesiastical character of preaching is guaranteed so long as it is inspired by the sacrament and is faithful to Scripture.

ARCHBISHOP OSCAR ROMERO

A Pastor's Last Homily

Oscar Arnulfo Romero (1917-1980) was born in an isolated mountain village in eastern El Salvador. He left home at age thirteen to study for the priesthood; at twenty, he was sent to Rome for his theological studies and was ordained a priest there in 1942. During the next twenty-five years he gained renown among the people of El Salvador as a priest, journalist, and social organizer. He was ordained an auxiliary bishop of the San Salvador archdiocese in 1970. His tenure in the small diocese of Santiago de Maria opened his eyes to the repressive conditions in which Salvadoran peasants lived and plunged him into dangerous controversies over poverty and land reform. After the murder of a socially active rural pastor, Romero ordered that one unified mass be celebrated in San Salvador. During the next three years, five more priests would be murdered. Romero's identification with the peasants intensified, and he found himself at the vortex of unrelenting conflicts and threats of violence. In his Sunday homily on March 23, 1980, he called upon the troops and national guardsmen to obey the law of God rather than the orders of officers who might instruct them to kill their brothers and sisters. On Monday, March 24, 1980, as he preached in the chapel of the Divine Providence cancer hospital, Romero was shot and killed by a gunman standing in the rear of the sanctuary. The following selection adds local density to the abstraction, "liberation theology," and illustrates how one preacher gave homiletical voice to his theological convictions. In its treatment of Lent and resurrection, the homily also discloses the connection between political resistance and liturgical time.

Oscar Romero, "A Pastor's Last Homily," trans. Nena Terrell and Sally Hanlon, *Sojourners* (May 1980): 12-16.

We want to greet the entities of [radio station] YSAX, which for so long have awaited this moment which, thanks to God, has arrived. We know the risk that is run by our poor station for being the instrument and vehicle of truth and justice, but we recognize that the risk has to be taken, for behind that risk is an entire people that upholds this word of truth and justice. . . .

We give thanks to God that a message that doesn't mean to be more than a modest reflection of the spoken Word finds marvelous channels of outreach and tells many people that, in the context of Lent, all of this is preparation for our Easter, and Easter is a shout of victory. No one can extinguish that life which Christ revived. Not even death and hatred against him and against his church will be able to overcome it. He is the victor!

As he will flourish in an Easter of unending resurrection, it is necessary to also accompany him in Lent, in a Holy Week that is cross, sacrifice, martyrdom; as he would say, "Happy are those who do not become offended by their cross!"

Lent is then a call to celebrate our redemption in that difficult complex of cross and victory. Our people are very qualified, all their surroundings preach to us of cross; but all who have Christian faith and hope know that behind this Calvary of El Salvador is our Easter, our resurrection, and that is the hope of the Christian people. . . .

Today, as diverse historical projects emerge for our people, we can be sure that victory will be had by the one that best reflects the plan of God. And this is the mission of the church. That is why, in the light of the divine word that reveals the designs of God for the happiness of the peoples, we have the duty, dear brothers and sisters, to also point out the facts, to see how the plan of God is being reflected or disdained in our midst. Let no one take badly the fact that we illuminate the social, political, and economic truths by the light of the divine words that are read at our Mass, because not to do so would, for us, be unChristian. . . .

I know there are many who are shocked by this word and who want to accuse it of having left the sermon of the gospel to insert itself in politics; but I don't accept this accusation, for I am making an effort so that all that the Vatican Council II, the meetings of Medellin and Puebla have wanted to impel us to is not just held on the pages as we study it theoretically, but so that we live it and translate it into the conflictive reality of preaching the gospel as it should be for our people. That is why I ask the Lord during the whole week as I go gathering up the clamor of the people and the aches of so much crime, the ignominy of so much violence, that he give me the suitable word to console, to denounce, to call for repentance; and even though I may continue to be a voice crying in the desert, I know that the church is making the effort to fulfill its mission. . . .

Isaiah 43:16-21

The readings of Lent tell us how God applied his project in history in order to make the history of the peoples their history of salvation. And in the measure that those peoples reflect that project of God — to save us in Christ by conversion — in that measure the peoples are gaining salvation and are happy. For that reason, the history of Israel is in the first reading of all of Lent. A paradigm people, an example, exemplary even in their infidelities and sins, because in them we also learn how God punishes the infidelities, the sins; and also there is in them a model for bringing the promise of God's salvation. . . .

It is a history that each nation has to imitate; for every population may not be the same as Israel's, but there is something that exists in all peoples: the group that follows Christ, the group of the people of God which is not the entire population, naturally, but which is a group of the faithful. . . .

John 8:1-11

The figure of the adulteress before Christ: There we have the gospel. I find no more beautiful example of Jesus saving human dignity than this sinless Jesus face to face with an adulteress, humiliated because she has been caught, and facing being stoned. And Jesus, after casting to the earth without a word the sin of her very judges, asks the woman, "Has no one condemned you?" "No one, Sir." "Well, neither do I condemn you. But do not sin again." Strength but tenderness. Human dignity before all else. . . .

The witnesses, in looking at their own conscience, found that they were witnesses of their own sin. . . . Personal sin is the root of the great social sin: This we must be very clear on, beloved brothers and sisters, because today it is very easy, as it was for the witnesses against the adulteress, to point out and beg justice for others; but how few cast a glance at their own conscience! How easy it is to denounce structural injustice, institutionalized violence, social sin! And it is true, this sin is everywhere, but where are the roots of this social sin? In the heart of every human being. Present-day society is a sort of anonymous world in which no one is willing to admit guilt and everyone is responsible. We are all sinners, and we have all contributed to this massive crime and violence in our country.

Because of this, salvation begins with the human person, with human dignity, with saving every person from sin. And in Lent this is God's call: Be converted! Individually there are among us here no two sinners alike. Each one has committed his or her own shameful deeds, and yet we want to cast our guilt on the other and hide our own sin. I must take off my mask; I, too, am one of them, and I need to beg God's pardon because I have offended God and society. This is the call of Christ: Before all else, the human person!

How beautiful the expression of that woman upon finding herself pardoned and understood: "No one, Sir. No one has condemned me." Then neither do I, I who could give that truly condemning word, neither do I condemn; but be careful, do not sin again. Do not sin again! Let us be careful, brothers and sisters, since God has forgiven us so many times, let us take advantage of that friendship with the Lord which we have recovered and let us live it with gratitude.

How wonderful a chapter on the promotion of woman by Christianity would fit here! If woman has achieved heights similar to those of man, much of this is due to the gospel of Jesus Christ. In the time of Christ, people were shocked that he should speak with a Samaritan woman, because woman was considered unworthy of speaking with man. And Jesus knows that we are all equal, that there is neither Jew nor Greek, man nor woman, but that all are God's children. . . .

Jesus' attitude is what we must focus on in this Gospel and what we must learn: a delicacy with reference to the person, however sinful that person may be, is what distinguishes him as the Son of God, image of the Lord. He does not condemn; rather he pardons. Nor does he tolerate sin. He is strong in rejecting the sin, but he knows how to condemn the sin and save the sinner. He does not subordinate the human person to the law. And this is very important in our own times. He has said: "The human person was not made for the Sabbath, but the Sabbath made for humanity."

Let us not try to call upon our country's constitution to defend our own personal selfishness, trying to use it for our own interests when it has been trampled upon everywhere. The law is for the benefit of the human person, not the person for the law. And so Jesus is the source of peace when he has thus given human dignity its rightful place. We feel that we count on Jesus, that we do not count on sin, that we must repent and return to Jesus with sincerity. This is the deepest joy that a human being can have.

Philippians 3:8-14

In today's New Testament reading we have another example of a sinner who went about fooling himself for a long time, but who in coming to know Christ was saved by him and now places all his dreams, the aim of his whole life, in reaching Christ. "And everything else has become as nothing to me" the epistle says to us today. When the things of earth are no longer idolatrized, but we have come to know the true God, the true Savior, all earthly ideologies, all worldly strategies, all the idols of power, of money, of things become as nothing to us. Saint Paul uses an even stronger word, they become "like garbage," "like manure" to me, "as long as I can win Christ."

So as not to hold you too long, I won't read, brothers and sisters, the whole rich content of the Puebla document on one of its theological foundations. . . . As bishops of the continent we signed a commitment there in Puebla when we spoke about the false earthly visions that people have had based on their own selfishness, above all those visions which make of the human person an instrument of exploitation, or those visions which make of the person in Marxist ideologies but a cog in the machinery, or those which make [of the person] in national security a servant of the state, as if the state were lord and humanity the slave, when it is the reverse. It is not humanity for the state, but rather the state for humanity. The human person must be the summit of all human organization to promote humanity. . . .

Our personal accounts with God, our individual relationship with him, set the stage for everything else. False liberators are those who hold their souls slaves to sin and because of this are many times so cruel because they do not know how either to love or respect the human person.

The second idea passes on from the individual to the communitarian. This is put beautifully in today's readings, which show how God desires to save people as a people. It is the whole population that God wants to save.

The first reading today, the famous songs of Isaiah, present God speaking with a people. It is the dialogue of God with what the Scriptures call "a collective personality," as though he were speaking with one person. God speaks with a people and to that people. God makes them his people because he is going to entrust them with promises, revelations that soon will serve for all the rest of the peoples. . . .

And when I, as pastor, address the people of God, I don't pretend to be the master of all of El Salvador, if not the servant of a nucleus that is called the church, those that want to serve Christ and who recognize the bishop as the teacher who speaks to them in the name of Christ. From them I expect respect, obedience. With them I feel so united that it doesn't bother me that those who are not of the church, although they may be within it, criticize me, murmur at me, pick me apart.

They are no longer the people of God. . . . Even though they may be baptized, even though they may come to hear the Mass, if they don't join in solidarity with the exacting teachings of the gospel, the concrete applications of our pastoral thrust, then, brothers and sisters, we well know how to discern in order not to toy with that name so sacred: the people. We call to the people of God, to the nucleus of Salvadorans who believe in Christ and want to follow him faithfully, and who are nourished by his life, his sacraments, by means of his pastors.

This people of God exists throughout history. Did you notice what today's reading has said so beautifully? "You glorify the first exodus when I took you out of Egypt, when you crossed the desert. What many wonders were made on that journey with Moses! But glory no longer in that past. That has already become history, I make things anew." What a beautiful phrase from God! It is God who makes the new; it is God who goes with history.

Now the exodus will be from another direction, from Babylon, from exile. The desert through which they are going to pass will flower like a garden, the waters will gush forth symbolizing the passing of God's pardon, the people reconciled with God on the way to Jerusalem. . . .

Today El Salvador is living its own exodus. Today we too are passing to our liberation through the desert, where cadavers, where anguished pain are devastating us, and where many suffer the temptation of those who were walking with Moses and who wanted to turn back. . . . God desires to save the people making a new history. . . .

What is not repeated in history are the circumstances, the opportunities to which we are witnesses in El Salvador. How dense is our history, how varied from one day to another! One leaves El Salvador and returns the following week, and it seems that history has changed so categorically. Let us not rest our stability on wanting to judge things as they were once judged. One thing, yes: may we have firmly anchored in the soul our faith in Jesus Christ, God of history. That does not change; but he has, as it were, the satisfaction of changing history, playing with history: "I make things new."

The grace of the Christian, therefore, is to not be braced on traditions that can no longer sustain themselves, but to apply that eternal tradition of Christ to the present realities. Change in the church, dear brothers and sisters, above all for those of us who have been formed at other times, in other systems, we have to have, and we have to ask God for that grace to adapt ourselves without betraying our faith. . . .

History will not perish; God sustains it. That is why I say that in the measure that the historical projects attempt to reflect the eternal project that is God's, in that measure they are reflecting the kingdom of God, and this is the work of the church. Because of this, the church, the people of God in history, is not installed in any one social system, in any political organization, in any party. The church is not led on a hunt by any of these forces because she is the eternal pilgrim of history and is indicating at every historical moment what does reflect the kingdom of God and what does not reflect the kingdom of God. She is the servant of the kingdom of God.

The great task of the Christian has to be to absorb the kingdom of God, and with that soul filled with the kingdom of God to work on the projects of history. It's fine to be organized in popular organizations; it's all right to form political parties; it's all right to take part in government; it's fine as long as you are a Christian carrying the reflection of the kingdom of God and trying to establish it there where you are working, and not becoming a toy to the ambitions of the earth.

This is the great duty of the people of today. My dear Christians, I have always told you, and I will repeat, that from here, the Christian group, from the people of God have to come those who are going to be the true liberators of our people. . . .

That is why you have to be grateful for the church, dear political brothers and sisters, and not manipulate the church to bring her to say what we want, but to say ourselves what the church is teaching. The church doesn't have interests. I do not have a single ambition for power, and because of that, I tell power, with all liberty, what is good and what is bad, and I also tell any political group what is good and what is bad. It is my duty.

And from that freedom of the kingdom of God, the church (which is not only the bishop and the priests, but all of you, the faithful, the religious, the nucleus of believers in Christ) should unify our criterion. We should not disunite ourselves, we should not appear dispersed. Many times it's as though we are inhibited by the popular political organizations, and we want to please them more than the kingdom of God in its eternal designs. We don't have to lie to anyone about anything because we have a lot to give to everyone. And this is not arrogance but the grateful humility of one who has received from God a revelation to communicate to the rest.

Finally, the third thought drawn from today's readings: this project God has for liberating his people is transcendent. I think that I may even repeat too often this idea, but I'll never tire of doing it because we run the risk often of wanting to get out of present situations with immediate resolutions, and we forget that haste makes waste, that quick answers are patches but not true solutions. The true solution has to fit into the definitive plan of God. Every solution we seek — a better land distribution, a better administration and distribution of wealth in El Salvador, a political organization structured around the common good of Salvadorans — these must be sought always within the context of the definitive liberation.

Recently I was offered a very meaningful schema: that one who works in politics looks at temporal problems such as money, land, things, and can be content with but solving these problems; but the politician who has faith rises to God, and from God's point of view looks at how this present message that political people of today are trying to decipher should be regarded from God's perspective. . . .

Beautiful is the moment in which we understand that we are no more than an instrument of God; we live only as God wants us to live; we can do only as much as God makes us able to; we are only as intelligent as God would have us be. To place all these limitations in God's hands, to recognize that without God we can do nothing, is to have a sense, my beloved brothers and sisters, that a transcendent meaning of this time in El Salvador means to pray much, to be very united with God. . . .

We must continue to be mindful of how liberation must free us from sin. All evils have a common root, and it is sin. There are, in the human heart, egotisms, envies, idolatries, and it is from these that divisions and hoarding arise. As Christ said, "It is not what comes out from a man that defiles him, but rather what is in the human heart: evil thoughts." We must purify, then, this source of all slaveries. Why does slavery exist? Why is there margination? Why is illiteracy rampant? Why are there diseases? Why do people mourn in pain? All of these things are pointing out that sin does exist. . . .

That is why the transcendence of liberation lifts us from our sins, and the church will always be preaching: repent of your personal sins. And she will say as Christ did to the adulteress: I do not condemn you; you have repented, but do not sin again. How much I want to convince you, brothers and sisters, all those who see little importance in these intimate relations with God, that these things are important! It is not enough to say: I am an atheist, I don't believe in God; I do not offend him. Because it's not a question of what you believe, but objectively you have broken off relations with the source of all life. As long as you don't discover this, and you don't follow him, and you don't love him, you are a dislocated part away from the whole: and because of this you carry within yourself disorder, disunity, ingratitude, lack of faith, of community spirit. Without God, there can be no true concept of liberation. Temporary liberations, yes; but definitive, solid liberations — only people of faith can reach them. . . .

Paul says of Christ: "To know him and the strength of his resurrection and the communion with his sufferings, dying with his same death that I may arrive one day at the resurrection of the dead." Do you see how life recovers all of its meaning? And suffering then becomes a communion with Christ, the Christ that suffers, and death is a communion with the death that redeemed the world? Who can feel worthless before this treasure that one finds in Christ, that gives meaning to sickness, to pain, to oppression, to torture, to margination? No one is conquered, no one — even though they put you under the boot of oppression and of repression, whoever believes in Christ knows that he is a victor and that the definitive victory will be that of truth and justice!

440

Church Events

The first thing I announce to you today is that next Sunday we begin Holy Week and because of the present situation we will celebrate it here, in this basilica.

. . . I want to tell you ahead of time that we'd like to give our Good Friday Way of the Cross its full meaning of amendment, of renunciation, and of solidarity with which a Christian should meditate on the passion of Christ among a people who shoulder their own heavy cross. . . .

In Aguilares we celebrated the third anniversary of Fr. Rutilio Grande's assassination. It is obvious that the repression is having its effects — there were few people present; there is fear. It is an area martyred in the extreme. The message was that Christ's messenger must always find what Fr. Grande found, if he would be faithful.

In Tejutla, in the village of Los Martinez, we celebrated the village feast day. And there they told me of a terrible violation of human rights: on March 7 about midnight a truck filled with military men in civilian dress and some in uniform opened doors, pulling people out in a violent way with kicks and blows from rifle butts; they raped four young women, beat up their parents savagely, and threatened them that if they said anything about it they would have to bear the consequences. We have learned the tragedy of these poor young girls.

[Archbishop Romero recounted the incidents of torture and repression throughout El Salvador for each day of the week preceding his homily, listing the dead by name whenever possible. He followed this with a description of the daily ongoing events of the church.]

. . . And a pleasant note from our diocesan life is that a composer and poet has made for us a pretty hymn to our divine savior. We will start to learn it soon: "The explosive songs of joy vibrate. I'm going to the cathedral to join my people. A thousand voices are united on this day. To sing in celebration of our feast day." And so the stanzas go in whole heart with the people. The last one's very pretty: "But the gods of power and of money oppose that there be transfiguration. That's why you, Lord, are the first to raise the arm against oppression. . . ."

[The archbishop continued with a report on the severe violence of March 17 in response to a national strike, which made a strong statement against the military repression by paralyzing the economic activity of the country.]

The least that can be said is that the country is going through a prerevolutionary and by no means transitional stage. The basic question is how to come out of this critical stage in the least violent way. And on this point the main responsibility is that of the civilian, and notably, the military rulers. Let us hope that they will not be blinded by what they are doing with land reform; it may be a ruse that will block their view of the problem in its entirety. . . .

Beloved brothers and sisters, it would be interesting to analyze, but I don't want to abuse your time, what significance there is in these months of a new government that precisely wanted to draw us out of these horrible situations. And if what it wants to do is leave headless the organization of the people and obstruct the process that the people want, no other process can thrive. Without its roots in the people, no government can be effective — much less so when it seeks to impose itself by the force of bloodshed and pain.

I would like to appeal in a special way to the men of the army, and in particular to the troops of the National Guard, the Police, and the garrisons. Brothers, you belong to our own people. You kill your own brother peasants; and in the face of an order to kill that is given by a man, the law of God should prevail that says: Do not kill! No soldier is obliged to obey an order counter to the law of God. No one has to comply with an immoral law. It is time now that you recover your conscience and obey its dictates rather than the command of sin. The church, defender of the rights of God, of the law of God, of the dignity of the human person, cannot remain silent before so much abomination.

We want the government to seriously consider that reforms mean nothing when they come bathed in so much blood. Therefore, in the name of God, and in the name of this long-suffering people, whose laments rise to heaven every day more tumultuous, I beseech you, I beg you, I command you in the name of God: Cease the repression!

The church preaches your liberation just as we studied it today in the Holy Bible. A liberation that holds, above all, respect for human dignity, the salvation of the common good of the people, and the transcendence that looks above all else to God, and from God alone derives its hope and its strength.

GEOFFREY WAINWRIGHT

Preaching and Eucharist

In some Protestant traditions preaching plays so dominant a role in worship that liturgy and sacraments appear as preface or appendix to the sermon. Barth criticized the lack of proportion in Protestant worship, insisting that preaching derives its substance from the sacrament and means the same as the sacrament, "but in words." Geoffrey Wainwright, a British Methodist, professor of systematic theology at Duke Divinity School, and author of *Eucharist and Eschatology* and *Doxology*, underscores Barth's point and elaborates it. He draws an even closer parallel between preaching and the Eucharist in order to demonstrate that the homily is not merely located in the context of worship, but that it is a liturgical act itself. Such preaching is doxological, for it understands itself as a "reasonable service" to God, its primary "audience." In its concern to hear the Scripture, preaching is an exercise in anamnesis, or remembering. Just as the eucharistic anamnesis recites the mighty acts of God culminating in the resurrection, so preaching never forgets the story that shapes the church's life and hope. In the *epiclesis* [calling down] the celebrant (and preacher) invokes the power of the Holy Spirit on that which is to be enacted and said. Like Calvin, Wainwright assigns to the Holy Spirit the task of joining the remembered word to the present moment of faith. Throughout his analysis, Wainwright draws on the thought of John Chrysostom, the Eastern church's greatest exegete and preacher. The following is taken from the St. John Chrysostom Lectures delivered at the Holy Cross Greek Orthodox School of Theology, Brookline, Massachusetts, in November 1982.

Geoffrey Wainwright, "Preaching as Worship," *The Greek Orthodox Theological Review* 28, no. 4 (Winter 1983): 325-36.

The Second Vatican Council, in its Constitution on the Sacred Liturgy, restated what had always been in principle true: the homily is part of the liturgy itself. . . . The Easter narrative of the Emmaus pilgrims may already reflect a regular Sunday liturgy of the primitive church, in which the presence of the risen Lord is experienced through the reading and exposition of the Scriptures and the divine Stranger is known in the breaking of the mysterious bread. In my own Methodist tradition, the Wesley brothers took St. Luke's story in that way and made a present liturgical application in their *Hymns on the Lord's Supper:*

> O Thou who this mysterious bread
> Didst in Emmaus break,
> Return herewith our souls to feed,
> And to Thy followers speak.
>
> Unseal the volume of Thy grace,
> Apply the gospel word,
> Open our eyes to see Thy face,
> Our hearts to know the Lord.

Certainly word and sacrament belonged together in the Sunday assembly of the Christians by the time of St. Justin Martyr in the middle of the second century:

> And on the day called Sun-day an assembly is held in one place of all who live in town or country, and the records of the apostles or writings of the prophets are read for as long as time allows. Then, when the reader has finished, the president in a discourse admonishes and exhorts us to imitate these good things. Then we all stand up together and offer prayers; and as we said before, when we have finished praying, bread and wine and water are brought up, and the president likewise offers prayers and thanksgivings to the best of his ability, and the people assent, saying the Amen; and there is a distribution, and everyone participates in the elements over which thanks have been given; and they are sent through the deacons to those who are not present. (*Apol.* 1, 67)

In the vicissitudes of Christian history, the sermon has sometimes been shifted from its proper place within the liturgy and may even, in certain degenerate periods and places, have disappeared altogether from use, while in Protestantism the service of the word has often been robbed of its sacramental counterpart and context. But since the teaching and practice of the early church indicate that the homily is an integral component of the liturgy, it will be appropriate for us to consider preaching in the same theological categories as we use for Christian worship as such; and it may in return be the case that the sermon sheds light on the whole enterprise of Christian worship. Let us, therefore, try to examine preaching under four aspects which characterize the church's liturgy but which modern writers rarely bring to bear on the sermon. I want to suggest that preaching is, first, doxological; second, anamnetic; third, epicletic; and fourth, eschatological. In the first case, the most explicit divine reference will be to God the Father; in the second case, to the incarnate Word; in the third case, to the Holy Spirit; and the fourth and final part of this first lecture will unite these various hypostatic accents in a suitable trinitarian harmony which will have been implicitly present throughout to sensitive ears. At all stages we shall seek help from the Eastern church's greatest preacher, John Chrysostom.

The Doxological Character of Preaching

In his treatise *On the Priesthood* [6,5], St. John Chrysostom declares that "all these various [duties of the priest] have one goal in view: the glory of God and upbuilding of the church." Elsewhere this twin aim is ascribed by him to the preacher in particular, who as God's servant must have his mouth opened, and the word supplied, "for his glory and your edification." Such texts find their broad ecclesiological grounding in the liturgically framed passage of 1 Peter 2:4-10: By the very fact of being "built into a spiritual house, to be a holy priesthood, to offer spiritual sacrifices acceptable to God through Jesus Christ," Christians are "declaring the excellencies of Him who called you out of darkness into His marvelous light." And contrariwise, by proclaiming the mighty acts of God we are constituting a living temple for worship of God. It is, however, not to St. Peter but to St. Paul that the preacher of Antioch and Constantinople looks for an example in his own priestly duty of preaching; and we may go with John Chrysostom to his apostolic instructor.

The Apostle to the Gentiles several times envisages his evangelism in liturgical terms. At the very end, he wrote to Timothy: "I am already on the point of being sacrificed; the time of my departure has come" (2 Tim. 4:6). The martyrdom which St. Paul expected was but the culmination of an apostolate marked by "afflictions, hardships, calamities, beatings, imprisonments, tumults, labors, watching, hunger" (2 Cor. 6:4-5). He bore on his body the marks of Jesus (Gal. 6:17). In the trials of apostleship Paul believed that he was "carrying in the body the death of Jesus": "While we live we are always being given up to death for Jesus' sake, so that the life of Jesus may be manifested in our mortal

445

flesh. So death is at work in us, but life in you" (2 Cor. 4:7-12). The cultic roots of this sacrificial language become unmistakable when the Apostle writes to the Philippians: "Even if I am to be poured out as a libation upon the sacrificial offering of your faith, I am glad and rejoice with you all" (Phil. 2:17). The self-spending of the gospel-preacher is part of the larger offering that includes the converts' faith. . . .

The Apostle's personal sacrifice finds its verbal counterpart in his preaching. To the Romans St. Paul says: "On some points I have written to you very boldly, by way of reminder, because of the grace given me by God to be a minister *(leitourgon)* of Christ Jesus to the Gentiles in the priestly service of the gospel of God, so that the offering of the Gentiles may be acceptable, sanctified by the Holy Spirit" (Rom. 15:15-16). In interpreting that text, Chrysostom places these words in the Apostle's mouth: "My priesthood consists in preaching and proclaiming; this is the sacrifice I offer"; and he develops the image by borrowing from Ephesians 6:17: "the sword of the Spirit, which is the word of God." The offering of the Gentiles — it matters little exegetically whether the genitive is objective or subjective — is their "obedience," which is "the obedience of faith" (Rom. 1:5). When, in response to the preacher's message, conversions are made, the eucharistic chorus is thereby augmented (see 2 Cor. 4:13-15).

John Chrysostom rightly concludes from the presence of the verb *latreuo* that St. Paul in Romans 1:9 conceives of his evangelizing activity as itself the worship of God: "For God is my witness, to whom I render spiritual worship in proclaiming the gospel of his Son, that without ceasing I mention you always in my prayers. . . ." In the sermon he preached at his ordination to the presbyterate, it is not on his prayers for the congregation that Chrysostom concentrates; and the future "doctor of the eucharist" does not so much as mention the sacrament. Rather the sermon itself, which God has put into his mouth, is returned to God as "an offering of first fruits," "a sacred hymn of praise": "What kind of a sacrifice is the word, someone may ask. It is a great and august sacrifice, better than all others." Elsewhere he calls the closing doxology of the sermon a "fitting end." It is so because it recalls the direction of the whole sermon toward God.

No more than the Apostle is the later preacher alone in his sacrifice. Just as St. Paul's sacrificial evangelism drew the Gentiles into the obedient offering of themselves to God, so it would be fair to see John Chrysostom — by now preaching to the at least half converted — as leading the congregation in and into the "sacrifice of praise, the tribute of lips that acknowledge God's name" (Heb. 13:15). The *sacrificium laudis* is traditionally identified with the Eucharist proper, but it may also be appropriate to notice here some words of Chrysostom concerning the Psalms as used in Israel's and the church's worship: "At one and the same time, God receives praise and the singers receive an instruction to guide their life and lead them to exact knowledge of the truths of faith." Just so with preaching. Not only are the sermons of Chrysostom hymns of praise; they are constantly concerned to help his hearers confess the true faith in the face of heretics and unbelievers and, perhaps above all, to lead a Christian life.

In this last way, preaching is also indirectly doxological in that it is an encouragement to doxological living. Immediately after speaking of the sacrifice of praise, the Letter to the Hebrews continues: "Do not neglect to do good and to share what you have, for such sacrifices are pleasing to God" (13:16). According to St. Paul, "your body is a temple of the Holy Spirit within you, which you have from God. You are not your own; you were bought with a price. So glorify God in your body" (1 Cor. 6:18-20; cf. 2 Cor. 6:16–7:1). Conversely, the Apostle identifies sin with idolatry in Romans 1:18-32, Colossians 3:5, and Ephesians 5:5. The most classical of the texts on ethical sacrifice, however, is probably Romans 12:1-2: "I appeal to you therefore, brethren, by the mercies of God, to present your bodies as a living sacrifice, holy and acceptable to God, which is your spiritual worship *(logikēn latreian)*. Do not be conformed to this world but be transformed by the renewal of your mind, that you may prove what is the will of God, what is good and acceptable and perfect." Preaching has its part to play in the renewing of minds to discern the will of God for the living of lives acceptable to God. The transformation of the believer means an end to conformity with this world. Ethically distinguishable behavior contributes to the Christian witness in a pagan environment. John Chrysostom, who often exhorted his hearers to works of charity, would doubtless have approved of the use of Matthew 5:16 at the almsgiving in the communion office of the English Book of Common Prayer: "Let your light so shine before men, that they may see your good works, and glorify your Father which is in heaven." There we move into the area of what contemporary Orthodox theology has started to call "the liturgy after the Liturgy."

For the moment, however, we must return to the Liturgy itself and consider the anamnetic moment of preaching.

The Anamnetic Character of Preaching

The earthly church needs constantly to be reminded of the gospel on which it is founded and which continues to shape its life. That gospel is embodied in the teaching, person, and work of Jesus Christ, the incarnate Word of God and now the exalted Lord; and the definitive written testimony to the gospel is contained in the prophetic books of the Old Testament and the apostolic books of the New.

The Scriptures continue to be read in church; and in and through their reading, as Chrysostom recognizes, the Lord makes himself present. But just as the incarnation itself and the provision of the Scriptures represent a divine condescension and accommodation to the human condition, so a further *sunkatabasis* takes place in the preaching. For while the Scriptures are, Chrysostom holds, in themselves perspicuous, yet human slowness to understand requires the Lord to speak even through the interpretive words of the preacher [see R. Kaczynski, *Das Wort Gottes in Liturgie und Alltag der Gemeinden des Johannes Chrysostomos* (Freiburg im Breisgou, 1974), pp. 283-86].

The first task of the preacher, as far as his human audience is concerned, is to expound the Scriptures in their witness to Christ. Modern people will sympathize with Chrysostom's stress — typical of the Antiochene school of exegesis — on the historical sense of the text. Postmodernists will perhaps welcome his recognition, from time to time, that the historical sense may itself have been metaphorical from the first. What will scare our critical scholars in their concern for a narrowly conceived academic integrity is the patristic insistence that faith, prayer, and conversion, as well as careful study, are necessary for the understanding of the Scriptures: "Both a thorough search and persistent prayer are needed," Chrysostom tells the expositor [*Homilia* 21 (20), 1 *in Joannem*]; and he requires of the congregation that they first confess their sins, for otherwise their eye of faith will be dimmed and their ears blocked for the hearing of the word of God.

Certainly the preacher himself must go on learning from the Scriptures, just as Timothy needed to continue learning from St. Paul. But he will not do this in an isolated way. Doubtless the preacher will spend time in private preparation of his sermon; but it will be as one who participates regularly in the liturgy and is steeped in its spirit, and as one who must deliver the sermon precisely in the framework of the liturgy. The liturgy is the connatural context for the interpretation of the Scriptures [*Doxology*, ch. 5]. So much of the Bible originated in the worship of Israel and of the primitive church.

It was, above all, their reading in church which secured the recognition of these particular writings as canonical. It is only by their continued use in the worship of the church that the Scriptures have retained their status as holy books rather than now being treated, if at all, as more or less interesting pieces of ancient literature. The worshiping community supplies a living continuity down the centuries for transmitting the great images and themes of Scriptures which might otherwise have become unintelligible through external cultural changes. The constant features and qualitative wholeness of the liturgy also provide the stability and unity within which to come to terms with the highly diverse material of the Bible.

John Chrysostom was in fact deeply concerned for the integrity of the Bible. Selective exegesis was the mark of heretics. He himself delighted in drawing instruction from the seemingly most unlikely passages of Scripture. He aimed at making his hearers familiar with the biblical material. He complained that some of them knew the names of the horses at the local racetrack better than the names of the churches to which St. Paul wrote his epistles. In discovering the riches of the Scriptures the congregation needed to cooperate with the preacher. The preacher digs for the hidden treasures, draws the water from the well, prepares the table and offers the food and drink, sows the seed. The congregation must come hungering and thirsting, must prepare the ground and allow the fruit to grow in their lives, must put what they have acquired to work with interest.

This devotion to the entirety of Scripture and the determination to exploit it in every part nevertheless raises certain questions. By Chrysostom's time it appears that certain biblical passages or books had become traditional reading at appropriate feasts or seasons; but at other periods of the year and on other occasions it was the preacher's choice of text which determined the public lessons. This latter responsibility has been much prized in some Protestant circles; but while the circumstances of a congregation or an event in its life can call for an appropriate text from Scripture, there is a real danger that the congregation's exposure to the Bible will be limited to a particular preacher's preferred passages, perhaps idiosyncratically interpreted. Protestant moves toward the long-standing practice in the more catholic churches of following a lectionary cycle are therefore welcome. Lectionaries themselves, however, do not drop down directly from heaven, and their choice of texts is not immutable. Luther's key to the Scriptures — *"was Christum treibt"* [that which promotes Christ] — has not only an objective side to it but also a more subjective: it appears that in different times and places, different parts of Scripture serve better than others to advance Christ. After the thoroughgoing revisions of the lectionaries in the Roman and other Western churches in the past two decades, which were much influenced by the biblical theology movement of the 1950s, it is interesting that the 1977 Prague consultation on "The Role and Place of the Bible in the Liturgical and Spiritual Life of the Orthodox Church" should declare an openness to the "examination of possible changes in the pericope of evangelical and apostolic readings prescribed for Sundays and feasts of the year. For in these days multitudes of God's people assemble who, because of the incompleteness and monotony of the pericope, are deprived of the possibility to listen to the Word of God and its interpretation in its fullness" (Ion Bria, ed., *Martyria/Mission*, pp. 235f). It is not only a question of the amount of Scripture that can be absorbed over a recurring cycle of time. It is also — if I may say so as a preacher

— a matter of the *combination* of the readings from the various parts of Scripture; for new juxtapositions can cause freshly illuminating sparks to fly among the appointed texts.

In this second section of the lecture we have been concentrating on the preacher's business with the Scriptures in their witness to the historic self-revelation of God in Jesus Christ; but this irreversible given is only one pole in the hermeneutical ellipse. The preacher must interpret the gospel *in the present situation*. The word needs the vivifying Spirit. Anamnesis requires elaboration.

The Epicletic Character of Preaching

The preacher's connection with the Scriptures and his connection with the present situation are different in kind and quality. He is *bound* to the Scriptures but he need only *refer* to the present situation. . . . If, as Karl Barth hinted, one almost has to preach with the Bible in one hand and the newspaper in the other, yet there is no doubt that the Bible weighs heavier than even an American Sunday newspaper. No single sermon can conceivably count as much as the definitive witness to Christ in the Scriptures. No human situation has the permanence of the word of God. Nevertheless the same Holy Spirit who rested upon the incarnate Son and who presided over the composition of the Scriptures is appropriately invoked upon the preacher and his sermon.

St. John Chrysostom more than once recalls the gift of the Holy Spirit which the preacher presbyter has received through the laying on of hands at his ordination. He takes the exchange of greetings between preacher and people at the start of the sermon to echo that gift: "The Lord be with you"/"And with thy spirit." Chrysostom frequently begs his congregation to pray for their preacher. The people's prayer for the preacher is finally to their own advantage, since his words are intended for them. The Holy Spirit's help is needed in order to discern *which* word from Scripture needs to be proclaimed at a particular time, and in order that it may be preached with a power that transcends human words (cf. 1 Thess. 1:5).

Effective preaching to a concrete situation demands a "reading" of that situation. Here the cooperation between preacher and people is most valuable. Since Pentecost, there is a sense in which all the Lord's people have indeed become prophets (cf. Num. 11:29). The faithful have the responsibility to read "the signs of the times." Through their very multiplicity and variety, believers have the opportunity to penetrate to levels and areas of human society which cannot be reached by the individual preacher or even by a whole college of preachers. By a service of information and discussion, all the members of the church can help their preacher to see the straws in the wind, the smoke that betokens a fire. The preacher then has the responsibility of bringing the word of God to bear on the great issues of the age, particularly as they affect the company of believers. John Chrysostom's series of sermons after the storming of the statues by the turbulent population of Antioch in 387 may serve as an example of sound pastoral advice in a difficult political situation. He was later removed from the see of Constantinople when he incurred the displeasure of the Empress Eudoxia by rebuking her imperial conduct.

Times may change, but the joys and sorrows, the hopes and fears of human beings remain fairly constant. Like many less important figures in the history of the church, Chrysostom was subjected to the complaint that, though he was a fine preacher, he failed to visit his people. What a preacher lacks in rhetorical skills may often be made up in sensitive pastoral care. That experience, in which the Holy Spirit is also present, will likely enhance the preacher's power to touch hearts and minds with a simple statement of the gospel. To interpret a difficult world for a troubled soul is often to change that world by the transfiguring light of God's kingdom.

The Eschatological Character of Preaching

In an essay "Towards a Catholic Use of Hermeneutics," Edward Schillebeeckx has criticized Bultmann for treating the Bible as simply a text, a closed "deposit," on which we draw again and again in the narrow point of the present for the existential possibilities it expresses. The Flemish Dominican writes:

> Everything to which the Bible bears witness is directed towards the fulfillment in the future of God's promise, the history of which has been narrated in faith in the Bible. It is possible to express our understanding of the Bible this way: we should not look back at the Bible, but rather look forward, with the Bible, to a future which is given us to be achieved — to be achieved, but also *given us* to be achieved. . . . What biblical interpretation "points to" . . . must be orthodoxy (the correct interpretation of the promise insofar as it has already been realized in the past) as the basis of orthopraxis whereby the promise realizes a new future in us. It is only in the sphere of action — of doing in the faith — that orthodox interpretation can be inwardly fulfilled. . . . There certainly is a "deposit of faith," but its content still remains, on the basis of the promise already realized in Christ (realized in fact, but nonetheless still really a *promise*), a promise-for-us, with the result that interpretation becomes orientated to praxis. The Bible

451

reminds us of God's faithfulness in the past, precisely in order to arouse our confidence in God's faithfulness in the future. [*God, the Future of Man* (London, 1969), pp. 1-49, esp. pp. 36f]

In the anaphora of St. John Chrysostom, the *anamnesis* opens out to the final advent of Christ and the fullness of the divine kingdom:

We therefore, remembering this saving commandment and all the things that were done for us: the cross, the tomb, the resurrection on the third day, the ascension into heaven, the session at the right hand, the second and glorious coming again; offering you your own from your own, in all and through all: we offer you also this reasonable and bloodless sacrifice, and we beseech and pray and entreat you, send down your Holy Spirit on us and on these gifts set forth; and make this bread the precious body of your Christ, changing it by your Holy Spirit, and that which is in this cup the precious blood of your Christ, changing it by your Holy Spirit, so that they may become to those who partake for vigilance of soul, for forgiveness of sins, for fellowship with the Holy Spirit, for the fullness of the kingdom, for boldness toward you, and not for judgment or for condemnation.

John Chrysostom the preacher was well aware of the trinitarian origins of the teaching office. The preacher is called by God to a ministry stemming from Christ, into which one is set by the Holy Ghost. As the herald and ambassador of God, the preacher has the task of building up the faith of the eucharistic community to the glory of God. Through the Eucharist, believers are sacramentally maintained in the communion of the Holy Spirit whom they received in their baptisms as the *arrabōn* of their promised inheritance. In the eucharistic communion they experience by anticipation the final *parousia* of Christ and enjoy a foretaste of the messianic banquet in the kingdom. In the anaphora they join with the whole company of heaven in worship before the throne of God.

At the last judgment, the preacher, priest, and pastor will be called to account for their ministry. Who is sufficient for these things? The preacher stands under the same word as his hearers. He must dare to hope that the grace of which he has been the unworthy minister will not be denied him either.

WILLIAM H. WILLIMON

Baptismal Speech

William Willimon is Dean of the Chapel at Duke University and Professor of Christian Ministry at Duke Divinity School. He is a generalist in his approach to theology and ministry. A prolific author, his wide-ranging expertise includes topics as diverse as Christian worship, the sacraments, pastoral care, marriage, Bible study, prayer, and preaching. Perhaps no other contemporary author enjoys the confidence of rank-and-file pastors as fully as Will Willimon, whose *Worship as Pastoral Care* was selected as one of the ten most useful books for pastors by the Academy of Parish Clergy in 1979. He is also the author of *Acts* (a commentary), the co-author of *Resident Aliens,* and the co-editor of the *Concise Encyclopedia of Preaching.* He is a longtime editor-at-large for the *Christian Century,* where his lively articles and commentaries have won him a faithful readership. Willimon has spent the past eighteen years preaching in a university chapel to a "mixed" congregation of townspeople, tourists, academics, and students. In both his preaching and his contributions to homiletics, Willimon has sought to defamiliarize Christianity, that is, to strip it of its cultural associations in order to depict its distinctive or "peculiar" character. That character is threefold: (1) the sermon is about God and not human experience; (2) the message is conveyed in its own language and not "translated" into the idioms of psychology or politics; (3) its authority is grounded in the worshiping community and not in the privacy of individual opinion. Using irony and humor, Willimon skillfully separates the hearer from his or her most cherished religious assumptions, thereby preparing his audience for the surprising shock of the Good News.

William H. Willimon, *Peculiar Speech: Preaching to the Baptized* (Grand Rapids: Eerdmans, 1992), pp. 4-11.

It has long been said by the church that, because worship is an act of the church, and because the church is before all else a community at worship before God in Christ, worship precedes theological reflection and subordinates it. Worship is not an "authority" or "source for theology"; it is the ontological condition of theology, the font out of which proper understanding of the *kerygma* (proclamation) arises. This was expressed in the old patristic position, *Legem credendi lex statuat supplicandi.* (The law of prayer precedes the law of belief.)

The church's worship is nothing other than the church's faith in motion, both in its most sublime and on its most practical levels. The worship of a church does not merely reflect the church's faith but actualizes it concretely in a sustained manner across the generations and in an irreducible way. Worship is the scripture's home rather than its stepchild. The Bible is the church's first liturgical book. Preaching is best conceived of as an act of worship, the precedent of and a commentary upon baptism.

To speak among the baptized, those who are dying and being raised (Romans 6:4), is to enter into a world of odd communication and peculiar speech. Baptismal speech need not conform to the reasons of this world (Romans 12:2). Conversation among the baptized is ecclesial in nature, political. A peculiar *polis* is being formed here, a family, a holy nation, a new people where once there was none (the images are all baptismal, 1 Peter 2:9).

Forgetting the baptismal context of our preaching, we risk distorting the gospel into an intellectual dilemma: how can modern, twentieth-century people believe a first-century Jew? It becomes a matter of subjective affirmation ("this seems right to me"), or of nodding whenever our particular gender, racial, or cultural button is pushed. But the gospel is none of these.

Rather, in baptism, we are subsumed into a story of water and the word. A story of creation formed out of dark waters. A story of a God so righteous that he was willing to make war on the world he created, only to hang up his bow and to promise never to give up on us again. A story of a people, created out of nothing, by a God determined to be worshipped rightly, led through waters into the desert as imperial chariots foundered. A story of a Jewish woman visited by God in a way that confounded her fiancé, but caused her to sing. A story of a crazy man out in the desert proclaiming a new kingdom coming in water and fire. A story of one who saved by an issue of water and blood.

As Augustine noted, water is water. "The word is added to the element, and there results the Sacrament, as if itself also a kind of visible word." Water set next to the word, next to *this* story, is called baptism. Luther, following Augustine, emphasized that baptism "is not merely water, but water used according to God's command and connected with God's word."

Christian preaching brings out or brings into view the mystery inherent in the waters of baptism. Baptismal preaching names the reality to which we have all been exposed, that is, the peculiar salvation of this crucified God. Therefore baptismal preaching is not so much a matter of being didactic, of explaining something, as it is of testifying to something, struggling to describe an event that has already happened to the congregation, bringing into view the significance of our baptism with words.

The theology of the church is the church's attempt to speak of the change wrought in itself through baptism. As Thomas C. Oden has said, "Christian theology fundamentally began as a lengthy set of footnotes on the baptismal formula which preceded all deliberate Christian doctrinal formulation. All the heresies against which early pastoral care had to struggle were essentially offenses against the baptismal formula" (*Ministry through Word and Sacrament,* Crossroad, 1989, p. 110).

One of the reasons why "the language of preaching is essentially metaphorical" (David Buttrick, *Homiletic,* Fortress, 1987, p. 125) is not just that people enjoy the use of metaphor but rather that an act like baptism sets the tone and determines the mode for Christian communication. Speech must fit that which it attempts to describe.

To preach among the baptized or the being baptized is to operate within *a domain of distinctive discourse.* We talk differently here, work within a certain "language game" to which everyone here subscribes for the duration of the conversation. The language is rooted in the elemental narrative testimony: "Do you not know that all of us who have been baptized into Christ Jesus were baptized into his death? Therefore we have been buried with him by baptism into death, so that, just as Christ was raised from the dead by the glory of the Father, so we too might walk in newness of life" (Romans 6:3-4).

A distinctive identity arises from this distinctive community of discourse. There is politics in our preaching. I am troubled by preaching that won't come clean on its politics. We speak of expository preaching, or narrative preaching, story preaching, inductive, deductive preaching as if preaching were mainly a matter of method, of style, as if nothing political were at stake in the mode of our communication, as if no particular people were congregating due to our speaking, as if being Christian were synonymous with being a good human being who speaks conventional imperial English but with a certain accent.

No matter our style of preaching, there is no way for us preachers to weasel out of the baptismal truth that we preach within a distinctive universe of discourse. We talk funny.

Last fall we had a panel discussion on "Homosexuality and the Church." (Who told us to call people "homosexual"? A nineteenth-century Viennese psychotherapist who wrote a book arguing that there were males, females, and a third sex, homosexuals. What on earth are we talking about when we talk this way? Why would the church be interested in such labeling of people?) After the discussion, a young man came up to me saying that he was "a baptized Episcopalian" and "none of you have a right to tell me who I am. I define myself."

I noted that if his first declaration were true ("I am a baptized Episcopalian"), his second was false. In baptizing this young man the church was quite clear, or at least should have been clear (false advertising is so wrong), that we were telling him who he was, namely a cherished child of God who was washed, gifted, chosen, called, and named.

Not knowing who names us is a tragic plight. The uncalled life is an empty one. Identity is too important a matter to be left to individuals. Why we believe this to be true requires the telling of a story that is baptismal.

Our speech becomes corrupted, not only by Viennese psychotherapists but also in church assemblies. What are we to do with a church that speaks to people on the basis of their gender or race, all the while baptizing them on the basis of Galatians 3:28? "Before faith came, we were confined under the law, kept under restraint. . . . But now that faith has come, we are no longer under a custodian. . . . For as many of you as were baptized into Christ have put on Christ. There is neither Jew nor Greek, there is neither slave nor free, there is neither male nor female; for you are all one in Christ Jesus" (Galatians 3:23, 25, 27-28, RSV).

When Christians are invited to say something about social justice, we begin by saying "church," which is to say "baptism": "For indeed we were all brought into one body by baptism, in the one Spirit, whether we are Jews or Greeks, whether slaves or free, and that one Holy Spirit was poured out for all of us to drink" (1 Corinthians 12:13, NEB). Poured out for *all* to drink, no matter race, gender, class, or sexual orientation. "Now that faith has come" (Galatians 3:25) we speak differently to one another than when we were kept under restraint by the custodian of quotas, gender issues, and ethnic pride.

In the words of John Alsup, by these baptismal texts "we are invited to imagine the New as life in the flesh where the latter is not the dominant reality for the people of faith" ("Imagining the New: Feminism, Galatians 3:28 and the Current Interpretive Discussion," *Austin Seminary Review,* pp. 92-108). In baptism, it is not so much that worldly labels like race or gender are washed away as that we recapitulate creation and become new as if in the primal waters of creation, dying to our old selves and rising to newness of life.

We preachers need not be embarrassed by the distinctiveness of our speech. It is rooted in primordial narrative. "The sea roared," "the wind of God moved over the face of the waters" (Genesis 1:2). "The waters prevailed. . . . everything on the dry land in whose nostrils was the breath of life died" (Genesis 7:20, 22, RSV).

At the university, when we attempt to address the factors that divide us we must rely on language speaking of "multiculturalism," or "the value of diversity," or "pluralism" in an attempt to put a happy face on our fragmentation. Though such speech is devoid of power to transform or even adequately to describe the depth of our divisions it's the best we can do at a place like the university, which knows not the baptismal phenomenon behind Galatians 3. You stay out of my "culture" and I'll stay out of yours. We call it "tolerance," but it is another name for loneliness.

So the preacher need not always be looking over her shoulder, justifying pulpit rhetoric according to some other criterion. Lacking confidence in the power of our story to effect that of which it speaks, to evoke a new people out of nothing, our communication loses its nerve. Nothing is said that could not be heard elsewhere, nobody need die and be raised to assimilate the speech of the Empire or its universities.

Unfortunately, most of the theology I learned in seminary was in the translation mode. Take this biblical image and translate it into something more palatable to people who use Cuisinarts. The modern church has been willing to use everyone's language but its own. In conservative contexts, gospel speech is traded for dogmatic assertion and moralism, for self-help psychologies and narcotic mantras. In more liberal speech, talk tiptoes around the outrage of Christian discourse and ends up as an innocuous, though urbane, affirmation of the ruling order. Unable to preach Christ and him crucified, we preach humanity and it improved. As Walter Brueggemann said, when the preacher is uncertain about speech, a great deal of energy is expended reassuring the listener that nothing will be said that would require conversion in order to be understood, certainly nothing that would be regarded by cultured despisers as either foolish or weak. By the time most of us finish qualifying the scandal of Christian speech, very little can be said by the preacher that can't be heard elsewhere.

To categorize preaching as distinctive baptismal speech is to part company with advocates of linguistic accommodation like David Tracy, who argues (in his books like *Plurality and Ambiguity*) that our speech must bow to what he calls "public criteria." Tracy says, "the demand for public criteria for truth-claims remains both the initial impetus and the great hope for all contemporary theology" (*The Christian Century,* Oct. 10, 1990, p. 901). He is surely right about the desire for "public speech" as the great hope of contemporary theology. Yet Tracy is surely wrong in his claim that when ecclesial speech takes its own distinctiveness seriously it becomes private and introverted in a way in which Tracy's speech is not. Tracy claims to fight "obscurantism" and "mystification" — two terms not used by too wide a "public," I daresay. In reality his is the privileged talk of the academy, and one branch of the fragmented academy at that. All energy is expended upon consideration of method as if we could find a method of talking that would enable us to bypass having to admit that, as Christians (or as university professors), our talk arises out of our account of the world, out of a story that is not universal.

So when Tracy speaks of the need to defend "reason" he acts as if there really is some innate, noncontingent, universal human attribute called "reason" as opposed to contingent, story-dependent activities like baptismal speech. No. Tracy's "reason" is a way of talking about the world in the hope that our communities, our traditions, our stories don't matter. (If that were true, why doesn't Tracy's reason sound more "reasonable" outside the confines of The University of Chicago?) We keep hoping that we could find some universal speech, some universal, contextless attribute like "reason" that would enable us to organize the world without having to take our differences seriously.

When Christians are asked to say something "reasonable," we say something like, "Repent!" or "Join Up," or "You must be born again." Why we speak thus is rationality that can only be understood by reference to a story that is baptismal. We must not degrade those who misunderstand us by claiming that they are dumb or unreasonable. They simply have not yet heard the story that makes our Christian speech intelligible.

Baptismal speech is every bit as "public" as Tracy's Chicago "analogic imagination." It's just that, when we talk in public, we Christians expect to be honest about the narrative, communal basis of our speech, whereas most advocates of "reason" do not. Baptismal speaking reminds us that very little speech makes sense apart from a narrative and a community that makes it make sense.

CHARLES L. CAMPBELL

Building Up the Church

Charles L. Campbell is Associate Professor of Homiletics at Columbia Theological Seminary in Decatur, Georgia. He obtained his theological training at Yale and Duke universities, where he fully integrated his interests in theology, ethics, and homiletics. These studies culminated in his important first book, *Preaching Jesus*. Campbell's homiletic is strongly reflective of the "Yale School" of theology, especially the work of Hans Frei (1922-1988) and George Lindbeck, both of whom exposed the shortcomings of theological liberalism and historical biblical criticism and pointed the church in a new direction. Frei radically criticized the historicist quest for the "real" Jesus, as if Jesus enjoys some other life outside that which is rendered by the church's narrative Scripture and its worship. Those renderings mediate his presence to the church (and preacher) in a way that liberalism never quite divined. The point of theology (and preaching) is not to find analogies or illustrations of Jesus in the world, as if the essence of Jesus lies just beyond our experience, but to *render* him and his presence among us, much as the four Evangelists do. Hence the title of Campbell's book is not *Preaching "About" Jesus*. It is not the preacher's job to find words that correlate with or substitute for the language of faith — the modernist enterprise of Tillich, Bultmann, and many others — but to contribute to the formation of the church by teaching it to speak its *own* language, which is its distinctive witness in the world. This was Lindbeck's argument for the "cultural-linguistic" mode of theological discourse outlined in *The Nature of Doctrine*. Armed with these theological principles, Campbell conducts a searching critique of popular "narrative preaching," finding that for the most part it has remained within the orbit of historicism, psychology, and personal experience and thereby failed to render the narrative identity of Jesus Christ.

Charles L. Campbell, *Preaching Jesus: New Directions for Homiletics in Hans Frei's Postliberal Theology* (Grand Rapids: Eerdmans, 1997), pp. 221-25, 228-31, 232-34, 236-37.

459

[E arlier] I discussed the individualistic orientation of the contemporary homiletical emphasis on experiential events. Contrary to this general tendency, Hans Frei's cultural-linguistic model of Christianity moves preaching in a more communal direction. Guided by Frei's work, the preacher's task must be seen not as that of creating experiential events for individual hearers, but rather as that of building up the church. In "grammatical" terms, one might say that God in Jesus Christ is not primarily the predicate of individual human needs or experience, but rather the active subject who gathers and builds up the eschatological people of God in and for the world. Within the context of Frei's postliberal theology, this grammar governs the peculiar speech of preaching. The function of preaching is not that of locating individual human needs and then offering God as an answer or solution to them — the issue in liberal, problem-solving preaching (including some of its newer narrative and inductive forms). Rather, the sermon moves from the identity of Jesus Christ to the "upbuilding" of the church.

Before delineating the ways in which Frei's work moves homiletics in this communal direction and suggesting some of the concrete implications for preaching, I need to clarify my choice of the image "building up," which I am intentionally using instead of the more popular term, "formation." "Building up" *(oikodomein/oikodome)* is an important image in the biblical idiom; it is part of the peculiar speech the church needs to learn to speak. Because of its communal, messianic, eschatological, and apocalyptic dimensions, *oikodomein* is not translated very well into the more domesticated term, "formation."

Although it is not my purpose to provide a complete exegetical study of *oikodomein,* a general look at some characteristics of the use of the word in Scripture may be helpful. The Old Testament roots of the image go back to the prophets, particularly Jeremiah, and emphasize the building up of the people of Israel, usually within an eschatological context. The image is often used in parallel to the image of planting and in contrast with that of tearing down or pulling up.

In the Gospels, which draw on this Old Testament background, the image is thoroughly communal and takes on strong messianic and eschatological dimensions. *Oikodomein* is an eschatological act of the Messiah, who will build up the future temple and the new community. The stress is on the activity of the Messiah, with some tension between the final building up at the time of *parousia* and the present building up through the eschatological power of the resurrection. This tension is the eschatological tension between the "already" and the "not yet."

In Acts the image takes on a strong "ecclesiastical ring" and is used somewhat differently from the Synoptics. The messianic emphasis is not as strong;

God, rather than the Messiah, does the building; and the image of the "heavenly building" is not central. Nevertheless, the communal and eschatological dimensions remain. "The subject is God and the object is Israel or the community. The reference is to a fellowship. The totality grows and is built up with a spiritual and eschatological reference" [*Theological Dictionary of the New Testament,* vol. 5, p. 139].

The image really comes to the fore in the Pauline literature, where it not only serves as an image for Paul's apostolic activity, which involves establishing and building up the community, but also is highlighted as a task of the entire church. The gifts of the Spirit are given for the upbuilding of the church, and the image is used particularly with reference to preaching and exhortation. This "building up" is "the content and purpose of the [church's] liturgical life and its meetings." Here the tensive character of *oikodomein* is evident. "Building up" is not only the work of God through the power of the resurrection and the activity of the Spirit, but also the task of the community of faith through the gifts of the Spirit. Another frequent translation is "edification," but this term, because of its associations with individual spiritual growth, also fails to capture very well the eschatological and communal dimensions of *oikodomein.* While the object of this building up includes the individual, its purpose is the incorporation of that individual brother or sister into the life of the community.

Recently, a growing body of literature dealing with the ecclesial "household" *(oikos/oikia)* has highlighted the social, economic, and political dimensions of the community of faith. The upbuilding of the church thus should not be considered simply a spiritual matter, but rather involves the building up of a concrete, publicly enacted society — a genuinely political community, or *polis.*

My use of "building up" thus seeks to capture the richness of preaching in an eschatological, communal context, which is precisely the context in which preaching takes place among the baptized people of God gathered for worship on the Lord's Day. In addition, my use of "building up" serves as a reminder of the richness and distinctiveness of the biblical idiom, which is not easily translated into contemporary terminology. "Building up" is an image that finds its proper use not in the language of American culture, but in the particular story of God's active creation of a people — past, present, and future. Engaging in this "building up" is one of the primary ways the church participates in and carries forward that story.

In addition, the image of "building up" helps to clarify the practice of preaching at its most basic level. Preaching is basically a "practice of constituting a people." As Alasdair MacIntyre writes, ". . . the creation and sustaining of human communities — and of households, cities, nations — is generally taken to be a practice in the sense in which I have defined it" [*After Virtue,* 2nd ed.

(Notre Dame, Ind.: University of Notre Dame Press, 1984), pp. 187-88]. Approaching preaching as this kind of communal practice will go a long way toward reshaping homiletical theory and Sunday-morning sermons.

Moreover, Frei suggests that this upbuilding of the church is the central function of preaching. In *The Identity of Jesus Christ* Frei moves immediately from his rendering of the identity of Jesus to a discussion of the publicly enacted identity of the church. Jesus' presence and action in the world, which is the presence and action of God, is indirectly embodied in the church through the presence and action of the Spirit. The church is now the spatial and temporal basis of the presence of Jesus in the world. The church, that is, embodies Jesus' indirect presence in and for the world. Or, as Frei thinks is better, "the church is simply the witness to the fact that it is Jesus Christ and none other who is the ultimate presence in and to the world. . . ." In Frei's thought there is an integral, narratively rendered relationship between Jesus and the church. . . .

This intimate, narratively rendered relationship between the identity of Jesus and the church can be seen in the way Frei applies the same categories of identity description to the church that he uses in his identity description of Jesus. The church's identity is derived from Jesus' identity and is enacted publicly in the world as Jesus' was. Although Frei does make two important distinctions between Jesus and the church, each of these distinctions actually serves to emphasize the inseparable relationship between the two and to highlight Frei's move from Jesus to the community of faith. First, the church must be a follower, rather than a complete reiteration, of Jesus. Jesus has enacted the good of all people on their behalf once and for all; the church has no need to play the role of Christ figure. Rather, the church is called to be a "collective disciple," to "follow at a distance" the pattern of Christ's intentional action that is narrated in the Gospels. Second, the church's intention-action pattern differs from that of Jesus because the church's story is not yet finished.

Frei thus moves from the narratively rendered identity of Jesus to the church, which is the embodiment of and witness to Jesus' indirect presence in and for the world. Frei does not move to the private, affective life of individuals; indeed, he says almost nothing about individuals. Nor does Frei turn to general human experience as the key correlate of the gospel message. Nor, except through the church's relation to humanity as a whole, does he move to society at large. Rather, Frei moves from the narratively rendered identity of Jesus Christ to the publicly enacted "collective discipleship" of the church. The church, as the embodiment of the indirect presence of Jesus Christ in and for the world, becomes a central character in the ongoing story of Jesus. Further, according to Frei, Word and sacrament "constitute" the church; they provide the temporal and spatial basis for Christ's indirect presence and for the church's ongoing role as a publicly enacted character in the story.

Homiletically, Frei's move is crucially important. Grammatically, God in Jesus Christ is not simply the predicate of individual human experience or needs, but is an active subject building up a people to embody and witness to Jesus' presence in and for the world. . . .

Frei's work thus directs preaching beyond individual, experiential events to the building up of the church as a people who embody and witness to Jesus Christ's indirect "presence" and thereby God's reign in the world. This orientation is further emphasized and clarified in Frei's turn to a cultural-linguistic model of Christianity in his later work. . . .

In this regard Walter Brueggemann has written that preaching helps to provide an "infrastructure" for the corporate life of the community.

> I use the term "infrastructure" to refer to the system or network of signs and gestures that make social relationships possible, significant, and effective. The social infrastructure is the almost invisible system of connections that gives life functioning power and provides connections and support systems. I take it that the most elemental human infrastructure is a network of stories, sacraments, and signs that give a certain nuance, shape, and possibility to human interaction. An evangelical infrastructure is one that mediates and operates in ways that heal, redeem, and transform. [*Texts Under Negiotiation* (Minneapolis: Fortress, 1993), p. 27]

Within Frei's cultural-linguistic model of Christianity, this communal function of helping to "build up" a distinctive "infrastructure" within the church becomes fundamental to preaching — and leads to a quite different understanding of preaching from that which focuses on private, individual, experiential events.

The implications of this different understanding of preaching may be seen by looking at a couple of concrete ways in which this communal approach can inform the actual practice of preaching. One concrete way this "upbuilding" can take place through preaching is when the preacher redescribes theologically the common practices of the church, usually in contrast to the descriptions offered by the culture. For example, American culture would describe the welcoming of a new member into the church through baptism as the addition of an individual to a voluntary institution, which is a collection of individuals. In contrast to this description, the preacher's task is to redescribe the practice of baptism as an episode in the ongoing story of God's active gathering and building up of an eschatological people who carry forward

Jesus' story in and for the world. Such repeated redescriptive use of the church's peculiar speech is vitally important for building up "a visible people who have listened to a different story from that of the world."

Moreover, only as the church is built up in this way will believers begin to see the character of the world in a truthful light. Only in relation to the church can the world be known as world, as a realm that is disobedient to God. For example, only as the Eucharist becomes a meal where barriers are broken down between races, classes, and genders will Christians see the world clearly as a place of domination where, in opposition to the way of Jesus, these barriers distort and corrupt human relationships. In this way the redescription of the church's practices inevitably includes a redescription of the world and shapes the church's service and resistance to the world.

Another concrete implication of this communal approach can also be noted. It consists quite simply of letting the church be the "middle term" as the preacher moves from text to sermon. Rather than asking how texts connect with predetermined individual needs or how they connect with "general human experience" or how they are relevant to American society, preachers should quite consciously ask what the Spirit is saying to the *church* through the church's Scripture. The focus is not simply on what a text "means" but on how a particular passage of Scripture functions to "build up" the people of God in and for the world. The movement, again, is from the narratively rendered identity of God in Jesus Christ to the identity of the church as a character in that ongoing story.

This approach may sound rather simple, but it is foreign to many preachers in an individualistic, liberal society. Most of the sermons I hear focus either on the needs of individuals in the congregation or on issues in American society. This twofold movement is typical of American liberalism, reflecting a story that divides life into the "private" and the "public," with no room for the church (and with Christianity increasingly relegated to the private realm because of its lack of influence on the public). In ethical terms, such liberal preaching moves between an "ethics of interiority" and an "ethics of society." In contrast, the move to the church is radically different, placing both preacher and congregation in a different story from that of American liberalism. Learning to ask the "hermeneutical question" in this communal way is another crucial element in a "hermeneutic of suspicion," which preachers need to remember in a liberal, individualistic society. Such communal interpretation provides one concrete means of building up the church as an alternative community. . . .

Within a postliberal, cultural-linguistic model, then, faith is not primarily an individual, existential, experiential event, but rather a journey into the language and practices of a particular community. People enter this distinctive community through the practice of baptism, which inaugurates their journey into the language and practices of the church. And on the Lord's Day the people of God are gathered as this distinctive community in a peculiar time — the eschatological day of resurrection and new creation. Within Frei's postliberal theology, this distinctive cultural-linguistic community becomes crucial to the Christian faith — and to preaching.

Within this model, preaching does not seek primarily to present cognitive propositions; here a postliberal homiletic accepts the criticism of cognitive-propositional preaching that has been developed by contemporary narrative homileticians. However, unlike much of contemporary homiletics, the postliberal alternative also does not emphasize the individual experiential event. Rather, the focus is on learning the distinctive language and practices — the infrastructure — of the Christian community, which then makes certain ideas and experiences possible.

The differences between a postliberal homiletic and one focused on the individual experiential event can be seen clearly in the emphasis on language *use* in the cultural-linguistic model. As George Lindbeck has noted, within a cultural-linguistic model, language is not understood primarily as a collection of symbols that are expressive or evocative of private, affective experience. Rather, language is fundamentally a public instance of communally ruled behavior. As [Nancey] Murphy and [James William] McClendon have argued, this "postmodern" understanding of language focuses not on its representational or expressive dimensions, but on the public, communal *use* of language:

> How may we use the word "God," and how does this use restrain or shape ideas about God and even our experience of God? Putting it in an oversimplified form, whereas for classical Greek thought, *ideas* determined both reality and language, and for moderns, at least with the rise of empiricism, *experience* determined ideas, which determined language, in postmodern thought the tables are turned and *language* makes possible both ideas and experience. ["Distinguishing Modern and Postmodern Theologies," *Modern Theology* 5 (April 1989): 202-3]

This language use is shaped by the beliefs, institutions, and practices of the community, as Alasdair MacIntyre has demonstrated:

> The conception of language . . . is that of a language as it is used in and by a particular community living at a particular time and place with particular shared beliefs, institutions, and practices. These beliefs, institutions, and practices will be furnished expression and embodiment in a variety of lin-

guistic expressions and idioms; the language will provide standard uses for a necessary range of expressions and idioms, the use of which will presuppose commitment to those same beliefs, institutions, and practices. . . . Moreover, the learning of the language and the acquisition of cultural understanding are not two independent activities. [*Whose Justice? Which Rationality?* (Notre Dame, Ind.: University of Notre Dame Press, 1988), pp. 373-74]

Within the cultural-linguistic view of language, learning a community's "peculiar speech" and being initiated into that community's traditions, beliefs, and practices are one and the same initiation.

When language is thus understood as a public, communal instance of ruled behavior, rather than as a collection of evocative and expressive symbols, the implications for preaching are significant. In general, the purpose of preaching becomes not to explain the meaning (much less prove the "truth") of the Christian gospel in terms of cognitive propositions. Nor does preaching seek primarily to create an existential, experiential event for individual hearers (though there is nothing to prevent this from happening from time to time). Rather, preaching models the use of Christian language and thereby plays a role in nurturing believers in that language usage. Sermons become a means through which the Christian community enters more deeply into its own distinctive speech, so that Christian ideas, beliefs, and experiences become possible. Preaching seeks to re-create a universe of discourse and put the community in the middle of that world — instructing the hearers in the use of the language by showing them how to use it. . . .

At the heart of learning this distinctive language is the ability to "go on," as Wittgenstein puts it, the ability to use the language innovatively in all its richness in new situations and contexts. . . .

As an exemplary part of the Christian community's language-in-use, preaching should be understood as modeling appropriate Christian speech based primarily on the Scripture that functions as the canon of the church. Preaching models ways of "going on," as the richness and "semantic depth" of the language are developed in new contexts and new situations. The preacher thus needs to be a person who preeminently knows the language of faith and is able to "go on" with it — a consideration that might shift the teaching of preaching away from learning certain methods and techniques to nurturing preaching in the language of the Christian community through immersion in Scripture.

Preaching, in this sense, is something like jazz improvisation. Starting with a basic "text" of music, jazz musicians do not translate that text into a new language, but rather "go on" with the language of the text in new ways for new contexts. Whether improvising rather conservatively on the theme of a piece of music or engaging in a more radical, nonthematic improvisation based on the chord progressions, jazz musicians develop the basic language of the "text" in new ways. Consistent with MacIntyre's description of language, jazz musicians often learn the art of improvisation by immersing themselves in the language and spirit of the tradition and by imitating classic pieces from the tradition. Through such immersion and imitation, jazz musicians are prepared to improvise, or "go on," with the music in new and creative ways. Improvisation is not simply spontaneous, but is the fruit of years of immersion in the "language" of jazz. Not surprisingly, African-American preaching, which improvises with the biblical idiom in such powerful ways, has been closely related to the jazz tradition.

This kind of "going on" with the language of Scripture and tradition is what preaching (and the training of preachers) involves in a cultural-linguistic model. Week after week the preacher uses distinctive Christian speech both paradigmatically and innovatively as an instance of communal, public, ruled behavior within the language game of the worship of the baptized on the Lord's Day. While private, affective "experiential events" may occur from time to time for some members of the congregation, at a deeper and more significant level people are repeatedly hearing a peculiar speech used to redescribe contemporary life. In the process, preacher and hearers alike are learning how to use this language more richly and faithfully.

Further, learning Christian speech is not simply a conceptual or cognitive activity. Rather, it involves disposition and behavior as well. Preaching is not just an abstract language, but is embodied in the character of the preacher, the tone and inflections of speech, and the manner of delivery, just as a piece of jazz improvisation is inseparably related to the character and spirit of the musician. . . .

The crucial role of preaching in a cultural-linguistic model is thus not that of offering cognitive-propositional information, nor that of creating private, affective experiential events for individual hearers. Rather, the crucial role of preaching is the use of Christian speech so that the community may learn to use its language rightly. The focus of preaching is on learning a language, which is not simply a series of discrete existential "events," but a long, slow process of use and growth. In a time when the church is struggling with its identity within a secular society, this postliberal, cultural-linguistic model is a crucial one for the contemporary pulpit to take seriously.

ACKNOWLEDGMENTS

The author and publisher gratefully acknowledge permission to include material from the following sources:

Epigraph

James Weldon Johnson, "Listen Lord — A Prayer," from *God's Trombones,* © 1927 The Viking Press Inc., renewed © 1955 by Grace Nail Johnson. Used by permission of Viking Penguin, a division of Penguin Putnam Inc.

What Is Preaching?

Alan of Lille, *The Art of Preaching,* Cistercian Fathers Series, Number 23, trans. Gilian R. Evans, © Cistercian Publications 1981. Used by permission.

Friedrich Schleiermacher, *Praktische Theologie, Samtliche Werke,* part 1, vol. 13, © 1850 Walter De Gruyter. Used by permission.

C. H. Dodd, *The Apostolic Preaching and Its Developments,* © 1936 Hodder and Stoughton.

Dietrich Bonhoeffer, *Worldly Preaching,* ed. Clyde E. Fant, © Thomas Nelson, 1975. Used by permission.

Carl Michalson, "Communicating the Gospel," *Theology Today* 14, no. 3 (October 1957): 321-34 (with several paragraphs omitted). Used by permission.

Barbara Brown Taylor, *The Preaching Life,* © Cowley 1993. Used by permission of Cowley Publications, 28 Temple Place, Boston, MA 02111 (1-800-225-1534).

The Preacher

John Chrysostom, *Six Books on the Priesthood,* trans. Graham Neville, © 1977 St. Vladimir's Seminary Press. Used by permission of St. Vladimir's Seminary Press, 575 Scarsdale Road, Crestwood, N.Y., 10707.

Gardner C. Taylor, *How Shall They Preach,* © 1977 Progressive Baptist Publishing House. Used by permission.

Acknowledgments

Proclaiming the Word

Martin Luther, *Luther's Works,* vol. 35, ed. E. Theodore Bachmann and Helmut Lehmann, © 1960 Fortress Press. Used by permission of Augsburg Fortress.

Henry H. Mitchell, *The Recovery of Preaching,* © 1977 Harper and Row. Used by permission.

Walter Brueggemann, *The Prophetic Imagination,* © 1978 Fortress Press. Used by permission of Augsburg Fortress.

Biblical Interpretation

Augustine, *Teaching Christianity* [*On Christian Doctrine*], trans. Edmund Hill, OP, ed. John E. Rotelle, in *The Works of Saint Augustine,* © New City Press 1990-97. Used by permission.

John Cassian, *John Cassian: The Conferences,* trans. Boniface Ramsey, OP, in *Ancient Christian Writers,* ed. Walter J. Burghardt et al., © 1997 Paulist. Used by permission of Paulist Press.

Martin Luther, *Works of Martin Luther,* vol. 3, © Muhlenberg Press 1930. Reprinted with permission.

Rudolf Bultmann, *New Testament and Mythology,* © 1984 Fortress Press. Used by permission of Augsburg Fortress.

Gerhard Ebeling, *Word and Faith,* © SCM Press 1963. Used by permission.

Paul Ricoeur, *The Conflict of Interpretations: Essays on Hermeneutics,* © Northwestern University Press 1974. Used by permission.

James A. Sanders, *God Has a Story Too,* © Fortress 1979. Used by permission.

Nicholas Lash, "Performing the Scriptures," in *Theology on the Way to Emmaus,* © SCM Press 1986. Used by permission.

Katharine Doob Sakenfeld, "Feminist Uses of Biblical Materials," from *Feminist Interpretation of the Bible,* © Westminster 1985. Used by permission.

Justo L. González and Catherine G. González, *The Liberating Pulpit,* © Abingdon 1994. Used by permission.

Richard B. Hays, "Salvation by Trust? Reading the Bible Faithfully," *The Christian Century,* © 1997 Christian Century Foundation. Reprinted with permission from the Feb. 26, 1997 issue of *The Christian Century* (P.O. Box 378, Mt. Morris, IL 61054).

Rhetoric

Augustine, *Teaching Christianity* [*On Christian Doctrine*], trans. Edmund Hill, OP, ed. John E. Rotelle, in *The Works of Saint Augustine,* © New City Press 1990-97. Used by permission.

Robert of Basevorn, *The Form of Preaching,* trans. Leopold Krul, O.S.B., in *Three*

Medieval Rhetorical Arts, ed. James J. Murphy, © University of California Press, 1971. Used by permission.

Amos N. Wilder, *Early Christian Rhetoric: The Language of the Gospel,* © 1964 Harvard University Press, 1971 by the President and Fellows of Harvard College. Used by permission.

David Buttrick, *Homiletic: Moves and Structures,* © 1987 Fortress Press. Used by permission of Augsburg Fortress.

The Hearer

John Calvin, *Institutes of the Christian Religion,* Library of Christian Classics, ed. John T. McNeill, © Westminster 1960. Used by permission of Westminster John Knox Press.

Philip Jacob Spener, *Pia Desidera,* © 1964 Fortress Press. Used by permission of Augsburg Fortress.

Harry Emerson Fosdick, "Pastoral Counseling and Preaching," in *Harry Emerson Fosdick's Art of Preaching,* ed. Lionel Crocker, © Charles C. Thomas, 1971. Used by permission of Charles C. Thomas, Publisher, Ltd., Springfield, Illinois.

Fred B. Craddock, *Overhearing the Gospel,* © 1978 by Fred B. Craddock. Used by permission.

Preaching and the Church

Karl Barth, *The Preaching of the Gospel,* trans. B. E. Hooke. English translation © S.C.M. Press 1963. Published in the U.S.A. by Westminster Press. Used by permission of Westminster John Knox Press.

Oscar Romero, "A Pastor's Last Homily," *Sojourners.* Reprinted with permission of *Sojourners,* www.sojo.net.

Geoffrey Wainwright, "Preaching as Worship," *The Greek Orthodox Theological Review.* Used by permission of *The Greek Orthodox Theological Review.*

INDEX

Aeschylus, 39

Affections, 120, 375, 384

Africa, 149-50

African Society, 76

Alan of Lille, 3

Allegory, xiv, 173, 180, 183, 188, 192, 195, 197, 212-13, 215, 216, 255, 299, 319. *See also* Biblical interpretation

Allen, Richard, 75-76, 78

Alsup, John, 456

Ambrose of Milan, 255, 257

Anagogy, 183-84, 192, 216

Analogy, 317, 342, 376, 416; dynamic 226

Anamnesis, 443, 450, 452

Anselm of Canterbury, 57

Apostles, 26, 41, 92, 117-19, 135, 171, 193, 266, 307, 363, 367, 385, 413, 415, 421, 424-25, 431, 444

Aristotle, 71, 311, 355, 385

Arminius, Jacobus, 298

Arnold, Thomas, 393

Art, 88, 99, 234, 277-78, 281, 283, 302, 314-15, 382; of grammar, 180, 279; of preaching, 293, 312, 315, 338; of speaking, 59

Audience, 3, 6, 46, 58, 99, 155, 277, 281, 284-86, 294-95, 302, 318-19, 338-40, 355, 380, 388, 389, 391-92, 395, 400, 443; diversity of, 356-61. *See also* Congregation; Hearer(s)

Auerbach, Erich, 328

Augustine, xiv, xvi, 3, 143-44, 169, 188, 190-92, 257, 277, 304, 305, 331, 355, 368, 393, 454

Authority, 7, 59, 101, 175, 222, 236, 246, 279, 281-82, 303, 305, 381, 388; external and internal, 102; of the church, 170, 230, 265; of Scripture, 156, 169, 172, 188, 239, 243, 247, 250, 277; of texts, 211; of women, 241

Awakenings, 120

Azusa Street, 417, 418-19

Baldwin, Charles, 305

Baptism, 161, 171, 342, 374, 429-30, 452, 454-56, 463, 465. *See also* Sacrament(s)

Barth, Karl, xv, 98, 126, 423, 443, 450

Bartleman, Frank, 417

Basil of Caesarea, 255, 257

Baxter, Richard, xiv, 69, 369, 393

Beecher, Henry Ward, 109

Beecher Lectures, 15, 98, 104, 108, 109, 142, 149, 311, 331, 411

Beethoven, Ludwig von, 233, 235-36

Benedict, 182

Bennet, John, 129

Bernard of Clairvaux, 215, 294, 309

Beza, Theodorus, 304

Bible, 10-11, 35, 42, 50, 70, 76, 79, 99-100, 123-24, 169, 188, 192, 202, 215-16, 218, 219-25, 227-29, 234, 238, 239-47, 248, 249-52, 260-62, 265, 266-67, 272, 294, 362, 370-72, 397, 399, 406, 420, 423, 425, 431, 442, 448-51. *See also* Biblical interpretation; Scripture

Biblical interpretation, xiii, 14, 182, 196, 218, 231-37, 238, 251, 262, 267, 272, 298, 417, 448, 451; allegorical and figurative, 169, 170-81, 188; feminist, 239-47, 261-63; historical and spiritual, 183-87. *See also* Exegesis; Hermeneutics

Black preaching. *See* Preaching, African-American

Bonhoeffer, Dietrich, 31, 38, 204, 224, 411

Bornkamm, Günther, 329

Brastow, Lewis, 389

Broadus, John, 311

Brooks, Phillips, 15, 104, 142, 389, 395

Brueggemann, Walter, 156, 463

Buber, Martin, 142, 144

Bultmann, Rudolf, xv, 38, 98, 196, 204, 207, 211, 214, 219, 248, 451, 459

Burke, Edmund, 333

Bushnell, Horace, 15, 83

Buttrick, David, 337, 455

Buttrick, George, 108

Calvin, John, 224, 266, 362, 417, 430, 443

Campbell, Charles, xv, 459

Canning, George, 392

Cardenal, Ernesto, 248, 259-60

Cervantes, Miguel de, 40

Chalmers, Thomas, 69, 393

Chekhov, Anton, 44

Christ. *See* Jesus Christ

Church, xiii-xvi, 3, 8, 18-20, 23-24, 26, 29, 39, 41-42, 45, 53, 64, 66, 70, 72-73, 77, 79, 99-100, 103, 115, 136-37, 140, 156, 171, 183, 192, 218, 227, 230, 235, 237-38, 241-42, 245-47, 249-57, 262, 265, 268, 271, 277, 279, 286, 296, 298, 301, 324-25, 327-28, 341, 344-47, 363, 366, 369-70, 373, 386, 395, 398, 404-7, 414-16, 420-21, 428-32, 434, 437-42, 444-52, 459-60, 462-65

Cicero, Marcus Tullius, xiv, 213, 305, 309-10, 311, 315

Civil rights, 104, 110, 165

Clarke, James Freeman, 93

Clement of Alexandria, 255

Coleridge, Samuel Taylor, 83

Communion. *See* Eucharist

Community, 105-7, 152, 215, 217, 222, 230, 234-35, 237, 239, 244, 249, 267, 269-70, 406, 408, 413, 455, 461, 463-67; and individuals, 110; of interpretation, 45; prophetic, 157, 159-62; worshiping, 43

Cone, James, 149

Congregation, 9, 14, 33, 35, 47, 51, 58-59, 73, 79, 81, 123, 127, 136, 141, 149, 151, 155,

250, 292, 317, 319, 339, 341, 355, 370, 389, 390-94, 396, 398-99, 411, 418-19, 449-49; and the minister, 10-11, 139. *See also* Audience

Constantine I, 33, 255

Craddock, Fred B., xv, 401

Creed(s), 33, 100-101, 161

Cross, 76, 80, 91, 98, 101, 194, 197, 214, 270, 294, 368, 412-14, 434, 441, 452

Cyprian of Carthage, 257

Dante Alighieri, 57, 326

Deissmann, Gustav-Adolf, 333

de Lubac, Henri, 214

Demosthenes, 88, 309, 313, 315

Deposit of faith, 451

de Vitry, Jacques, 296

Dewey, Joanna, 261-62

Dibelius, Martin, 98

Dilthey, Wilhelm, 207, 212

Dodd, C. H., 23, 31, 38, 98, 142

Doddridge, Philip, 69

Dodwell, Henry (?), 94

Donne, John, 42

Dostoevsky, Fyodor, 40

Downes, John, 129, 131

Earnestness, 382-84

Ebeling, Gerhard, xv, 204, 331

Edwards, Jonathan, xv, 120, 126, 132, 136, 375, 417

Eliade, Mircea, 149

Eliot, T. S., 273

Eloquence, 58, 62, 89, 278-86, 290, 308-9, 383, 424

Emerson, Ralph Waldo, 83

Emser, Jerome, 188-93

Epiclesis, 443

Erasmus of Rotterdam, 304

Ethics, 253, 265, 324, 447, 459

Eucharist, xvi, 51, 161, 171, 184, 227, 230, 237, 342, 374, 429-30, 443, 446, 452, 464

Eudoxia, 451

Eusebius of Caesarea, 94, 253

Exegesis, xiv, 46, 196, 197-98, 200-203, 204, 206, 213-15, 242, 252, 425, 449; Antiochene school of, 448. *See also* Biblical interpretation

Farmer, Herbert H., 142
Fénelon, François, 305, 401
Finney, Charles Grandison, xv, 132, 142
Formation (and preaching), 3-5
Forsyth, P. T., 98, 411, 423
Fosdick, Harry Emerson, xv, 104, 395, 401
Foucault, Michel, 266
Fowler, James, 107
Francis de Sales, 380, 384
Fredrickson, Paula, 270
Freedom, xv, 100-101, 146, 162-63, 165, 171, 227-28, 243, 439. *See also* God, freedom of; Liberation; Liberty
Frei, Hans, 265, 459-60, 462-63, 465
Fuchs, Ernst, 204, 326, 329
Fuller, Thomas, 317

Garrick, David, 140
Geraldus Cambrensis (Gerald), 295
God, xiv, 21, 25, 27, 31, 39, 40-42, 45, 47, 50-51, 53, 67, 69, 72-73, 77-79, 81, 87, 93-95, 105-8, 110-11, 117, 119, 122, 128, 131, 134-38, 154, 162, 170-71, 177, 184, 190, 192, 194, 199, 202-3, 208, 218, 224, 226, 228, 234, 239, 243, 245-47, 251, 267-74, 287-88, 290-92, 295, 301, 313, 328-29, 331-32, 334-36, 342, 368, 376-79, 388, 396, 399, 412-16, 429-31, 435-40, 442, 446, 454-55, 457-59; act(s) of, 29, 327, 424, 443; authority of, 17, 102-3; enjoyment of, 149, 173; existence of, 424; experience of, 8; faithfulness of 160-61, 224, 268-69, 452; the Father, 16-17, 26, 36, 42, 68, 82, 91, 367-68, 445; fear of, 361; feminine characteristics of, 238; foreknowledge of, 26; freedom of, 218, 224-25; future of, 208-9, 408; glory of, 445; goodness of, 152; graciousness of, 158, 163; image of, 256; knowledge of, 40, 71, 120, 169, 172, 230, 362, 363-65, 371, 421; judgment of, 66, 158; love of, 6, 78, 82, 120, 127, 172, 175-76, 194, 255, 283, 297, 374; majesty of, 67, 225; messenger of, 17; mind of, 367; mystery of, 232, 237; name of, 322; obedience to, 96, 178; people of, 249-50, 299, 303, 341, 438; and personal relationships, 142, 143-48; power of, 80, 82, 140, 153, 198,

418, 420, 422; praise of, 150, 152, 372; presence of, 52, 67, 151; providence of, 84, 155; purpose of, 109, 143, 259; self-revelation of, 265, 426-27, 450; service of, 64; the Son, 21, 34, 68, 77, 82, 112, 116-17, 154, 295, 335, 436, 446, 450; sovereignty of, xv, 139, 164, 426; speech of, 159-60, 425, 448; will of, 254, 329, 373; work of, 86, 134, 227, 236, 252, 375, 461; wrath of, 121, 124, 179, 188, 378. *See also* Jesus Christ; Word of God
Goethe, Johann Wolfgang von, 415
González, Justo L. and Catherine G., 248
Gospel, xvi, 17, 20-21, 25, 28-29, 38-39, 40-45, 76, 94, 99-101, 105, 109, 112, 115-17, 119-20, 122, 124, 128-31, 135-36, 139, 152-53, 154, 185, 193, 195, 208, 213, 215-17, 242, 244, 247, 253, 264, 267, 270, 277, 305, 318, 321, 324, 326-30, 332, 340, 342, 364, 368, 392, 396-97, 399, 403, 405, 412-15, 424, 429, 434-37, 446-47, 451, 466. *See also* Kerygma
Grace, 47, 70, 74, 91, 97, 108, 115, 126-28, 132, 169, 179, 183-84, 193-95, 224-25, 228, 254, 266-67, 271-72, 274, 302-3, 336, 342, 362, 373, 379, 385, 388, 411-12, 415-16, 427-29, 431, 438, 446, 452
Great Awakening, the, 375; Second, 132
Gregory I (the Great), 257, 355, 385
Gregory Nazianzen, 356
Gregory of Nyssa, 256-57
Gunkel, Hermann, 198

Handel, Georg Friedrich, xiii
Haughton, John, 129
Hays, Richard B., 265
Hearer(s), xiii, 5-6, 74, 138, 215, 250, 284, 288, 294, 297, 299, 305, 308, 310, 313, 315, 358, 373, 381-83, 385-88, 401, 402-7, 424, 452. *See also* Audience; Congregation
Hegel, G. W. F., 44
Heidegger, Martin, 196, 207
Hell, 377-78
Helmholtz, Hermann Ludwig Ferdinand von, 39
Helps, Arthur, 391
Hemmingius, Nicholas, 304
Herbert, George, xiv, 64, 69, 369

Hermas, 254-55
Hermeneutics, 196, 204, 205-8, 210, 211, 212-17, 218, 219-21, 223-25, 230, 331; of suspicion and trust, 266-74. *See also* Biblical interpretation; New Hermeneutic
Hermogenes, 66
Herodotus, 223
Historical method, 197-201
History, 144, 157, 198-201, 215-16, 234, 236, 253-54, 335, 343, 398, 408, 428, 435, 438-39, 451; of the church, 188; of Jesus' life, 39, 188; outer/inner, 38; of salvation, 435; as sense of Scripture, 183-84, 213
Holiness, 21, 57, 64, 66-67, 69-70, 72, 90, 98, 126, 140, 174, 302, 318, 323, 336, 369, 417
Holy Spirit, xiv, 26-27, 34, 36, 45, 53, 68, 70, 73, 75, 80, 82, 90-93, 95, 118, 121, 132, 133-35, 151, 171, 179, 180, 186, 189, 191-95, 205, 227, 271, 277, 283, 300-302, 328, 362, 368, 371, 374, 375, 376-79, 382, 406, 416, 417, 418-21, 424, 443, 445-47, 450-52, 461-62, 464; testimony of, 362, 364-67. *See also* God
Homer, 223
Homiletics, 23, 31-32, 38, 46, 169, 265, 277, 298, 311, 315, 324, 337, 340-41, 395, 396, 401, 459, 460, 465
Homilia, 315
Homily, 33, 51, 105, 443, 444-45
Hope, 157, 159-64, 172, 237, 243, 268, 406, 408, 427, 434, 442, 443
Horace, 311
Hughes, Sarah, 75
Hyperius, Andreas Gerhard, 304

Ignatius of Antioch, 254, 326
Ignatius of Loyola, 384
Illustration. *See* Sermon, illustration in
Illyricus, Matthias Flacius, 304
Imagination, 331-36
Incarnation, 31, 34, 48, 95, 332, 336, 389, 393, 426, 448
Innocent I, 182
Interpretation. *See* Biblical interpretation
Isocrates, 309
Israel, 26, 67, 108, 157, 161-65, 171, 184, 226-27, 238-29, 243, 267-71, 326, 329, 414, 431, 435, 446, 448, 460-61

Jarrett-Kerr, Martin, 328
Jerome, 189, 192, 372
Jesus Christ, 4, 5, 16, 19, 20, 23, 26, 29, 32, 34-39, 41-42, 45, 48, 49, 67, 70, 73, 74, 78, 90, 94-95, 97, 100, 108-9, 111, 115-17, 119, 121, 123-24, 126, 128-31, 135, 138, 152, 165, 169, 173-74, 179, 183-86, 189-95, 197-98, 209, 212, 215, 222, 226-27, 236-38, 231-32, 234-35, 238, 241-43, 246-47, 250, 254-55, 261-65, 266-72, 290, 294-95, 300, 307, 321, 323, 325-26, 328-30, 334, 336, 345, 366-67, 374, 389, 396-98, 400, 405, 407, 411-16, 423-27, 431, 434-40, 445-49, 450, 469-60, 462-64; death and resurrection of, 24, 26, 127; as event, 41-42, 44, 224; as example, 115, 117-18; as gift, 115, 117-18; historical Jesus, 34-35, 38, 459; knowledge of, 16, 127, 301; love of, 128; mind of, 420; mystery of, 213; passion of, 441; preaching of, 41, 89, 98, 304; return of 452; work of, 71. *See also* God, the Son; Logos; Word of God
John Cassian, 182
John Chrysostom, 57, 93, 182, 256-57, 315, 355, 393, 443, 445-52
Johns, Vernon, 108
Johnson, James Weldon, xviii
Jones, Alan, 52
Junius, Franciscus, 304
Justin Martyr, 32, 94, 444

Kähler, Martin, 34
Keats, John, 326
Kernan, Alvin, 273
Kerygma, 23, 24-28, 32, 38, 41, 98, 115, 196, 212-13, 215-17, 269, 426; and *didache*, 23. *See also* Preaching, apostolic
Keys, Martha Jayne, 75
Kierkegaard, Søren, 38, 40, 45, 344, 401, 405-7, 424
King, Martin Luther, Jr., 104, 110, 120
Kingdom of God, 28, 31, 100, 174, 212, 286, 367, 382, 424, 438-39, 451-52; of heaven, 186, 376
Kroner, Richard, 333

Lake, Kirsopp, 28

Lamb, Charles, 412

Language, 83, 213, 232, 325-30, 341-42, 351, 405, 465-67; of the gospel, 38

La Rochefoucauld, François, 392

Lash, Nicholas, xv, 230, 265

Law, 82, 128-29, 185, 193-95, 208, 295, 433, 436, 443; and gospel, xv, 126-31, 188, 300, 364, 370, 426, 431

Lee, Jarena, 75

Lee, Robert E., 311

Lentricchia, Frank, 272-73

Leo I (the Great), 182

Leonard, George, 151

Libanius, 57

Liberation, xv, 433, 439-40, 442

Liberty, 80-81, 100-101, 127. *See also* Freedom; Liberation

Lindbeck, George, 230, 265, 459, 465

Listener. *See* Hearer

Liturgy, 35-36, 64, 229, 248, 311, 341, 443, 444-45, 447-48

Locke, John, 92, 120

Logos, 34-35

Longinus, Dionysius Cassius, 40, 311

Lord's Supper. *See* Eucharist

Lucretius, 7

Luther, Martin, xv-xvi, 37-38, 41, 43, 98, 115, 126, 142, 188, 191, 196, 200-202, 204, 218, 266, 431, 449

Macaulay, Thomas Babington, 392

MacIntyre, Alasdair, 461, 465, 467

Maddern, John, 130

Marcel, Gabriel, 39

Marcion, 213

Marx, Karl, 266

Matthias, Jacobus, 304

McClendon, James William, 465

Memory, 226-27, 310, 343, 345, 348, 406, 408

Michalson, Carl, 38

Milton, John, 18

Minister, 9, 11, 13-14, 91, 93, 121-24, 133, 135, 323; and education, 301; as co-worker with Christ, 123; as theologian, 10. *See also* Preacher

Mitchell, Henry, 149

Moody, Dwight, 15

Murphy, James J., 3

Murphy, Nancey, 465

Narrative, 46, 116, 211, 401, 405-8, 459

Nelson, John, 130-31, 400

New Hermeneutic, xv, 38, 204

Newman, John Henry, 380

New Testament, xvi, 10, 17, 27, 29, 32-33, 39, 41, 43-44, 98, 115, 145, 193-95, 198, 206, 209, 214-17, 219-20, 27, 231-34, 236-38, 241-42, 245-46, 265, 266, 277, 324, 325-27, 329, 370, 427-28, 447. *See also* Bible; Scripture

Niebuhr, H. Richard, 107

Niebuhr, Reinhold, 162

Nietzsche, Friedrich, 266

Oden, Thomas C., 455

Old Testament, 25, 115, 118-19, 156, 169, 177-78, 188, 193-95, 199, 206, 209, 213-16, 219, 220-21, 227, 231, 238, 250, 326, 388, 414, 428, 447, 460. *See also* Bible; Scripture

Oman, John, 142

Oratory, 57, 61-62, 99. *See also* Rhetoric

Origen, 33, 182, 188-89, 191-93, 213

Palmer, Phoebe, 75, 90

Palmer, Walter C., 90

Paul, 5-7, 24-25, 28-29, 41, 67, 77-78, 92-93, 111, 116, 189-94, 197, 213-14, 231, 241-43, 265, 267-71, 273, 288, 299, 300, 329, 331, 332-36, 345, 358, 366-68, 371-72, 382, 388, 393, 414, 424, 437, 440, 445-49, 461

Perkins, Benjamin, 106

Perkins, William, 298

Perpetua and Felicitas, 94

Personality, 15-17, 20-21

Peter the Hermit, 391

Philo of Alexandria, 197, 213

Photius, 315

Plato, 305, 404

Potominia Ammius, 94

Preacher: and the audience, 6-7, 294-97, 356-61, 448, 452; authority of, 48, 98-103; Black, 108, 149; calling of, 64, 75-82, 106, 452; competency of 58-63; and the congregation, 47-48, 371, 390-94, 396, 449-51; and gender, 238; as herald, 105; and ideological suspicion, 257; individuality of 8, 20, 395; insufficiencies of 70, 302; as messenger, 18; personal qualities of, xiv, 58-63, 302, 415-16; as prophet, 85, 99, 156; as representative, 49; and Scripture, 37, 196, 425, 447-50; strengths of, 112; temptations of, 58-63; training of, 69, 71-74, 86

Preaching: act of, 42, 316; African-American, 149-50, 467; anamnetic character of, 447-50; apostolic, 24-30, 217, 414, 426; as celebration, 149, 150-55; and the church, 411, 412-16, 423, 428-32, 440, 443, 444-52, 460-67; definitions of, xiii, 3, 4-7, 15-16, 34, 49, 53, 86, 381; as divine gift, 85; doxological character of, 445-47; as encounter, 142, 143-48; epicletic character of, 450-51; eschatological character of, 451-52, 461; as event, 115; expository, 370, 398-99; grammar of, 460-67; manner of, 138-41; method of, 87, 298, 314, 399; New Testament expressions for, 32; objectives of, 33, 381, 397; patristic, 33; as performance, 230; and personal counseling, 395, 396-400; as prayer; 52; and relationships, 143-48; renewal of, 69, 369; rules for, 381; styles of, 284-90, 298, 315, 324; talents for, 84-89; topical, 398; in worship, 99, 430, 443, 445. See also Kerygma

Preunderstanding (in interpretation), 201-2

Proclamation, 41, 94, 105, 205, 210, 423. See also Preaching

Propaganda, 325, 450

Prophecy, 91-92, 95, 157, 162, 184

Prophet(s), 24-25, 66, 116, 118, 135, 156, 157-66, 171, 174-75, 190, 192, 209, 239, 299, 307, 322, 329, 363-65, 424-25, 431, 444

Proust, Marcel, 43

Pseudo-Dionysius the Areopagite (Dionysius), 189

Race/racism, 108-9, 110, 259, 273, 428, 464

Raitt, Thomas, 161-62

Ramus, Peter, 305, 311

Reformation, the, 200, 212, 232, 293, 430

Resurrection, 77, 96, 171, 214, 269, 271, 336, 407, 433-34, 440, 452, 460-61, 465

Revelation, 5, 41-42, 99, 105, 183, 236, 266, 327, 332, 342, 362, 365, 412-13, 423, 424-32, 439

Rhetoric, xiii, 58, 87-88, 99, 104, 277, 278-81, 283, 293, 305, 310, 311, 312-15, 324, 325-27, 331, 337, 341-43, 382, 385-86, 401, 404

Ricoeur, Paul, 204, 211, 218, 407

Rimbaud, Arthur, 326

Robert of Basevorn, 293, 305

Robertson, Frederick W., 104, 393

Romero, Oscar, xv, 433

Ruether, Rosemary, 243-44

Rule of faith, 170, 279

Russell, Letty, 243-44

Sacrament(s), xiv, 43, 161, 171, 237, 423, 429-32, 438, 443, 444, 446, 454, 462; of the word, 37; preacher as, 411, 412-13. See also Baptism; Eucharist

Sakenfeld, Katherine Doob, 238

Sanders, James A., 218

Savonarola, Girolamo, 393

Scherer, Paul, 104

Schillebeeckx, Edward, 451

Schleiermacher, Friedrich, xiv, 8, 33, 83, 196, 207, 248

Schüssler Fiorenza, Elisabeth, 238, 244-46, 266-67, 271

Scripture(s), 4, 8, 10-13, 26, 33, 36, 43, 51, 66-67, 72, 77, 79, 82, 90, 108, 115, 116, 118-19, 123, 128, 133-35, 169, 182, 189-90, 202-3, 205-6, 209-10, 212-13, 216-17, 221, 230, 232, 234-35, 237, 239, 241, 244, 249-50, 253, 258, 265, 266-67, 270-74, 279-81, 299, 301, 304, 305, 327, 333, 349, 362, 363-65, 370-71, 395, 403, 406, 408, 423, 425, 431-32, 437, 443, 444, 448-50, 459, 460, 464, 466-67; application of, 307; dialogue with, 10-11; figurative sense of, 170-81; fourfold sense of, 182, 183-87, 188, 192, 214-16; literal sense of, 170-81, 182, 189-95, 216; perspicuity of, 37;

spiritual understanding of, 189-95, 214-15, 302

Sermon, xiv-xv, 3, 6, 10, 12, 37, 48, 52, 58, 64, 66, 72, 74, 79, 86, 120, 205, 229, 301, 385-88, 429-30; as art, 51; Black, 149; as a communal act, 47; design of, 293-97, 320, 337, 338-51; faults of, 306-9; as God's creation, 48; illustration in, 294-97, 317-23; inductive, 401, 402-8; inspiration for, 362; mission of, 115; as narrative process, xv, 460-67; and the needs of the parish, 9; origins of, 33; place in worship, 430, 444-45; preparation of, 50-51, 209-10, 448; and rhetorical style, 287-92; as sacrament, 413

Shakespeare, William, 273

Sidgwick, Henry, 144

Sin, 117, 124, 127, 172, 176, 194-95, 250, 269, 300-301, 338-40, 343, 375, 378, 387, 397, 416, 426, 431, 435, 440, 442, 447

Sittler, Joseph, 331

Smith, Amanda, 75

Somoza, Anastasio, 260-61

Spener, Philip Jacob, xiv, 69, 90, 369, 401

Spirituality, 64, 69

Spurgeon, Charles Haddon, 69, 316

Stoddard, Solomon, 120

Stuhlmacher, Peter, 271

Suckling, John, 129

Swindells, Robert, 130

Taylor, Barbara Brown, xv, 46

Taylor, Gardner C., 104

Taylor, Hudson, 420

Tertullian, 213

Text, the, 50, 209-10, 231

Theology, 5, 8, 69, 71-72, 73, 98, 101, 193, 206-7, 223-24, 233, 234-35, 248, 253, 257, 264, 311, 380, 390, 398, 405, 423, 455, 459, 460, 465

Theophylact Simocatta, 93

Tillich, Paul, 459

Tracy, David, 457-58

Trathan, David, 130

Trible, Phyllis, 238, 245-46

Trinity, the, 169, 288, 294. *See also* God

Tropology, 183, 184, 195

Truth, 15-18, 21, 40, 58, 121, 133-34, 172, 291

Virgil, 191

Wahlberg, Rachel Conrad, 262

Wainwright, Geoffrey, xvi, 443

Warrack Lectures, 142

Webb, Thomas, 130

Wesley, John, xv-xvi, 90, 126, 142, 400, 417; and Charles, 69, 444

Wheatley, James, 129-30

Whitefield, George, 136

Wigandus, Johann, 304

Wilder, Amos, xvi, 277, 324, 331

Wilder, Thornton, 324

Williams, Richard, 78

Willimon, William, 453

Witness, 15, 17-18, 32, 36, 39-44, 215, 217, 328, 423, 425, 435, 447-48, 450, 462; apostolic, 45, 431

Wittgenstein, Ludwig, 466

Women: in the Bible, 238, 260-64; in the church, 92-94; in the Old Testament, 91-93; ordination of, 75; right to preach, 90

Word, the, 17, 100-101, 105, 142, 232, 237, 249, 299, 302, 344, 362, 384, 386, 462; and the congregation, 35, 415; as event, 208, 428; of God, xiii, xv, 6, 31, 36, 41, 45, 48-49, 51-53, 66, 115, 121-24, 153, 184, 191, 204-5, 208-10, 215,-16, 218, 250, 253, 262, 266, 269, 291, 295-98, 306-7, 327, 331, 334-35, 363-38, 370-74, 403, 413, 423, 424-46, 448-51; incarnate, 36, 243, 445, 447; proclaimed, 34-37, 300-301, 372-73, 423; response to, 375; spoken, 146-48, 204, 210, 434. *See also* Bible; God, the Son; Scripture

Worship, 149, 171, 227, 230, 249-50, 318, 337, 369, 374, 412, 446-48, 454, 459, 461, 467

Xavier, Francis, 42

Yeats, W. B., 39

ABOUT THE EDITOR

Richard Lischer is James T. and Alice Mead Cleland Professor of Preaching at Duke Divinity School. Before joining the Duke faculty, he served as pastor of Lutheran congregations in Illinois and Virginia. A graduate of Concordia Senior College and Concordia Seminary, he also holds an M.A. in English from Washington University in St. Louis and a Ph.D. in theology from the University of London. His many lectureships include the Sprunt Lectures at Union, Richmond, the Macleod Lectures at Princeton, and the Lyman Beecher Lectures in Preaching at Yale Divinity School. He is the author of numerous books on preaching, theology, and ministry, including *A Theology of Preaching: The Dynamics of the Gospel* and the prize-winning *The Preacher King: Martin Luther King, Jr. and the Word That Moved America*. He is also co-editor of the *Concise Encyclopedia of Preaching*. The story of his first pastorate, *Open Secrets: A Memoir of Faith and Discovery,* was published by Doubleday/Broadway Books. He lives in Durham, North Carolina.